BARBARA JORDAN
AMERICAN HERO

BARBARA JORDAN

American Hero

MARY BETH ROGERS

BANTAM BOOKS

New York   Toronto   London
Sydney   Auckland

BARBARA JORDAN *American Hero*

A Bantam Book / December 1998

BOOK DESIGN BY GLEN M. EDELSTEIN

Library of Congress Cataloging-in-Publication Data
Rogers, Mary Beth.
Barbara Jordan : American hero / by Mary Beth Rogers.
p.   cm.
Includes bibliographical references and index.
ISBN 0-553-10603-1
1. Jordan, Barbara, 1936–1996.   2. Afro-American women legislators—Biography.
3. Legislators—United States—Biography.   4. United States. Congress. House—
Biography.   I. Title.
E840.8.J62R63   1998
328.73′092—dc21
[B]   98-19996
CIP

Photo on page ii courtesy of Frank Wolfe, Lyndon Baines Johnson Library Collection.
Photo on page 357 courtesy of Texas Senate Media Service.

Excerpts from FOR THE INWARD JOURNEY: THE WRITINGS OF
HOWARD THURMAN by Anne Spencer Thurman, copyright © 1984 selected by
Sue Bailey Thurman, reprinted by permission of Harcourt Brace & Company.

Published simultaneously in the United States and Canada

Bantam Books are published by Bantam Books, a division of Bantam Doubleday Dell
Publishing Group, Inc. Its trademark, consisting of the words "Bantam Books"
and the portrayal of a rooster, is Registered in U.S. Patent and Trademark Office
and in other countries. Marca Registrada. Bantam Books, 1540 Broadway,
New York, New York 10036.

PRINTED IN THE UNITED STATES OF AMERICA
BVG   10 9 8 7 6 5 4 3

For my parents
Frank and Anita Hicks Coniglio

CONTENTS

WHEN I WAS involved in political campaigns in the early 1990s, we often asked focus group participants to name their heroes. We hoped to determine the core beliefs that might influence how they vote. Most of the time, there would be a puzzled silence, then someone might venture the name of a sports figure, a favorite teacher or family member, or perhaps even someone in the news. But if we pressed for a name of an admired public figure, or someone who had moral stature, only two names emerged with any regularity: Mother Teresa and Barbara Jordan.

Mother Teresa's saintly deeds in Calcutta clearly accorded her the honor of becoming a moral hero. But Barbara Jordan? Why did her name appear so often? What allowed this African American woman from Houston, Texas, who served only six years in the U.S. Congress, to retain public admiration and acclaim almost twenty years after she left the national arena? How did she gain her status as an American moral hero at the end of the twentieth century, when so few of her political compatriots were able to stand at her side?

After Barbara Jordan's death at the age of fifty-nine in January 1996, those questions intrigued me. Some of the answers were obvious. Her riveting Watergate testimony in 1974, when she juxtaposed the intent and words of the Constitution against the behavior of the president of the United States, earned her America's trust. "'We, the People' . . . is a very eloquent beginning," we heard her say. Then she evoked our painful national legacy of slavery in a most personal and poignant way.

But when that document was completed on the 17th of September in 1787, I was not included in that "We, the People." I felt

somehow for many years that George Washington and Alexander
Hamilton must have left me out by mistake. But through the
process of amendment, interpretation, and court decision I have
finally been included in "We, the People."

As a result of that inclusion, she told us, "My faith in the Constitution is whole, it is complete, it is total. I am not going to sit here and be an idle spectator to the diminution, the subversion, the destruction of the Constitution."[1]

We were startled. In the managed speeches about Watergate, many of which were intelligent and heartfelt, we—the spectators—were passively absorbing the shock of what we saw and heard. But when Barbara Jordan spoke, she created what the poet Adrienne Rich has called a "poetic rift," a lapse in the prevailing mood.[2] Jordan's language, her unquestionable logic, her polyrhythmic speech, her aura of authority, and her very presence caused thousands of Americans to say, "Wait a minute. This is my country, my Constitution, and I won't have it treated this way."

The Constitution was not subverted. The president of the United States resigned before he could be impeached. And Barbara Jordan became a symbol of everything that was right about America at a time when so much seemed so wrong. The moment she started to speak in that distinctive voice, giving new meaning to the "old, beaten, worn stones of language," we knew that she was more than a mere member of Congress.[3] She vindicated the nation's hard-fought commitment to civil rights and racial equality. How could the United States of America have ever had laws that shut out people like Barbara Jordan?

Then, in 1976, seventy million of us saw her again during the Democratic National Convention in New York City. As a band played "Deep in the Heart of Texas," Robert Strauss escorted her to the platform. She wore a chic three-piece dress the color of lime sherbet. She was thinner than we remembered her, and she walked with a slight limp. But she was smiling radiantly, and the crowd jumped to its feet at the sight of her. Walter Cronkite told CBS viewers, "This is the first time this convention has come alive."

There was a rare hush in the crowd as she began to speak. "It was 144 years ago that members of the Democratic Party first met in convention to select their presidential candidate. . . . There is something special about tonight. What is different? What is special?"

After a significant pause, her thunderous voice gave the answer. "I, Barbara Jordan, am a keynote speaker."[4]

That said it all. The television cameras caught cheering Democrats wiping tears from their eyes.

To Americans who had been curious in 1976 to know more about the woman who had mesmerized them two years earlier with her lessons on the Constitution during the House Judiciary Committee hearings on Watergate, Barbara Jordan that night interpreted her own role in history. She told Americans what they should believe about her, about democracy, about the promise of racial equality, and about something she called our national community. She articulated a belief in equality and she reaffirmed public hope for ethical leadership and racial harmony. She made Democrats—and Americans—feel good about themselves. A Democratic president emerged from that convention, and Barbara Jordan chalked up another "first" in her remarkable career. Besides being the first African American to give a key-note address at either major political party's convention, she had also been the first African American to serve in the Texas State Senate since Recon-struction and the first black woman elected to the U.S. Congress from the South. So many firsts. But do they matter? Are they the basis of her moral heroism?

Studs Terkel has said that a hero is someone who "breaks through."[5] Until Martin Luther King Jr., the twentieth century's only authentic break-through black heroes were sports figures—first Joe Louis, then Jackie Robinson. An entertainer, Lena Horne, had broken the color barrier in the movies to become the first African American symbol of beauty and glam-our, a feat that generated enormous pride within the black community. We know from the stories of King and other civil rights leaders, and of black sports and entertainment figures, that breaking through, or being the first, requires enormous courage, fierce determination, and bold action—univer-sally recognized qualities of traditional heroic behavior. Heroes also have a streak of altruism, and most, in some way, face physical risks or challenge death. They meet life's perils head-on, moving forward where most of us would shrink backward. When they break through seemingly impenetrable barriers to change our perceptions or point of view, they open a new world to us. That is what Barbara Jordan did.

Barbara Jordan was the first African American *elected* official to be-come an American hero. She broke through previously impenetrable barri-ers to beome an "inside" political player who was taken very seriously by the white politicians in power. What made her unique, however, was her "out-side" following, a national audience of admirers who looked to her for guidance and inspiration. In late-twentieth-century America, the combina-tion was a rarity—for either whites or blacks.

Jordan was comfortable with only three labels: patriot, politician, and teacher. She loved the Constitution of the United States, and she loved politics. The Constitution made politics possible, and politics made the Constitution a reality. For Jordan, one had no meaning without the other. Politics was akin to freedom. People who are not free have no politics. Slaves or subjects of authoritarian regimes are denied a political life, but so are people beaten down by poverty or discrimination.

So, for Jordan, politics was the activity necessary to make sure that ordinary people could participate in the public life where society's essential priorities are worked out. Politics could also be fun and totally enjoyable, and Jordan loved the excitement and give-and-take of political life, both the campaigning and the governing. She tested her mettle in the complex world of politics. Her successes showed up in vote tallies, new laws and policies, respect from colleagues, favorable press clips, and fame in the classical sense—as a reward for good deeds, not just for being well known or the celebrity du jour.

Several other characteristics set Barbara Jordan apart from other modern politicians or patriots. She had a remarkable gift of voice. She learned to use the incomparable tone and tenor of her voice to her advantage. Both her mother and father were noted speakers, and she came from a proud tradition of oratory among African Americans—from Sojourner Truth and Frederick Douglass to the thousands of unheralded black preachers whose voices carried hope over hundreds of years of struggle. With her natural gift for oratory, she stepped into that tradition and "traveled on her tongue," as the Tammany Hall politician George Washington Plunkitt used to say. At her best, Jordan let her voice convey the analytical powers of her mind to explain complicated legal and moral questions to people hungry for her insights.

The sound of her voice may have been her supreme gift, however, because, like music, it evoked an emotional response in her listeners. Barbara Jordan's music-based gift of speech communicated her own experience in a way that gave her listeners a glimpse of the truth of the American black experience. If for one moment white men and women could move out of their skins and into the experience of the commanding black woman speaking to them from the podium, then they might see the necessity of her belief in *e pluribus unum*—in unity we are one—the American motto she used in almost every major speech. And if for one moment black men and women could rest nobly in their own skins as they listened to her, they, too, could believe in the quintessential American hope for one community, one nation, one people.

Barbara Jordan felt she was an American first and foremost; an American who happened to be black. And although she recognized and experienced the plague of racism, she believed that the American political system was sound enough and strong enough to allow its legacy to be worked out in personal relationships among people of all races, and that someday we would become one people in fact as well as in theory. She did not come by that belief easily. W.E.B. Du Bois in 1898 was the first to articulate what he felt to be the duality of African American existence. While other Americans might move beyond their ethnic identity as Irish or Poles or Italians to become American, Du Bois believed that African Americans would always be defined by their skin color: "One ever feels his two-ness—an American, a Negro; two souls, two thoughts, two unreconciled strivings; two warring ideals in one dark body, whose dogged strength alone kept it from being torn asunder."[6] Early in his career, Du Bois held out hope that these two ideals could coexist as antagonistic yet complementary paths. He came to believe, however, that African Americans must either reject America, in a nationalistic effort to promote their race, or vanish into a vast system that would ignore it.

By the time Barbara Jordan was thirty years old and entering the all-male, all-white Texas State Senate, she had decided to embrace America, not reject it. She also intended to merge with it, and in so doing she moved beyond Du Bois's notion of two-ness. For Barbara Jordan never felt marginal to anything, and she clearly did not intend to vanish in order to become one with America. For the remainder of her life, she did everything she could to obliterate the tension between the two worlds, black and white. Perhaps this is one reason she was a rarity among American political leaders. She could speak to both worlds and be respected, understood, and admired by each.

Yet with all of this talent and acclaim, with all of her insight and brilliance, she gave up public life before her forty-fifth birthday. Barely into her third term in Congress, she decided to withdraw from the national political arena and to return to private life. African American residents of Houston's Fifth Ward, the poor area where Jordan grew up and which she represented in Congress, were devastated. When Jordan had opened doors for herself in the white world of the 1960s and 1970s, many of her constituents felt she was also opening doors for them. Her firsts were their firsts. Her victories were their victories. But many whites also were shaken by the news of her retirement from Congress. One white Houston lawyer said privately that he went into a mental depression that lasted months; without Barbara Jordan in public office, he did not think it would ever be possible to bridge the chasm of racism, heal the legacy of slavery, or realize the promise of the civil rights movement.

Most people simply wondered why she would give up such a promising public career at the height of her powers, at the peak of her influence. There were rumors of a mysterious illness, of her disillusionment with being a junior member of Congress without seniority—both partially true. After making a statement that she was leaving the nation's capital, she stayed silent and left most questions unanswered. Thereafter, she would pop up occasionally in news interviews or by taking on interesting assignments, such as serving on a United Nations task force to end apartheid in South Africa, but she was generally out of the limelight. Yet every year she would show up on some magazine's "most admired" list and receive dozens of new honors. The National Women's Hall of Fame named her one of the twentieth century's most influential American women, along with Eleanor Roosevelt, Helen Keller, and Rosa Parks. And in 1994 President Bill Clinton presented her with the nation's highest civilian honor, the Medal of Freedom, for her work in advancing civil rights and ethics in government. Jordan's acclaim, however, seemed to go deeper than celebrity lists and high honors from magazines and presidents.

Up until her death, she continued to receive hundreds of letters every year from people all over the nation. Children sent her birthday cards and love notes. In 1986 a woman from Pennsylvania wrote that she wanted to lead a "Republicans for Jordan" presidential effort. In 1988 a retired veteran from Maryland wrote that although he was in his seventies, he had fallen in love with her during the Watergate hearings. In 1989 children in a fifth-grade class in Flushing, New York, wrote Jordan, telling her they had voted to study her over Janet Jackson and Mother Teresa. One child wrote, "I'm glad no other woman was chosen. We made a giant banner that said, 'Barbara Jordan, The Great Lady From Texas.' "[7] When she died, hundreds of ordinary people stood in front of feed stores, service stations, and tractor dealerships with their hands, or their cowboy hats, over their hearts as the small motorcade carrying her body made its way from Houston to her burial site in Austin 150 miles away.

Why did she have such an impact on average Americans? She was big and black, and not very fashionable. She made no attempt to be endearing—or even accommodating to the public's interest in her. Comporting herself with a reserve and dignity that demanded respect, she seemed to embody an ancient ideal of nobility. Jordan had the audacity to believe her life was nobody's business. Deeply stoic, she never talked about her troubles or let anyone know when she felt pain or discomfort. Her strong personal boundaries, shielding and protecting her, were impenetrable for groupies, politicians, the press, or colleagues. Her circle of intimate friends was small, and even they were never sure whether they knew everything that was going on behind those boundaries. Many people who considered themselves close friends never knew the details of her upbringing and had no idea that her mother was a maid or that her father was a Teamsters union steward as well as a Baptist preacher. Still others never had a conversation with her about her illness, multiple sclerosis, even after she was confined to a wheelchair.

George Christian, who was President Lyndon Johnson's press secretary and who became a friend of Jordan's after she began teaching at the University of Texas, said he never knew the nature of her disability until the day she died. In the last year of her life, Christian had driven Jordan to an Austin event. "I'll never forget lifting her from the wheelchair to my car. . . . Oh, brother . . . it was hard, and I realized she was a lot sicker than she let on," he remembered. "But I didn't know what it was. Then her lawyer, Bill Hilgers, asked me to help with the press calls the day she died, and I had to call her doctor and ask him what she had, and what caused her death. He said she had everything."[8] The range of physical ailments Jordan had experienced was staggering: multiple sclerosis, leukemia, diabetes, hypertension, pneumonia, and more. Yet she never talked about any of it, and her close friends rarely asked. If friends wanted to stay close, they never disclosed the few personal things they had learned about her.

Jordan's notion of integrity was grounded in her idea of privacy, and one did not violate it. She would not allow it. She believed that neither public officials nor private citizens should parcel out bits and pieces of their lives for entertainment or titillation, and she refused to do so.

But her penchant for privacy was often misunderstood, and it fueled a certain kind of malicious speculation. What was she hiding? The question seemed to be most intriguing to those who sought personal gain at her expense, or those whose stock in trade was unsubstantiated gossip—particularly in the area of sexual relationships. Speculation on the sex lives of public figures is a popular pastime. I declined to do that in my work on Barbara Jordan, and decided to tell her story factually, as best I could. Until quite recently, single American women in public life have usually been gossiped about by their detractors in two ways: either they "slept around" with men or they "slept around" with women. Sometimes both claims have been made about the same woman. Few women who entered public life prior to the 1990s were spared such gossip. And neither was Barbara Jordan. Yet in two years of research for this book, there was one clear fact that emerged from almost every experience or relationship in her life: Barbara Jordan was soulmates with no one but her self and her God, and even her concept of God was truly her own private territory. She was emotionally self-contained and, for much of her adult life, physically incapacitated.

The significant truths in Barbara's life, I believe, revolved around her single-minded pursuit of achievement and power during the first part of her life; and her efforts to cope with her serious illnesses and physical disability in the second part of her life, which began when she left Congress in 1979. Illness, frailty, pain, vulnerability: *these were the secrets Barbara Jordan kept from the public.* An intense pride was at the root of her desire for privacy, which represented for her the essence of her integrity, or a wholeness that should not be broken by unwelcome intruders.

I came to believe that there was something quite fragile beneath Jordan's bull-like strength and essential stoicism. Like all of us, she had a human vulnerability to life's blows that made her heroism even more interesting. There was something admirable about her discipline and persistence. There was something daunting about her physical courage. What most of us never knew about Barbara Jordan was that for the last twenty years of her life almost every day encompassed a physical struggle. Multiple sclerosis progressively weakened her body, and she spent most of her life after 1988 in a wheelchair. She underwent many experimental treatments, and sometimes the new medicines created even more problems. There were so many medical and maintenance activities she had to complete every morning that it would take her at least two hours to get ready to leave the house. If she had an early flight to catch, she would wake up at two or three o'clock in the morning to start the process. Yet she went on, keeping up a heavy speaking schedule in the weeks immediately before she died, planning another trip even as she was rushed to the hospital for the last time in mid-January 1996.

Over the years, various physical therapists and caregivers had to help her function each day. One morning she was so weak from recent surgery that her therapist told her she couldn't possibly go to the University of Texas to teach her class. She insisted. He was furious that she would take such a physical risk, and went to class with her, sitting in the back of the room, certain that she would not make it through the three-hour seminar without collapsing. But she did make it that day, and many others. She called on every ounce of the tenacity and discipline she had accumulated over a lifetime of hard work. A few close friends remembered visits to her home when they would hear her in another room, talking to herself, psyching herself up to go on. "Come on, Barbara," she would say. "Get going, move . . . push . . . don't stop now. . . ." And then she would appear and smile and be ready for whatever the day offered. "She just never wanted to have to explain any of it, or have people feel sorry for her," a close friend said. Aside from a few very intimate friends and the physicians and therapists who worked with her, no one ever knew how physically debilitated Jordan was. It was a matter of intense pride for her to keep going.

Even though she had no intention of ever revealing anything about her disabilities during her lifetime, she realized that her full story could never be told without some understanding of the difficulties she had encountered. When she knew that her death might be only a few months away, she pointed to the folder of medical records that her physician and friend Dr. Rambie Briggs was holding and told him, with a smile on her face, "Well, you won't have to keep all that a secret much longer." Indeed, Briggs believed that "Barbara wanted people to know just how hard it had been for her."[9]

For all of her stoicism, Barbara Jordan was no martyr, and certainly no saint. In her early years, she was ambitious to a fault, single-mindedly driven to advance her political career at almost any cost. She was drawn by a need to be where the political action was, more than by causes or idealism. She had a tendency to put aside old friends as she moved on, and they learned that once out of her sight, they were quickly out of her mind. Easily bored, she could be stubborn, impatient, mocking, and sarcastic. Because she made no effort to hide these attributes, Jordan had her share of public detractors. Most of them complained that she was too much of a deal-maker, that she never did anything important in the Texas Senate or in the U.S. Congress, that she was cold and calculating, that she put herself first, before causes, issues, or personal loyalties. Was any of this true? Was this the Barbara Jordan loved and admired by millions of Americans?

Believing that Jordan was human and flawed as well as human and magnificent compelled me to try to understand her life. I was fascinated with her story: ghetto girl rises above it all, moves in powerful political circles, gives up a promising career, inspires the American people, and becomes a public hero. Yet I let years go by without ever asking her the questions that came to fill my mind.

I had watched Jordan from afar in the 1960s in Texas. My husband was a journalist who handled communications for the Texas AFL-CIO, and Jordan was organized labor's star. I would see her at receptions and meetings, and while she knew and got along with my husband, I was just "Mrs. Rogers," a spectator at the gatherings who was juggling work, young children, and my own volunteer interest in politics. Later I worked more closely with her when she became Governor Ann Richards's counsel on ethics and I was the governor's chief of staff. And still later, when I began to teach at the LBJ School of Public Affairs, Jordan welcomed me warmly because she was happy to have another "practitioner" join her in the often stuffy and stifling world of academe. But even though she was exceptionally kind to me and invited me to be a guest in her home, Jordan was not an easy person to know. I felt I came to know her better through my research than I had in real life, and I was consoled somewhat by the realization that even people who claimed to know her well really did not know her deeply.

Nevertheless, having the opportunity to know her at the end of her life helped me to understand just what she had to deal with, and just how much she had given up. I remember the jolt of surprise I felt one time when I put my hand on her shoulder and felt delicate bones instead of the fleshy pad of skin or muscle I expected. And her hands—how they changed over time. When she was a young woman, Barbara's hands were enormous and noticeable, with long tapered fingers, slender and delicate in contrast to her commanding size and presence. As the multiple sclerosis progressed, her fingers began to arch and close. When you shook her hand, if you dared, it was not a palm-to-palm shake. Rather, you clasped her fingers and withdrew your hand quickly, lest you hurt her surprisingly fragile hands, a reminder of human mortality—hers, and your own.

But what had it really been like for this magnificent speaker, this defender of our Constitution? What shaped her? How important were her achievements? How did she integrate her flaws and frailties into her strength and integrity? How did she become a moral hero, a woman of character? Who was this black star, this beacon for the light of democracy?

These were the questions I wanted to answer as I sorted through thousands of news clippings, hundreds of her speeches, the four hundred boxes of papers from her congressional years that she gave to Texas Southern University, the once all-black college that had been her alma mater. I read again and again the most complete set of interviews she ever gave, to the novelist Shelby Hearon, her coauthor for *Self-Portrait*. I talked and listened to people who knew and loved her, and to some who knew and didn't love her. I worked to come to terms with this remarkable woman who survived the complexities of public life and the realities of racial politics, turning away from them both with surprising contentment. And, of course, as a white woman, I had to come to terms with her blackness, with what it meant to her—and to me.

Any white biographer who tries to peer into the life of a prominent black person must ask this question: Can I cross the color line and understand what the life of this individual was really like? I wrestled with the question because I knew that no matter how many causes, friends, or political affinities we shared, Jordan and I were shaped by totally different experiences. The reality of skin color in American life is central to perception and purpose. How can we understand the experiences of the "other"? Could I push through the barrier that American culture and law have shaped from mere human physical *difference*? Sometimes I felt the answer was yes, sometimes it was no. I finally settled the dilemma by asking myself: What would Barbara say? Would she think a white woman could understand the life of a black woman? Did she believe that black and white Americans could ever hope to know each other? And I could almost hear her bell-like voice answer, *"Ab-so-lute-ly!"* I could imagine her impish smile when she added a challenge: "Try it." For that was the reigning belief of her life—that we have to get over the notion of "otherness" and come to the point of "togetherness." That was her view of America—one people, diverse but bound by a common belief in the Constitution and the ideal of America. One community. *E pluribus unum.*

The last time millions of Americans got a glimpse of Barbara Jordan on prime-time television was at another Democratic convention. In 1992 she gave a keynote address again, and once more a Democratic president emerged—Bill Clinton. Near the end of her address to the 1992 Democratic convention, Jordan spoke of the need for an "ethic of love" in public life, and as the applause began, her voice kept repeating the words "love . . . love . . . love. . . ." What did she mean by "love" in the hurly-burly of public life? Soft, sentimental statements rarely sprang from her steel-trap mind. Was this an exception? Or had Barbara Jordan locked into some deep strain of public hope that still abides in the hearts of Americans of goodwill? What did she know that had the power to move us so? That is what I wanted to learn.

I believe Barbara Jordan's story reflects both the American dream and a fundamental human hope for a sense of community. She lived an interesting life in interesting times. She enjoyed her life, and we enjoyed her presence and performance. Nevertheless, Jordan's life was full of lessons learned through hardship—the hardships of racial discrimination, economic and educational deprivation, political disappointment, personal loss, and physical illness. If we understand her lessons, then we will know that the making of an American hero is a rare—and wondrous—event.

PART I

In the long way that we take, in our growing up, in the
vicissitudes of life by which we are led into its meaning and
its mystery, there are established for us, for each one of us,
certain landmarks. They represent discoveries sometimes
symbolizing the moment when we became aware of the
purpose of our lives; they may establish for us our membership in the human frailty; they may be certain words that
were spoken into a stillness within us, the sound thereof
singing forever through all the corridors of our being as
landmarks; yes, each one of us has his own. No communication between people is possible if there is not some mutual recognition of the landmarks. There are no reverences
that bind us together as people that can be meaningful if
the landmarks are profaned. To understand a man is not
merely to know his name and the number of his thoughts,
to be acquainted with how he acts or what he does. To
know a man is to know, somewhat, of his landmarks. For
these are his points of referral that stand out beyond and
above all the traffic of his life, advising and tutoring him in
his journey through life and beyond. In the language of
religion, these are the places where the Eternal has been
caught and held for a swirling moment in times and years.
Think twice before you move your neighbor's landmarks.

—HOWARD THURMAN,
FOR THE INWARD JOURNEY

CHAPTER 1

COLOR

BARBARA CHARLINE JORDAN was born February 21, 1936, the third daughter and last child of Benjamin Meredith and Arlyne Patten Jordan. The fortunes of Ben and Arlyne were good enough to pay Dr. Thelma Patten, a relative of Arlyne's father, John Ed, to deliver the baby at home instead of in Houston's charity hospital, where the first two Jordan girls had been born. Ben Jordan saw his daughter almost immediately after the delivery, and his first comment was, "Why is she so dark?"[1]

From that moment, skin and body—color, hue, texture, size, condition—began to determine who Barbara Jordan was and how she reacted to her life. She learned quite early that the degree of blackness for a black child mattered. It mattered to her father, and it mattered in the white world, which would be beyond her imagination until she was almost an adult. It also mattered in the black world, her world, the Fifth Ward of Houston, Texas, and would hit her with full force when she was in the all-black Phillis Wheatley High School in the early 1950s. There, her color, her size, her hair texture, and her features would determine and limit her choices. "Color-struck" teachers favored light-skinned students, who were given the honors and awards, the opportunities for college and jobs. They even escaped the harshness of encounters with the white law. A common saying in the African American neighborhoods was, "The lighter the skin, the lighter the sentence."[2]

By the time she was a teenager in the early 1950s, Barbara Jordan had been confronted by all of America's negative messages about skin color: pitch-black, charcoal, cocoa, bronze, copper, chestnut, mahogany, smoke, milky brown, high yellow—so many shades and variations, but one consistent message. "The world had decided that we were all Negro, but that some of us were more Negro than others," Jordan remembered. "The whole system . . . was saying to us that you achieved more, you went further, you had a better chance, you got the awards, if you were not black-black with kinky hair. Black was bad and you didn't want to be black, and so the message we were getting was that you were really in tough shape and it was too bad that you were so unfortunate that your skin was totally black and there was no light there anywhere."[3] It was a particularly tough message to get from your own father.

Barbara looked like her father's father, Charles Jordan, who was dark and strong-featured, with a ridge of bone over his eyes that gave him the appearance of stubborn strength. Ben Jordan did not resemble his father. He had lighter skin and the finer features of his mother, Mary. Tall, handsome, of medium color, and imbued with the pride of a Tuskegee man, Ben Jordan wanted his daughters to represent his success and God's glory. In the African American community in the 1930s, light skin and delicate features were the visible marks that divided the educated from the ignorant, the well-off from the poor, the attractive from the plain.[4] Black was not beautiful. It was a burden. For a girl-child, the degree of melanin pigmentation in her skin and the turn of her features mattered. The shape of her nose or the texture of her hair determined acceptance, opportunity, and status. Ben Jordan knew all of that, and he knew he would have to demand much more of his new baby girl to compensate for her blackness. Mind, will, discipline, work, achievement—those attributes would be the hope, and the challenge, for this child.

The pain of being a dark-skinned female goes back to slavery and intensified with Reconstruction. The preferential treatment of lighter-skinned, mixed-race African Americans by whites had "laid the groundwork for a pattern of color classism in black America."[5] It was the lighter-skinned African Americans who had the first opportunities for education and the benefits of freedom in post-Reconstruction America. Certain churches, neighborhoods, colleges, sororities and fraternities, social clubs, even political clubs, harbored a light-colored elite. At one time African Americans had their own "Blue Vein Society"; admission to this Nashville group depended on skin color. An applicant had to be fair enough for the spidery network of purplish veins at the wrist to be visible to a panel of expert judges.[6]

The separate social and educational paths taken by light-skinned and dark-skinned African Americans during Reconstruction divided their world. By the turn of the century, the light-skinned mulattos were the intellectual and political leaders. They were the doctors, lawyers, teachers, writers, and entertainers, admired and emulated by the rest.

The prevalence of skin prejudice began to weaken after the Harlem Renaissance of the 1920s, and all but disappeared in the African American community with the resurgence of black pride in the 1960s and 1970s. But even before black pride, before "Black is beautiful," before "I am somebody," Barbara Jordan got comfortable with herself. By the time she was in the third grade, in 1944, she knew in her guts that she was somebody special. It did not matter to her how black she was. If someone didn't like her because of her color, she just thought, "Well, those are stupid people, and I don't have time to deal with them."[7] Quite early, she had the self-confidence to transcend the limits of her body, whether imposed by color, culture, physical capability—or stupidity! It was a pattern of being and behavior that stayed with her until the day she died. To all who thought that black was not as good as white, her retort was, "That's a colossal *lie!*"

All of her life, she was determined to discredit the naysayers, the people for whom color determined quality or human worth, "the people who thought you were inferior . . . because you were born in certain economic conditions, because you're a certain race, because your hair is a certain texture—that because of that you are not as good as the person seated next to you with blond hair and blue eyes." Quite early, she adopted a belief, with all of the considerable passion she could muster, in a fundamental human truth: "You've got to be able to love yourself—love yourself strongly, and not let anybody disabuse you of your self-respect." When anyone, black or white, challenged her—or even really looked at her—they knew it was true. She had worked very hard, however, to create this deep reservoir of self-respect and belief in herself.

She often quoted the former slave Frederick Douglass, who taught himself to read and write and who decided that education was the key to his success. "Education unfits a man to be a slave," he said.[8] Jordan would tell her audiences, "If you want to be free . . . free in your heart, free in your mind, free in your movement—free!—that means get something in your head."[9] And that was always her driving force—to get something in her head in order to be free.

The character, certainty, and command at the core of Barbara Jordan, the powerful woman whose voice could move men and women to tears, insight, inspiration, or action, came from that blackness and from her acceptance of it. She took pride in her own inner power. "The greatest motivation . . . has to come from inside you. . . . If you don't think very much of yourself then you are not going to succeed."

The person who taught her to be proud of herself, to be proud of her blackness, was not her father, Ben Jordan, or his father, the dark-skinned Charles Jordan, but her maternal grandfather, John Ed Patten. Her relationship with this old man, and with all of his problems, taught her to be free within herself, even within the confines of her segregated, color-constrained world in Houston, Texas.

"Grandpa didn't want me to be like the other kids. . . . He would say this very directly. There were kids who lived just behind my grandfather's house . . . that he did not want me to associate with," she said. John Ed Patten told her, " 'You just trot your own horse and don't get into the same rut as everyone else.'" She always believed that Grandpa Patten considered himself "quite different, just a little cut above the ordinary man, black or white. That was continually driven into me in those years: Look, this man can make it, my grandfather. He can put together whatever combination of things necessary and just kind of make it."

Knowing John Ed Patten is essential to understanding Barbara Jordan, but his story is so rooted in and covered up by the troubles of the past that we can glimpse only snatches. It begins, of course, with the enslavement of African Americans in the South. Slavery, war, freedom, Reconstruction, Jim Crow, and all of the political struggles that flowed from these events shaped Jordan's Grandpa Patten—and through him, her.

Barbara Jordan knew little of her Grandpa Patten's story, except that it combined hope and failure, triumph and tragedy. It certainly shaped, however, her view of black history in general. In 1981 she told the Urban League: "History may have consigned to blacks race as an unending negative which will support failure and oppression. That does not have to be the case. Blacks can reject history's negatives and call upon the strengths endemic to us and make America work for *us*." And then she asked, "But is it possible?"[10]

Barbara Jordan's life was her answer to her own question. Did America work for her? Did she reject history's negatives? Could she transcend race as an unending negative? Her personal answer was a resounding *yes*! Her patriot's belief in the American Dream was grounded in *e pluribus unum*. "We are diverse, and yet we can be one," she believed. "Each person must be willing to tolerate the other person in their differences and in their inner souls."[11]

Barbara Jordan's path to her inner soul—and to America's—was laid for her before she was born. We see her first "landmark" in 1891, forty-five years before her birth—appropriately, in the legislative chambers of the state Capitol Building in Austin, Texas. There, a script unfolds that Barbara Charline Jordan would star in, win acclaim for, and complete. There, her personal story begins.

CHAPTER 2

THE ANCESTORS

ON FEBRUARY 20, 1891, State Representative Edward A. Patton of Evergreen, deep in east Texas, rose to make his maiden speech in the Texas legislature. He was the only black man among the 150 members, and a Republican, one of the despised holdovers from what whites called the "nigger party" of the radical reconstruction of the southern states after the Civil War.[1]

Edward Patton was able to summon his courage to speak on this day to members of the twenty-second Texas legislature because his very right to be there was under siege. The issue was the disfranchisement of some 40 percent of the Texas electorate—eighty thousand black voters as well as ninety thousand poor white tenant farmers. Up for a vote was a proposed amendment to the Texas Constitution to institute a poll tax: citizens would have to pay a fee to vote in Texas. The poll tax was the most serious volley in the systematic legal war to reverse the gains made by African Americans since the Civil War. The end of Reconstruction and the gradual withdrawal of federal troops from Texas beginning in 1871 had started the restoration of the Democratic Party, and the only obstacles to its completion were the thousands of black voters who could tip the balance of power in key elections.[2] The resurgent Southern Democracy (as the Democratic Party was called) intended to strip African Americans of the right to vote.

For the Texas Democracy, the issue was power as well as race. If Negroes could be stopped from voting, white Democrats could regain public office and the political patronage they had lost. It was particularly important to recapture the sixteen east Texas counties where black voters outnumbered whites. In these "black belt" counties adjacent to the border of Louisiana, African American voters had elected their own to be sheriffs and tax assessors. Blacks held all of the government posts in Walker County in 1872, and African Americans in Marion County that same year held three of the five county commissioners' seats. By 1880 Fort Bend County had a black majority in public office, as did Gregg County by 1885. Most of the African American officeholders were Republicans, and a few were Populists.

The state's anti-Republican, anti-Populist newspapers complained incessantly of the corruption of African American voters and officeholders. Some defined corruption as the mere presence of blacks in public office, or even as participants in elections at all.[3] One Houston newspaper editorial asked the question that shaped many of the arguments for white supremacy: "Must the low, groveling, equal-before-the-law, lazy, purchasable negro, who pays no taxes, have the privilege of neutralizing the vote of a good citizen and taxpayer?"[4] Inflamed by such rhetoric, white leaders of the Texas Democracy did not wait for legal segregation or black voter disfranchisement before acting to restore their pre–Civil War authority. To dilute the impact of black voters, they tried various reapportionment schemes, combining predominantly black counties with larger white counties, a form of racial gerrymandering that would be perfected years later. Reapportionment, however, could not entirely erase the impact of so many African American voters. Moreover, in statewide elections the Greenback Party, the Populists, and other groups courted the black vote and promoted fusion efforts with the Republicans to keep the Democrats out of power.

Edward Patton had been elected state representative from San Jacinto County in November 1890. None of the other African Americans who ran for the legislature from east Texas, or anywhere in the state that year, had been as lucky. By 1890 groups like the White Man's Union, the Citizens White Primary, and the Jaybird Democratic Association had engaged in a series of planned acts of intimidation, including the infamous "night rides," which involved abductions, beatings, even murder. Many blacks were forced to leave their homes, accused of "obnoxious conduct"—often defined as too much interest in politics. The "K.K. Resurectionists [sic]" in Kaufman County in 1885 "advised" several politically active African Americans to leave the county or suffer the consequences. In Red River County, a group called the "white caps" publicly whipped several Negroes and ran them out of the county. In some parts of Titus County, which had a large black population, newspapers reported that the intimidation had worked so well in some areas that "not a Negro man, woman or child remains."[5] Black participation in Texas elections declined in direct proportion to the level and nature of such intimidation.

Even white Republican leaders, seeking voter legitimacy after they had lost control of the Texas legislature in 1874, were determined to shed the label of "nigger party." By 1890 a Republican "lily-white" faction had broken "Negro power" within the party hierarchy.[6] Black politicians had once controlled the party machinery and dispensed federal patronage in Texas, but now not a single African American held party office. One Grimes County Democratic candidate put the popular sentiment into verse:

> 'Twas nature's laws that drew the lines
> Between the Anglo-Saxon and African races,
> And we, the Anglo-Saxons of Grand Old Grimes,
> Must force the African to keep his place.[7]

By the 1890s, ascendant southern politicians had forced three themes into public consciousness, not only in the South but in the North as well: (1) white superiority versus black inferiority; (2) white moral purity versus black moral impurity; and (3) the need to keep the races separate.[8] These themes formed an ideology that was used to justify everything from lynchings to legislation. The poll tax strategy, a legal means to "force the African to keep his place," was perhaps the single most effective tactic to fulfill this ideology. After it was first proposed in Texas in 1874, a coalition of Republican and Populist-leaning legislators had managed to block the poll tax. By 1891, however, power had shifted. Democrats had gained enough strength to win the governor's office, and Republicans were in disarray. Populists, strong only in a few areas, were beginning to be divided by the race issue themselves.

Thirty-two-year-old Ed Patton, a farmer and a teacher, felt he must speak to members of the Texas legislature that day in February.[9] Yet he was restrained. He recognized his position of weakness in this body of lawmakers. He saw clearly that his moral outrage would not be an effective tool to block the poll tax. He wanted to persuade his fellow members on the basis of reason, their reason, by pointing out that they would harm their own people in an effort to prevent blacks from voting.

The *Galveston Daily News* reported that Ed Patton "appealed to the house in a manly way against all measures calculated to create and nourish race prejudices in the state. He held that it would disfranchise many whites and that the white property holders, having the power, the wealth and the intelligence, should not disfranchise the young and poor white men through race prejudice."[10] The argument that white voters would be harmed as well as blacks convinced enough lawmakers that day to withhold their votes from the measure. Although the poll tax amendment received a majority of House votes, it fell fifteen votes short of the two-thirds approval needed to go on the ballot for voter approval to amend the Texas Constitution. Representative Ed Patton had won the day.

Because of the efforts of Ed Patton, and others, it would be twelve years (1903) before the poll tax became Texas law. Meanwhile, the night riders continued their campaign of intimidation and terror. Each year, fewer

African Americans made it out to vote on Election Day. The fear finally reached into Patton's district just north of Houston, the "piney woods" forest counties of Polk and San Jacinto. When Ed Patton ran for reelection in 1892, he was defeated. Insult and injury were added to his ignominy when the sheriff of San Jacinto County took a shot at him. Even though he was not wounded, Ed Patton did what thousands of other blacks were starting to do. He left. He fled for his life, leaving a wife and two sons behind. Ed Patton was virtually forgotten, as were most of the thirty-seven African American Reconstructionists who served in the Texas legislature from 1870 to 1898. When one of Ed Patton's sons was grown and living in Houston, all he could tell his grandchildren about his own father was that he left Texas to go to Washington, D.C., to be a lawyer. But no one ever knew for sure.

Edward A. Patton was one of the last Reconstruction African Americans to hold public office in Texas and to serve in the Texas legislature. It would take the modern civil rights movement, the passage of the Civil Rights Act of 1964 and the Voting Rights Act of 1965, plus numerous court cases to end the poll tax and racial gerrymandering, to make it possible for African Americans to be elected to public office in Texas again. Seventy-five years after Ed Patton had been run out of Texas, the old Texas Democracy finally began to crack. Because of federal court–ordered reapportionment in 1966, African American voters in Dallas were able to elect a black state representative for the first time. In the same election, Houston's heavy concentration of African American voters sent not only a black state representative to Austin but a black *female* state senator as well—the first in Texas history. Her name was Barbara Charline Jordan, and although she never knew it, she was Edward A. Patton's great-granddaughter.

GRANDPA PATTEN AND THE EARLY HISTORY OF HOUSTON

It would not have been unusual for a black child growing up in a segregated city neighborhood in the South to know little or nothing about her ancestors—even those who might have been famous in their day. And Barbara Jordan knew nothing about Edward A. Patton, her maternal great-grandfather. In the 1930s and 1940s, when Jordan grew up in Texas, tales of sorrow and slavery, separation and abandonment, were still too fresh or humiliating to take on mythic or symbolic importance. Many families did not dwell on the painful stories of the past, with the result that their children often grew up with little more than vague images of suffering brought down on their slave ancestors by beatings, family separations, or the shame of sexual exploitation.[11]

The period immediately after the end of the Civil War was even more difficult to explain because southern slave expectations of freedom and emancipation clashed with brutal economic and political realities. Emancipation had transformed the economic life of African Americans from one of bond slavery to a form of peonage. If they stayed on the land, they became tenant farmers and deeply indebted to the landowners. If they moved to the cities, they worked at "slave wages," when they could find work. The homes of most former slaves, rural or urban, were shanties, with sometimes only a shed serving as a kitchen, and an outhouse for a bathroom. Starvation was always a possibility.[12]

Stripped of voting rights and terrorized by night riders and other vigilantes, many African Americans were soon dispirited because freedom had not lived up to its promise. The lack of progress was internalized as guilt or shame for some, as if they could or should be doing something to improve their own condition. But what? Oppressed peoples do not always place the blame for their condition "squarely on the doorsteps of the oppressor."[13] People often blame themselves, or God, for their suffering and hardships. So, for many families, some of the stories from the past remained untold. It was best to focus on the future, and the opportunities that were bound to come. That was the case with the Texas descendants of Edward Patton. His son John Edward knew little about his own father. Or perhaps he did not tell all he knew to his favorite granddaughter, Barbara Charline. He told her only that his father was *somebody*—somebody important, a Washington, D.C., lawyer, as if that made up for growing up without him. Barbara Jordan said her grandfather was "very proud of his family, and he would talk about his father, who was a lawyer in Washington, and I didn't know about that, what that meant, but it just sounded fine."

John Ed Patten grew up in the all-black former slave community of Evergreen in San Jacinto County, sixty-five miles north of Houston.[14] By the time his father, the legislator, had left Evergreen, fewer than one hundred former slaves or their descendants remained. John Ed believed that his father had gone to Washington, D.C., to become a lawyer. And Edward A. Patton did indeed go to Washington, where he was registered in the census of 1900. He may have worked for the federal government, as one Texas historian believed, but there is no record of him as a licensed attorney, although his legislative experience in Texas could certainly have qualified him to "read" for the bar.[15] Edward Patton had a wife with him in Washington, and it was not John Ed's mother, who had remained in Evergreen. Census records reveal that Edward Patton and a woman named Ruth lived on Cleveland Place, with two children. His other wife, the young woman who was John Ed's mother, was left behind, with her two boys. Soon she was involved with the demands of family—a new husband and a quick succession of six more children, including a set of twins. The circumstances of her abandonment by one of the leaders of the black political community in Texas were never fully revealed. But she did raise John Ed to believe that his father was a man of distinction. And it was that belief that sustained John Edward as he made his way from Evergreen to Houston.

In its first decades, Houston grew as a commercial and marketing center that supported the plantation agriculture in the area—cotton, sugarcane, and timber. By 1860 there were hundreds of slaves in Houston proper, and the metropolitan area was about half black.[16] Many slaves hired out as day laborers, paying their owners the larger portion of their wages but keeping enough money to live independently in the city. Black laborers worked in the sawmills and in the new rail yards, while both men and women hired out as gardeners and domestics for the growing number of white households. There was even a small colony of free blacks, Freedman's Town, along Buffalo Bayou, although the city's white leaders had made it illegal for free blacks to enter the city after 1839.[17] Laxly enforced, the law did not prevent the growth of a relatively free African American community. Even slaves operated with a degree of freedom in Houston unheard of on the east Texas plantations. One visitor to Houston in 1849 reported seeing a number of well-dressed blacks, some using their owners' carriages for pleasure.[18]

Within weeks of the end of the Civil War, hundreds of liberated slaves began moving into Houston to look for work. The newly freed slaves came mostly on foot, bearing heavy burdens of clothing and other belongings on their heads. They were weary, hungry, homeless, and jobless. Still they came. Although no reliable numbers exist, the influx of former slaves increased the African American population of Houston to almost 40 percent of all residents in the 1870 census. The federal Freedman's Bureau set up shop in Houston in 1865 to address the former slaves' most immediate needs for food and housing, but most of them had to figure out how to find work and survive on their own in the years immediately after the war. Most former slaves continued doing much of the same kinds of work they had done before and during the war: domestic work, or the menial labor of cleaning the rail yards and loading and unloading cargo from the freight trains, as well as from boats along the docks of the Trinity River.

Because of restrictions on suffrage for former Confederate soldiers, African American voters actually outnumbered white voters in Houston by 1870. The black leader Richard Allen was elected street commissioner in 1878, and soon thereafter, black laborers could find construction jobs; they built the first major streets, roads, and bridges in Houston. The first federal jobs were opening up as well. Houston's U.S. post office hired African Americans who could read and write. Some also found jobs with the railroads, primarily Southern Pacific and Missouri Pacific.

Republicans who controlled Texas state government appointed a Republican mayor of Houston in 1869, Thomas H. Scanlan. They also named several black members to the city council. The victory of Democrats at the polls in 1874, however, ended both Republican and African American influence in Houston's municipal government.

When John Ed Patten came to Houston, shortly after the turn of the century, the city had already outgrown its original five-mile township site, which had been divided into five pie-shaped voting wards or districts, with the downtown corner of Main and Congress as the keystone. The voting districts were abolished when the city went to a commission form of government in 1906, but the cultural boundaries of the wards and their well-defined neighborhoods remained. Although African Americans originally lived throughout the city, most were concentrated in the Third Ward, to the south and east of downtown, and in the neighborhoods on the fringe of the Fourth Ward, west of downtown. The Fifth Ward, which eventually housed most of the city's African American population, was virtually cut off from the city, connected only by an iron drawbridge over Buffalo Bayou until the Elysian Viaduct was built in 1955.

Houston's black citizens were, for all practical purposes, politically disfranchised by the early 1900s. The use of the poll tax for the first time in 1903 cut off most African American voting, as did the racial gerrymandering of election districts and the imposition of literacy and property requirements for voting. When the U.S. Supreme Court in 1896 abrogated the intent of the Fourteenth Amendment by declaring in *Plessy v. Ferguson* that "separate-but-equal" facilities for blacks and whites did not violate the Constitution, southern states were free to enact laws that kept the races separate, creating a dual system of public and private facilities. By 1907 new Texas laws, as well as Houston city ordinances, had resulted in segregated hotels, restaurants, theaters, and other public facilities. In 1913 railroad officials for the first time created segregated waiting rooms at the city's train station, and in Houston's city hall blacks could not drink from water fountains designated for whites.

As poor, white east Texas sharecroppers poured into Houston after 1910 because the farm economy could no longer support them, the black percentage of the population began to fall. Nevertheless, the intensity of white hatred for blacks began to rise. The Jim Crow segregation laws allowed race to dominate class, and the constant reinforcement of the white superiority/black inferiority theme through the newspapers, the clubs, the schools, and the pulpits allowed the poorest whites to believe they were superior to the most well-off blacks. Newspapers regularly used the term "nigger," and news stories compared black men to apes. Articles emphasized "white" as a synonym for purity and innocence and "black" as a synonym for wickedness and death.[19]

It was in this atmosphere of restriction, racism, and retrenchment that John Ed Patten came to Houston. Yet while the new segregation laws cut African Americans off from white social, political, and economic activity in the city, they inadvertently spurred the creation of a new economic and cultural life for the growing black community. John Ed Patten found black-owned and -operated beer halls, funeral parlors, pawnshops, barbecue stands, and beauty and barber shops. And there were churches everywhere.

While there had been some all-black churches prior to emancipation, the freedom to worship without the interference of whites created a passionate outpouring of religious activity in the 1870s. Most of the new congregations were Baptist and Methodist, the two most active Protestant denominations in the South. The church was the only institution after the Civil War that could be totally black-controlled, not dependent for survival on anything or anyone from the white world. The churches were not only centers of worship and inspiration but social centers, informal places of learning, even health clinics and food pantries when people needed help. In Houston's Third and Fourth Wards, churches quickly became the focal point of community life.

Professional and social clubs also began to develop. After the 1870s, African American Masonic orders flourished, and the Grand United Order of Odd Fellows occupied an impressive building in the Third Ward. There were "Married Ladies" societies, drama and arts groups, and civic associations that focused on community betterment projects. The Art and Charity Club had teas for prominent visitors and in 1911 entertained Mrs. Booker T. Washington. There were businessmen's associations and at least two African American newspapers. Small businesses that provided services to the isolated black population flourished, as did the small number of doctors and lawyers. No Houston hospital, however, would allow an African American doctor to treat patients until the first black hospital opened in 1910.[20] Lawyers were limited to performing notary public services or writing briefs for white attorneys.[21] Houston's African Americans could not use the white public library and had no access to books until an African American civic association obtained a Carnegie grant to open its own library in 1907. The Colored High School opened in 1893, but by the early 1920s it had room for only five hundred students when more than one thousand wanted to enroll. The Houston School District was forced to take on a massive building program to add two new high schools and increase the number of all-black elementary schools to sixteen.[22]

The new schools, churches, libraries, hospitals, and civic clubs represented the aspirations of the leaders of the African American community, the people who had been lucky enough in the days after emancipation to get an education, start a business, or hold a family together. But there was another world in African American neighborhoods—a freewheeling nightlife, with jazz clubs, liquor stores, cheap wine, all-night bars, illicit gambling parlors, and readily available prostitutes. It had enormous appeal, for here there could be freedom from everything! White rules, white laws, and white sanctions rarely applied. Houston's white police generally looked the other way when they saw petty crime, drunkenness, even knifings or shootings in

African American neighborhoods—as long as it was black against black crime and did not threaten to spill over into white neighborhoods.

By the turn of the century, two distinct cultures began to emerge within Houston's African American community: one was built on church-going, education, and respectability, and the other on escape and immediate pleasure. Music, dancing, drinking, and having fun became a way to escape from the daily grind of poverty, to shut out the constant bombardment of contempt from the white world. For many, however, the night culture was both easygoing and going nowhere, for it trapped men and women in the addictive grip of alcoholism, overlaying a new despair on poverty and discrimination.

Newly arrived in Houston, John Ed Patten, resourceful, smart, and ambitious, initially chose the world of respectability and work. Early on he met and married Martha Ann Fletcher, and their first child, born in 1909, was a daughter, Arlyne, who would become Barbara Jordan's mother; then there was another daughter, Johnnie; and finally an adored baby boy, Ed. John Ed and Martha Patten rented a frame house in a Fourth Ward segregated neighborhood. Martha turned their front yard into a garden with collards, turnip greens, marigolds, and zinnias. To earn a living, John Ed Patten first tried preaching but soon soured on church life and began a variety of business ventures.

Barbara Jordan said that while some people thought Grandpa Patten was eccentric, she thought he had a pure streak of independence. "He never wanted a boss, as he always wanted to be his own boss," she said. As a result, John Ed Patten "went through several business ventures." At one time, he owned a café on West Dallas Street in the Fourth Ward. According to his daughter Arlyne, Patten let people buy meals on credit, and "the folks just ripped him off . . . and he never got paid."[23] Later he opened a confectionery store on San Felipe Street, selling cookies and candy to neighborhood residents. All was fine for a while, but both political and personal troubles would intervene in John Ed Patten's life. The issue of race was at their center.

In 1917, during World War I, a northern unit of black soldiers was sent to Camp Logan in west Houston to provide security for army property. The northern soldiers were unaccustomed to Houston's rigid racial segregation, enforced by an all-white police force, and the Houstonians were unaccustomed to African Americans in uniform who exercised any kind of authority. One sultry August evening, two white police officers raided a dice game in which all of the participants were black. In the ensuing melee, they beat up a black soldier and were taking him and a woman to jail when a black military police colonel protested that military law, not the Houston police, had jurisdiction over the soldier. That argument made no difference to the white officers, who struck the black colonel and whisked him off to jail, too. Rumors spread that the black officer had been killed. Within a few hours, more than one hundred black soldiers, determined to get revenge, broke into the Camp Logan armory. They armed themselves with Springfield rifles, shotguns, pistols, and machine guns and marched into downtown Houston toward the police station. Houston police, in the meantime, had set up a barricade outside the station where they awaited the soldiers. When the black soldiers arrived, a gun battle raged for several hours, and one thousand white U.S. Army troops were brought in to bring the siege to a halt. The city of Houston was placed under martial law the next day.[24] Police conducted a house-to-house search of black neighborhoods to confiscate all firearms owned by African Americans.[25]

White and black accounts of the midnight gun battle differed. There were casualties, both civilian and military. More than one hundred black soldiers were court-martialed in the largest military trial in American history. Thirteen black soldiers were hanged after an exceptionally speedy trial, which one observer called a "legal lynching."[26] Dozens of others were imprisoned. The Houston violence was the largest race riot in American history and was a forerunner of riots in Chicago and Detroit the following year. Everywhere black soldiers were returning from World War I with heightened expectations of greater equality. Conditions in the South, however, had changed little since Jim Crow replaced Reconstruction as the law of the land.

Houstonians reacted to the 1917 military riot with fear, panic, anger, and a determination to make sure hometown blacks didn't get any rebellious ideas from the northern soldiers. A new mood of resentment and repression took hold. Houston's police took so many "preemptive" actions against blacks that a pattern of harassment became entrenched and would not finally be dislodged until the mid-1980s with the appointment of a black police chief.[27] Houston's most respected citizens began calling for a more rigid system of housing and work segregation of the races.[28] As a result, all new residential developments throughout the city were off-limits for blacks. Because African Americans could not expand out of their existing neighborhoods in the Third and Fourth Wards, newcomers were increasingly forced to settle in the Fifth Ward, which had no paved streets or public water supply. In the Fifth Ward, white developers built and rented out block after block of "shotgun" houses, so named because you could fire a shotgun through the front door and hit everything in the house. The houses were about sixteen feet wide and five feet apart, with a center door and small porch. Sometimes two or three generations of a family would crowd into one house.

To enforce the new segregation decrees, the Houston police were helped by the first chapter of the Ku Klux Klan in Texas, organized in Houston in the early 1920s. In 1921 the Klan brutalized a black dentist, and four years later a Klan mob tarred and feathered a black doctor.[29]

THE PATTEN FAMILY IN TROUBLE

The whole system came crashing down on John Ed Patten in May 1918. On a warm spring night, Patten was closing up his candy store and clearing out his cash register at midnight when he was startled by a black man who rushed into the shop and grabbed the money he had counted out on the counter. Patten was outraged, got his gun from a storeroom, and ran into the street after the man, cursing, not sure what or how much had been stolen.[30] Patten chased the man into a late-night café but lost sight of him in the crowd. When he came back out on the street, he heard a voice shout, "Catch that nigger, he's got a gun." Patten realized he was the target of the voices as a pair of assailants started to chase him. Shots were exchanged, and Patten started running. At the end of the block, he crouched in the dark at the corner and looked back at his pursuers. To Patten's dismay, he saw that two white policemen were running toward him. Patten threw up his hands and surrendered, suffering a gunshot wound in the hand. One of the police officers was bleeding, apparently hit by bullets from Patten's gun.

John Ed Patten was taken into custody and indicted by a Houston grand jury for assault with intent to murder. He was brought to trial and defended by a court-appointed lawyer he had never seen before. Patten testified at his trial that he didn't know who was chasing him and that he was running for his life. "I do not remember shooting. . . . I was so excited when they shot my hand I don't know what I did," he told the court. One of the white police officers, who was hit by three of Patten's bullets, testified that "I shot only twice, and . . . this darky shot six times." His partner could not exactly corroborate his story, testifying that he did not know who had shot first. But the officer said of Patten and the chase, "He was a Negro, and I knew from my experience that I could not outrun one of them. I did not see who fired the first shot. . . . I fired two shots myself . . . and the darky was running."

Patten's defense lawyer called in a physician to testify that the bullet had entered Patten's hand through the palm. The lawyer argued that Patten must have had his hands up in a gesture of surrender, as he claimed. White business owners, who had shops along San Felipe near Patten's store, swore that Patten was a man of good character, never known to act violently. Yet Patten's lawyer forgot to call to the stand two eyewitnesses seated in the courtroom who could have backed up Patten's account of the incident. The presiding judge thought the evidence submitted was sufficient to convict Patten, and he instructed the all-white jury to return a guilty verdict. The jury duly complied. In the tense racial atmosphere after the Camp Logan riots, the presiding judge issued a ten-year penitentiary sentence for John Edward Patten.

Patten frantically tried to get his white attorney to protest his innocence and move for a reversal of the sentence, only to have the lawyer withdraw from the case. A black attorney, J. M. Gibson, came to Patten's assistance and feverishly worked around the clock to present a motion for a new trial the next day. White shopkeepers put up $5,000 bail to keep Patten out of jail until his appeal could be heard. Gibson's written appeal made the points that the judge had not charged the jury correctly, that the all-white jurors were racially biased, and that witnesses present in the courtroom had not been called. The state court in Austin affirmed the original decision, however, and John Ed Patten went to the Huntsville State Penitentiary in February 1919.

Conditions for prisoners were barbarous there, with rats running freely through the cells and mess halls. Prisoners worked in the fields, shackled together by metal chokers attached to chains, and they were whipped by guards with bullwhips and blackjacks for the slightest infraction. Food was meager, and the men were so weak, they were always in danger of serious illness or death. John Ed Patten's only goal in prison was to survive. Survival was also the goal for his young family. Martha Fletcher Patten's life with her three children was almost as difficult as her husband's. Her baby boy, Ed, died of malnutrition while his father was in the Texas prison system. In 1925, six years into his term, life seemed at its bleakest for the Patten family. But luck and politics finally turned in John Ed Patten's favor.

One of Texas's most colorful governors, Jim Ferguson, had been impeached by the Texas legislature in 1917 on several charges, including misapplication of state funds, in what Ferguson charged was a "kangaroo" court of impeachment. Barred from running for office again, the popular Ferguson got his wife, Miriam, to run instead, and she was elected in 1925. The Fergusons were anti-prohibition and anti–Ku Klux Klan, and they were heroes to poor tenant farmers because they wanted to limit the rent paid to landlords. They supported tax increases on the wealthy to pay for new state services, such as the first mental hospitals, state aid to rural schools, and the creation of a state highway system. The state's establishment press hated the Fergusons and derisively dubbed them "Pa and Ma." But "Ma" was elected on her own to be governor for two different terms. During her first few months in office, she issued a record number of pardons, including many for black convicts.

John Ed Patten was among those released in 1925 on a full and unconditional pardon. He returned to Houston penniless. Reunited with Martha and his two daughters, he set up a salvage junk business, an appropriate symbol for the salvaging of his life and family in Houston's increasingly crowded African American neighborhoods. His family, however, was moving on beyond him. His oldest daughter, Arlyne, was beginning to make a name for herself in the Good Hope Missionary Baptist Church. By the time she graduated from the Fourth Ward's Booker T. Washington High School (the old Colored High School), she was an orator of some repute in the youth revivals and missionary meetings of the church. It was there she caught the eye of young Ben Jordan, a Tuskegee student whose father, Charles Jordan, was a deacon at Good Hope. Ben Jordan was clearly a catch for Arlyne. He was handsome, educated, respectable, and steeped in the religious culture and traditions of the venerable Good Hope Baptist Church. Yet Patten did everything he could to discourage the union when Ben Jordan proposed to Arlyne. Patten had come to loathe the pious pretensions of the Baptist churches, and he thought Arlyne was too talented to tie herself down within the strict respectability of a prominent Baptist family. But she wasn't going to listen to her father, the ex-convict. When she married Ben Jordan at the Good Hope Baptist Church, John Ed Patten stayed away, sulking in the confines of his fenced-in junkyard.

CHAPTER 3

THE COMMUNITY

BARBARA JORDAN WAS raised in a cocoon of respectability in the heart of Houston's Good Hope Missionary Baptist Church. It was home to her father, Ben Jordan, and to his father, Charles Jordan, who was chairman of the board of deacons. Ben's mother, Mary, was a missionary who traveled to small communities across Texas, giving her testimony and seeking to convert others to the Baptist version of Christian life.

Mary Jordan was drawn to the dream of Booker T. Washington and urged Ben to aspire to Tuskegee, the Alabama college founded by Washington. The Tuskegee dream was not one of academic or intellectual attainment; at that time the school put no emphasis on literature, the classics, history, or languages. Booker T. Washington had believed that such studies were foolish endeavors for the first and second generations of free African Americans. He believed, and Tuskegee taught, that the descendants of slaves should equip themselves with the specialized skills of low-level laborers and artisans, as well as basic reading and arithmetic. Washington wanted his students to internalize the white Protestant work ethic with an attitude of respect toward whites and a demeanor of respectability for themselves. "Uplift through enterprise" was one of Tuskegee's mottoes. Carpentry, animal husbandry, secretarial studies, and other vocational courses formed the curriculum. Washington also eschewed politics and discouraged African American participation, lest it arouse the ire of whites. The conservative moral atmosphere of the black Baptist churches reinforced a dream of limited aspiration. So Ben Jordan went to Tuskegee to learn an antiquated trade—blacksmithing—and to play football and become respectable. When his mother fell ill and could no longer work, there was not enough money to keep Ben in Tuskegee, and he returned to Houston, a year shy of his college degree.

Ben Jordan got a laborer's job at the Houston Terminal Warehouse and Cold Storage near the Southern Pacific rail yards. The enterprising young man soon began lending money to his coworkers, and the paybacks, with interest, allowed him to become a dapper dresser and striking figure, much admired by the young women at Good Hope. Ben sang in the Junior Male Quartet as well as the Senior Choir. When Mary Jordan died shortly after Ben returned home, he and his father took their death insurance benefit and made a down payment on a new two-bedroom brick house on Sharon Street in the Fifth Ward. Charles Jordan drove a truck for Southwestern Paper Company, and he would park the big red vehicle in his driveway, sit on the front porch, and visit with neighbors on the treelined street, which was paved—a rarity in Fifth Ward neighborhoods. Two years after he and Ben bought the house, Charles Jordan remarried and moved his bride, a prominent schoolteacher, into the house.

Alice Reed, Ben's new stepmother, was the daughter of Good Hope's senior pastor, H. C. Cashaw. Few individuals had their roots sunk deeper into the social soil of black Houston than a Good Hope preacher. Good Hope Missionary Baptist Church, founded in 1872, was one of Houston's first free African American churches. Its original members were the former slaves who had streamed into Houston from east Texas. Good Hope was such a force for stability in Houston's black community that it had only four pastors in its first hundred years of existence. The church held services in a number of buildings, one of them overlooking the 1917 Camp Logan riot scene. It was Alice's father, Reverend Cashaw, who managed to pull together enough resources during the 1930s depression to build Good Hope's first permanent home, a brick building in Houston's Fourth Ward.[1] H. C. Cashaw had become Good Hope's pastor in 1922, and he so valued and encouraged education as the key to advancement for members of the black community that his congregation began to develop a reputation as the "bourgeois" Baptist church. Good Hope attracted many college-educated residents of the Third, Fourth, and Fifth Wards, the teachers, physicians, postal workers, and small-business owners who formed Houston's black middle class. With her father's encouragement, Alice Cashaw Reed had become a high school English teacher, earning her master's degree from Prairie View College, the state's only black public college, about fifty miles northwest of Houston. She even had earned credits for a Ph.D. Alice had been married before and had a daughter, Mamie, who was away at school.

The domestic bliss of Charles and Alice Reed Jordan appealed to the younger Jordan, and only a year after his father and stepmother were married, Ben married Good Hope's star orator, Arlyne Patten. They, too, set up housekeeping in the Sharon Street house. Within a few years, Ben and

Arlyne added three baby girls to the household: Rose Mary, born in 1932; Bennie in 1934; and Barbara Charline, named for Ben's father, Charles, in 1936. Alice Reed Jordan quickly became "Grandmother Gar" to the girls, and Alice's daughter, Mamie Reed, became their idol. Aunt Mamie was a "beautiful, vibrant woman" who had gone to both the University of Iowa and Westminster Choir College in Princeton, after earning her degree from Prairie View College. She taught music in high school, and she spent the summers going to voice workshops at Columbia University, as well as the Fred Waring Clinic in Pennsylvania. The joining of the Jordan and Reed-Cashaw families ensured that music, as well as religion, would fill the crowded brick house on Sharon Street. Grandmother Gar played an upright piano, and the children would crowd around her to sing. Bennie was her special favorite and learned to play the piano while still a toddler. Mamie Reed, well traveled and sophisticated, taught the little Jordan girls to develop their singing voices and to speak clearly, always enunciating their words carefully. "I was a diction specialist," she said. "I taught them that you have to memorize the words to each song because you've got to be able to paint a picture to whomever you're singing."[2]

In such a household of achievers, the cream of Houston's African American middle class, Arlyne Patten Jordan began to fade. She had never attended college, felt lucky to have completed high school, and did "day work," the euphemism for being a maid. Initially attracted to the respect and respectability of the combined Jordan-Reed-Cashaw family, Arlyne now felt overwhelmed. She was acutely aware of her background as the poverty-stricken daughter of an ex-convict turned junk dealer who refused to set foot in church. Arlyne was ill at ease within her own house, which she never really felt belonged to her. It was too full of Charles and Alice and Ben.

Ben Jordan, the dashing suitor, had become a stern and demanding husband. He had firm ideas about being the head of his family: his word was law with Arlyne and the girls. He was tight with his money and austere in the pleasures he would allow his wife and children. Because Grand-mother Gar taught in a rural school outside of Houston, and was away during the week, Arlyne did all of the cooking and cleaning—washing the family's clothes in three black washtubs, which had to be heated over an open fire in the backyard. Ben wanted his khaki work pants pressed in a certain way, and his meals served at exact times. Although he always seemed to have money and drove a nice car, Ben was not generous with extras for Arlyne. Household expenses were kept to a minimum. Ben dominated, Arlyne acquiesced.

There seemed to be no fight in Arlyne, only rare, occasional hints of independence. Shortly after Barbara was born, Arlyne took a bus into downtown Houston to get fitted with a diaphragm at a public clinic. She had decided that at least she would bring no more children into that crowded home, where the three girls slept together on a rollaway bed in the dining room. She continued her maid's work so she would have her own money to buy a few extras for the girls—for instance, fancy matching Easter outfits, which Ben disapproved of heartily. She would get up earlier than Charles and Alice Jordan so that she could fix and serve breakfast to her own little family, separately. The rest of the time, however, she was subsumed into the larger family, both at home and at church, where she soon dropped her oratorical activities and settled into the solid respectability of regular attendance, choir singing, and devoted motherhood. Her daughters never heard her speak in church. "She didn't really speak after we came along. The neighbors used to tell us how good she had been, but we never heard her," Arlyne's oldest daughter, Rose Mary, said.[3]

Sunday morning before church was a time for Charles and Ben to quiz the little girls on Bible verses and for the family to join hands and pray before heading off to Good Hope. After church, they would have a big lunch at Grandma and Grandpa Patten's run-down rented house in the Fourth Ward, and then return to church in the late afternoon for another round of lessons, praying, and singing. To the consternation of Charles and Ben, as well as Arlyne, Barbara Charline, from the time she was only a little tot, much preferred to spend her entire Sunday with Grandpa Patten in his junkyard. Because she was the baby, developing a will soon to be as strong as her father's, Barbara Charline almost always got her way. She skipped evening church services and traipsed around Houston on Sunday afternoons with eccentric, independent, plain-speaking Grandpa Patten, who had seen enough of life to know that church respectability was not all that mattered.

John Ed Patten had two mules and a large wagon, which he kept in his junkyard in the heart of the old Fourth Ward, by this time merging with downtown Houston. It was an eyesore, and city health officials hassled him frequently to clean up the rags, paper, scrap iron, and manure. Barbara Jordan said her grandpa was never cowed by the white people coming to tell him he couldn't keep mules and manure in downtown Houston. "He'd kind of shore it up and make it look presentable," she said. Patten made a fence out of tin and cardboard to cover up the junk, then went on about his business.

Grandpa Patten made five-year-old Barbara his business partner in the junkyard. "Part of my Sunday experience was to go out into his yard and help him sort out the rags and get them bundled up and get the papers stacked and tied and the metal piled. . . . My grandfather always gave me part of the money. . . . He gave me a money belt which had a little zipper area. You wore it under your clothes and around your waist. . . . And Grandpa would give me money to keep for him. I was his bank. And I tell you, it would be a great wad because we had a successful business."

John Ed Patten doted on little Barbara, who was unafraid of the dirt and junk, or of him. He thought she was beautiful and didn't care if she was the blackest of black. He wished she had been named for him instead of her other grandfather, Charles, and he even called her "Barbara Ed-ine." He once gave her a pair of diamond earrings. "I was just a little kid . . . and I didn't have much appreciation of a pair of diamond earrings at that time," she said. A self-admitted tomboy, she was far more thrilled with the three bicycles he got for her—two from his junk collection and one brand-new blue-and-white Schwinn from Western Auto. But Grandpa Patten did more to win his granddaughter's heart than give her money, diamonds, and wheels. He gave her his undivided attention and love that was total and unconditional. What's more, he talked to her, and he listened to her. "It was part of the ritual on those Sunday evenings that when the others had left, we would talk," she wrote in *Self-Portrait.* "In those early years it was certainly the case that he was the only one who talked to me—because mostly what adults do to children is to give them catechism in some form or another. But in terms of instructions about how to live, that is missing."

The old grizzled man and the little pigtailed girl sorted junk and counted their money. Ed Patten made it clear that he did not want Barbara to be like the other kids. He told her that she was different. She could do better, she could *be* better. "That came through loud and clear. . . . He really catered to me in every way," she remembered.

Although Patten was not a church man, he was religious, and in his Sunday evening conversations with Barbara, he always pulled out his Bible, full of inserted scrap papers on which he had scrawled in red crayon his favorite sayings. His "sayings" became for Barbara the "Gospel According to St. John," which is what he called himself, and she loved them as well as his irreverence, a far cry from anything she might hear on Sharon Street. Jordan remembered one of his sayings in particular because he made her memorize it, but also because she came to believe it so fervently:

> *Just remember the world is not a playground, but a school room.*
> *Life is not a holiday, but an education. One eternal lesson for us*
> *all: to teach us how better we should love.*[4]

Jordan said she got a better understanding of Jesus and God from "St. John" than from the preachings in Good Hope Missionary Baptist Church or the Bible drills and scripture readings at home. "He taught me that if I followed his standards, and did what he said, and just followed the plan of action that he set out for me, I would be moving in the path of following Christ," she wrote in 1979. "And his path was an overwhelming degree of self-sufficiency—that's a present-day term, but that's the way I perceived it at that point. Grandpa was saying that the message of Jesus is: Don't get sidetracked and be like everybody else. Do what you're going to do on the basis of your own ingenuity. He was also saying that you couldn't trust the world out there. You couldn't trust them, so you had to figure things out for yourself. But you had to love humanity, even if you couldn't trust it. That's what he said the message of Jesus is."

THE CULT OF RESPECTABILITY AND THE
BLACK MIDDLE CLASS

It is tempting to romanticize the influence of the junk dealer John Ed Patten in Barbara Jordan's life. While he did instill in her a sense of humor, a bit of irreverence, and a healthy skepticism, John Ed's day-to-day influence paled in comparison with the unyielding rules and respectability of Ben Jordan. Yet it was Grandpa Patten's gift of acceptance for who she really was—black, smart, different, special—that she internalized. By believing in herself, as John Ed Patten taught her to do, Barbara Jordan had the strength to absorb her father's influence, rather than be overwhelmed by it.

In his determination to have his daughters eschew the easy path to sin and pleasure, to learn to walk the "straight and narrow," Ben Jordan instilled in all of them a discipline, a sense of purpose, and a demand for excellence beyond the experience of Grandpa Patten. There were daily chores, lessons, scripture readings, exhortations, and lists of "thou shalt nots" that were as staggering for the little girls as they were stifling for their mother. It was a sin to go to movies. It was a sin to dance or drink. It was a sin to waste your time or your talent. It was a sin to sass your mother or father. Ben Jordan also taught his daughters to save their money, dress neatly, be on time, and be respectful to their elders by listening quietly, observing carefully, being polite and "mannerly."

"We were not even allowed to go into other people's houses," Rose Mary remembered.[5] As the oldest daughter, Rose Mary took the exhortations to heart. She studied, minded her parents, and became the quintessential "good girl" in the family. Rose Mary's good behavior made her feel that Ben Jordan was actually pleased with her, because he would single her out for conversations about serious moral issues. Of all the girls, Rose Mary was probably most like Ben—tall, attractive, and reserved, with a serious bent. The middle daughter, Bennie, found her release in music. She was Grandmother Gar's favorite. Talented, energetic, affectionate, and bubbly, Bennie loved to sing and made a name for herself as a gifted pianist in the church. Bennie was also close to Mamie Reed, who inspired rather than terrorized her to do well in school.

Rose Mary and Bennie accommodated themselves to the demands of their father without question. Barbara merely complied—and not always willingly. There was something about Ben Jordan, however, that made open rebellion unthinkable. Formidable and unyielding, he was also physically imposing, a tall, broad-shouldered man who held himself straight and was as exacting with his appearance as he was with his language. Clear and precise in his diction, Ben Jordan wasted no words. He knew how to make a point quickly and forcefully. And there was his own daily example. Because he worked so hard himself, he felt justified in demanding that his daughters do the same. He often held two jobs, and the girls knew it was for them that he labored. Ben Jordan wanted his daughters to rise above the crowd, to achieve, to make him—and themselves—proud. He repeatedly told them that the rules, the discipline, the prohibitions were for their benefit, for their advancement in a harsh world.

Moreover, he provided for them materially; even though their lives were difficult and not luxurious, they were almost privileged in comparison with most Fifth Ward residents. The Jordans lived in a brick house on a paved street and had indoor plumbing and a big Oldsmobile. From 1938 on, Ben Jordan's warehouse job was protected by a Teamsters union contract, which gave him regular wages and job security. He was a pillar of the church and respectable in the community, and that mattered enormously in the Fifth Ward.

The concept of respectability within Houston's African American community was more than a matter of "manners and morals." It also conveyed self-esteem and racial pride.[6] Because Ben Jordan was respectable, he was accorded respect from the entire community, and that respect allowed the Jordan girls to have opportunities *within* the community that Grandpa Patten could never have provided.

Barbara could not escape Ben Jordan's focus on respectability and hard work, no matter how much she loved the junkyard life of Grandpa Patten. The notion of respectability was too ingrained in the Fifth Ward's middle-class families and in the Good Hope Baptist Church. Both the great accommodator Booker T. Washington and his nemesis, the writer and founder of the National Association for the Advancement of Colored People (NAACP), W.E.B. Du Bois, had emphasized respectability—social behavior acceptable to whites—as one way to break racial barriers and dislodge the superiority/inferiority ideology that permeated social, economic, and political life and was so psychologically damaging to young black men and women. Thoughtful, respectable, educated African Americans could not bear being thought of as inferior, or as sexually promiscuous, lazy, thieving, fun-loving, childlike, or somewhat stupid. Yet, they, too, suffered the indignities of being so labeled. Promoted in the popular press, these labels quickly became the stereotypes against which all African American men and women, educated or not, struggled.

The stereotype of out-of-control sexuality was the most odious, and for African American men it could be life-threatening. A mere misunderstood glance at a white woman could get a black man beaten or lynched, so convinced were whites that black men were sexual predators. The sexual stereotyping also affected black women, and one result was a heavily repressive impulse within the black community, and particularly within the black

Baptist church. From the days of slavery until well into the twentieth century, white assumptions about black women's innate promiscuity prevented
legal redress, even in the case of rape. Under Jim Crow laws in Mississippi,
the courts would not convict a white man for the rape of a black female
after she had reached puberty.[7] In the popular and academic literature,
black women were even held responsible for the "sexuality run rampant" of
black men.[8] The major thrust of the cult of respectability in the black
community was to overcome this pernicious racial stereotype and the
themes of white purity versus black impurity, white superiority versus black
inferiority, civilized versus barbaric, and ultimately human versus animal.

That so much of the cult of respectability within the black community
was directed at women made Ben Jordan all the more strict with his girls.
He would not allow his daughters to engage in any action that could provoke anyone—white or black—to question their moral reputation. He
would brag to his friends, "I'm raising three girls in the heart of the city.
And they don't drink, they don't smoke, they don't dance, they don't play
cards, they don't go to the movies. I tell you it's hard, friends, to do that
with three young girls in the heart of the city."[9] When young Barbara heard
him say things like that, it caused her to get what she called "the squeemies
of the gut." She would wonder how he could go around bragging "about the
fact that he has three freaks."

Few of her friends' parents were as strict as Ben Jordan. Barbara
chafed at the rules, believing them to be both unreasonable and unnecessary, but she kept her mouth shut. "It was unthinkable to have a hot exchange of words with him," she later said of her father. "It was unthinkable
for me, for my sisters or my mother. So one does develop quite a bit of
control that way."[10] Rose Mary said that her father never had to use force to
make his point. "The way he talked to us when he was displeased was more
of a punishment than Mother's spankings. Just to have him question you
frightened you to the point of never doing it again."[11] The Jordan girls can
remember disobeying Ben Jordan only once when they were little children.
They desperately wanted to see a Shirley Temple movie at the Lyons Avenue Theater in the Fifth Ward, and Arlyne conspired with them to get a
cousin to take them to a matinee. Barbara thought it was a "great adventure," but the girls didn't try anything quite so daring again until they were
teenagers.

Ben Jordan's tight rein held. It was important for him not only to meet
the standards of the white community but to honor the social codes of the
black community as well. White society lumped all blacks together in one
undifferentiated mass and attributed to all alike the kinds of behavior common only within the bottom segments of society; the reality of life inside
the African American community was quite different from the white stereotypes. Isolated in segregated neighborhoods, away from the white world
that regarded them with such disdain, African Americans began to experi-

ence a growing class cleavage among themselves. It was important to Ben
that he and his family never be lumped at the bottom.

Houston's small African American upper class consisted of lawyers,
educators, physicians, and ministers. Their common bond was education,
and they were at the high end of a class stratification that began immediately after emancipation. The lighter-skinned first generation of slaves and
their children, many of them half-white, were among the first to have an
opportunity for education after the Civil War. The former slaves who could
already read and write, and who were exposed to the behavior patterns of
white owners through house work rather than field work, could move more
quickly into the first schools established by abolitionists, missionaries, and
the Freedman's Bureau. They became the first generation of teachers, ministers, and physicians who served the black community.

W.E.B. Du Bois called the nation's African American college graduates and professionals, most of whom lived in the Northeast, the "Talented
Tenth," because he thought the elite of black America could be expected to
represent about one-tenth of the total black population at the time. For Du
Bois, the Talented Tenth had a responsibility to lead and teach the rest. In
the South, however, the number of college-educated African Americans
never came close to reaching one-tenth of the population. In Houston as
late as 1940, less than 5 percent of the black population were college-
educated. The African American business owners who provided the services
blacks could get nowhere else were probably more influential. These largely
self-made men—and quite a few women—most without benefit of a college
degree, were insurance agents, morticians, barbers, restaurant owners, dry
cleaners, beauty operators, hat makers, and proprietors of mom-and-pop
grocery stores or service establishments.[12] They represented the hope of
upward mobility within the black community. As early as 1915 in Houston,
there were four hundred such business owners, compared with only seven
attorneys and four physicians.[13] At the lowest extreme of the social spectrum were the vagrants, gamblers, criminals, drunkards, and prostitutes
whose lifestyles transgressed both white and black social norms and whose
loose behavior became the basis of the white-held stereotypes and their
justification for Jim Crow segregation laws.[14]

Most black Houstonians did not fit into any neatly defined category.
Of the more than sixty-five thousand African Americans who lived in
Houston in the 1930s, the vast number worked steadily in the menial jobs
open to them and struggled as best they could to get by with limited educational and economic opportunities. Most lived without the basic amenities
of indoor toilets, running water, electricity, or heat. As late as 1940, almost
one-fourth of Houston's black population had no running water. In addition, most had little opportunity for schooling beyond the first few grades.
As late as 1910, no southern black community could claim a single public
school offering more than two years of high school.[15] Only after two new

African American high schools, Jack Yates and Phillis Wheatley, were opened in the mid-1920s did Houston offer a standard high school curriculum for black students.

Although Ben Jordan's lack of a degree from Tuskegee prevented him from moving into Houston's small professional class, he was a Tuskegee man from head to toe, taking to heart Booker T. Washington's philosophy that the way to self-improvement was hard work and clean living. The values of respectability—religion, education, and hard work—played a far more important role in achieving status than money or position.

Ben Jordan's anchor of respectability was the Good Hope Baptist Church. Good Hope was affiliated with the National Baptist Convention, a loose confederation of African American Baptist churches that had met annually since 1892. By 1900 the National Baptist Convention represented almost two million church members, mostly in the South. The pronouncements of the convention reflected a complicated mix of conservative and radical impulses. Convention teachings emphasized biblical authority for man's dominant role in the household. There was honor for a man who held his family together—respect in the community and glory in heaven. For Ben Jordan, this was an important source of the self-affirmation he would never receive in any encounter in Houston's white world. In the wider world, all African American men were called "boys," perhaps "uncle" if they were old and gray. Men could be janitors during the week but deacons on Sunday, thus acquiring dignity and status in their communities. The church did for Ben Jordan what no other institution could: it affirmed his humanity, his relevance, and his right to "see himself in the image of God."[16]

The National Baptist Convention's notion of respectability assumed a political dimension, too. The emphasis on respectable behavior and attitudes became both a goal and a strategy for reform of the entire structure of American race relations. Public behavior was equated not only with individual self-respect but with the advancement of African Americans as a group.[17] Within the convention, however, and in the preaching from the pulpit at Good Hope, there was a reading of scripture and interpretation of Christian tradition that heartily rejected white supremacy. Through the filter of the reality of everyday black experience in a hostile world, black churches interpreted in a radical way the biblical stories of liberation and justice in the Old Testament and the message of equality and concern for the "least" in the gospel of Jesus in the New Testament. The church thus always provided hope, if not a blueprint for action. Within the African American church, ministers preached the message of human equality and the dignity of the individual. And that message was in direct conflict with the Jim Crow segregation laws, which had marginalized even elite African Americans in the North and relegated African Americans in the South to almost subhuman conditions. The central question was always: What can be done about it?

SEEDS OF CHANGE

Within Good Hope Baptist Church in the 1930s, there was a growing recognition that respectable behavior was not enough to convince white people that something had to change. The seeds for a new activism had been planted with the founding in 1910 of the NAACP, which provided the first collective action to force the issue of African American civil rights into public consciousness and undo the damage of Jim Crow.

To say simply that African Americans were either "accommodationists" who accepted their plight or "activists" who resisted oversimplifies the complexities of African American life in the 1920s and 1930s. Black people, inside the church and out, were dealing with issues of survival. Of necessity, most men and women incorporated whatever behavior seemed to work best at the time and place where they found themselves. In the late 1930s and early 1940s in the Fifth Ward in Houston, Texas, and particularly within the Good Hope Baptist Church, the emphasis on conservative personal behavior was beginning to mix with a growing political awareness that would eventually lead to more direct intervention in the oppressive political system.

The year before Ben Jordan's last child, Barbara, was born, Good Hope Baptist Church called a new minister. Ben's step-grandfather, H. C. Cashaw, had died, and in 1935 Reverend Albert A. Lucas took over the ministry at Good Hope. Lucas was active in the National Baptist Convention, serving for a period of years as its president. Lucas was a "race pride" man, and he was considered the kingpin of Houston's Baptist ministers.[18] He quickly became a conciliator among diverse factions within the African American community.

Good Hope took on a new mood of political activism under Reverend Lucas, whose philosophy was that "prayer without action isn't worth a dip of Scott's snuff."[19] In 1936, the year Barbara Jordan was born, Lucas helped organize the Texas State Conference of Branches of the NAACP. By 1940 he was the state president of the NAACP, and eventually he would lay the groundwork that made the Houston NAACP the largest chapter in the South. With Lucas at the helm, the Houston NAACP grew from only a few hundred members in the late 1930s to almost six thousand in 1943. Virtually every member of Good Hope Church also belonged to the NAACP, making up half of the Houston chapter. By 1945 membership had doubled to twelve thousand. The state conference of NAACP chapters was the second largest in the United States, expanding from 6 to 104 branches.[20]

The NAACP Legal Defense Fund attorney Thurgood Marshall was a frequent visitor to Good Hope during the 1940s. It was at Good Hope that Marshall found his plaintiff to challenge the whites-only primary election laws in Texas, a suit that eventually led to a Supreme Court decision outlawing them. The Democratic Party in 1898 had barred African Americans from participating in primary elections to choose candidates who would appear on the ballot at general elections. Because the Republican Party had been virtually wiped out in the period immediately after Reconstruction, winning the nomination in the Democratic primary guaranteed victory in the general election for the next sixty years. African American voters had thus been shut out of the electoral process in Texas. When Good Hope's Reverend Lucas initiated the development of a ten-year agenda for the Texas NAACP, a challenge to the all-white primary was his top priority. In 1940 Lucas recruited one of his church members, the dentist Dr. Lonnie Smith, to try to vote in the Democratic primary election. When Smith was denied the right to vote, Marshall started the federal court challenge. After the Supreme Court, in *Smith v. Allwright*, declared the whites-only primary illegal in 1944, an estimated seventy-five thousand African Americans voted in the next state Democratic primary in 1946.[21] For the first time in more than half a century, black Texans had enough votes to influence close elections, and they could not be totally ignored by state Democratic leaders. White candidates began appearing before black audiences and placing political advertisements in African American newspapers. The poll tax and other election law restrictions, however, prevented a dramatic increase in the number of African American voters.

Albert Lucas's activism, like that of Thurgood Marshall, was conducted totally within the framework of the legal system; both men filed lawsuits based upon denial of constitutional rights. The protests and picketing that would characterize the civil rights movement after the Montgomery bus boycott in 1955 would have been unthinkable to Reverend Lucas and Thurgood Marshall. The NAACP strategy was to use the law to change the law—to use the system to beat the system.

The whole Jordan family was as deeply involved in Good Hope under Reverend Lucas as it had been under Reverend Cashaw. Charles Jordan became one of Lucas's most fervent deacons.[22] Ben Jordan was a tenor in Good Hope's choir, and Bennie and Rose Mary were the little "penny-collection" girls in blue capes who took up one of the three offerings during the service. Barbara sat with her mother in the congregation. Arlyne would carefully spread her handkerchief on her left knee so that when Barbara went to sleep in her lap during the long service, the Excellento on the child's hair would not spoil her dress.

The NAACP activism of the Good Hope Baptist Church was a backdrop rather than a centerpiece in Jordan family life, however. It was part of the atmosphere, something young Barbara imbibed but was not directly involved in or even more than vaguely aware of. Childhood pursuits and school were so engrossing that civil rights and lawsuits to end discrimination did not pierce her consciousness. But the Reverend Lucas's emotional sermons, which led to loud shouts of "Hallelujah!" and strong "Amens!" did reach her. Although she had promised her Grandfather Patten that she would not join the church until she was at least twelve, Barbara broke her vow one Sunday morning when she was only ten and marched straight up to the railing when Reverend Lucas issued the call for sinners to be born again. Jordan later said she decided to join that Sunday, without telling Arlyne or Ben or Grandpa Patten, because while playing a kids' game that separated the Christians from the sinners, she had tired of always being a sinner.

When Barbara headed down the aisle, Arlyne was shocked and Barbara could hear her say, "Where is she going?" But Ben Jordan was glowing, particularly as Reverend Lucas took Barbara's hand, turned to the choir, and said, "We have a little sister as a candidate for baptism; we have a little sister, Barbara Jordan." And then he addressed Ben specifically. "Ben, I think this is the last button on your coat." And Ben beamed with pride, saying, "Yeah, yeah!" Reverend Lucas then turned to little Barbara, whom he called Barb, and told her to make her statement. And Barbara Jordan said, "I want to join church to be baptized and become a Christian." Someone offered a motion that she become a candidate for baptism, which occurred a few weeks later.

The little sister Jordan came more and more under the influence of her father after she became an official Christian, and a newly serious student as well. Barbara was at first a cutup in school, talking and laughing, passing notes, disrupting the class with her jokes and pranks. She even got spanked in front of her class one day at Atherton Elementary School. "My teacher, Mrs. Johnson, told us all to line up to go back in after recess. Well, I was too busy playing and I didn't line up." The teacher spanked her when they got inside the building. Barbara had already had her share of spankings from Arlyne's leather belt and later said, "I knew how to draw in my buttocks so I didn't feel a spanking." She could never misbehave at school too much, however, because of fear of her father. When one of her teachers told Aunt Mamie that Barbara was being a problem in class, Mamie talked to Barbara. "She never was heavy-handed—she would just say to me: 'Well, you ought not to do that, because I don't want to tell Ben about your behavior.'" That settled it, and "after a while I got it under control," Barbara said.[23]

From third grade on, Barbara was larger than most of the other kids. Instead of shrinking inwardly, however, as many girls who are larger than their classmates do, Barbara's personality seemed to *expand* with her body. Her height and bulk were beginning to give authority to her presence. She was clearly the "boss," but her friends accepted her bossiness. That was "just Barbara." Her strong sense of herself added to the aura of specialness that enveloped her from the beginning. Her playmate Mary Justice York remembers that Barbara was "very sure of herself." In those days, she said, "the kids who were the leaders were usually slim and pretty, with nice, long hair and pretty brown skin . . . but Barbara—it wasn't that she tried to be the leader or strove for it . . . we just recognized her."[24]

Barbara herself recognized fairly early that she might be smarter than some of the other children. When a teacher confirmed it for her, she began to take her studies more seriously. And, of course, Ben Jordan was there pushing her along, none too gently. "I would come home with five A's and a B and my father would say, 'Why do you have a B?'" she lamented.[25] Barbara Jordan knew from the beginning that Ben Jordan had certain standards that he expected his children to adhere to. "You knew that, you just knew that," Barbara said. "I hated for him to assist me, in my arithmetic in particular, because he made me feel so dumb . . . I didn't think it was such a great experience while it was taking place, but hindsight tells me he really did have the greatest influence on my life."[26]

Ben Jordan was rarely affectionate or approving of what Barbara did, but he was present in her life. He went to her school programs, watched over her homework, and conveyed to his youngest daughter something that would ultimately become an important lesson. "One expression that he always used was, 'I'll stick with you and go with you as far as you want to go.' Now that let me know that I had a decision-making role in that little encounter because he said, 'I'll stick with you as far as *you* want to go.' He had not set any limits for me. He left that up to me. Whatever I sought, he was standing back there ready to help," Jordan said.[27]

The strength and determination that Barbara, her sisters, and the church community saw in Ben Jordan was one thing. What he himself was experiencing was something else. Ben Jordan had to struggle to meet his own high standards. His own upbringing had been centered in the respectability he imposed upon his family. The strain of middle-class respectability and fatherly responsibility, however, was sometimes too much for him. Respectability was an external standard, imposed on his increasingly empty internal spirit. Something was missing for Ben. He worked constantly. He had always done more than was expected of him, and he was beginning to feel weary. He kept himself tight and rigid at home with Arlyne and the girls because he felt that was the right thing to do. But there were times when he just wanted to let go, to relax. He wanted something more. The life of the night world had a belated appeal for him. Ben was still a handsome man when his daughters entered high school. He liked to spend time with friends, swapping stories, even bragging a bit. Women had always liked him, and he chafed at the restrictions of his married, monogamous life. He had started drinking and caused a serious accident when his big Oldsmobile struck a pedestrian while he was speeding down Lyons Avenue. He agonized over such slips from respectability. He was guilt-ridden because of his sins. He prayed for guidance, for help and deliverance from his weakness. For the longest while, however, he received no comfort or relief.

Ben Jordan's battle with his own demons was totally within himself.

Neither the girls nor Arlyne was privy to his struggle. Ben Jordan set the tone and standards for behavior in his home. If he was silent, so was his family. If he did not reveal his worries or concerns, they did not ask. His silence within his family preserved his self-respect. His pride was on the line at home. He was the father, the husband, the head of the house. He had a role to play. It would be unseemly to reveal that he had moments of doubt or weakness. He did not allow his daughters to whine or complain, and neither would he. He wrapped himself in a cloak of proud stoicism, and so his reserve held steady at home. Ben Jordan sought guidance only from Reverend Lucas, and in prayer. Finally he felt that God had answered him. But the answer placed a new demand on him.

In 1949 Ben Jordan felt the call to become a preacher himself. He was forty-seven years old. His oldest daughter was a senior in high school, and his youngest daughter was thirteen. The call would disrupt their lives, but he knew he would have no peace if he failed to answer it. So he let his call lead him in a new direction—to the ministry of a church of his own, the Greater Pleasant Hill Baptist Church in the Heights neighborhood, which had once been an independent black community in northeast Houston. Because Ben made his reluctant family attend his new church with him— even on Sunday evenings—Barbara's days with Grandpa Patten were over.

CHAPTER 4

THE GIFT OF VOICE

THE YEAR 1949 was one of massive change for thirteen-year-old Barbara Jordan. Church, home, school, her relationships with her sisters and Grandpa Patten, even her own body—everything began to change that year.

When Ben added preaching to his regular job at the Houston Terminal Warehouse and Cold Storage, Jordan family life shifted dramatically. The Greater Pleasant Hill Baptist Church was small, old, and inconsequential. While Ben was paid for preaching only every other Sunday, he was expected to preach every week, conduct home and hospital visits, and minister to the flock. Ben wanted his whole family to leave Good Hope and join him at the new church, and it was a wrenching experience for all of them. Good Hope was a warm cocoon of love for them, a safe haven of activity, meetings, music, fellowship, friends, and support—a second family. Bennie played the piano at some of the services, and Rose Mary, Bennie, and Barbara, as the singing Jordan Sisters, had given warmly received concerts at Good Hope. Now Ben expected them to leave and go to a tiny, rundown church in another part of town. For a brief moment, Barbara and Bennie considered refusing to go. Rose Mary simply cried all day the first Sunday they were expected to attend Greater Pleasant Hill. Ultimately, however, the girls had no choice in the matter. They followed their mother and father across town to the small church, which had only about a dozen members. Seventeen-year-old Rose Mary escaped the confines of her father's church in the fall when she went away to Prairie View College to study to be a music teacher, fulfilling Ben Jordan's dream for her. But thirteen-year-old Barbara and fifteen-year-old Bennie were stuck.

The new church was dreary and uninspiring compared to Good Hope. Moreover, it was disconcerting, particularly for Barbara, to see Ben in the

pulpit with his moral exhortations taking on the greater authority of the
Baptist Church. She concentrated so hard on his first sermon in her attempt
to figure out what this change meant in her father's life that she remembered the biblical text, and most of his words. Ben based his sermon on a
passage from Philippians: "I press toward the mark for the prize of the high
calling of God in Christ Jesus." She liked the notion of "pressing toward the
mark." That seemed to be a continuation of what her father had always
done and what he was teaching her to do. In fact, Ben's sermon included
the idea that his call was merely an "extension," a "fulfillment" of Christ in
him. Barbara decided that her father was saying that God could issue a call
to anybody, and that if God calls you, you must do whatever He was telling
you to do. She could accept that. She could believe that her father was
simply doing what he had to do, in answering this call. But it was still hard
for her to accept the Greater Pleasant Hill Baptist Church. It was not *her*
call.

With Rose Mary away at college, Barbara and Bennie drew closer to
each other. They adapted to the change at church by forming a new singing
group. Bennie and Barbara teamed up with two sisters, Odessa and Lillian
Counts, to create a girls' quartet—the "Counts and Jordan Sisters," although the Counts were hardly girls any longer, being almost as old as
Arlyne. Barbara didn't think the new group was very good, but they were
warmly received in the church community. In fact, the group was appealing
enough that they soon had singing engagements lined up at churches
throughout the Third and Fifth Wards. Barbara even did recitations as part
of their program, memorizing religious or sentimental poetry for the occasions. Later she said that she must have recited James Weldon Johnson's
words a "thousand times":

> Thus Great God,
> like a mammy bending over the baby,
> Kneeled down in the dust
> Toiling over a lump of clay
> Till He shaped it in His own image;
> Then into it He blew the breath of life,
> And man became a living soul.
> Amen. Amen.[1]

Barbara used her most dramatic flourish to repeat the words "Amen.
Amen." The best thing for her about the Counts and Jordan Sisters was
being paid for their programs. Having extra money pleased Barbara Jordan
enormously. She didn't have to ask, or answer to, Ben Jordan when she
wanted something. Sometimes what Barbara wanted that she couldn't get
from Ben was simply meat. One of the ways Grandpa Patten had spoiled
Barbara, her parents felt, was to fill her up on barbecue every Sunday eve-

ning—ribs, sausage, and beef. Most of the meals in the Jordan family, despite Ben's two jobs, were meatless. Arlyne fixed beans, every kind imaginable, and collard greens or rice. She also cooked wonderful fruit cobblers and mouthwatering yeast rolls, but what Barbara craved was the taste of beef or sausage. When she complained, Ben Jordan snapped at her and told her that if she wanted meat so badly, she could buy her own. When she had extra money, that's exactly what she did. "I would bring home a serving of hot sausage which I did not share with Bennie or Rose Mary," she said.

Ben Jordan demanded that Barbara attend the Baptist Young People's Union (BYPU) on Sunday evenings, and she was required to affirm the words of the Baptist Covenant. The covenant had been part of her Sunday school instruction at Good Hope and was recited repeatedly in the Jordan home, as a guide to living. As Barbara progressed through her teen years, it was the standard by which she sometimes measured herself, but felt she could never reach. These words from the covenant had the most impact on her:

> [We engage] to seek the salvation of our kindred and
> acquaintances; to walk circumspectly in the world; to be just in our
> dealings; faithful in our engagements; and exemplary in our
> deportment; to avoid all tattling, backbiting, and excessive anger;
> to abstain from the sale of and use of intoxicating drinks and
> beverages; and to be zealous in our efforts to advance the kingdom
> of our Savior.[2]

Teenage Barbara Jordan derived no joy from the covenant, nor from the other trappings of religious obligation, which for the Jordans could be manifested only within the Baptist church. But it was there, ingrained in her, producing a mixture of rebellion and guilt. "I do not recall any message of joy or love or happiness generated out of this experience," she wrote in Self-Portrait in 1979. "It was a confining, restricting mandate. I did not feel free to do anything other than what was being presented to me as the way one must proceed. . . . So, on balance, my church relationship was, without doubt, a very imprisoning kind of experience."

Changes and restrictions for Barbara at church were echoed by changes at home. Ben and Arlyne finally moved out of the Sharon Street house they had shared with Charles and Alice Jordan for more than seventeen years. Ben bought a pink frame home on Campbell Street near the Southern Pacific rail yards in the heart of the Fifth Ward shotgun houses. The Jordan home was not a shotgun house, but it was in a poorer neighborhood than the Sharon Street residence. Immediately behind the houses on Campbell Street were the Southern Pacific freight yards. They were the largest train yards in the South, covering 359 acres and extending four and a half miles long. Sixty trains a day moved through the yards—six thousand freight cars. And there were thousands of trailer trucks moving day and night, taking cargo in and out of the yards. The neighborhood was noisy and dusty. In many ways, moving from a brick house in a middle-class neighborhood to a frame house on an unpaved street was as disconcerting for Barbara as leaving the warm, protective cocoon at Good Hope Church. "It was a bit of an embarrassment to me to have to tell my friends . . . that I lived on a street that wasn't paved," she said.[3]

The one positive change in young Barbara's life that year came when she entered Phillis Wheatley High School. Wheatley was Houston's third and newest all-black high school and was considered one of the "best physical plants in the South for Negroes."[4] Barbara felt that Bennie had paved the way for her, since she had gone to Wheatley the year before, and Barbara was eager to join Bennie and their friends there. Once she got to Wheatley, however, Barbara discovered that her old playmates were interested in boyfriends, parties, and dancing—most of the activities she was forbidden to engage in. If she wanted to be part of her "gang," as she called her friends, she had to do the same. Barbara started taking part in activities for teenagers at Hester House, a community center a few blocks from her home on Campbell Street. Hester House, modeled after a Jane Addams–type settlement home, provided a range of sports, recreational, and educational activities for children in the Fifth Ward. It was a place to go after school and on the weekends, and Barbara and Bennie were Hester House regulars. On Friday nights, black soldiers from nearby Ellington Air Force Base would come in for a canteen dance. All the teenage girls would dress up to flirt with the airmen. The Reverend Ben Jordan didn't want his girls to be seen at these public dances, and they were forbidden to go. But both Bennie and Barbara began slipping away to attend the dances whenever they could. Barbara went not so much to dance as to sing. She didn't even know how to dance—she had never been allowed to! She loved the music and the attention of the crowd, however, and she would get up to belt out rhythm-and-blues hits like "Dance with Me, Henry" or "Money, Honey," which she considered her "specialty."

Barbara also experimented with smoking—again, behind her father's back. She was the only one in her crowd of girlfriends who had the nerve to venture into the neighborhood store to buy a pack of Pall Malls, which all the girls would share. Now that she was a high school girl, Barbara became more adventuresome in breaking away from her father's stern commandments. What she did with her free time, she felt, was no longer his business—or anybody else's. She was growing up, and taking to heart Grandpa Patten's admonishment to trot her own horse. She was not quite strong enough, however, to risk an open confrontation with Ben Jordan, so her acts of defiance were silent and secret.

Barbara was also growing up physically. Having reached her full height of more than 5'8" and weighing about 175 pounds, Barbara was already an imposing presence. She didn't always know how to handle it. She loathed the physical education classes, which required her to wear a short-sleeved, short-legged gym suit. Full-busted and wide-hipped, with long thin legs, she was beginning to develop the physical features that would characterize her looks in adulthood. She was a big girl, but her bigness reflected a solid bull-like strength, rather than the soft flabbiness of someone who was merely overweight. The lump of bone across her brow added an intensity and fierceness to her gaze, broken only by her smile, big and wide, showing perfect, if slightly protruding, teeth. And she smiled a lot, because that is what the popular girls at Wheatley did.

Trying to feminize her broad, strong facial features, Barbara began to curl her hair in the then-fashionable pageboy bob. She wore earrings, fake-gold jewelry, and bobby socks to fit in with the other girls. Her gang would not miss a Wheatley High School football game, so she followed the team and loved the competitive rivalry between the Fifth Ward's Wheatley and the Third Ward's Jack Yates High School. The big event of the year was always the Wheatley-Yates football game on Thanksgiving Day at Jeppesen Stadium. Barbara felt that everybody who was anybody was at that game, and she threw herself into the spirit of the event. "I felt I did a better job of leading the cheers than the cheerleaders," she said, believing that she should have been a cheerleader. But the cheerleaders and popular girls at Wheatley were slim and petite, and *very* light-skinned. Skin color influenced the teenagers' choice of who would be the most popular and sought-after girls and boys, and to Barbara's dismay, it influenced how teachers felt about their students.

"There was one teacher I didn't like too well, because I felt that she was *color-struck*—that's what we called it," Jordan remembered about those days. "I felt that she favored all the people who had fair skin and good hair. Teachers of her bias favored those who had hair that wasn't nappy, hair that didn't require Excellento, straighter hair. That's what it was: a better grade of hair. This was a really big factor that all of us could see clearly, and one reason that I could always detect when favoritism was being shown by the teacher to the half-white kids was that they became the attendants of Miss Wheatley, the student elected as the symbol of the high school." Some of Barbara's darker friends started using bleaching cream. "It would have been desirable [then] to pass for white if you could have, but few had enough features of a white person to do that," Jordan said.

Barbara Jordan did not have light skin, delicate features, or a petite body—all the features that seemed to matter most for girls at Wheatley High School. But she wouldn't use a bleaching cream. Grandpa Patten had taught her to cultivate pride in herself. That included her deep blackness, even her bigness. And Ben Jordan had taught her to cultivate her intelligence and preserve her dignity, at all costs. Pride, dignity, and intelligence—those were the attributes that Barbara Jordan had in abundance, not feminine wiles.

By the time she was fifteen, her wide diaphragm and broad girth were supporting a gift that began to compensate for her dark skin and lack of beauty: the voice. Jordan's voice had always been loud. But as she matured, it expanded to a depth that eliminated shrillness. It was almost as if there were a clear, single sound coming from her throat that encompassed a harmonic blend of a dozen tones, round and complete. Her father's insistence on precise diction, Aunt Mamie Reed's emphasis on memorizing and melody, and the example of Reverend Lucas's powerful rhythmic cadences and visual words to paint his moral pictures—all of these influences had already begun to shape her speech patterns. Now she had the strength in her voice that could connect her words to her listeners and hold them transfixed. When Barbara and Bennie would go to Prairie View on the weekend to see Rose Mary, the girls in the dormitory would crowd into Rose Mary's room just to hear Barbara speak. She would embellish her stories with dramatic flourishes, lowering her voice in pitch for effect, speaking in hushed tones for emphasis, just as she had heard the preachers do. The college girls loved it. Barbara loved the attention, and wanted more. She was beginning to realize that her voice could be the trumpet that might bring her admiration and acclaim. She still carried with her Grandpa Patten's notion that she was special, better than the rest. At the same time, she was beginning to agree with her father that discipline and hard work, plus a willingness to use her brain and this new gift of voice, could get her what she wanted.

What Barbara wanted most was to be popular in high school. Since she wasn't going to get there by the beauty or cheerleading route, she started looking at other options. At Wheatley, Barbara began to develop an ability to size up a situation, figure out what she wanted, plot a course to get it, and stay focused on her effort until she succeeded. She was beginning to develop the skill of a strategist and the instinct for single-minded pursuit. Her strategy in high school—and later—was to look for a way around an obstacle rather than to try to move it or hit it head-on. She began a pattern of looking for ways to maneuver within the system, rather than change the system. At Wheatley, she wasn't going to be able to change her size, so she would make it work for her. She wasn't going to change the color-struck teachers, so she would seek out the others. She wasn't going to be able to use her voice to lead the football cheers, so she would find other uses for it.

One teacher who was not color-struck was Evelyn Cunningham, the dean of girls at Wheatley. When Barbara was in the tenth grade, Cunningham suggested she run for election as an attendant to Miss Wheatley. Barbara demurred, having already figured out that she was too black to beat the color system that prevailed at Wheatley. "I am not the right light color," she told Cunningham, "and I don't have the clothes, the whole thing." Barbara had decided instead that when she was a senior she wanted to be Wheatley's "Girl of the Year." Since the Girl of the Year was not elected by the students but selected by a national black sorority that looked over a roster of senior girls to select the most outstanding one, Barbara thought she had a better shot at that honor. All she had to do was *become* the most outstanding girl in her class. That, she felt, was within her reach. "But I didn't tell this to anybody at the time," she said. Barbara Jordan, the strategist, was learning to conceal, rather than reveal, her feelings and ambitions. What had started as a defense mechanism against her father's stern criticism was becoming a pattern for dealing with her world. Safety and success would come from keeping her own counsel.

Barbara's strategy to be named Girl of the Year was to become the best public speaker at Wheatley High School. Because of her poetry and speech recitations in church, someone suggested that she participate in the oratorical contests and debate team activities in which students from black schools competed. Immediately Barbara liked that idea, and she began to speak at various meetings around school whenever she could get an audience. When the sponsor of Wheatley's declamation oratorical contests, Ashton Jerome Olivier, heard her, he asked her to join his team.

The oratorical contest circuit always began with competitions at each school, with the winners meeting those from other schools in regional and district meets. Each year, the statewide public school contest for winners from black schools was held at Prairie View. Barbara started winning at the local, regional, and district levels immediately, and she made it to the state finals every year of high school. Students would be assigned a topic to develop into a memorized speech. Judges awarded the prize to the most effective speaker. "I would be the winner and bring home the medals," Jordan remembered. "Then we would have a ceremony and a presentation of the trophies to the school. And we declaimers and debaters felt self-important with the little box of three-by-five-inch index cards on which we kept our notes. These were our badge of superiority over the others who could not do things like that."

Barbara's main oratorical triumph in high school, however, was winning a church-sponsored contest and all-expenses-paid trip to Chicago to participate in the National Ushers Convention Oratorical Contest. She had won the fifty-dollar first prize at the Texas contest in Waco, and Arlyne and Ben were so proud of her that Arlyne decided to make the train trip to Chicago with Barbara for the national contest, sponsored by black Baptist churches. It was Barbara's first time out of Texas, and she and Arlyne stayed at the Greater Bethesda Baptist Church in Chicago where the contest was to be held. On the night of the speeches, Barbara wore a pink evening dress, and she gave the same memorized speech that had brought her a first prize in Waco, "Is the Necessity for a Higher Education More in Demand Today Than a Decade Ago?" She belted it out with the passionate intensity of "Money, Honey." When she finished, she knew that she had given the speech, just the way she wanted to, and thought that if she didn't take first place here, she never would. She did win, and after that, she said, "I was riding on a great big high." She told one of the African American newspapers in Houston, somewhat immodestly, "It's just another milestone I have passed; it's just the beginning."

By the time she was a senior at Wheatley, Barbara was well on her way to being selected Girl of the Year. She was the star of the high school speakers' circuit, she sang in the All-Girls' Choir, and she had joined all of the important clubs, particularly those whose faculty sponsors were influential within the school and the community. Even Ben Jordan's prodding about homework and grades paid off when Barbara was named president of the scholastic honor society her senior year.

High school had turned out to be a happy adventure for Barbara Jordan. Her achievements brought admirers, and she and Bennie had a regular gang of friends who hung around together. Bennie and Barbara, Evelyn and Mary Elizabeth Justice, Charles White, the grocer's son, and a few others would amble along their walk home from Wheatley to the house on Campbell Street, normally a fifteen-minute walk that the gang managed to stretch into well over an hour. Along the way, they would stop at Ben Jordan's new soft-drink stand, "Your City Soda," which he and a friend from church had invested in. There they would load up on soft drinks and candy and meander along laughing, gossiping, and telling stories.

Ben's venture into full-time preaching had not lasted long, primarily because it placed such a great financial strain on the family. Most of the small Baptist churches willing to hire a newly called fifty-year-old minister were too poor or desperate to attract anyone else. They paid little, and demanded much. Wrangling over time and salary had worn Ben down within a year at Greater Pleasant Hill. He had briefly taken on two other small churches in rural areas outside of Houston, and he was on the road constantly when not working at the warehouse. He was determined to send Bennie and Barbara to college, as well as Rose Mary, but he quickly learned that his religious calling could not provide the extra income he needed. When Reverend Lucas, his mentor at Good Hope, asked him to come be a part-time staff member and return to the Good Hope flock, Ben jumped at the chance. Bennie and Barbara did, too. The whole family rejoined the church, and Reverend Lucas especially welcomed the girls back, even as he admonished Ben: "You're not going to take away my chaps again. They are here to stay." When Barbara heard those words resounding in Reverend Lucas's strong, clear voice, she said a silent prayer of thanks.

Something else happened to Barbara in those years at Wheatley that gave her a motivation to succeed that had nothing to do with popularity, the Baptist Covenant, or Ben's admonitions. A brief encounter with a black woman who operated in a wider arena than Barbara's segregated world of church, neighborhood, and school opened a new door of imagination for her.

The noted African American lawyer Edith Spurlock Sampson of Chicago spoke at a career day program at Wheatley.[5] In speeches to black high school students all over the country, she was urging young men and women to consider the law as a career. Sampson had been born in Pittsburgh and attended school in New York and Chicago. She received her master of law degree from Loyola University in Chicago, the first woman of any race to receive that degree from the institution. Sampson had begun her law practice in Chicago in 1926. She specialized in criminal law and domestic relations. In 1947 she had become the first African American woman to be appointed an assistant state's attorney in Cook County. President Truman had recently appointed her an alternate delegate to the United Nations. Edith Sampson was so impressive in her dress, her demeanor, her accomplishments, and her speech that Barbara Jordan was starstruck. She had never seen anyone like Edith Sampson in Houston—even among the middle-class lawyers and physicians who were members of Good Hope and active in Houston's NAACP.

Otis King, a Wheatley student who would become Barbara's college debate partner and the first black attorney for the city of Houston, said Sampson set the students "on fire." "It wasn't so much what she said," he remembered. "She was just so self-assured. She had been involved with the UN, she had been to Africa. She had done all of these wonderful things, and she was a very eloquent speaker, with such poise and self-assurance. All of us felt . . . there was some change going on, and there were some things we could legitimately reach for. Before Edith Sampson, we saw teaching or being in the ministry as 'it.' We didn't think about being lawyers or anything like that. But here was this person in front of us doing these things. Our horizons as to the things that were possible expanded."[6] Otis King decided to become a lawyer that day at Wheatley High School. And so did Barbara Jordan.

She said it was like a conversion experience. "That's it," she said. "That is what I'm going to be. Of course my homeroom teacher said, 'Fine, fine, we'll see.' "[7] Texas had only sixteen black lawyers in 1936, the year Barbara Jordan was born. Until 1949, there was no school in Texas where an African American could study law. When Barbara announced to her parents that she had decided to become a lawyer, their reactions were cautious and mixed. Of course, they had seen the NAACP lawyer Thurgood Marshall when he came through Texas to bring the all-white primary lawsuit.

Nevertheless, being a lawyer was a bit beyond their expectations for Barbara. Arlyne was quite skeptical, thinking that it was a passing fancy. Ben Jordan had seen what Barbara could do, however, both in the oratorical contests and in earning the A's on her report card, and he told her to aim for whatever she thought she could achieve. Although Barbara had no idea exactly what being a lawyer meant, she did now carry an image of a self-possessed woman who was different, better somehow than the rest, just as Barbara felt she was. Grandpa Patten approved of her goal, too. After all, he reminded her, he thought his own father had been a lawyer.

So Barbara pushed ahead now with two goals: to be Girl of the Year and to go to law school. Of course, she had to go to college first. She had seen enough of Prairie View, where Rose Mary was about to earn her degree, to know that she did not want to be there. Bennie had enrolled in Texas State University for Negroes in Houston in 1949, where the state of Texas had established a law school in an attempt to keep African Americans out of the University of Texas law school. Barbara decided to join Bennie at TSU and live at home. Her sights were clear, and her first goal was within reach by the time she began the last semester of her senior year. Adult judges selected Barbara Jordan Wheatley's Girl of the Year. When the announcement was made, however, Barbara panicked. Although she had planned for this moment for three years, she now realized that she had failed to take into account that she would need a new dress to wear to the award ceremony. Ben and Arlyne, with Rose Mary and Bennie both in college now, had no extra money for a fancy new dress. Arlyne, too, agonized over how to outfit Barbara for the ceremony. Aunt Mamie Reed resolved the crisis when she offered to lend Arlyne the money to buy Barbara a new dress. That was an acceptable solution, and Barbara bought a long, off-white lace dress from Houston's then most fashionable store, Sakowitz. The dress cost thirty-five dollars, and Barbara loved it. When she appeared in her new dress to accept the Girl of the Year award, Ben and Arlyne came to the ceremony, and Barbara wanted to wow them more than anyone else in the audience. "My acceptance speech was really super. . . . I had people in tears. It was so moving that my father couldn't stand it." Arlyne paid Mamie Reed five dollars a month until the debt for Barbara's dress was repaid.

For all of Barbara Jordan's first-place finishes and achievements at Wheatley High School, however, it was a second-place finish in another oratorical contest sponsored by the Elks Clubs of Texas for black students that turned out to be the true milestone. Tom Freeman, the TSU debate coach and one of the contest judges, told Barbara that he had voted for her for first place. It thrilled Barbara to be noticed by Tom Freeman. She was grateful and decided she would look him up once she got to college. It was a fortuitous decision, for Tom Freeman would teach her how to use the gift of her voice.

SEPARATE . . . NOT EQUAL

How could it be possible that this southern black high school girl in Houston, Texas, in the 1940s and 1950s would not have the issue of racial discrimination front and center in her life? How could she not be obsessed with the inequalities, injustices, and barriers that restricted her? How could she not question the limitations imposed, even on her imagination?

At Wheatley High School, Barbara Jordan did not develop a racial consciousness or an obsession with her "plight" and "the race question." While she was intellectually astute enough to notice and judge the disparities she saw, she was too safe, too tucked away in the cocoon of Ben Jordan's all-encompassing morality, too well protected by the very real sense of community that prevailed in the Good Hope Missionary Baptist Church and the Fifth Ward itself, with its mom-and-pop stores, its community centers, and the watchful eyes of its neighbors. She knew that there was this beast called racism, and that because of the deep blackness of her skin there were things she could not do or hope for. She knew she was affected by a wall of separation that made her world different from downtown Houston, but she was affected by it only in a general way, the way all African Americans were. Her skin color was more of a problem in the African American world of Wheatley High School than it ever was for her in the white world of downtown Houston. In her daily, lived experiences, she rarely even saw white people, except on her infrequent trips downtown.

"In the middle of downtown were the five-and-dimes—Kress, Woolworth," she remembered. "We would go into them to buy paper and pencils for school and see white kids sitting at the counter having sodas and hamburgers. It never occurred to me that I might want to sit down and eat a hamburger there. That was part of some other world. . . . When you were in a store you had to ask, 'Where is the basement colored restroom?' We didn't question those things then."[8]

When Barbara Jordan was in high school, the segregation of lunch counters in five-and-dime stores was not personal or particular to her. It was impersonal and general. She didn't expect to sit there, she didn't want to sit there, she didn't try to sit there. So she experienced no specific rejections, no direct humiliations from white people. "I did not think it right for blacks to be in one place and whites in another place and never shall the two meet," she wrote in *Self-Portrait*. "There was just something about that that didn't feel right to me. And I wanted that to change, but I also had those feelings that it was going to be this way for a long, long time, and that nobody was going to be able to do anything to change it. . . . So it was massive and I felt that it was something bigger than anyone I knew. . . . It was everywhere."

When the adult Barbara Jordan looked back on those years, it was almost as if she were trying to figure out why she did not feel some surge of righteous indignation, and the only thing she could come up with was that "it was just too big." She had grown up in a supportive—if strict—home. She had the sense of being cared for, and being taken care of, in a fundamental way. She developed a belief that if she worked hard and did her part, everything would turn out okay, because it always had. She had no sense of urgency about social or political problems. They were not *personal.* Rosa Parks had to ride the bus to work every day and had to sit at the back behind the color bar until she got sick and tired of it. For her, segregation *was* personal. By contrast, young Barbara Jordan took only occasional trips on the bus. She got to drive her father's Oldsmobile. She knew the larger system was wrong, but she was managing quite nicely within the smaller system that was her community. She could discuss segregation or integration quite dispassionately, even debate it in formal tournaments at Wheatley High School. She was detached from its reality, however, and had a certain fatalistic view of its longevity.

Her notes for a high school debate on racial integration were orderly, logical, and virtually without emotion: "While to be sure we are students in a segregated institution, and while certainly we must work within the framework of the laws of our state, let it be realized by every student that the challenge facing us is not the defense of any system, be it segregated or integrated; the challenge facing us is to so equip ourselves that we will be able to take our place wherever we are in the affairs of men. . . . Integration is a process whose end will probably not be fully realized in our generation." These were reasonable views, given what she saw and knew, and they certainly represented the conventional wisdom of the Fifth Ward at the time. Perhaps understandably, her remarks lacked a fiery spark of rebellion, but they also revealed no hint of outrage at the injustice of a system that excluded her. The debate notes of this sixteen-year-old Fifth Ward girl are full of acceptance of the limits of her world. Jordan's acceptance, however, was quite different from the passivity of a victim, or the apathy of one who withdraws from the world in despair or defeat. The author of these debate notes, in fact, is clearly someone who believes in herself, who believes she must equip herself for whatever might be possible in her world, no matter how limited. She reveals a remarkable sense of responsibility for her own self-development, but little for society as a whole. Personal change was possible and could be immediate. Society's change was desirable, but distant.

In 1951 there was nothing in Barbara's experience to counter her gradualist approach to change. The NAACP, thoroughly enmeshed in the activities at Good Hope Baptist Church, pursued a slow but steady antisegregation strategy. Because the organization knew that southern legislators would never take Jim Crow laws off the books voluntarily, it had begun to mount court challenges to segregation in Texas—all within the framework of existing laws. Case by case, the NAACP would chip away at segregation laws. Change would come in increments, a step at a time. Desirable, but distant.

The NAACP Legal Defense Fund attorney Thurgood Marshall spent an extraordinary amount of time in Texas in the 1940s and 1950s, and some of his most far-reaching legal victories came from his Texas cases, like *Smith v. Allwright,* which brought an end to the all-white primary. But Marshall had come to believe that "segregation and discrimination are one."⁹ Legal segregation, he believed, gave a "halo of respectability" to the judgment that African Americans were inferior. The NAACP in 1948 had taken the position expressing its "unalterable opposition to segregation in any form" by stating that it would not "undertake any case or cooperate in any case which recognizes the validity of segregation statutes"; nor would it take part in any case that had as its "direct purpose the establishment of segregated public facilities." In other words, any NAACP assault on *Plessy v. Ferguson's* separate-but-equal doctrine would have at its core the contention that separate could never be equal.

Even though Pastor Lucas and the Good Hope Baptist Church were in the thick, the lawsuits and debates and issues of discrimination were rather removed from Barbara Jordan. As long as her contacts with the white world were limited, whites were truly "other"—unknown, out of bounds, not worthy of her time or thought. "There was nothing you saw to indicate that a black person and a white person could be together on a friendly basis," she wrote. "You saw the porters and the maids, but to see a black person in some other capacity, in a white shirt with a tie, was nonexistent. The idea of a black going to a hotel for any purpose other than for a backdoor delivery was impossible. And looking at how widespread this was, my feeling was, well this is just it. I guess it's always going to be this way."

It's always going to be this way. Period. Barbara Jordan felt no special anger or bitter resentment about having to live in a segregated world. The psychological roots of anger are related to fear, insult, injury, or denial of something to which you feel you are entitled. Barbara Jordan on the eve of entering college in 1952 felt no entitlement to anything other than what she had known in her Fifth Ward community. While she had developed personal ambitions and aspirations, they were always in relation to what might be possible for a *black* person, rather than what might be possible for *any* person.

"As a student at Phillis Wheatley High School, seeing all of that, I decided that if I was going to be outstanding or different it was going to have to be in relation to other black people rather than in some setting where white people were. . . . At the time I decided that I was not going to be like the rest, my point of reference was other black people. It seemed an impossibility to make any transition to that larger world out there."

If Barbara Jordan felt any sense of entitlement denied, it was within her own family. She wanted to have fun. She wanted to have things—

material possessions. She wanted to have money enough to be independent. She wanted freedom to do what she wanted. And Ben Jordan's stern morality always stood in the way. When Barbara wanted to go to her senior prom, Ben Jordan refused to let her go. "I quoted the Bible at him," Barbara said. "I told him the Bible said that there is a time to mourn and a time to dance. He didn't argue Scripture with me, but simply said 'No.' "[10] Yet even Ben Jordan could be gotten around, or ignored, if she was careful and discreet. By the time she entered college, Barbara had learned to shut out people or events that disturbed her. She had begun to compartmentalize her life—to keep some areas unknown and unprobed, even by those closest to her, and especially by Ben Jordan.

THE OPENING WEDGE

Barbara Jordan entered Texas Southern University in 1952, along with more than two thousand other African American students. It was still a relatively new all-black university, created by the Texas legislature in March 1947. Originally called the Texas State University for Negroes, the school was renamed Texas Southern University in 1951, the year Barbara's sister Bennie entered.

TSU was born in compromise and confusion—the product of the efforts of white segregationists to buy time and hold off unfavorable court decisions to integrate Texas colleges and universities as the NAACP marched through federal courts challenging the separate-but-equal doctrine of *Plessy v. Ferguson* in higher education. In 1946 an African American mail carrier from Houston, Heman Sweatt, had tried to enroll in the University of Texas Law School and was denied admission. Thurgood Marshall felt it was the perfect test case to integrate higher education in Texas because there was no black law school in the state and a suit could penetrate the sham of the whole separate-but-equal system. The University of Texas had recognized its untenable legal position and hastily decided to open a law school for Negroes in the basement of a building in downtown Austin. Law school administrators planned to have faculty members come downtown to teach law courses to one black student—Heman Sweatt. The plan was presented to Marshall and Sweatt, in an attempt to get the suit dropped, but the arrangement was not acceptable to Sweatt or the NAACP, and the legal battle was enjoined.

By the time the *Sweatt* case arose, the political and intellectual climate in the nation made the commitment of Texas—and the South—to segregation increasingly abhorrent. President Franklin Roosevelt had ended race discrimination in federal employment and among defense contractors during World War II with an executive order mandating fair employment practices. And Gunnar Myrdal's massive study of race relations in 1944, *An American Dilemma*, created a consensus among liberal intellectuals that segregation was wrong and oppressive. For years, the NAACP had been pointing out the same inconsistency that Myrdal described between segregation and the nation's commitment to democracy.[11] Now the rest of educated opinion in the country seemed to have caught up with the NAACP. In 1946 President Harry Truman had appointed the prestigious fifteen-member Commission on Civil Rights to study and recommend new legislation to end racial discrimination. But Texas was determined to protect its all-white law school. In the first round of the legal battle, a Texas trial judge gave the state six months to come up with a "substantially equal" law school for Negroes to bring the state into compliance with *Plessy*.

The Texas legislature hurriedly appropriated $2 million to create the Texas State University for Negroes in Houston, complete with a law school. The bill establishing the new college was an attempt to protect the University of Texas, not only from the presence of Heman Sweatt but from all Heman Sweatt *imitators* who might flood into the state's all-white university system in the future.

Once Texas had created a real law school for African Americans, the context of the litigation changed: the separate-but-equal doctrine became the central question in the case. Marshall threw himself into the case because he wanted to experiment with the evidence that might be useful in an all-out attack on segregation in *all* areas. His goal was to construct a record that would provide a good basis for evaluation of the NAACP's claim that separate facilities could never be equal. Marshall's task was to show that segregation had no "line of reasonableness."[12] He brought a team of expert witnesses to the second Texas trial to show that segregation inhibited education by generating mistrust and preventing students from learning about other groups. Assertions of the equality of the TSU law school were countered by NAACP lawyers who pointed out the small size of the segregated law school, the lack of extracurricular activities, such as a moot court or law journal, and the inadequate library. But the Texas trial court rejected Sweatt's plea for admittance to the University of Texas, and the appeal process began. By the time the case got to the Supreme Court, the TSU law school was fully operational. President Truman's solicitor general of the United States filed an amicus brief supporting the NAACP in the case, stating that *Plessy* should finally be overturned and putting the executive branch of the federal government squarely on the line for the abolition of the separate-but-equal doctrine.

The Supreme Court heard the case on April 4, 1950. Marshall waged a full assault on *Plessy*, creating a dilemma for the Court. Overruling the separate-but-equal doctrine would end segregation in public schools as well as in higher education. The high court's justices, including Tom Clark of

Texas, thought that such a decision would unleash chaos and perhaps violence in the nation, which they felt was not yet ready for full-scale racial
integration. The justices were willing to see *Plessy* undermined, but not
overruled. In a compromise decision handed down in June, the Court stated
that Sweatt had to be admitted to the University of Texas Law School so
that he could obtain his full "constitutional right," but stopped short of
overruling the separate-but-equal doctrine of *Plessy* in its entirety.

Marshall was satisfied, however. He believed the *Sweatt* decision was
"replete with road markings" showing that *Plessy* had been gutted and that
"we have at last obtained the opening wedge."[13] Unfortunately, the case put
a strain on the NAACP in Texas from which it never fully recovered.[14] The
four-year battle over the *Sweatt* case and the opening of Texas State University for Negroes created tensions among three rival groups of African Americans within the NAACP: (1) the men and women whose careers and
interests were closely tied to Prairie View College, and who saw the new
TSU as a threat to their prestige and longtime dominance in the African
American community in Texas; (2) the practical Houstonians who were
now vitally interested in the new school and wanted to build its programs,
secure more state funding, and cautiously refrain from alienating powerful
Texas politicians who could dismantle the school by shutting off state support; and (3) the NAACP lawyers and key officials who were interested in
the *Sweatt* case as a vehicle to integrate all of higher education in Texas and
dislodge *Plessy* once and for all. Carter Wesley, the publisher of the African
American *Houston Informer,* resigned from the NAACP because he wanted
black efforts focused solely on building up TSU. The NAACP organizer
Lula B. White and the attorneys Maceo Smith and W. J. Durham wanted
to downplay TSU and push for integration of the University of Texas. The
positions were irreconcilable, and the solidarity that had prevailed within
the leadership of the African American community in Texas prior to 1947
was broken.

The case created strains within the conservative white political community as well. Once the court case was over, the expense of creating the
black equivalent of the University of Texas began to cloud the entire enterprise. The legislature never appropriated enough money to run the school
smoothly, and the failure to give any thought to an appropriate curriculum,
other than within the law school, created massive headaches for TSU administrators. In 1950 the school had four fully equipped shops for training
in cleaning and pressing, shoe repair, tailoring, and auto mechanics, and
only one small chemistry classroom for the 119 students who signed up for
the course. The physics department had $30,000 worth of uncrated equip-
ment, with no space available to use it.[15]

Yet African American students flooded the all-black school instead of
the University of Texas. It was the scenario state officials had planned. An

alternative all-black university would ease the pressure to integrate the University of Texas. Barbara Jordan was typical of Houston and east Texas students who had never once considered applying anywhere but TSU. By 1950, when the Supreme Court was hearing the *Sweatt* case, more than fifteen hundred students were enrolled at TSU, with almost three hundred of them in graduate programs.

The white superiority/black inferiority motif still prevailed, however. Control of the all-black TSU was vested in a board of regents that, *by law*, had to have a majority of white members. The school's business and financial manager was required to be white as well. The NAACP leaders who wanted to develop TSU realized that they would not have a free hand in directing the affairs of their new university after all. In an effort to quell the tension surrounding the *Sweatt* case and the opening of TSU, however, the white board members acquiesced to their black colleagues and appointed the noted African American educator Dr. Raphael O'Hara Lanier as TSU's first president.

Dr. Lanier was easily recognizable as one of W.E.B. Du Bois's Talented Tenth. A graduate of Lincoln University in Pennsylvania, with graduate degrees from Stanford and postgraduate work at Columbia and Harvard, Lanier had taught at Tuskegee and been a dean at both Florida A&M and Hampton Institute in Virginia. When he served for a brief time as acting president of Hampton, he was the first African American to serve in that capacity for the all-black school. Mary McCleod Bethune had recruited Lanier to be her assistant director of Negro affairs in President Roosevelt's National Youth Administration of the New Deal. In 1946 President Harry Truman had appointed Lanier to be the minister to Liberia. He came home from Liberia to accept the TSU job. The African American community in Houston was indeed placated by Lanier's appointment. He had served a stint as dean of the old Houston College for Negroes in the 1930s and was known and admired in the city. But in segregated Texas, Lanier was never given full authority to run the school. White legislators were not about to turn over state-appropriated money or management of a new institution to a black man—even to run an all-black college.[16]

Yet it was the all-black law school at TSU that Barbara Jordan was interested in when she enrolled as a freshman in 1952. The TSU law school, however, was far from being well organized. When Jordan sought pre-law academic counseling about her undergraduate course work, she was told to take anything she wanted. It didn't matter. She thought: "Fine. I'll play around three years." And her first act of play was to run for freshman class president, an election in which she was soundly defeated by Andrew Jefferson, a pre-law classmate who would become a lifelong friend. For Barbara, however, the loss was a reminder that TSU could be a repeat of her Wheatley experience. She was not going to win the popularity contests as long as the students voted. The TSU yearbook was full of photographs of stylish African American beauties, with clear eyes, light skin, smooth hair, and slim bodies. These were the popular girls. She was taller, broader, blacker, with not one girlish or cute feature. So she moved into other arenas at TSU, just as she had at Wheatley. First came a sorority.

Within its first few years, TSU had already seen the influx of the black sororities and fraternities that invaded black education after the turn of the century, just as the social organizations had gained a foothold in white institutions of higher education. Barbara pledged Delta Sigma Theta her first semester. The Deltas were less color-conscious than the other sororities, and Bennie was a Delta. Barbara thought it would be fun to go to the Delta parties, perform in the skits, wear the Delta colors of red and white, and sing the Delta song. But Ben Jordan could not abide the idea of his daughters in that "hell-fire" sorority, and he refused to give them money for dues or other sorority activities. So Bennie used the money she made playing the piano at church, and Barbara got jobs baby-sitting and housecleaning to finance her social activities.

By the time Barbara and Bennie Jordan became Deltas, the sorority had begun to develop a legacy that combined social action with service in the African American community. The first act of the sorority's initial twenty-two members, shortly after organizing in 1913 at Howard University, was to carry the Delta banner in a suffrage demonstration, marching down Pennsylvania Avenue on the eve of Woodrow Wilson's inauguration. Both in college chapters and within its growing alumnae network all across the country, the Deltas focused on leadership training for young black women. Many of the earliest Delta chapters had been organized to support young black women students at white colleges in the Northeast, and within the sorority the emphasis had always been more on achievement—both academically and professionally—than on social events. The Deltas, like most black women's clubs, felt the need to prove their acceptability to the white world. Scholarship and achievement offered proof to the white world of the intellectual ability of African American women in a society that doubted that blacks had the capability. From the beginning, black sororities, especially the Deltas, were more than imitations of white social sororities. According to Delta's historian, Paula Giddings, they also had distinct feminist leanings, which provided a contrast for Barbara and Bennie Jordan to the subservient and obedient role assigned women in conservative black churches like Good Hope. W.E.B. Du Bois had spoken to those first Delta women at Howard, telling them that economic conditions demanded a "change in the role of women," and that women were entitled to a career the same as men.[17] For the first time, Barbara Jordan was beginning to get some reinforcement for her ideas about herself, her ambition, and her desire for independence from Ben Jordan and all that he had come to represent for her.

A NEW LOOK AT THE WORLD

An even stronger affirmation came to Barbara Jordan when she sought out Tom Freeman, TSU's debate coach. Her voice and oratorical skills seemed to provide the surest way to build a record of outstanding achievements, as she had done at Wheatley. Freeman's debate team would provide the opportunity.

Tom Freeman was a jaunty, handsome man with a thin mustache who could have been mistaken for a slimmer version of the entertainer Cab Calloway. He grew up in Virginia and attended Andover Newton Seminary in Boston. He had also taken courses at Boston University and Harvard and received his doctorate at the University of Chicago. Freeman had colleagues, friends, and relatives all along the East Coast and throughout the Midwest, and he scheduled debate tournaments for his TSU students at prestigious colleges that most of them had never dreamed they would see. The trips attracted students to debate, and Freeman had his pick of TSU's most talented young men and women. Otis King, Barbara and Bennie Jordan's classmate at Wheatley High School, remembers that the trips outside of Houston were a lure for him. "Most of us had never been out of the ghetto, although we probably didn't know what a ghetto was then," King remembers. "The trips just seemed exciting to me."

Otis King and Barbara Jordan gravitated toward each other in the first weeks at TSU. They had been friends at Wheatley and were part of the same gang of teenagers that would drive to Galveston on summer afternoons to spend the day at the city's still-segregated beaches. They tried out for debate at the same time, and Tom Freeman paired them as debate partners from the beginning. Their first competitions were in intramural contests at TSU. Freeman thought that Barbara was good at projecting herself, but not as good at thinking about her arguments and rebuttals. So initially he would only allow her to lay out the "constructive affirmative," or the presentation of the case. Otis King, who was quick at thinking on his feet, took on refutations of the opponent's argument. Barbara Jordan and Otis King complemented each other. "With her dramatic flair and my straightforward style, we could cover all the bases," King remembered. As freshmen, they debated TSU's seniors and won.

Tom Freeman had a dramatic style himself that impressed his debaters, and they sought to imitate him. He had earned his Ph.D in "homiletics," or preaching, and he peppered his conversation with quotations from Shakespeare and the King James version of the Bible. He had a sense of speech as a form of music—rolling, rhythmic, and emotion-laden. He orchestrated hand gestures and facial expressions to complement and enrich the words his students would memorize for their debate presentations or rebuttals. He made sure his students were always mindful of their audience and choreographed presentations to generate applause or laughter, or even tears. Tom Freeman was a showman as well as a debater, and his TSU teams put on a good show. "All of us would mimic him when we were speaking," King remembered. "I didn't have the deep booming voice that he had, but Barbara did, and we copied his mannerisms and inflections. Barbara picked up a lot of that, a lot of Dr. Freeman's flair. She was a very effective speaker. She was the absolute best orator we ever had. As part of a team, I thought I was as good or a better debater than she because I had the ability to make the key debating points. I used to tell people when we were debating, 'I have to listen to *what* Barbara says, so I can defend her positions. I can't be listening to *how* she says it.' She had the sense of the dramatic even before coming to Tom Freeman. But he certainly influenced all of us."

Initially Freeman did not want Barbara to travel with the team for their out-of-town tournaments. The cult of respectability for female students was very much alive at TSU in 1952, and Freeman did not want to compromise the reputations of his young women debaters by having them drive all night to the tournaments with a bunch of young men. Barbara was determined to go on the trips, however, and waged a campaign to persuade him to let her go. She abandoned the ingenue look she had worked so hard to perfect in high school. She gave up her scoop-neck dresses and earrings. She cut her hair short and began to wear bulky, boxy jackets and flat shoes. Because she had also gained twenty pounds during her freshman year at TSU, she took on what the novelist Shelby Hearon called the "squared lines of androgyny." She had a new look. She became someone it was all right to take across the country in a car full of males without a chaperone.[18] Freeman relented and allowed her to travel to some of the freshman debate tournaments at other southern black schools. When the TSU freshmen went to Southern University in Baton Rouge and Arkansas A&M in Pine Bluff, the team of Jordan and King came back winners. Their confidence level was high. Nevertheless, their skills had been tested that first year only against other African American college students; King remembered that their confidence was shaken when Freeman scheduled them against white teams when they were sophomores in 1953. "We had not yet had the experience of debating the 'better' schools, and that was how we thought of the white schools," he said.

Baylor University hosted the Southern Forensic Conference, a full forensic tournament, with public-speaking and other oratorical contests as well as debate, in the spring of 1953. TSU broke the color bar for the first time in college debate in the South when Freeman arranged for TSU to be invited to the meet. Freeman entered Barbara in an oratorical contest as well as the debate tournament. The TSU students were both excited and apprehensive as they filled two cars to make the almost two-hundred-mile trip from Houston to Waco, where they would spend the night and compete in the contests. Freeman drove one car full of students, and Otis King drove the other, with his partner Barbara and other students. The cars got separated on the way to Waco, and King and Jordan didn't know where they were supposed to go when they got there. "As we went into Waco, we didn't know where Dr. Freeman was, or where we were going to stay. We knew we wouldn't be staying at any of the nice hotels or on the Baylor campus, and we didn't know what to do," King remembered. They drove to the Baylor campus and tried to find out where the TSU team would be lodged for the night, but no one knew. So King drove into downtown Waco, and he and Barbara walked into the biggest hotel they saw and found a registration table for the forensic tournament. Once again they asked where the Negro students were supposed to go and were directed to a motel on the outskirts of town, in the "colored" section. "When we got out there, Dr. Freeman was already there. And Barbara and I were kind of upset that he hadn't told us where to go," King recalled. "But Dr. Freeman took the attitude that we were smart enough to figure things out. And it was like he would stage these kinds of little experiences along the way so he could tell us, 'You're bright people. You can figure it out.' Dr. Freeman had confidence in us, and the best experience for all of us was the confidence we gained as we came into contact with the rest of the world."

The Baylor tournament was a turning point for Barbara Jordan in other ways as well. For the first time, she was matched one-on-one with white students in a speaking contest. Tom Freeman watched her from the back of the room, and when the crowd hushed as Jordan began her recitation—"We are poor little lambs who have lost our way. . . . We are little black sheep who have gone astray. . . . Lord, have mercy on such as we"—he knew his confidence in her was justified. She took first prize in the declamation contest. Jordan herself had a revelation in the middle of the contest. She thought, "Why, you white girls are no competition at all. If this is the best you have to offer, I haven't missed anything."

Debate filled a major portion of Barbara Jordan's life at TSU; in addition to developing her speaking skills, she was developing her ability to conduct research and organize information. The debate team had to research all of its own topics, organize the arguments for and against, lay them out in a logical way, memorize key points, and figure out how and what would impress the judges. Jordan became quite adept at rebuttals, too, as if to prove to Tom Freeman that she could master anything the males could do. During Jordan's junior year, Freeman took his team on swings up through the Midwest, as well as along the East Coast. Barbara Jordan and Otis King were Freeman's star debaters, almost unbeatable in collegiate tournaments and, in retrospect, probably the best debate team TSU ever had.

"On one trip, we drove to Florida. We rolled on up the East Coast to Baltimore, then on up to New York," King said. The trips opened a new world to King and Jordan, whose encounters with whites had been limited to a few bus trips into downtown Houston. Both came from secure, church-going families in the Fifth Ward. Both had never known a world that was not segregated, and now here they were, bombarded with a whole new set of experiences. They debated at the University of Chicago, Purdue, New York University, Howard, and other well-known colleges. Two things began to change for both of them, King believed.

"As we did well, we started to realize that if we had the same opportunities as the white students . . . that if we had a level playing field, we could do just as well or better than they could. In debate, if we knew what the topic was, we had the same abilities to go to the libraries, to get the readings to prepare, to use our minds. And when we met for debate, we thought we were really meeting on equal terms, regardless of the advantages or disadvantages we all brought. That was very, very rewarding to us. We felt that, to win, we had to be so clearly better than the white team so that a judge who wanted to rule for the white team, based upon his own prejudice, just couldn't do it. We worked really hard when we went to those kinds of tournaments. We had to make our case so clear that we could not lose."

TSU's debate team was gaining a national reputation, partly because of the novelty of an all-black school producing championship debaters, but also because they were smart and quick and could easily score high enough on all the debate points to win the judge's approval. White schools started seeking out Freeman to get debates scheduled for their schools. The high point came when the Harvard debate team showed up in Houston to debate TSU. Jordan and King, and especially Tom Freeman, were elated when the debate ended in a tie. Years later, when she was awarded an honorary Harvard degree, Barbara Jordan said she considered the tie a "win."

The good showing against Harvard, plus the numerous other wins, were beginning to reinforce Barbara Jordan's view of herself as special and different from the rest. But now she was beginning to see herself in relation not only to other African Americans but to whites as well. She was beginning to think that she could hold her own in the white world, as well as in her black world. For both Jordan and Otis King, the revelation that they were as capable as white students began to dislodge the white superiority/black inferiority message they had received their entire lives. There was no doubt for King, Jordan, and Freeman's other debaters that it was *they* who could be superior if the playing field was truly level. "The self-assurance began to develop within us when we went to New York University or the University of Chicago. Those folks weren't that different from us, and some of them weren't even real sharp. You start to realize that there's more out there that we might reach for," King said. And as this revelation opened them to wider possibilities, the realities of the discrimination they encountered in their travels made them realize for the first time how forceful the barriers were against them in the South, and at home.

On their travels to various tournaments, sometimes they would have to drive eighteen to twenty hours without stopping to sleep until they got out of the South. "There was no place to stay," King said, other than with relatives or friends. "Dr. Freeman would arrange for us, plan our trips so that we would be at his brother's house one night, or at his sister's another, or with a friend. Sometimes we would drive all night long, and we really had to plan our trips, including gas stops. We would buy food at a grocery store and eat in the car and just keep moving. We didn't think a lot about it at the time because we just had to do what we were doing. But looking back, you really get angry about it."

Tom Freeman was angry about it at the time. He let the students see his rage at gas station attendants because the "colored" restrooms were often outhouses in a field, while there were separate indoor facilities for white men and women. One night when the home-packed food was gone and his students were hungry, Freeman and the students went into a barbecue place to try to buy food. The owner refused to serve them but told Freeman that if he brought the kids to the back door of the kitchen he would let them eat there. Dispirited and angry, Freeman took what he could get. There was no other choice that night. In New York, Boston, or Chicago, at least the team could walk into the front door of a restaurant. "We didn't eat at any fancy restaurants," Freeman said. "We didn't have that kind of money to spend. But we could at least go in front doors to get something to eat. That was the main point: we could go in the front door."[19]

Tom Freeman's anger reflected a changing mood among a growing number of African Americans in the South in the 1950s. The NAACP's slow, sometimes tortuous assault on segregation through the court system generated the hope, if not the actuality, of change. And each new court victory—the defeat of the all-white primary, the higher-education cases—heightened both expectation and frustration. The changes were so slow, so incremental, that they were barely noticeable. The Jim Crow laws in public facilities and public school education were as strong as ever. For southern black students like Barbara Jordan and Otis King, their education and travels in the North were exposing them to the absurdities of the South's Jim Crow system. Jordan's northern exposure to white students, white restaurants, and white water fountains began to create within her the first glimmers of race consciousness.

In 1954, during her junior year at TSU, the Supreme Court ended the myth of "separate but equal" in education by overturning *Plessy v. Ferguson* and declaring in the case of the century—*Brown v. Board of Education of Topeka*—that segregated schools in Topeka, Kansas, were unconstitutional. The Court finally agreed with Thurgood Marshall and the NAACP and stated unequivocally that, in the field of public education, the separate-but-equal doctrine had no place. "Separate educational facilities are inherently unequal." The integration of the nation's public schools was mandated to proceed with "all deliberate speed."

But *Brown* laid out no specific timetable for change, and instead of school integration, a furious reaction set in. Three segregationist referenda that Texas governor Allan Shivers placed on the ballot for the Democratic primary in 1956—preserving school segregation, prohibiting intermarriage, and supporting local rule over federal "intrusion"—won voter approval.[20] Members of the Texas legislature began enacting all sorts of segregation measures—from laws against "miscegenation" to prohibitions against the burial of whites and blacks in the same cemetery and the staging of interracial sporting events. One bill even required "integrationists" to register with the secretary of state. Critics called it the "thought-permit" bill. Yet it and all the segregation bills passed overwhelmingly. Race became a litmus test in Texas politics, as it had not been since the end of Reconstruction. And it got mixed in with the cold war "Red Scare," the anti-Communist hysteria spreading nationally with Senator Joseph McCarthy's tirades against "Communist fellow-travelers." In Texas the Red-baiting took an even uglier tone. High-level Texas Democrats, such as Attorney General John Ben Shepperd, charged that racial integration was a "Communist plot" to destroy American—and Texan—society.[21] The notion of the "co-mingling" of the races had become, in the eyes of political extremists, part of a Communist conspiracy to overthrow the U.S. government. It spilled over into mainstream politics as well. The most common epithet thrown at any white office-seeker who refused to take a firm stand against school integration— no matter what office was sought—was "nigger lover." If you were a "nigger lover" in Texas in the 1950s, you could not be elected dogcatcher.

Jordan's travels, her sense of specialness, and the furious reaction to *Brown* made her look at the world differently now. Being most popular at her all-black college, winning debates and oratorical contests, no longer seemed to matter. She had been elected editor of the yearbook. She was an officer in her sorority and a member of the student council, as well as a number of other organizations. Her activities changed nothing. It was beginning to appear to her that it was going to take more than the U.S. Supreme Court to bring about an end to segregation. Two years after *Brown,* not a single Texas school had even begun the process of racial integration. It weighed on her, and she decided that her carefully plotted course of action, her safe haven in the Fifth Ward and the Baptist Church and segregated Texas Southern University, might have to be shifted if change was ever to be possible in her lifetime.

"I woke to the necessity that someone had to push integration along in a private way if it were ever going to come," she wrote in *Self-Portrait.* "That was on my mind continually at that period—that some black people could make it in this white man's world, and that those who could had to do it. They had to move."

She decided to look at TSU's law school a little more closely. She had to examine her own academic record as well. Having taken electives and any course that struck her fancy, she was afraid she was not qualified to go anywhere *but* TSU. She decided to stay an additional year at TSU to take enough academic courses to qualify her to leave Texas, to go to a law school outside of the state. She felt she had to move away from the environment at TSU, away from the Fifth Ward community, and, most important, away from segregated Houston if she wanted to make a difference in her own world, and in the larger world of black people in relation to white society.

The pride she and her friends felt in holding their own with the Harvard debate team made her consider applying to the Harvard Law School. It must be the best, she thought. Tom Freeman discouraged her, however, telling her she would never make it; no student from TSU ever had. Instead, Freeman suggested she apply to Boston University Law School. Freeman himself had been a student at Boston University, and he thought that if she still wanted to go to Harvard, it would be easier to transfer from the school across the Charles River than to be admitted fresh out of a college created to avoid racial integration in Texas. So Jordan, quietly and without telling her family, sent away for catalogs and admission forms from Boston University. When she received them, the reality of financing an education outside of Texas hit her. If she wanted to leave Texas or to go to Boston University, she had no choice but to summon up her courage and ask for Ben Jordan's help.

Ben Jordan had always told his daughter he would stand behind her. But Boston University was truly a test for him. He believed she had an obligation to go as far as she could in achieving excellence, in becoming someone important and respectable. He did not say no immediately, as he did to many other requests. Instead, he, too, studied the catalogs and admission forms to Boston University. It was one of only two universities in America that had been open to people of all races since its founding by a group of Methodist ministers in 1839, when slavery was still an entrenched national institution.[22] Its early faculty and students had been active in the abolitionist wing of the Methodist Church, which split from its coreligionists in the South over the issue of slavery. Over the years, Boston University had become a beacon of tolerance and acceptance for bright young African Americans from all over the country.

Perhaps as Ben Jordan pondered his daughter's desire to go to Boston, he recognized his own deferred dream to be a Tuskegee graduate. He began to sense how important it was for Barbara to leave Texas to study law, and if it was that important to his youngest daughter, it would be that important to him. To make her law school dream come true, Ben Jordan pledged to Barbara all that he had. He told her, "This is more money than I have ever spent on anything or anyone. But if you want to go, we'll manage." That was all she needed to hear.

CHAPTER 5

THE TRANSITION

BARBARA JORDAN FELT lonely and lost in Boston. The pain comes through in *Self-Portrait*, written more than twenty-two years later. Yet she recognized the experience as one of those difficult but necessary life passages that are full of obstacles and tests of character. If you are lucky, they can transform you. Jordan was both lucky and prescient in her loneliness in Boston. She transformed herself from a bright schoolgirl, who relied upon a narrow range of instinctual reactions to life's experiences, into a fully realized adult, capable of reflection, insight, reason, and judgment.

In Boston, Jordan had to reflect on everything she had taken for granted—her community, her race and religion, her family, and, most important, herself. She realized for the first time how damaging segregation had been for her and her family. In Boston, she began to see the relationship of whites and blacks in terms of power. Segregation and Jim Crow laws could exist only in a relationship between the strong and the weak, a relationship between two groups unequal in power and control. She saw clearly that the position of the weaker—her position—was powerless, fixed, indeed frozen, limiting imagination as much as physical movement or economic advancement. Once in Boston, she saw that *everything* in her segregated world had been limited—her education, her experience, her religion, even her achievements, and certainly her imagination. While she had always evaluated her success and ambition in relation to other black students—except for those brief moments of triumph against white collegiate debate teams—she was now forced to measure her worth on a daily basis against students as ambitious as she, but with degrees from Harvard, Brown, Yale, Dartmouth, and other Ivy League schools. She watched them, marveling at their abilities in class and their savvy in all sorts of social activities outside of class. Then she examined herself. She did not always like what she discovered. While she still believed she was their equal in innate intelligence—Grandpa Patten had taught her that—she saw plainly that she was not their equal in knowledge or experience. "I realized that my deprivation had been stark," she said. She now understood that segregation had affected her *personally*. The realization tore a rip in the veil of detachment that had shielded her from the other world, the white world.

"I realized that the best training available in an all-black instant university was not equal to the best training one developed as a white university student. Separate was not equal; it just wasn't. No matter what kind of face you put on it or how many frills you attached to it, separate was not equal," she wrote.

She also faced for the first time the dynamics of social interaction when two groups—white and black—are relatively equal in legal rights yet separated more or less by a voluntary arrangement. While Boston had no Jim Crow laws to enforce segregation of the races, it did have patterns of culture and custom that kept blacks and whites apart, and it was these patterns that Jordan also encountered for the first time. In Boston, she was thrust into a more confusing social milieu, never knowing whether she would be welcomed, shunned, or merely ignored by the white people she met. Boston University had a tradition of religious and ethnic diversity, and that continued as it changed from a commuter school to a more residential institution throughout the 1950s. Interracial and interfaith events abounded on campus. The dormitories were fully integrated, as were all facilities. But when she was engaged with white students, observing their activities and social events, she experienced another awakening. She discovered they had a world of books, music, art, and ideas totally unfamiliar to her. She was fascinated by that cultural world and eager to be part of it, but she also felt a wave of discouragement because the patterns of conversation, interest, and experience among the white students had evolved over a lifetime of exposure to a world she had never known existed. "I knew I could not catch up," she said. "I'd have to be born again and just come from another mother's womb and have a totally different kind of upbringing. My whole life would have to be different."

The stark realization of the limitations of her experiences was a shock to Jordan. In Boston, no one knew or cared that she was a member of the Good Hope Baptist Church, or Girl of the Year, or star debater, or Ben Jordan's daughter. No one saw her within the context of the respectable Fifth Ward community that had shaped her. In Boston, she was just another black woman, from an obscure black college in Houston.

As a teenager, Jordan had developed a protective ability to shut out from consciousness anything that tended to get under her skin. She had learned to block Ben Jordan's exhortations. She had learned to ignore her fellow students' preference for lighter skins. She had refused to think about the white world beyond Houston's Fifth Ward because it was too "big," too overwhelming. She always found ways to divert her attention or to shift her focus. In Boston, there seemed to be nothing else but law school and the dormitory, and no one seemed to care whether she made it or not. Facing this, Jordan became introspective for the first time in her life. She could see that she was out of place, out of *her* place. It was disorienting. And lonely.

Jordan's first three days in Boston had been spent alone in a campus guest house because her room in the graduate women's dorm was not yet available. As she checked out the location of her housing accommodations in relation to the law school where she would have classes every day, her doubts shifted to full-fledged anxiety. Jordan realized that she would have to ride the subway from her dormitory to the law school in Isaac Rich Hall on Ashburton Place. The problem was that neither she nor Ben Jordan had figured the cost of transportation into her tight budget. Riding the subway would cost her forty cents a day, two dollars a week. Her money was so tight that two dollars a week would make a difference. Law school tuition was six hundred dollars a year, and living accommodations, meals, fees, and other necessities added another thousand dollars to the bill. Ben Jordan had come up with close to the full amount, but the tuition and room and board were such a financial strain that he and Barbara agreed that there could be no trips home during the year, even at Christmas. Ben Jordan's salary at the Houston Terminal Warehouse was $350 a month. He made extra money from preaching and other odd jobs, and Arlyne could pick up day work now and then. But they simply could not scrape up another dollar. Rose Mary had paid for Barbara's textbooks, and Rose Mary and Bennie were going to send her ten dollars each a month from their teaching salaries to provide spending money. So when she subtracted her transportation costs from the twenty dollars a month she would have to spend on herself, she realized she would have to get by with about twelve dollars a month. That would have to do.

When Jordan finally moved into her room in the women's graduate dormitory on Railey Street, she found that she had been assigned an African American roommate, LaConyea Butler, who was working on a master's degree in education. On her first day in the dorm, she met a friendly and outgoing white graduate student, Louise Bailey, whose father, John Bailey, was chairman of the Democratic National Committee. Louise seemed to like and accept her, and Jordan was delighted. While Barbara valued the security of her friendship with LaConyea, she very much wanted to have a close white friend. That was one of the reasons she decided to get away from Houston and TSU—to know and experience relationships with white people. But she soon came to view Louise as a "typical rich white girl." The friendship was limited to coffee and gossiping in their dormitory rooms. Louise seemed unable to grasp the vast differences in their circumstances.

Once when she wanted to go home to Connecticut for the weekend and had run out of cash, she asked Barbara for a loan to tide her over the weekend. All Barbara had was one of her ten-dollar bills, and she didn't know what to do except hand it over to Louise. "I just had to lend her the money," Barbara said. Fortunately, Louise paid her back, but Barbara spent an anxiety-filled weekend in the dormitory wondering how she would get through the month if Louise forgot to pay her back.

Jordan's anxiety extended to her studies as well. Her courses in law school were more difficult than anything she had encountered at Texas Southern University. Immediately she felt that her achievements thus far—graduating from TSU magna cum laude, being editor of the yearbook and a star debater—had prepared her for nothing that now mattered.

When she entered Boston University Law School in the fall of 1956, there were about 250 students in her first-year class. Only six were women, and only two were black women. The other black woman was Issie Shelton, also from Houston. Shelton was a graduate of Wheatley's football rival, Jack Yates High School, and she also had been a Girl of the Year. Barbara and Issie expected to find a hospitable environment at Boston University. Women had been BU students since the 1840s, and in 1877 the university was the first school in the nation to award a Ph.D. to a woman.[1] As early as 1842, the college had admitted a young black woman to its seminary, and even integrated its living and dining quarters then. African American students and women had been present in the School of Law almost from the beginning, although there were usually only five or six women who enrolled in each first-year class, along with about the same number of African American men.

Because Issie Shelton had earned her undergraduate degree at Indiana University and spent most of the previous four years away from Houston's segregated neighborhoods, she was a little more streetwise than Barbara. When they went to law school orientation together, and the *Law Review* was mentioned as a top honor for students, Barbara, with her characteristic bravado, said, "I'll make the *Law Review*. I'll take care of that." Issie just laughed at her, and Barbara was puzzled. But they busied themselves with orientation, getting supplies, books, and assignments.

All first-year students took the same courses: contracts, criminal law, business organization, procedure, property, and torts. The law school curriculum was based on the idea that the law should be taught as a series of related and integrated parts rather than as detached units. Courses were also organized around three essential skills its graduates were expected to master: to understand the theory behind the law; to analyze the materials encompassed by the law; and to apply certain tools in the practice of the law. While other schools might emphasize only the analytical component, or only the theoretical component, BU insisted on all three, combining traditional legal reasoning with interdisciplinary learning. The school placed a unique emphasis on written problem work in order to develop in the student the power of original thought, as well as accurate expression.

By the end of her first week of classes, Barbara understood exactly why Issie had laughed at her cocky boast about making *Law Review.* "Everything was so different to me," she wrote later. "*Contracts, property, torts* were strange words to me. Words I had not dealt with. And there I was. It appeared that everybody else's father was a lawyer . . . and they talked about working in their father's office in the summer, and what they did there. . . . Can you understand how strange this was to my ears? This was a language that I had not heard before. How could I hear it? . . . To them it was so familiar, it was just like mother's milk."

Barbara Jordan's first classes provided an appalling revelation for her. Law students were not expected to regurgitate back to their professors memorized readings or rote recitations of the law. Law professors presented cases, and students were supposed to derive principles from them. They were expected to *think,* use logic, develop arguments, and arrive at judgments. It was a new experience for her. She knew how to make a presentation in class. She knew how to memorize, maneuver, recite, entertain, even mesmerize. But she did not know how to think.

"In the past I had got along by spouting off. Whether you talked about debates or oratory, you dealt with speechifying. Even in debate it was pretty much canned because you had in your little three-by-five box a response for whatever issue might be raised by the opposition. The format was structured so that there was no opportunity for independent thinking," she said.

Jordan realized that until she sat in those first classrooms in Boston, her opinions had never been challenged. "You couldn't just say a thing is so because it might not be so, and somebody brighter, smarter and more thoughtful would come out and tell you it wasn't so. Then, if you still thought it was, you had to prove it. Well, that was a new thing for me. I could no longer orate and let that pass for reasoning, because there was not any demand for an orator in Boston University Law School," she said. "You had to think and read and understand and reason. I really cannot describe what that did to my insides and to my head. I thought: I'm being educated finally. . . . I was doing sixteen years of remedial work in thinking."

Remedial work meant extra work. Jordan realized that if she was going to survive—and survival was more critical to her now than success had ever been at TSU—she would have to work harder, read more deeply, and study longer hours than her classmates. She had to find a way to compensate for what she had missed, to become used to new patterns of study and thought. Her recognition that she did not know what her fellow white students knew did not shake her basic belief in herself, or her fundamental self-confidence. She simply recognized a *fact* and coupled it with a determination to make it otherwise. Jordan wrapped herself in the family cloak of pride and stoicism, just as her father had always done, and kept her anxieties to herself. She admitted later that she did not want her fellow students to know what a tough time she was having "understanding the concepts, the words, the ideas, the process." So she did not study at the law school library, where her struggles might have been witnessed. Instead, she found a little-used study room in her dormitory, and each night after dinner she would take her books there, hide out, and read until the early morning hours. "I didn't get much sleep during those years. I was lucky if I got three or four hours a night, because I had to stay up. I had to. The professors would assign cases for the next day, and these cases had to be read and understood or I would be behind, further behind than I was."

Jordan's first exam came in December. It was in her criminal law course, a half-year course. While taking the test, she was unable to focus on the questions because she realized it was not a specific answer the professor wanted from her, it was the *reasoning*. She was not sure she could pull a coherent line of reasoning from her brain. She felt she was miserably inept at developing the stages of thought that might lead to what the professor wanted: several interpretations of the law involved in the complex case, rather than one correct answer. She felt confused while writing out her explanations, and she thought she had flunked the exam. Afterward, she was so upset she did not want to see or talk to anyone. She took the few dollars she had, went to a movie, and sat in the dark. "I sat there for three hours wondering how I was going to lay it on my father that I had just busted out of law school." She would not know her grade until after the Christmas holidays. And, of course, she could not go home. To add to her misery, she also had to move out of her graduate dormitory room into the only campus dorm open over the holidays for foreign students and others, like herself, who would not be going home. In the strange room in cold wet Boston, she felt alone and isolated among the Korean, Greek, and Liberian students there with her.

It was a bleak time for Barbara Jordan—the first Christmas she had ever been away from her father and mother, from Rose Mary and Bennie, from Grandpa Patten, Aunt Mamie, and the other relatives. She missed balmy Houston with its seventy-degree winter days. She missed the Christmas tree in the Campbell Street house. There was nothing for her to do in Boston but study and slip away to the movies as long as her money held out. Her friend Louise called on Christmas Day to wish her a Merry Christmas, and Jordan thanked her for "inquiring about my well-being." But the reality of her relationship with her first white friend stung so deeply over that first holiday away from home that the wound was still festering more than twenty years later. "If Louise was my very good friend, why didn't she invite me to go to Hartford?" she asked rhetorically years later in *Self-Portrait*. But she knew the answer. "I didn't expect that I was going to be tottling off to their big house. I knew I was not to do that."

Things looked better shortly after New Year's Day when Jordan got her grade in criminal law. She had not flunked. She made a 79 on her exam, and she was elated. She had passed the course and survived the holidays.

Jordan's second semester went more smoothly, although she was still not sure she could master either her subjects or the process of learning the law. She joined a study group composed of about six other African American law students. None of them had been invited to participate in the small work review sessions with white students, and they decided they needed to start their own. Issie Shelton, Bill Gibson, a Rutgers graduate who was dating one of Jordan's friends, and Morehouse graduate Maynard Jackson, plus a few others, began to meet regularly to help each other out. They would talk through the cases and ask each other questions. "One thing I learned was that you had to talk out the issues, the facts, the cases, the decisions, the process," Jordan said. "You couldn't just read the cases and study alone in the library as I had been doing; and you couldn't get it all in the classroom. But once you had talked it out in the study group, it flowed more easily and made a lot more sense," she said.

Jordan struggled with her classes again that second semester, as well as with the late-night readings and study group sessions. But as the end of the semester and finals approached, she was also desperately homesick. She made a rare telephone call to her father and told him how hard her struggle had been and that she was in a real hurry to get back to the family she had not seen in nine months. So Ben Jordan found the money to buy her a plane ticket to fly home to Houston the day after completing her finals. She studied furiously for her exams, but with the assurance that she would be going home just as soon as they were over. After her exams, she was exhausted, but also excited by the prospect of her first airplane ride and going home to see her family. She used the savings from her allowance and some gift money to buy a new navy blue Lili Ann suit with a blue-and-white stand-up collar. She added a big yellow wide-brimmed hat to her new outfit. She wanted to look her best when her parents met her at the airport. Jordan's excitement, however, was tinged with just a little bit of apprehension. She was nervous about the flight, concerned about her final grades, and eager to impress her family with her new clothes and stories about life at Boston University. She recited the Lord's Prayer to still her frayed nerves as the Eastern Airlines turboprop jet sped down the runway. The irony of her situation struck her when she reached Houston. "There I was greeting my family in the Houston airport in my new suit and my yellow hat, and I did not know whether I had flunked out of Boston University Law School."

During the weeks she waited for her grades back at home on Campbell Street, Jordan tried to prepare her father for the shock if she didn't make it. The grades came, and to her great relief, she had a 78.4 average in the six courses she had taken—3.4 points above the minimum 75 she needed to stay in school. It had been the most difficult year of her life, and there was no one who knew it. Her Jordan family stoicism was intact. Years later, she confessed, with both resignation and disdain, "Of course my folks did not understand what I had been going through."

Barbara Jordan's self-assurance began to reemerge during her second year at BU. Her difficulties the first year had stemmed in large part from the need to reorient herself and adjust to an entirely new atmosphere—one where the competition was fierce and praise, which she had always received, was absent. Nevertheless, once she understood how the new system operated—both at school and in society—she figured out what she needed to do to succeed, and then she buckled down to do it.

During her second year, one of Jordan's professors finally recognized her abilities and told his very surprised student that he thought she had some potential as a lawyer. He encouraged her to go see Boston's most prominent black attorney, Edward Brooke, who would become a U.S. senator from Massachusetts in 1966, the first African American to serve in that body since Reconstruction. After meeting him, Jordan would stay in touch with Brooke over the years, but their first meeting was secondary to the recognition from her law professor. "The point was that here was a professor who had said to me that I was finally on top of the thing."

Jordan's social life also opened up. Her study group began to throw parties, and she felt she was also learning how to get to know white students without being vulnerable to the insensitivity they sometimes exhibited. "I had learned that you see what works and you see what gets turned down. It's a sense of how you are received," she wrote in *Self-Portrait*. "You drop by a room, or you walk into a study group, or you suggest that you have a cup of coffee together—and that is either accepted or rejected. So it's just trial and error. I learned that white people love to stop doing whatever they're doing and go have a cup of coffee. That was always a sure one. You knew you could do that. So I did that in the dorm. Went by and invited people to stop by and have a cup of coffee. In the big world out there it might sound trite, but people discussed issues and ideas of substance in general conversation. They were very well read; they could discuss books, and, of course, a lot of our conversation focused on law school and legal issues and points of law, and we would get into discussions about that. I learned to do that. . . . And if I can pinpoint anything . . . the most important lesson was that you always had to be prepared. You were a dodo if you were not prepared. Whatever you were talking about, in class or your private discussion, you had to be prepared."

Many years later, Jordan told an interviewer: "*The Man,* as many of our young people call him, writes the books, knows the rules and makes the decisions. And so I decided in order to cope with the world as it is and not as we would like for it to be, in order to cope . . . it was necessary to find the door for getting inside just a little bit to find out what *The Man* is doing and how he acts and how he thinks and how he reaches decisions, and then to try to get a little corner at the decision-making table where you can hang on and maybe get a word in here or there. . . . From the days of Boston University Law School, which was my first predominantly white situation to be thrown into and [to] cope with . . . I suppose I was in the process of learning."[2]

The social chitchats with white students were learning experiences for Jordan, as much as class discussions and case-study note-taking. This serious, now very studious young woman, acutely aware of her shortcomings, was preparing for conversations with white friends—and becoming quite good at it. Her encounters with them were performances, just as Tom Freeman's debates had been, and she could always master a performance. She spent the initial moments of an encounter sizing up the individual, deciding how far she could go with him or her, how much of herself to reveal. She felt safer holding back, waiting to see what might work. The Fifth Ward and the Good Hope Baptist Church upbringing were safely tucked away, out of public view. By the time Jordan could ease up a bit on herself during the second year, she had observed enough of white student society to have figured out how she might fit in. Once her self-assurance began to return, the gregarious Barbara of high school soon followed, and her circle of acquaintances took on the trappings of easygoing camaraderie and friendship.

Barbara Jordan also made time during her second year to attend Sunday services at Marsh Chapel, the religious center of Boston University. She was drawn to its preacher, Howard Thurman, who served as dean of the chapel and as a professor in the Boston University School of Theology. She heard in Thurman's sermons a way to change how she thought about and experienced religion, a way to free herself from Ben Jordan's harsh interpretation of the scriptures and his narrow path to living a Christian life.

Thurman was the first African American appointed dean of Marsh Chapel. Boston's forward-looking president, Dr. Harold Case, had named Thurman to the post in 1953—before *Brown*, before the civil rights movement, before the breakup of segregation in the South. Case wanted to build an interracial, interdenominational religious center on campus that would also be open to the African American community in Boston. Born in Daytona Beach, Florida, and raised by his grandmother, who was a former slave, Howard Thurman found respite from the humiliations of segregation when he was a boy by seeking solace in nature—the palmetto forests, the ocean, the tropical rivers. His love of nature and his sense of a God who speaks through nature provided many of his religious insights, some quite mystical.[3] Thurman developed into an academically brilliant student and graduated from Morehouse College in Atlanta and the Rochester Theological Seminary. He was a Baptist pastor at a church in Oberlin, Ohio, before he became a professor at the School of Religion at Howard University in Washington, D.C. Thurman began to publish widely and speak in churches and colleges across the country. In the 1930s and 1940s, he was considered one of the three greatest African American ministers in the United States, along with Mordecai Johnson and Vernon Johns.[4] In 1935, the YMCA and the YWCA asked him to lead a pilgrimage to Burma, Ceylon, and India, where he spent a memorable day with Mahatma Gandhi. Thurman came back from India with a sense of the "oneness" of all religions and the power of love to transcend racial barriers of hatred, suspicion, and fear. In 1943 Thurman created the first racially mixed church in the nation in San Francisco, under the auspices of the Presbyterian Church. The Interdenominational Church of the Fellowship of All Peoples had a racially mixed board of directors, staff, choir, and Sunday school. Huge crowds flocked to its services, which blended Christian theology, Buddhist mysticism, Negro spirituals, even modern dance. Boston University president Dr. Harold Case wanted Thurman to create a similar experience on the Boston campus.

Once in Boston, Thurman immediately changed all of the services and programs at the moribund Marsh Chapel, and he preached from the pulpit every Sunday. His preaching style was restrained, with the choir often singing softly a cappella behind him. His sermons were usually followed by a time of meditation. The five-hundred-seat chapel was soon full every Sunday, with an audience two-thirds white and one-third black. Thurman attracted ordinary Boston residents as well as students. It wasn't his meditative approach alone that brought the crowds to Marsh Chapel. Thurman's sermons were woven out of what he called an "ethic of love." Instead of hellfire and damnation, he preached a way of living life with love as the organizing principle. He also preached about the root causes of racism, hatred, and evil:

> *The setting for hate often begins in situations where there are contacts without fellowship. That is, contacts that are devoid of the simple overtones of warmth, fellow-feeling, and genuineness. There is some region in every man that listens for the sound of the genuine in other men. But where there is contact that is stripped of fellow-feeling, the sound cannot come through and the will to listen for it is not manifest.[5]*

Howard Thurman's first year at Boston in 1953 coincided with Martin Luther King Jr.'s first year as a doctoral student at the Boston University School of Theology. King sought out Thurman for long conversations and attended Thurman's services as often as he could. The two men became friends, both of them Baptist preachers transplanted into the academic world. King was struggling to overcome the strict Baptist fundamentalism of his upbringing, to develop the ideas that could sustain him. He was interested in Thurman's sermons and writings, as well as his travels and impressions of Gandhi. He saw in Thurman a worthy role model: preaching for a number of years, then writing and settling into a respected academic life.[6]

By 1957, when Barbara Jordan began attending Thurman's Marsh Chapel services, she, too, was dissatisfied with her Baptist fundamentalist upbringing, but most of her frustration was personalized and focused on her father. The strictness, the emphasis on punishment and sacrifice, on sin and its avoidance, had always repelled her. Her doubts, however, filled her with guilt. Until she heard Howard Thurman, she had no idea there might be another way to be a Christian. Thurman's motivation for action in the world was love for your neighbor, not fear of damnation in a future world. He wrote:

> *The experience of love is either a necessity or a luxury. If it be a luxury, it is expendable; if it be a necessity, then to deny it is to perish. So simple is the reality, and so terrifying. Ultimately there is only one place of refuge on this planet for any man—that is in another man's heart. To love is to make of one's heart a swinging door.*[7]

Yet Thurman kept his message of love within the Christian tradition, within the context of the life and teachings of Jesus. Jordan did not have to reject everything she had been taught at the Good Hope Baptist Church to accept the truths she found in Thurman's teachings.

> *The sins, bitterness, weakness, virtues, losses, and strengths are all gathered and transmuted by His love and His grace, and we become whole in His Presence. This is the miracle of religious experience—the sense of being totally dealt with, completely understood, and utterly cared for. That is what a man seeks with his fellows. That is why the way of reconciliation and the way of love finally are one way. The building blocks for the society of man and for the well-being of the individual are the fundamental desire to understand others and to be understood. The crucial sentence is "Every man wants to be cared for, to be sustained by the assurance of the watchful and thoughtful attention of others." Such is the meaning of love.*[8]

These were welcome words to a lonely, searching law student whose inherited religion provided no comfort in her struggles. She also found in Thurman a way to put into practice the kind of love he envisioned.

> *I must find the opening . . . through which my love can flow into the life of the other, and at the same time locate in myself openings through which his love can flow into me. Most often this*

involves an increased understanding of the other person. This is arrived at by a disciplined use of the imagination. . . . But the imagination shows its greatest powers . . . in the miracle it creates when one man, standing on his ground, is able to put himself in another man's place. To send his imagination forth to establish a point of focus in another man's spirit, and from that vantage point so to blend with the other's landscape that what he sees and feels is authentic—this is the great adventure in human relations.[9]

After hearing such words Sunday after Sunday, Jordan said that she came to believe that it was not necessary to adhere to her father's ritual prohibitions. "God really is caring," she said. "He wants me to live according to the preachments of His scripture, but He doesn't mean for me to be hounded into heaven. He just wants me to live right and treat other people right. I decided that then, and it was very comforting."

One of the appeals of Thurman's sermons to Jordan was their focus on how to live here and now, on how to deal with what was happening in modern society. "He did not try to get us to live because of the great lure of something beyond," she said. Life was not a preparation. It was an experience. She liked that. It seemed more realistic than anything she had heard at Good Hope.

Jordan was so taken with Thurman's sermons that she literally preached them herself. She would take the program from church services back to her dormitory and preach Thurman's sermons anew to her roommates, "whether they wanted to hear them or not. I was making sure I had it all," she said. "If I could preach it again, I really did have it." Thurman's messages made so much sense to her that she considered enrolling in the School of Theology. She wrote her father and told him so. Ben Jordan was ecstatic. Too much so, for Jordan. He made an uncharacteristic long-distance telephone call to her to say he was excited about her decision, that he saw it as her following in the footsteps of his mother, Mary Jordan, who had been a missionary. "When he said that, that sobered me," she said. "I knew that what he had in mind was not what I had in mind," she said. And that ended her temptation to become a theologian.

Jordan's new social and religious activities took just enough time away from her studies to lower her scholastic average during her second year. Her grades were high enough to remain in school (a 77.8 average), but she was still disappointed that she was not doing better. The *Law Review* was out of the question now, and so was any hope of graduating with honors. The financial strain was also taking its toll on the Jordans. Rose Mary had gotten married, and although she still sent Barbara money every month, she was beginning to have other obligations. Bennie was also planning to marry soon, so there would be another wedding to pay for in the future. Jordan applied for a scholarship to help with her final year's expenses, but was turned down. During her last year in law school, she and Issie Shelton were the only two remaining women in her class. Jordan buckled down to complete her course work. She did manage to bring her grades up and finished her last year with an 80.86 average. Her class of almost 250 entering law students had dwindled to 128. Jordan ranked 84th in the class, not quite making the top half. But it was over, and Ben and Arlyne, Rose Mary and Bennie, were so proud of Barbara that they drove to Boston in Ben's Oldsmobile to see her receive her law degree in the graduation ceremony in June. Jordan, too, was proud, and relieved, when she put on BU's traditional bright red tam and flowing gown. She had done it—on her own. She felt good.

Jordan stayed in Boston over the summer to prepare for the Massachusetts bar exam because she was not sure whether she wanted to return to Houston to practice law. She considered settling in Boston, where, she said, "the air was freer." She even applied for a job at the huge John Hancock Insurance Company, but after looking at the rows of cubicles for claims-processing lawyers, she realized, "They won't even know your name there." By the end of the summer, she was ready to go home. There was a different mood in the country. The Russian satellite *Sputnik* had been launched in 1957, changing perceptions about human possibilities. The Montgomery bus boycott had kicked off the civil rights movement, and lunch counter sit-ins and other protests were raising both consciousness and expectations in the African American community. The Congress had even passed a mild civil rights bill in 1957, and the federal government had begun to enforce school integration in Little Rock and other southern cities. President Eisenhower's term was about to end. People were beginning to talk about the 1960 presidential campaign, only about a year away. The world of politics was beginning to interest Jordan, and she had been watching the young Massachusetts senator John F. Kennedy, who might become a presidential candidate. She liked what she saw.

After three years in Boston, Barbara Jordan had a new maturity. She was less oblivious to the world around her, and she was better equipped to deal with it. She had proven herself in the white world, and in her final year at law school she had survived the loss of someone she loved.

She had received an emergency call from home. There had been an accident. Grandpa Patten was dying. She was horrified as she listened to the story. The old man had taken to drinking himself into a stupor every afternoon, and he had been wandering aimlessly near his Fourth Ward home when he fell across the railroad tracks. When he heard the blasting whistle and the whoosh and click of the iron wheels of an oncoming train, he had been unable to move fast enough to pull himself completely off the tracks. The engine descended on him with an explosive noise, shattering his frail old body and severing his legs at his hips. When the train came to a halt, railway workers rushed to John Ed Patten. Miraculously, he was alive in the bloody heap along the tracks. An ambulance whisked him away to Jeff Davis Hospital, where the family hurriedly gathered. He floated in and out of a morphine daze, and when he was aware enough to recognize his daughter Arlyne, he begged her not to let Barbara see him like this. But Ben had already wired Barbara the money to fly home. When she arrived at the hospital, she held Grandpa Patten's hand. He opened his eyes, looked up at his "Barbara Ed-ine" one last time, and then let go of his life.

In *Self-Portrait*, Jordan reminisces with great affection about John Ed Patten. The format of the slender book is alternating sections written by Jordan and her coauthor, Shelby Hearon. The section about the death of John Ed Patten was written by Hearon, not Jordan. Stoicism and guarded silence prevailed again. At the time of the book's publication, however, almost twenty years after his death, Jordan said she still carried two photographs of John Ed Patten in her pocketbook. They were still there, along with her palm-sized copy of the U.S. Constitution, the day she died.

CHAPTER 6

THE JOY OF
POLITICS

HOUSTON WAS BOOMING when Barbara Jordan returned in the fall of 1959. It was hard for her to believe, but Houston's phenomenal population growth in the 1950s made it a larger city than Boston, which had seemed so overwhelming to her only three years earlier. Houston's population was nearing one million, a whopping 57 percent increase since 1950. It was the seventh-largest American city, bypassing not only Boston but other established cities like Cleveland, St. Louis, Washington, Milwaukee, and San Francisco. Houston's wealth was in the pipelines and refineries that carried and processed oil and gas, the lifeblood of the region, but it had also become a manufacturing center for chemical products and the tools and equipment used in the petrochemical industry.[1]

While Jordan found the Fifth Ward much the same as it had always been, downtown Houston had taken on a new sheen. The banks were growing, and investors were financing the construction of a new generation of high-rise office buildings. Both residential and commercial development had spurred the growth of new white suburbs ringing the city, and new highways connected the sprawling suburbs out in Harris County to jobs in the refineries and the port. The lawyers, CPAs, and financiers who did the paperwork on Houston's megadeals were getting rich. The Houston Chamber of Commerce bragged that Houston was a model of free enterprise, an example of what could happen when government kept its hands off business development. Yet, business leaders did not hesitate to encourage governmental intervention when it improved commerce and profit. Houston had low taxes and a good business climate, with no zoning laws and very few restrictions on any kind of business activity.

By the 1950s, Houston's prosperity owed a great deal to one entrepreneur—Jesse H. Jones, who had seen the strategic importance of the city's Gulf of Mexico access during World War II. Jones was probably one of the nation's greatest finance capitalist visionaries. He headed the Reconstruction Finance Corporation during the Depression and spent billions of federal dollars to bail out the nation's banks and businesses. Later, as Franklin Roosevelt's secretary of commerce, he directed $450 million in federal capital expenditures to the Houston area for manufacturing enterprises and infrastructure improvements for World War II–related efforts. The industrial development of Houston can be traced to Jones's federally directed subsidies for synthetic rubber development, which opened doors along the Texas Gulf Coast to the manufacture of all sorts of petrochemical products. Jones also had a superb knack for large-scale *private* business ventures. He built Texas Commerce Bank into a major banking operation, owned the *Houston Chronicle,* built the first wave of high-rise buildings in downtown Houston, financed the development of major real estate ventures, and was one of the leaders of the famous Suite 8F crowd, the dozen or so members of Houston's elite who met in Jones's Rice Hotel on a regular basis to discuss and decide the fortunes and future of their city. Jones and the Suite 8F crowd represented Houston's big money, and its influence determined not only the actions and leaders of Houston's city council but those of the state legislature and the U.S. Congress as well.[2] No ambitious Houston—or Texas—politician could afford to ignore the impact of the Suite 8F crowd. Nevertheless, there was so much money produced by Houston's growth in the 1950s that one did not have to be a Suite 8F insider to profit.

A new generation of wealthy entrepreneurs had begun to emerge in the late 1950s. Typical of the new generation was the young Midland oilman George Bush, who moved to Houston and joined with Hugh Liedke to found Zapata Energy, later to become Pennzoil. Houston's new business entrepreneurs followed the pattern of their elders in figuring out how to use government money to finance their fortunes. In the mid-1950s, they invented the taxpayer subsidy for professional sports. A consortium of business and government leaders, led by Mayor Roy Hofheinz, persuaded voters to approve $35 million in bonds and other government subsidies to build the $45 million Astrodome, the first indoor sports arena in the nation. It was billed as the eighth wonder of the world, and Houston basked in the national and international attention it brought.

Yet there was another Houston, one that bore the social costs of the city's good business climate, with its low taxes and paltry public services. The city faced serious problems with flooding, street maintenance, and sewage and was beginning to experience the effects of toxic wastes and water and air pollution from the heavy concentration of refineries. One-fifth of the city's population—about 227,000 people—lived on annual incomes of less than $3,000, the national yardstick for defining poverty in 1959.[3] Most of Houston's poor were concentrated in twenty-three census tracts in the inner city—now the old Third, Fourth, and Fifth Wards, home to most of the African American population.

Barbara Jordan returned to a Houston that was still racially segregated in 1959. The African American leadership in Houston was fractionalized and unable to come up with a workable strategy to provoke change. The local chapters of the NAACP were wracked by pettiness, factionalism, and turf battles among minor leaders that took up time and energy. The NAACP had lost its ability to serve as the united voice for Houston's black community, and most African Americans who wanted to accomplish anything simply paid their dues and found other outlets.

The unchanging racial conditions in Houston had been one of the factors that made Jordan consider staying in Boston. She knew in her heart, however, that it still made "more sense to go home where people will be interested in helping you." And Ben and Arlyne Jordan wanted to help. When their daughter did come home, Ben demonstrated his delight by buying her a car, a small light-green Simca, with the understanding that he would make the monthly payments until she became established as a lawyer. It would be many months before that could happen, however. Barbara had to take the Texas bar exam and wait for the results before she could set up a law practice. Although Bennie was planning to get married the next year to Ben Creswell, the two young women, living at home with their parents, resumed their old social life, cruising the neighborhoods and going to the clubs with friends. Bennie had her teaching job, but Ben Jordan continued to support his Boston-educated daughter in her first year home after law school. Fortunately, he was under less financial pressure than at any time in his life. His longevity and interest in the Teamsters union had won him the post of shop steward; he now represented other workers in grievances or disputes with management. His pay was steady, his benefits were good, and he still drew income from his ministerial duties. For the first time in eleven years, he was not paying college expenses for his daughters. He was proud of Barbara and happy to have his youngest daughter at home. They enjoyed watching the Sunday afternoon televised football games together, and Ben seemed to relax his stern manner in her presence at long last. Barbara, too, eased back into her old life, feeling quite comfortable once again in the neighborhood and in the Good Hope Baptist Church where she accommodated herself to the fundamentalist preachings by accepting them as symbolic rather than literal interpretations of the Bible.

At twenty-three, Barbara Jordan had the appearance and demeanor that would characterize her adult years. Her commanding voice carried just a hint of a Boston accent, the inflection that would become familiar to Texans the next year when John F. Kennedy campaigned there for the presidency. To be fair, she had had traces of the accent even before she went to Boston. Her TSU mentor and debate coach Tom Freeman had picked up the clipped Boston accent himself while a student at Andover Newton

Seminary, and Jordan had taken on Freeman's dramatic speech characteristics while at TSU. After law school, her old friends barely noticed any change. That was "just Barbara," always a little different. New acquaintances, however, would be immediately caught off guard by the sound of her voice, her clipped words and precise diction.

Jordan's physical presence was also striking. She had developed a distinctive walk that resembled a lateral roll. She ambled from side to side as she shifted her bulk on thin legs, knees turned inward and feet thrust outward. She dressed neatly in boxy suits and wore high-heeled shoes that thrust her body slightly forward when she moved. The walk and her increasing weight, which had reached over two hundred pounds, reflected a proud bearing and a distilled self-confidence. People noticed her. And then when they heard her voice, the power of her physical presence was overwhelming. She had only to speak a few words to capture attention. Jordan also had a way of looking at people that kept them locked in her force field. Her gaze could be penetrating, and her eyes sometimes took on a fierceness when she wanted to focus on the person in front of her. Yet when she released her welcoming smile, her formidable demeanor eased, although never completely. People were drawn to her, interested in her, and they usually struggled to say something intelligent, or at least not foolish, in her presence. By the time she returned to the Fifth Ward, Jordan was fully invested in her physical as well as her intellectual being. She was a woman who knew and accepted herself—her size, her color, and her capabilities. As such, she carried an aura of power unusual for one so young.

When Jordan passed the Texas bar exam in the late fall of 1959, she was only the third female African American attorney licensed to practice law in Texas, along with about three dozen African American men.[4] Jordan had taken the three-day Texas bar exam in Austin with some of her old friends from TSU days, including Andrew Jefferson, one of a small group of African American students who had managed to graduate from the University of Texas School of Law after Heman Sweatt's pioneer days there.

When she got word that she had passed the bar and was now licensed to practice law in Texas, Jordan, for all of her self-possession, had no clear idea of exactly what she wanted to do. With prodding from her father, she had some business cards printed and started handing them out on Sunday mornings at Good Hope Baptist Church.

"One day a man called me, a member of my church, and he had my card. I had to learn then and there to draw up a will," she said. "The second client was a lady, a friend of my sister, who had been separated from her husband for years. But now that she had a lawyer, she decided to get a divorce."[5] Little by little, Jordan began to build a practice, largely by providing legal services to Good Hope members. She used her parents' dining room table and the family telephone to conduct her law business. She drove back and forth to the courthouse in downtown Houston to file papers for wills, divorces, adoptions, and occasional probate cases. Once she learned the procedures, the cases were neither demanding nor challenging. They did not require the analytical thinking or reasoned judgment she had struggled to develop in Boston. By the fall of 1960, she was already bored with her law practice, and as a result she had plenty of time on her hands. The presidential campaign was heating up, and she went down to the local Kennedy-Johnson campaign headquarters to volunteer her services.

The labor lawyer and Democratic Party leader Chris Dixie remembered vividly the day Jordan came in to volunteer. "Barbara Jordan walked into the headquarters and said she wanted to help. I told her she could either lick stamps or stuff envelopes, and she elected one or the other, and she went to work, right at the bottom rung. I don't think I had ever heard of her, but it didn't take many minutes to realize that here was a quality person, and we should cultivate her. And we did."[6] Dixie was one of the organizers of the Harris County Democrats, a group of liberal party activists who controlled the party machinery in Houston. The Harris County Democrats were one of the first racially integrated political organizations in Texas, and Chris Dixie himself had long been recognized as one of a handful of white friends the black community could count on.

Dixie immediately assigned Jordan the task of working with him, Versie Shelton, and John Butler to develop a block-worker program for the forty black precincts in Harris County. Jordan threw herself into the operation and was immensely proud of her efforts. The way in which she would make her greatest contribution to the local campaign effort, however, was discovered almost accidentally. "One night there was a speech at a black church in the Fifth Ward . . . and the speaker who usually gave the pitch was sick and couldn't show up. I was selected to do the pitch, and I was startled with the impact I had on people. Those people were just as turned on and excited as if some of the head candidates had been there to talk about the issues. When I got back to the local headquarters that night—we would usually close up about twelve or one o'clock—they said, 'Look, we are going to have to take you off the [mailing] lists and the envelopes and put you on the speaking circuit,'" Jordan recounted.[7]

Once on the speaking circuit, rallying mostly African American groups, Barbara Jordan came to be noticed by some of Houston's most prominent black citizens. Mack Hannah, the owner of Standard Savings and Loan Association, the only black-owned S&L in Houston, began inquiring about her. "Mr. Mack" was *the* recognized African American "ambassador" to the white political establishment. As such, he was a conduit for information and a mediator of disputes. Ever since the institution of Jim Crow laws, men like Hannah had become brokers with the white community on behalf of blacks. In return for small favors, they were expected to keep the lid on potentially explosive situations that could spill over into the white community. After the end of the whites-only primaries, these "ambassadors" would usually line up with a prominent white Democratic politician. Mack Hannah was considered a Lyndon Johnson man, and he had access to Houston's downtown establishment. Hannah was one of the African American business leaders who wanted to build Texas Southern University into a great institution, and because of his connections he had been appointed to its board of regents. Later he would become its chairman. Hannah's main base of support in the African American community came from the churches. Standard Savings and Loan, which Hannah advertised as the "largest Negro owned and controlled business" in Texas,[8] bought most of the church bonds issued to finance the construction of their buildings. So Hannah was particularly close to the ministers of the one hundred or so African American churches in the Third, Fourth, and Fifth Wards. When Mack Hannah found out that Barbara Jordan had grown up in A. A. Lucas's Good Hope Missionary Baptist Church, and that Reverend Lucas personally vouched for her and her family, Hannah paid even closer attention, spotting Jordan as a talented future community leader. At his instigation, even more churches and civic clubs invited her to speak.

Chris Dixie also arranged for Jordan to speak to white Democratic groups and labor union rallies. Her combination of wit and inspiration wowed some of the white groups. She hit it off immediately with members of District 37 of the United Steelworkers, one of the first Texas labor unions to fully integrate its membership. The beefy, macho men who worked at Armco, U.S. Steel, Hughes Tools, and other manufacturers couldn't seem to get enough of her. The first time Jordan was invited to speak to the Steelworkers, she asked Dixie what she should say. "I told her they were a bunch of proud people, and all you have to tell them is that if you were a workman in a factory, you would want to belong to the Steelworkers union." Barbara Jordan did exactly that, and "they all promptly fell in love with her," Dixie remembered. Other industrial unions, such as the Communications Workers, the Longshoremen's Association, and the Oil, Chemical and Atomic Workers (OCAW), also warmed to Jordan and put her on their agenda to help get out the Democratic vote on Election Day.

As the campaign built momentum, Jordan realized how much she loved what she was doing. Politics was giving her the opportunity to shape her identity in a way her fledgling law practice had not. Inspiring or entertaining an audience was not a new experience for her. She had been doing that since high school. But seeing something *happen* as a result of her public speaking was new. When a crowd of elderly black precinct workers decided to walk an extra block to get people out to vote because of something she had said, or when a group of union officials added another shift to a get-out-the-vote telephone bank because she gave them compelling reasons to act, she felt that she could influence events, perhaps even bring about change. She felt she really mattered. And people acted so grateful to her for speaking to them. They told her they were moved by what she said. Jordan began to see herself as a person who had power. That was different from merely being a star.

The African American orator Frederick Douglass had made a similar discovery one hundred years earlier. Douglass was a former slave who escaped to the North and became one of the nation's most effective spokesmen for abolition. Realizing the power of his own speech, wrote Christopher Lasch, "gave him access both to the inner world of his own thoughts and to the public world in which the fate of his people would be decided for better or worse."[9] Barbara Jordan's power of speech in her initial political efforts gave her similar access to both worlds. The surprise reaction from the white world to her voice and words certainly allowed her to add new value to her own inner thoughts. People *responded.* Their eyes shone, their faces smiled, their voices cheered. *Her* words produced an effect. It was more than adulation, however. The audiences could be moved to action, and it was action that could generate the votes that would allow the fate of her people to be decided. This discovery whetted her political appetite.

"By the time the Kennedy-Johnson campaign ended successfully, I had really been bitten by the political bug," Jordan recalled. "My interest, which had been latent, was sparked. I think it had always been there, but that I did not focus on it before because there were certain things I had to get out of the way before I could concentrate on any political effort. I recall I had been keenly interested in the Stevenson-Eisenhower contest, but my interest had been unfocused. Now that I was thinking in terms of myself, I couldn't turn politics loose."

Jordan was indeed thinking in terms of herself. As she watched the presidential campaign and went to the rallies for local Democratic officeholders, she could envision herself as one of them. In the 1960 campaign hustings, she had broken through to white Houstonians for the first time. Not only did the labor unions, the political activists, and the liberal organizations treat her with respect, but some of them were plainly in awe of her. She saw reflected in their eyes a new sense of possibility for herself. Although she had been paying close attention to the activities of Martin Luther King Jr. and civil rights protesters, she had never been able to see herself as one of them. Her upbringing had been too conservative and her Baptist notion of respectability was too ingrained to violate the law deliberately—even if the law was unjust. She had personally seen the effects of a jail term on her Grandpa Patten, and she knew she would have none of that. But she had also been influenced by A. A. Lucas's approach to righting the wrongs inflicted upon her race: Use the system to beat the system. For Lucas and the NAACP, the courts opened the door to change. Now, for the first time, she could envision herself taking on a prominent role *within* the system. Instead of using her skills as a lawyer in the courts, however, Jordan could see herself as a politician and an officeholder. That would feel comfortable. Being a civil rights protester would not.

For all of Jordan's efforts and enthusiasm, the Democrats still lost Harris County in the 1960 presidential election, but the huge margins in the forty black precincts Jordan organized helped the Kennedy-Johnson ticket carry Texas by slightly more than forty-six thousand votes, out of more than two and a half million votes cast statewide, a 50.5 percent majority. Houston had the largest African American vote of any city in the South in the 1960 election.[10]

Ministers, politicians, and precinct workers gave Jordan a large share of the credit for being able to channel enthusiasm in the African American community into actual votes on Election Day. Her reputation for solid work, as well as her charm and ability to inspire a crowd, kept her name alive. Speaking invitations continued to come in after the election. Jordan spoke to any group that wanted her. "If they wanted somebody to talk about flowers, I'd be the one out there to talk about flowers," she said. She was beginning to be noticed. Her name showed up in the *Houston Informer* and the *Forward Times,* the two African American community newspapers. Jordan was delighted but modestly offered an explanation: "There was the novelty of my being a black woman lawyer, and graduating from a law school in Boston, and sounding different. That got attention."

Jordan joined the Harris County Democrats, the NAACP, and the Harris County Council of Organizations (HCCO), which had replaced the NAACP as the dominant political organization for African Americans. Formed in 1949 to bring together all of the city's black civic, social, and political clubs, the HCCO took on a decidedly more political bent than the NAACP. One of its goals was to recruit black candidates to run for political office. It had mounted a massive poll tax drive in 1958 in Houston's Third and Fifth Wards that made it possible for Mrs. Charles White, an African American former schoolteacher and civic leader, to be elected to the school board. The Harris County Council of Organizations underwrote a series of meetings to bring together all the black organizations, and "a united effort to run a Negro candidate was crystallized."[11] While there had been other Negro political aspirants before, this was the first time that a candidacy was more than a personal action. With HCCO serving as coordinating agent within the black community, as well as liaison to the liberals and to organized labor, Mrs. White won. Her election in November dispelled the notion that it couldn't be done. The wider Houston black community began to see the significance of the ballot, and of the need for unified action.

Barbara Jordan saw it, too. She was flattered after the 1960 presidential elections when the Harris County Council of Organizations sought her out and the organization's venerable leader, Moses LeRoy, invited her to become an HCCO officer. Chris Dixie began to encourage her to think about running for the Texas legislature on a liberal-labor-minority coalition ticket in 1962. The coalition had never supported an African American candidate for the legislature, and Dixie thought it was time. Jordan was still practicing law, however, on her parents' dining room table. If she was ever going to run for office, she felt, she would need to have a more professional operation.

Jordan had begun to see her career as a sequence of steps: law practice, community involvement, political campaign, and officeholding. She felt she had only just begun, and she did not yet have the funds to open a real law office. The few dollars she picked up for handling wills and divorces did not allow her to accumulate any savings. Jordan thought that if she temporarily gave up the nickel-and-dime law practice and taught school during the summer she might save enough to open a law office in the Fifth Ward. So in the spring of 1961, she applied to six black colleges for a summer teaching position. Tuskegee Institute, her father's alma mater, offered her a job teaching political science. She accepted and went off to Alabama for the summer. It was not a pleasant experience. Tuskegee's conservatism and its Booker T. Washington legacy of accommodation seemed out of sync with the tide of history as the civil rights movement was gaining steam. After her own experiences in Boston, even in Houston's Fifth Ward, she found the atmosphere repressive. "Tuskegee disturbed me," she said. "I think it was the most frustrating summer I've ever spent. I got the job because they had just fired the political science professor for activities that they considered to be against the best interests of Tuskegee. Teaching political science, I understand he had the students reading things like Karl Marx, and they were quoting him, and that kind of disturbed folks at Tuskegee. I stepped into that situation and stood it as long as I could, which was one summer. I could not have been in the permanent employ of that school."[12]

Nevertheless, Jordan "saved every nickel" Tuskegee paid her, and in January 1962, she opened a law office in the heart of the Fifth Ward—in the 4100 block of Lyons Avenue where a dark, knotty pine–paneled stairway led to an office over a drugstore. She shared the space initially with an old friend from Wheatley, Asbury Butler, and later James Muldrow joined them. Each of the three attorneys kept a separate law practice but shared the rent and expenses of one secretary. Jordan's portion of the rent was seventy dollars a month. Ben Jordan went with his daughter to pick out office furniture; even with her Tuskegee money, she still needed his help with the expense. She bought a white Formica desk with black trim and a secondhand white leather swivel desk chair. She found a file cabinet and two "squatty cream-colored chairs" for her future clients to use. She also bought a typewriter on credit. That was it. Prospective clients began to call after she placed an ad in the Yellow Pages. "I didn't have to sit and admire my desk all day," she said. Sometimes a white person would call as a result of her Yellow Pages advertisement, and Jordan would ask, "Are you aware that I am a Negro?" They would say, "No," or, "Thank you, anyway," and hang up.[13] Jordan never represented a white client in those early days.

Barbara Jordan's Lyons Avenue office put her on the Fifth Ward's main street, the center of commerce and activity. The travel writer Richard West called Lyons Avenue "Soul Street" because it so captured the flavor and community spirit of the Fifth Ward.[14] There were shops, theaters, cafés, weekend flea markets. It was like a small-town Main Street. If you wanted to see or be seen by people who mattered in the Fifth Ward, you went to Lyons Avenue. And that's where Barbara Jordan was—in the thick of it. She became a fixture in her little green Simca, stopping to buy cigarettes in the drugstore, always carrying a briefcase full of legal papers. People came to know her as the "Boston lawyer," or that "fine speaker," or the "Reverend Ben Jordan's girl" out of Good Hope and Wheatley, or simply "our Barbara." People noticed her, and Jordan began to build a record as a community leader. She was active in the Delta Sigma Theta alumnae organization, served as an officer of the Harris County Council of Organizations, and became president of the all-black Houston Lawyers Association, whose members included Mack Hannah's son-in-law, Harrel G. Tillman; and Otis King, Jordan's former TSU debate partner who was teaching at the TSU law school.

Jordan also intensified her public-speaking schedule in early 1962, addressing PTA groups on the importance of paying the poll tax. The deadline for registering to vote by purchasing a $1.75 poll tax was February 2, and the Harris County Council of Organizations was mounting a poll tax selling campaign with Jordan as the star speaker. The Democratic primary elections would be in May, and as the filing deadline approached, Chris Dixie began pressing Jordan to file her name. She hesitated, telling him frankly, "I don't know whether I want to make this move at this particular point in my career." Jordan's goal to hold political office had been clear since she experienced the joys of politics in the Kennedy-Johnson campaign, but she wasn't sure whether 1962 was the year. Now Dixie was offering her the opportunity to have a place on the liberal-labor ticket. "It was a plausible offer," Dixie said later, "because in 1958 the entire Harris County Democrats' slate of supported candidates swept the legislative delegation— sending six liberals to Austin." In the primary of 1960, however, all but two had been defeated when conservatives came back with a well-financed slate of their own. Nevertheless, Dixie was confident that the liberals could win once again. In 1962 they had some money, and their organization had been invigorated by the Kennedy election victory.

Jordan finally decided that a 1962 timetable could be reconciled with her goal; she told Dixie she would run. But she still had one concern— money. Jordan told Dixie, "Well, Chris, I make enough money to eat and buy my clothes and gasoline for my little Simca, but I certainly don't make enough money to run a political race." Dixie told her not to worry, because she would be carried on the ticket of the Harris County Democrats, which would absorb a significant cost of the campaign. Dixie himself and a wealthy Houston socialite turned political activist, Mrs. Frankie Randolph, were financing precinct organizing and materials for most of the candidates supported by the Harris County Democrats.

Another factor in Jordan's decision to run in 1962 was the strong support and encouragement she received from an association of black ministers, influenced by Reverend A. A. Lucas. Barbara Jordan was their ideal—a respectable, churchgoing young woman from a good Baptist family. Many of them had known her as a young girl, when she gave her recitations, or when she and her sisters sang for various congregations. The ministers committed to raising the first five hundred dollars to give to Jordan for her filing fee. As the deadline approached, however, the ministers did not yet have the funds. Jordan had to go back to Dixie and explain that she did not have the money for her filing fee. "Chris loaned me the five hundred dollars. Five crisp new one-hundred-dollar bills. And I liked that," she said. She filed her election papers, along with the fee, and set about to organize her campaign. When the ministers came through with their pledge a few weeks later, she paid Dixie back.

To get her campaign organized, Jordan first went to see Aloysious Wickliff, an African American law professor at TSU who had run for the legislature and lost in 1956. Wickliff had run Mrs. Charles White's successful school board campaign. He knew all of the precinct leaders and understood how to organize a campaign in the forty-plus black voting precincts that mattered. He agreed to be her campaign manager. Jordan's aunt Mamie Reed and her husband, Wilmer Lee, had been active in Fifth Ward politics, and they introduced Jordan to other key people. Uncle Wilmer took Jordan to meet the richest African American in Houston, Hobart Taylor, who owned a taxi franchise. Taylor gave her twenty-five dollars for her campaign, but his blessing was more important than the money. With Taylor and the banker Mack Hannah behind her, plus the ministers, the Deltas, Al Wickliff's precinct leaders, and the Harris County Council of Organizations led by Moses LeRoy, Jordan had the unanimous backing of Houston's black leadership. Chris Dixie then began to prepare the way for her with the liberal Democrats and labor union members who made up the Harris County Democrats.

The Harris County Democrats' organization was the brainchild of Mrs. Frankie Randolph, the legendary figure among Texas liberals who had put up the money to start the crusading *Texas Observer* in the early 1950s. She represented the liberal-loyalist faction of Texas Democrats, who by 1962 were hopelessly estranged from conservative Democrats and the Texas financial establishment. The election of the conservative Democrat Lyndon Johnson to the vice presidency under the liberals' adored John F. Kennedy enormously complicated the liberal-conservative split in Texas. The relationship between Johnson and the liberal wing of his party in Texas had been one of mutual expediency and mutual suspicion, and the tension between them extended down to party activists at the precinct level in major Texas cities.

The midcentury split between Democratic Party liberals and Democratic Party conservatives in Texas would complicate Barbara Jordan's entire political career, and any criticism of her that emerged from within the state would usually derive from this intraparty feud. Jordan was just a little girl when the split began in 1944. The Texas supporters and opponents of President Franklin Roosevelt had broken into open political warfare. The conservative faction, calling itself the Texas Regulars, was part of a movement among well-to-do Democrats throughout the South to reassert their strength within the party. The Regulars did not like the direction taken by Roosevelt and the national party, and when the NAACP lawsuit *Smith v. Allwright* ended the whites-only primary, they decided to put up a separate slate of unpledged Democratic electors. In combination with other unpledged electors from the South, the Texas electors would withhold votes from FDR and throw the election into the House of Representatives, which was dominated by southern members. Roosevelt's supporters in Texas, however, organized at the precinct level and elected enough delegates to the party's state convention to unseat the Regulars. The fight over Roosevelt's fourth term brought together the party's liberals and loyalists and constituted the beginning of the modern liberal movement in Texas.[15] The loyalists began to develop grassroots activists who would support the national Democratic Party against the states' rights Regulars. But the liberal-loyalists lost control of the party when their candidate for governor, Homer Rainey, a former president of the University of Texas, lost the primary in 1946. Once the Regulars were back in power, they discouraged grassroots electoral participation by minorities, workers, and less affluent Texans.

When the Texas Regular Allan Shivers became governor in 1947, he purged the remaining liberals and Roosevelt loyalists from the state party's offices and stacked the party's executive committee with his own appointments. In 1952 the loyalists' worst nightmare came true: the "Shivercrats" defected en masse to the Republican presidential nominee, Dwight Eisenhower, over Democrat Adlai Stevenson and took the entire Democratic Party apparatus with them. The party structure was now in the hands of the most conservative elements in the state—and delivered over to the Republican presidential campaign. Many of the party's large contributors, including some of Houston's Suite 8F crowd, had joined the Republican presidential camp as well. After the liberal-loyalist judge Ralph Yarborough unsuccessfully challenged Governor Shivers in the Democratic primary that spring, Yarborough supporters decided they needed a permanent organization to retake the party structure. They established precinct organizations in major cities, coordinated by an umbrella group at the state level, the Democratic Organizing Committee, later to become the Democrats of Texas (DOT).

Frankie Randolph, heiress to a lumber and banking fortune and a daughter of Houston's wealthy establishment, was a central figure in these insurgent groups. When she stayed with the loyalists against Allan Shivers, her former friends called her a "traitor to her class."[16]

With the organizing skills of women like Billie Carr, who would become the statewide leader of the liberals, and funds from liberals like Mrs. Randolph and Chris Dixie, plus the AFL-CIO's Committee on Political Education (COPE), the loyalists began to build precinct organizations across Texas. From the beginning, they welcomed African American and Mexican American supporters into their ranks. It was unprecedented at the time for blacks and whites to meet together in the same room and plot a mutually beneficial strategy. That is exactly what the liberal-labor loyalists initiated, creating an even more vehement opposition to their movement from the die-hard segregationists within conservative party ranks. In spite of that opposition, the coalition of liberals, labor, and minority voters had become strong enough in Houston, Galveston, San Antonio, and a few other places to elect several liberal members to the Texas legislature. They and loyalists from across the state joined forces with U.S. Senate majority leader Lyndon Johnson and Speaker of the House Sam Rayburn in 1956 to take back the state party apparatus from Governor Shivers. For these two national leaders, it was an embarrassment to have the Democratic Party machinery in their home state in the hands of the Texas Regulars and the "Eisenhower Democrats" who supported the Republican Party nationally.

While the Johnson-controlled party maintained contact with some African American businessmen like Mack Hannah, it kept its distance from many of the black precinct activists who formed the base of NAACP activities in Texas. Black organizations like the Harris County Council of Organizations were solidly in the liberal-loyalist camp, as was the Texas AFL-CIO, which already was beginning to develop grassroots political organizations. But unions were anathema to the Suite 8F crowd, and particularly to some of Lyndon Johnson's network of supporters, who continued to shut labor out of party deliberations, as well as minorities.

In 1962, if Barbara Jordan wanted support from white Democrats for a state legislative race, the liberal-loyalist organizations would provide her only hope of finding it.

CANDIDATE JORDAN

Barbara Jordan was an ideal candidate for public office. During the three-month primary campaign in the spring of 1962 she traveled throughout Harris County (which covered 1,747 square miles), holding candidate forums and political rallies. It took only one or two Jordan speeches before the candidates for each of the twelve legislative seats allocated to Harris

County, as well as the crowds, recognized her appeal. At her first outing, Jordan talked about how she was going to change state budgeting procedures and break up the cash-rich University of Texas endowment to spread some of its money around to other Texas colleges, such as the University of Houston and Texas Southern University. She also argued that Texas had an obligation to use its welfare programs to take care of people who couldn't take care of themselves. Jordan thought her first speech "sounded wonderful." And her first audience agreed. People jumped up and applauded her.

"That was the first standing ovation I ever received," she said. It occurred to Jordan, however, that she needed to know whether they were standing because she was the only black, she was the only woman, she sounded different, or she said such fantastic things about state reform. "I didn't know what had really turned them on, what had given them the spark. And I needed to know so that I could keep doing it throughout my campaign. There they were, all on their feet just cheering and cheering. And after that response the last two speakers . . . were just wiped out." For the remainder of the campaign, the standing joke among candidates was: "Let's get there early so we can get on the program before Barbara Jordan." Jordan was thrilled when she heard the others speak about her that way.

During all of those gatherings—almost nightly—she got a good chance to size up Willis Whatley, her white opponent in the Democratic primary Place Ten legislative seat. Whatley had resigned his office as assistant district attorney to make the race. A 1956 graduate of the University of Texas law school, Whatley had spent his entire career as a prosecutor for his mentor, Frank Briscoe, the Harris County district attorney. Briscoe was connected to the business community and to conservative Democrats, and he paved the way for Whatley's inclusion on the conservative ticket. As Jordan listened to him speak, she would say to herself, "Anybody in his right mind will vote for me against this fellow. . . . I've got a better case to present." And some of her old boastfulness returned as Election Day approached. She said she would look at Whatley and think, "You ought to just forget it, Willis, and go back to the practice of law."

She had sound reasons to feel confident. She was part of the Harris County Democrats' endorsed ticket, as well as that of the Harris County AFL-CIO. What being part of these slates meant for Jordan was that her name would be included in mailings and hand-cards distributed to more than ninety thousand union members in Harris County, as well as to the precincts organized by the Harris County Democrats. It meant a surge of volunteers putting up signs and distributing handbills, as well as precinct block-workers and telephone canvassers—more support than any black candidate for public office in Harris County had ever had. She was still responsible, however, for raising her own money for radio or television advertisements. She would also have to conduct her own activities in the black community and participate in rallies and events throughout the remainder of the county. Jordan had her own campaign headquarters in the Atlanta Life Insurance Company building on Prairie Street, and it became a hub of family and church activity on her behalf. Rose Mary and her husband, John McGowan, and Bennie and her husband, Ben Creswell, were there almost every evening. Arlyne and Ben, Aunt Mamie and Wilmer Lee, and a host of other relatives, church members, and friends kept the office open around the clock. In the beginning, however, the usually confident Jordan found it difficult to ask for contributions. "I just couldn't do that," she said. "So I took my father along with me, and he asked for the contributions."[17] Ben Jordan also accompanied his daughter to many evening political functions for the sake of "propriety."

Both African American newspapers endorsed Jordan's candidacy and covered her campaign extensively. She spoke at any church that would invite her, and because she was so heavily supported by the ministers' associations, she had church-speaking engagements almost every day of the week. There was a buzz in the middle-class African American community about her candidacy, a real excitement about this extraordinary young woman who was about to break the barriers. By the midpoint of the campaign, Fifth Ward residents were bringing their nickels, dimes, and quarters into headquarters to help Jordan. And after her campaign manager, Aloysious Wickliff, made a special appeal for funds through the *Informer*, people started coming up to Jordan at church functions to press their crumpled one-dollar bills into her hands or pockets. She had to start carrying a large envelope in her purse to hold the loose change. The church ladies and auto mechanics and store clerks raised her spirits enormously, and Chris Dixie was also keeping her pumped up, telling her, "You're great. You're going to win."

Jordan even went before the editorial boards of the *Chronicle* and the *Post* to seek their endorsements, becoming the first African American candidate to try to reach Houston's news elite establishment. Although she didn't receive their endorsements, the newspapers began to assign reporters to follow her progress.

The liberal candidates were not alone in slating up. The conservative faction of the local Democratic Party also ran a slate of candidates for the twelve legislative positions. It was heavily financed by Houston's business community, which attacked the labor-liberal ticket as a collection of "radicals," "integrationists," and labor "goons." "The crowd on the West Side were calling us 'nigger-lovers' and all that ugly stuff," Chris Dixie recalled.

Liberal optimism still prevailed on Election Day. As the lines started forming early in the morning at Fifth Ward polling stations, both Jordan and Dixie were excited. African American voters were coming out in droves to vote for "that lady." Dixie thought Jordan would pull 90 percent of the black vote and at least 30 percent of the white vote, enough to push her over the top. But he began to have some concern when he saw the difficulty that black precinct judges were having processing the huge numbers of voters. "We didn't have enough voting machines, and the precinct judges were not trained to handle the crowds. We saw voters leave in frustration after waiting two or three hours to cast their ballot." He was convinced that many of Jordan's supporters never actually voted.

There were two other problems as well. One was with Jordan herself: she was black and female and big. The Rice University professor and political pollster Richard Murray was helping in Jordan's campaign and early on sounded its only discordant note when he told her, "People don't really like your image." What he really meant was that *white* people didn't like her image. Because of the demographics of Harris County, she had to attract white votes to win the election. She reacted defensively at the time, telling him, "Well, I can't do anything about the first two elements—black and female." She later said that she didn't feel those were factors she had to overcome. "I felt that the *black* and *woman* stuff were just side issues, and that people were going to ignore that. Now, that was naivete on my part, but it seemed to me that no one would care at all about such factors, that those were extraneous issues, that they were neutral." This was Houston, however, not Boston, and Houston was still bitterly segregated by both custom and law. In 1962, the year of Jordan's campaign, John F. Kennedy's assistant secretary of labor, George Weaver, had been turned away from the famed Shamrock Hilton Hotel because he was black.

The second problem Jordan faced would make victory even more illusive: she had to run countywide. Her base of support was among black voters, largely concentrated in the center of the city. She could also count on the support of some of the blue-collar precincts, which would vote for organized labor's slate of candidates down the line. Jordan did run exceptionally well in those areas. As the votes started coming in election night, however, she was swamped by the white vote in the remainder of the county. The at-large system of electing legislators through a countywide vote, rather than a single-member district encompassing only the precincts where most black Houstonians lived, virtually assured her defeat. In 1962 Harris County voters, as a whole, would not vote for a black candidate—male or female, big or little. Jordan drew only 23 percent of the white vote. Willis Whatley defeated her, winning more than sixty-five thousand votes countywide to Jordan's forty-six thousand.[18] She didn't know what hit her.

"How could everybody else do so well?" she asked. "How could the other liberals make it and not me?" Jordan drew record votes in the all-black precincts but lost virtually everywhere else. "The [white] people would come to hear me and be very polite. But they didn't give me their votes. The votes were just not there from these fine white people. That was very puzzling to me and disturbing. I spent a lot of time trying to figure out what did happen in that race."

Jordan's analysis reflected her hurt feelings, rather than cold reason. She placed most of the blame on the liberal friends like Chris Dixie who had encouraged her to run. "The feeling I had was that I had been used to get black people to vote. And that nobody else on the ticket brought that kind of strength to me in return," she said. Six white liberals on the Harris County Democrats' slate won the primary, helped enormously by the huge black turnout.

"Those fine people, I thought, all the Harris County Democrats, they had me come to teas and coffees in their areas in the southwest part of town . . . but they didn't give me their votes," Jordan complained. But she never expressed her frustration with the Harris County Democrats openly to Dixie.

"In her book [*Self-Portrait*], she was a little bit sour toward me and the Harris County Democrats," Dixie remembered. "I didn't know that until I saw it in her book. She felt she was being used. And in one sense of the word, that's absolutely correct. I did see in Barbara the chance to wake up the black community, and it did work. . . . Barbara excited the black community and brought about what I was anxious to get done, which was to get more and more people in the black community attached to the electoral process."

Another complicating factor in the 1962 Democratic primary contributed to Jordan's loss, and to Dixie's misplaced optimism about her chances from the beginning: the hotly contested Texas Democratic primary election for governor. Texas liberals thought they had an excellent chance to win the governor's race because the field was so crowded with prominent conservatives. There were six major gubernatorial candidates—one liberal and five conservatives, including John B. Connally, who would ultimately win—and the strong field generated a huge turnout among conservative voters in Harris County. Every conservatively inclined voter in the county came out to vote for a candidate for governor, and they swamped liberals further down on the ballot. Jordan was aware, however, that first-time white liberal candidates managed to win. She struggled to find the reasons.

Even with her loss, Jordan had become a beacon to Houston's black community. Her speaking ability, her intelligence, her demeanor—everything about her indicated that she was a natural leader. By late 1962 most of Houston's black community was ready to follow her wherever she wanted to go.

CHAPTER 7

THE RIGHT TO VOTE

"IT'S TIME TO think about getting married."

That's what Barbara Jordan heard again and again from her family and friends after her defeat in November 1962. It was as if they were saying to her that she had indulged in this interesting diversion of running for political office, but now it was time to get on with the business of ordinary life. But *ordinary* was the last thing Barbara Jordan wanted. In fact, she felt that a marriage would be not only ordinary but stifling, limiting, and prohibitive for any kind of political success she might eventually have.

A nascent, unnamed feminism was stirring in the twenty-seven-year-old Jordan. Old John Ed Patten had planted it, and Ben Jordan had inadvertently nurtured it by generating within his daughter a fierce reaction to his role as demanding husband and father. Arlyne Patten Jordan's choice to marry into the pious Jordan family and give up her individuality, as well as all prospects of developing her talents as a public speaker, had always left a bitter taste with Grandpa Patten. He repeatedly told his granddaughter, "Do not take a boss. Do not marry. Look at your mother." Even Ben Jordan admonished his daughter never to let a man "take away your brain."[1] Giving up her brain was exactly how Barbara Jordan saw a woman's traditional role in marriage.

"People didn't expect a woman to make rough decisions," Jordan wrote in *Self-Portrait.* "She was the ward of her man; she was always to be available at her husband's side no matter where he had to go or what he had to do. She must always be prepared to turn and kiss his puckered lips." Disdain and sarcasm infused Jordan's remarks as she described her state of mind some fifteen years earlier. It is difficult to know whether her views were as definitive then as they became when she was the more experienced forty-two-year-old woman writing *Self-Portrait*. Yet it is clear that the very idea of marriage was problematic at the time.

"My mother wanted me to be married, and my father wanted me to be married and so did everybody else. But they also wanted me to be successful." In 1963 Jordan perceived the dilemma as an either-or choice: either marriage or career, not both. She did not think the choice was fair. "Where a man was concerned, the public perception was that he was supposed to get out there and lead and do and make decisions and the rest of it; and no one said to him that he needed to care for the babies, or iron the curtains or clean the johns. That was not expected of him. What was expected was that he'd marry a woman to do it for him." Jordan simply could not see herself in that kind of subservient role.

The discussion at this point in Jordan's life, however, was purely theoretical. She had never had a serious boyfriend, or even the kinds of dates that Rose Mary and Bennie had enjoyed. In high school she was both bigger and smarter than most of the boys, not the type of "cute," light-skinned girl who got asked out. In college, she focused on accumulating accolades and awards. And in Boston she studied all the time. "I never knew Barbara to go out on a date," said Otis King, who had known Barbara in high school and, as her college debate partner, spent an extraordinary amount of time with her. King remembered that Jordan had many male friends and frequently went places with them, but there was never a special boyfriend in her life. It was the same story once she came home to Houston. After getting her law degree, she plunged into the world of politics. "Barbara was never interested in any man in that way as far as I could tell," Chris Dixie said. "Or any woman, either, for that matter. Barbara was too interested in her political career to be diverted by anything like that." She would joke about her single status, telling a friend one time, "When I find someone as smart as I am, I'll get married."[2] She told Otis King that she didn't see how any man would put up with her career and activities. Nevertheless, King said, "she expressed some concern about living the public life and not being able to have a private life as a result."

In her own mind, she had settled the matter. "I made the decision, and it was a fairly conscious one, that I couldn't have it both ways. Politics was the most important thing to me. I reasoned that this political thing was so total in terms of focus that, if I formed an attachment over here, this total commitment would become less than total. And I didn't want that. I did not want anything to take away from the singleness of my focus at that time," she wrote. But just as she had withheld from her family and friends her struggles with so many other life-changing decisions, Jordan kept this one to herself, too. She decided that she would not confront the issue directly with her parents, her sisters, or her friends. So when they asked, "When are you going to start thinking about getting married?" she would tell them, "Down the road a piece. . . . Just let me get it all organized, and then we'll see."[3]

Barbara Jordan was clearly going to run for political office again. Even after the bitter surprise of her election loss, Jordan knew she was caught up in the magnetic force field of political life. Running for political office had been the most exciting experience of her life. Forty-five thousand people had voted for *her*, for Barbara Charline Jordan. People recognized her now and called out to her on the street: "Hey, Barbara," or, "Way to go, Barbara," or, "I voted for you, girl." Articles about "Miss Barbara Jordan" appeared with some regularity in the *Forward Times* and the *Informer*, Houston's two African American newspapers. She was in demand as a speaker at the black churches and civic clubs. White Houston, too, recognized her. In 1963 the *Houston Post* ran a photograph and feature story about her in which she said that politics was "my forte," and that "many of the problems Negroes demonstrate against, protest and negotiate for could be solved by an effective and powerful use of the ballot."[4] On the basis of such statements, people expected her to run again. They saw her as a leader, and she became a Fifth Ward celebrity.

In 1963, because of civil rights activities throughout the South, Jordan had ample opportunity to expand her sphere of influence. People wanted to hear what she had to say, but her ideas were still developing.

A few years later, Jordan would tell Texas journalists that during that period she had faith that white Americans would respond to the needs of black Americans once they were fully aware of the conditions and restrictions under which they lived. "The Negro in the main, the majority of black people in this country, still have faith in white America. Don't forget that. Even those who shout the loudest and those who talk the longest, if you could get them in the quietness of their conscience they would hope not to destroy America but to make America own up to their involvement in it in a meaningful way. The Negro has always had the faith, and almost blind faith, in what this country promised to become."[5] What Jordan was also saying was that *she* had always had faith in what America "promised to become." A part of her recognized that Martin Luther King Jr. was helping the nation become what it should be. Even though she could never bring herself to take on the kinds of struggles that King engaged in, or generate the civil disobedience and protests that were finally forcing decent Americans to confront the problem of racial discrimination, she recognized their value. The question for her was how best to deal with the problems of discrimination in Houston. And there were problems.

In Houston, no African American was yet immune to segregation's sting. In 1963 the Nobel Prize winner and undersecretary-general of the United Nations, Ralph Bunche, had been picketed by white segregationists when he spoke at Rice University. The public reaction of Houston's established black leadership was one of shock and dismay. A younger generation of students and activists decided it was time to act.

A group of Texas Southern University students, who called themselves the Progressive Youth Association, had begun to hold protests and demonstrations to integrate downtown movie theaters and lunch counters. In 1963 African Americans had even picketed the First Baptist Church in Houston after three Negroes were denied membership. The Houston protests on the whole were mild, however, poorly organized and sparsely attended in comparison to those in other areas of the South. Houston's business leaders proved to be far more adept in dealing with the protests than other white southern leaders; they successfully employed a strategy of accommodation or avoidance. No prominent business leader in Houston wanted to let anything happen to disrupt the economic boom. So if Houston's black people wanted to eat at a dime-store lunch counter downtown, let them! The integration of a few restaurants or public facilities did not matter to the city's white leaders, since most of their important business and social affairs took place in private, segregated neighborhoods and clubs—the Ramada Club, the Houston Club, and the River Oaks Country Club.

The Reverend Bill Lawson, a civil rights activist in the 1960s, believed that the white business leadership acted out of its own self-interest. "They did not want to have the economic growth stopped because of racial confrontation," he said. A member of the Houston Council on Human Relations agreed: "The white community [is] afraid of what demonstrations might do to business and the Houston image. So they give just what they seem to need to give."[6] The "giving" worked to forestall serious demonstrations or disruptions and contributed to a lack of sustained militancy among Houston's black population. Some activists found that troubling, given the tone and tenor of the times. The *Houston Post* reporter Saul Friedman was frustrated by the low level of activism in the black community. "For all their numbers . . . for all the voting power they wield, the Negroes of Houston are among the most politically docile and backward in the south, if not the nation," he wrote.[7] Yet by 1963 some downtown restaurants were integrated, and Houston opened its public swimming pools on an integrated basis for the first time that summer. By 1965 Mayor Louis Welch could confidently tell a national conference of mayors, "We have no race problem in Houston."[8]

The African American community saw it differently, as did Barbara Jordan. For Jordan, two issues were of primary importance in the struggle for civil rights: jobs and schools. Each issue would allow her to take on the kind of civil rights work she felt most comfortable with—meetings, negotiations, and behind-the-scenes efforts to bring about change. Yet, the lure of elective office still permeated her work for the NAACP and other organizations.

In 1963 she made a trip to Austin for the NAACP to testify before a legislative committee hearing about the impact of some key education bills on Negro students. While she was there, Jordan visited the gallery in the state Capitol Building to watch the House of Representatives in action. She looked down on the man who had defeated her in 1962, Willis Whatley, and thought, "I ought to be in his place. I deserve it."

Barbara Jordan felt that the tide was turning and that conditions might be improving enough by 1964 to make another run for the legislature. Texas legislators had to run for office every two years, and all twelve legislative seats would be up for grabs again in a countywide election. Once more, Jordan began to set a campaign in motion. Although candidates ran for a specific "place," all voters got to vote for their choice in each of the twelve "places." Conservative lawyer Willis Whatley had defeated Jordan for the Place Ten seat in 1962. In 1964, Jordan considered that it might be easier to run against a weaker candidate than Whatley, who had the solid backing of the downtown business community and plenty of money for his campaign. She picked a place where she thought the incumbent was more vulnerable. But a white candidate, John Ray Harrison, who had run and lost on the same liberal slate with Jordan in 1962, called Jordan to his office shortly before the filing deadline and told her that he planned to run against the weaker incumbent. Harrison convinced Jordan that it made "better sense" for her to run again for the Place Ten spot, against Whatley just as she had done before. "He [Harrison] made me feel that it was the thing to do, so I agreed to that," Jordan said. But almost immediately after leaving Harrison's office she realized that she had made a tactical mistake. She had allowed herself to be manipulated into taking on the more difficult campaign against a powerful incumbent while Harrison would have a relatively easy race. "I knew that, and I took a deep breath and said to myself: 'Well, you made a mistake.'" When expensive billboards and television ads began appearing in April for Willis Whatley, Jordan's feeling that she had been snookered was confirmed. Yet she still hoped for an election victory.

She bought new, more feminine clothes to try to improve her appearance. She spoke to enthusiastic crowds all across the county, but this time she drove to the meetings in a new light-blue Oldsmobile Cutlass, the first car she ever owned in her own name. She worked hard to get out the vote in the black precincts, but the 1964 Democratic primary campaign was essentially a repeat of 1962. Nothing had changed. White voters dominated the countywide elections, and no matter how many black voters turned out to cast their ballots for Jordan, they were a numerical and racial minority. Because more than 70 percent of all white voters still refused to vote for a black candidate, no matter how well qualified, there was no possibility that Barbara Jordan or any other black person could win a legislative seat in Harris County.[9] Although Jordan increased her white vote by 50 percent and pulled 97 percent of the black vote, it was not enough. She lost to Willis Whatley again. Her vote-gathering strength, however, was becoming evident. In 1962 she pulled a total of forty-five thousand votes. By 1964 that number had grown to sixty-five thousand.

While Jordan believed she had been more realistic about her chances in 1964, she was still devastated by the loss. More importantly, she was confused. Somehow, she felt, she should have been able to overcome all of the obstacles that were present before. She had worked harder and put in longer hours. What was wrong? Again she turned her frustration on the very people who had helped her—those liberals in the Harris County Democrats who could not deliver what they had promised her: enough white votes to put her over the top. She had a hard time accepting the fact that her hard work, a reinvigorated black electorate that had bought poll taxes in record numbers, and the endorsements of the largely white Harris County Democrats and the Harris County AFL-CIO were not enough to win an election for her. Jordan was only beginning to grasp that it was the very structure of the at-large system of countywide elections in which she was forced to run that was responsible for her defeat. The at-large system in Harris County, and almost everywhere else in the South, would always ensure that no black candidate could be elected as long as white voters had a sizable numerical majority. In 1964 African Americans made up less than 25 percent of Harris County's population. The 1962 and 1964 election results were totally beyond her control, and ultimately outside the sphere of influence of groups like the Harris County Democrats.

The real meaning of her losses began to come clear by the time the U.S. Congress passed the Civil Rights Act in July 1964. The majority of white voters in Houston and the Texas political establishment were dead-set against legal or structural changes to ensure racial equality, and most opposed the legislation. President Johnson had been able to persuade only four of the twenty-four members of the Texas congressional delegation to vote for his civil rights legislation.[10] Opposition to integration in Texas was intransigent. On the eve of the civil rights vote, Governor John Connally made a speech in Florida opposing the public accommodations section of the bill. Chris Dixie called Jordan to ask whether she'd seen Connally's remarks on television. "Did I see it? I cried all night about it," she told Dixie. Connally also gave Jordan a more personal reason to cry that fall at the state Democratic convention when he vetoed her nomination to serve on the party's executive committee on the grounds that it wasn't ready for a Negro.[11]

Jordan was beginning to understand that it would take federal intervention to alter the political reality for black political aspirants like herself in Houston and Texas. So she put aside her frustrations with her liberal friends; as weak as she perceived them to be, they were the only allies she had in her efforts to build a political future.

A few days after the passage of the Civil Rights Act, Chris Dixie and key officers of the Steelworkers union called Jordan to invite her to dinner.

"Barbara, we all want to go to a restaurant together to try out *your* new civil rights," he recalls telling her. She laughed and told him she would be delighted to go. Dixie pulled together a group of labor, liberal, and minority leaders to celebrate the passage of the Civil Rights Act in one of Houston's finer restaurants. The owner nearly "broke his neck trying to get enough tables together to take care of our entourage," Dixie said, "and we had a wonderful time laughing and celebrating Barbara's newfound freedom." By that time Jordan had decided she was going to stay involved in politics one way or another. It had not been an easy decision. She had considered leaving Texas and going somewhere else to establish herself and run for office, but she dismissed that notion. Once she fully grasped the nature of the discriminatory electoral structure that prevented her from winning elections in Houston, she reasoned that something could be done about it. For her, the passage of the 1964 Civil Rights Act was proof that change might be possible. Moreover, President Johnson's commitment to guaranteeing civil rights under federal law gave her hope. His landslide victory over Republican Barry Goldwater in November 1964 seemed to infuse her with a new political energy.

The loss of the 1964 legislative race, however, left an indelible mark on Jordan that would stay with her the remainder of her political life. She made up her mind that she had to preserve her political independence at all costs. "I couldn't let anyone else get in my head and make my decisions any more," she said. While she might seek the advice of others, she would *never* accept their direction, or put herself under their control. Never.

PUBLIC ACTIONS

Barbara Jordan was offered a unique opportunity in early 1965 to expand her work outside of the Fifth Ward and develop more contacts in the white political community. Harris County judge Bill Elliott offered her a job as his assistant. She became the first African American to work at the Harris County Courthouse in a position other than janitor. "Courthouse" politics had long been the centerpiece of political organization and deal-making in Texas. While that was beginning to change as Texas shifted from a rural to an urban state, the "courthouse crowd" in many Texas cities could still dominate political life. The Harris County Courthouse crowd could not be ignored in the politics of the city of Houston, or even in the state of Texas. Being on the inside of Harris County government was a true breakthrough for an African American.

Judge Elliott was considered a liberal and had been elected as the liberal-labor coalition was establishing its firm organizational base in 1958. He was so popular that he had managed to win reelection in 1960 and 1964. He won support of the business communities by putting funds into the construction of the Astrodome and Houston's new international air-port—both projects enormously popular with Houstonians—but he also had strong ties to organized labor. At one time he had been a union member, and people like Chris Dixie and members of the Harris County Democrats considered him a strong friend. Early on, Elliott had spotted Barbara Jordan as a new type of political leader. "Bill really gave Barbara her start and really encouraged her, giving her time off to build a political base," according to Texas Supreme Court justice Oscar Mauzy, a former state senator and a friend of Elliott's.[12]

Under Texas law, a county judge like Elliott in reality had few judicial functions. His main responsibility was to preside over the county's governing body, called a commissioners' court, which served as the administrative arm of the state—running county jails, maintaining roads and law enforcement in unincorporated areas, running the state's health and welfare programs, keeping public records, and overseeing the state's system of courts and dockets.

Both of Houston's daily newspapers ran big photographs and news stories about Jordan's appointment, which they labeled a "first" for the Harris County Courthouse; in fact, they noted, she was the first Negro to hold any high position in *any* county in Texas.[13] Jordan was tremendously excited about her job, which was to coordinate the "diverse interest" the county had in welfare agencies, and projects such as the Community Council, the Action for Youth, and the Council on Alcoholism. She felt that she had a position of real responsibility, and that she was not merely a "head Negro in charge of nothing," she said. "I must look into each agency program and evaluate its effectiveness and see how the county can help in implementing the program," she told reporters proudly. She also talked to the press about "revising" the American philosophy of welfare based on handouts. Instead, she called for policies to "eliminate the causes of poverty" and to "help unfortunates return to a productive role."[14]

Jordan was grateful to Elliott for giving her an opportunity to get out of her Fifth Ward "rut" and to begin to move in the wider world of Houston. His tolerance for her "off-the-clock" volunteer activities—she continued her speaking schedule and even spent a few hours every day at her law practice—enabled her to become active in the very center of Houston's community and political life. In 1965 Jordan undertook her only significant public civil rights protest activity. She used her new high profile for the benefit of Houston's black community in the civil rights battle that still mattered most to it: school integration. While Houston's city fathers had acquiesced on the integration of public facilities, the actions of board members of the Houston Independent School District were an entirely different matter. Two years after the *Brown* decision, the Houston school board had made no effort to begin integrating the schools.

In the fall of 1956, Barbara Jordan's aunt Mamie Reed Lee had escorted a young Good Hope Missionary Baptist Church member, Beneva Williams, to an all-white school for enrollment. When she and another student, Delores Ross, were turned away, the NAACP filed the first of its lawsuits in federal district court to begin the enforcement of the *Brown* decision in Houston. In 1957 the district court ordered the school district to admit children to schools on a nondiscriminatory basis with "all deliberate speed," but the Houston school board still took no action. The NAACP, on behalf of the plaintiffs, filed a motion for further relief, and on April 8, 1960, the court ordered the board to present a plan for desegregation by June 1. But the board immediately minimized the court order by deciding to integrate only one grade a year. In September 1960, only 12 African American children were admitted to the first grade in all-white schools. Six years after *Brown,* they were the first black students to integrate Houston schools, which had 168,000 students in 170 schools. In 1961, 33 African American students would enter previously all-white schools, but by 1962 Houston still would have only 63 black students in integrated classes, in only six schools in the district.

Parents of black students who had been denied admission to all-white schools once again filed discrimination suits in federal court. The Fifth Circuit Court of Appeals ordered the desegregation of schools through the sixth grade to begin immediately. By 1964 slightly more than 1,000 African American children were in integrated classrooms from kindergarten through the fifth grade. They represented, however, only 3 percent of the 39,000 black students who were eligible to integrate all classes up to grade six.

In the meantime, the NAACP was pushing for integration of all grades, including Houston's high schools. Black parents filed a petition with the U.S. District Court asking that advanced vocational education classes at San Jacinto High School be opened to Negroes. Finally feeling the pressure, the school board voted to admit Negro students to vocational courses at San Jacinto, "if a similar course was not available" at any Negro high school. Once again, however, the policy was on paper only: school administrators stalled the admission of black students to San Jacinto High School.

Houston's African American community had finally had enough. "It was an insult to us," said Reverend Bill Lawson, who at age thirty-six was a leader of several community youth groups that had been working with the NAACP to integrate the schools. The NAACP sent the president of the school board a letter, signed by Barbara Jordan and four others, protesting this latest inaction; when they received no response, the younger leadership met to plan a protest action. "We decided to have a [Martin Luther] King–type march, and Barbara was one of the five of us who took the lead," Lawson remembered. They called their group "PUSH," People for Up-graded Schools in Houston.

Jordan, Lawson, and the others planned to organize a Negro student boycott. The mass absence of minority students would be costly to the Houston schools because state money allocated to the schools was based on average daily attendance. Lawson issued a public call for the black community to "combine forces for a show of strength that would mean demonstrations where needed, but negotiations where possible."[15]

Lawson was overjoyed when he arrived at the South Central YMCA on the day of the event and found three thousand teenagers ready to march to the main administrative offices of the school district. As the children, the five organizers, and a dozen or so NAACP leaders made their way to the administration building, they chanted, "All we want is freedom, and we want it now." The orderly student march shocked school and city leaders. Moreover, there were many students who did not march but also did not attend class. Eighty-five percent of the school district's African American students stayed home that day, creating a huge financial loss for the district. School officials realized they could not ignore PUSH. Its leaders represented a new group of young "respectable" professionals in Houston's Negro community, not the shouting, angry Texas Southern University students who had staged earlier protests. City leaders recognized that the PUSH march and threats were serious, and that the older leaders like Mack Hannah might be out of touch with the undercurrents of tension and frustration engulfing the black population.

Members of the school board, which was now divided by a four-to-three conservative majority, offered to set up a meeting with PUSH to discuss its demands. By June, and under additional pressure from the U.S. Department of Justice, the board had finally accelerated its desegregation program. A few months later, a federal judge ordered that the twelfth grade in Houston schools be desegregated by 1966. With its goals largely met, PUSH was disbanded, although Lawson and others continued to bring lawsuits to put pressure on the school district in other areas of race discrimination.

The student march and PUSH's successful negotiations were significant events in Houston's school integration efforts in the mid-1960s, and they helped turn Barbara Jordan into a hero, one loved and admired in the African American community. When she wrote *Self-Portrait* in 1979, however, she never mentioned the episode. Reverend Lawson, who remained a friend and admirer of Jordan's, acknowledges that although she was a leader in the effort, and an effective negotiator with the school board, "her enthusiasm for marches was never great. . . . This was not her thing. You have to look at her background, the structure of her life to know that she would always want to make the system work, rather than confront it."

Several years after the PUSH experience, in 1970, Jordan came closest to explaining her feelings about protest actions to the *Houston Post* reporter Charlotte Phelan: "All blacks are militants in their guts, but militancy is expressed in various ways. Some do it quite overtly, while others try to work their way through the system, trying to bring about changes in race and human relations. That's the way I like to work. Disruptive or divisive behavior is of no help."[16]

By 1965 the system was finally beginning to work on a number of fronts that would ultimately help Jordan reach her political goals. First, the federal Voting Rights Act of 1965 provided federal oversight of any phase of the voting process that might discriminate against African American voters—including voter registration. The purpose of the act was to enforce the Fifteenth Amendment guaranteeing the right to vote to anyone regardless of race. The act abolished literacy tests and prohibited any state or local political jurisdiction from applying voting prerequisites to deny or abridge the right of citizens to vote on account of color or race. It gave the attorney general and the Justice Department discretionary power to appoint federal officials as voting "examiners" who could oversee voter registration. Federal observers were also authorized to watch the polls to guarantee that voting procedures followed the law. Although the most restrictive sections of the law—the freeze on state changes in voting laws or procedures pending federal approval or "pre-clearance"—did not apply to Texas, the law did put the state and local governments on notice that their actions would be closely watched and subjected to lawsuits if racial discrimination appeared to be a factor in elections. Texas and Houston election officials had to make certain that black voters were not turned away from the polls on Election Day because of a lack of voting machines or poorly trained election officials, as had occurred in black precincts when Jordan ran for the legislature in 1962 and 1964.

Although the Voting Rights Act did not outlaw the poll tax in state elections, it did "instruct" the attorney general to challenge the constitutionality of the poll tax in state and local elections.[17] President Johnson's attorney general, Nicholas Katzenbach, did so, and in 1966 federal courts struck down the use of a poll tax in Texas, Alabama, Mississippi, and Virginia.[18] For the first time since 1903, poor and minority Texans would not have to pay for the right to vote.

These significant changes in federal law and state practice would open the doors for a massive entry of African Americans into the political system for the first time since Reconstruction. But none of the changes were as important to Barbara Jordan as the court cases on reapportionment.

The whole area of how states created voting districts came under review by the U.S. Supreme Court for the first time in 1962 when it heard *Baker v. Carr*. Before 1962, the high court had not allowed cases dealing with redistricting to come before it because they were so highly political. But the civil rights movement raised all sorts of new concerns that ultimately changed the course of judicial review. The Court decided to hear *Baker v. Carr* because it dealt with the arbitrary apportionment of state legislative seats without regard to the numbers of people represented. In its decision, the Court enacted an equality standard that set a precedent for the review of redistricting controversies under the equal protection clause of the Fourteenth Amendment. Two years later, the Court followed its own logic in *Baker v. Carr* and ruled that Georgia's state congressional redistricting plan was unconstitutional because Georgia's Fifth Congressional District had three times as many constituents as other Georgia districts. The Court's opinion in *Wesberry v. Sanders* established the principle of "one man, one vote." Although this case applied to congressional redistricting, the liberal lawyers Oscar Mauzy of Dallas and Bill Kilgarlin of Houston, both future justices of the Texas Supreme Court, filed challenges in federal court to the "Texas way" of redistricting its *state* Senate and House of Representatives. They had good reasons to act.

Pro forma redistricting with each census had not significantly changed election district boundaries in Texas since 1921. By the early 1960s, major metropolitan areas in Texas were grossly underrepresented in the state legislature. Houston, Dallas, San Antonio, and Fort Worth were limited to thirty-five of 150 seats in the House of Representatives and four of thirty-one members of the Texas Senate. Equal representation on the basis of population would have yielded them fifty-four House members and ten senators.[19] The Texas Constitution even had a provision limiting the number of representatives allowable per county. As long as districts remained apportioned in favor of rural areas, conservative Democrats could fight off repeated challenges from urban liberals and the increasingly urban-based Texas Republican Party, which had been revitalized because of the influx of new residents from other parts of the country who had no ties to the old Texas Democracy. The Eisenhower presidential victories in the 1950s had also brought a new respectable look to the Republican Party in the state, but it was a political party all dressed up with no place to go.

In 1964 the Supreme Court handed down four decisions that changed all of that. The most important for Jordan was the case of *Kilgarlin v. Martin,* in which the Court invalidated Texas districting schemes for both the House of Representatives and the Senate and threw out the restrictive section on county representational limits in the Texas Constitution. As a result of the decision, the Texas legislature had to abolish the old "at-large" system and draw new geographic-specific Senate and House districts in urban areas in time for the primary elections in 1966. On the basis of population, legislators had no choice but to shift six Senate seats from rural areas to urban districts. Harris County picked up three of the new seats, bringing the total number of senators who would represent the county in the legislature from one to four. One of those new districts just happened to be in the heart of the city—taking in the downtown business district, the Houston ship channel, the rail yards, and the Third, Fourth, and Fifth Wards. When Barbara Jordan overlaid the new inner-city Senate district on the voting precincts where she had carried 50 percent or more of the vote, she saw that under the new lines African American voters would make up 38 percent of the district's population. Working-class white voters and a small group of Mexican American voters made up the rest. With her history of having carried almost every voting precinct within the new Senate district boundaries, she thought she finally had an election district that she might be able to win.

THE TURNING POINT

By December 1965, Jordan was telling friends she would run for office "one more time," this time for the new Senate District 11. But there was one serious complication. A white liberal Democratic incumbent state representative, who had always had the support of organized labor and the Harris County Democrats, decided he wanted to run for the same post.

Jordan was in Judge Elliott's office talking about the race when she got a call from J. C. Whitfield Jr., who had served eight years in the state House of Representatives. Charlie Whitfield asked Jordan whether she planned to run for the new Senate seat. She told him she was considering it. "Barbara," he said, "I thought I ought to let you know I'm going to run." "Well, good luck, Charlie," she replied. But when she hung up, her discussion about the campaign with Judge Elliott became much more urgent. Whitfield did not live in the newly created district but had just bought a house there and was planning to move into it. She told Elliott that if Whitfield was getting a head start, she thought she had better quit her county job and begin campaigning. She could not be a political candidate and remain on the county's payroll at the same time. Elliott offered to let her stay on the county payroll until the filing deadline in February, but Jordan decided to quit immediately.

Because she had scaled down her law practice, Jordan needed a source of income in the absence of her county paycheck. Her old debate partner, Otis King, was the director of the Crescent Foundation, a nonprofit corporation that had a $360,000 manpower contract with the Department of Labor to line up businesses to train unemployed welfare recipients for jobs. King offered Jordan a $10,000 contract to be a project director. When Jordan sought to clear her status as a state political candidate holding a federal contract with the U.S. Labor Department, she was told there was no obstacle as long as she did the work required under the federal contract. With the question of her work and income settled, Jordan set out to solve the Whitfield problem.

When Jordan called Chris Dixie, he told her that he and the Harris County Democrats would support her in the Senate race, even though Whitfield had friends within the organization and would put up a battle for the endorsement. She also called her Steelworkers friends, Jim Ward, Jim

Smith, Eddie Ball, and others, who told her they could block a labor endorsement of Whitfield and swing labor's support her way.

Jordan's first test was with the executive committee of the Harris County Democrats, who would meet behind closed doors to make a recommendation for a vote by the membership as a whole. Democrat Bob Eckhardt, who had been elected to Congress two years earlier with the endorsements of labor and the liberals, said the group plainly had a dilemma. "Whitfield had good credentials. It was a pretty hard choice to make. What it got down to was institutional fairness. We had a pretty good tripod after 'one man, one vote' got put into effect: labor, blacks, liberals. . . . But you couldn't expect blacks to be one part of that tripod without their having a leader of their own. We couldn't say: 'You ought to support us but we won't support you.' "[20] The committee voted to recommend Barbara Jordan's endorsement.

Charlie Whitfield was furious and felt betrayed. He had been a loyal supporter of liberal causes. "He had a perfect voting record as far as we were concerned," Chris Dixie said, "but we just had to go with Barbara. She was a star." Whitfield sent word to Jordan that the battle was not over. "I'll fight to overturn the committee recommendation and I'll win on the floor," he warned her.[21] "Well, I'll be there, too," Jordan let him know.

Eight hundred people showed up for the membership meeting on March 9, 1966, in a crowded public school auditorium. Chris Dixie presented the executive committee report to the members and told the crowd, "If Charlie Whitfield gets elected, he's going to be another fine senator in Texas. But if Barbara gets elected, that's going to be the beginning of the modern history of Texas. And that's why we made the recommendation we did." Then it was time for Whitfield and Jordan to speak for themselves. Whitfield emphasized his record, his name identification, and his vote-getting power, and he received a warm response. When Jordan spoke, however, she was interrupted by applause four times. "I was born in this district. I live in the district and these are the people I am representative of," she began. "I ran a race in 1962. You endorsed me and I lost," she told the crowd. "I ran a race in 1964. You endorsed me and I lost. I want you to know that I have no intention of being a three-time loser."[22] The crowd applauded wildly and voted overwhelmingly to grant her the endorsement.

Jordan's endorsement by the Harris County Democrats, and later by organized labor, threw Whitfield into a rage, and he immediately launched into bitter personal attacks on Jordan, even injecting racial overtones into his campaign. First, Whitfield charged that Jordan's arrangement with the Crescent Foundation involved a conflict of interest, and he fired off telegrams to U.S. Attorney General Nicholas Katzenbach and Secretary of Labor Willard Wirtz, demanding an investigation. But because Jordan had prudently cleared her work with the Department of Labor before she even filed for office, nothing came of the episode except for a few headlines in the daily newspapers.[23] Neither the Justice nor the Labor Department even responded to Whitfield. So he formulated another attack—this one with racial overtones.

Whitfield sent a flyer out to African American voters telling them they *had* to vote for him or they would "fail the test" of racial prejudice. "My opponent has indicated that she will achieve ninety-five percent of the Negro bloc vote. . . . But I think there will be far too many of you who will remember your old friend, who have cast aside race prejudice, and will in this instance vote for me even if my skin does happen to be white." Then Whitfield asked, "Can you vote for a white man? . . . In this decade you have seen some great decisions go through an all-white Supreme Court, granting unto the most humble person of the Negro lineage equal justice under law. So I say to you that the White Man has passed his test, and this race is going to be your test. Can you pass *your* test?"[24]

Black voters were incensed when they received the flyer. And white liberals who had supported Whitfield in the past were both angry and embarrassed. The statewide liberal newspaper, the *Texas Observer,* whose financial angel, Mrs. Frankie Randolph, had been one of the founders of the Harris County Democrats, editorialized:

> *Whitfield is trying now to make Negroes who are proud of Miss Jordan as a Negro somehow ashamed of their wish to elect one of their own race to high office. Not just for Negroes, but for us all, it would be a very good thing to have a qualified Negro in the Senate. Even if Whitfield and Miss Jordan were equally qualified, the* Observer *would be for Miss Jordan for the larger reason, the need to break the race barrier in the still all-white legislature; but they are not equally qualified: Miss Jordan is better qualified. . . . She has better political judgment than Whitfield, she makes better speeches, and she's more liberal. The coalition of labor, the minorities, and the unattached liberals in Houston is backing her all-out. One supposes Whitfield thinks they all fail the test. It's he who fails it. Let us hope that Miss Jordan is elected.[25]*

Jordan also took on Whitfield directly, picking up his flyer and using it regularly in her speeches. Disputing his claim that a mindless bloc of black voters would vote for her solely because she was black, she brought her audiences to their feet when she told them, "Look, don't tell us about *black* bloc votes. You know white folks have been bloc-voting for the past century. We don't have to apologize. Our time has come!" And she would finish her speech by repeating Whitfield's question: " 'Can a white man win?' I say to you, No. Not this time. Not . . . this . . . time!"[26]

Barbara Jordan knew better, however, than to rely on rhetoric alone in this campaign. This time she left nothing to chance. She took over her own precinct organizing and sent a mailing to thirty-five thousand black voters in her district, showing them exactly how to vote for her. The mailing featured a big photograph of Jordan seated at her desk, with the American flag behind her, and big bold letters at the bottom saying, "I need your help this year." When the votes were tallied in the Democratic primary Saturday night, May 8, Barbara Jordan had won 64 percent of the vote. Because there was no Republican challenger on the ballot in November, Miss Barbara Jordan had just been elected the first black female state senator in Texas history, and she would become the first black person since 1883 to serve in the Texas Senate.[27]

Jordan's election party was mobbed with cameras, microphones, news reporters, white politicians, ministers, Good Hope church members, Delta sisters—hundreds of people crowded in for a glimpse of their new senator. Cars streamed out onto Lyons Avenue, with people hanging out of the windows and honking their horns. When Jordan got to the party, a scream went up from the crowd. She was beaming. Ben and Arlyne were crying. Judge Elliott told reporters, "This is just a first step for her. We will be hearing a lot more from Barbara Jordan. In the Senate, she will be a credit to the Negro race, the white race and all the races. We're extremely happy to see her win."[28] Both the *New York Times* and *Time* magazine ran her photo in the days immediately following the election, and Barbara Jordan told reporters, "I'm still kind of numb. But it feels great, just great."

PART II

Behold, I send you forth as sheep in the midst of wolves: be ye therefore wise as serpents, and harmless as doves.

—MATTHEW 10:16

THE PURSUIT OF POWER

IN 1967 THE massive and majestic pink granite Texas Capitol Building dominated Austin—physically as well as politically. By midmorning on Tuesday, January 10, the first day of the sixtieth biennial session of the Texas legislature, chartered buses began turning off Congress Avenue into the curved drive of the Capitol's parklike grounds. They stopped at the south steps of the Capitol Building to unload their passengers: hundreds of African Americans dressed in their church finery. The parking guards, re-tired veterans who fed the squirrels and shooed tourists away from the parking spots reserved for high public officials, did not know what to make of it. They had never seen so many black people at the Capitol.

Young kids from the Fifth Ward's E. O. Smith Junior High School Band were lining up at the south entrance of the building to form an honor guard. By noon the upstairs gallery overlooking the Texas Senate chamber was packed with more than 450 black people from Houston, many of whom had risen at 4:00 A.M. to make the 150-mile trip to Austin. The crowd was jubilant, excited, and some were even tearful. One retired man who had come to Austin on a chartered bus with the Houston Metropolitan Senior Citizens Club told a reporter, as he stuck his chest out proudly, "I'll never forget this day. You don't know how hard I've worked for this."[1]

Precisely at noon, Barbara Jordan walked onto the Senate floor and through the brass railings that formed an enclosure around the thirty-one desks and chairs for members of the Texas Senate. She wore a white orchid pinned to her pastel suit, and her family walked in behind her: Ben and Arlyne, Bennie and Rose Mary, Uncle Wilmer and Aunt Mamie Reed Lee.

Jordan's friends and constituents in the gallery broke into wild ap-plause as they watched other senators reach out to shake her hand on her way to her desk. Jordan looked up into the crowd, smiled, and waved, but she knew that Texas Senate rules prohibited demonstrations or applause from the gallery. So as she looked up, she placed her index finger over her lips and mouthed a gentle "shush" to her people. The crowd immediately became quiet, but she felt their joy and pride in the continuing smiles and shy waves. A few minutes later, Jordan, too, was ebullient as she was sworn into office by Lieutenant Governor Preston Smith.

STORMING THE CLUB

In 1967 members of the Texas Senate still prided themselves on being a club, a very exclusive club for white men. They met in the Capitol's elegant Victorian chamber with mahogany desks and lavish inlaid moldings on the imposing three-story-high ceiling. With portraits of Texas heroes on the walls and a brass-railed visitors' gallery above, they gloried in the trappings of exclusive elitism. Their showy formality, even gallantry, masked actions, however, that were often reactionary or brutish. The Senate's main function, as always, was to sustain, shore up, or enhance the interests of the state's most powerful individuals and industries. In the 1950s the petrochemical industry and the manufacturers' association, the insurance companies and banks, the real estate developers and highway builders—and the law firms that represented them—had replaced the cotton, cattle, and railroad barons of the previous century.

By the mid-1960s, the U.S. Supreme Court apportionment decisions and the growing political strength of organized labor were challenging the business stranglehold on the Senate. The 150,000-member Texas AFL-CIO, along with African Americans in the largest Texas cities and Mexican Americans in San Antonio and south Texas, were beginning to exert enough political clout in some areas to tip elections their way. Moreover, the same one-man-one-vote reapportionment court decisions that had allowed minorities and liberals like Jordan and the labor lawyer Oscar Mauzy to be elected also benefited the growing Texas Republican Party. The Senate now had three urban Republicans, the highest number since Reconstruction.[2]

Yet the slight power shift in the Senate did not dampen the traditional public camaraderie that prevailed, even among bitter enemies. Senate collegiality was based on coy politeness and exaggerated flattery, often with a raw edge or an ironic morbidity. One conservative senator broke down and cried on his deathbed because he was so touched when an old liberal enemy from the Senate came to see him. "I've carried water for the Dallas bankers, the insurance guys, the deal-makers for years, and made them millionaires ten times over, and not one of them has come here to see me. Only you," he said to his old colleague. "Now, don't go getting sentimental on me, Sena-

Above, Barbara's Great-grandfather Edward Patton, who
served in the Texas legislature during Reconstruction.
[Courtesy of the State Preservation Board, Austin, Texas]

Below, Barbara's Grandpa John Ed Patten.
[Courtesy of Rose Mary McGowan and Bennie Creswell]

Above left, Barbara (center) and her sisters, Bennie (left) and Rose Mary (right). *Above right*, Barbara, age ten. *Below*, shotgun houses in Houston's Fifth Ward. Built in the 1930s and 1940s by white developers, the houses were so small that if someone stood at the entrance and fired a shotgun, the pellets would hit every corner of the house.

[Courtesy of the Texas Historical Commission]

[Courtesy of the Provost Studio, Houston]

Above, Barbara was president of the National Honor Society at Phyllis Wheatly High School. She is seated fourth from the left in the front row. *Right*, the Good Hope Missionary Baptist Church. *Below*, the high point of Barbara's college career came when she and her Texas Southern University debate partner, Otis King, tied the Harvard debate team in 1956.

[Courtesy of Thomas Freeman]

The Sixty-first Texas State Senate Legislature.

Above, Barbara with some of her Senate colleagues, 1967.
Below, Barbara casting her "aye" vote in the Texas Senate, 1969.
[Courtesy of the Texas Senate Media Service]

Above, Barbara at her desk on the Texas Senate floor with her colleague Senator Oscar Mauzy of Dallas. *Below*, Barbara on the dais in the Texas Senate, with Lt. Gov. Ben Barnes on her far right, and fellow Senators Jim Willace, Chet Brooks, Don Kennard, and A. M. Aiken.

[Courtesy of the Texas Senate Media Service]

Left, Barbara was the first African American to serve as governor of any state when she assumed the role of Texas Governor for a Day, June 10, 1972. *Below*, Barbara presiding over the Texas Senate, chatting with Senator William Patman, the son of one of the U.S. Congress's most powerful Texans at the time, Wright Patman, who headed the House Banking Committee.

[Courtesy of the Texas State Library and Archives Commission]

[Courtesy of the Texas Senate Media Service]

Barbara standing in front of her campaign headquarters during the 1972
race for a seat in the U.S. House of Representatives.

tor," his visitor told him. "I just came by to make sure it was true that you were really dying."[3]

How on earth would the thirty-one-year-old black woman from Houston's Fifth Ward fit in with the Texas Senate? How would she deal with its clubbiness, its cutting banter, its notorious deal-making? What would she make of its secret meetings in the Headliners Club or the Austin Club, the capital city's favorite white male–only watering holes? Senate members and lobbyists were renowned for their stag hunts and weekend getaways. Would Barbara Jordan want to go? The Senate in 1964, immediately prior to Jordan's election, had one female member, Neveille Colson of Navasota. Mrs. Colson, who had been defeated when she ran for reelection in 1966, conveniently declined to participate in events away from the Senate chamber and never confronted "the Club" about being excluded. She even had to go to the third floor of the Capitol to find a bathroom, since there was no facility for women near the Senate floor. Barbara Jordan would be no Mrs. Colson. Most of the thirty white men who would be her colleagues were sure of that. The first order of business before Jordan was sworn in was a hasty remodeling of a committee room off the floor of the Senate chamber to turn it into a ladies' lounge, with pastel carpet, comfortable sofas, and big mirrors. One Senate wag called it the "Barbara Jordan Memorial Bathroom," a label that stuck for years.

Only ten or so of the senators who were considered liberal, by Texas standards, were genuinely overjoyed to serve with Barbara Jordan. "Her victory excited us, cheered us on," one member said.[4] Most of the other twenty-one senators were dismayed. They represented the old Texas—white, racist, conservative, either rural or big-business-oriented—and they had stayed aloof from Barbara Jordan after her much-heralded victory. They were like one-legged, one-armed George Parkhouse, who in 1957 had helped pass a dozen new segregation laws to protect the state from the "NAACP and the Communists." At the other end of the conservative spectrum was the sixty-eight-year-old gentlemanly "dean" of the Senate, A. M. Aiken of Paris. Aiken had never had a conversation with a black person as an equal, saying simply that he "had been raised differently." Some were as blunt as the master of Senate rules, crusty Dorsey Hardeman of San Angelo in west Texas, who told Senator Oscar Mauzy, after the hoopla of Jordan's swearing-in on opening day, that he "wasn't going to let no nigger woman tell him what to do."[5]

"Some of the people she dealt with in the state Senate were the most racist people you could imagine," George Christian emphasized. Christian had been Governor John Connally's press secretary before going to Washington to serve in the same role for President Lyndon B. Johnson. "They resented the hell out of a black woman showing up in the Texas Senate, and they did everything they could to block her out," he said.

Yet Barbara Jordan from the beginning felt she could handle it. She confidently told a newspaper reporter that she expected no difficulty in dealing with the Senate, even though "I know I will be a novelty." Jordan believed the state's leaders had recognized the historical inevitability of a Negro being elected. "They are psychologically prepared," she told friends.[6]

They were not prepared socially, however. Claude Wild Sr., the Gulf Oil lobbyist, always gave a dinner dance for members of the Senate and their wives the opening week of the legislative session.[7] He plainly didn't know what to do about the Senate's first black member. That she was a woman made it even more difficult. He called one of the Senate liberals, Fort Worth senator Don Kennard, for advice.

"Don," Wild said. "I've got a little dilemma with Senator Jordan."

"What's that?" Kennard asked.

"Well, it's about Parkhouse and Mrs. Parkhouse, not to mention some others. What if Senator Jordan brings along a big black man from Houston? How will everybody react? What if her date tries to dance with Mrs. Parkhouse? What then?"

To solve Wild's immediate problem, Kennard invited Jordan to go to the dinner dance with him and his wife. Kennard believed they were breaking such new ground that no one knew what to do. The rules started changing that night, however, according to Kennard. "Within three minutes after she arrived, she was at the center. . . . Just by being so gracious and charming she literally compelled even the biggest racists to be gracious and charming, too. . . . She didn't make them feel evil or guilty. And they had never been confronted with an intelligent, imposing, witty black person before so they warmed to her."[8]

George Christian believed it was probably the first time most Senate members had ever had any sort of a professional relationship with a black person, much less a black woman, whom "they probably thought of as a maid in a kitchen." Christian thought that Jordan recognized, even empathized, with their predicament. "She knew those folks were having a learning experience, just like she was. 'I need to help them learn,' is how she probably felt. She was half the age of some of them, and totally different, and yet she worked her way in. I believe she was helping them get adjusted to the fact that this was a new time. They wanted to go to their graves with things just the way they were and always had been. And they couldn't quite do it. She was the clear demonstration to them that they were facing some change, and she helped walk them through that change."

Jordan spent a lot of time thinking about how she might bring them along. She knew she would be stereotyped, and she worried that she would be cloaked in an all-encompassing mantle of black militancy. Despite her publicly expressed confidence, she worried that her presence would set off an equally militant reaction. "I wanted them to see me firsthand," she said. "I wanted them to know I was coming to be a Senator and I wasn't coming to lead anything. I was not coming carrying the flag and singing 'We Shall

Overcome.' I was coming to work and I wanted to get that message communicated personally."

Jordan deliberately set out to woo and win the Senate's toughest members during the opening days of the four-month legislative session, when ceremony and lobby receptions—not lawmaking—were the order of business. Jordan spent January and February studying the rules, learning Senate procedure, letting the Senate get used to her, and basking in the clubbiness of the body. She went to the parties, shook all the hands, smiled, and charmed the lobbyists. She knew the Capitol crowd wanted to see her and size her up. And she wanted to be seen, but she was sizing them up as well. Jordan quickly figured out who made a difference in the Senate, and in the state. She made friends with the Senate's presiding officer, Lieutenant Governor Preston Smith, a friendly, unassuming, yet visionless west Texan. She crossed the massive Capitol rotunda to the House side of the building to get to know the dynamic young speaker of the House, Ben Barnes, the Connally protégé whom the Texas political establishment was openly grooming to be governor, even president, someday. She spent most of her time, however, getting to know each senator individually and doing favors for them whenever possible. She took the time to speak to their hometown constituents who came to Austin and wanted to see the new phenomenon—the black woman senator.

It was important to Jordan, however, that she not be considered a mere decorative ornament, one more stop on the Capitol tour. She once told a reporter, "To be effective I had to get inside the Club, not just inside the chamber." A few weeks into the session, Jordan had seen enough to know she was the equal of the smartest senator in the Club. This was no Boston University for her, making her feel inadequate or lacking in specialized knowledge. "You must understand that I have a tremendous faith in my own capacity," she said.[9] Jordan's growing self-confidence propelled her to seek out the most influential and powerful members of the Senate. "I was determined to gain their respect."[10]

Dorsey Hardeman was at the top of her list. Rural, conservative, feared, even hated, the sixty-four-year-old Hardeman loved and understood the uses of political power. Hardeman was one of the few Senate insiders who could best Governor John Connally in legislative maneuvering, and Connally bitterly resented Hardeman's stranglehold on the Texas Senate.[11] Hardeman, a lawyer, had been in the Senate since 1947, after serving as mayor of San Angelo in the heart of the west Texas sheep and goat country. He once got so angry when he saw the United Nations flag flying above the Texas flag on the campus of the University of Texas that he introduced legislation to prevent any flag flying above the Texas banner except Old Glory. He got into a feud with the Texas Bar Association and sponsored a bill every session to abolish it, although he plainly wanted to harass the bar, not destroy it. Lively, always smiling, quick-witted, and tenacious, Hardeman became the master of the Senate's "local and uncontested" calendar, where unopposed, noncontroversial bills were placed. Hardeman would take the chair to preside over floor action when the uncontested calendar was called, and put bills through final passage at the rate of one every fifty seconds. Not surprisingly, quite a few of Hardeman's own bills, some of them quite controversial, managed to slip through on the uncontested calendar.[12] Yet, over time, he went unchallenged. He was by far the dominant personality in the Senate. He could wipe out a million-dollar appropriations with a "head shake or a pencil stroke."[13]

Hardeman was a master of techniques never revealed in government textbooks. If he didn't have the votes to defeat a bill in committee, he would sometimes simply put the bill in his pocket and walk out, leaving the committee with nothing to vote on. But Hardeman was not simply crafty; he had real power in the Senate. He always managed to seal an alliance with the lieutenant governor, who was the presiding officer and arbiter of power in the Senate.[14] Hardeman, over the years, rotated his duties as chairman of either the Senate's state affairs or finance committees, through which all major bills had to pass. In her own search for power, Barbara Jordan understood the importance of Dorsey Hardeman.

"Senator Hardeman knew the rules of the Senate better than any other member. In order to gain his respect, I, too, had to know the rules. So I learned the rules," Jordan said. Jordan did more than learn the rules, however; she began a slow, tedious process of relationship-building with the people who mattered in the Senate. She was as intrigued by the conservative A. M. Aiken as she was by Hardeman. Aiken, at sixty-eight, was the oldest member of the Senate, a prim and proper, diminutive man whose looks suggested he would be more comfortable playing dominoes on a rural courthouse square than serving in the Senate. Yet his tenacious willpower had brought about the first modern overhaul of public education in Texas in 1948, resulting in higher scholastic standards and the distribution of state funds based on average daily attendance in local school districts, significantly shifting state aid from rural to big-city districts.

Jordan felt she had to establish personal relationships with people like Aiken, Hardeman, even the old segregationist George Parkhouse. "They held the power with their seniority and conservatism. I knew it would be well if I could work my way to them, if they could see me as a legitimate member of the Senate. I don't mean bowing and scraping and shining their shoes. I mean doing my work on the committees, asking the right kinds of questions that make good law. I wanted them to respect me for my ability as a member of that body."[15]

State representative Jake Johnson of Houston, who had become friends with Jordan when they campaigned for office together in Houston, was concerned about how the clubby Senate was treating her. Midway in the legislative session, he crossed the Capitol rotunda to the Senate side of the building to check on her. He first went to the Senate floor, but she wasn't there. Then he went up to her fourth-floor office, but she wasn't there either. Someone suggested that he check in Senator A. M. Aiken's office. Johnson thought that a little strange, since Aiken had been uncomfortable about Jordan's presence from day one. But when Johnson stuck his head into Aiken's office, "there was Barbara, with Aiken and Dorsey Hardeman, and a little scotch drinking was taking place," he said. Johnson recounts that the three senators were in an intense discussion about how to break a filibuster.

"Hardeman laid out a series of steps they could take, and looked over at Barbara and said, 'Isn't that right, Senator?' 'Yes, Senator,' Barbara said, and then she pointed out some additional parliamentary maneuver they could take. And Hardeman jumped up and said with great enthusiasm, 'Oh, *yes*, that's right!' "

Johnson was amazed. "Here they are planning and plotting, and I realize that not only has Barbara been accepted in the Senate, she's been accepted in the inner sanctum sanctorum. And that's a stunning thing. Freshmen don't get anywhere in the Senate, much less a woman and a black woman at that!" When the meeting broke up, Jordan left with Johnson to walk back to her office, and Johnson confronted her about what he had seen. "I'm a little taller than Barbara, and I'm senior to Barbara because I'd been in the legislature two years longer, and I look down my nose at her and say, 'What were you doing in that den of iniquity?' And she looks at me with a half-smile, and also an impatience that turned up the corner of her mouth, and says to me, like it was elementary finesse bridge, stupid: 'They have the votes.' And I shut up because Barbara was not one to tolerate criticism of her methods."[16]

Senator Oscar Mauzy of Dallas also learned that lesson. Mauzy, too, was troubled by Jordan's courtship of Hardeman. "She tried to be so accommodating. I just don't understand that kind of thinking, and she would tell me, 'Of course you don't understand it. You're not female, and you're not black.' " Yet it was precisely because she was female and black that Mauzy and the liberals thought that they would be able to count on Jordan whenever they needed her.

"When we got to the Senate, we had eleven votes, and that was enough to block anything," said Oscar Mauzy, who would become the strategist of the Senate liberals, who called themselves the "Good Guys," a label that the news media adopted as well. "Because of my labor background, the first thing I wanted to do is get all the Good Guys in the room and give assignments and get organized. Barbara kind of held back, right from the beginning. She would come to the meetings and talk, but she always made it real clear that we were not to speak for her."

Jordan also made it clear to Mauzy and the other liberals that she would never merely be part of their group, no matter how philosophically close she might feel to the liberals. After her two losing races for the legislature on the liberal-sponsored ticket, she had decided that liberal politicians would never control her fate again. Yet Jordan still considered her views to be aligned more with the liberal wing of the Democratic Party than with the conservatives. Liberals initiated the kinds of programs that were designed to ease the problems of blacks and minorities who lived in places like the Fifth Ward and other stigmatized areas. Jordan was also interested in the process of power, however, the inside games of the players, the demeanor and stories of those who held and used power. The liberals didn't seem to have much power, or know how to use it, she felt—at least during her initial months in office.

It was March before Jordan spoke for the first time on the Senate floor. A. R. "Babe" Schwartz of Galveston and Charles Wilson of Lufkin in east Texas were leading Senate liberals in filibuster against a local-option 1 percent city sales tax. Texas had enacted a statewide general sales tax of 2 percent in 1961, with the heavy support of the business community. Liberals had fought the sales tax, then believing it to be regressive: poor people always end up paying a larger percentage of their income in sales taxes than the wealthy. But sales tax revenue had exceeded all expectations, and now financially strapped Texas cities wanted a cut. Jordan wanted to join the fight on the side of the liberals against the proposed city sales tax. Not only did she think it was bad policy, she thought it bad politics. On the day Jordan's friend Jake Johnson voted for the bill in the House, she warned him that Houston voters would seek vengeance. "You just voted your retirement, Jake," she said. Then she smiled at him and joked, "But then, you're probably a better lawyer than a legislator anyway."[17]

Schwartz and the Senate liberals quickly figured out that they didn't have the votes to kill the bill, so they decided to hold it up as long as possible, generate some press coverage, and put a little political heat on their opponents. Schwartz and Wilson were delighted to have Jordan join them.

Jordan started off by asking Schwartz a question. "Isn't it true, Senator, that Texas is number one in poor people because of its regressive tax structure?" Then, in the dance that keeps filibusters alive, Jordan and Schwartz engaged in the traditional banter of questions and answers that ties up floor debate. Nevertheless, Jordan made her key points. "The poor people of this state pay approximately 30 percent of their income in taxes. If we only had more time to consider the details of this city sales tax, we could find an alternative to it. Where is the equity," she asked, "when the people who make the most pay the least and the people who make the least pay the most?"[18] Later she would warn that the people most adversely affected would be "the underprivileged Negroes and Latin Americans of Texas."[19]

Jordan's remarks on the floor had been eagerly anticipated, and many House members came to the Senate chamber to watch the first full-scale filibuster of the session. The gallery was full of legislative staffers, lobbyists, and others who wanted to hear the black woman speak. She did not disappoint them with her oratory. Schwartz praised her eloquence and complimented her for "choosing this subject for your maiden speech in the Senate." And although Dorsey Hardeman was publicly complimentary as well, he whispered to Mauzy disparagingly, "So that's her *maidenhead* speech!"[20]

Hardeman and the Senate conservatives broke the filibuster after almost nineteen hours of nonstop talking, and the Senate joined the House in authorizing a local-option city sales tax. A shift had taken place in the Senate, however, and in Texas politics in general. Barbara Jordan was an important part of it. "For the first time," Schwartz said, "liberals had an organized, planned strategy. We had a significant number of people to do what needed to be done. We stayed together."[21]

The message conveyed by the Senate liberals was that there was a group that could cause real trouble for the old conservative Democratic establishment, and that on some issues down the line they might even be able to bring others along to vote with them. Twelve senators had helped with the filibuster. Yet none, perhaps, had considered his role with the seriousness of Barbara Jordan. The city sales tax was the right issue for her, at the right time in the legislative session. Her stand would thrill her Houston constituents and accurately represent their needs and opposition. She could also show the liberals that she was true to the causes they felt compelled to promote. For all of Schwartz's boasting about the power of the liberals, Jordan knew her vote on the city sales tax was in reality no threat to her newfound conservative friends in the Senate. The conservatives knew they had the votes to pass the city sales tax bill, and it really did not matter to them what the new black member from Houston said or did about it. She could do whatever she wanted, without losing the political capital she was so carefully accumulating. Hardeman said he even told her that she could *not* vote with him. "You just don't represent people that think like I do."[22]

With her participation in the filibuster and vote against the sales tax, Jordan was gingerly charting an independent role for herself. She could be *with* the liberals on key issues, but not *of* the liberals. They could perhaps count on her vote, even when they could not count on her unquestioned loyalty or support for their political maneuvering. They could use her enormous popularity to buttress their case, but only when she allowed herself to be used, and then only on her terms. Jordan's evolving legislative strategy revealed a focused determination to play the middle, to work with the leadership, and to vote the interests of her constituency. She did not attempt to conceal her own political beliefs or trade them away, but she was selective in how she applied them. Jordan's actions followed a logic that she felt was both ethical and effective. It was a strategy that ultimately, and most importantly, moved her agenda forward; it accomplished things.

Years later, Jordan would teach her graduate students that officehold-ers have a moral imperative to be effective.[23] And to be effective in the Senate in 1967, Jordan believed, she had to be on the inside, not outside with the liberals. In the sparse, no-nonsense, martyr-rejecting approach she was developing, she felt it was morally wrong to waste time on issues or maneuvers that ultimately had no chance of making a difference. Yet Jordan was not so calculating that she would not be moved by the same emotional sentiments that motivated her more liberal Senate colleagues. In fact, within an hour after the city sales tax filibuster ended, Jordan encountered in the Capitol hallway some of the state's poorest people—a group of Texas migrant farmworkers who had come to testify on a proposed state minimum-wage bill. The filibuster had delayed the public hearing on the minimum-wage bill, and the Mexican American farmworkers were being shunted from room to room in the Capitol, all but ignored by the official Senate hierarchy. Jordan was appalled.

During the previous summer, Mexican American migrant laborers from the rich fields of the Rio Grande Valley in south Texas had gone on strike to protest their abysmally low wages and working conditions. Led by the Texas affiliate of Cesar Chavez's United Farm Workers union, they had been staging a march from the valley to Austin, three hundred miles to the north. They wanted a state minimum-wage law. The march and *la causa* had ignited the imagination of the state's growing Hispanic population, and organized labor, church groups, and ordinary citizens had joined in an effort to help them. The Senate Labor Committee had scheduled a hearing on the minimum-wage bill the day of the city sales tax filibuster. Because of the filibuster, it had been postponed once, but was rescheduled immediately upon Senate adjournment when the filibuster ended. Weary and bone-tired from staying up all night for the filibuster, Barbara Jordan was joined by only one other senator, Joe Bernal from San Antonio, at the 8:30 A.M. hearing. The committee chairman, conservative David Ratliff of west Texas, used a Dorsey Hardeman trick and made off with the original copy of the bill, without which the hearing could not be held. The other two committee members did not show at all. Without the bill, or a quorum, there could be no hearing. After waiting hours and traveling long distances to be in Aus-tin, the farmworkers and their supporters were angry. Jordan was visibly upset at the Senate treatment of the farmworkers, and she stayed in the hearing room to talk with them individually. She pledged to the several hundred witnesses and supporters that "before the session ends, there will be a hearing on the Fair Wage Bill in the Senate." Jordan had already agreed to cosponsor the minimum-wage bill with Senator Bernal. But now she expressed a greater sense of urgency. "You've been waiting a long time to get a fair wage in Texas," she told the farmworkers. "This minimum wage is just going to be the start of a great new movement. . . . One more night of waiting won't make any difference because we're going to finish this job."

The crowd cheered her and shouted out cries of "Barbara for President." With her concern that evening, Jordan endeared herself to the state's Hispanic community in a way no black leader had ever done before.[24] When the hearing was held a few weeks later, however, Jordan and Bernal lost a three-to-two vote and were unable to get the bill voted out of committee. It was dead for the session.

Filibusters were still the order of the day in the Senate; during lengthy proceedings in the Senate, the lieutenant governor would leave his chair periodically and one of the senators would preside. When Lieutenant Governor Preston Smith handed Barbara Jordan the gavel to preside over the Senate for fifteen minutes on March 21, 1967, it was a history-making event. Texas television stations covered the event, and the *Dallas Morning News* ran a front-page story announcing "State Senate Marks First As Negro Woman Presides." The novelty of a black woman presiding for the first time over the conservative Texas Senate was too rich to ignore. An Associated Press wirephoto of Jordan holding the gavel was carried in newspapers across the country, including the *Washington Post*. Jordan was inundated with congratulatory letters and telegrams, including one from Houston's ambitious new Republican congressman, George Bush, who told her he was happy she had a "D.C. press agent at work."[25]

Barbara Jordan was becoming an important symbol of racial progress, the poster child of the New South. Requests for speeches began coming in from all over the country. Invitations descended from the White House, the Democratic National Committee, the NAACP, local chapters of her sorority Delta Sigma Theta, all-black colleges like Grambling in Louisiana, trade and professional associations, and chambers of commerce. She even spoke at the fiftieth anniversary of the Mt. Zion Baptist Church in Los Angeles. Jordan would take weekend trips to attend meetings and make speeches and collect honoraria, which supplemented her meager Senate salary of four hundred dollars a month.

Jordan was also organizing meetings across Texas to encourage greater black participation in the electoral process. The Southern Regional Council, one of the first integrated organizations in the South, had been funding voter education workshops since the 1960s, and Jordan headed up one of its efforts in Texas. She and other African American leaders, as well as the Texas AFL-CIO, created the Texas Leadership Conference, which received grant money to encourage blacks to register and vote. Vernon Jordan was the director of the Southern Regional Council's Voter Education Project, and he remembered meeting Barbara Jordan during this time. "I gave Barbara money to run a seminar, and she had organized a terrific meeting, which I came to keynote. That was the first time I had seen her at work. I had obviously heard about her before, because in the black community everybody who finished high school seemed to know each other. She had a presence in the community that we all knew about. But what I was able to see was her performance. That was really quite impressive. Presence *and* performance. That was unique."[26]

Barbara Jordan was an important public figure; she represented a rising political tide in Texas. Black voters in Houston, Dallas, and even in some parts of rural east Texas could not be ignored in statewide contests. Jordan's Senate victory had established her as *the* black political leader in Texas, easily replacing the local ministers and NAACP leaders who hovered at the edges of Democratic Party political action. Jordan's demeanor, her charm, her captivating voice, her growing national recognition, and even her liberal voting record were difficult to criticize publicly. None of the senators would dare make any disparaging comment. They didn't want to risk a confrontation with her. Despite her conciliatory approach, they could never be sure that she would not turn her bulky form their way, fix them with a cold stare, or skewer them with her precise words. Her surprising formidableness frightened them; they were especially fearful of being publicly confronted by her. And with good reason. "No one can drip contempt like Jordan can drip contempt," wrote Molly Ivins, who in the mid-1960s was covering the legislature for the liberal *Texas Observer*. Ivins had watched Jordan go after a hapless lobbyist who used bureaucratic jargon and sociological double-talk in testifying against an air pollution control measure she supported. "Your statement bothers me," she told the witness, "because of its weasel words. It is full of weasel words. I hope you will rethink your whole philosophy. I hope there will be some point in time when 'socioeconomic factors' don't count when a human life is at stake."[27]

INSIDE THE CLUB

As Jordan got more press exposure, the public's interest in her seemed limitless. Whether she was accepted for herself or for her perceived political power did not really matter to her. By the end of the first four-month Senate session, she felt she had established herself inside the Senate Club, and she relaxed enough to give vent to her sense of humor in public as well as in private.

One of the most popular Senate stories about Jordan involved her colleague and ally on the minimum-wage bill, Joe Bernal. Bernal was carrying a bill to require the posting of a warning sign wherever alcoholic beverages were served to notify customers that it was a felony to carry weapons in such places. The bill included a list of ten weapons. Because Jordan rarely got up to speak on a bill, Bernal was surprised when she signaled that she wanted the floor.

She began by complimenting his bill. "But I am concerned about certain sections," she continued.

Bernal thought, "Uh-oh, here it comes."

"Senator, I know what a dagger is," she said. "And I know what a rifle is. But do you mind telling me what you mean by a *slungshot*? I am not acquainted with that term, Senator."

Bernal said he didn't know why the word *slingshot* was misspelled in the bill, but he was immediately aware of the danger point in Jordan's question, as was the entire Senate membership. The slingshot had a nickname in the South that was, to say the least, inflammatory. "I guess she was going to push it until she got me to say it was a 'nigger-shooter,'" Bernal said. Instead, he responded by disarming her. "Well, Senator, in south Texas we refer to this as a Mexican-shooter." The Senate erupted in laughter, with Barbara Jordan leading the pack.[28]

Jordan's blend of "intellect and impishness" disarmed the more conservative Senate members, just as liberals like Bernal, Mauzy, and Schwartz delighted in it.[29] She busted all the stereotypes of race that old-timers like Aiken, Hardeman, and the others had so carefully constructed over the years. She was witty, smart, crafty, and, on occasion, every bit as irreverent as the legislative veterans. She went on the weekend deer hunts with the senators and lobbyists. She acquired a taste for Cutty Sark, and she even took up guitar-playing. Her singing became part of after-hours gatherings of senators and Austin politicians.

"Barbara wanted to be accepted," Oscar Mauzy believed. "She wanted to be considered one of the boys. That's the reason she learned to play the guitar. A bunch of us used to go to her place and sing and drink. Sometimes we would go on all night. Then sometimes we would go off for the weekend. That first year it was out at J. Frank Dobie's Friday Mountain Ranch. It was a big deal, with lots of whiskey-drinking, poker-playing, cooking, and food. Barbara was the first woman to do that. Neveille Colson never would go. But Barbara said to us right from the beginning, 'Hell, I'm going to go.'"

Jordan became as adept at mastering the parliamentary maneuvering of the Senate as she was at relationship-building. She loved the art of vote-trading, the "I'll scratch your back, you scratch mine" deal-making, even though she used it only rarely. When she did, she was not above bragging about her newfound skills.

Toward the end of her first four-month legislative session, Jordan was determined to kill a bill by Midland's senator Tom Creighton, who wanted to put severe restrictions on the Texas voter registration process, with the net effect of making it more difficult for blacks and Mexican Americans to vote. Ever since the courts threw out the poll tax in 1966, old-line conservative Democrats had been looking for new ways to restrict the voting franchise, just as the Texas Democracy had done seventy-five years earlier when Jordan's great-grandfather was in the legislature. In the 1960s conservative Democrats were haunted by the specter of new black voters, labor union members, Mexican Americans, and other "undesirables" voting in large enough numbers to dislodge them from power. Conservative Democrats had been squeezed out—liberal Ralph Yarborough held one U.S. Senate seat, and Republican John Tower held the other—and were desperately seeking a way to hold on to their power within the party itself, as well as to the state offices they monopolized. Now, with a powerful black woman and a bunch of liberals tying up Senate action, they felt something had to be done. Creighton's bill would have eliminated mail-in voter registration cards and required people to go to their county courthouses to register in person. The bill was more restrictive than existing laws because it would require voters to reregister every year and prove they not only could write their names but had no physical disability that would prevent them from marking a ballot. Barbara Jordan wanted to kill this bill. The bill aroused her anger as perhaps no other bill that session had. Under Senate rules, Creighton needed twenty-one votes to bring it up on the floor for debate. Jordan went looking for senators to join her in blocking the bill.

"I made a list of ten senators who were in my political debt," she said. "I went to each one and said I was calling in my chit. I needed their votes in order to keep the Creighton proposal from Senate deliberation." Armed with ten commitments, Jordan then went to Creighton and asked when he planned to bring the bill to the floor. Jordan said Creighton looked her square in the face, then smiled. With resignation in his voice, he told her, "I, too, can count, Barbara. The bill is dead."[30] Jordan was thrilled. Her maneuvering, vote-trading, deal-making strategy could pay off. So could her race, her bulk, and her metamorphosis into a political symbol. One conservative senator told a colleague, "I just couldn't vote for that voter registration bill when the Negro lady asked me not to."[31]

During her first session as a member of the Texas Senate, Jordan developed what would come to be a pattern. She would do favors for those she thought she might need someday. She would quietly observe the personal and political dynamics of a situation to size up the relative strengths and weaknesses of the players. She would vote the interests of her poor, mostly black constituents, but without bluster, bombast, or bragging. She would mingle and vote with the liberals most of the time. She would use her enormous charm and wit to win over the conservatives, or anyone inclined to stereotype her as militant, lazy, or dumb. Her tone with her colleagues was conversational and relaxed. She believed that an angry, confrontational tone indicated a feeling of weakness, and she knew she was not weak. If Jordan ever showed anger, it arose from the particular and present situation—not from the baggage of either real or imagined hurts. And so there was an authenticity to her, unique for one so young, so black, and so female in the macho world of Texas politics. Because she had no need to justify herself, she spoke out or initiated legislative action only on issues that really mattered to her. In that first session, nothing was more important to her than the voting franchise. When she needed to act, she had already carved out a space that would allow her to do so. To kill Creighton's voter registration bill, she moved without hesitation or second guesses. Little by little, in the myriad other small matters that never saw the light of day in the Senate, her small acts enlarged her space for effective action—a moral imperative she took most seriously.

By mastering the games of the Senate Club, Jordan believed she was making a difference and changing the Texas Senate forever. "It will not revert back to the old ways regarding black people," she promised.[32]

The Senate, as an institution, *was* changing. Before Jordan came to the Senate, the only African Americans working in the Capitol were janitors and porters. Jordan hired the first black administrative employees to work on her own staff, and she proudly announced at the end of the session that "as a result of my efforts, there are now employed at the State Capitol sixteen Negroes who would not otherwise have been hired."[33] Yet the changes only went so far, even for Barbara Jordan. One night at the Broken Spoke, a favorite country-western night spot for politicians, the crowd was lively and noisy, people were drinking beer and dancing, and Jordan was sitting with Rosa Walker, a tall blond lobbyist for the Texas AFL-CIO, whom Jordan had gotten to know when Walker lived in Houston. Every woman there, including Walker, was asked to dance by some senator or lobbyist—except Jordan.

Segregation was still a fact of life in Texas. A Barbara Jordan didn't get asked to dance, and a Barbara Jordan still could not eat dinner at the segregated Austin Club favored by lobbyists. Even in Houston there were places she could not go. Near the end of her first session, the former legislator and beer lobbyist Homer Leonard held a party for the white members of Houston's legislative delegation at the private, segregated Astro Club in the Astrodome. When confronted about it, Leonard claimed that he had not invited the delegation's two black members, Jordan and House member Curtis Graves, because they were "out of town."[34] Jordan refused to comment on the event, but only a few weeks before the party, she was telling students at her alma mater, Texas Southern University, that the "marching and singing phase of the civil rights movement should give way to calm, realistic progress in the arena of legislation."[35]

In the arena of legislation, Barbara Jordan had become so sure of herself that she wasn't going to dwell on the few public slights from lobbyists like the hapless Homer Leonard. Nevertheless, she did keep a mental "forgive and remember" list of those who had not shown her respect, and she didn't hesitate to consult it when legislation was concerned.

"Personal control is what is important, and that is not always easy," she said. "If you explode along with your exploding adversaries, all you have is a shouting match and nothing is resolved. In situations of that nature, you just hold on to your insides as tightly as you can and hope that others will simmer down, quiet down. The worst thing you can do is respond to a personal attack with a counterattack that is personal. Try to keep your side from being an attacker and hope that by holding on to your insides and as time passes by, sooner or later you will have a chance to get even, and I do."[36] And she did.

Outwardly Jordan always remained calm and never complained about the insults, insensitivity, or ignorance she encountered in the intensely competitive atmosphere of the Texas State Capitol. By the end of her first legislative session in May, most of the senators were singing her praises publicly. In an unusual gesture, the Senate named her outstanding freshman member and honored her with a resolution expressing its "warmest regard and affection" for her. At the conclusion of the speeches and ceremony, Dorsey Hardeman moved that the names of all the senators be added to the resolution.

ON BEING A SYMBOL

When Barbara Jordan began to prove herself in the Texas Senate, a different kind of racism took hold. It was the racism of "the exception." To whites, she was so different from most blacks, or at least from their perception of blacks, that she became not only acceptable but desirable. The minions of the Texas political establishment *wanted* to be with her, to claim her for a friend, to have her as their "pet."

The great orator and former slave Frederick Douglass experienced racism of the exception and described it succinctly. "When prejudice cannot deny the black man's ability, it denies his race, and claims him as a white man. It affirms that if he is not exactly white, he ought to be," Douglass said. Born to a slave mother and a white father, Douglass was so brilliant an orator and writer that his very *being* was an argument against slavery, and white abolitionists sent him on the speakers' circuit, even to England, to galvanize sentiment against slavery. As Douglass became more famous, however, he also became isolated from his own people. His coworkers were white, his friends were white, his audiences were white. Douglass came to resent his role as the Northern politicians' "official Negro." He often felt patronized, as if whites felt his abilities came only from "intellectual" association with them—and, "by implication, from genetic association as well." Douglass also recognized the source of his appeal to white leaders. "The mind of man has a special attraction towards first objects. It delights in the dim and shadowy outlines of the coming fact," Douglass wrote in the fall of 1865.[37]

Now, slightly more than one hundred years later, Barbara Jordan also had a special attraction as an important "first object." Like Douglass, she had a powerful voice and practical political judgment that made her a valued commodity among white politicians. Shunned by Texas conservative white politicians only a few months earlier, unable to win elective office in a system unprotected by civil rights laws, unable to attract the attention of the news media in Houston or of the powerful men who ran the city, unable even to hold a ceremonial office in her own Democratic Party, Senator Jordan now was receiving the kind of accolades reserved for the truly "exceptional."

She *was* different. And different not only from the stereotype of sullen, shuffling blacks that whites had created to justify segregation, but from the new militant civil rights leaders demanding immediate change. She was not like Martin Luther King Jr., whose new calls in 1966 for economic equality scared Texas business and political leaders; she was not like the black power advocates H. Rap Brown and Huey Newton, who were intent on turning the civil rights movement into a "get whitey" revolution; she was not like the dashing New York congressman Adam Clayton Powell Jr., who had figured out how to make money in the political system; she was not like Malcolm X, who had been assassinated in 1965 but whose stern dignity had carried a fierce rebuke of white culture and racism. Barbara Jordan was a politician, and her colleagues—liberal and conservative—felt she was rational and responsible. In her first session, she was on her way to becoming an insider. The doors to the inner sanctum of power began to open for her because she seemed to understand white people and to have some empathy for what they were going through. She seemed to want to work *with* them, without condemning them. She was not marching in the streets or angling for a confrontation. She was using their own insider system to *deal* with white politicians. And that was okay with the politicians who worked with her because she didn't humiliate or bully them in the process. The initial wonderment she generated among her political associates quickly gave way to a grudging admiration and then to outright adoration.

At the end of her first term, United Press International named Jordan one of the ten most influential women in Texas, along with Nellie Connally, the governor's wife, and other socially prominent women. A black woman had become *respectable* in the eyes of Texas! In some ways, this was a symbol as important in the black community as Jordan's political victories. Barbara Jordan had transcended the post-Reconstruction, segregation-justifying themes of black inferiority and impurity. It was a true breakthrough.

White politicians everywhere wanted to know Barbara Jordan, to be where she was, to have a story to tell about her. It was as if an association with Jordan in 1967 would prove not only that they were not racists but that they were also the "exceptions" within their own culture. White leaders sought every possible public occasion to praise Jordan. It was so unusual for some of them, however, to praise a black person that they didn't always get it right. After Jordan's spectacular first Senate session, former Dallas senator Jim Wade was speaking at a campaign rally at a black club in Dallas. Anxious to ingratiate himself with the audience, Wade praised Jordan expansively. "Why, that nigger girl is the smartest member of the Senate," he said.[38]

Most white politicians were more circumspect, however, when they began to claim her as one of their own. "That's our Barbara," became the more common tribute. She was *our* girl. Even the Houston newspapers, the *Post* and the *Chronicle,* began to brag editorially about all the marvels *"our* Senator Jordan" was achieving.

Houston's white establishment was beginning to recognize the value of Senator Barbara Jordan. When business leaders and city officials made their pitch to the Democratic National Committee to hold the 1968 presidential nominating convention in Houston, they flew Jordan to Washington on a private jet for a conspicuous appearance with them and then flew her back to Houston the same night so that she wouldn't have to miss a speaking engagement. In May, when Vice President Hubert Humphrey made a speech in Texas, *Air Force Two* made a special stop in Austin to pick up Jordan to fly to Houston for the occasion. Everyone wanted a "piece" of Barbara Jordan.

Andrew Young, who would later serve with Jordan in Congress, had it figured out. "It used to be southern politics was just 'nigger' politics, who would 'outnigger' the other—then you registered ten to fifteen percent in the community and folks would start saying 'nigra' and then you get thirty-five to forty percent registered and it's amazing how quickly they learned to say 'neegrow,' and now that we've got fifty, sixty, seventy percent of the black votes registered in the South, everybody's proud to be associated with their black brothers and sisters."[39]

Sometimes the cost of political "brotherhood" and "sisterhood" could be too high—particularly for the unsophisticated or ego-driven leader who might succumb to the flattery or fawning. Jesse Jackson once claimed with some bitterness that whites always try to take the best blacks away, to remove them from their culture, leaving the black people exactly where they were before—with neither leaders nor change in their lives. Barbara Jordan was clearly one of the best, and the pull away from her culture was strong. Jordan was observant enough, however, to know when she was being used or selected to be the black token among whites. She spoke openly about it. "I have been a token representative in many gatherings and . . . I don't necessarily resent this," she said. "But I want to know that is what's going on. Don't lie to me and say, 'We want you to come to this because we want you to enter into some intellectual discussion with somebody who's going to be there.' If you want a black representative, just come out and level with me and say, 'Well, you know, we've got to really put on a show here now, and will you come and be my Negro for a night?' " What Jordan most resented was obvious hypocrisy. "I fully resent, *fully resent,* an employer, business, industry, group, church, and the like deciding, 'We're just going to have a token here,' and then fooling themselves . . . into believing that they really have done something when they really haven't."[40]

Far more seductive than obvious tokenism for Jordan, and a more tempting factor in the pull away from her culture, was the prospect of real friendship, with genuine feelings of affection, reciprocity, and loyalty. A noted white Texas civil rights lawyer once warned his associates never to become friends with the conservatives they had to deal with politically because when it came time to confront the opposition on serious political issues, they would lack the toughness and courage needed for a protracted struggle. An enemy galvanizes you into action. A friend can open the door to compromise before it is strategically wise; or worse, a friend can co-opt you into minimizing the issue altogether.

Barbara Jordan had been influenced by two traditions that made the civil rights lawyer's advice seem absurd to her. First, there was the model of civil rights leadership in front of her every day at the Good Hope Missionary Baptist Church under the direction of the NAACP leader A. A. Lucas. In Houston, Reverend Lucas and the NAACP would challenge, then quickly accommodate and compromise to win incremental improvements. And second, at Boston University Jordan had been influenced by Dr. Howard Thurman's teaching that the essence of racism's evil was the notion of the "other," because it permitted an abandonment of moral responsibility toward those human beings "outside the pale." Thurman said that when he was growing up in the South, it never occurred to him to "regard white persons as falling within the scope of the magnetic field of my morality. [Whites] were in a world apart . . . to lie to them or deceive them had no moral relevance; no category of guilt was involved."[41] Thurman felt the legacy of slavery had given blacks as well as whites the tendency to see each other as outside the pale of moral behavior.

> *The fact was that the slave owner was regarded as one outside the place of moral and ethical responsibility. The level of high expectation of moral excellence for the master was practically nil. Nothing could be expected from him but gross evil; he was—in terms of morality—amoral. . . . There is no more tragic result from this total experience than the fact that even at the present time such injunctions as "love your enemies" are often taken for granted to mean the enemy within the group itself.*[42]

Like Thurman, Barbara Jordan did not see white politicians, even conservative white politicians, as "outside the place of moral and ethical responsibility." In that first Senate session, nothing was out of bounds for Jordan. She *wanted* to break through the boundaries of her group. Her religious tradition and beliefs, modified, shaped, and matured by Thurman, provided a moral framework that made it possible. And her experiences, as well as her ambition, made it necessary. Take Dorsey Hardeman. "Dorsey Hardeman enjoyed the worst of reputations," said Jordan's friend Jake Johnson. "The liberals hated Hardeman; even Connally couldn't stand him. But I doubt that Barbara ever listened to any of it. . . . She could identify with anybody on anything and was never phony about it. Never phony. Barbara had a constitutional absence of bias."

Yet, there was a danger. While authentic bonds between Jordan and her white friends might erase the notion of "other," they might also cause her to lose an edge to her energy or diminish the urgency of her causes. The danger, too, was that she might abandon those causes altogether. Jordan was so steeped in the Baptist biblical tradition, however, that she could not escape the prophetic call of the Old Testament book of Daniel, in which the prophet pointedly demands that the successful exiles in the land of the enemy take responsibility for the less fortunate, asking: "What about the rest?" Jordan's religious upbringing was a constant reminder to her that because she *was* the successful exception, the glowing symbol of progress to her community, she had a definite responsibility to "the rest."

"One's religion is personal and private in terms of how that religion or that belief impacts on one's actions," she said. "It was not until I reached . . . adulthood that I could personally actualize the feeling and impact of Christianity on [myself]. . . . We live in this world in order to contribute to the growth, the development, the spirit, and the life of the community of humankind. . . . I know there are some things which I must under any circumstance do. Christ, for me, is love, caring, sharing, peace, hope. I cannot live my life not caring for my fellow man and continue to say I am a Christian. I cannot live my life not loving the people who surround me and call myself a Christian."[43]

Jordan said that when she went into politics she wondered whether it would be possible "to perform in a political capacity and remain true to my Christian heritage." She said she "consulted scripture, as well as my innermost feelings and quickly recognized that . . . politics does not represent a divorcement from Christianity. . . . It is the basis for my acting out my commitment to myself and to all humankind."[44]

For Jordan, "the rest" were always represented by her mother's generation of hardworking black women: silent, suffering, invisible, working as maids and sacrificing to raise their children and serve their church. It was those elderly churchgoing black women, many of whom lived in Fifth Ward shotgun houses, who had pressed into her hands their precious quarters and crumpled dollar bills when she appealed for campaign contributions over the past few years. It was those elderly women who had knocked on their neighbors' doors to get them out to vote for her on Election Day. It was those old women who depended on a government check to pay their rent and buy their groceries. It was those old women who needed her voice and who wanted her to be inside the "Club" they would never be able to enter themselves. Jordan's morality held those old women inviolate. They represented for her the people who needed just a little help from their government to supplement their own hard work and efforts to survive. And they trusted *her*, Barbara Jordan, to do right by them.

Jordan made sure her newfound white political friends understood that she would not betray "her people." But everything else was on the table—at least worth talking about or negotiating. In the booming Texas economy of the late 1960s, it appeared to be possible to get a little something for everyone—rich, poor, and in-between, even if the scales tilted a little more toward the rich and powerful. They always did, the realist in Jordan reminded herself.

CHAPTER 9

FRIENDS IN HIGH PLACES

BARBARA JORDAN WAS not the only African American officeholder in the Texas Capitol in 1967. Two black men had been elected to the Texas House of Representatives at the same time Jordan was elected to the Senate. Houston's new representative, New Orleans–born Curtis Graves, was dashing, articulate, and militant, with a take-no-prisoners rhetoric that was a real shock to many Texas House members. Dallas voters elected the more conservative Joe Lockridge, a lawyer and onetime roommate of the civil rights leader Vernon Jordan. Lockridge was killed in a plane crash shortly after taking office, however; his successor in a special election was also black, the widely respected Dallas AME minister Dr. Zan Holmes.

The three Texans were part of the first wave of African American politicians elected nationwide after the passage of the Voting Rights Act. One million new African American voters cast ballots in 1966. As a result, there were six African American members of Congress and ninety-seven African Americans in state legislatures throughout the country. Most of them were elected in northern states, where blacks already had more than rudimentary political organizations.[1] Several future African American mayors and members of Congress won lower-level posts for the first time in the 1966 elections. Most of them, like Barbara Jordan, were ready to leave the streets and demonstrations—or the sidelines—of the civil rights movement for a chance to grab the power of political office. They represented the maturation of the movement, and many of them were motivated by personal ambition as well as by the cause of civil rights.[2]

National Democratic Party officials saw the emergence of these new political leaders as a plus, a vindication of the party's support of civil rights legislation. The Democratic National Committee invited them to Washington during the summer of 1966 for the National Conference of Elected Negro Democrats and sent them to the White House to meet President Johnson at a reception in the Rose Garden. Barbara Jordan was thrilled to be part of the delegation and got to shake the president's hand.

President Johnson's staff wanted to develop a more substantive relationship between the White House and the new African American leaders. In particular, key staffers wanted Johnson to reach out to the new African American officials with leadership potential. The presidential aide Harry McPherson began urging Johnson to have a meeting of mainstream civil rights leaders after the fall elections in 1966. McPherson felt that the civil rights movement was "obviously in a mess," with white resentment growing and the "Negro community . . . fragmented." McPherson was also worried about the increasing age of those he felt were the "responsible Negro leaders." A. Philip Randolph was in his seventies. Roy Wilkins was in his sixties. McPherson felt that Whitney Young and Martin Luther King, in spite of their youth, "have been around so long that they seem old school to the young militants."[3]

"When you look at where the greatest unrest is, among the teenagers and people in their twenties where unemployment is disastrously high, you know that the young on the streets will not always respond to advice from middle-aged and elderly men. Our lines of communication run generally (and from the White House, only) to the older establishment. We have very few contacts with younger Negro leaders. We *must* develop those contacts," McPherson wrote to Johnson.[4] He felt that the old black student groups like SNCC (Student Non-violent Coordinating Committee) and CORE (Congress of Racial Equality) were ineffective and irresponsible, and he was looking for some new entity to represent the younger generation of civil rights leaders.

But Johnson's assistant attorney general Nicholas Katzenbach believed the only way the president could reach the younger generation of black leaders was through "results"; he felt that if such a meeting were held at that time, "even the most conservative civil rights leaders would find it politically necessary to take issue publicly with the President on our failure to deliver sufficient results in any of the areas in which the problems are obvious." Katzenbach also warned that although he saw merit in the establishment of a militant but peaceful organization of young people who could successfully compete with SNCC, "to launch it at the White House would be to kill it before it was born."[5] No White House meeting was held in 1966.

President Johnson was beginning the turbulent last two years of his presidency. Vietnam had soured his dealings with both Congress and the public, and the legacy he cared most about—civil rights—was losing its luster. Part of the problem was that as profoundly meaningful as the Civil Rights Act of 1964 and the Voting Rights Act of 1965 were for southern blacks, and as symbolically important as they were for African Americans in other parts of the nation, the harsh conditions of daily life for most blacks had not changed much.[6] There had been little progress in education, housing, or employment. Political equality was closer to reality than economic opportunity because economic "rights" were harder—and more costly, in terms of both money and politics—to achieve. Only a few days after Johnson had signed the Voting Rights Act in 1965, an incident between white police and an African American driver ignited the Watts riots in Los Angeles. Five days later, thirty-four people were dead and more than one thousand injured. Both Watts and the escalation of the war in Vietnam changed the mood of the country from one of optimism to pessimism about dealing with the nation's problems. Yet just when the success of the civil rights movement had raised expectations among African Americans, funding for Great Society programs was being cut to pay for the escalation of the war. Threats from conservative Democratic senator John Stennis to block defense spending forced Johnson to cut loose Mississippi's independent Head Start program just as it was on the verge of making breakthrough changes in the lives of poor black children in the Delta. The problems for "old Democrats" like Stennis, as well as for some big-city mayors like Richard Daley of Chicago, was that War on Poverty community action programs were providing jobs for a new political class of militant activists who were threats to their political machines. When Daley and others began pressuring the president to scuttle community action programs, the idea of a presidential meeting with civil rights leaders was revived.

Jordan was amazed when she received a telegram early in February 1967, inviting her to a small meeting of civil rights leaders at the White House. "I was just aghast at getting this kind of wire," she said. "A telegram from the President of the United States is a summons, and certainly you must go," she thought. It would require missing a workday in the Texas Senate, so she decided she would fly to Washington early in the morning, attend the meeting, and return to Austin that night. She agonized over what to wear and how to make the arrangements, because this time she would be the only Texan (except for President Johnson) at the meeting. The nation's mainstream civil rights leaders would be there: Roy Wilkins, executive secretary of the NAACP; Dorothy Height, president of the National Council of Negro Women; Whitney M. Young Jr., director of the National Urban League; Reverend Walter E. Fauntroy, the influential minister of the New Bethel Baptist Church in Washington, D.C.; and Clarence Mitchell, director of the NAACP's Washington office. Representing the administration along with the president would be Vice President Hubert Humphrey; Attorney General Ramsey Clark and Nicholas Katzenbach and John Doar from the Justice Department; Health, Education, and Welfare secretary John W. Gardner; Housing and Urban Development secretary Robert C. Weaver; and the White House staffers Joseph A. Califano Jr., Harry McPherson, Larry O'Brien, and others. The aging A. Philip Randolph was ill and unable to attend, and Martin Luther King Jr. would be out of the country.[7]

Jordan was thrilled to be included with such luminaries, and excited to be going to Washington on her own, not as part of a Texas entourage. When she got to the White House, she joined the dignitaries as they gathered around a conference table, and when the president came into the room, he shook hands with each of them. Jordan wondered whether Johnson had any idea who she was, or if some aide had said to him: "Look, we ought to include that black woman who got elected down there in Texas."

After Johnson explained the 1967 civil rights initiative that he would be sending to Congress—it would include proposals concerning fair housing, federal and state jury selection, cease-and-desist authority for the EEOC (Equal Employment Opportunity Commission), extension of the Civil Rights Commission, and the addition of more than one hundred new FBI agents for civil rights enforcement—he asked his guests for their advice. The president went around the table calling on various people to comment. Then he stopped and looked at the state senator from Texas. "Barbara, what do you think?" he asked. Jordan felt her heart flutter. "I didn't know the president knew me, and here he's looking down at me saying, 'Barbara,' and . . . I'm startled. I got myself organized . . . and I gave a response."[8]

Jordan was so nervous that she could barely remember later how she had replied; she thought she may have talked about the fair housing proposals. But according to the White House minutes, she urged that the jury bill contain a "ban on sex discrimination" because "this would help us get the Negro women of the country mobilized."[9] Whatever she said, she impressed President Johnson. A week later, in the *Washington Post,* the political columnists Rowland Evans and Robert Novak, who had a direct pipeline to Johnson's staff, reported that the "White House was far more impressed with her than the usual run of civil rights leaders."[10] Jordan said that when she saw the column she knew it was a White House "plant," and for the first time she was aware that President Johnson might be taking an interest in her.

"I think he viewed her as a pioneer," George Christian said. "President Johnson liked people who got out and did things in the political arena, and she proved his point, I think, that folks like Barbara could be a success."

In the 1960s, it was hard to get civil rights activists to think about using the electoral process as an organizing tool. The Mississippi activist Bob Moses said the commitment in the movement was to "leadership more than organizing—media leadership."[11] Lyndon Johnson knew the limits, however, to that kind of civil rights leadership. For him, the route to power had to be through the electoral process, and Barbara Jordan was someone who not only understood that but had succeeded at it. By the time the White House invited her to the meeting of civil rights leaders, she was viewed as the "absolute" black leader in Texas. George Christian said, "President Johnson was just proud of her. Pure and simple. He used to brag about her. Whenever he got a chance, he used to talk about her."

Johnson was eager to give Jordan some national exposure after the meeting with civil rights leaders, and he began to look around for something he might do for her. He had established the Commission on Income Maintenance to undertake a two-year study of proposals to guarantee a minimum income for poor people. Its job was to look at the possibility of combining all the federal cash–payment programs, from Social Security and veterans' benefits to welfare and disability payments, into a single income maintenance program. The commission was to be composed of "heavyweights": economists, business leaders, three governors, cabinet secretaries Robert McNamara and Wilbur Cohen, and other distinguished individuals, such as the IBM heir Thomas J. Watson Jr. Johnson had put Joe Califano in charge of the project, and because it had the potential to be politically explosive and financially complex, Califano had selected the participants with great care. When he submitted his list to the president, it came back with the "approve" line checked and a handwritten note: "Add Barbara Jordan."

Califano said he had no idea who Barbara Jordan was. When Johnson's appointments secretary told him that Jordan was a state senator from Texas, Califano was appalled. "I waited for the appropriate moment to question the president's note," Califano said. "It came a couple of nights later at dinner alone with him. I reminded him of the task force and how complicated and controversial the topic of income maintenance was. I suggested that if he wanted to do a political favor for a Texas crony, we could find something less demanding and more interesting."

Johnson exploded. With his left elbow leaning on the arm of his chair and his right finger aiming between Califano's eyes, the president said, "You mark this good. Barbara Jordan is the smartest member of the Texas Legislature, and she's going to be the first black female elected United States Senator from Texas. She's got more compassion and common sense than that whole damn group of experts you put together." Califano put her on the list.[12]

Johnson wanted to issue the invitation to Jordan personally. A little after seven o'clock in the evening on January 3, 1968, the president called Jordan at home in Houston. "It upset my mother to no end," Jordan said. "I mean, upset her in a good way; she just couldn't quite handle the President of the United States being on the telephone at her house. When I walked in she said almost breathlessly, 'The Ranch is calling.' I said, 'The Ranch . . . ?' And she said, 'The President is calling from the Ranch.' So I got on the phone and I said, 'Hello, Mr. President,' and that is when President Johnson asked if I would serve on the Income Maintenance Commission. . . . That was the second conversation that I had with the President."[13]

The next morning she ran into attorney James Muldrow when she went into her Lyons Avenue law office. "You'll never guess who called me last night, Muldrow," she told him. "It was Big Daddy!" To Muldrow's quizzical look, she reiterated, "Yes, it was *the* Big Daddy in Washington. The *Man* himself." Muldrow said Jordan was as happy as he had ever seen her.[14]

Jordan was captivated by Lyndon Johnson and totally in awe of him. Of course she accepted the presidential appointment, and it was the beginning of a warm, affectionate, even adoring relationship between them. In some ways, President Johnson was as delighted with Jordan's attention as she was with his. In Nicholas Lemann's insightful book about the War on Poverty and the civil rights movement, *The Promised Land*, he points out that Johnson

> . . . *wanted to be loved—not by the old Southern crocodiles on Capitol Hill, whom he knew he would alienate, and not by bosses like Mayor Daley, whose implacable air of control made him uncomfortable, but by all the people whose wholehearted admiration he had not been able to win before: the little people; the blacks and the Mexican-Americans. . . . These were the people for whom Johnson was doing more than any president had. When he began to sense, in 1965, that they did not love him . . . it tore him apart.*[15]

When Johnson found his admiration returned from the rising black star in Texas, he was delighted and began to do everything he could to open doors for her.

Whenever there was a ceremonial event at the White House that Johnson thought would interest Jordan and help her make connections with people she might need to know, he made sure she was invited. He would single her out to gossip about people in the Texas legislature, tease her gently, or ask her advice on whatever civil rights matter had most recently come across his desk. They particularly enjoyed wagering on when the legendary University of Texas football coach Darrell Royal would see fit to put a black player on his team, which was one of the last segregated hold-outs in intercollegiate sports. Neither the president nor the state senator had been able to attend the University of Texas, and both enjoyed this particular dilemma for the most prestigious college in the state. Once when Johnson was to make an appearance at a fund-raising reception for Senator Ralph Yarborough in Texas, the organizers of the event asked the White House who should introduce the president. Johnson sent back only one name: Barbara Jordan.

THE CONNALLY-JOHNSON BOYS

Barbara Jordan initially came to Lyndon Johnson's attention because she had made three powerful friends during her first term in the Texas Senate: Ben Barnes, Speaker of the Texas House of Representatives; Robert Strauss, Dallas attorney and member of the Texas Banking Board; and Frank Erwin, who was chairman of the powerful University of Texas Board of Regents. Each would become her champion, and each would open doors for her that she could never have on her own. All of them told Lyndon Johnson to keep an eye on her. But Jordan's friendship with Barnes, Strauss, and Erwin would generate the first serious criticism of her political career from liberals, and the complicated nature of the relationships would frustrate her—and them—over the next ten years.

All three men came from the Lyndon B. Johnson wing of the Texas Democratic Party. But their first political loyalty was to John B. Connally, who was elected governor in 1962 after a brief stint as secretary of the navy. Connally was the conduit to political and economic power for all of them.

Money and power were the "twin pillars" of John Connally's life, and the men he attracted both wanted money and loved power.[16] He brought an exceptionally talented group of young men into government with him, and many drifted back and forth between Austin and Washington, sometimes working for Connally and sometimes working for Lyndon Johnson. George Christian affectionately called them the "Connally-Johnson boys," and he was one of them. Almost without exception, these young men eventually made money and acquired political power; quite a few ended up as respected elder statesmen of the Texas political establishment.[17] Barnes, Strauss, and Erwin were typical of this group in their intelligence, ambition, and charm. More driven than most, and more caught up in the pure joy of winning, each man was also a born deal-maker. While they were loyal beyond doubt to John Connally and Lyndon Johnson, each had his own ambitions and agenda beyond Connally's political future. And Connally's agenda was changing.

By 1967, when Barbara Jordan entered the Texas Senate, Connally was already tired of being governor. He had accomplished most of what he wanted by dramatically increasing state funding for the state's colleges and universities (paid for by consumer-based sales taxes). After he had been wounded by an assassin's bullet while riding in an open car in Dallas with President John F. Kennedy in November 1963, the pettiness of some of the Texas legislature's squabbles was almost beyond his endurance.

When Connally's attention began to wane, his indifference to the new political star Barbara Jordan was evident—but she was black and female, and she didn't represent anyone Connally cared about. It was no secret that he had national ambitions, but he had not made the connection between Barbara Jordan's recent election and the important demographic and political changes in the state. Moreover, Connally did not see, as Lyndon Johnson did, the changes already beginning to take place within the national Democratic Party as a result of the civil rights movement; he had not yet taken the mental leap that compelled Johnson to embrace civil rights. In 1964, when Johnson was twisting arms to get votes for his landmark civil rights bill, Connally was speaking out in opposition to it. He compounded his problems with national civil rights leaders by making intemperate remarks after the assassination of Martin Luther King Jr., who, he said, "had contributed much to the chaos, and the strife, and the confusion, and the uncertainty in this country, but whatever his actions, he deserved not the fate of assassination." Sharing a platform with Connally during ceremonies at the new Hemisfair '68 in San Antonio, Jordan had been stunned when she heard his statement, and later she said she "grieved" at Connally's "insensitivity." Jordan left the Hemisfair celebration in San Antonio to rush back to Houston to be with "her people" and arrange a memorial service for King. Her ire with Connally remained. The state's NAACP demanded an "apology for such a dastardly statement."[18]

Ben Barnes, Connally's protégé, would have never made such a statement. He was much more prescient and in tune with the state's younger leaders. Barnes was the boy wonder of Texas politics in the 1960s. Elected to the Texas House of Representatives at age twenty-two, Barnes became speaker at twenty-eight and was openly touted by Lyndon Johnson as a future president of the United States. Barnes's star rose because of his association with Connally, and as Connally lost interest in state government, Barnes picked up the slack. He immersed himself in both policy and politics, and he was in perpetual motion, much like an oscillating fan.[19] His instinct for legislative maneuvering, deal-making, and consensus-building enabled him to build alliances with liberal as well as conservative members of the legislature, labor as well as business leaders. By the time he was thirty years old, Barnes had run statewide and been elected lieutenant governor, just as Connally left office. Standing over 6'4", with red hair and a Howdy Doody smile, Barnes exuded the energy, charm, and intelligence of a young man destined for success. Women found him attractive, and men were drawn to him because he understood and used the games of power. Lyndon Johnson had a gut-level rapport with Barnes, and saw in him a worthy Texas successor to his legacy.

Ben Barnes may have been the most purposefully gregarious man to hold executive office in Texas. As House speaker, he regularly invited the freshman senator Barbara Jordan to come over to the House chamber to sit and gossip with him on the dais while he presided. And he made sure

Jordan was among the regulars included in after-hours rounds of drinks in the speaker's Capitol Building apartment. Talking constantly, Barnes would tell Jordan stories of one member's sexual dalliances or another's drinking problem, or yet another member's lock-step votes with the highway lobby. He absorbed political information like a big red sponge, and he shook off tidbits of political intelligence it would have taken Jordan twenty years to learn on her own.

"Barbara was not an immediate .300 hitter," Barnes said. "She didn't come to spring training and start knocking the ball out. But she was young and bright. She was a good listener, and Barbara was always listening. Sometimes you might not think she was listening, but she was." Barnes believed one of Jordan's greatest strengths was her practicality. "Barbara was a very practical person. She was able to understand politics from the standpoint that if someone had the votes, even if you were against them, you'd let them have it. She and I had a good understanding and an ability to communicate. She never asked for advice about how to vote, but she would ask me how to handle certain situations."[20]

Barnes eagerly gave Jordan advice on how to deal with certain senators and how to be effective within the Senate Club. "We talked one time about how she didn't need to talk a lot because everybody listened to her anyway, and the less she talked the more people would listen. I could talk to her about things like that. We'd talk about one another's weaknesses and strengths. I pushed Barbara a lot. I thought she was an able person. I thought Texas needed her. I thought President Johnson needed her. I thought she would be a great team player."

Barnes immediately began singing Jordan's praises to two key Connally operatives: Bob Strauss and Frank Erwin, who had been instrumental in getting Connally elected in 1962.

Bob Strauss, John Connally, and Frank Erwin were all involved in Lyndon Johnson's campaign to win the Democratic nomination for the presidency in 1960. Devastated by Johnson's failure to gain the nomination, the three men nevertheless strode into the political arena without looking back. In 1962 Connally, with the help of Strauss and Erwin, was elected governor of Texas. All three went on to embrace state politics wholeheartedly.

Strauss remembers getting a call from Barnes about Barbara Jordan during the spring of 1967. "Barnes was smitten with her," Strauss said. "He told me, 'You need to get to know her, not just for her sake or your sake, although that would be important, but for *my* sake.'" Barnes had the right instincts about what was happening, about what government ought to be doing. He saw Barbara as part of the future, and she was necessary to his future as well as to Texas, and the nation. Barnes wanted to be governor and president, and he knew that to be a national Democrat he had to have the support of blacks. This was in 1967. Barnes saw in Barbara more than others did. He also saw how she could help him in his national career. "After I got to know her a bit . . . I thought we had a winner," Strauss said. "Barbara brought a dimension we desperately needed. She had charisma, political instinct. She had something I can't quite define. But it was extraordinary, and we got to be friends, not intimate, but we certainly had a good friendly relationship."[21]

Strauss said he also got calls about Jordan from Frank Erwin. Little-known outside of Texas, Erwin had been Connally's fund-raiser, Lyndon Johnson's drinking buddy, and Ben Barnes's mentor. Connally had given Erwin a key appointment—membership on the board of regents of the University of Texas. As chairman of the university board, Erwin became one of the most powerful men in Texas politics in the mid-1960s, handing out contracts for everything from building construction and architecture design to legal services, bond deals, and investment management of the university's billion-dollar endowment. He presided over a system of governance so broad and influential that it was the de facto executive branch of state government. He held court every night with legislators, lobbyists, and journalists at the bar in the Quorum Club, less stodgy than the more formal Headliners and Austin Clubs.

After Barnes introduced them, Erwin was immediately taken in by Barbara Jordan's charm, her willingness to laugh at his off-color jokes, and her ability to match him drink for drink when they got together at Barnes's apartment in the Capitol. Erwin taught Jordan what mattered in state politics—or, at least, what mattered to him.

When Jordan had first run for office in 1962, she called for the breakup of the Permanent University Fund, the university's cash-rich endowment from oil revenue that had been set aside to fund a "university of the first class." She wanted to "spread the wealth" and allow schools like Texas Southern University to benefit. "Erwin got her off that immediately," according to George Christian. "I'm sure he told her, 'You want a future, you'll get off that right now.' Erwin gave her the *lecture* that the University of Texas is the most powerful thing in the state. He gave it to everybody." Jordan took Erwin's advice on the Permanent University Fund, and he became one of her champions in Austin.

THE DEMANDS OF FRIENDSHIP

Lyndon Johnson's withdrawal from the 1968 presidential campaign in the midst of heated challenges from the antiwar activist Senator Eugene McCarthy of Minnesota and New York senator Bobby Kennedy generated an onrush of political activity among the Connally forces. Connally immediately announced his intention to become a "favorite son" candidate to ensure that state delegates would be pledged to him. It was an effort both to block Texas liberals and to hold Texas for a candidate of Johnson's choosing, or even to give Johnson the option of reconsidering his decision not to run.

When Barbara Jordan found out what Connally intended to do, she told her friends, "Why, that son of a bitch. How does he think he can be anyone's favorite anything?" With the presidential primary contests under way between Vice President Hubert Humphrey, Robert Kennedy, and Eugene McCarthy, the age-old conservative-liberal tug-of-war for party control continued. However, the assassination of Robert Kennedy on June 5 left the liberals in disarray. The Connally forces seized the moment when the Texas State Democratic Party convention began six days later. They shut the liberals out of power to eliminate any influence they might have at the upcoming Democratic National Convention in Chicago. However, bowing to Johnson, as well as to Frank Erwin, Bob Strauss, and Ben Barnes, Connally had allowed Barbara Jordan to be one of five Negroes named to the Texas delegation to the national convention, which also included six Mexican Americans and four representatives from organized labor, a concession to the national AFL-CIO.

The Connally Democrats went to the convention confident they were in control. But they could not foresee that events on the streets of Chicago would overshadow and influence what Democrats did inside the hall.

The antiwar demonstrators battling police and booing the Texas delegates as they made their way into the hall signaled the virtual breakup of the Democratic Party. The Humphrey-Johnson forces (often at odds with each other) tried to maintain control inside the hall, but it was increasingly difficult with war on the streets outside. Many of the delegates sympathized with the protesters and wanted to disassociate themselves from the war, from Johnson, and from anything Texan. The first challenge to Johnson loyalists came on the convention's first night. It was a resolution to free all delegates from the unit rule (requiring the votes of the entire delegation to reflect the majority's wishes, thus negating any dissenting minority's votes).

Jordan was firmly opposed to the unit rule and it took only a few minutes for the entire convention to vote to abolish the unit rule in all future Democratic Party proceedings. Erwin was furious and said if the Connally Democrats had known the unit rule would not be in effect at the convention, they would not have included liberals, like his good friend Barbara Jordan, on the delegate slate. "We put them on there because we knew we could control them under the unit rule."[22]

Far more serious to the Johnson-Connally forces, however, was the scheduled vote on the party platform's plank on Vietnam—it was the critical vote at the convention for Lyndon Johnson, far more important to him than the nomination of Humphrey. Johnson's hold on the Texas delegation was so strong that, even free from the unit rule, the delegation cast all of its 104 votes for the majority report, essentially affirming the Johnson policy on Vietnam, which passed the convention with a comfortable margin. Barbara Jordan felt some ambivalence about the war, but her loyalty to Johnson was so secure by the summer of 1968 that she had no qualms about her vote. She told reporters, "There really isn't enough difference in the two planks to make a major fuss about it."[23] Jordan broke from the Texas ranks, however, on the balloting for the presidential nomination. Loyal to Johnson, the Connally delegates gave one hundred votes to Humphrey on the roll call. Three liberals on the delegation voted for McCarthy, and Jordan cast the state's lone vote for a black candidate whose name had been placed in nomination—a minister from Washington, D.C., the Reverend Channing Phillips.

PRIVATE LIFE

Barbara Jordan was always working. During her entire time in the Texas Senate, from 1966 to 1972, she had an apartment in Austin but still went home to Houston on the weekends and lived with her parents on Campbell Street. She had a law practice to take care of, constituents who wanted to meet with her, speeches to make. The whole time she was growing up, her private world had included activities with her sisters, Rose Mary and Bennie, and the Justice sisters. But now these young women were caught up in their own work, families, and church service. There was no cruising the neighborhood in a big car, no dropping in at the bars or clubs. Even if there had been time, Barbara Jordan was so widely recognized in the Fifth Ward that there were few places she could go without being mobbed.

Even in the most casual encounter, people expected her to smile, to say something clever or profound, no matter how she felt or what she was doing. The strain of always having to perform was beginning to wear on her. She knew she had to begin taking breaks from the work, but it was increasingly difficult to find them. "You can't maintain a public face all the time," Jordan lamented. "You need friends you can be with who don't care what your title is."

Well into her second legislative session, Jordan finally found a small group of women friends who just enjoyed being with her and never asked anything of her. The first was Azie Taylor, an investigator and conciliator for the U.S. Equal Employment Opportunity Commission (EEOC) in Austin. Taylor was one of the few female African American professionals whom Jordan came across when she went to Austin. Azie and Barbara were exactly the same age, their birthdays only weeks apart. Their experiences and meteoric careers were similar, and they shared a love of politics—and political gossip. Their paths would cross often over the years. Azie went to Washington to be Bob Strauss's assistant at the Democratic National Committee in 1972, and after her marriage in 1977, Azie Taylor Morton was appointed by President Jimmy Carter to be the first African American treasurer of the United States.

Barbara Jordan also got to be close friends with a small group of white women. When she had been getting her career established in Houston, one of the organizations she was active in was the YWCA. There she met Anne Appenzellar, director of the Austin Y. Whenever Barbara had to go to Austin to make a speech, Anne would meet her plane, take her to meetings, or help her run errands. They would often have dinner together. Through Anne, Barbara got to know Betty Whitaker, who was a social worker, and Nancy Earl, who worked in the Measurement and Evaluation Center at the University of Texas. Anne's group of friends liked to camp out at the lakes in the hill country surrounding Austin. After Barbara had served for some time in the Senate, Anne persuaded her to come along with them. For a Fifth Ward girl who had never been exposed to freshwater lakes, hundred-year-old oak trees, or scrub cedar on rugged hillsides, a camp-out was a delightful new experience. Anne's friends were easy to be with. They were smart, and they cared about ideas and issues. Around the campfire, they liked to sing, tell good stories, and have a few drinks. They were so far removed from life at the capital, they barely recognized the names of the men Barbara considered powerful. Neither did they kowtow to Barbara, or try to flatter her. She found that interesting—and refreshing! Barbara had such a good time on her first outing that she decided to join the group whenever she could get away. "We would camp out in tents and light fires and get dressed in the morning and sleep on air mattresses and all that sort of business," Barbara wrote later. "Sometimes we would fish and troll in the streams. And I thought: it's nice for me to be associated with all these people with these outdoorsy interests." These outdoor weekends seemed to sustain Barbara, keep her relaxed, and provide some balance in her life, which revolved totally around her work and career. Anne Appenzellar's group of friends became Barbara Jordan's friends—the first deep friendships she had outside of her sisters and the Justices.

"I knew friends like the Justices were always going to be my friends," Jordan said. "They would follow me anywhere and they did not ask for anything, because they were there in the beginning. But out here in the white world it took a long time to decide the criteria for whom you could trust, and it was a judgment call every time. . . . Some people fit, and some people didn't, and you learned over the passage of time which ones would and which ones wouldn't." Anne, Nancy, Betty, and a few others "fit."

One weekend, Bennie and Rose Mary came to Austin for a big party at Nancy's house, amid huge cypress trees and wildflowers on Onion Creek, just south of Austin. Barbara thought Nancy was a particularly "fun person to be with." Blond, lithe, and exuberant about life, Nancy also had a Pennsylvania practicality that exceeded even Barbara's. She wasn't overly impressed with Barbara's position or status as "the first black woman who ever did this or that. . . . I don't know why, but I was never intimidated by Barbara," Nancy said. "I just treated her like anybody else. I think if you didn't let Barbara run all over you, she came to respect you."[24]

Jordan came to feel secure in her new circle of friends. "I liked to be part of those parties. I had discovered I could relax . . . where I was safe." She needed the safety of close friends because she was increasingly distancing herself from her family—and particularly from Ben Jordan.

From the time she was a teenager, Jordan had liked the way she felt after drinking a beer with her buddies. She had been sneaking cigarettes since she was about fourteen. In the Senate, she had discovered a taste for fine scotch, and she found that sitting down with her colleagues to swap stories with a cigarette and a good stiff drink was a good way to establish the relationships she felt she needed in order to be effective. In those after-hours gatherings, she had also learned to be a pretty good poker player.

Jordan's drinking, smoking, singing, card-playing, and all-night parties would have sent Ben Jordan reeling if he had known the details. But all he knew, or wanted to know, at this time in his daughter's life was that she was a state senator, a hero to her people, the proud daughter of Good Hope, the Fifth Ward, and *him*. He was proud. *He* had produced this wonder woman. Ben Jordan believed he deserved the credit because he had worked so hard and sacrificed so much to give Barbara the opportunities to succeed. And he wanted her to acknowledge it. He had written to Barbara when she was in Boston to remind her of all that he had done for her and to tell her that she should recognize it and let others know that she would not be there without his help. He continued to remind her when she was in the Senate that she should let people know how much he had sacrificed for her. When she did recognize his influence publicly on several occasions, Ben was satisfied. He rarely asked what she did in her free time.

Barbara had moved beyond caring what Ben Jordan thought or cared about. For years, she had resented her father. She felt he had sucked the energy and will, the very life force, out of her mother. She hated that. Her mother's passivity had always disturbed her, and she blamed Ben for intimidating and dominating Arlyne. She had decided from the time she was a little girl that she would not let Ben Jordan do that to her. Even when she was a teenager, however, Ben was too overwhelming, too powerful, too harsh for her to think of open rebellion. She learned to hide things from him, keep secrets, sneak off. As she developed her powers of observation and ability to strategize, Barbara Jordan also learned how to get around her father.

Beneath his stern exterior, Ben Jordan concealed a sentimental soul. When his daughters made him proud by fitting into the mold he had so carefully constructed for them, he would be so moved, so confirmed in the rightness of his control over them, that he would cry. Seeing his girls sing in front of Good Hope's congregation always brought tears to his eyes. Seeing Barbara win a declamation contest would make him so emotional he could not speak. He sobbed when she was named Wheatley High School's Girl of the Year. At first, Ben's tears confused Barbara. How could it be that someone so strong, so stern and sure, could cry when a little girl made a speech? Maybe he wasn't so strong after all.

Barbara soon learned that when she put Ben in one of his prideful, teary states, his no might soften into a yes. By the time she was in college, she had figured out, plain and simple, how to manipulate Ben. Then her fear of Ben Jordan had turned to contempt. She saw his emotional breakdowns and crying, his bragging and need for recognition as fundamental weaknesses, which she did not like.

Until her second year in law school, Barbara had always felt guilty about her anger toward Ben, as if by challenging or manipulating her father she was also challenging or trying to manipulate God. Once Howard Thurman had given her a new way to look at God and religion, however, rebellion against Ben no longer had a religious dimension. It was all personal. It was Ben she was angry with, not God. Barbara's emotional split from Ben was deep by the time she was elected to the state Senate.

After she had run for office in Houston something about Ben's behavior began to arouse her suspicions. He was often away from home, leaving Arlyne alone to watch her soap operas and late-night shows. One night when Ben left the Campbell Street house in his Oldsmobile, Barbara decided to follow him. He drove straight to the home of a woman she knew. Barbara parked her car down the street and waited. And she put it all together. Ben Jordan—preacher, husband, father, moralist, naysayer, disciplinarian—was apparently involved with another woman!

Barbara Jordan closed her heart to her father that evening. Like so much else in her life, however, she did not talk about it at the time. Years later, when stories about Martin Luther King Jr.'s sexual activities became widespread, she shocked some of her closest friends by discussing Ben's behavior quite openly—with the hint of outrage still in her voice. One of her friends said that Barbara was a one-person morality squad, both judge and jury in regard to her father, and that she stayed furious with him for years. But it was a silent fury. Ben Jordan never knew it existed.

CHAPTER 10

THE OPPORTUNITY

IN 1968 BARBARA Jordan gave a prophetic speech to newspaper publishers entitled "Who Speaks for the Negro?" It was a few weeks after the assassination of Martin Luther King Jr., a time of turmoil and despair. In her speech, it was clear that she was speaking for herself as well as for her race, and in fact she was *explaining* herself and her motivations.

> *The Negro has always had the faith, an almost blind faith, in what this country promised to become. . . . The question that we've asked . . . is, Who speaks for the Negro? Well, I'll answer that question: No one. No one can. You see, the Negro stands, silhouetted against a thriving and abundant America and his presence, his very presence on the American scene speaks for itself. . . . What does he want? He wants "in." The Negro wants "in." He wants you to hear him, understand his condition. He feels that if you do this—if you really listen to him as he speaks through his presence and understand his condition—he feels that you'll save him. And that in the process of saving him you will also save this country. And in the process of saving this country you save yourselves.[1]*

When Jordan began her second term in the Texas Senate in 1969, not only had she gotten *in*, she had become a consummate *insider*. That would set her apart from most other African American leaders in the 1960s and 1970s.

The eloquence of Martin Luther King Jr. would certainly have been on her mind as Jordan gave her speech to the newspaper publishers. And she would have recognized that King's mark on history came from his role as an *outsider*. Like a biblical prophet calling a nation to righteousness, King had stood outside the political system, pointing out its injustices, challenging its institutions, evoking shame among its leaders, and inspiring its downtrodden to speak out and to organize. But Jordan could never see herself in that role. Her path led to the inner circles where key relationships were the tools that allowed deals and laws to be hammered out and shaped—long before they became a part of a system of laws, which in turn would shape human experience.

In 1969 Barbara Jordan's insider status allowed her to be directly responsible for two major changes in Texas law: the state's first minimum-wage law and the first increase in benefits in twelve years for workers injured on the job. Both bills required extensive negotiation, arm-twisting, vote-trading, chit-calling, and the kinds of compromising that only political insiders are capable of managing—indeed the kind of *effective* deal-making that is the mark of a political leader.

Jordan was especially proud of the passage of her $1.25/hour minimum-wage bill, which had died in an unfriendly legislative committee during her first session. Along with her cosponsor, Senator Joe Bernal of San Antonio, she extended minimum-wage coverage to two and a half million Texans who had never been included under the federal minimum-wage law, which in 1969 defined minimum wage as $1.60 an hour. Jordan and Bernal's bill included the state's poorest people, such as the Mexican American farmworkers in the Rio Grande Valley and the black laundry workers in the Fifth Ward.

"The $1.25 an hour was an embarrassingly low figure, in my judgment, for working people," Jordan said. The original bill had called for a state wage of $1.60 an hour, but opposition was too strong, and Jordan had to compromise. Still, she felt, "it was a major victory to get the two words *minimum wage* as part of statutory law in Texas. . . . I was pleased with that."[2]

The liberal *Texas Observer* called the passage of the minimum wage by the Texas legislature a "near miracle."[3] And it was. But it was also the result of realpolitik in Texas, where changes in policy reflected changes in power. After the 1968 general election, in which Richard Nixon defeated Hubert Humphrey for the presidency and Barbara Jordan was reelected unopposed for a full four-year term in the Senate, old political alliances in Texas were so destabilized that neither the liberal nor the conservative faction was comfortable with the previous terms of engagement.[4] Everything was different.

Lyndon Johnson was back home in Texas for the first time in thirty-five years, and Texas no longer had a powerful presence in Washington. Of the state's two U.S. senators, one was a liberal Democrat, Ralph Yarborough, and the other was a conservative Republican, John Tower. Internal

Texas politics were changing, too. With civil rights laws on the books, minorities were voting in record numbers. In addition to Barbara Jordan, Texas now had twenty-one black elected officials, most serving on city councils and school boards. Yet, the old Texas Democracy continued to hold power in the Texas legislature, and its hope was centered on Ben Barnes, who was now lieutenant governor. By the beginning of the 1969 legislative session, however, even Ben Barnes was boasting about his new liberal, labor, and minority friends. That was as disconcerting to some old-line conservatives as it was puzzling to many suspicious liberals. Barnes was only following Lyndon Johnson's advice: "Be as liberal as possible without offending or disturbing your money base."[5] In addition to liberal senators, Barnes had also courted organized labor, establishing warm personal relationships with key labor leaders.

But the Yarborough liberals, like Barbara Jordan's friends in the Harris County Democrats, were fearful of Barnes; they saw him as a potential challenger to Senator Yarborough's reelection in 1970.[6] They watched warily as Barbara Jordan and labor union officials seemed to move closer to him.

Jordan's early white supporters in the liberal organizations didn't know what to make of her after she was elected. It was as if they were uneasy with her success—and her independence. They didn't recognize that once new voting districts allowed minorities to win elections in their own right, white liberal influence might diminish. They were thrown off balance when people they considered their "own" hobnobbed or worked inside the political system with the "enemy." And most liberal activists considered Ben Barnes the enemy because of his ties to John Connally. It was hard for liberal stalwarts like Chris Dixie or the *Texas Observer* to understand how their heroes—Jordan, Mauzy, and the others—could be so close to Barnes. But for the liberal senators, who now numbered fourteen, working with the lieutenant governor was the way to pass the laws they cared about.

Yet, Barbara was quite sanguine about Barnes because she saw him clearly. "Ben Barnes is . . . a man on the move with his eye someplace. . . . He wants to innovate and be resourceful . . . and wants to be, I think, the most powerful figure in state government. But Ben has the danger of burning himself out. When you start so young so fast, there is that danger that you can move too fast and wear the people out. . . . He's constantly on the move. . . . It seems as if he always has an eye on the next political campaign. And it's difficult to stop and say, 'Well, what is this man substantively?' This, I think, is a question that would have to be answered if Ben ever got into a serious campaign, and he hasn't had one yet."[7]

A NEW DAY IN TEXAS

In 1969 Ben Barnes's and Barbara Jordan's interests coincided on minimum-wage legislation. Since most of the state's major businesses were already covered by the federal minimum-wage law, the only significant opposition to the measure came from agriculture, small-business groups, and traditional Texas conservatives who in principle were against any government-imposed minimum-wage law. Because of a fiasco several years earlier, when Connally had angered and insulted Mexican farmworkers, Barnes desperately needed to bring liberals and labor back into the tent.[8] Backing Jordan's minimum-wage bill would certainly help.

At the beginning of the 1969 legislative session, when Barnes told Jordan that he was as committed to passing the bill as she was, she worried that even if the Senate passed the bill, they would never get enough votes to win approval in the House. But Barnes told her, "Don't worry, I'll find something that [Speaker Gus] Mutscher's got to get through the Senate, and you wait and see if the House doesn't pass it." Jordan's job was to find twenty-one votes in the Senate. She went to work in her focused, efficient way, cajoling, arguing, charming. When she had managed to pull *all* of the swing-vote moderates her way, she told Barnes she was ready for a vote. With Barnes's swift use of his presiding officer's gavel, Jordan managed to avoid a conservative filibuster against the bill. To the amazement of political pundits, the business lobby, and the state's major newspapers, Jordan passed the minimum-wage bill in the Senate, twenty-one to ten. A few weeks later, on the day before final adjournment, moderates in the House of Representatives teamed up with the liberals to pass the bill, eighty-nine to sixty, sparking incredulous jubilation. The vote seemed to herald a new political era for Texas.

The feeling was compounded because another Jordan-sponsored, pro-labor bill to help injured workers had also passed both houses. Jordan herself told reporters that the liberals had "arrived." Her workers' compensation bill, however, required far more intense legislative maneuvering because it affected all of the big Texas employers—the "money base" for Barnes.

In Texas, as in most states, employers were required by law to buy workers' compensation insurance to pay medical costs and compensatory damages for workplace-related injuries. The Texas weekly benefit of only thirty-five dollars for an injured worker was among the lowest in the nation, and the Texas AFL-CIO had made "workers' comp" reform its top priority. Labor leaders had asked Barbara Jordan to sponsor the bill.

Ben Barnes felt obligated to the Texas AFL-CIO for its support in his election, and he also wanted to help Jordan on a major piece of legislation that she cared about. Workers' comp proved to be the issue that would allow him to do both. Barnes and Jordan huddled to figure out a strategy to pass the bill. Three key lobby groups had a direct interest in the issue: the Texas

AFL-CIO, the Texas Manufacturers Association, and the Texas Trial Lawyers Association, whose members represented injured workers. Barnes and Jordan knew that if they could get the three groups to reach an agreement, they might be able to overcome the rest of the opposition and pass the bill. They began to meet secretly with key leaders of the groups, first separately, and then in larger meetings where all were present.

While Jordan had carried other bills and been involved in negotiations and Senate deal-making before, this was the first time she had been the leader in closed-door meetings where the stakes were so high for people she cared about. According to Barnes, the 1969 negotiations on workers' comp also represented the first time labor leaders had ever been invited inside any room in the Capitol where a deal might actually get made. For the Texas Senate, it was an unprecedented negotiation between labor and management, led by a black woman. The meetings were intense and initially hostile. But Jordan was amazingly adept at calming fears, staying focused on the issues, and pulling out a consensus from the diverse group. Within a few weeks, they struck a deal. The three groups agreed to support legislation that would raise an injured worker's weekly benefit to forty-nine dollars, increase payments to survivors in the case of a fatal injury, and accomplish a number of other significant reforms.[9] Because it was such an unusual agreement among three antagonistic interest groups, Barnes advised Jordan to move the bill through the Senate without accepting *any* amendments, which might shift the tenuous balance and unravel the compromise. A few of the Senate's most vociferous liberals, however, were unhappy with the compromise. They were resentful, first, because they had not been included in the negotiations, and second, because they believed that the weekly benefits should be higher.

"I was the guy who fought Barbara hardest on this," said her friend and Senate colleague Oscar Mauzy. "I had the votes on the floor for higher benefits, and if Barbara hadn't told the guys not to go with me, I could have won it. But the deal had been cut. Labor was in on the deal, and labor could be wrong, too, and they were. I just thought we could do better." Mauzy, a labor lawyer, was not included in the negotiations on the bill. Neither was Senator Babe Schwartz. "After having carried labor's water all these years, I think I should have been consulted," Schwartz complained.[10] Jordan held her votes during the Senate debate, however, and defeated amendments by Schwartz and Mauzy to raise benefits. The bill eventually sailed through the Senate on a thirty-to-zero vote, and it passed the House, too.

"Some of my friends didn't like it because it didn't go far enough," Jordan admitted. "It was a compromise measure. I wasn't happy with it, but I was pleased that we did increase benefits by the amount that we did. . . . It was an easy job to get that through with everybody compromising on that figure. And, of course, that's the way you do. You compromise."[11]

In any compromise, a deal is a deal. Jordan had given her promise, and she stuck by it, although she found it uncomfortable to vote against higher benefits for injured workers when she had to fight off the Mauzy and Schwartz amendments. And the criticism from her liberal friends stung. Years later, when she taught a seminar on ethics at the LBJ School of Public Affairs at the University of Texas, she acknowledged the built-in instability of compromises such as her workers' compensation bill. She believed a politician could maintain a moral stance through compromise if he or she acknowledged the reality of the problems that remained *after* the compromise, and acknowledged them *publicly*.[12] Jordan did not try to hide the wrongs left uncorrected by her bill. The weekly payments to injured workers were still abysmally low. Nevertheless, she publicly recognized the remaining problems, and because she could only cajole or persuade, not dictate to, the other interested parties, she felt that she had achieved the best she could under the circumstances. She felt that her action reflected a moral as well as a political realism.

In many ways, dealing with liberal criticism of her role in the workers' comp legislation sharpened—rather than dampened—Jordan's propensity for deal-making. The liberals had made her angry as well as defensive. She had a strong belief in the reliability of her moral compass to warn her if she was close to violating her own integrity or hurting her core constituency in the Fifth Ward. The workers' comp compromise triggered none of those warning signals. "I just maintained a sense of who I am and what's important to me," Jordan said. "You need a core inside you—a core that directs everything you do. You confer with it for guidance. It is not negotiable. No amount of money will make you violate the core. If you don't have that, then forget about elective politics. If you do, then it will guide you well."[13] Jordan's moral core was quite simple. "The core of morality is to do unto others as you would have them do unto you. If you make that the central theme of your morality code, it will serve you well as a moral individual."[14]

Jordan was quite proud of her workers' compensation deal because she had gained something for workers no one else had been able to do in twelve years. Only a purist, or a fool, she thought, would spoil such a deal for a few more dollars a week. Because she had been criticized by some of her liberal friends for being willing to negotiate and compromise on legislation in the Senate, she developed a tolerance, even an empathy, for other officeholders who were similarly criticized for their lack of political "purity."[15]

THE PATH TO PRAGMATISM

By Texas standards—if not liberal standards—the Texas legislature was remarkably progressive during Jordan's remaining term. In addition to the minimum wage and the new workers' compensation law, the legislature also gave teachers a pay raise, created state-funded public kindergartens for five-year-old children, created three new state universities, and provided funding for two new medical schools. Jordan worked on passing other pieces of legislation that were also quite amazing for Texas. She won approval for the state's first Fair Employment Practices Act, which made it unlawful for employers or labor unions to discriminate against their employees on the basis of race, color, gender, or creed. She successfully sponsored a 10 percent increase in retirement benefits for Texas schoolteachers and persuaded her colleagues to pass legislation creating a "sheltered workshop" bill, which provided state funding for organizations that hired handicapped persons. She even succeeded in getting the legislature to repeal the Texas law requiring segregated burials in cemeteries, as well as all of the other 1957 segregation laws that had been passed in reaction to federal court orders on school integration.

Barbara Jordan took part in dozens of legislative skirmishes and initiatives that established her credentials as one of the Senate's key players. In August 1969, the most important was a tax bill—the governor called a special legislative session to deal with it, so that the Texas government would not run out of money when the next fiscal year began in September.

Liberals, including Barbara Jordan, were adamantly against more consumer taxes, and conservatives were adamantly against business taxes. But someone had to pay for the new universities, the teacher pay raises, and other legislative initiatives. The House bill was pro-business and heavy with consumer taxes, while the Senate bill was more balanced, with an even split between business and consumer taxes.

In the liberal "Good Guy" caucuses, Jordan had always advocated a state income tax, but she was realistic enough to know that an income tax would never pass the Texas legislature—or even pass muster in her own district. Instead, during the Senate debate, she had sponsored a 10 percent corporate profits tax. Business groups were so united in their opposition that she could get only ten votes. Nevertheless, corporate chieftains were finally beginning to realize that the business lobby's traditional lock on the Texas legislature could be broken if something were not done quickly. When the House and Senate were hopelessly deadlocked over their different versions of the tax legislation, key business lobbyists came out with a proposal to place a sales tax on food, which would raise almost $500 million in new tax revenue, solving the state's perennial money problems for years to come.

Ben Barnes became the chief proponent of the food tax, and the wheels were greased for speedy passage.[16] But on Friday evening, August 23, Senate liberals kicked off a filibuster. While they knew that Barnes had the votes to pass the food tax, they were hoping to stall until it would be too late to take any action.

Barbara Jordan took her turn to keep the filibuster alive that evening, holding the floor for more than an hour, even though she told colleagues she did not feel well. She criticized the tax bill for exempting fertilizer and farm animal food, while taxing "people" food. "If we're going to compromise on the mouths of babies, why not compromise on the mouths of horses and mules?" she argued.[17]

By Saturday afternoon, eighteen hours after it had begun, the filibuster was still going. Barnes was obviously having trouble cutting it off, and it looked like he was losing his own votes, too. Then, with the help of the business lobby, Barnes engaged in some heavy arm-twisting and Texas-style theatrics. He flew one seriously ill senator into Austin on his sickbed to be ready to cast his pro-tax vote. And there was a Saturday night showdown in the lieutenant governor's living room, in which Barnes drew an imaginary line in the carpet, just as William B. Travis had done at the Alamo.[18] With pressure, promises, and parliamentary maneuvering, Barnes began to lay plans to cut off the filibuster. That meant putting pressure on his liberal friends. Oscar Mauzy said Barnes and the business lobby pulled out all the stops Saturday afternoon and evening. "I'm convinced, after their little soirees over there the other night, that they could get sixteen people to vote to repeal the Bible, the Constitution, and Newton's laws of physics," Mauzy said.[19] Barnes persuaded two liberals to leave the Senate chamber and "take a walk" when he was ready to call for a procedural vote to end the filibuster a little after midnight.

The Senate finally passed the food tax, fifteen to fourteen, in the early hours Sunday morning. Barbara Jordan was one of the fourteen liberals who voted against the bill. It was summer in Texas, however, and the only news of significance was the Saturday night action of the Texas legislature. By breakfast time Sunday morning, stories about the new "bread tax" were displayed prominently on the front page of every newspaper in the state. And Senate food-taxers got the surprise of their lives.

Texans were outraged. In one of the most spontaneous grassroots uprisings Texas had ever seen, ordinary citizens began calling their legislators all day Sunday to complain. By Monday morning, the crush of incoming protest calls had jammed the Capitol's telephone lines. And by noon, telegrams from all across the state were stacked high on members' desks. Consumer and labor lobbyists also pulled their members into the protests, and the Capitol was full of angry taxpayers. By late Monday afternoon, support for the measure had faded. The House had rejected the Senate bread tax, 147 to 0. An uncomfortable Ben Barnes and his Senate colleagues were left dangling. They had gone on record for an unpopular tax that set off the first modern tax revolt in Texas.

What had been Barbara Jordan's role in the Senate food tax fight? On the record, she had been against the food tax. Barnes had pressured her to help him, however, and she did. Jordan's colleagues knew that she had given Barnes one record vote late Saturday evening on a failed motion to end the filibuster. That was as far as she went, publicly. More than twenty-five years later, Barnes said she helped him secretly in the parliamentary maneuver that finally cut off debate. At the point late Saturday evening when Barnes felt his votes were secure, he persuaded Jordan to ask filibustering senator Don Kennard a question. While she had the floor, on a prearranged signal, one of the conservatives "moved the previous question," a parliamentary tactic that requires a vote and effectively cuts off debate. The motion to cut off the debate carried on a fourteen-to-thirteen vote, with several liberals conveniently off the floor, also at Barnes's instigation. The parliamentary vote cleared the way for final approval of the bill. Was this a smooth maneuver on Jordan's part? Or merely a turn of the head at the wrong moment, a momentary lapse of attention, the blur of fatigue after more than thirty hours of filibuster? The motion could have prevailed when *anyone* had the floor, and no one ever blamed Barbara Jordan for the Senate passage of the food tax bill. Yet Barnes was adamant that it was Jordan's cooperation that brought the matter to a head. "Barbara Jordan enabled me to stop the filibuster on the food tax," he insisted.

Why would Jordan have aided in the passage of a bill that she personally detested? Barbara never talked publicly about her role in the food tax episode. It was well known, however, that she had little patience for fighting futile battles. If Barnes had the votes to pass the bill, as he ultimately did, why put off the inevitable? If she could not change the final outcome, which is what mattered to her, she probably saw no moral dilemma in helping with a procedural matter that would simply move things along.

Mauzy remembered a similar incident during Jordan's first session. The liberals were filibustering a bill dealing with ownership of mineral rights; they did not have the votes to defeat it. After three or four votes with the liberals, Jordan balked. "Enough is enough," she said. "I think this has gone on just about long enough, and I'm not going to go with you anymore."

It would have been consistent with Jordan's beliefs and behavior to agree with Barnes's assessment of the food tax filibuster: "There wasn't any reason to stay in session any longer and get people all mad." And it would not have been uncharacteristic for Jordan to help shut off a futile filibuster. Being in the Senate Club had taught her to be a political realist. That meant measuring the obstacles to political change, taking opportunities where she found them, and acquiescing when she was blocked rather than fighting to the bloody end. Not only was that the path to power inside the legislative system, but to her that was moral as well as political realism.

Reinhold Niebuhr, the Protestant theologian whom Jordan later often quoted in her speeches, saw a relationship between political realism and what he called "moral realism." For Niebuhr, both political and moral realists understood the use of power, and the moral realist was willing to use political power to achieve some human "good." Jordan had become a Niebuhr-style moral realist, with an understanding that if she wanted to promote human good, then she had to have enough power to operate effectively. When she was on the losing side of an issue, she tried to preserve enough room to maneuver, always saving enough power for the next piece of legislation, the next debate, the next cause. In the Texas Senate, she perfected her approach to finding, preserving, and using power. It was an approach she had used her whole life.

Even as a little girl, Barbara Jordan seemed to understand the idea of power as a tool rather than a possession. Power was simply the ability to make something happen, to change the course of events. She had been influenced by her Grandpa Patten's view of power, reflected in his understanding of God. "*Power* was the word that stuck in my mind when I thought about Grandpa Patten speaking about God. He definitely did not present God as a father image. He was always *power*. That was the operative word," she wrote. She had also learned about power in the Good Hope Missionary Baptist Church, where Reverend Albert Lucas, her grandfather Charles Jordan, even her father Ben Jordan wielded power, if only in their own little spheres. And there was Mack Hannah—*the* power in the black community. All of these men could speak sparingly and strike hard. Jordan could see that the powerful men in her community always aligned themselves with a source of *outside* power in order to increase their own influence and effectiveness. For Reverend Lucas, it was the NAACP and the National Baptist Convention. For Mack Hannah, it was the combined clout of the black community of churches and his association with Houston's white business leaders. For Grandfather Jordan, it was the prominent Cashaw family. For her father, it was both the church, which gave him prestige, and the union, which gave him economic security. If you didn't have money, which could always buy political power, you had to have an association with something or someone else beyond your natural community. You always had to have an alliance with a source of *organized* power.

By the time Jordan made it to the Texas Senate, it was second nature for her to look for, and align herself with, those who had power. From watching Lyndon Johnson she had learned to practice the art of political favors. The writer William Broyles believed that in fact it was Jordan, not John Connally, who was "the true heir to Lyndon Johnson's wheeling and dealing skills."[20]

The operative word for a political favor is *chit,* a voucher that allows its holder to claim something of value. Favor-trading is how trust is developed among political colleagues. Inside players have always helped each other by doing favors, trading votes, providing information, keeping secrets, helping on procedural matters, being available, and above all being realistic about vote counts and the prospects for victory or defeat. By the end of her second legislative session in 1970, Jordan excelled at inside politics, an arena in which loyalty to colleagues, despite philosophical or policy disputes, is one of the highest values. Without it nothing ever gets done.

"Barbara was a team player with me," Ben Barnes remembered. "When I needed her to do something, she did it." In the Senate Club, members protected one another. Most of these favors were never discussed, and many were never visible. The favors and loyalties built a trust, however, and paved the way for reciprocal actions or rewards. That was the nature of the Barbara Jordan–Ben Barnes relationship. And the payoff was still to come for Barbara Jordan.

SURVIVAL OF THE FITTEST

In politics, only the fit—the fleet, smart, strong, and persistent—survive the decennial process of redistricting. In the 1971 reapportionment of congressional boundaries in Texas, Barbara Jordan was the fittest of them all.

The reapportionment of the election district boundaries is one of the most emotional, contentious, and important activities that can occur in the American political system. It determines not only who will serve but who will be represented. The 1970 census revealed that the population of Texas had grown sufficiently to warrant a new seat in the U.S. Congress, bringing the total number of Texas representatives to twenty-four. Lyndon Johnson, now living at his Johnson City ranch in the hill country west of Austin, wanted Jordan to have it. So did she, but it all depended on how the lines were drawn.

During Jordan's first term, when the Senate liberals had stayed up all night drinking, singing, and musing about their ambitions, several of them talked openly about wanting to go to Congress. Charlie Wilson from east Texas was quite frank about his ambitions, as were Oscar Mauzy, Fort Worth's Don Kennard, and Galveston's Babe Schwartz. Joe Bernal was waiting only for a new district to be created in San Antonio so that he would not have to run against the legendary Mexican American local hero, Congressman Henry B. Gonzalez.[21] In those early days, Barbara was reticent, as usual, about revealing what she might want. Mauzy remembered that Jordan "didn't talk about Congress very much in those early days. I think she wanted to serve a few terms in the Senate and go back to Houston to make some money and continue to be active in things." All of that changed, however, when the possibility of a congressional seat came up. It looked like it would be possible to create a district that Jordan could win. "I think that's when she got interested," Mauzy said.

In 1971 Houston's population dominated three congressional districts: a safe Republican seat held by W. R. "Bill" Archer, and two other Democratic seats, one held by the liberal Bob Eckhardt and the other by the conservative Bob Casey.[22] Jordan and the scholarly Eckhardt had been allies, and Jordan had said publicly that she would never consider running against him. But after preliminary 1970 census reports indicated Houston

would get a new seat, she began telling reporters that she might be interested. She had some powerful allies in her quest.

By the end of Jordan's first term, three of Houston's most influential
business leaders had determined that they could live with her: Searcy
Bracewell, a former state senator and the premier lobbyist for Houston's
major industries;[23] the *Houston Chronicle*'s powerful publisher, Everett Collier; and Ben Love, the city's most important banker, who ran Texas Commerce Bank.[24] By the 1971 redistricting session, these men did not want to
stand in Barbara Jordan's way for a congressional district. Because the
Houston "money" usually followed the lead of these men, Jordan had the
blessings of the city's most powerful conservatives. That made it possible for
Ben Barnes to be quite open in his efforts to carve out a safe district for her.

"The business community was convinced that Barbara was an asset,"
said Barnes. While still holding the presidency, President Johnson had
made calls advising his Houston political and financial supporters to avoid
stereotyping Barbara Jordan, get to know her, and give her a chance to get
to know them. So when Mayor Louis Welch put together the prestigious
Human Relations Council to advise him on race relations, he appointed the
noted attorney Leon Jaworski as its chairman and made Jordan a member.
Business leaders soon began to feel the effects of Jordan's presence and
charm.

Ben Love, the leader of the new generation of suave, efficient money
managers who succeeded the Suite 8F crowd as Houston's primary establishment power brokers, believed that Jordan's intelligence won over the
initially resistant Houston business community. "Barbara was a fabulous
listener. . . . Just by looking into her eyes . . . there was an intelligence
that just was visible in those eyes. I think she understood that for everyone
to prosper, business had to create jobs."[25] By 1971 Ben Love had become a
fan of Barbara Jordan's, and her graciousness and charm as well as her
intelligence had alleviated the fear and trepidation that Houston's business
elite felt about the growing political power of minorities and liberals. Jordan
put them personally at ease, letting them know, "This is not going to be as
bad as you think it is." Lyndon Johnson had been telling them the same
thing.

As early as 1968, Lyndon Johnson had told key leaders in Houston
that they should invest in Jordan. And later, when some of them sent
contributions to her, they would send Johnson copies of their checks so that
he would know they were doing what he suggested. Ben Barnes, too, was
telling Houston's conservative leaders, "The greatest thing you could do is
build Barbara Jordan, send her to Congress. She's going to have more
influence than anybody else you could possibly send." Barnes said that after
her first legislative session Houston's business elite was "knocked out" by
Jordan personally and came to tolerate her liberal votes.

While calls from the president in Washington and the lieutenant governor in Texas obviously opened doors for her, "Barbara had to have other mentors besides President Johnson to accomplish what she wanted to do," George Christian believed. "She had to have the white establishment on her side, and I think she worked very hard to get it there. . . . Some of them had spent years trying to fight integration. And all of a sudden, she began to push that envelope, and they began to back away. . . . It may have been calculated, but it was important for her to do because she was the leader. And a leader, in her view, was somebody who brought people together and tried to find solutions." Houston's business community always paid attention to leaders.

DRAWING THE LINES

"Don't go for it unless it's already in your pocket," Lyndon Johnson had advised Jordan about running for Congress. Ben Barnes did his part by making her vice-chair of the Senate redistricting panel, the small committee that would direct the action. "Go get your precinct lines set, and then we'll build the other Houston districts around what you want," Barnes told her. He added, "If you don't go to Congress, it's only going to be your own fault. You're in charge of creating your district."

Jordan consulted with her old friend Dr. Richard Murray of the University of Houston, who had become one of the expert witnesses in challenging election districts on the basis of racial discrimination. Murray knew the demographics of Houston—the racial composition of neighborhoods, census tract data, and precinct lines—better than anyone in the state. He helped Jordan draw a district she could win—right in the center of Houston. Blacks made up 52 percent of its population, whites were at 25 percent, and Mexican Americans at 25 percent.

"We took that district and drew the rest of the districts around it," Barnes said. By refusing to dilute the minority vote in central Houston and spread it among a number of districts where it might be expected to help liberal white Democrats, Jordan's district would be safe. However, Jordan's district created a lot of problems for other senators, and, indeed, Houston Republicans were prevented from picking up a second seat in west Houston, which their numbers probably warranted. "The problem was that Barbara's district was taboo. I could be real sanctimonious and say I thought it was great for Texas, and I did, but also I looked on Barbara Jordan as one fine political ally," said Barnes. Lyndon Johnson was looking over Barnes's shoulder to make sure Jordan got what she wanted. "Barnes was committed to doing whatever Johnson wanted him to do to help create a district so that Barbara could get elected to Congress," Oscar Mauzy asserted.

Barbara Jordan was so totally absorbed in the redistricting process that she pushed no major bills during her last legislative session, with one exception. When the Equal Rights Amendment to the U.S. Constitution had been proposed in 1969, Jordan in the Senate and Frances "Sissy" Farenthold, the only woman in the House, cosponsored its passage, then took it one step further. They proposed and passed an amendment to the Texas Constitution guaranteeing equal rights for women.[26] However, except for their successful joint passage of the ERA, Jordan and Farenthold had little contact with each other during their overlapping terms in the Texas legislature. In the beginning, it puzzled Farenthold, who assumed that, because they were both liberals and the only women in the legislature, they would become friends. Jordan was a consummate *insider,* however, and Farenthold was a passionate *outsider.* "I used to smile at myself and think, 'Well, you know, what's the story that the white woman is outside throwing rocks and the black woman is inside working with the system?' "[27] In the meantime, Farenthold, as the leader of a band of ethics reformers, had a rebellion to lead in the House, and Jordan had a bill to pass and a congressional district to develop.[28]

Jordan's close attention ensured that her proposed congressional district remained intact, and even survived a court challenge. Yet, her safe seat had a price. When it was all over, Barbara and Charlie Wilson from east Texas were the only two liberals who might win in congressional districts they had helped draw. Mauzy, Schwartz, Kennard, Bernal, and many others came away from the process with nothing. Jordan finally seemed to have a safe congressional district in her "pocket." Her election to Congress seemed such a certainty that Houston's mayor Louis Welch proclaimed October 1, 1971, "Barbara Jordan Appreciation Day." Lyndon Johnson was the honored guest at a dinner for her that evening, and he called Barbara the epitome of the new politics in Texas. Johnson said, "Barbara Jordan proved to us that black was beautiful before we knew what it meant. Wherever she goes, she is going to be at the top. Wherever Barbara goes, all of us are going to be behind her."[29]

Lyndon Johnson's presence at her appreciation dinner was one of the high points of Jordan's life. "Barbara was beside herself when she learned at the last moment that he would be coming," said her friend Stan McClelland, a lawyer and energy executive who helped in Jordan's campaign and became one of her closest lifelong friends. The dinner event was packed with excitement—some planned and some unplanned. McClelland remembered that "Barbara was wearing this gold sequined gown . . . and the Secret Service had called to let us know that President Johnson was on his way. Frank Erwin . . . had just refreshed his Cutty Sark and soda when he came over to hug Barbara. They kind of met in midair, and Erwin spilled his drink all over her. . . . Everyone was just beside themselves and all hell broke loose. . . . Erwin was so apologetic, just effusive. Only Barbara was calm. She said, with clear phonetic emphasis, 'Well, Frank. That's all right. I'm just glad you're not hooked on Blood-y Mary-ys.' "[30]

McClelland was convinced that the president was "in his cups" that evening, too. When Johnson came to the podium, he said, "Well, I'm going to tell you the real story of the Civil Rights Act." He began to tell the story about how when he was in the Senate he tried to persuade his "nigra" man to drive his dog, "Little Beagle Johnson," to Texas, along with the family's belongings so that Johnson, Lady Bird, and their little girls could fly home for a congressional recess. But Johnson's servants, Gene and Helen Williams, had demurred and done everything they could to get out of the trip. When Johnson finally confronted Gene Williams, he told the president: "It's hard enough for a nigger to find a place to stay in the South, but a nigger with a dog can't stay anywhere." The president said he was shocked, because he had never before considered the problems of being black in the South. And he told the story often to explain his conversion to the need for new civil rights laws. But at the appreciation dinner, Johnson greatly embellished the story, telling it in a white southerner's imitation of black dialect. He told the crowd that he decided then and there that if it ever came within his power to end segregation in public accommodations, he would, so that no one would ever have trouble finding a bathroom or a place to eat, "or driving my dog from Washington to Texas." And "that's the story of the Civil Rights Act," he said.

"It was a colorful story, in the sense that everybody was amused," McClelland remembered. "But we were really embarrassed by it. We had a black audience. It was a low-dollar event to show support, and we had all these black people around there, and he was talking like this."

Jake Johnson says he, too, was embarrassed, but that Barbara Jordan clearly was not. The next day he asked her what she thought. "Did you really believe that story about the 1964 Civil Rights Act?" Jordan looked at Jake, put her hand over her heart, and said, "With all my heart." Then she explained to her skeptical friend, "What people don't realize is that great movements start with just one person, not crowds and cheers . . . so, yes, I believe that experience changed Lyndon Johnson."

Barbara Jordan was riding high after Johnson's appearance at the appreciation dinner. Immediately afterward, however, she had to face the reality of a bitterly contested congressional election. The district was not in her pocket after all. State Representative Curtis Graves had decided he was going to run for Congress, too. He was angry. In fact, he was furious with Barbara Jordan. And the appreciation dinner had only made him more determined to take her down.

CHAPTER 11

RUNNING FOR CONGRESS

BARBARA JORDAN'S 1972 campaign for Congress established her as a political master of two very different constituencies. Each represented political experiences as far apart as the poles.

African American voters overwhelmingly reaffirmed their trust and pride in her, and Houston's downtown business community adopted her as their champion and personal guide to appropriate race relations in tumultuous times. With both constituencies, the African American activist Curtis Graves became the foil against which all of Jordan's attributes were measured, allowing her to solidify an amazingly broad range of support—as no politician in Houston had been able to do before, or has done since. It was not exactly what Curtis Graves intended to do for Barbara Jordan.

Graves had assumed he would move up to the state Senate when Jordan moved up to Congress. But the *Houston Chronicle*'s publisher Everett Collier—one of Houston's most powerful white business leaders—drew up a plan on behalf of the Houston Chamber of Commerce that carved up the solid black Senate district that had elected Jordan and split the black vote among five state Senate districts, making it virtually impossible for an African American to win—just as in the old days. Graves blamed Ben Barnes and Barbara Jordan. He was particularly angry with Jordan. He believed that in order to get a safe congressional seat, she had made a deal to sacrifice a black state Senate seat to keep him from moving up. He denounced her as the "Aunt Jemima of Texas politics."[1] And he told a group of African Americans that Jordan had sold them out. "She traded your black Senate seat for her own seat in Congress. Redistricting was an attempt to cut down any black man from ever having any power. I say that the white man has used our women too long . . . now, they are using them in Congress."[2]

Curtis Graves, who had been elected to the state House of Representatives at the same time Jordan was elected to the state Senate, was quick and eager to speak out about anything he perceived as an injustice. Arrested in one of the early 1960s sit-ins to integrate the coffee shop at Houston's train station, he viewed his arrest as a civil rights badge of honor. He waged a constant verbal war against Houston's police chief, Herman Short, the symbol of police brutality in the black community after Short's troops fired six thousand rounds of ammunition into two student dormitories to quell demonstrations by Texas Southern University students in 1967.[3]

"There was an element of the community that found Graves attractive," according to Stan McClelland, "but downtown Houston was scared to death. Ben Love and those people could not tolerate the downtown business community being represented by Curtis Graves."

The contrast between Curtis Graves and Barbara Jordan was stark. Former congressman Craig Washington, who represented Jordan's old congressional district in the late 1980s, said that in a way Graves's presence in the Capitol allowed Jordan to be more effective. "It was like the Mutt and Jeff routine policemen use—when you have a belligerent cop and a sympathetic one working over a suspect together. After the confrontational politics of Graves, they were all too happy to receive a Barbara Jordan."[4] Graves was always *demanding* something—investigations, firings, hearings, or just attention. Once he had even jumped on a table in the House chambers to get members' attention. But he had little to show for his four and a half years in the legislature. One black politician said of Graves, "He didn't know when it was time to put his dashiki in the closet, stop raising hell and start getting things done."[5]

Now that he did not have a winnable state Senate seat, Graves was furious. He believed Barbara Jordan was the beneficiary of the business community's largesse, while he was its victim. He wanted revenge.

Most participants in the 1971 redistricting battles agreed twenty-five years later that Barbara Jordan played no role in any "get Graves" campaign. "There really was no big deal about Barbara's old Senate seat," Oscar Mauzy remembered. "We didn't think we did anything. Barbara's seat was never a majority black seat, and Curtis wanted a district that was 75 percent black, and that wasn't going to happen." Liberal congressman Bob Eckhardt agreed. "I was in Ben Barnes's office when he said the Senate was determined not to let Graves in. It was not Barbara's trade-off. Graves was rather flamboyant and they didn't want him."[6] Jake Johnson also insisted that "Barbara didn't mess with anybody else. She didn't trade off that district." Graves and an assortment of white Houston liberals, however, always believed that if Jordan didn't actually draw the lines, she did nothing to block them.

Graves's campaign attacks on Jordan were brutal. After the "Aunt Jemima" charges failed to dent her support, he began to call her an "Uncle Tom." Either way, aunt or uncle, he denounced her as a "sellout," saying she would be the best black congressman money could "buy."

Barbara Jordan was running scared. She was concerned about how black Houston would react to the attacks on her, but Graves's charges that she had "sold out" simply did not ring true. Otis King, Jordan's former debate partner and a onetime roommate of Graves's, believed people *wanted* Jordan to get along with the business community. "I think basically there was an understanding that because she was the first in so many things that she had to go along. The symbol of her being there and presenting a shining image was enough. There are different ways of going about accomplishing what you're trying to get. Sometimes it calls for using a meat ax, and there are times when something else is called for. The important thing is to try to have some results. Politics is the art of the possible, and I think that is the way Barbara thought about it. I don't think she considered that she was selling out. I don't think she even thought she was compromising very much. She was just doing the things that are required. There were some things that were just owed to Barbara, and people felt the seat in Congress should be hers."

Jordan took the high road in the campaign and never attacked Graves personally. She was not above using puns, however, as when she talked to the Teamsters union about the "Graves they were going to dig on May 6— election day."[7] She told one audience, "It's not enough to say, 'right on, brother' or 'we shall overcome' . . . you must become part of the decision-making process."[8] She was refining her core of morality. "The issue is, who can get things done. Who is the most effective?"[9]

After one political rally, where Jordan sat tight-lipped and silent while Graves heaped abuse on her, she told a reporter: "Certainly, I resent it. Maybe the public would enjoy a free-for-all, but not in my campaign. I like to conduct a campaign based on issues rather than attacks and counterattacks. Not a negative campaign designed to discredit my opponent. I don't think the black community has any leadership to sacrifice. It's in scarce supply and I would have preferred this not happen. But what you have to do in public office is get on the inside and chip away at the way people think."[10] Yet, despite her confidence in her own efforts on behalf of her people in the Fifth Ward, Graves's attacks were still upsetting. Particularly to Jordan's family.

Ben Jordan's health was failing. Because of high blood pressure and recurring heart problems, he had been so sick he couldn't even attend the dinner when President Johnson paid tribute to Barbara. Ben could not bear to hear Curtis Graves attack Barbara at the political rallies and speakers' forums. It was as if he himself were being assailed, and he no longer had the strength to absorb blows aimed at his daughter. Arlyne remained Ben's quiet shadow, taking care of him now that he was ailing and limiting herself to cooking fulsome meals for Barbara to keep her going during the campaign. But sisters Rose Mary and Bennie, other relatives, and friends plunged wholeheartedly into the campaign. Bennie's husband, Cres, drove his sister-in-law to all of her campaign events, serving as a kind of bodyguard anytime she was around the unpredictable Graves. The family was terribly upset about Graves's continuing attacks on Barbara.

No one had ever criticized Barbara Jordan before, and she had achieved almost as revered a presence in her family as she had in the Fifth Ward community. The sisters, like their father, took it personally, as if they were also under attack. As adults, each of the sisters reflected different facets of Barbara. Rose Mary had Barbara's distinct, careful voice, without the drama or deep tone. She also had the bearing, dignity, and elegance of manner that Barbara possessed. Rose Mary made a concerted effort to forgive Graves because that is what Christians do: forgive their enemies. But it was harder for Bennie. More impulsive than her sisters, she had Barbara's skepticism and critical judgment. She could spot a phony a mile away. Bennie also represented Barbara's light, fun-loving side, and her sense of humor could break the tension still evident whenever Ben Jordan was around. But Bennie was furious with Curtis Graves. She knew that Barbara was angry, too, "but she didn't let it get to her the way it did to me. She just never would show her anger," Bennie said. "Barbara just wasn't that type. She was so even . . . that was just her demeanor. Barbara even told me not to be angry with Curtis, but I was."

Although there were three other African American men in the race against Jordan in addition to Graves, early polls for the May election showed that she was far ahead of all of them. The money helped. In the critical election period from February 18 to April 15, Jordan had already outspent Graves five to one—some $32,000 to Graves's $6,700. The Dallas millionaire Ross Perot even sent her a check. The conservative *Houston Chronicle* endorsed her, as did the more moderate *Houston Post,* the first time either paper had ever endorsed an African American for anything. And prominent national African American leaders were offering to help her, too. U.S. Congressman Charles Rangel of New York, who had defeated Harlem's Adam Clayton Powell two years earlier, offered to come in and help. The respected civil rights leader Bayard Rustin, head of the AFL-CIO's A. Philip Randolph Institute, sent her a note wishing her a victory and offering to help. Winning looked so certain that Jake Johnson told her, "It looks like you've got it in the bag, so just don't blow it." But Jordan told him, "You know, people have always refused to discuss the issues with my people. And my people deserve to know, so I'm going to respond and talk about what is important to them." She continued to speak at the meetings and shake as many hands as she could. She spoke to stevedores in union halls and beauticians in church halls, and everywhere she went in central

Houston people were thrilled to see her. Every other car in the Fifth Ward seemed to have one of her bumper stickers on its tailgate. Even in the supermarket, people mobbed her. One woman told her, "I've never seen you before in my life, but I just love you."[11] Her campaign headquarters was a storefront office in the Fifth Ward, decorated with red, white, and blue bunting and blown-up photos of the candidate. From it, volunteers had distributed more than twenty-five thousand signs, which were plastered in almost every neighborhood.

As Graves's situation seemed more desperate, some of his supporters began spreading rumors about Jordan's sex life.[12] While there was nothing specific, "it was absolutely vicious on a personal level," according to Jake Johnson, who was involved on a daily basis in the campaign. "Panic rushed through our group. We got together and decided to run a full-page ad in both the *Chronicle* and the *Post* that listed the accomplishments of each of the candidates. And here's Barbara's name with all this stuff—her accolades and accomplishments. And here's Curtis Graves, and there is nothing."

"The people in the general community supported her so solidly—the people in the churches, the people who would come out to vote, they supported her," Otis King said. The ministers stayed with Jordan, and the Harris County Council of Organizations, which by 1971 represented sixty-five black organizations, gave Jordan its endorsement, with a backhanded slap at Graves. "Mr. Graves, while considered effective in bringing issues out into the open, often antagonizes people so badly that he cannot get results. Senator Jordan on the other hand has been effective in getting meaningful bills passed in the legislature. The feeling was that if Mr. Graves was ineffective in Austin, there was no reason to send him to Washington."[13]

In spite of this support, there were other problems for Jordan during her campaign. Ben Barnes was in the middle of his long-planned campaign for governor, and Jordan's old friends in the Harris County Democrats did not like her friendship with him. When Jordan went to the Harris County Democrats' endorsement session in April, a month before the primary, she was prepared for charges from some of the liberals that she had "sold out" to the establishment. Graves had a lot of friends there, but she didn't see how the group could do anything other than adopt a joint endorsement—of both herself and Graves. She was somewhat surprised when the discussion about her congressional race turned to the governor's campaign. One of the candidates for governor in the Democratic Primary was Frances "Sissy" Farenthold, whose leadership of the "Dirty Thirty" reformers in the lower house during the Sharpstown Bank scandal had made her a liberal hero. A few members demanded to know where Jordan stood: Farenthold or Barnes? The discussion quickly shifted to a not-so-subtle challenge: Choose us or choose "them." In fact, it was put to her directly: If she wanted the group to stay neutral in her race, then she had to endorse Farenthold for governor. Jordan was exasperated. All of her misgivings about the impracticality of white liberals rang out. What did one political race have to do with the other? In politics, Jordan believed the liberals would fall on their swords rather than compromise, while she herself would almost always compromise and save her sword for another day. And that is exactly what she did. Without mentioning Farenthold by name, she agreed to support the entire slate endorsed by the Harris County Democrats.[14] Then she left, disgusted by the whole affair.

Ben Barnes was devastated. "Barbara was for me," he believed, "but when she went down to Houston a bunch of those people got after her, and they just started burning her, calling her everything . . . and Barbara just took off her Barnes button," he remembered.

While they did not talk at the time—each was busy trying to win an election—they did talk later, after it was all over. Barnes was indeed squeezed out of the governor's race—running a distant third behind Farenthold and Dolph Briscoe, who would eventually win after a runoff election with Farenthold.[15] Jordan commiserated with Barnes about his fall from favor among Democrats. She had anticipated that he might falter in a heated campaign. "I don't know where Ben Barnes is philosophically. I don't know what makes his guts comfortable, you know. . . . I have talked to him . . . but I never get to where he is. I don't feel that I've ever got to where he really is."[16]

While Barnes lost his bid to ascend the political ladder, Jordan, on the other hand, *trounced* Curtis Graves. She got 80 percent of the total vote and 90 percent of the black vote. Jordan's win over Graves was an important triumph for her. Graves and his accusations had been soundly rejected in the black-dominated district. Barbara Jordan was the undisputed leader of black Houston. When asked whether the results meant that Houston's blacks preferred a moderate over a militant, she said, "It shows that black people want representatives who get things done."

Stan McClelland said his deep friendship with Jordan really began that May 6 election evening. "We had all had a little too much to drink, and I got into political arguments with the family," McClelland remembered. "They thought Barbara could do anything and they were fixing to run her for the United States Senate in two years. I told them, 'You people are crazy. Texas is not anywhere close to electing a black to the Senate, much less a black woman.' And they were furious. I thought they were going to lynch me there." But Barbara had been very quiet, listening to the arguments.

"Now, wait a minute," she finally said. "Stan is right. We are not going to get carried away over this." The discussion continued in a quieter vein until the early Sunday morning sunlight began to fill the room.

GOVERNOR FOR A DAY

In the summer of 1972 between the Democratic Primary victory day and the certain win in November, the Texas Senate bestowed one more honor on Barbara Jordan. By electing her president pro tempore of the Senate, her colleagues made her third in succession to the governor's office. With this election, she became the first black woman elected to preside over a legislative body in the United States, and the first black to preside over the Texas legislature. She told her colleagues: "Nothing can happen in my lifetime that can match the feeling I have for my service in the Texas Senate, and nothing that can happen to me in the future will mean more than receiving this high honor."[17] Tradition called for both the governor and the lieutenant governor to be out of the state on the same day so that the president pro tempore of the Senate could assume the duties of the governor's office, which involved signing a few ceremonial bills while being honored with a huge party at the Capitol, Texas-style, complete with speeches, bands, barbecue, tributes, and gifts.

"Governor for a Day" was a quirky Texas tradition, traditionally used to shake down the lobby and its rich clients by forcing them to shower gifts and money on the Senate's reigning member. But it was different at the state Capitol on June 10, 1972, when Jordan took the governor's chair and addressed a joint session of the Texas legislature. For one thing, the official administering the oath of office to her was black—her old friend from TSU days, Andrew Jefferson, who was now a judge in Houston. Her security guard for the day was the only black member of the Texas Department of Safety's Capitol security force. And the galleries were full of black people. In fact, the audience was predominantly black, a sight seen only once before—the day Jordan had been sworn into the Senate some five and a half years earlier. Someone had even been thoughtful enough to remove the Confederate flag from the Senate chamber, where the main ceremony was being held.

With joyful irony, Barbara Jordan called her historic celebration a "black day" for Texas. African American leaders from all across Texas attended. Delta sorority sisters were there in force. Bands and choirs from predominantly black high schools gave concerts all during the day. Barbara joked to one friend, "We blacks don't take long to get used to things. If one more person calls me Governor, I may just want to keep the title for a long time."[18] But the ceremony in the Senate chamber turned serious when Leon Jaworski, then the president of the American Bar Association, introduced her to the crowd.

"Governor Jordan stands before you as the central figure of a new page in Texas history," he said. "I am wondering how many of us have given thought to the reasons for her high achievement. First of all, and most important of all, she became a good citizen. She was not only indoctrinated in the principles of American citizenship but she practiced them without deviation. She gained the respect and the admiration of members of her community and her state, not merely because she is an articulate and a brilliant woman, but because she believes in the processes of a democracy, upholding the standards that made this country great and deploring those which would erode its greatness."[19]

Roy Evans, who had just become president of the Texas AFL-CIO, added to the accolades when he said, "We look at Governor Jordan and we see what we wish we could see in every politician in this land, a person who believes in building, who believes in love instead of hate."[20]

Jordan, too, was serious when she took the podium to respond to the praise and adulation. "I've thought about a lot of things today," she said. "I thought about the Fifth Ward in Houston. Who would have thought ten years ago that a product of Phillis Wheatley High School and Texas Southern University could become governor of Texas, even for a day? Who could have predicted even ten years ago that this would be *our* day?"

She went on in her most reflective and serious voice: "I want you to celebrate this day as a day of new commitment when a new idea and a new sense of future is to be born in Texas, a new commitment that Texas will not tolerate difference based on race, a day when Texas will fight injustice and inequity whenever it finds it.

"Man must be judged on the content of his character, not where he was born. . . . Texas must be a state where love overrides hate. . . . We must try to see whether it's humanly possible for man to love his fellow man anymore."

And then she spoke primarily to the black people in her audience. "I want to be a voice for you . . . wherever I can be a voice. I want to lead the great coalition that makes us tell the truth when we say we are *one* nation under God, *indivisible* with liberty and justice for all. . . . I want to give every Texan a place to grow . . . and a place to be . . . and a place to dream . . . and a place to think. One day we will be able to sing in a great chorus, 'Freedom has come' . . . but no man is free until all men are free. It doth not yet appear that we shall be."[21]

People in the gallery were blotting their wet faces when Jordan finished, and she had succeeded in bringing tears to Ben Jordan's eyes once again. Even though Ben had to be helped to his feet for the standing ovation the crowd gave Jordan, he could still stand tall and proud behind her.

However, almost immediately after the ceremony, on his way out of the Capitol, Ben Jordan collapsed. A nearby state trooper with a walkie-talkie summoned an ambulance, which rushed him to Brackenridge Hospital, about ten blocks from the Capitol. Barbara dispatched her friend Anne

Appenzellar to the hospital to size up the situation. In the middle of the afternoon festivities, with bands from Wheatley and Jack Yates High School playing, the TSU choir singing, and young kids doing the bugaloo on the Capitol steps, Anne reported back to Barbara that her father had suffered a stroke. Barbara went to the hospital before she changed her clothes for the evening party.

"I walked into the room and there he was on the bed with all of his teeth showing. Just the most wonderful smile imaginable," she wrote years later. "He didn't say much, because at that point his speech was somewhat impaired, but he had that wonderful expression on his face."

"Chief, you almost made the day . . . ," she told him. "You got to see me be governor." When Barbara left the room, he was still grinning.

Ben Jordan died on Sunday morning, June 11, 1972, the day after his youngest daughter took the governor's chair. Barbara accompanied the body, and her family, back to Houston. The funeral was scheduled for the next Wednesday at Good Hope Missionary Baptist Church. Arlyne was full of grief, and Barbara was especially solicitous of her. When Rose Mary urged her mother to pull herself together and stop crying, Barbara told her mother, "No, you cry. You've lost your man." And she told Rose Mary, "This is her man who's gone."

Barbara went back to Austin before the funeral to "settle down," she later said. She consoled herself somewhat with the thought that "if my father had the option of choosing a time to die, he would have chosen that day."

Ben Jordan had been the driving force in his daughter's life. For so many years, everything she had done had either been a reaction to him, a rebellion against him, or an effort to impress him. For her whole life, she had been engaged in a struggle with him. He pushed her, he goaded her, he controlled her, he shaped her, and he supported her in every venture that would bring her success. Yet it was always a contest between his will and her will, his stubbornness and her stubbornness, his notion of discipline and her internalized discipline, his sense of excellence and her demonstration of excellence. She was like him in so many ways, yet she was harder, less forgiving of him than anyone else she encountered in her whole life. She resisted him, she resented him, and she removed herself emotionally from his grasp. She was determined to surpass him in every way, to show him, to best him—this person who was so critical, so strict, so moralistic in his approach to her life, yet so human in his failings and ultimately so proud to be seen as her father. Now he was gone.

Senator Edward Brooke of Massachusetts sent her a clipping from the *New York Times* about Ben Jordan's death. The headline read, "Father Sees Daughter Sworn In, Dies Next Day." When Barbara showed the obituary clipping to her mother, Arlyne was consoled, even happy that recognition had finally come to Ben. "He died at a time when everybody knew it. In New York they know that he died," she said proudly.

Arlyne Jordan knew better than anyone what that little bit of newsprint would have meant to "her man." When Ben insisted on going to Austin to see Barbara sworn in as governor for a day, he had told her, "I wanted to see this day . . . that Black Girl!"[22]

PART III

Politics is . . . an activity . . . a complex activity; it is not simply the grasping for an ideal, for then the ideals of others may be threatened; but it is not pure self-interest either, simply because the more realistically one construes self-interest the more one is involved in relationships with others. . . . The more one is involved in relationships with others, the more conflicts of interest, or of character and circumstance, will arise. These conflicts, when personal, create the activity we call "ethics" . . . and such conflicts, when public, create political activity. . . .

There are two great enemies of politics: indifference to human suffering and the passionate quest for certainty in matters which are essentially political. Indifference to human suffering discredits free regimes which are unable, or which fear, to extend the habits and possibility of freedom from the few to the many. The quest for certainty scorns the political virtues—of prudence, of conciliation, of compromise, of variety, of adaptability, of liveliness—in favour of some pseudo-science of government, some absolute-sounding ethic, or some ideology, some world-picture in terms of either race or economics. . . . A free government is one which makes decisions politically, not ideologically.

—BERNARD CRICK,
IN DEFENSE OF POLITICS (1982)

CHAPTER 12

THE U.S. CONGRESS

ARLYNE JORDAN RODE the bus from Houston to Washington, D.C., to see her thirty-six-year-old daughter sworn into Congress on January 3, 1973. The A. Philip Randolph Institute of the national AFL-CIO had chartered a plane from Houston to take one hundred of Barbara Jordan's friends and supporters to the capital for opening-day ceremonies, but Arlyne had never been on an airplane before, and she would not start flying now.

With her mother there, her sisters, neighbors, and friends from Houston and Austin, Barbara Jordan thoroughly enjoyed her first day as a member of Congress. Her self-confidence was reflected in the simplicity of her dress: a basic black suit, with a small white orchid pinned on her shoulder. She was the center of attention and loved every minute of it. And when it was over, she was ready to go to work.

Her work for the next two years would be shaped by events that unfolded four days later in the court of Judge John Sirica. Five men who were linked to Richard Nixon's reelection campaign pleaded guilty and were given prison sentences for breaking into Democratic Party headquarters at the Watergate complex on June 17, 1972. Two other men went on trial for the same offense. Like most Americans, Barbara Jordan paid little attention to the trial.

Jordan had trounced her nominal Republican congressional opponent, Paul M. Merritt, on November 7, 1972. She won more than eighty-five thousand votes to his nineteen thousand. Although her election to Congress had been a foregone conclusion after she defeated Curtis Graves in the Democratic primary in May, the national news media in November hailed her as the new star on the scene: the first black woman from the South ever elected to Congress. Immediately after the election, everyone wanted a piece of Barbara Jordan for speeches, interviews, awards, receptions, and photographs. Lyndon Johnson had first claim, however, and early in December 1972, he invited her to be with him for the ceremonies and speeches celebrating the opening of his civil rights papers to the public. Of course she went. Although she would talk to him a number of times in the weeks before she took the oath of office, the December 16 meeting with Johnson at his presidential library in Austin would be the last time she saw him.

Johnson was clearly ailing at the civil rights symposium, which had drawn about five hundred old friends, staffers, and civil rights leaders. His health had steadily deteriorated since his return to Texas in early 1969. He had suffered another heart attack in the spring of 1972. It was an effort for him to climb the steps to the rostrum to speak, but when he did, it was as if his heart were reaching out to the crowd. With a profound sadness, he told the audience, "I'm kind of ashamed that I had six years and couldn't do more." Out of all the thirty-one million papers in the library, he told the group, the record of his civil rights work "holds most of myself within it and holds for me the most intimate meanings."[1]

The meeting showcased dozens of Great Society veterans and civil rights leaders, and their words revealed a mix of pride and poignancy, as well as a sense of foreboding, as they assessed the past and looked to the future of civil rights. Roy Wilkins retraced the great trials and victories of the movement. Wilkins and other speakers recalled the sense of promise when Johnson had passionately laid out his civil rights bill in 1964. The president had so electrified the joint session of Congress and the civil rights community that Martin Luther King Jr. reportedly wept when he heard Johnson utter the rallying cry of the movement, "We Shall Overcome." Former chief justice Earl Warren even "obliquely warned President Richard Nixon not to allow the country to slip back into a period of oppression and neglect where blacks were concerned."[2] But in December 1972, the world had changed. Among the old Johnson staffers and civil rights veterans there was obvious regret and nostalgia for what "might have been." School integration had been stopped by the outcry against busing. The attack on systematic causes of poverty that Johnson envisioned for his Great Society programs had been sacrificed for Vietnam. The national Democratic Party had been in disarray so long that Richard Nixon's 62 percent, second-term win over George McGovern a few weeks earlier was as predictable as it was humiliating. And now the spirit of racial "brotherhood," and the liberal hope for a true integration of American society, seemed to be dying, as was Lyndon Johnson.

At the conclusion of the speeches, the president was obviously exhausted. As people were leaving, Barbara Jordan walked over to him, and when he smiled at her, she took him by the hand and gently led him over to view Lincoln's Emancipation Proclamation, which had been put on display for the occasion. They stood together, shoulders touching as they read it. When Lincoln presented the document to his cabinet before releasing it, he had told them, "I know very well that many others might, in this matter, as in others, do better than I can . . . but I must do the best I can, and bear the responsibility for taking the course which I feel I ought to take."[3] Lincoln had to endure the criticism of those who felt his great document had not gone far enough, as well as the complaints of those who felt it had gone too far. The double burden of political responsibility and public criticism was something that the former Texas president and the new member of Congress, each in his or her own way, could understand.

A few weeks later, Lyndon Johnson died, and Jordan reflected on not only what Johnson had done for her but what he had *meant* to her. "Lyndon Johnson made me believe I could be president of the United States," she said. "I believed it because he believed it. Can you imagine what such faith does for one's self-concept? No limits. Free to soar. A level playing field. No artificial barriers. He was saying to me, believe in yourself, as I believe in you."[4]

It was a remarkable gift from a master politician to a young black woman from Houston's Fifth Ward. He believed in her potential and she believed in his wisdom, so much so that when he advised her to switch her congressional committee choices, from Armed Services to Judiciary, she did so without hesitation, and by so doing, she embarked on a path in Congress that allowed her gifts to transcend her own ambition.

HARVARD

Immediately after the election, Jordan had been one of four new members of Congress selected to be fellows in the congressional "Head Start" program at the Institute of Politics at Harvard's Kennedy School. The program was designed to help the brightest members of each new freshman class get acclimated to their new role early so they could be more effective in their work once Congress convened. In addition to Jordan, Yvonne Braithwaite Burke from California, Alan Steelman from Dallas, and William Cohen from Maine rounded out the small group.[5] The briefings focused on the workings and current issues of various federal agencies, the scope and structure of congressional power and leadership, and the mechanics of constituent services and office management. It was a thrilling time for Jordan. She thought Harvard represented the pinnacle of academic excellence, as well as the ultimate in acceptance from the white political establishment. President Johnson had often told her stories about the arrogance of "those Harvards" in government, and now she could test his theories about their "overrated" authority. She found the whole experience interesting, even helpful. She met imminent Democratic Party luminaries such as former Speaker of the

House John McCormack and the Harvard economist John Kenneth Galbraith, who had been President Kennedy's ambassador to India.[6] And she renewed her acquaintance with Yvonne Braithwaite Burke, the other African American and female fellow in the Harvard program.

Yvonne Braithwaite Burke had been elected to the California legislature at the same time Jordan was elected to the Texas Senate. She and Jordan had seen each other periodically at various state legislative conferences and civil rights gatherings. Once, at Dr. Martin Luther King Jr.'s invitation, they had traveled together to Atlanta to speak at a Southern Christian Leadership Conference meeting, where Burke remembered Jordan starting off her speech by singing a gospel song. "They loved it, and I think Dr. King really enjoyed having her there," she said. Jordan had also shown Burke and her husband around Austin when they attended the opening of the Johnson Presidential Library the year before. "Barbara and my husband used to kid around. He liked to tell jokes, and she liked to tell jokes, and they would have a great time together. Barbara had a great sense of humor then."[7] Jordan had both warm feelings and political respect for Burke, whose polite and gracious public demeanor reflected the way Jordan believed public officials should act. Burke's light-skinned beauty and poise had impressed television viewers when she presided at the Democrats' 1972 summer national convention, and political observers expected her to be one of the stars of the forty-five member freshman class in Congress. The women became frequent lunch companions in their early days in Congress.

In January 1973, Jordan and Burke joined the largest group of African American members of Congress since Reconstruction.[8] The House of Representatives would have sixteen black members in 1973—twelve African American men, Jordan and Burke, and Congresswoman Shirley Chisholm of New York, who had been the first and only African American woman in Congress since her election in 1968. Cardiss Collins from Chicago would join the group in February after winning a special election to fill the seat of her late husband, George Collins, who had died in a car accident in December 1972. Senator Edward Brooke of Massachusetts was the only African American in the Senate. Barbara Jordan and Andrew Young, who had also been elected in 1972, were the first black members from the modern South. They represented a true breakthrough for black southerners in American politics. Members of the Congressional Black Caucus were ecstatic to add the southerners, Jordan and Young, to their ranks because their reputations had already been well established in the civil rights community. Jordan was a sought-after speaker, and Andrew Young was the respected lieutenant of Dr. Martin Luther King Jr. Jordan and Young also brought a new luster to the Congressional Black Caucus, as did Yvonne Burke as a result of her television exposure the previous summer, and the Caucus expected a lot from its new members.

Until the early 1970s, there had been no extended African American influence in Congress since Reconstruction. In 1928, Oscar Stanton DePriest, a Republican from Chicago, had been the first African American elected to Congress after Reconstruction. He was defeated in 1934, and it was not until 1942 that another African American was elected: Democratic representative William Dawson of Chicago. The next term, Adam Clayton Powell of New York joined him, and for ten years they were the only black members of Congress. Steadily, after 1954, when Charles Diggs of Michigan was elected, the numbers increased each year. It was not until the 1970 elections, however, that there were even a dozen African Americans among the 435 members of the House. Buoyed by their numbers and alarmed by the rollback in civil rights initiatives by President Nixon, they had formed the first formal Congressional Black Caucus in 1971, with Representative Diggs as chairman.[9]

During its first year of operation, the Caucus saw itself as the primary voice for the "national black community" because no single African American leader had been able to fill the vacuum left by the death of Martin Luther King Jr. Much of the Caucus's visibility during its first year came from a series of hearings held around the country on health, education, black enterprise, the mass media, Africa, and racism in the military. However, the Congressional Black Caucus was without staff or significant funding. Its members had neither the time, the resources, nor the breadth of a constituency to assume a national role. Prior to 1972, the African American members of Congress had all been elected from inner-city neighborhoods in Detroit, Cleveland, New York City, Chicago, and Los Angeles. Most black Americans still lived in the South, however, where conditions were still drastically different from those in the cities, which had escaped the brunt of Jim Crow segregation laws. So there was little real connection between the large masses of black citizens and the black members of Congress.

By 1972 it was obvious that Congressional Black Caucus members, as a group, had not filled the leadership void in the black community. Some recognized that reality and decided to concentrate their energies on legislative matters within Congress. Representative Louis Stokes of Cleveland had become the chair of the Caucus in 1972, and he tried to refocus the goals of African American members: "If we were to be effective, if we were going to make the meaningful contribution to minority citizens in this country, then it must be as legislators. This is the area in which we possess expertise—it is within the hall of Congress that we must make this expertise felt."[10]

Barbara Jordan, too, felt that the Caucus's primary role should be legislative. "As members of Congress, we are *legislators,* and we ought to remember that is our role," Jordan believed. "I have told my Black Caucus colleagues that we cannot try to be the Urban League, the NAACP, the Urban Coalition, the Afro-Americans for Black Unity all rolled into one. We have a commonality of issue—blackness—but we cannot do what the other organizations have been designed to do through the years. There are bills which come up and which affect black people directly, and in my judgment the Black Caucus ought to be looking for those pieces of legislation and seeing to it that amendments are offered which would change the impact if that impact would be negative or adverse to black people."[11] Jordan's forthright views, delivered in her preaching style, immediately set her on a collision course with several Caucus members, who did not want to be eclipsed by this new star from the South, particularly when it became obvious she did not intend to follow the lead of members who had greater seniority.

Jordan first departed from Caucus plans for her shortly before she took office. With its increasing numbers and the addition of some strong personalities, veteran Caucus members were eager to spread African American influence among the House's major committees. So before she even arrived, Caucus leaders had selected Jordan to serve on the Armed Services Committee, which had no African American member. Jordan believed the Caucus was trying to help its new members, and at first she welcomed its attention. In fact, she wanted to demonstrate her solidarity with the Caucus because she felt it was the right thing to do. In addition, Jordan also thought she might really be interested in Armed Services. It was a powerful and important committee, and she was quite eager to take a seat there. She also had to specify a second choice for her committee assignment, and because she was a lawyer, she picked the Judiciary Committee. When she was discussing her committee choices with Mark Talisman, who directed the Congressional "Head Start" program, at Harvard's Kennedy School, he suggested she enlist Lyndon Johnson's help in securing the posts she wanted.

So Jordan wrote President Johnson to ask for his help in getting on the Armed Services Committee, and she specifically requested that he call two key congressmen on the Ways and Means Committee, which would make the appointments: Omar Burleson from west Texas, whom Jordan did not know well; and Wilbur Mills of Arkansas, who was chairman of the committee.

When Johnson got the letter, he immediately called Jordan and told her, "You don't want to be on the Armed Services Committee. People will be cursing you from here to there, and the defense budget is always a sore spot, and people don't want to spend the money. You don't want that. What you want is Judiciary. If you get the Judiciary Committee and one day someone beats hell out of you, you can be a judge."

Judiciary it would be, she agreed. Just like that. Johnson had already made the calls she requested, both to Burleson and to Mills, and he assured her she would get what she wanted. Johnson said he had to track down Mills on his vacation, "but I interrupted his fishing and told him he had to get on your committee assignment right away."[12]

Wilbur Mills, the powerful House Ways and Means Committee

chairman, told colleagues that in all of his years of working with Lyndon Johnson, this was the first time Johnson had ever called him about a committee assignment for a member. The call made Jordan Wilbur Mills's top priority, but the vagaries of electoral politics made her placement on Judiciary downright easy. Texas traditionally had two seats on the thirty-seven-member Judiciary Committee. Representative Jack Brooks of Beaumont was the second-ranking Democrat on the committee, but the other Texan, John Dowdy of Athens, had not run for reelection. So there was a "Texas" seat just waiting for Barbara Jordan, although she had to go through the formality of an interview with the new committee chairman, Peter W. Rodino of New Jersey. Lyndon Johnson left nothing to chance: he dispatched his former aide Jack Valenti, who had just become president of the Motion Picture Association of America, to call Rodino on Jordan's behalf.

"Jack told me what a tremendous asset this young black woman lawyer would be to the Judiciary Committee," Rodino remembered. "He described her in superlatives . . . and when Barbara first came to my office in the Rayburn Building to introduce herself, I immediately realized that Jack's superlatives had been carefully chosen, and I knew then and there that Barbara would be a great addition to our committee—that she would make a difference. I lost no time in recommending her to the Democratic Steering Committee for membership on the House Judiciary Committee."[13]

Jordan's rejection of the Congressional Black Caucus's suggestion that she seek the Armed Services Committee post ruffled a few feathers. Caucus members John Conyers of Michigan and Charles Rangel of New York already served on the Judiciary Committee, which reviewed civil rights issues as well as civil and criminal judicial proceedings, constitutional amendments, espionage and other activities affecting the internal security of the United States, and just about anything relating to the legal system and structure of the states and the federal government. With Conyers and Rangel already on Judiciary, the Caucus felt its interests were well represented there. Barbara Jordan's independence raised a few more eyebrows in the Caucus when the House organized itself in January and she cast her vote for Carl Albert of Oklahoma to be House Speaker, rather than for Caucus member John Conyers, whose protest bid for the post drew no more than twenty votes. Since Jordan clearly had powerful Texas allies in the Congress, Caucus members quietly tolerated her choices.

When committee assignments were announced in the first weeks of the session, Jordan not only got the Judiciary assignment but was the first named so that she automatically had more seniority than the other new members. The House leadership also named her to the Standing Committee on Government Operations, whose diverse activities included general revenue-sharing and federal energy policy.

Lyndon Johnson had clearly pushed open some heavy doors for Barbara Jordan, but there was actually little resistance. In fact, many of the

Democratic congressional leaders were so pleased to bask in the publicity glow that surrounded Jordan that they bragged about how much they were helping her along. Jordan knew better. When she got word that Lyndon Johnson had died on January 22, she reflected, "Other people are always talking about what they had done for me. But Lyndon Johnson wasn't like that. He just did it and he didn't take credit for it." Barbara felt a real sense of loss when Johnson died. She realized that she was all on her own, just as she had been when she entered the Texas legislature. This time, however, she had the experience to know what she needed to do.

It did not take long for Jordan to hit her stride. One of her black colleagues was amazed at how she operated. "You should just see how everybody, including the old rednecks who've been running things in Washington for decades, are now bowing and scraping to Barbara. . . . Her friendliness with the big boys from Texas just adds to the whole thing. She's with them all the time, meeting with them, having lunch with them, making a contact here and another one there. And they can't help noticing her, not just because she's black and a woman, but mainly because they know she's so much smarter than most of them and there's no way they can pull the wool over her eyes on *anything*. Whether they like her or not, they've got to respect her, and in Washington your contacts and the respect you get are mighty important things."[14]

THE DEMOCRATIC NATIONAL COMMITTEE

Before she took the oath of office in January, Jordan had to take care of a purely partisan obligation. She was a member of the Democratic National Committee, and it was going to elect a new chairman. In Texas, when the liberal Democrats had finally garnered sufficient voting strength to win battles at their state party conventions, they had elected Jordan to be one of the state's six representatives on the national committee. She was the unanimous choice of the Black Caucus in Texas. Now, after the debacle of the McGovern defeat in November, a move was under way to dump McGovern's hand-picked chair of the Democratic Party, Jean Westwood, and replace her with someone who could rebuild and reunite the party after the devastating 1968 and 1972 presidential losses. The Democratic National Committee would make its decision on a new chair in late December. Jordan's old Texas friend, Robert Strauss, was a candidate for the job, and he thought Barbara Jordan would be his secret weapon to win the party chairmanship.

Strauss had become treasurer of the Democratic National Committee in 1970, and most recently he had been the chief fund-raiser for the Democrats' fall congressional campaigns. In those posts, the outgoing Strauss had made key Democratic friends all across the country. His home-state senator, Lloyd M. Bentsen Jr., who had presidential ambitions of his own, was the first to urge him to make the race for party chairman. Strauss also had the support of organized labor. But the "reformers," who were systematically dismantling the party's convention and delegate selection system, wanted nothing to do with Bob Strauss, even though the liberal *Texas Observer* once described him as a man so charming that he seemed to "suffer from an inability to be unkind about anyone."[15] George Mitchell from Maine entered the race for party chairman, as did Californian Charles Mannett.

"The 1968 and 1972 campaigns had left a lot of scars in the party—among women, liberals, and minorities," Strauss said. "All of that left me with almost no support in the black community. I was looked on as a Johnson-Connally fellow—not too favorable a description at the time. But no one knew about my friendship with Barbara Jordan, and I thought I had an ace in the hole."

Strauss called Jordan and asked her how many votes she could round up for him among the African American members of the Democratic National Committee, who had formed their own caucus. She told Strauss she would check it out and call him back. After a few days went by, and then a week, with no word from Jordan, Strauss called her back.

"Bob, I can't vote for you," she told the stunned Strauss. "I am going to have to be against you. The Black Caucus is against you, and I cannot cast my first vote in Washington against the Black Caucus."

Strauss was so upset that he argued for a while with Jordan. "I think you're wrong, Barbara," he told her. "It's going to be embarrassing and tough for me not to have your vote." But Jordan wouldn't budge, in what Strauss describes as a very uncomfortable conversation. "The race for party chairman was terribly important to me. I saw the race as important for everything I wanted to do," he admitted.

Strauss went to see Aaron Henry, the NAACP leader from Mississippi who was a member of the Democratic National Committee, and he asked Henry to talk to Jordan on his behalf. Henry had impeccable civil rights credentials, having been arrested for protests more than thirty times in the South, including one time on the floor of the Mississippi legislature. Strauss and Henry had developed the kind of teasing, easy camaraderie that can exist between white and black southerners and is so puzzling to those outside of the South. Henry intended to cast his vote for Strauss, even though the Black Caucus was against him. Strauss said that Henry "called Barbara for me, but reported back that he couldn't get her to vote for me."

The main objection to Strauss from liberals and minorities was his long association with John Connally, not Lyndon Johnson. Connally's outspoken opposition to the 1964 Civil Rights Act, as well as his insensitive statement after the assassination of Martin Luther King Jr., had permanently alienated the nation's African American leaders. Liberals were freshly incensed because Connally, who had served as President Nixon's secretary of the treasury in 1969, headed up a nationwide "Democrats for Nixon" fund-raising operation during the 1972 elections. Still calling himself a Democrat, Connally had not yet formally switched political parties. Connally put fire on the flames with his endorsement of Strauss for the DNC post. He joked, "I haven't known whether to endorse him or denounce him. I don't know which will help him the most, and I'm prepared to do either if it will help him." The Connally endorsement clearly hurt, however, and Strauss told friends privately that it would have been better if Connally had kept quiet. Nevertheless, Strauss refused to denounce Connally, as liberals plainly wanted him to do. "I belong to no man," Strauss told DNC members the day of the vote. "I have gotten this far without denouncing my friends and I will not start now."[16]

Strauss had enough organizational support from across the country to win the party post, but he won it without Barbara Jordan's vote or help. "It hurt not to have Barbara with me," he said. "We never lost our relationship over this. But it changed it. She always seemed a bit uncomfortable with me after this, although we saw each other and were on friendly terms."

Bob Strauss was the second conservative white Texas politician who had been disappointed when friendship with Barbara Jordan did not accrue to his benefit at election time. Strauss said Ben Barnes reminded him that Jordan had not helped in his own losing governor's race. "Barnes reminded me that although she was a magnificent personality, she always took care of Barbara Jordan's business first." Yet Jordan obviously saw her actions in regard to Strauss and Barnes very differently. Although always on friendly terms, she had never made a specific commitment to either one of them. She felt that she had always been clear with them that she would *always vote the interests of her constituency*. So what did they expect?

The civil rights leader Vernon Jordan, who headed the National Urban League at the time of Barbara Jordan's election to Congress and later became one of Bob Strauss's law partners at Akin, Gump, Strauss and Feld, thought the Texas congresswoman made the right decision in staying with the Black Caucus over the Strauss election. "Why should she stick her neck out in the very first week in the very first term of her congressional career?" he pointedly asked. "Strauss was not exactly a flaming liberal. I would think that Barbara made a *political* decision, not a personal decision, and she was very capable of doing that. But I also suspect that she was right. Strauss won and still had to deal with Barbara. You could not *not deal* with her. She was a formidable politician, in the sense that she was principled and that she stood up for her principles. . . . She took her politics seriously. When you sat down and had a conversation with her, you knew you were dealing with a power person. It had to do with her blackness, it had to do with her size, it had to do with her voice. It had to do with her determination. And it had to do with her ability to say to whomever: on this issue, I'm like the tree planted by the rivers of water . . . I shall not be moved."

Nevertheless, turning away from Bob Strauss when he needed her vote must have rankled Jordan. She never talked about it or even mentioned it in her autobiographical *Self-Portrait*. Maintaining public silence about issues of political complexity was her practice. As she had done so many times before, she had voted her constituency. That was always a given with her. That was her core from which she rarely deviated. Whatever her personal feelings were, she represented a predominantly black constituency in the Texas and national Democratic parties. She was the representative of *black* people, chosen by the Black Caucus of Texas Democrats, to serve on the national party committee. Her constituency did not want Bob Strauss in charge of their political party, and so she did not vote for him. But she very much wanted to keep their relationship alive, as did Bob Strauss. Both knew that the next time he asked for something, she would try to oblige. On the day she was sworn into office, Strauss attended a reception honoring her, and their relationship, albeit strained, was officially "on" again.

SETTLING INTO CONGRESS

Jordan approached her first weeks in the U.S. Congress the same way she had the Texas legislature: look, listen, and learn before acting. It didn't take more than a few hours on the floor of the House to realize it was a totally different operation. First, it was fourteen times the size of the Texas Senate. "There were so many members," she said. "It became obvious to me that it was going to be difficult to make any impact on anybody with all of these people also trying to make an impact, in order to create the impression back home among their constituents that they were outstanding." But Jordan was not discouraged. She would just work harder.

Jordan organized her office early. For her top position, she had wanted someone thoroughly familiar with the capital scene, and she settled on Rufus "Bud" Myers, who had worked for Representative Andrew Jacobs, one of the Democrats who lost his seat in the Nixon landslide. Myers was one of the few experienced African American capital staffers at the time. Bespectacled, with a modified Afro haircut and modest sideburns, and slightly shorter than Jordan, Myers was somewhat in awe of her. He wasn't even sure how he should address her. Their first meeting after Thanksgiving, however, was friendly and open as Jordan quizzed him about how things worked, and how he could get her office to function smoothly.

"We talked about an hour and a half, and she offered me the job on the spot," Myers remembered. "There were other people waiting outside to be interviewed. But when I left her, I knew I would have the job in January.

So I started preparing things for her to get ready for the session."[17] Although Jordan would always maintain a certain formality with Myers and her staff, by the time Congress convened she had put them all at ease by telling them to call her "BJ," instead of fumbling around with titles or honorifics. Jordan was satisfied that Myers knew his way around the Hill. "My thinking was, if I had a black and a man, that would satisfy everyone," she later said. Myers set up her office, which, by the bad luck of the draw, was rather small and about as far away from the House floor as a member's office could be: on the fifth floor of the Longworth Office Building, across the street from the Capitol.

As Jordan began to review the situation and the sheer size of the place, she gave careful thought to where she should sit—something most members approached only casually. It was extremely important to her, however, and to how she perceived her new role. She came to Congress to be a lawmaker, and laws were passed on the House floor. That was where she thought she should be whenever Congress was in session. But the House floor was also a fifteen-minute walk from her office in the Longworth Building through the tunnel to the Capitol. She didn't intend to make that long walk more often than she had to. She had begun to feel an occasional numbness in her feet and a weakness in her legs that she thought might be the beginning of arthritis. So once she got to the House each day, she planned to just stay there. And she wanted to be comfortable. Jordan always wanted to be physically comfortable. "My conclusion was that you can hear better on the center aisle, and you can catch the eye of the presiding officer better on the center aisle, as you are in his direct line of vision. So I decided that is where I would always sit, leaving one seat next to me on the aisle vacant for those people who might want to stop and visit from time to time."[18]

Every day Jordan took up her chosen seat just off the aisle in the center section about three rows from the back in the House. She made that spot her "office" away from the office. That immediately set her apart from most House members, although Massachusetts representative Thomas "Tip" O'Neill, who was the Democratic majority leader and second in line to House Speaker Albert, also ran most of his operation from his seat on the House floor. Former House Speaker Jim Wright, one of Jordan's Texas colleagues at the time, remembered that O'Neill "was almost like a priest in the confessional because members would come to him to tell him their problems. They would sometimes just line up. Tip used the House floor in that way to do his case work, to be the ombudsman for the members."[19] But as a freshman, a woman, and an African American, Jordan was not quite at the same level as the Democratic majority leader. Almost immediately there was some grumbling in the Congressional Black Caucus because Jordan was not sitting with them as a group. Her seemingly innocuous choice of a place to sit would reverberate back to her in various forms of criticism during her entire stay in Congress. She brushed off the immediate criticism, however, and said that her seat choice was simply "the exercise of plain, ordinary, good, practicable judgment."[20]

Jordan felt that her most important task during those first few weeks in Congress was to "get in good with my colleagues from Texas."[21] There were twenty-four members of the Texas congressional delegation. She was the only African American and the only female. Henry B. Gonzalez, the Mexican American leader from San Antonio, and Kika de la Garza of Mission in south Texas were the only other minority members. With the exception of her friends from the Senate's liberal caucus, Charles Wilson of Lufkin in east Texas and Houston liberal Bob Eckhardt, Jordan had no more than a passing acquaintance with most of the other members of the delegation.

The Texans were among the most powerful members of Congress. With its antiquated seniority system still intact, long-tenured conservative Texas Democrats chaired most of the House's major committees: Appropriations, Banking, Agriculture, Veterans Affairs, Government Operations, and even the House Democratic Caucus, where conservative Olin "Tiger" Teague of College Station had managed to win the post over liberal Dan Rostenkowski of Illinois in 1971. Tiger Teague was by far the most personable member of the delegation and represented the Texas good-old-boy back-slapping stereotype in the extreme. "Tiger was raised in that Texas tradition where everyone is running for Miss Watermelon Thump and trying to be the most popular person imaginable," said one Texan.[22] There was a little bit of Tiger in most of the older members, however, and the personalities, as well as the power, of the Texans set them apart. Barbara Jordan carefully observed the dynamics of the group and began to cultivate individual members, just as she had in the state Senate.

"Barbara's attitude was that she was a Texan," Yvonne Burke said. "Her closest colleagues were the Texans. She never sat with the rest of us. She and Charlie Wilson usually sat together. But let's be honest. It was tough for a black person of the South then. They had to keep their own caucus members happy. Andy Young had to get along with the Georgia delegation, and Barbara had to get along with Texas."

W. R. "Bob" Poage of Waco, who was chairman of the Agriculture Committee, was fairly typical of the old-timers, most of whom were in their sixties or seventies when Jordan arrived in Congress. A few years earlier, when President Johnson was trying to push his War on Poverty legislation through the Congress, a staffer was explaining it all to Poage and using such bureaucratic buzzwords as "coordinated service delivery" and providing opportunities to the "disadvantaged." Poage looked at him with "blank incomprehension," until finally a light seemed to go on in his head, and he said, "Oh, I see! You're talking about the niggers!"[23]

By the time Jordan came to Congress, the language of the delegation was more temperate, but the underlying feelings had not changed much.

The Texas delegation also had a reputation for being quite "sexist," although that term was not yet in use. The delegation held weekly stag luncheons where important business often took place. But the males-only rule held firm—even for wives and special guests. The veteran news reporter Sarah McClendon used to stand outside the door each week, partly to taunt the group, and partly to make the point about how provincial the Texans were in the nation's capital. "She was like some Carry Nation, and that, ironically, caused the members to say, 'Hell no!' to *any* woman," Representative Wright remembered. Wright of Fort Worth and Jack Brooks of Beaumont, moderates in the delegation, thought the delegation's males-only stance was ridiculous and outdated. After Jordan was elected, but before she took office, they decided to bust up the group on her behalf. "I went and asked [Congresswoman] Leonore Sullivan of Missouri to be my guest at the Texas lunch, and she agreed to be our 'blockbuster,'" Jim Wright remembered. "Jack got someone, too, and we walked into the luncheon with the ladies, and Kika de la Garza looks up and sees what we're doing, and he runs over to the public dining room across the hall and finds some woman he knows and brings her back to be his guest. We had a great time, and Texas was ready for Barbara when she came to lunch in January."

With all of its power and folklore, the Texas delegation was as fascinated with Barbara Jordan as the rest of the nation was. Its members, even the crusty old mossbacks, went out of their way to get on her good side. As a freshman member, she was already more sought out by the news media than most of them. One Texas lobbyist in the capital said Jordan was so imposing to the Texas members, with her bulk and blackness, that she "looks like she might be God, if God turns out to be a black woman."[24] Jordan's bearing and manner of dress only reinforced their awe. At an early Democratic caucus meeting, she wore a black dress with white cuffs and a broad white collar. The effect was like an El Greco portrait, emphasizing her face and hands to make her even more imposing.[25] At one reception, she entered the room on the arm of her aide, Bud Myers, and circled the room shaking hands with members like some regal queen. One Texan said that in those first weeks Jordan had an awesome power over all of them. "She is one of the few people in the city with the power to destroy other politicians; imagine the impact of Barbara Jordan labeling someone a racist! She is able to exploit in a very shrewd way people's admiration and fear."[26]

This mix of admiration and fear had prompted the entire Texas delegation to stand around Jordan when she had been sworn in. One member worried that the group might take attention away from her, but she was so delighted to have the Texans with her that she told him, "Don't worry, I think they'll be able to figure out who I am." Then the Texans elected her secretary of their delegation.

Of all the Texas members, Jordan was perhaps closest to Charlie Wilson, her old buddy from the Texas Senate. Four years older than Jordan,

Wilson was so flamboyant, unconventional, and eccentric that he became known as "Good Time Charlie," a nickname he enthusiastically adopted. Much was made of the "odd couple" friendship between Wilson, the lanky raconteur who casually skipped committee meetings and missed key House votes, and the solid, serious Jordan, who worked all the time and kept a near-perfect attendance record. Yet the two shared a sense of humor and an understanding of their own limitations. Some of the Texans were a little jealous of the friendship because they seemed to be having such a good time, huddled around Jordan's station on the House floor.

"Usually we were talking about some stuffed shirt making too long a speech," Wilson said. Jordan agreed. "We get so ticked at the folks who act as if they were in sole control of the ship of state. We can't resist sticking a pin in such puffery." Wilson said they also reserved the right to tell each other "what's what and keep ourselves on the level." Wilson said he believed Jordan was "one of the few *real* people in a profession that is known for its phonies. I have a high regard for her because she is a no-nonsense person who votes compassionately and tries to do for her people. But she doesn't wear it on her sleeve. She's not a grandstander." And Jordan was equally complimentary about Wilson. "He's open, free, a rare person with no illusions or delusions about what his role is. And he's very competent."[27] Competency always meant a lot to Jordan, but her closeness with Wilson was a political relationship, not a personal one. He never had her unlisted home telephone number. Neither did anyone else in Congress. Aside from her family and a few Texas friends, plus her key staff aide, Bud Myers, no one bothered Jordan after hours unless she specifically invited their attention. During her first two years, Jordan focused her entire attention on the work she felt she was sent to Washington to do: building relationships, voting her constituency, and getting things done. Her view of her job was uncomplicated: "I am here simply because all those people in the Eighteenth District of Texas cannot get on planes and buses and come to Washington to speak for themselves. They have elected me as their spokesman, nothing else, and my only job is to speak for them."[28] Jordan showed up at her office at 8:45 A.M. and rarely left before 9:00 P.M., and even then, she took work home with her. She and Andrew Young lived on the same floor in the same high-rise apartment building in southwest Washington, but they rarely saw each other because Jordan worked all the time. Just as had happened in Texas, Jordan's deliberate attention to detail and careful relationship-building with key leaders contributed to her aura of uniqueness. She tried to explain to a newspaper reporter why she was always at the center of attention, and why such diverse people always sang her praises. "I try to respect the humanity of everybody—no matter who they are or how they think or how they feel," she said. "Their position on anything is not relevant to the way I can relate to them as a human being. *That* we have in common."[29]

Jordan's attitude was unusual enough among members to turn heads, because her method of reaching out to white members definitely did not include saccharine sweetness, nor was it even remotely close to the extremely gregarious approach of her colleague Tiger Teague. "Barbara doesn't try to play possum on you," one Texas congressman said. "She doesn't mind letting you know that she's got a very, very high I.Q. But she doesn't embarrass you by making you feel that you're nowhere close to being as smart as she is. It's an amazing thing how she can be standing there schooling you about something and still make you feel that you knew all that right along. Not all smart people can do that; some of them love to make you feel right ignorant. Another thing about Barbara is that she's not the type that comes on with a lot of feminine charm and that kind of thing, so you often forget that she's a woman. She's not one of those delicate beauties, yet she's far too young to be one of those 'motherly' types. You think of her as, well, *just Barbara,* because she fits in so well."[30]

The conservative Texas Democrat George Mahon, who was chairman of the largest congressional committee, Appropriations, said of her, "I've been here for forty years, and I've never known anyone to capture so quickly the response of the House."[31] It was a sentiment reflected by other southern white men as well. The conservative Democrat John R. Rarick of Louisiana believed Jordan to be the "best congressman" Texas had. When a female reporter chided him for using the word congress*man* to describe Jordan, he fumbled around with congress*woman* for a minute, then he explained that he didn't think Barbara acted like a woman, a black, or a liberal. "She just acts like a representative in Congress."[32]

Barbara Jordan had another constituency, in addition to the Texans and African Americans: women. She was one of five new women members elected to Congress in 1972, bringing the total to fourteen, the largest number ever to serve. Jordan and Yvonne Burke were joined by Patricia Schroeder of Colorado, Marjorie Holt of Maryland, and Elizabeth Holtzman of New York. After winning a special election in Illinois, Cardiss Collins would bring the total to fifteen in February.[33] The National Women's Political Caucus had been formed in 1971, representing a new political thrust by an emerging women's movement. That caucus had focused on getting women to run for political office.[34] The impact of so many new women in Congress was stunning. "It was like an invasion," Pat Schroeder remembered. "Many of the women who were already there had been elected to fill their husband's term, so there was a big difference for us. The whole world adopted you as their spokesperson. You represented *all* the women. You got so much mail and so many requests, and everybody who came to Washington wanted to see you. They would bring in baskets of mail from all over the country . . . and, of course, Barbara got that from black groups, too. I got to where I felt sorry for her . . . there was just so much to do." The women set up an informal caucus and tried to have lunch on a regular basis, but Jordan did not always attend. "You know African

American women were caught in a bind," Schroeder said. "The women's movement was white . . . and although I think Barbara approved of it, she probably had to be careful. Barbara had some demands on her that the rest of us did not."[35]

By 1972 Barbara Jordan had definite feminist views, although, as with other labels, she did not apply the word *feminist* to herself. She supported the main tenets of the women's movement for full legal equality—and she always had. She had been a sponsor of the Equal Legal Rights Amendment to the Texas Constitution, and she backed the Equal Rights Amendment to the U.S. Constitution that was winding its way through the state approval process. She was also encouraged when, shortly after she was sworn into Congress, the U.S. Supreme Court affirmed a woman's right to choose an abortion in the landmark *Roe v. Wade* decision.[36] Nevertheless, just as Jordan's dawning awareness of racism and injustice in a segregated society had both an intellectual and experiential component, so did feminism and the issue of discrimination against women. On the intellectual level, she automatically rejected discriminatory features in any law that relegated women to one course of action and men to another. But because she had always been able to break through almost every barrier to achievement in her own life, the women's movement never had the personal urgency with her that it did with many feminist leaders. Jordan's experience, however, always seemed to catch up to her intellectual awareness. It did with segregation. And it did with special concerns about women's issues.

After Jordan's mother was widowed in 1972, she received a small widow's benefit because Ben Jordan had always contributed to the Social Security system. It was a pitifully small amount for an elderly woman to live on. Arlyne was sixty-six years old, and because she had been primarily a homemaker she was ineligible for any kind of Social Security benefit on her own. As Jordan looked around at Good Hope Baptist Church members and other elderly women in Fifth Ward neighborhoods, she realized that most of them were in the same boat. She believed there was a need for some special federal recognition in the Social Security system of "homemaker" status, which for most women in 1972 was still the primary role. Before the end of her first term, Jordan had joined with veteran Democratic representative Martha Griffith of Michigan, whom she admired, to cosponsor a bill to provide Social Security benefits to homemakers. After the bill went nowhere, however, other issues soon absorbed Jordan's attention.

RICHARD M. NIXON

President Nixon dominated Barbara Jordan's first two years in Congress. In 1973, long before the climactic activities of the Watergate scandal reached crisis proportions, Nixon had dramatically challenged congressional authority in three ways: he refused to spend appropriated money; he refused to let certain members of his administration appear before congressional committees; and he refused to stop the bombing of Indochina despite protests from both houses that it was illegal.[37] Congressional leaders spent the first few weeks of Jordan's initial session considering new rules that could be used to block Nixon. Jordan began to focus on him almost immediately.

The first confrontation came when Nixon "impounded" funds by refusing to spend what Congress had appropriated. In other words, he arbitrarily and unilaterally, without benefit of law or legal sanction, cut specific programs Congress had authorized. Nixon's impoundment of funds in early 1973 ended the Office of Economic Opportunity (OEO), the Hill-Burton hospital funding programs that benefited poor rural and urban communities, and a number of housing assistance, health training, and federal aid to education programs—programs that communities like the Fifth Ward of Houston, Texas, depended upon. That bothered Jordan, and it prompted her to undertake her first public action as a House member.

Jordan was concerned that the Democratic leadership of the House seemed to be unwilling, or unable, to stand up to the president, who talked repeatedly about the mandate he had from the American people after winning forty-nine states in his crushing defeat of George McGovern and the Democrats in November. Jordan was particularly upset because the Democratic congressional leadership, with most committees headed by elderly southern congressmen, had simply rolled over and accepted the Nixon breakup of OEO, which she felt had benefited minorities and poor people. In April, after the House failed to override two Nixon vetoes on spending measures, Jordan and another freshman Democrat, Edward Mezvinsky of Iowa, decided to organize the freshmen to challenge their own party's leadership. Quietly they and other first-term Democratic members decided they would try to act as a catalyst to convince the House Democratic leadership to resist the will of the White House. "In the ninety days that I've been in Congress, I find that Congress is having difficulty finding its back and its voice," she observed. Jordan and Mezvinsky had decided to ask for four hours' time on the House floor in mid-April for the freshmen to make their plea. They went to see Speaker Carl Albert to discuss their desire to prod the House into reasserting its authority.

Albert was less than enthusiastic, but Jordan used the considerable force and focus she was capable of mustering and pointedly told him that "the inability of the Democratic majority to decide on a course of action and to move on it . . . has caused a deep sense of depression, not only among freshmen, but among some of the most senior members of Congress." More serious in Jordan's mind than the psychological depression in Congress was the imbalance between the executive and legislative branches of the government that threatened the most basic parts of the Constitution. As freshmen, Jordan said, she and her colleagues didn't expect to wield a great amount of power in Congress, but "we do not expect powerlessness of Congress as an institution."[38]

Wanting to keep peace in his own party, Albert scheduled the unprecedented floor action for April 18. About half of the new members of Congress—all Democrats—joined the action. Jordan and Mezvinsky coordinated the speeches and wrote a resolution, signed by most of the Democratic freshmen. Jordan, the lawyer, took as her speaking assignment the constitutional issues involved in Nixon's impoundment of funds, although she also challenged the idea of a Nixon mandate to do whatever he wanted.

"As freshmen members of Congress, we have a unique perspective on this," she said in her first speech on the floor. "We are here because the American people voted against monolithic government in the 1972 elections. They clearly wanted some restraint on executive branch power, and they hoped to get it by electing Democrats to Congress while a Republican president maintained control of the White House."[39] She believed the Democrats had a countermandate, or a voter-imposed check on the powers of the executive branch of government.

Jordan's remarks on the House floor about the sacredness of the Constitution were a preview of the views she would develop and articulate more fully during the House Judiciary Committee's hearings the following year. As she had always done, she prepared thoroughly. For her initial speech in Congress, she went to the Library of Congress to read the history, the law, and the relevant court cases relating to the constitutional separation of powers between the executive and legislative branches of government. She reviewed the Federalist Papers on the topic. But, practical as she always was, she also calmly assessed all of the political reasons that should tempt Congress to go along. She came to the conclusion that the Nixon impoundment was a "trampling perversion of the Constitution that cannot be permitted."[40]

In her speech, Jordan quoted from both the Constitution and the Federalist Papers about the balance and separation of powers:

These few words, encrusted with traditions, customs and statutes over the years, provide the basis for two co-equal branches of the federal government, with the federal courts supplying the third balancing force. . . . In 1973, this delicate balance has been destroyed. The President, flouting the Constitution, laws and tradition is attempting to completely dominate all decisions about how and where the federal government is to spend money. . . . The President goes even further, however, by dismantling agencies and programs of which he disapproves. . . . I do not think that the founding fathers intended faithful execution of the laws to encompass death of legislation by execution.[41]

Jordan also identified the central issue that would haunt the Judiciary Committee's impeachment hearings the next year: Richard Nixon's contempt for the law. "These impoundments reflect an unparalleled contempt for the laws of Congress, as the President ignores appropriation laws which he has sworn to faithfully execute."

Speaker Albert had missed most of the freshmen speeches because he was attending the Smithsonian's ceremonial unveiling of a bust of the late Speaker Sam Rayburn, but he rushed back to hear Jordan's remarks. His response was so enthusiastic that listeners might have believed the whole freshmen speak-out had been his idea from the beginning. "I concur with everything that has been said. . . . The old statement we sometimes hear that new Members are to be seen and not heard is simply hogwash."[42]

The freshmen action was one of a series of events that did help galvanize congressional leadership into action—eventually.[43] Congress finally responded to the Nixon challenge to "the very root of its authority" by coming up with sweeping procedural revisions known as the Budget Control and Impoundment Act of 1974.[44] It not only outlawed presidential impoundments but established the House and Senate Budget Committees, the Congressional Budget Office, and specific machinery for across-the-board budgetary control by Congress. Senator Sam Ervin called the legislation the most significant law on which he had worked during his twenty years in the Senate.

Jordan introduced sixty-four bills or resolutions during the Ninety-third Congress, but almost all of them were overshadowed during her first year by the atmosphere of crisis unfolding in Washington. Nevertheless, by August 2, 1973, she had managed to pass what she felt was significant legislation for a freshman member: adding a civil rights provision to the Omnibus Crime Control and Safe Streets Act, which provided funding for the Law Enforcement Assistance Administration (LEAA).

As a subcommittee of the House Judiciary Committee began considering the reauthorization of the 1968 Omnibus Crime Act early in March, Jordan saw an opportunity to attack a festering problem for urban African Americans. One of the lingering grievances in the civil rights community was the unequal and heavy-handed enforcement of criminal laws against African Americans. In Houston, police chief Herman Short continued to be the focus of black anger because of the all-white police department's record of brutality against African Americans. In major cities across the country, many police forces—like Houston's—remained all white; Jordan and other civil rights leaders felt that if more blacks served on local police forces, such practices would decline. LEAA had distributed more than $2 billion to state and local police departments since 1968, including some $92 million to Texas, and Jordan wanted to leverage the money to force police administrators to hire more black police officers.[45] By adding a clause that barred discrimination by any program receiving LEAA funds on the basis of race, color, national origin, or sex, she thought the situation would improve.

The major battle over LEAA, however, had always been between state governors and big-city mayors over who would control the distribution of the federal money. The reauthorization in 1973 was no simple matter. Because of the swirling controversy over President Nixon's misuse of the FBI, the bill also provided for the Senate confirmation of a president's choice for FBI director for the first time. Issues over many of its provisions were fought over the months in subcommittee, in full committee, and on the floor. Although Jordan's nondiscrimination amendment was a side issue in the LEAA negotiations, she still had to fight off opposition to it. State governors forced a compromise in committee that provided that any violation of the nondiscrimination ban had to be dealt with first by the governor; only if the governor failed to bring about compliance within a "reasonable" time would LEAA terminate funds. The measure was further weakened by a provision added by a 231–161 vote on the House floor that the LEAA grants could not be conditioned on a quota system or other program to achieve racial balance. Jordan hovered over her amendment to keep it intact until the legislation finally passed the House on June 18. The Senate passed its own version of the bill on June 28 and sent it to a conference committee presided over by Democratic senator John McClellan of Arkansas, chair of the Senate's Judiciary Committee.

Although House Judiciary Committee chairman Rodino had put Jordan on the conference committee, Senator McClellan ignored her—and her amendment—for weeks. She sat next to him every time the committee met, and she finally wore him down, even when he tried to disparage her amendment by asking her, "Now, we're not going in there and just cut off money for a lot of people, are we?" Jordan promptly replied, "The way they avoid getting any money cut off is just obey the law, Senator." Her amendment prevailed, and she achieved her first legislative victory when both houses passed the conference committee compromise on August 2.

Jordan had started working on her amendment in March, and it took five months for the bill to finally pass both the House and the Senate. She was appalled at the snail's pace of legislative action. In the Texas legislature, she had learned how to make something important happen in a matter of weeks, if not days. She was discovering that in the U.S. Congress it would take months, even years, to accomplish what she wanted. Jordan struggled to be patient, but patience was not her strength. So she just worked very hard to push it along. It was a good way for her to learn to move a piece of legislation through the byzantine congressional process of rules, committees, egos, and interests. It was different from the Texas legislature only in that there were more steps to take, more agencies to deal with, more people to see, more local communities affected. Instead of one governor, there were many, all with different agendas. And of course, there was the White

House, represented by both its own staff and the Justice Department. In the beginning of the conference committee negotiations, Jordan also had to deal with the glaring disparity between her status as a freshman, female *black* member of the House trying to operate with equanimity in relation to a veteran, conservative southern *white* senator like John McClellan, who carried the weight of Senate autocracy like some sterling silver shield from the family heirloom collection. But knowing how to shift that kind of social status psychologically as well as politically was Jordan's primary strength. The prospect of moving some old southern senator challenged and stimulated her, even encouraged her to use her size and blackness, her booming voice, and her powerful stare to throw him just slightly off balance. Once that happened, she always felt she could connect with the humanity of the person—if it was there to begin with. So as she looked at the process, the procedures, and the pomposity of some of the members, Jordan saw that action in the Congress was indeed slower and slightly more complicated than it had been in the Texas legislature. But more difficult? Absolutely not! It was just different.

A YEAR OF CRISIS

Barbara Jordan maintained an incredibly hectic schedule during her first six months in Congress. She was present for 99 percent of all roll call votes, a feat unsurpassed by her colleagues. She introduced bills to provide five hundred thousand public service jobs, to put bilingual translators in all federal courts, to give cost-of-living increases to Social Security recipients, to establish a consumer protection agency, to improve veterans' education benefits and review the discharges of Vietnam-era veterans, to keep public beaches open, and myriad other measures that put her in the ranks of the most liberal members of the House. She scored perfectly on the vote tallies of both the national AFL-CIO and the League of Women Voters, and the much-maligned liberal Americans for Democratic Action (ADA) gave her a 92 percent rating. Despite a bumpy start, there were few votes on which she and her colleagues in the Congressional Black Caucus differed. Even Shirley Chisholm, the grande dame of the Congressional Black Caucus, who had never taken to Jordan's southern style of operating, admitted that the freshman congresswoman did her homework. "She's intelligent. There is no doubt that she is the star of the three new black congresswomen elected last year [Jordan, Burke, and Collins], and if she stays around she will outshine me."[46]

During her first year, when Congress was not in session, Jordan was on the road. She went home to Houston every other weekend and made speeches around the country as well, maintaining ties with civil rights leaders by preaching in places like Reverend Ralph Abernathy's church in Atlanta, and extending her national audiences by speaking to new groups like the National Association of Broadcasters and dozens of colleges and universities. Everywhere she went in 1973 people wanted to know what on earth was going on in Washington. A sense of crisis was in the air, and three words, Jordan felt, summed it up: war, oil, and Watergate.

The Paris Peace Accord, signed January 27, ended the fighting in Vietnam, although President Nixon continued the bombing in Cambodia he had begun in December, an action many considered unconstitutional because the Congress had not been consulted. The War Powers Act was the first action taken by Congress to stop U.S. military involvement in the Indochina war. The House—and Barbara Jordan—voted on May 10 to bring U.S. bombing of Cambodia to an end. The Senate agreed, and the president reluctantly signed the bill. The bombing did not end until August 15, however, more than eight years after it had started in North Vietnam and more than four months after the last American troops had left Vietnam.

There was a domestic crisis, too. In 1973 the Arab nations placed an embargo on the oil they had been exporting, and within weeks the U.S. economy felt the effect of its dependency on foreign oil. Domestic oil and gas prices soared. The nation was embroiled in its first serious energy crisis, which precipitated job layoffs and the highest unemployment rates since the Great Depression. Interest rates were also soaring, reaching double digits for the first time since World War II. Recession loomed.

Meanwhile, Congress was becoming more deeply involved in the third crisis of 1973. Watergate. When Judge Sirica read the letter of the Watergate burglar James W. McCord Jr. in court on March 23, 1973, the date of McCord's sentencing, it was the beginning of the end of the White House cover-up. McCord had been director of security for Nixon's reelection committee, and his letter to the judge stated that others had been involved in the break-in, the purpose of which was to place a telephone listening device in the office of Democratic Party chairman Larry O'Brien; that pressure had been applied to remain silent; and that perjury had been committed during the trial.

In February 1973, the Senate had decided to look into campaign irregularities related to the break-in by creating its own bipartisan, seven-member select committee, chaired by Democratic senator Sam J. Ervin of North Carolina. Although most of the puzzle remained unsolved in the early spring of 1973, it was beginning to look like the president was involved in a cover-up about the break-in. There were also indications that the FBI, the CIA, and the IRS had all been directed to undertake certain illegal actions at the request of the White House. By April, the Watergate break-in was becoming recognized for what it was: one small piece of a larger White House plot involving espionage and sabotage against individuals or institutions that the president or his advisers considered political "enemies."[47]

White House officials were implicated in illegal activities that had been carried out with hundreds of thousands of dollars in secret and illegal campaign funds. By the time the Senate committee began its formal, televised hearings in May, twelve administration officials had already resigned or been fired, including President Nixon's top aides H. R. Haldeman and John Ehrlichman, Attorney General Richard G. Kleindienst, White House counsel John Dean, and acting FBI director Patrick Gray. Nixon's new attorney general, Elliot Richardson, had appointed a special prosecutor to look into the events, the former solicitor general and Harvard law professor Archibald Cox. In May, Nixon brought his friend and former treasury secretary John B. Connally back into the White House as a special, part-time, unpaid adviser. The previous week Connally had finally announced his switch to the Republican Party. The same week, a grand jury had indicted on obstruction-of-justice charges Nixon's former attorney general, John Mitchell, and his campaign fund-raiser, former secretary of commerce Maurice Stans. On July 29, Connally himself was indicted on charges that he accepted a $10,000 bribe from the Associated Milk Producers for recommending an increase in milk price supports and thwarting an investigation into the payoff. He was also accused of perjury and conspiracy to obstruct justice.

Jordan told the American Society of Newspaper Publishers that the "explosion of Watergate has completely obscured the view" of the Nixon presidency. "The Watergate affair clearly tarnishes whatever mandate this administration thought it had because of its widespread and illegal disruption of the political process."[48]

By early August, the administration was virtually paralyzed by Watergate. Some twenty investigations were under way. When the existence of White House tape recordings, which could reveal what actually took place, had been disclosed in the middle of July, the stage was set for a constitutional confrontation, with Congress and the courts on one side and the White House on the other. Both the Senate committee and Special Prosecutor Cox had subpoenaed the tapes, and Nixon refused to release them.

Jordan paid close attention to the calls for impeachment proceedings against the president because any such inquiry would have to originate in her Judiciary Committee. The first call came as early as April 30, when Haldeman and Ehrlichman resigned. By July 31, Father Robert F. Drinan, Barbara's colleague on Judiciary who was the former dean of the Boston College Law School, introduced the first impeachment resolution against the president for "high crimes and misdemeanors."

The saga went on, even when members of Congress began their summer recess on August 3. Jordan had gone back to Houston, and she spent time in Austin with her women friends. During the summer break, the Justice Department announced that Vice President Spiro Agnew was under investigation for bribery, extortion, and tax fraud related to the awarding of federal building contracts in Maryland while he was vice president in 1969, plus the awarding of state contracts while he was governor of Maryland. When Jordan returned to Washington for the start of the session on September 21, the final seven weeks of the 1973 congressional session were enmeshed in crisis.

Vice President Agnew resigned on October 10, and two days later the president nominated Gerald Ford to replace him. Under the Twenty-fifth Amendment to the Constitution, which deals with presidential succession and had never been used before, Ford had to be approved by both the House and the Senate. Hearings would be held before the judiciary committees in both bodies. The Congressional Black Caucus immediately opposed the nomination of House minority leader Ford. After poring over thousands of pages of investigative work into the background of the Michigan congressman, Jordan agreed with the Congressional Black Caucus. She did not like his civil rights record at all.

There would be still another October crisis—Nixon's famous "Saturday Night Massacre" on October 20. The president ordered his attorney general to fire Special Prosecutor Cox, over his zealous pursuit of the White House tapes. When Elliot Richardson refused to do so, and resigned, as did his deputy, William Ruckelshaus, Solicitor General Robert Bork carried out the action. Almost 250,000 telegrams flooded Washington over the next few days. Newspaper editorials began calling on Nixon to resign. Edward Brooke in the Senate became the first Republican to ask his president to step down. To settle the furor, White House aides persuaded Nixon to fill the vacancy of special prosecutor immediately. This time Nixon chose Leon Jaworski of Houston.

Leon Jaworski, one of Houston's most conservative lawyers, was part of the city's political and business establishment. His firm represented the public utilities and oil companies. Jaworski had a sterling reputation, largely because he had served as a prosecutor at the Nuremberg war crimes trials after World War II. But his Houston business ties must have made him seem a safer choice to Nixon than the dismissed Archibald Cox.

Jordan was puzzled by Nixon's choice. She knew Jaworski well. They had served together on Houston's Council on Human Relations in the mid-1960s to work out racial tensions in the city. Jaworski had been the master of ceremonies at a fund-raising event when she first ran for Congress. Jordan knew him to be both fair and honest. The day after the appointment was announced, she pulled Democratic Party whip Jim Wright aside on the House floor and asked him whether he thought Nixon knew what he had done.

"One of two things, Barbara," Wright replied. "Either President

Nixon honestly believes in his innocence; or else he doesn't know Leon Jaworski."

"I think it's the latter, Jim," she said.[49]

When the House Judiciary Committee began its hearings on the nomination of Gerald Ford late in November, Jordan was dogged in her questioning of Ford. She quoted one of his own speeches back to him: "In politics, when the train is moving, you'd better jump on because you don't get a second chance." Then she fixed him with one of her powerful glares and asked, "Would it be fair to characterize your voting record on civil rights as trying to stall the train as long as you can and then jump on when you know it will keep on going no matter what you do?"[50] Ford politely disagreed, telling her that he believed every American was entitled to equal treatment. But Jordan clearly did not believe Ford was qualified to be president. She thought that he was a plodding naysayer, and that his nine years as House minority leader for the Republicans had been undistinguished. "Mr. Ford has not been an innovative or imaginative congressman," she said, and she feared that "he could be expected to work towards weakening civil rights bills as they move through the legislative process."[51] When the Judiciary Committee voted on his confirmation on December 1, hers was one of eight nay votes.

One of the reasons Jordan was so careful in her consideration of Gerald Ford was that she believed at some point President Nixon would resign, and that Gerald Ford might actually become president, "whether he is ready to be president or not." She told a group in Houston that she "expected additional revelations from the Watergate investigations and that at some point President Nixon will recognize that the country will not be able to survive a continuation of leadership in which the people have no confidence." She reported that "there is an underlying feeling in Washington that the government will not be able to continue from crisis to crisis."[52] Yet she very carefully refrained from calling for Nixon's resignation, and she criticized colleagues who did.

The House Democratic leadership finally decided it was time to act on the chorus of calls for impeachment. Judiciary Committee chairman Rodino announced plans for the committee to "proceed full steam ahead" with an impeachment investigation. After meeting with the committee, he set a target date of April 1974 for completion of the staff investigation. The committee would begin holding meetings immediately after the first of the year. Barbara Jordan knew her most important work was ahead of her.

PERSONAL CRISIS

Jordan did not feel well during the summer and fall of 1973. At first she thought it was just fatigue, or standing on her feet too long every day, or the heat and humidity of Washington. She had experienced a tingling sensation in her toes and feet for several months, and occasionally she felt a weakness all the way up to her knees. Sometimes her feet just felt numb, like they were "asleep," with pins and needles jabbing them. Occasionally, late in the afternoon or early evening when she made the long walk back to her office in the Longworth Building from the House floor, she felt as if she were dragging weights in her shoes—feet of bricks instead of bones.

She didn't like the feeling one bit. She switched to low-heeled shoes, thinking it might help. Some days were better than others. She assumed she had gained too much weight, and perhaps that was the problem. She now weighed over two hundred pounds. In November, when the tingling appeared in her fingers and hands, making it difficult to clutch the handle of the heavy briefcase she carried with her all the time, she decided she had better check it out. She went to see the House physician. Although he could not detect a specific problem, he was alarmed enough by her description of the symptoms to suggest she undergo some tests at the Bethesda Naval Hospital in Maryland. Jordan initially resisted. She did not want to miss her chance to question Gerald Ford before the Judiciary Committee, and she needed time to prepare. So she delayed. Throughout the Judiciary Committee hearings, however, she felt more and more uncomfortable. On December 3, two days after she had voted against Ford in committee and only three weeks before the end of her first year in Congress, Jordan gave up her goal of a perfect attendance record and checked herself into Bethesda. She wanted to get to the bottom of this. Whatever *this* was.

When the *Houston Post* ran a brief notice of the congresswoman's hospitalization, she was furious with her staff for letting the word out. But her absence from her regular seat on the House floor was as obvious as her daily presence, and her office had been besieged with calls from members and news reporters who wanted to know where she was. Jordan was not in the mood to answer questions or talk to anyone. She imposed a wall of secrecy between herself and her Washington staff, as well as her colleagues and friends in Congress. By her second day in Bethesda, old friends from Houston were calling, and the Texas Senate Ladies' Club from Austin even sent flowers. But Jordan did not respond to anyone, and she instructed her staff to tell well-wishers that everything was fine, and nothing more— which, for all she knew, might be the case. She did not allow anyone to come see her, but she did talk to her aide Bud Myers every day so that he could brief her on what was happening in the office. The legislative aide Bob Alcock would also call to tell her about the votes she missed—including the House's overwhelming vote of approval of Gerald Ford for vice president.

"It was made clear to us, I guess by Bud, that we just shouldn't ask too many questions about this," Alcock remembered. "It almost became a test of staff loyalty not to raise any questions about it. You were told she was okay, and she insisted she was okay, and that was all there was to it, thank you very much."[53]

Jordan was tested for a number of neurological and muscular disorders. The numbness in her feet and hands and the feeling of pins and needles in her legs could have indicated any number of problems: a spinal tumor, a pinched nerve, an infection like viral encephalitis, compression of a nerve root by a slipped disk, thyroid disease, diabetic neuritis, or even lead poisoning. Jordan had been treated in Austin in 1969 for a mild hypertension, and her father's death had been caused by the complications of severe hypertension and its effects on his heart, as well as the stroke it induced.

One by one the tests began to eliminate certain possibilities. A myelogram, the process where dye is injected into the spinal column, revealed that she had no spinal tumor or obstruction. And that was a relief. As doctors began a process of elimination with the remainder of the tests, one of the physicians suspected that Jordan had multiple sclerosis, an autoimmune disease that produces some of the symptoms she was experiencing. In multiple sclerosis, for some unknown reason, the body produces antibodies that attack its own healthy cells. The central nervous system's myelin sheath, which surrounds and insulates nerve fibers in the brain and spinal cord, seems to be the focus of the immune system attack by the body's T cells, as if it were a hostile invader.[54] But there were few reliable tests in 1973 to confirm a multiple sclerosis diagnosis. Doctors told patients that only an autopsy could absolutely confirm the diagnosis, by revealing the presence of lesions in the brain.[55]

Jordan did have two tests that indicated multiple sclerosis might be the problem: a spinal tap and a heat bath. The tap indicated the presence of increased antibody formation, suggesting some type of immune abnormality. Increased antibodies in the spinal fluid, however, could also indicate other diseases, such as lupus, meningitis, or encephalitis. Since the spinal tap was inconclusive, a heat bath was ordered. It was a rather primitive device in use for only a few years because it was not reliable. The intense heat of the hot water was suspected to bring on some of the symptoms of multiple sclerosis. Jordan was immersed in a swirling hot bath that raised her body temperature to over 103 degrees Fahrenheit, and when that happened, her speech became slurred and her vision blurred. Out of the water, her speech and vision returned to normal in a short time. Because the heat produced a temporary worsening of neurological symptoms, it was a strong indication of the nature of her problems.

At that point, the Bethesda doctors told her that it was likely she had multiple sclerosis. Multiple sclerosis! Jordan had never heard of it, and now these doctors were telling her she might have it. They also told her that no one knew what caused it, or how to cure it. It was not contagious, and it was not directly inherited, although there might be certain genetic patterns that made the myelin sheath more vulnerable, resulting in more than one family member having the disease. No one knew for sure. The symptoms might be mild or severe. They might come or go. No two people with MS experienced it the same way. It was not fatal, but it did cause disabilities. And it was not rare. Almost a half-million Americans had it; many people had suffered its symptoms for several years before being correctly diagnosed. When multiple sclerosis attacks are under way, the electrical connections in the brain that stimulate movement from nerves to muscles cannot be transmitted. An attack may strike anywhere in the body and last for days or weeks; the body may recover, or not. Each attack leaves lesions in the brain that can progressively block nerve impulses—and the ability to walk, see, swallow, urinate, pick up a telephone, hold a milk carton, change a baby's diaper. Because it is such an idiosyncratic disease, each patient follows his or her own path.

The specific diagnosis for Jordan was the "onset of distal paresthesia related to multiple sclerosis"—the numbness and weakness in the legs that constitute one of the most common early symptoms of the disease. Doctors also believed that Jordan's multiple sclerosis might be progressive rather than "episodic": it might move more rapidly than it did for the majority of multiple sclerosis patients, who often experience years of remission between attacks. One physician told her it was like a "smoldering mattress" that would slowly and eventually "burn up." But no one could tell Barbara Jordan exactly what path her multiple sclerosis would take. The symptoms she might expect included tingling sensations, numbness, slurred speech, dizziness, blurred or double vision, muscle weakness, poor coordination, tremor, unusual fatigue, muscle tightness or spasticity, problems with bladder or bowel function, and paralysis. The symptoms might occur in any combination, they might come and go, and they might range from very mild to very severe.

Well! She had certainly not expected *this*. She was calm, however, when she received the diagnosis. Calm, thoughtful, and *very* serious. Her first question to the doctors was: "What are you going to do about it?" It was as if she were lobbing the whole problem back into their court. What were *they* going to do? What were they going to do with her body, which apparently was attacking itself?

Fortunately, the Bethesda neurologists had an answer—at least for the time being. Treatments did exist to relieve or prevent symptoms, although they could not repair the underlying damage to the myelin sheath. Certain drugs could temporarily suppress the immune system and halt an attack by the T cells. Yet there was no known drug that could prevent a new attack, and each attack would leave still more damage, perhaps causing greater disability to the muscle group to which the damaged myelin was to transmit signals from the brain—hence the progressive nature of the disease.[56] Corticosteroid drugs could usually halt the course of an acute MS attack—particularly in the early stages of the illness. Doctors immediately gave

Jordan prednisone, a powerful steroid, which suppressed the immune system and seemed to stop the attack on the myelin sheath. Within a few days, her numbness was gone, her energy had returned, and her legs felt almost as strong as ever. She left the hospital on Saturday and was back at work on Monday.

She had sworn the Bethesda staff to secrecy, and she had made an important decision. *No one* was to know that she had this thing called multiple sclerosis, which she knew very little about and did not even want to ponder.

She wanted to join her colleagues on the House Judiciary Committee as they prepared to investigate whether sufficient grounds existed for the House of Representatives to exercise its constitutional power to impeach Richard M. Nixon, president of the United States of America. That was what was important to her. And the other? The body? Well, for now, she felt just fine. She would figure out the rest of it later.

CHAPTER 13

WATERGATE

WE HAVE TO ask our heroes at the moment their challenge is thrust upon them, with its trials and the possibilities of greatness on the other side: Are you ready? Can you handle it?[1]

When we ask these questions of Barbara Jordan in January 1974, she was just thirty-eight years old. The droning days of the closed House Judiciary Committee meetings had begun, and the multiple sclerosis diagnosis was both fresh and absolutely secret. The American political system was breaking down in front of her, mirroring the breakdown of her own body cells. She had the intellectual capacity and political experience to assess the governmental crisis, but how would she deal with her own body? Was this illness in the same category as the deep blackness of her skin, or the broad features of her face, which had once threatened to limit her but which she had managed to surmount, even extol, and finally put aside? Or would it be different? Would MS limit her in a way she had simply not allowed her blackness to do? She did not think so. She truly did not.

The very nature of multiple sclerosis helped her push its seriousness aside in those first few months. It is an illness that lends itself to denial, which may be psychologically important and necessary. Its onset is quirky, and the early symptoms are easy to obliterate—at least temporarily. After the initial attack and treatment, the body once again seems fine, although the underlying defect of demyelination may continue. There is a physical respite. The episodic nature of multiple sclerosis seems to defuse its early impact and block the perception of its unpredictability, its fluctuating course, and its progression over time to a deeper level of physical disability. And so it was with Jordan. She simply did not let herself dwell on the diagnosis or the disease. Her public persona remained intact: strong, stoic, and very matter-of-fact. In a January letter to friends who inquired about her health and hospital stay, she attributed her illness to a "vitamin deficiency, which precipitated the numbness in my leg."[2] She said that there were "indications" that her hectic congressional schedule and "overwork" contributed. She *was* telling the truth, or at least part of it: extreme fatigue can contribute to the onset of multiple sclerosis symptoms.

Bud Myers, however, without knowing about the diagnosis, stretched the truth when he told a *Houston Post* reporter that Jordan had been treated for an "infection" of the nerve endings in her "extremities" and that her physician "had prescribed medication and physical exercise to ease the problem."[3] Myers's statement initiated a pattern of public comment that Jordan herself, as well as friends who never knew the truth, would perpetuate over the years. A number of excuses would be presented to account for the multiple sclerosis symptoms: a "bum" knee, "torn" cartilage behind her knee, arthritis, high blood pressure, stress on her knees caused by weight—but never multiple sclerosis. In January 1974, Jordan wanted neither to think about it herself nor to call attention to it publicly. Yet the luxury of ignoring her MS lasted only a short while. The illness would fester, just as the Watergate crisis had festered.

As she absorbed the changes in her physical well-being, and as she pondered the disturbing disclosures in the Watergate hearings, all of the patterns of Jordan's life seemed to converge. On a personal level, her reserve, sense of privacy, and decision to keep the multiple sclerosis diagnosis secret would serve to protect her from the pity-servers, the curious, and those who, sensing her physical weakness, might plot the end of her political career. Her past stoicism and determination to maneuver around the obstacles in her path also provided the resolve to deal with this new and threatening obstacle of illness. Her ability to compartmentalize the different aspects of her life in order to concentrate on the task at hand allowed her to put the disease out of her mind so that she could concentrate on what she was beginning to believe was a constitutional crisis for the nation. That was what she wanted to do—focus on Watergate and her work on the House Judiciary Committee. That is what she intended to do. The actions of President Nixon and his associates had violated her fundamental belief in the rule of *law* and her respect for the American constitutional *system* of laws.

The Watergate revelations hit Barbara Jordan at such a deep and personal level that her emotions and her intellect combined to imbue her with an extraordinary moral clarity. It was that morality, and her precisely defined patriotism, that millions of Americans would glimpse for the first time the following summer. She seemed to recognize the fragility of the rule of law at the same time she recognized the fragility of her own body. This awareness of personal and national vulnerability created in her a somber determination to protect and defend all that was important to her.

THE DELIBERATIONS

On February 6, the House of Representatives voted overwhelmingly, 410–4, to direct the Judiciary Committee to "investigate fully and completely whether sufficient grounds exist for the House of Representatives to exercise its constitutional power to impeach Richard M. Nixon, President of the United States of America."[4]

"I still could not take in that it was really going to happen," Jordan said. "I have the same high regard for the office of the President as the majority of Americans. He is a figure who towers above all other figures in the world. Certainly no one could seriously consider forcing the President to leave office before his term expired. This feeling stayed with me a long time."[5]

Jordan also had doubts about how her colleagues on the Judiciary Committee would handle the process. The House Judiciary Committee was not a particularly distinguished group of members of Congress, consisting, for the most part, of obscure, "suspected second raters and partisan politicians."[6] One-third of its thirty-eight members were freshmen, including Elizabeth Holtzman of New York, the only other woman on the committee besides Jordan. Even Chairman Peter W. Rodino was new at the job. He had become chairman only in January 1973, by virtue of his twenty-four years' seniority in the House. With the exception of the two freshman women, few names of Judiciary Committee members would have been recognized outside of their own districts. One reporter said, "There was hardly a statesman in the bunch."[7]

Chairman Rodino determined privately, and then announced publicly, that he would not play politics with something as serious as the possibility of removing a sitting president from office by a means other than a national election. Rodino was determined that his committee would rise to the occasion and not let the impeachment proceedings degenerate into the kind of sordid, partisan mess that had for one hundred years clouded the House of Representatives' only other impeachment against a president of the United States—Andrew Johnson. That proceeding in 1868 was attacked by historians, politicians, and constitutional lawyers as so enmeshed in political partisanship and emotionalism that the members of Congress seemed unaware of the seriousness of their task or the implications for the nation. The House had voted to bring impeachment charges against Johnson, but the Senate trial acquitted him. The nation was both torn and embarrassed by the ordeal.

Rodino had his work cut out for him. He had to prevent partisan Democratic colleagues from launching into vitriolic attacks on Richard Nixon, whom they plainly hated, and he had to placate partisan Republicans—even win them over to a belief in the process itself. Jordan agreed with Rodino's concerns and supported him by casting her votes with him on almost every action taken in committee. She clearly sympathized with his plight. "Rodino has had to sit on the Democrats pretty hard to keep this from looking partisan," she said. However, each new revelation of White House wrongdoing made it even more difficult. She told the *Dallas Morning News*, "I don't know how long he can keep the lid on."[8]

In closed sessions, from February to July, the committee spent most of the time hearing evidence organized in three general areas: Watergate, election abuse, and the misuse of government agencies. Huge black notebooks contained copies of all the briefs that had been filed in the various court actions, copies of testimony before the select Senate committee, and depositions and other information turned over to the committee by Special Prosecutor Jaworski. The bipartisan legal staff engaged in an in-depth investigation of everything that had been said and done and in lengthy discussions of whether the acts constituted a violation of the law. The staff investigations concentrated on seven broad areas of allegations against the president—among them, the burglary and cover-up, domestic surveillance, and the president's personal finances.[9]

For once, Jordan was patient with the slowness of the process, although the tedium of the early committee meetings, when procedures were being worked out, nearly drove her crazy. There were twenty-one Democrats and seventeen Republicans on the committee, and some members of each party questioned every procedural move. Others seemed determined to speak at every session, jockeying for prestige, influence, or simply notice in the news media. Jordan was silent and contemplative. She did not need attention, nor did she feel the need to prove anything to other members of the committee. She leaned back in her high leather chair and listened or perused the briefing papers.

The committee's Republicans were suspicious from the beginning, united in their belief that the whole venture was a partisan effort concocted by the House Democratic leadership to do in Nixon and the Republican Party. It took an enormous amount of haggling over procedural details to convince them that the process itself would be fair, that the materials involved in grand jury proceedings could be kept secret, that staff could be trusted, that members would not precipitously leak secret information, and that the rights of the president and his staff would not be trampled on. Moreover, the lead Democratic counsel, John Doar, and the minority counsel, Albert E. Jenner Jr., worked in such harmony and were so united in their bipartisan approach that the degree of staff professionalism was raised to an extraordinarily high level. Exceptional efforts were made to maintain the integrity of the process of inquiry and protect the rights of the president, including allowing Nixon's lawyer, James D. St. Clair, to sit in on all of the closed meetings. The examples of Doar, Jenner, and Rodino himself motivated most of the other members of the committee to also operate at a higher level. Just keeping track of the data was a monumental task. "I gave credit for most of that to John Doar, who was an organizational genius," Jordan said.[10]

Jordan was especially guarded, even protective, about the information provided to her in the committee. She never discussed the privileged information with her staff or political friends. She kept the notebooks and materials given to her in committee hearings in a locked safe in her office. She essentially kept her own counsel during the months of closed-door testimony. She wouldn't even say to friends over dinner whether she thought the president was guilty or not.[11] She wrote a letter in the spring chastising the student newspaper at the University of Houston for what she felt was an inaccurate headline, "Jordan Works to Impeach." She complained that it was "highly misleading. . . . I will not make a decision on the impeachability of the President until all the evidence has been reviewed by the Committee."[12] Jordan thought discretion and confidentiality were essential to the final outcome of the investigations. "We are determined to do a job that is defensible—not only by those who agree with our conclusions, but by people who disagree. We cannot afford partisanship," she said. For once she was grateful to be in the presence of so many lawyers. "There are thirty-eight lawyers on this committee. Every member is a lawyer, and the approach is a very lawyer-like, legal-like approach."[13]

A lawyerlike approach, however, is also adversarial. As early as February it was clear that the Nixon defense and the key Republicans on the committee had a strategy to keep the members tied up with the very definition of an "impeachable offense." The Constitution itself is not specific. It says only that the president can be impeached for "treason, bribery or other high crimes and misdemeanors." The phrase "high crimes and misdemeanors" has traditionally been considered a "term of art," like other constitutional phrases ("levying war," "due process"). The Supreme Court has held that such phrases must be construed not according to modern usage but according to what the framers meant when they adopted them.[14] The committee's Democratic majority said that high crimes and misdemeanors meant serious offenses against the "system" of government.

Jordan initially was troubled by the vagueness of the definition. Wanting advice from a wiser head, she called Senator Sam Ervin of North Carolina, who had conducted the Senate's select committee hearings on Watergate and was a constitutional scholar. Ervin had impressed her the previous summer, and she felt she could trust this elderly southern conservative who so obviously loved the Constitution.

"I said [to Senator Ervin], Just tell me now: failure to take care, to see that the laws are faithfully executed . . . that couldn't be an impeachable offense, could it? That couldn't fall under the aegis of high crimes and misdemeanors, could it?"[15] Senator Ervin told Jordan that it was the constitutional duty of the president to uphold the laws, and "if he doesn't do it, he ought to be impeached." That satisfied her somewhat, but she began to read and study on her own everything that "had ever been written, said, or uttered about impeachment." In addition to the 650 statements of information—7,200 pages of supporting evidentiary materials—Jordan wanted more. She studied the history of the twelve impeachments in the United States that had been voted on by the House and sent to the Senate. Of these, there were four convictions—all federal judges. She read the deliberations of the debates of the Constitutional Convention in Philadelphia in 1787 and studied the constitutional ratification proceedings of various state legislatures.

While Jordan had taken the required course on constitutional law at Boston University School of Law, this was the first time she had really delved into the intellectual arguments of American constitutional discourse. Her independent research convinced her that the founders were "hard-nosed, practical men determined to reject aristocracy and found a nation in which reason would be its guide."[16] James Madison's writings in the Federalist Papers helped crystallize her thinking about the law. "The law is supposed to be the configuration of rules and regulations, which if implemented, will lead to justice. The question is not if the law will win, but will justice be served," she later said.[17] The rule of law is important, she observed in 1990, because it teaches us the "ways of liberty: tolerance for opposing arguments, decisions based on reason and articulated to persuade rather than simply overpower, a willingness to respect the other person's point of view and to refrain from the 'short cut' to a goal, the commitment to listen and then make up one's mind based on what has been heard and thought and not on what one has been instructed to do. These are the lessons of the rule of law which, by repetition and example, infuse us with the habits of liberty. It was the spirit of liberty that placed the rule of law about government and, I trust, will keep it there."[18]

Jordan went to the National Archives twice and stood in line with the tourists to look at the Constitution in its airtight glass casement. As she stood in the magnificent marble Exhibition Hall built especially to house the Constitution, the Declaration of Independence, and the Bill of Rights, she had to ask herself: Is the living, breathing ideal that we are a nation of laws—the ideal that has held us together as a people—as fragile as that document on parchment? As she gazed at the Constitution in that hall, along with Americans of all colors and nationalities who had also come to see or study those precious charters of liberty, she realized that the answer was yes. The ideal was as fragile as the document. The realization brought a new understanding of her own role as a member of Congress.

In politics, Jordan's inner moral compass had as its magnetic lodestar the interests of poor black people in the Fifth Ward of Houston, Texas, and particularly the elderly, hardworking women like her mother. She had always felt it was her duty to protect them. Now she believed she had an additional responsibility.

As a member of Congress, as a citizen, she had a responsibility to be the protector of the Constitution. *She* was a shield—just like that glass case protecting the document. Her duty was to protect the ideal from lawless people, lawless activities, or a lawless president of the United States. And so she came to agree with Senator Sam Ervin, and the staff of the Judiciary Committee, that impeachment was a constitutional remedy addressed to serious offenses against the *system* of government.

What did it mean to commit a crime against a system? The Judiciary staff had tried to answer that very question in one of its memos to members. The crimes with which the president was charged could be considered constitutional wrongs if they "subverted the structure" of government or "undermined the integrity" of the office, or of the Constitution itself, and thus could be considered "high offenses" in keeping with the historical use of the term, which went back four hundred years in English common law. The most troubling question, however, was whether an impeachable crime had to be an offense that could be indictable under the criminal law, or whether it was something else. The bipartisan staff of lawyers concluded that it was something else. They went back to the intent of the framers of the impeachment provisions of the Constitution and concluded that an impeachable "high crime" was intended to reflect grave *misconduct* that injured or abused "constitutional institutions" or the form of government itself. Barbara Jordan agreed that the historical meaning of "high crimes" in the impeachment process was very different from the modern concept of ordinary "crime."[19]

The Republicans did not accept such a broad interpretation. Charles Wiggins of California, Nixon's earliest and most staunch defender on the committee—who reluctantly came out for impeachment only after all of the facts were known—said he believed the Republicans were justified to insist on a narrower definition. "The definition the majority wanted was so broad that anything a president did that was simply *wrong*, whatever that might mean, could be grounds for impeachment. In short, they had almost a standardless basis of accepting evidence."[20] Wiggins believed the president could be impeached only for an outright crime. Indications that President Nixon *had* committed a crime were present by March, when the Watergate grand jury indicted seven White House aides and named Nixon an "unindicted co-conspirator."[21]

As she read the notebooks night after night, Jordan's belief that Richard Nixon should be impeached became firmer. The cumulative evidence had the same effect on other committee members. "When we began to sift through this whole morass, this mountain of information, that is when it all began to jell. I can't point to any specific revelation which caused the mood of the committee to shift, but around mid-April, the partisan acrimony was reduced. People started to listen and look and make decisions," she said.[22]

The committee requested the White House tapes in February. When they had not received them by April, the committee issued the first of several subpoenas. Instead of the tapes, however, they received more than one thousand pages of heavily edited transcripts. Committee members—Republicans as well as Democrats—were not pleased. The president had ignored a subpoena issued by the U.S. Congress. Nixon's defiance of the Judiciary Committee's subpoenas later became the basis of one of the articles of impeachment.

By the time the staff presentations of evidence began on May 9, the president's supporters on the House Judiciary Committee were wavering. The committee was meeting in all-day sessions three times a week, beginning about nine-thirty in the morning and breaking only for roll call votes on the House floor. The staff presentations took more than two months. Members went through the court transcripts and other documents line by line, and they listened to the tapes the White House had previously turned over to Special Prosecutor Jaworski, although key tapes that had been subpoenaed had not yet been forthcoming. When the committee members realized there were discrepancies between parts of the transcripts the White House had given them and the actual conversations on tape, the new evidence of White House perfidy infuriated many of them. The White House was *still* defying the subpoena.

Jordan rocked back and forth in her leather chair and rarely spoke as she listened to both the majority and minority counsels discuss the evidence. "I felt that it was more important that I hear the evidence which was being presented to me than that I start speaking. I think it is unwise to say anything until you have an adequate accumulation and understanding of the facts of the matter, and when I had the evidence I would have something to say."[23] But sometimes Jordan couldn't resist pushing the discussion along. She would sum up two or three hours of discussion in two or three sentences, leaving committee members shaking their heads and saying, "That's right, Barbara . . . that's right."[24] It was a "funny" time, she felt. "Every day when we would leave those closed-door sessions, the media people would chase us down the hall asking: 'Have you found the smoking gun?'" What *was* the "smoking gun"? Why was Nixon holding back the remaining tapes? What was he trying so desperately to hide?

Jordan told the *Christian Science Monitor* that she realized that much of the country was confused about what was happening with all of the congressional investigations, but she said flatly that she was not confused. "First, everybody ought to regret 'the Watergate' and all that word has come to mean. Nobody ought to take comfort in what we are going through in terms of investigation and indictments and trials. One should regret that it happened—then try to find out why. What is it about the American political system which allowed this kind of event to occur? If you find out what it is which allowed it, then maybe we can prevent it in the future. It ought to be an opportunity for a cleansing experience for the political process, and I view it that way."[25]

By early July, Rodino was sure that eighteen of the twenty-one Democrats would be for impeachment, and he counted Jordan's vote among them. It would take two more votes to win a simple majority. Three Democrats, all southern conservatives, were undecided—Walter Flowers of Alabama, Ray Thornton of Arkansas, and Jim Mann of South Carolina. To ensure that the American public believed that the committee's deliberations had been fair and unbiased, Rodino needed Republican votes, too. He targeted Hamilton Fish of New York, William Cohen of Maine, Tom Railsback of Illinois, and M. Caldwell Butler of Virginia, one of the committee's most conservative members.

The committee scheduled its first public hearings to discuss the evidence and possible articles of impeachment for July 24. Rodino had worked out a format for public presentations—granting each member fifteen minutes to make an opening statement, which he wanted to get out of the way before the committee laid out any charges.

Jordan thought that was a bad idea. "There were thirty-eight of us. And I recall that when Rodino said that, I thought: I don't think that's necessary. I said: 'Let's deal with the issue and make a decision on the basis of the facts we have accumulated to this point. We don't need speech-making.'"

"But I did not have much support for that position," she said. "The reaction from the other committee members was: 'You must be out of your head.' It seemed they all wanted that fifteen minutes on television." Despite her off-the-record objections to individual statements by members, Jordan had voted with the majority of the committee to allow television coverage—in prime time.

On the evening of July 24, when the members were to speak, television cameras and news reporters crowded the small committee room in the Rayburn House Office Building. Spectators had waited in line all day to be admitted. The packed committee room was shaped like a crackerbox, with the thirty-eight committee members sitting in two tiers on platforms higher than the staff, the press, and the audience, which faced them. Behind them was a backdrop of heavy green velvet curtains. Jordan sat on the lower level, with the other freshmen members of the committee. For most of the proceedings she was out of direct camera range because she was on Chairman Rodino's far right, near the end of the table. Ray Thornton of Arkansas, one of the swing-vote Democrats, took the end seat at her right, and Charles Rangel of New York was on her left. Elizabeth Holtzman, the other woman on the committee, was front and center, directly below Rodino, and visible most of the time to the television audience.

"The day we went public there were members who had been working on their opening statements for weeks, and I didn't have a word," Jordan said. "I was still just reading my sources and trying to be sure that I understood the charge and the offenses. I was not going to vote to impeach Richard Nixon because I didn't like him."

Rodino gaveled the meeting to order a little before 8:00 P.M. His opening remarks emphasized the gravity of the occasion. "Throughout all of the painstaking proceedings of this committee, I as chairman have been guided by a simple principle, the principle that the law must deal fairly with every man. . . . We have deliberated, we have been patient, we have been fair." Rodino was solemn as he concluded. "Now, we make up our minds. . . . This is a turning point, whatever we decide."[26]

The months of meetings and hearings, the mounds of information, the cascade of revelations, and the seriousness of the charges weighed on most of the committee members. Rodino hoped the members would lay out all of the evidence in their opening statements, but he had made no effort to organize them, leaving it up to each member to say what he or she wanted. As the senior members of the committee began to speak first, the seriousness with which they viewed their task was evident, and their reactions were as emotional as they were factual. The fifteen-minute statements Jordan had feared would degenerate into mere grandstanding turned out to be full of passion, even eloquence. Conservative Democrats like Jim Mann and Walter Flowers, whose districts had voted overwhelmingly for Richard Nixon only two years earlier, knew they were risking their political futures if they spoke out for impeachment. Yet their emotion and sense of morality pushed them in that direction. Mann pleaded with the president to release all of the tapes. Republican moderate Tom Railsback described his agony over the proceedings as he narrated the sequence of events that had brought the committee to this point: the White House attempt to contain Watergate, the payment of hush money, the lying, the withholding of evidence, the misuses of the FBI and the CIA, the turning over of grand jury testimony to H. R. Haldeman.[27] And Railsback, too, pleaded with the president, who was his friend and had campaigned for him twice in his Illinois district. "I wish the President could do something to absolve himself. I wish he would come forward with the information that we have subpoenaed. I must say I am very, very concerned."[28] But Caldwell Butler, the conservative Republican from Virginia, was just angry at the disregard for the law exhibited by the White House, and expressed his outrage by outlining Nixon's disregard of committee requests and subpoenas. It was an emotional evening, and Rodino called a recess shortly after 10:00 P.M. The remainder of the members would make their presentations the next morning.

On Thursday, Jordan still did not have a prepared statement ready. "But it became apparent at some point that . . . they would get around to me, as we were proceeding by seniority. I was going to have to make a statement." All during the day, her colleagues kept coming up to her, making comments like: "I just can't wait to hear your opening statement. I want to hear what you have to say. I know you're going to let Nixon have it." One woman called the office and told Jordan she had it figured out that Jordan would be speaking around nine o'clock in the evening and that she was having people over to watch her on television.

The Judiciary Committee was to convene for its evening session at eight-thirty on July 25. About six o'clock, Jordan was in her office talking with Bud Myers, who finally asked: "Well, what are you going to say?" Jordan had been so noncommunicative about the whole process that Myers didn't know whether she was going to be for or against the impeachment of Richard Nixon. She told him, "Yes, I'm going to come out for impeachment. I have decided I am going to do that, and I am going to say why."

Jordan's secretary, Marian Ricks, was due to leave work at six-thirty, but Jordan asked her to stay to type up a statement. Jordan began to pull together all of the "little disjointed notes that I'd written from all of my reading on impeachment." She had been thinking about other members' statements all day. Walter Flowers had quoted from the preamble to the Constitution during the morning session: " 'We, the People of the United States' . . . surely there is no more inspiring phrase than 'We, the People.' "[29] As Jordan began working on her remarks, she recalled his statement, and the others. "It occurred to me that not one of them had mentioned that back then the Preamble was not talking about *all* the people. So I said: 'Well, I'll just start with that.' " Jordan's lifetime experiences and her months of serious study had by now convinced her that the Constitution was a "living" document—not something static, or delivered whole. "We, the people," are always becoming the people—a whole people—one people. The process goes on and on and must be protected. That is what she wanted to convey.

Jordan began to jot down sentences in longhand and sent each page out to Ricks to type. She had already had Bob Alcock prepare parallel statements on impeachment—historical documents, Constitutions of the Confederacy, wherever "impeachment had been talked about"—against some of the Nixon offenses that had been detailed in the committee. "So I had that chart, that comparison about what had been said and what it was that Richard Nixon had done." When the typing was finally complete, Bud Myers rushed to get Jordan to the hearing room before Rodino gaveled the meeting to order. They barely made it.

"When I got in there, the Judiciary Committee was all seated and the camera was right there on us," she recalled. Again the committee room was packed. Because there was no place to sit, Myers had held back at the door, but Jordan found a place for him and motioned him to come down in front where the press was.

Jordan was scheduled to be the third speaker of the evening, after Representative Charles Rangel and Republican representative Joseph J. Maraziti of New Jersey. Just before nine o'clock, the hour when most Americans are in front of their television sets, Rodino called on her: "I recognize the gentlelady from Texas, Ms. Jordan, for the purpose of general debate, not to exceed a period of fifteen minutes."

It was then that millions of television viewers saw Barbara Jordan for the first time. What they saw was a massive, heavy black woman, in a pumpkin-orange knit dress, with a black-and-white polka-dot scarf at her neck. She was such a large woman that there seemed nothing unusual about her round and puffy face, swollen from the prednisone. Pearl earrings were visible under her short, smooth hair, but she wore no makeup or lipstick, and her eyes were shielded by glasses in heavy black frames that reflected the television lights back into the cameras, making her eyes almost impossible to see. Her elbows were on the table, with her right hand holding the edge of her glasses. She leaned into the microphone and started to read her remarks. The magic of her voice began to obliterate her appearance. Its clear, rapid, bell-like tones and rhythmic patterns made most viewers pause. Within a mere fifteen seconds, no more than fifty words into her text, both the sound and the content of her words began to engage, even captivate, her audience.

> *Earlier today we heard the beginning of the Preamble to the Constitution of the United States, "We, the People." It is a very eloquent beginning. But when that document was completed on the 17th of September in 1787, I was not included in that "We, the People." I felt somehow for many years that George Washington and Alexander Hamilton must have left me out by mistake. But through the process of amendment, interpretation, and court decision I have finally been included in "We, the People."*
>
> *Today, I am an inquisitor. I believe hyperbole would not be fictional and would not overstate the solemnness that I feel right now. My faith in the Constitution is whole, it is complete, it is total. I am not going to sit here and be an idle spectator to the diminution, the subversion, the destruction of the Constitution.*[30]

Jordan then began to explain—in effect, to teach—what the whole crisis was about: the rule of law and a president who put himself above the rule of law. What the tapes and testimony, the evidence, revealed was a presidential scandal like never before (and never since). The president of the United States had knowingly directed his underlings to raise illegal funds to finance illegal activities designed to destroy the Democratic Party and key individuals. Then he had abused the powers of his office and federal agencies like the FBI to cover up his activities. This abuse extended to denying to the Congress and the courts information they were constitutionally entitled to have. What galled Jordan the most was the lying—the president's lying about his own involvement and that of his staff. To Barbara Jordan, it was contempt and disregard for the law in extreme. She wanted her remarks to get to the center of that issue. She wanted to answer the questions people *wanted* answered.

First, what *was* impeachment? It was like an indictment, she told us, an accusation that still had to be proven. "In establishing the division between the two branches of the legislature, the House and the Senate, assigning to the one the right to accuse and to the other the right to judge, the Framers of this Constitution were very astute. They did not make the accusers and the judges the same person." Without "playing games," she also began to lay out a respectable constitutional position for those committee members who had not yet made up their minds. She was telling them, in effect, that they could vote to impeach without having to judge beyond a shadow of a doubt the president's guilt. That would be up to the Senate.[31]

To the American people, Jordan explained why the misdeeds of the president were crimes against the Constitution. She went back to the proceedings of the various states' debates during the process of ratifying the federal Constitution. She quoted from the Virginia Ratification Convention, from the South Carolina Ratification Convention, from Alexander Hamilton's words in the Federalist Papers, and particularly from James Madison's reasoning at the Constitutional Convention of 1787.

We know the nature of impeachment. We have been talking about it awhile now. "It is chiefly designed for the President and his high ministers" to somehow be called into account. It is designed to "bridle" the Executive if he engages in excesses. "It is designed as a method of national inquest into the conduct of public men" (Hamilton, Federalist No. 65). *The Framers confined in the Congress the power, if need be, to remove the President in order to strike a delicate balance between a President swollen with power and grown tyrannical and preservation of the independence of the Executive. The nature of impeachment is a narrowly channeled exception to the separation of powers maxim; the Federal Convention of 1787 said that. It limited impeachment to high crimes and misdemeanors and discounted and opposed the term "maladministration." . . .*

Common sense would be revolted if we engaged upon this process for petty reasons. Congress has a lot to do. Appropriations, tax reform, health insurance, campaign finance reform, housing, environmental protection, energy sufficiency, mass transportation.

*Pettiness cannot be allowed to stand in the face of such
overwhelming problems. So today we are not being petty. We are
trying to be big because the task we have before us is a big one.*

Then Jordan juxtaposed a few of the impeachment criteria with some of the
president's actions:

*Impeachment criteria: James Madison, from the Virginia
Ratification Convention. "If the President be connected in any
suspicious manner with any person and there be grounds to believe
that he will shelter him, he may be impeached."*

*We have heard time and time again that the evidence reflects
payments to the defendants of money. The President had
knowledge that these funds were being paid and that these were
funds collected for the 1972 Presidential campaign. We know that
the President met with Mr. Henry Petersen[32] twenty-seven times
to discuss matters related to Watergate and immediately thereafter
met with the very persons who were implicated in the information
Mr. Petersen was receiving and transmitting to the President. The
words are, "if the President be connected in any suspicious manner
with any person and there be grounds to believe that he will
shelter that person, he may be impeached. . . ."*

*The South Carolina Ratification Convention impeachment
criteria: "Those are impeachable who behave amiss or betray their
public trust." Beginning shortly after the Watergate break-in and
continuing to the present time, the President has engaged in a
series of public statements and actions designed to thwart the
lawful investigation by Government prosecutors. Moreover, the
President has made public announcements and assertions bearing
on the Watergate case which the evidence will show he knew to be
false.*

*James Madison, again at the Constitutional Convention: "A
President is impeachable if he attempts to subvert the
Constitution." The Constitution charges the President with the
task of taking care that the laws be faithfully executed, and yet, the
President has counseled his aides to commit perjury, willfully
disregarded the secrecy of grand jury proceedings, concealed
surreptitious entry, attempted to compromise a Federal judge while
publicly displaying his cooperation with the processes of criminal
justice.*

As she had done throughout her remarks, Jordan repeated a key phrase for
emphasis, also the words of James Madison: "A President is impeachable if
he attempts to subvert the Constitution."

It was pure Barbara Jordan common sense when she concluded: "If the impeachment provision in the Constitution of the United States will not reach the offense charged here, then perhaps that 18th century Constitution should be abandoned to a 20th century paper shredder."

The audience had been spellbound during her brief remarks. Chairman Rodino had tears in his eyes. Barbara Jordan took a deep breath when she finished. The committee heard the remaining six speakers after Jordan's presentation and did not adjourn until almost 11:00 P.M. Jordan was exhausted, and Myers was waiting to take her to the car outside the Rayburn Building. There was a crowd waiting for her as she made her way, and people started cheering when they saw her. Someone shouted, "Right on!" One man grabbed her arm and told her he knew that "when you talked you were going to base whatever you were going to say on the law, if you had to go back to Moses."

Jordan was surprised. There had been such strict security during the proceedings, and there had been no applause or comment after each presentation, so she had no idea how her remarks had been received. She did not know that in his summation on the *CBS News* the reporter Bruce Morton had called Jordan the "best mind on the committee." Later, when she thought about it, Jordan felt that people must have "liked it that I didn't present a harangue." Maybe they knew "I was very serious about what I was doing. I felt that was what I was communicating. That here was a person who had really thought this through and had reached a decision, a considered, sincere, and sensible decision." Telegrams flooded into her office the next day, congratulating her. On Saturday, the *Washington Post* ran the full text of her remarks. By Monday morning, her mail was overwhelming.

One woman from Arkansas wrote: "I want to let you know how much I appreciated your address last evening. It was one of the finest presentations given by any member of the Committee and it clearly showed the effort and research you had put into its preparation. I think the reference to your race and sex was appropriate. Keep up the good work. The country needs to hear from people who are proud to be Americans and not afraid to express themselves in time of crisis."

An attorney from Cedar Rapids, Iowa, had this to say: "I thought it was a brilliant summary. . . . You might be interested to know that before last night I had considered myself a life-long Republican." From an eighty-year-old woman in Miami: "I sat here with tears in my eyes. . . . I am not a constituent of yours. I am an old woman of eighty years and will not be voting for anyone for very much longer, but I will die with renewed belief that there is still a vast store of honesty, truth and honor among the men and women we have elected to serve us—you have restored my faith in our government."

And from a man in San Francisco: "Thank you once again for helping to restore this country and its people to a pride in our form of government and those who govern." A woman in Camp Hill, Pennsylvania, wrote: "You brought the basic principles of the Constitution and the Articles of Impeachment alive." From another man in California: "Eloquence, forthrightness, incisive rationality, and dignity are rare qualities. Yet you, as a black woman from the South, vividly displayed these qualities. That a black woman from the South should have these qualities is no surprise; that the American political process should have progressed far enough to allow you to display these qualities to the entire country is a surprise."

She had notes from African Americans across the nation: "All of us who love all of the Mosaic of this precious land that is our own bless you for your Forceful, scholarly, Eloquent and Epic statement of the case. Now you belong to the ages. 'Free at last.'" Another: "I am 48 years old, black, female. I was born in a mining town in rural Alabama. This should give you an idea of some of the circumstances of my early years . . . nevertheless, I have earned a doctorate degree. . . . I have known many outstanding people—Mrs. Mary McCleod Bethune, Dr. Martin Luther King Jr., Whitney M. Young Jr., Roy Wilkins—all, in my estimation, the epitomes of the dedicated, concerned, active black. Last night, I met you."

And from a one-hundred-year-old black man: "Madam, after Listen to you in Impeachment committee which you speak so eloquence made me Happy. Because I was Born in Texas in 1874. . . . I know you had some Bad Days to make it where you are." He asked her for a photograph of herself, "that I mite keep it the Rest of My Life."

The letters came from naturalized citizens as well. "When you speak of that great Document the 'Constitution of our beloved United States' it brings tears to my eyes. You see I am European born and a citizen by 'choice.' I pledged to protect and pledge allegiance to it, not to the President, whoever he may be."

Many Americans were ready to run Barbara Jordan for president of the United States on the spot: "You have changed the minds of myself, my wife, our relatives and all our friends, for the good of our country, as before we watched you on T.V. we thought only a man should be the President, but all of us will vote for you or any black man or lady." And from another: "Your scholarship was breathtaking tonight; your logic convincing; your sincerity unimpeachable; your power and beauty and dignity overwhelming. When you run for President, you can count on my vote."[33]

Of the opening statements of the thirty-eight members of the Judiciary Committee, many were eloquent, some were agonizingly heartfelt, and others were scholarly and erudite. Yet Barbara Jordan's was the one that resonated with ordinary Americans. She became a national sensation overnight. Houstonians were so proud, they sent flowers and flooded her office with calls. One supporter bought twenty-five billboards all over Houston and plastered them with the message: "Thank you—Barbara Jordan—for explaining our constitution."

What was going on? What was so moving, so inspirational about Barbara Jordan's eleven minutes on national television? Was it the voice? The words? Her very blackness? Perhaps it was the sheer authenticity of this woman who had spent most of her life on the fringe of American mainstream society but was now inside and able to see—and explain—to all of the other Americans who would never be inside, or privy to the high secrets of politics, just what was right, as well as what was wrong, with the American system of law and the people sworn to uphold it. In one sense, Jordan was like the Old Testament prophet Jeremiah, who had a certain confidence in the moral coherence of a world in which justice and righteousness should not be violated, mocked, or nullified and who, like others who have spoken in the prophetic tradition, are passionate poets, moral energizers, and discerning social analysts.[34] Jordan's cadence and rhythm did give a poetic ring to her words, creating emotions that touched the hearts as well as the minds of her listeners. But her words conveyed information, too. Her analysis of the legal and moral issues was clear and instructional, and her obvious faith in the Constitution provided a moral energy sorely needed to deal with the whole morass of Watergate corruption. Her passion conveyed the clarity of righteousness and justice. Andrew Young said that when Jordan spoke, "It sounds like the heavens have opened up."[35] The writer William Broyles, the former *Newsweek* editor who had observed Jordan closely in Texas, believed the religious parallels were apt: her voice was "an evangelical voice, a voice designed to bring to the fold the presence of the Lord."[36] After a year of Watergate revelations, resignations, details, and denials, Americans clearly needed a voice of reason from "on high," and Barbara Jordan gave it to them.

The actual presentations of the articles of impeachment, the debate, and the votes were still to come. Jordan wasted no time in getting back to work.

THE VOTE

Friday, July 26, was a hard day for members of the committee. "We had great difficulty trying to frame the articles of impeachment," Jordan said. The staff had prepared early drafts that covered six different areas. But the seven swing-vote members—the three Democrats and four Republicans—didn't like them and began working behind the scenes to draft their own, with Rodino's encouragement. They were not finished when the opening statements were completed, and on Friday morning the plan of action was still not clear. Representative Paul Sarbanes of Maryland began laying out article 1, charging the president with obstruction of justice. Ten Republicans had defended the president during the opening presentations; Representative Charles Sandman of California had forcefully demanded "clear and convincing evidence." On Friday morning Sandman once again demanded "specificity" in the charges Sarbanes was laying out before the committee. Sarbanes and other Democrats were caught off guard. By the midafternoon recess, the pro-impeachment side was in trouble. They were so familiar with the evidence that their assumptions had led them to believe that certain acts could be considered a given when it came to impeachment, but they clearly could not.

"We kind of had a notion of 'high crimes and misdemeanors,' " Jordan said. "We thought the president had done some serious wrongdoing, but when it came time to offer articles of impeachment, we weren't ready on that score. Everything we would say, this congressman—Sandman—said, what you're saying lacks 'specificity.' *Specificity* was the word of the day. What you're saying is so general, you've got to have specificity. That word was haunting us."[37]

By the time the committee reconvened for the afternoon session, the Democrats had pulled themselves together to provide specific examples of wrongdoing. The Democratic speakers, now joined by Republican moderate William Cohen of Maine, went into detailed explanations of the evidence, and they were sarcastic when they did it. Jordan remembered: "We started saying before stating any article . . . *spe-ci-fi-cally* . . . and then we proceeded."

The advocates of article 1 were trying to establish a broad pattern of wrongdoing by the president. Nixon's defenders were demanding a single, stark incident, a "smoking gun" that would justify impeachment. Article 1 covered the basic obstruction-of-justice charge, which involved all of the White House activities in the cover-up of the Watergate burglary, particularly the president's failure to "take care that the laws be faithfully executed." Nine separate charges related to the cover-up: The president had lied to federal investigators and instructed others to lie, approved the payment of hush money, interfered with and misused the FBI and the CIA, and deceived the American people. The article itself had no evidence attached to it, although the evidence had been compiled; it would be presented to the House in a separate document. The president's defenders insisted, however, that the detailed evidence be listed in the article of impeachment itself. They complained that because the specific examples of wrongdoing were not listed in the articles, the president was being treated unfairly by the committee and denied his constitutional right to due process under the law. Democrats on the committee realized late in the afternoon that as this course of discussion proceeded, they were not only becoming bogged down but confusing the millions of Americans watching them on television; those viewers might end up believing the committee had not given the president a fair chance. Rodino was worried, and he called Jordan to his desk to give her an assignment: respond to the due process argument. He thought she was "articulate, balanced, not extremist," and he knew he could trust her to be "concise and precise, but not aggressive."[38]

Rodino wanted Jordan to explain how fair the committee had been to the president and how many times it had waited for his responses, and he wanted her to "do it in prime time that very evening . . . because the Democrats wanted the public to understand the proceedings."[39]

When the committee reconvened for its evening session, Rodino immediately recognized Jordan. Once again she explained—and taught.

> *It is understandable that this committee would have procedural difficulties, because this is an unfamiliar and strange procedure. But some of the arguments which were offered earlier today by some members of this committee in my judgment are phantom arguments, bottomless arguments.*
>
> *Due process. If we have not afforded the President of the United States due process as we have proceeded through this impeachment inquiry, then there is no due process to be found anywhere. Well, what did we do? The Judiciary Committee under all of the historical precedents available does not have to allow counsel to the President to participate in its proceedings, but this committee, because of its grace, because it wanted to be fair, because of its interest in due process, allowed—suffered, if you will— counsel to the President to sit in these proceedings every day.*
>
> *He was present. Was he gagged? Was he silent? No, because this Judiciary Committee cast a rule which allowed the President's counsel to speak.*
>
> *Now, one might say, well, certainly that is minimal due process. All I am saying is that the committee was under no compulsion to do that, but voted to do it. So, the President's counsel was here and received every item of information this committee received.*
>
> *The President's counsel suggested witnesses he wanted called and heard by this committee. They were all called. They were all heard. The President's counsel was afforded the right to cross- examine witnesses.*
>
> *. . . The subpoenas. We were very reluctant to issue a subpoena to the President of the United States. But the President asked us for additional time to respond to our first subpoena, and we said we want you, Mr. President, to have due process, so additional time is yours. And we gave him that time.*
>
> *Due process? Due process tripled. Due process quadrupled. We did that. The President knows the case which has been heard before this committee. The President's counsel knows the case which has been heard before this committee. . . .*
>
> *. . . We talked about a report. . . . That report will be filed and it will contain the rather detailed specific particularized*

information so that no one can question whether the President has been advised of the allegations against him.[40]

Jordan's remarks set the tone for the remainder of the evening's debate: sharp and specific. The committee would not actually vote on the first article until the next evening—after listening to another full day of debate. Finally, a little before 7:00 P.M. on Saturday, July 27, Chairman Rodino allowed the vote to proceed. The roll call took three minutes. It was somber and slow. While the clerk called the roll, Jordan and many other members had a look of profound gloom. Yet, when her name was called, Barbara Jordan voted aye.

"It was an awful moment," she said. "I was unprepared for how I felt. And it hit me so hard. After voting the first article, and after Rodino adjourned the committee, we were in back behind the main committee hearing room and several of us cried, absolutely shed tears. For Richard Nixon? No. But that the country had come to this."[41]

Peter Rodino called his wife as soon as the vote was taken. "I am unashamed to say that I cried," he said. So did conservative Republican M. Caldwell Butler, who had also voted to impeach his party's president. He was one of six Republicans who joined all twenty-one Democrats in approving the first article of impeachment—twenty-seven to eleven. The vote was a stunning experience for the committee, and the nation, but there was more to come. The committee would meet on Monday, July 29, to take up the second article, which dealt with abuse of power.

The weekend was a mix of emotion for Jordan. Because of her presentations before the committee, people congratulated her and clamored to be around her. But the committee's work was far too different and difficult to feel like a victory. "I didn't like the idea of working to impeach a President. I didn't like doing that; I wished that it had been unnecessary to do that. I really did." She told one reporter, "Listen, I salute the flag. I get goose pimples over the national anthem and 'God Bless America.' I don't apologize for it. I feel very keenly about the necessity for this country to survive as a republican form of government having as its supreme law a constitution which remains inviolate. I feel this quite strongly and that is what's operating with me."[42] This was no political victory for Barbara Jordan. She felt no jubilation, but she did feel anger. "Richard Nixon violated that basic, fundamental law that is the glue that holds us together. He took us to the abyss . . . almost over the chasm. I do not feel that any of these figures—Nixon, Haldeman, Mitchell—were to be pitied. Each of us are responsible for ourselves. We are a nation of laws. Anyone who violated those laws, knowing full well what the consequences are, we do not pity."[43]

Jordan felt it was a sensitive time for the country. "We are not a banana republic, but we are a government of laws, and not of men. To have the actions of a single individual violate so many of the sacred principles of government was a very serious occurrence. It hurt that we were about to take an act to try to remove from position someone who may be a premier leader of the free world. So, that is a very serious time. It can be very destabilizing for a government and for a people, so that made it very, very difficult. It would be most foolhardy for someone to take on a decision like a vote for impeachment cavalierly. It's just not something to be lightly treated."[44]

On Monday, July 29, the House Judiciary Committee approved, on a twenty-eight-to-ten vote, the second article of impeachment. It charged the president with using the powers of his office to violate the constitutional rights of citizens and of impairing the due and proper administration of justice in the conduct of lawful inquiries. And on Tuesday, July 30, the committee, on a twenty-one-to-seventeen vote, approved article 3, which charged the president with defying subpoenas of Congress and failing to produce papers and tapes directed by the Judiciary Committee. Two other articles, dealing with the president's tax evasion and with the illegal bombing of Cambodia, were not approved, although Barbara Jordan voted with the twelve Democratic members of the committee who supported them.

She was particularly upset because President Nixon had used federal funds to increase the value of his San Clemente and Key Biscayne private properties to such a "lavish degree" that he had effectively violated the emoluments clause of the Constitution. Moreover, she believed that he had deliberately violated the tax laws.[45] For two years, President Nixon had paid less than $1,000 a year in federal income taxes on an income of more than $250,000. Jordan was so indignant over this breach of ethics that she signed a joint statement with eleven of her colleagues that was attached to the committee's final report: "The integrity of the Office of President cannot be maintained by one who would convert public funds to his own private benefit and who would refuse to abide by the same laws that govern every American taxpayer."

The televised meetings were over. The committee prepared to send the articles of impeachment to the full House of Representatives.

When the White House, under order of the Supreme Court, released the last of its tapes on August 5, the smoking gun was finally revealed. One of the tapes showed that Nixon had been involved in the activities surrounding Watergate as early as the week after the break-in, and that he had indeed used the CIA to block an FBI investigation of the activities. This was the heart of the obstruction-of-justice charge in the second article of impeachment, and it was a crime—not a vague "wrong." It was this revelation that shook Richard Nixon's remaining loyal supporters and caused his staunchest backers on the Judiciary Committee to announce that they would support the articles of impeachment when the full House voted. On August 8, with the certainty that the House would vote to impeach him and that he would face a Senate trial, President Nixon resigned.

If the impeachment trial had proceeded, five members of the House would have served as prosecutors with the duty of presenting the charges, marshaling the evidence, and advocating impeachment. Chairman Rodino would have been the chief prosecutor, or manager, and he had selected Jordan to be one of his co-managers. The full Senate would have served as the jury, with the chief justice of the Supreme Court, Warren Burger, presiding. Rodino's selection of Jordan was a tribute to a freshman member of the committee. By the time the committee votes were taken, Jordan was clearly the committee's star. She knew what to say, and she knew how to say it. People listened to her, and they believed her. She was a logical choice. Jordan was obviously disappointed that she did not have the opportunity to make the legal case against the president in the Senate.

"When our articles of impeachment were voted ultimately by the Judiciary Committee and we were to present this indictment to the Senate, I wanted to be one of the managers . . . on the part of the House floor who did that. . . . But of course I never got a chance. Nobody did. Because Nixon resigned. Which was a mixture of relief that we didn't have to go forward with it, and disappointment because due process did not take place. And it should have."

Although the president had resigned, the Judiciary Committee presented its report on impeachment to the House on August 20. Richard Nixon was already in San Clemente, but the possibility of a federal court trial remained. Then, five weeks later, on September 8, the man Barbara Jordan had opposed for the vice presidency, Gerald Ford—now the president of the United States—pardoned Richard M. Nixon, removing the possibility of any further legal action. Before Gerald Ford issued the pardon, he made sure Barbara Jordan was out of the country—and out of the range of the television cameras.

Immediately after Ford took office, he had invited the Congressional Black Caucus to meet with him in the White House. It was the first time members had ever been asked to come as a group. Jordan had appreciated the gesture and in fact had helped Ford escape from the meeting as it droned on, with almost every Caucus member making a speech. Ford so appreciated Jordan's action in cutting off the meeting that he called to thank her the following day. So when she got a call from the White House asking her to make an "important" trip to China, she considered it. The State Department was putting together a bipartisan group of American officials to assure the People's Republic of China that the absence of Richard Nixon did not mean that his historic and successful diplomatic openings to the Chinese would be ended. The State Department wanted to show continuity in American foreign policy despite the domestic crisis. When Jordan was told that both former vice president Hubert Humphrey and former Senate Foreign Relations Committee chairman William Fulbright were going, she decided to make the trip, too.

"And there we were in China in some little province just at the foot of a mountain and sleeping on these slatted cots with straw mats," Jordan said, when she was summoned to the telephone to take a call from a Houston television station. The reporter asked her, "What do you think about Ford's pardon of Richard Nixon?"

"What the hell are you talking about?" Jordan asked. "Just repeat what you have said. Slowly." And when the reporter did, Jordan said she still could not get it straight. And then she realized that President Ford had sent "all of us as far out of the country as possible to this little province so this could happen." Richard Nixon was off the hook. Jordan felt cheated. "Something at least could have been resolved with the finality of a court decision, but now everything is wiped out. The country definitely got short-changed. I don't know whether it would have been the long, agonizing nightmare which Gerald Ford said it would be for the country if we had gone through the trial. But I do know that it would have been done with some finality."

The whole crisis for Jordan was about the rule of law, and about a president who put himself above the law. The eight months of Watergate hearings, with transcipts, testimony, and study during the Judiciary Committee's proceedings, had helped her focus on just why the law was so important to her, and to the unique concept of American nationhood. Her belief in the American system of laws and justice had been tested, examined, proven, deepened, and embedded as part of her core of morality. The Constitution became imprinted on her consciousness as the Bible had been when she was a child. The Constitution provided *the* way to achieve justice and fairness. She believed that Americans had to be united in a common bond of respect for the Constitution, and that no one—not even the president of the United States—was free to flaunt it. Her gift of voice had allowed her to explain that belief to the American people.

The sociologist Barry Schwartz, writing about the first American hero, George Washington, said, "Great men, like other sacred symbols, are created in times of crisis and collective enthusiasm, times when people enter into intense and effervescent relationships with one another."[46] The Judiciary Committee's impeachment inquiry was a time of crisis during which many Americans came to see Barbara Jordan as the symbol of the moral authority of the Constitution. The thousands of letters she received after her television remarks attest to the "intense and effervescent" relationship Americans from all walks of life felt they had with her. Her moral persona had taken hold.

Moral leadership happens in human minds—the mind of the leader and the minds of followers. It depends on how leaders characterize and resolve important issues in their own minds, and how, in turn, they attempt to alter the minds of their audiences to effect change.[47] Barbara Jordan became a national leader that week in July 1974. She also began her transition from a good political speechmaker to a great orator, a feat possible only when a leader finds the subject of her soul. Frederick Douglass, whom Jordan so often quoted, had made such a transition on the antislavery speakers' circuit in New England when his soul finally matched the power of his voice and passion. For Barbara Jordan it came together during the impeachment proceedings. As she talked about the Constitution, she began her transformation from a politician to a patriot, from an inside player who could get a law passed to an inspirational leader who could influence the beliefs and actions of an entire people. Through her discipline, concentration, and scholarship during Watergate, she uncovered the great belief of her life, her one true political passion—the love of the American Constitution. Now she had a message that matched her voice.

Yet for all of her intelligence and insight, it would take some time before she really understood what that meant to her and to Americans who wanted to follow her.

CHAPTER 14

"ONE OF THOSE TEXAS TRIBAL THINGS"

THE ARTIST EDSEL Cramer, who lived in Houston's Third Ward for twenty-five years, had studied Barbara Jordan's face. "Studying her up close you see exactly how intense she is," Cramer said. "There are fine lines etched around her eyes, the sort of lines that mean stress, hard work, and determination. Her head is like a bull's head; across her brow is a lump of bone that stands out like the forehead of a bull. That look of bull-like strength is part of her character. But the most impressive thing about her is she is simply so big—in size and personality."[1]

After Jordan went to Congress, the Texas Senate had commissioned Cramer to paint a portrait of her to be hung in the Texas Capitol along with Davy Crockett, Sam Houston, Jefferson Davis, and other Texas and Confederate heroes. During her first year in Washington, Jordan had gone to Cramer's Houston studio six times to sit for the portrait. She told Cramer, "My mother says not to make me pretty."[2] Cramer's use of muted blues, violets, and gray tones did not make Jordan artificially pretty, but they did soften her direct, clear gaze and coat her expression with a sheen of serenity as she sat with her hands gently clasped in front of her. Yet the softness could not diminish her overpowering presence. Cramer could not confine her to normal scale. "No matter how hard I tried, even though I prefer to keep the scale of my paintings down . . . her painting just kept coming out too big," he said. "I couldn't help but make her larger than life."[3]

After Watergate, Barbara Jordan did seem larger than life. She had won reelection in the fall with only token opposition, and she was invigorated, even slightly cocky, because of the Watergate accolades and attention. When she began the new session of Congress in January 1975, the national news media could not get enough of her. *Redbook* magazine readers named

Jordan one of six women who were qualified to be president. And the *Ladies' Home Journal* designated her one of its eight "women of the year." Requests for speeches came in from all over the country, and many of the nation's finest universities lined up to offer her honorary degrees, including her law school alma mater Boston University. House Speaker Carl Albert named her to one of ten spots on the House Democratic Steering and Policy Committee, giving her real influence with her party's members in Congress.[4]

When she began her second term, Jordan was so imposing that she dominated every situation or personal encounter she experienced. The veteran Washington journalist Meg Greenfield, who interviewed Jordan in February for her *Newsweek* column, wrote: "I can't remember being more apprehensive about an interview with a public figure than I was before (and, occasionally during) my talk with her. The message is conveyed in her every word and gesture: Don't tread on me. And she is also known for a certain brusqueness associated with another minority group to which she belongs: that of very smart people who see the point long before others have finished making it and who have a low threshold for muzzy argument or political blah."[5] That became clear on the House floor one afternoon when Maryland Republican representative Marjorie Holt proposed a constitutional amendment to ban school busing and raced over to Jordan to tell her "there was nothing racist in the bill." Jordan silently stared her down, making no effort to hide her contempt.[6]

In 1975, although a national arena seemed to be opening for Jordan, her orientation, views, ambition, and patterns of thinking and acting were still rooted in her desire to be a Texas insider, to be "let in" by those who held power in Texas. It was as if all of the national attention were simply one more tool to pry open the door to enter the room and be admired by the men who—outside of public view—wielded political and economic power at home. Early in 1975, she felt close enough to that power to remark, "I think I'm about to crack it."[7] In Texas, political and economic power still derived from oil and gas, and one of Jordan's first votes in the new Congress was to preserve tax favors for the men and industries that produced it.

Congress had been working since late 1973 to formulate a national energy policy that would end fuel shortages and lessen U.S. dependency on foreign oil. When the major oil companies began to reap windfall profits from domestic production in 1973 and 1974, as a result of the Arab oil embargo, Congress had put a tax on those windfall profits. Because ordinary people had to pay higher prices, the huge oil company profits had violated Jordan's sense of fair play, and she had voted for the tax. But in February 1975, the House scheduled a vote to repeal the 22 percent oil depletion allowance, a $2 billion tax subsidy to the industry for exploration and development costs. This time she voted for the industry by voting against repeal of the tax break, going along with almost the entire Texas delegation. But Jordan, the Texans, and the oil industry were on the losing side of a 248–113 House vote to repeal the tax break.

A few days later, Jordan cast another, far more important vote for the oil and gas industry. Once again, however, she and the Texans were on the losing side when they voted to end twenty years of federal price controls on natural gas. Natural gas was the primary source of heating fuel for more than half of the country, and producers were promoting higher prices and a deregulated national market as the way to increase exploration, development, and new production to deal with expected winter shortages of the fuel.[8] With a restructuring—and deregulation—of its pricing and markets, the industry would also be able to expand and generate larger profits. The Ford administration had joined the industry in support of deregulation, and early in the year Texas senator Lloyd Bentsen Jr. had managed to get the Senate to lift the price controls. But the House, under the influence of the new Democrats elected in the wake of Watergate, and others from the Northeast and Midwest whose constituents would have to pay the higher winter fuel costs, blocked the measure—but only temporarily. By 1976 the House would also approve deregulation.

Jordan's 1975 votes with the Texas delegation in favor of the oil industry represented her first major split from positions taken by the Congressional Black Caucus and liberal Democrats in the House. Houston's other Democratic member of Congress, Bob Eckhardt, was the only member of the Texas delegation who voted to end the oil depletion allowance, and he was also against deregulation of natural gas. Many doctrinaire liberals expected Jordan to follow his example, but just as she had not allowed herself to be taken for granted by her liberal colleagues in the Texas Senate, Jordan was not going to vote with liberals in Congress on key energy issues that affected her district. Houston was the petroleum capital of the nation. More than one hundred thousand Houston jobs were centered in the refineries and plants that produced petrochemical products. Jordan had concluded that her constituency included energy executives and refinery workers as well as poor people in Houston's central city. Besides, early in her term she had made a commitment to industry officials that she would support their efforts to deregulate natural gas.

"Natural gas was *the* critical vote for the industry," said Jordan's friend Stan McClelland, who would later become a top executive with Valero Energy, one of the Southwest's largest natural gas suppliers. "Deregulation was going to change the industry fundamentally, and it was much more important than something like the windfall profits tax break," said McClelland. "Barbara could separate the big victories that were important to the industry from those they would merely like to have but weren't critical for survival or profitability. This was critical—and Barbara knew it."

When Jordan first went to Congress, she had held a meeting with key Houston bankers and industry leaders and asked them in her most direct and forthright manner: "What is your bottom line? What is the vote you most want from me?" They told her: deregulation of natural gas. She promised they would have her vote on the issue.

It was that direct and very clear understanding with Houston's business, banking, and energy officials that "gave her some wiggle room" on other anti-business votes, her legislative aide Bob Alcock believed. "Natural gas deregulation was one of those monsters . . . but it was the one thing the oil and banking people really wanted from her, and because she gave it to them they left her alone on the other votes."

Stan McClelland agreed. "She voted against the business establishment on a number of things, but she gave them this vote on natural gas. She realized that her core constituency was the Fifth Ward, the black community, but she was also very aware that she represented downtown Houston. It was symbolic if nothing else. If Barbara Jordan from Houston, whose district included most of the oil industry in the country, was voting against the key energy issues, it gave everybody else a free ride."

Although there were some rumblings among her more liberal colleagues in Congress over her oil and gas votes, most members cut her some slack and did not criticize her on the issue. She *was* a Texan, after all. To some members of the Congressional Black Caucus, however, she was *too* Texan. "We just never feel that Barbara's heart is with us. She is first and foremost voting in the interests of Texas," said a Caucus member, who would not allow his name to be used, in a 1975 article in *Encore* magazine.[9] It was well known that when there was a conflict between a meeting of the Congressional Black Caucus and the Texas congressional delegation, Jordan always chose Texas.

In her first congressional term, Jordan had amassed more honors and more power than most members of Congress accumulate in a lifetime. Her rapid rise set off speculation about "Speaker" Jordan, "Supreme Court Justice" Jordan, even "Vice President" Jordan. It also set off a wave of professional jealousy among members who gossiped about her "almost limitless ambition." The resentment among some of Jordan's liberal, female, and black colleagues was undeniable by early in 1975. It was particularly virulent among some members of the Congressional Black Caucus, provoking one observer to contrast the styles of its three most prominent female members. "There is pretty Yvonne Burke, the glamour girl of the Black Caucus, reluctant to use the political muscle that would disturb her feminine image. Shirley Chisholm, principled and aggressive, projected the 'unbought, unbossed' image that ruffled a lot of the male feathers in the Caucus. And now there is Barbara Jordan, tough, cold, who makes it clear that she did not need them, nor would she follow their directives. When Barbara Jordan came to Washington, it was clear that the Black Caucus would never be the same again."[10] The criticism surfaced publicly for the first time in a front-page article in the *Wall Street Journal* in February. The article centered on Jordan's glowing introduction of West Virginia's senator Robert Byrd at the Democratic Party's midterm convention in Kansas City.

"What is the measure of one man?" she asked about Byrd in her speech. "Some will say that it is the depth of his intellect and capacity for human understanding and compassion. Others will say that it is his ability to lead other men and influence them to believe in the rightness of the cause he espouses. Some measure a man by the content of his commitment to a government of laws and others by his sense of justice." After quoting from Jordan's speech, the reporter John Pierson reminded readers that Robert Byrd had belonged to the Ku Klux Klan, called Martin Luther King a "self-seeking rabble-rouser," and voted against almost every major civil rights bill. Pierson wrote: "the incident shows a side of Barbara Jordan not fully perceived by the public: She is a very ambitious politician who uses her eloquence not only on behalf of high principle but also to get ahead. Whatever his views on race, Sen. Byrd is, after all, No. 2 in the Senate Democratic leadership."

Jordan defended her praise of Senator Byrd by telling Pierson, "I really do believe that people change and that you can help people change more quickly at times by defining them. He [Byrd] was obviously moved by the introduction and said to me later: 'You'll never be sorry that you introduced me.'"[11]

The rumbles about Jordan's "extraordinary" ambitions continued, although most of her critics insisted on anonymity and refused to go on the record with their complaints. One Republican member of the House Judiciary Committee told a reporter, off the record, that Jordan had a "Gothic preoccupation with power."[12] Colorado's former Democratic representative Patricia Schroeder brushed off such comments. "That's just one of those male assessments," she said. "Like women weren't supposed to be interested in power. . . . You wouldn't be in the Congress if you weren't interested in power, in having the power to do something."

Jordan barely hid her contempt for anyone who said she was preoccupied with power—particularly for those who expected her to sit on the sidelines, waiting for permission and political crumbs because she was a woman. "There is no place for women to be shy and retiring if they want to be leaders," she said. "Women have got to take an unwoman-like stance and be bold and aggressive. . . . There are no instances in history where people voluntarily relinquish or give you a gift of power. Power has to be seized."[13] Jordan felt that "one who feels that power is distasteful and to be disdained ought not to be in politics."[14]

The perception that Jordan was cold and aloof was given wider exposure in an *Ebony* magazine article that also appeared in February. When asked directly about it, Jordan told *Ebony*'s reporter, "Maybe some people have had experiences with me where I came through as 'cold' or whatever . . . I can't control [people's perceptions], and all I can say is that I am just the way I am and I am very comfortable with me."[15] Jordan's aide Bud Myers came to her defense. "Some people misunderstand her because they're so used to dealing with people who are not entirely serious when they're on the job. She just feels that when she is on the Hill taking care of the people's business she doesn't have time to try and please everybody by being what they might call 'nice.' She just wants everybody to state their business as briefly as possible so that she can have enough time to do her job. It's really as simple as that."[16]

Jordan gave her critics in Congress something new to focus on in April when she did a favor for the Texan most liberal Democrats loved to hate: John Connally. She appeared as a surprise character witness for Connally at his Washington, D.C., trial for bribery.

"Now, I never understood that," Pat Schroeder said. "But I just figured it was one of those Texas tribal things where everybody just circled the wagons. I thought Connally must have been just great to her somewhere along the way. But then, I didn't want to believe anything bad about her either."

THE CONNALLY-JOHNSON BOYS . . . AGAIN

John Connally had chosen the noted attorney Edward Bennett Williams to defend him against federal charges that he accepted a bribe for getting the Nixon administration to increase milk price supports in 1971 when he was secretary of the treasury. Williams, a shrewd lawyer who understood the power of symbolism, wanted Barbara Jordan to testify on Connally's behalf before his all-black jury.

Connally was hardly a sympathetic defendant. Arrogant, patrician, and notoriously insensitive to the feelings or interests of minorities during his entire career, Connally, by 1974, had also switched parties to become a Republican. He was accused of perjury, conspiracy to obstruct justice, and accepting bribes. Connally's selection of Edward Bennett Williams, who was treasurer of the Democratic Party and had represented it against the Republican Committee to Reelect the President over the Watergate break-in, was designed to counter the impression that Connally was involved with any of the Watergate activities.

Oscar Mauzy, Jordan's old friend from the Texas Senate, remembered watching Williams win over an all-black Washington jury when he successfully defended the Teamsters union chief Jimmy Hoffa against charges that he had tried to bribe FBI agents. "I sat in the courtroom and watched as

Williams arranged for boxing great Joe Louis to walk into the courtroom, go over to the defendant's table and shake Jimmy Hoffa's hand—nothing more. The jury walked Hoffa in eighteen minutes."

Edward Bennett Williams intended to put on a first-rate defense for John Connally, but he believed that Barbara Jordan, the new black hero of the nation, could be Connally's equivalent of Hoffa's Joe Louis. When he talked to Connally about it, Connally agreed that Jordan would be persuasive—if she would do it. Frank Erwin believed Bob Strauss should be the one to ask her. When he did, Jordan told Strauss, "I know he is a friend of yours, but . . . I don't like his character. I don't like what he stands for. I don't like *him*."[17]

Bob Strauss, full of charm and savvy—and insight into how Barbara Jordan's political mind worked—began his sales pitch: "You don't have to *like* him," Strauss told her. "You don't have to testify as to his character. Williams only wants you to testify as to Connally's *reputation* for truth and veracity in his home community. He doesn't give a damn whether you despise or love him. Now, would you deny that he has a *reputation* for truth and veracity in Texas?" Strauss asked her.

"No," Jordan responded.

"Well, would you deny that he has a *reputation* for truth in Houston—his and your home community?" Strauss pressed on. Again Jordan answered, "No."

"If they asked you those questions, wouldn't you have to answer just the way you answered me?" Strauss said this last question "stumped" her. "I knew she was softening. So then I told her that Mrs. [Lady Bird] Johnson was going to testify, that the Reverend Billy Graham was going to testify, and I told her that it was not Connally who was asking her to do this, it was Edward Bennett Williams—a Democrat! I asked her to think it over and to talk to Williams, and she agreed. I knew by the end of our conversation that she would do it."

Jordan also knew it. Strauss had shown her that there was a way she could do it—not for John Connally, but for Edward Bennett Williams, and for Bob Strauss! After all, she owed Strauss a big favor, a leftover chit for denying him her vote in his bid to become chairman of the Democratic Party. It was her turn to do something for him, and to put Strauss in *her* debt. Jordan had a lot of thinking to do, however, before she would say yes officially.

The charges against Connally had come from the Watergate special prosecutor's investigations into illegal contributions made to the Committee to Reelect the President during Nixon's 1972 presidential campaign. Watergate prosecutors had uncovered enough evidence to assert that the Nixon administration's decision to increase milk price supports in March 1971 was return payment for commitments by the Associated Milk Producers, Inc. (AMPI), to make massive campaign contributions of at least $2 million.[18]

The specific indictment against Connally charged that while he was secretary of the treasury in 1971 he had accepted two illegal gratuities of $5,000 each from the Texas lawyer Jake Jacobsen, who was the lobbyist for the milk producers, in return for having influenced the Nixon administration to increase the federal milk price supports. Indeed, Jacobsen was indicted for—and pled guilty to—making an illegal payment to a public official: Connally. Connally, however, maintained that the payment was never made.[19]

The Connally trial, and the controversy surrounding it, provided a national glimpse into the underbelly of Texas political power. Jake Jacobsen was one of the original Connally-Johnson boys, with such close ties to the Texas Democratic Party that later he went to the White House to handle all of Lyndon Johnson's personal business. But he was also a careless wheeler-dealer who was under federal investigation for embezzlement and was facing thirty-five years in jail for perjury during his grand jury testimony. Federal prosecutors were negotiating a deal with him when the Senate select committee's Watergate hearings began in the summer of 1973. Because of the unrelated federal charges against him, Jacobsen's credibility and motivation for testifying against Connally were questioned from the beginning. Washington insiders also tittered about the relatively small dollar amount of the alleged bribe. Ten thousand dollars seemed like small potatoes in the Connally-Johnson world, and if it had really happened, why would Connally risk so much for so little? And why would Barbara Jordan risk *anything* for John Connally?[20]

The choice to testify for Connally was an extension of Jordan's decision-making patterns in the Texas legislature, where every tit for tat had been calculated in terms of her own goals, ambitions, and advancement. To outsiders later, it looked like a step down from the high ground of defending constitutional principles during the Judiciary Committee's Watergate hearings only a few months earlier.

It had not yet occurred to her that Watergate might have thrust her into a different arena—that her clarion calls for political morality arising from the Watergate hearings had created a different set of expectations among her new fans, many of whom now thought her capable of more than mere Texas political horse-trading.

"I knew in my own head that I was being used," Jordan later recounted. "But I always made a distinction between when people used you and you didn't *know it*, and when you *knew* you were being used and agreed to it. I made that distinction then." Moreover, she did not *owe* Connally anything, and there was *nothing* she wanted from him. (Connally had, by this time, switched to the Republican Party.) Because her testimony would involve no quid pro quo with John Connally, she felt that her conscience could be clear.

Before she could feel comfortable with her decision, however, she had called her old friend in Houston, Jake Johnson, a man she trusted personally and politically.

"I want you to find out something for me," she told him. "Find out about that $10,000 milk money, find out what the deal really is." Johnson contacted a wealthy Houston businessman with ties to the Suite 8F crowd and the Connally-Johnson boys, someone he felt would be a truthful source. His source made calls to people very close to Connally, and Johnson said he received the message that "Connally did not take the money for himself. So I told Barbara what I had found out." Johnson felt strongly that his source would not lie to him. "Reputation and integrity—that's his stock in trade, and he would not have told me that if he had not been pretty damn sure. So I was willing to tell her to go ahead and testify."

Connally told prosecutors that Jacobsen had indeed *discussed* making available to him $10,000 provided by the milk producers to distribute to key members of Congress to "win points by helping in the members' congressional campaigns."[21] But Connally also said that "Jacobsen knew there was no way that he would dare suggest that I would take money for my personal benefit." But Connally denied that he had taken the money for this or any other purpose.[22] Jordan's friend Stan McClelland said that her decision to testify came from this assertion. "It wasn't that she felt he was a wonderful human being, or did or did not deserve to be acquitted. But I think she did believe that he wouldn't straight up lie."

Jordan asked Jake Johnson to check on one more fact. She wanted him to find out if Connally's law firm—Vinson, Elkins, Searls and Connally—one of Houston's oldest and most prestigious firms, which Connally had joined after leaving the governor's office—had ever contributed to one of *her* campaigns. "I want to know so if they ask me on cross-examination I can say for sure."

"Well, of course they have, Barbara," Johnson told her. And he reminded her of a two-hundred-dollar contribution she had gotten from the firm at her last fund-raising event. "Hell, I'll send you the contributors' list, Barbara, but they're not going to ask you that. They're not going to ask you anything." And then Johnson gave her some advice. "The one thing you need to do is to get Ed Bennett Williams—just for us troops down here—at least get him to ask you if you are a political supporter of Connally's. Connally is a Nixon deal, and as far as we're concerned, he's the enemy. At least make sure that they bring that out, because your testimony cannot be seen as an endorsement of Connally politically. It just cannot!"

THE TESTIMONY

"I sat there in that witness room with all of them—Lady Bird, Dean Rusk, Bob McNamara, Barbara Jordan . . . and Billy Graham, who was as nervous as a cat. He had never testified in his life," George Christian remembered. Christian, too, was a witness because Jacobsen had testified that Connally had returned the ten thousand dollars to him in front of Christian's house in Austin. But Christian was to directly refute that charge on the witness stand. "Everybody was nervous and tried to console everybody else," Christian said. "But Barbara was totally calm. She just sat there, hardly smiled, just conversed with everybody and didn't show any signs of nervousness. She was in total control . . . I'll never forget that. If I didn't know better, I'd say she was just showing off. She wasn't nervous. It was like she did it every day."

Edward Bennett Williams and his young assistant, Michael Tigar,[23] methodically demolished the prosecution's case, largely by discrediting Jacobsen's motivations and his character. Despite the evidence that had been presented, the whole issue still boiled down to whether the jury would believe Connally or Jacobsen. Jacobsen had been caught lying to a grand jury over a fraudulent bank loan, while Connally had been a magnificent witness on the stand—handsome, uncharacteristically humble, and outraged that his integrity had been questioned. Moreover, Connally had all of these prominent individuals ready to testify on his behalf.

The rules of the court were strict for the six witnesses who were to testify for Connally. Each would be asked only two questions: How long and how well had the witness known the defendant? What was his reputation for honesty and integrity? Robert McNamara was the first witness to testify, then Lady Bird Johnson, followed by Dean Rusk, James J. Rowe Jr., and Bob Strauss. But the only two witnesses who really mattered to the jury came last: Billy Graham and Barbara Jordan. When Graham responded to a question about the nature of his work by saying, "I am an evangelist, preaching the gospel of Jesus Christ all over the world," one female juror was heard to say "Amen!"[24]

When Jordan's familiar hulking figure strode to the stand as the last witness for Connally, her magnetic larger-than-life presence riveted spectators in the courtroom. She was the most famous black woman in America, and there she was, not five feet away from the twelve black jurors who held John Connally's fate and future in their hands. After stating her name and occupation, Jordan's voice was electrifying when she answered the question about Connally's reputation. "As far as I know from my personal experience, he has a good reputation for honesty." She started to say more, but prosecutors cut her off. She was on the stand less than five minutes.

On April 17, the jury brought in a verdict of "not guilty." Connally and his family celebrated in the Watergate apartment of the chairman of the Democratic Party, Bob Strauss. When Connally called to thank Jordan, she told him, "I wouldn't have done it if I didn't feel it was the right thing to do." Connally later wrote her: "I hope your future is filled only with good fortune which would never require a repayment in kind, but if it should, I will be there. Whatever the future, I shall be looking for opportunities to make you proud that you did what you did."[25]

Jordan felt just fine about her testimony. She got positive reinforcement from members of the Texas congressional delegation and from Texas newspaper editorial writers. Representative Jim Wright said, "I thought it was the decent thing to do. I knew that he and she were not of the same wing of the Democratic Party, but she knew him as an honorable man, and why shouldn't she say that? I think she did the right thing, and I admired her for doing it." Even her old liberal friend Oscar Mauzy approved. "There wasn't a damn thing wrong with what she did for John Connally." She received dozens of letters from prominent Texas conservatives who praised her courage in testifying for Connally. William Broyles wrote in *Texas Monthly* that Jordan's testimony put the Houston "establishment even deeper in her debt."[26]

Jordan later wrote in *Self-Portrait* that there was no big hue and cry in Texas about her testimony on Connally's behalf, but that was not entirely true. Most of the furor came from the old-line Ralph Yarborough liberals, to whom it seemed a betrayal to do *anything* for John Connally. One woman from Angelton wrote, "I've come to your defense time and time again, even against those who claimed you gerrymandered a district to insure your election as a U.S. Representative. . . . Will I come to your defense again? Never More, Never More." But the tone of most of the letters was disappointment. A man from west Texas wrote, "Your voting record and conduct during the Judicial Committee hearings are exemplary and highly commendable. If you have no regrets about John Connally, many of your friends do."[27]

The Texas writer Larry King, who had sat in the courtroom every day for an article he wrote on the trial for *Atlantic Monthly*, was blistering in his attack on Jordan in conversations with friends. He said he was "disgusted by the groveling of Barbara Jordan," and felt that she had "displayed the ultimate corruption of a black who had made it and then had betrayed her own people."[28] Some of that feeling was echoed within the Congressional Black Caucus. An article in *Encore* magazine said Jordan's testimony for Connally had also created a "fissure in the solid wall" of black loyalty to her.[29] And the national press, surprised by Jordan's testimony and certain that it had influenced the all-black jury in Connally's favor, took a few swipes at her, too. Myra MacPherson in the *Washington Post* wrote that Jordan was cynically "obeying the code of Texas political loyalty."[30]

Jordan, on the surface, was unmoved by the flap and kept moving forward, as she had always done. The politics of principles and issues was inextricably linked in her mind with the politics of deal-making. And both were necessary to get something done that really mattered to people. For Jordan, the Connally testimony was just part of the mix. The public acclaim from Watergate, however, had focused a media-filtered spotlight on her philosophy, which, to those who did not know her well, seemed to be precariously balanced between pragmatism and principle. The deals, trades, and friendships with ideological enemies were baffling to political purists who valued being right more than being effective. Jordan believed that her pragmatism was the tool to allow her to be effective in achieving justice—because it led her directly to the sources of political power, which could make something happen. She saw no incongruity in her actions. Achieving a balance between her pragmatism and her principles, the two strong elements in her nature, was preferable to falling off a political high wire into the pit of snarling, self-righteous irrelevancy she saw below.

Several years later she was able to explain her philosophy more clearly than when she had been in the direct line of fire during her time in Congress. "It is dangerous to enter the struggle to establish a civil society as a purist if, as a purist, you are unwilling to take in others and be flexible," she said. "You can have principles that are at the core of your position: we don't kill, we don't maim, we respect the dignity of the individual, and it is essential that we hate bigotry and intolerance. And on these principles I certainly advocate the purist position. But there are times when you must get off the purist position if you are going to come to a consensus or resolution of the issues. You cannot change the minds of even good men and women overnight—at least not on every issue. If you respect differences, you will also respect the ability of other thoughtful people to struggle internally with a problem and come to an answer that is somewhat different than your own."[31]

Meg Greenfield, writing in *Newsweek*, believed that Jordan was up to something far more complicated than mere political ladder-climbing.

> For a while ambition for any statewide or national office would require that she reach out beyond a minority constituency. The consistency of her record and the consistency of certain themes in her conversations suggest that her personal impulse has always been to enlarge the context of the civil rights and poverty battles she was fighting, and to make her own experience of hardship and injustice the basis of a more inclusionary, generous politics. The evidence is lying all around: in her concentration both in the Texas Legislature and in Congress on programs . . . whose benefits would cut across racial and sexual lines; in her flat-out rejection of the narrower, more vindictive and/or special pleading aspects of the black and women's movement; and in her insistence that those

minority causes for which she fights are only part of a larger and more generally applicable "people issue."[32]

Because Jordan had made the deals to climb the political ladder—and she clearly saw the Connally testimony in that light—she felt she was only developing the presence and power to take on causes that really mattered.

CHAPTER 15

THE VOTING RIGHTS ACT OF 1975

DURING THE SPRING of 1975, even when she was embroiled in the Connally testimony, Barbara Jordan was also at the center of congressional efforts to extend the Voting Rights Act. She had become the most prominent and powerful black member of Congress. Because of her close ties with Texas conservatives and other southern Democrats, she could probably influence as many as forty to fifty votes on a piece of legislation important to her. No other black member of Congress had that span of influence, and other than the Speaker or the minority leader, few white members had it either.

Jordan felt that the Voting Rights Act of 1965 was the most important—and effective—piece of civil rights legislation ever passed because it opened the doors for millions of southern blacks to participate in the American system. But the act would end August 7, 1975, unless Congress extended it. For Jordan, the right to vote was *the* paramount civil right. From this one right could come the political opportunity to acquire decent jobs and income, education, health care, housing, and the other goods people needed to live without systemic humiliation or private misery.

While the notion of exactly what constituted a civil right sometimes got lost in the movements, marches, struggles, shouts, and litigation, Jordan's penetrating mind always went straight to the heart of the concept of rights. A civil right, to her, simply meant having the freedom to carry out the ordinary activities of private or public life and enjoy the benefits of society. She believed that certain rights were "fundamental."

"The addition of 'fundamental' adds something . . . it is not surplus verbiage . . . it enhances the concept of right exponentially. . . ."[1] In Jordan's mind, civil rights were "entitlements" of citizenship. Citizenship depended on an unfettered right to vote, and to have one's vote count in a way that one could be represented. Jordan had always believed that if "her people" had full access to this right, they could make the *political* changes necessary to secure other rights and benefits.

President Johnson and the Congress had also recognized that voting rights were fundamental elements of civil rights protection. The 1965 voting rights law had prohibited state or other political jurisdictions from imposing voting requirements to deny or abridge the right to vote on account of color or race. Designed to end seventy-five years of discrimination against southern blacks, the law gave the attorney general and the Justice Department discretionary power to appoint federal officials as voting "examiners" who made sure that African Americans could register to vote without interference. The Voting Rights Act also abolished literacy tests, which seven southern states still used to keep blacks from voting. The most controversial provision of the law, however, required seven Deep South states to obtain federal approval, or "pre-clearance," of *any* change in law or procedure that might affect the rights of minority voters.[2]

When African Americans in the South had begun to participate in electoral politics in greater numbers as a result of the civil rights movement, recalcitrant white officials quickly figured out that they could minimize the impact of large blocs of black voters through structural changes like gerrymandered districts, at-large elections, and the consolidation of voting districts, which could dilute the power of the black vote to influence the outcome of an election.[3]

The pre-clearance section of the Voting Rights Act of 1965 halted many of the most blatant of these practices in the South. Representative Andrew Young's congressional seat in Atlanta was effectively spared by the pre-clearance requirement. After the 1966 elections, in which Young and Barbara Jordan became the first African Americans elected to Congress from the modern South, the Georgia legislature redrew the state's congressional district boundaries, effectively eliminating Young's district and replacing it with one in which the black vote would be so diluted that Young—or any black—would have no hope of winning. Because the new districts had to be submitted to the Justice Department for approval, however, the gerrymandered plan was thrown out and Young's district remained essentially intact.

The Voting Rights Act would expire in August 1975, and it was questionable whether the old civil rights community, with its fragmented leadership, could rally for one more battle for its extension. Many observers felt that the punch was gone from the movement, and that it might be difficult to pass a veto-proof law that would meet Republican president Gerald Ford's approval, or even to pass *anything* through the Senate, where Mississippi's conservative Democratic senator James Eastland was chairman of the Judiciary Committee. Yet if the act expired, the "New South" might revert back to its old ways. While it was unlikely that the most egregious abuses of the old days would be reinstituted, leaders in the civil rights community feared that structural changes could so dilute minority votes that the hard-fought gains of the past ten years would be lost. By 1974, there were approximately 3,200 black elected officials in the nation.[4] But that could change—particularly because a new reapportionment would be mandated after the 1980 census. Federal pre-clearance was the most valuable tool to prevent such structural forms of discrimination and exclusion.

Jordan's legislative aide Bob Alcock and her administrative assistant, Bud Myers, were enmeshed with the key Capitol Hill staffers and civil rights advocates who cared most about the extension of the Voting Rights Act. Alcock, in particular, was plugged into what he called the "Title Sixers," the advocates of applying the nondiscrimination clauses and enforcement powers of Title VI of the 1964 Civil Rights Act to a wide range of federal legislation, from revenue-sharing to law enforcement. The group included members of the staffs of the U.S. Civil Rights Commission, the NAACP Legal Defense Fund, the Mexican American Legal Defense and Education Fund (MALDEF), key executive agencies, and some House and Senate Judiciary Committee staff members. Alcock remembers that they began talking about the upcoming Voting Rights Act extension as early as 1973.

The U.S. Civil Rights Commission had accumulated enough evidence of voter intimidation in the Southwest to conclude that English-language-only election materials had been used as a means to keep Spanish-speaking people from participating in the political process. Its staff was preparing a recommendation that Mexican American voters be included in any extension of the Voting Rights Act. The consensus of the Title Sixers was that the extension was "something Barbara should be interested in," recalled Alcock. They wanted her to bring Texas into the full coverage of the act by adding Texas to the original seven states subject to pre-clearance.

"MALDEF was pushing bilingual ballots, and since my mother had been born in Mexico, I could see the logic of that, but when they talked about covering Texas, at first it was too big a leap for me," Alcock said. President Lyndon Johnson had deliberately not included Texas in the original legislation to placate his own political friends in the state. Now the Title Sixers wanted Barbara Jordan to do what Johnson had been unwilling to tackle. They left it up to Alcock to persuade her.

Alcock, a sandy-headed, affable Californian, had developed a solid working relationship with Jordan during her first session. He was a "heads-down, do-your-work" kind of guy who knew both the workings of the Hill and the peculiarities of Texas State government. Jordan hired him to be her chief legislative aide shortly into her first session in Congress and would delegate most of the detail work to him and Bud Myers. Jordan had a small staff, as congressional staffs go, but she expected a lot from them.

"We would take her mail and messages over to her, and sit in the Rayburn Room off the floor to go over things with her," Alcock remembered. "She was pretty insistent that everything be organized and in order. She wanted to be informed, and she didn't want surprises." Alcock had helped Jordan organize her research during the Watergate inquiry, and because he was conscientious and good at anticipating what she might need in the way of documentation, she came to trust both his work and his judgment. Extending the Voting Rights Act to Mexican Americans involved a host of legal technicalities, and Alcock said he was not sure he ever mastered it. "But she did," he said of his boss.

"She was intrigued when I laid it out for her," Alcock said. "Barbara initially really didn't understand the pre-clearance process because Texas had not been included in the original bill. Her political life didn't include this concept. So we sat down with her and tried to explain this in real terms so she would understand just how a Texas politician would feel about having to submit these election law changes to the Justice Department. And she didn't have any hesitation once she saw it." When Jordan realized that she might be able to end the practice of gerrymandering and at-large districts that had prevented her own entry into politics thirteen years earlier, she enthusiastically agreed to sponsor a bill that would bring Texas under the act. It would extend greater protection to black voters, "her people," but she wanted to be sure Mexican American voters would be included, too. She sent Alcock off to work out a formula to include Mexican Americans in the Southwest without a blanket coverage of all the southwestern states, which she thought would endanger passage of the bill.

The formula Alcock and the Title Sixers, along with U.S. Census Department officials, worked out for her was based on a mix of the relative percentages of low voter turnout and large concentrations of non-English-speaking voters. In any given area, a voter turnout rate below 50 percent and a 5 percent concentration of non-English-speaking voters would trigger the pre-clearance sections of the Voting Rights Act and mandate the use of bilingual ballots. The key legal justification for requiring bilingual ballots would be to establish that English-only ballots were in the same category as literacy tests.

Two issues had to be resolved: finding a legally acceptable term to describe Mexican American voters, and determining the exact trigger mechanism. The Fifteenth Amendment language protecting the voting rights of African Americans was based on "race, color, or previous condition of servitude." The logical constitutional question that had to be considered was: Do Mexican Americans, Cuban Americans, Puerto Rican Americans, constitute a race or color? As she always did, Jordan dug deeply into the constitutional issues. She came to the conclusion that Fifteenth Amendment protection "is not limited to blacks. *Any* denial of voting rights, on the ground of race or color, would contravene the Fifteenth Amendment."[5]

Jordan contended that because the phrase "race or color" did not have a precise, generally accepted meaning, it could be applied in a general way to Spanish-language voters. She produced a memo from the Justice Department stating that antidiscrimination laws were already being enforced as if "race or color" did in fact apply to Mexican Americans.

Another issue was whether *language* was the primary form of discrimination faced by Mexican Americans. Jordan said: "Probably not, but it *is* characteristic of the myriad of problems Mexican Americans face. Just as the Congress seized upon literacy tests as *characteristic* of the voting problems facing blacks in the South, so too are English-only ballots among a substantial Spanish-speaking population. Printing of Spanish registration forms and Spanish ballots will not cure voting discrimination in the Southwest . . . but I can think of no clearer alternative criterion which is both characteristic of Mexican American voting problems and provides clearer direction to the executive than the employment of an English-only ballot." Jordan's bill used the Census Bureau's legal term "mother tongue" to define those who would be covered under her bill, which called for the use of bilingual ballots when at least 5 percent of the population of a jurisdiction spoke a "mother tongue" other than English.

When Jordan presented her bill to the Subcommittee on Civil and Constitutional Rights, she used an exhibit Bob Alcock had prepared showing the proposed newly covered jurisdictions colored in pink on a U.S. map. All of Texas was included, as were counties with a heavy concentration of Mexican Americans in New Mexico, Arizona, Florida, and California. The surprises on the map—even to Jordan—were the pink-colored counties in Maine, Massachusetts, New Hampshire, Pennsylvania, and Vermont. Alcock's non-English "mother tongue" census categories, in combination with the low-voter-turnout criterion, had picked up German, Amish, and French ethnic communities that had *never* been discriminated against. Jordan was appalled and told committee members she would happily change her formula if they could come up with a better one. After the hearing, she admonished Alcock. "You've got me in a hole, Bob. Now go back and find a better trigger!"

Judiciary chairman Peter Rodino and the subcommittee chairman, Don Edwards, had introduced a simple extension of the bill for ten years. Some members, like Massachusetts representative Robert F. Drinan, wanted to add general election reforms and national voter registration procedures to the Voting Rights Act, but there was sentiment on the committee and within the civil rights community against turning the bill into a "Judiciary Christmas tree" by hanging every conceivable reform on the bill. There was even opposition among older African American civil rights leaders against extending protections to Mexican Americans. "It's not that the civil rights leaders don't want brown people, Mexican American people, included," Jordan explained. "They just don't want to jeopardize the possible extension of the act by an effort to expand it."[6]

Although Andrew Young favored inclusion of Mexican Americans in the bill, he wanted to keep general election and voter registration reform out of the extension arguments. Dr. Aaron Henry, president of the Mississippi State Conference of the NAACP and national lobbyist for the NAACP Leadership Conference on Civil Rights, did not want anything but a simple extension of the act. "I do not want to lose. I do not want to give anybody an excuse to vote against what we have got now under the ruse of trying to extend it. . . . If we have the votes for it, I am completely supportive of that idea. But I do not want to amend the act to perfection and then lose the whole thing."[7]

Barbara Jordan, with Bob Alcock at her side, outlined and explained her bill at the subcommittee hearings. "I know firsthand the difficulty minorities have in participating in the political process as equals. The same discriminatory practices which moved the Congress to pass the Voting Rights Act in 1965, and renew it in 1970, are practiced in Texas today."[8]

M. Caldwell Butler from Virginia, the leader of Republican efforts to block the extension, commented somewhat facetiously to her in the hearing that "if voting rights could have been protected four years earlier in Texas, by this time you would probably be President of the United States."[9]

When the subcommittee began its markup of the bill, the basic extension of the act for ten years was included in a separate Title I, which also permanently outlawed literacy tests. Jordan, along with two Hispanic members of Congress, Edward Roybal of Los Angeles and Herman Badillo of New York, and their staffs then sat down to work on sections of the bill that dealt with expansion of coverage to foreign-language-speaking minorities. They defined Spanish-language voters as persons of "Spanish heritage" and kept Jordan's 5 percent minority population trigger to require bilingual ballots for specific language minorities. Then they included American Indians, Asian Americans, and Alaskan natives in the bill. They added the preclearance requirement for the state of Texas and for certain counties in other states, and redefined English-only ballots and election materials in affected jurisdictions as a "test and device" that resulted in discrimination. "In its simplest form . . . my bill amends the definition of the phrase 'test or device' to make explicit the rulings of federal courts that the failure to provide bilingual registration forms and ballots constitutes the use of a literacy test," Jordan said.[10]

In the meantime, Jordan's actions were setting off a political furor among politicians in Texas who vehemently opposed Texas's inclusion in the federal law. The Texas legislature was so fearful of the possibility of having to pre-clear all of its voting and election laws with the Justice Department that it hastily passed its own bilingual ballot bill in the hope of forestalling inclusion in the bill. But the full House Judiciary Committee made no changes in Jordan's consensus subcommittee bill and reported it out on May 8. The committee's report to the House filled more than thirteen hundred printed pages with detailed evidence of discrimination against Mexican American voters to justify their inclusion in the act. The full House debate began on June 2, with Representative Edwards managing the bill and Caldwell Butler orchestrating the opposition. Jordan took up her customary place on the House floor to line up key votes to fight off seventeen crippling amendments, including one to remove Texas from the bill altogether. Ironically, it was proposed by the first Hispanic member of Congress from Texas, Democrat Henry B. Gonzalez of San Antonio.

"Henry B."—as he was often affectionately called—had been the first Mexican American in almost as many settings as Barbara Jordan had been the first African American. He was incensed that he had not been included in any of the deliberations about the inclusion of Mexican American voters in the bill. He bitterly resented Jordan's intrusion into his business—which he considered to be *anything* that had to do with Mexican American politics or power. Gonzalez had also been at war with the Mexican American Legal Defense and Education Fund over some local turf battles, and he was furious because Jordan had worked with MALDEF, which had submitted an annexation decision on San Antonio as a prime example of Mexican American vote dilution. He called the subcommittee's report, with the MALDEF exhibits, a "lie" and "an outright mendacious fabrication of the truth" about San Antonio.[11] He spoke angrily in defense of his amendment to drop Texas from the bill.[12] The debate degenerated when Gonzalez and Roybal got into a shouting match about the reality of discrimination against Mexican American voters. By this time, however, the voting rights extension had the full backing of the civil rights community, the Congressional Black Caucus, the Democratic leadership in Congress, a host of moderate Republicans, and Mexican American activists in the Southwest—minus Henry B. Gonzalez, whose amendment failed on a division vote. The House overwhelmingly passed the full bill on June 3 by a 341–70 vote. Jordan had persuaded two-thirds of the Texas delegation to vote with her on a bill that would subject Texas to the same federal oversight as the states of the Deep South. It was a remarkable feat considering the opposition to the measure at home. Gonzalez was recorded as present and not voting, still mad as a hornet at Jordan and his Hispanic colleagues in Congress.

The bill had a more difficult time in the Senate, however, because Mississippi senator Eastland refused to call a hearing of the Judiciary Committee. It took a cloture motion by Senate Democratic leaders Mike Mansfield and Barbara's new friend, Senator Robert C. Byrd, to call up the bill, and they still had to fight off a filibuster attempt by invoking another cloture vote to limit debate. Senator Byrd put together the compromise to get Senate passage, and President Ford signed the bill on August 6, 1975, one day before it would have expired. It was ten years to the day that Lyndon Johnson signed the first version of the landmark Civil Rights Act.

Jordan was so happy at the bill-signing ceremony that she asked President Ford to give her the big index cards from which he read his remarks before signing the bill. She wanted him to autograph them, too. Ford gave her the cards with his signature. She said that although she was not much of a collector, "this is my first big legislative victory and I wanted a memento."[13] She was also savoring her victory over the president. Gerald Ford had tried to stop the bill in the Senate, and Jordan took great delight in hearing him read from his cue cards "about how he had worked for its successful passage."

Jordan operated at her highest level during the Voting Rights Act deliberations. She did her research, spoke with eloquence, hammered out the details of the deal, made the necessary compromises, recognized the political consequences of carrying a good idea too far, bucked the politicians in her own state, and used her influence with House conservatives to get them to vote for something they would have normally voted against. It didn't hurt that she had made a friend earlier in the year with the Senate's second most powerful man, Robert Byrd, who was responsible for shaking the bill loose in the Senate.

Jordan was busy on several other legislative fronts during 1975. She sponsored and passed in July a consumer protection measure eliminating the practice of price-fixing among manufacturers of consumer goods, saving consumers an estimated $3 billion in excess payments. Judiciary Committee chairman Peter Rodino assigned her the responsibility of managing the floor debate on the bill, which she thoroughly enjoyed.[14] House Democratic leaders recognized both her abilities and her appeal and began to involve her in some of their deliberations. Jordan's influence on the ten-member Democratic Steering and Policy Committee had secured a second "black" seat on the powerful House Ways and Means Committee, which went to new Caucus member Harold Ford of Tennessee.

Jordan was also active in the Judiciary Committee's efforts to curb abuses by the federal intelligence agencies, both foreign and domestic. She was particularly interested in the issue because she had been the target of the U.S. Army's domestic intelligence program in the 1960s. The army maintained more than one hundred thousand files on citizens not connected with the armed forces. Barbara Jordan was one of them. She had not reacted publicly at the time, but when Congress took up the matter she was personally interested in making sure the practice had ended. In a newsletter to her constituents she wrote, "I reject the hypothesis that our civil liberties may be either strictly observed or blatantly ignored depending upon the whim of government officials."[15]

Although Jordan had refused to become involved in the internal struggles to build a women's political movement, or in the competitions between various feminist leaders and organizations to lead it, her beliefs about the need for equal protection under the law for women had now become clear in her own mind, and she did not hesitate to articulate them. She revived her bill to provide Social Security benefits for homemakers, this time cosponsoring the measure with Yvonne Burke. She gave speeches around the nation to help boost passage of the Equal Rights Amendment, which needed approval by four more states to become part of the Constitution. She told the Hollywood Chapter of Media Women that "this simple act of justice will not become a reality unless the myths and emotionalism being generated in debate on the amendment are exposed for what they are."[16]

Despite the periodic carping about her from a few members of the Congressional Black Caucus, Jordan was still the most sought-after African American speaker in the nation. She had started giving weekly television commentaries on *The CBS Morning News Show,* talking about everything in her one-minute segments from civil rights and democracy to the Public Disclosure Lobbying Act of 1975. Congressional Black Caucus members themselves wanted her to visit their home districts because she was such a tremendous draw. She made appearances at political fund-raisers for Representatives Ron Dellums and Yvonne Burke in California. Her Texas colleague Charlie Wilson believed that by 1975 she had become one of the most influential members of Congress. "I mean, if you're talking about the one person who is able to get to just anybody, I don't care who it is, and make them stop and listen to what she has to say and convince them that she's right, then you're talking about Barbara. . . . That's what *influence* is—persuading others to do what you want. . . . Along with all her superior intelligence and legislative skill she also has a certain *moral authority* and . . . presence, and it all comes together in a way that sort of grabs you. Maybe you're kind of intimidated by it, and you have to listen when she speaks and you feel you must try and do what she wants. What Barbara has is not something you learn and develop, it's something that God gave her and it's something you can't really describe."[17]

In 1975 Jordan was constantly being reminded of how important she had become. When U.S. Supreme Court justice William O. Douglas resigned, Texas senator Lloyd Bentsen suggested that Jordan be appointed to fill his seat on the Court. She was flattered by the gesture, particularly coming from the patrician Bentsen, the courteous, sophisticated voice of the Texas conservative political establishment. She had no illusions, however, about the prospects of such an appointment. After all, Gerald Ford was president, and she had voted against his vice presidential appointment in 1973. She was even more sanguine when people suggested her for the U.S. Senate seat in Texas held by Republican John Tower. With an arch of her eyebrows and an expression of mocking self-deprecation, she would laugh, "A black woman . . . winning statewide in Texas? You must be joking!"[18]

That same year Jordan began incorporating into her speeches some of the ideas that had gestated during her Watergate experience. New themes began to emerge: patriotism, ethics, human dignity—and an almost relentless criticism of the narrowness and selfishness she believed President Ford and the Republican Party embodied. Notwithstanding her liberal critics, Jordan had begun to articulate the essence of Democratic Party liberalism: a compassionate, activist government; a belief in the rule of law; a commitment to honest public service; and a respect for human dignity. She spelled it out in a California speech in October:

> *The human condition must be improved and government must help improve it. . . . Government is here not just to build roads and bridges. . . . Government is our appointed mediator, prosecutor, defender—our means of guaranteeing our freedoms and protecting our frailties. It is people, not things, that make this country great. It is the capacity for human kindness and compassion that gives depth and meaning to life in America. . . .*
>
> *It is our task to impress upon our leaders that people are the stuff of America; that simple human dignity is more important than tax-free bonds, exempt dividends on preferred stock, or larger investment tax credits. Compassion for the sick, the poor, the elderly is not anathema to the efficient functioning of a democratic government. . . . The Republic has weathered a constitutional storm, and our institutions have survived. Can we weather the economic, social, and political storms ahead? . . . The House of America must be put in order. . . . We must believe that human values are worth fighting for. . . . The wounds in the body politic can be administered to only by men and women of good conscience.*
>
> *I am a patriot. I believe that the world community does better when America leads from a position of strength and confidence. I believe that the people of America live better when Democrats occupy the seats of power. We are not frightened by big government. We use it as the paramount instrumentality to get things done for people.*
>
> *The people of America must send a message to Washington. The message should begin: "To the President and the members of the Congress of the United States: We recognize that you are mortal and ordinary men and women. However, we, the people of the United States, have entrusted to you our freedoms. Take care of them. We expect you to be honest in all you do. Tell the truth; don't lie; do justly; be fair; know the difference between right and wrong; and do what is right. Settle your disputes peacefully; adhere to the law as the great citizen-protector. Do this, Mr. President, Ladies and Gentlemen of the Congress, and a monument will be erected to you which no room can contain."[19]*

Jordan's reputation was soaring, and her congressional career was in high gear. But it was also beginning to take its toll. She was larger than she had ever been in her life. She wore a 24½ dress size and weighed almost 250 pounds. She was still going home to Houston every other weekend. She was smoking too much, and the Washington heat and humidity during the summer of 1975 had made her miserable. She kept the air-conditioning thermostat so low in her Longworth Building office that some of her staffers had to wear coats.

Once again she was putting in fourteen- and sixteen-hour days at the Capitol and returning home at night to her apartment, exhausted and alone. One evening her right eye was irritated and watery and the right side of her face was tingling. She was stunned when she looked into the mirror. The whole side of her face looked like it had dropped. When she tried to smile, the right corner of her mouth did not move. She was frightened and rushed in to see her neurologist at Bethesda the next day. He confirmed for her what she most feared. Her multiple sclerosis had returned—this time involving her main facial nerve, causing paralysis of the right side of her face. She began another regimen of steroid drug treatments, and the numbness and paralysis went away. But the realization of the random—and now certain—nature of her disease struck her like a blow to the heart.

This was Jordan's second major multiple sclerosis attack. As happens with many people with MS, this was when the deadening reality of the illness sank in. If she followed the pattern of most multiple sclerosis patients, the second attack would bring on shock, anger, and depression, until a sort of grudging acceptance could emerge. Jordan's multiple sclerosis had been diagnosed as chronic-progressive: after the second attack, she would probably not have long periods of remission between episodes. Her immune system's attacks on the myelin sheaths that carried nerve impulses to muscles would become fairly constant, but no one could tell her just where, or when, or how severely, they would strike. Her legs, her feet, her hands, and now her face had been affected. What would be next?

For the first time since her multiple sclerosis had been diagnosed, Jordan realized that she might need to make some adjustments in her life. She had to deal with her weight. She had to deal with the fatigue from her long hours and the daily grind of congressional life. And indeed, the recurrence of multiple sclerosis had shaken her. She seemed to have no control over the direction of her life. That was just plain unacceptable, however, to Barbara Jordan. Something had to change.

HOME

Barbara Jordan was notoriously tight with her money. So much so that it became a joke with her family and friends. "My family says that I am very stingy," she wrote in *Self-Portrait*. Jordan had learned to love handling a wad of dollar bills after being around her Grandpa Patten, who always had cash from his junk business. A roll of bills was tactile, physical, and real. "When I first started to earn money I used to carry around large sums of cash," she said. "I would carry hundred-dollar bills in my billfold. Did I spend it? No. I would just open my billfold from time to time and look at it." Money to Barbara meant freedom and independence. As a young girl, it represented the freedom to buy what she wanted—meat or a movie ticket; but most importantly, it meant a degree of independence from the control of her father.

When she was older, the motivation may have been more abstract, but the relationship for her between money and independence was just as strong. As a result, Jordan hoarded her money and only reluctantly parted with it when she needed to buy a car or the few basic suits she needed for work or to pay the $500 rent on her Washington apartment, which was furnished quite sparsely. Like her father, she was determined to pay cash for everything. She didn't want to be in debt to anyone or any institution. Because she lived inexpensively and had no financial obligations, Jordan had been able to accumulate a sizable savings account over the years—close to $100,000 by the end of 1975. Her congressional salary was just under $55,000 a year, and she collected an additional $12,000 to $15,000 each year in honoraria for many of her speeches, which brought her from $500 to $2,000 each.[20] She also received several thousand dollars each year from some old law cases and legal referrals. Her total annual income while she was in Congress averaged about $80,000 a year. The money, and the security it represented, was enormously important to her.

At the end of 1975, an exhausted, overweight, and sick Barbara Jordan finally decided to part with some of her money. When her friend Nancy Earl said she was going to buy five acres along Onion Creek on the southern edge of Austin, Barbara decided it was time she owned something substantial, too. So she joined with Nancy to buy the land, and Nancy spent the following year building a home on the property, which contained huge cypress trees, spreading oaks, and a mile-long view over open land to the creek bed, woods, and purple hills in the distance.

Nancy Earl was Barbara Jordan's polar opposite. Slender and blond with streaks of gray highlighting her softly styled short hair, she had the ruddy complexion of one who loved an outdoor life. Nancy bought her clothes from L.L. Bean catalogs, she hiked and swam, and she knew the names of birds and trees. Two years older than Barbara, Nancy had grown up in the rolling hills outside of Pittsburgh and was a graduate of a small college in upstate New York. Later she received a graduate degree in educational psychology from Indiana University. Nancy had moved to Texas in 1959 to work in the Measurement and Evaluation Center at the University of Texas, which handled academic and psychological testing for students.

Nancy had become active in the YWCA, and in a number of other "do-gooder" organizations. When Nancy and Barbara met during Barbara's last term in the Texas Senate, they had immediately hit it off. Like Barbara, Nancy had grown up in a musical family. She loved to sing, and her brother Jerry, who had followed her to Austin, was a popular pianist who entertained at many of Austin's finest social events.

Nancy was well-read and good with words, although she was extremely modest about her talents and accomplishments. But most importantly, she was not in awe of Barbara. She neither fawned nor hovered over her, and this was a respite for the congresswoman. When Nancy was around, Barbara felt no pressure to perform, to be profound or wise. She could just *be*—grumpy or sarcastic, silent, silly, or serious—or she could stretch out on a sofa and read. It did not matter. Nancy might be amused, angry, or indifferent to her antics, but she had few expectations. While Barbara loved being the center of attention, there were times when it was a burden. She had been spoiled by her family, even while Ben Jordan was alive. After his death, Rose Mary, Bennie, and particularly Arlyne doted on Barbara. They waited on her when she was at home in Houston, and they made her life the center of their own. In return, they expected her to reward them with tales of her adventures and political conquests. Nancy did not do that. She had her own life, and Barbara's stories were . . . just stories! The *equality* inherent in such a friendship resonated with a maturing Barbara, and she came to rely on Nancy's friendship to bring some balance and diversity, even quietude, to her own life.

After Barbara had been elected to Congress in 1972, Nancy moved back to upstate New York to counsel students at her alma mater, Keuka College. On weekends, she occasionally flew down to Washington to see Barbara. Nancy was a good writer, and when Barbara began making speeches more frequently all across the country, Nancy would help her flesh out her ideas and give her the language or key phrases that Barbara's voice would bring to life. After Watergate, when Barbara was in such demand to make speeches around the country, Nancy actually took on specific speech-writing assignments, earning the gratitude of Barbara's overworked legislative aide Bob Alcock, who was also drafting speeches.

Nancy did not enjoy living in New York in the 1970s the way she had as a college student twenty years earlier. She had forgotten about the severe winters in upstate New York, and after two seasons of snow and bitter cold she realized that she wanted to go back to Texas. She had come to love the rural atmosphere of the Onion Creek area, where she had rented a house before. When she found out that one of her former neighbors wanted to sell some of her land, Nancy decided to take her savings to buy a portion of it—almost five acres. When she discussed her plans with Barbara, she was surprised that Barbara suggested they buy the land jointly. "Look, I don't own any real property, and I would like to," Barbara said. "Why don't I go halves with you, and then I'll have a place to come to on the weekend." The land purchase represented a major shift in Jordan's thinking, and she agonized about it in a way she rarely did when making an important decision. "I guess I thought about that, and turned it over in my mind, for a month before I ever did it. It was a large expenditure. But ultimately I enjoyed spending the money on that, because then I could walk around those acres and say: 'This is mine.' I had to get it firmly fixed in my mind just what the dimensions of that property were."

Barbara's family also agonized over her purchase of the land in Austin. "My mother and family could not get ready for my becoming a co-owner of a house," Barbara wrote in *Self-Portrait*. Arlyne told her, "If you want a place, why don't you go out and find a place in Houston that's yours?" Barbara tried to explain that she wanted to get away from the demands of her constituents in Houston, and that this would be a retreat for her, a place where she could read and rest. "I tried to tell them the advantages of being out and away, of having someone who would be there all the time to see that the place didn't deteriorate while I was in the Congress. I explained that I would be one-half owner, which means they would certainly be free to come."

Barbara's family was still skeptical. For years her closest friends and her most intimate associations had been within the family, the Good Hope Missionary Baptist Church, and the Fifth Ward. They were worried that Barbara might be drifting away. Her Washington life was distant and unknown to them, and her experiences in Congress—particularly after Watergate—were hard for them to imagine. Barbara had kept the details of her illness from them, and they were unaware that it was going to require her to make some changes in how she lived. But they recognized her determination to do what she wanted. And she wanted a home of her own on the banks of Onion Creek outside of Austin. Nancy Earl was in charge of seeing that she got it.

Nancy hired an architect and began design work on the house, which would not be completed until the summer of 1976. The house would become a reflection of Nancy—open, tasteful, simple, with off-white walls complemented by rough-hewn cedar paneling and a native fieldstone fireplace. Natural wood doors and woodwork would give the place a warm contemporary look. The exterior of the house would be a mix of native fieldstone and cedar with a metal roof, a Texas hill country home in harmony with its surroundings. Nancy had the architect situate the house down a slope from the gravel road at the front end of the property, and she designed stone-terraced steps from the driveway to the house. The drop in elevation from the road to the creek was several hundred feet and the house was set about halfway from the road to the cypress trees on the creek bank.

A huge one-hundred-year-old oak tree spread in front of the house, its massive fifty- to sixty-foot branches bending to the ground. A narrow, rarely used one-lane road that led to the house was shaded under an archway of trees that gave it the feeling of an open-air tunnel, allowing glimpses of deer, rabbits, horses, or a Charlois bull in adjacent fields. The house was isolated and private and would be difficult to find without explicit directions—just the way Barbara wanted it.

Nancy wanted all of the windows across the back of the house to be uncluttered by drapes in order to enjoy the panoramic view down the sloping yard to the woods and creek. But Barbara would have none of it. Her one significant contribution to the house was to insist that her own bedroom have some window covering. She had lived so long in the city that the openness of a country view was disconcerting. So Nancy had vertical blinds installed in Barbara's room. But once she had moved in, Barbara, too, relaxed in the country atmosphere, and she never closed them. Nancy's bedroom and a small sitting room were on the east side of the house, with a large living and dining area separating it from Barbara's west side of the house. Floor-to-ceiling glass windows and sliding glass doors from the living area opened onto a covered porch that extended all across the back of the house. A thirty-five-foot-high hackberry tree shaded the ground around the porch. When finished, the house would indeed provide the refuge Barbara felt she needed. It was peaceful, quiet, and nourishing in its harmony with the natural world around it. Although it was Nancy's in vision and spirit, Barbara's commitment of her precious money to half-ownership made her feel like it was entirely her own.

Nancy Earl was one of the few people who knew about Barbara's illness. Despite her friend's early, apparent indifference, Nancy had begun to read everything she could find on multiple sclerosis. At the time there was a theory that a gluten-free diet might help, and so Nancy had encouraged Barbara to change her eating patterns. In late 1975, with Nancy spurring her on, Barbara decided to lose weight. She set some goals, a yearlong timetable to lose one hundred pounds, and Nancy made a chart so Barbara could plot her progress every day. For the first time in her life, Barbara began to pay attention to her eating habits, and she was relieved to figure out that "you don't necessarily have to stop eating for all time. You just have to eat differently. You stop running in for little midnight snacks, and you stop going to those cocktail parties and eating hors d'oeuvres and then coming home to eat a big dinner." When she began to eat regularly and sensibly, she saw some results. Each week she would be a few pounds lighter, and she would happily record her weight loss on the chart. By December 1975, she was beginning to feel a little better.

The decisions to lose weight and to buy a house had given her a sense once more that she could chart her own destiny, which had been threatened when she finally confronted the seriousness of her multiple sclerosis.

* * *

For all of the shifts in thought and action, however, that she had embraced in 1975, Barbara was still firmly anchored in the Good Hope Missionary Baptist Church and the Fifth Ward of Houston, Texas. It was evident shortly before Christmas, when Jordan's fellow church members honored her with a lavish banquet to which they also invited the public, and particularly "the poor, the lame, the outcast," whom Barbara Jordan served.

Good Hope's new pastor, Reverend Crawford W. Kimble, paid a tribute to Jordan that reflected the pride church members felt to be part of her life. Reverend Kimble spoke with the rhythm and eloquence associated with the preaching tradition of his church when he said of his most famous church member:

> *Wait a minute, World! We have a claim, too. We claimed her first. We claimed her when she was one among many tiny tots cutting her teeth on Baptist pews. World, we claimed her when you would suppress her, deny her, enslave her. . . . And listen, World, we don't claim her because she is famous . . . We claim her because she is family . . . sure enough, blood, born-again kinfolk. . . . And so we have come not so much to pay tribute to one of the most famous women in these United States . . . But we have come to this appointed place to lay claim on a Christian woman. . . . Our claim is kingdom-founded, and our claim is eternal! And here we are before a watching world . . . to claim her . . . not to hoard . . . not to possess, but to share. We share her because she is not ours to keep . . . she is ours to give.*[21]

When Barbara went to the podium to respond, more than five hundred guests gave her a standing ovation. With Arlyne beaming, Barbara told her fellow church members that of the many honors she had received, this was the "closest" to her heart. As her sisters, old friends, and "her people" looked up to her, she told them that she had always tried to follow an injunction in the book of Micah: "He hath showed thee, O man, what is good; and what doth Jehovah require of thee, but to do justly, and to love kindness, and to walk humbly with thy God."[22] And in their eyes, that was exactly what she was doing.

CHAPTER 16

DEMOCRATS

THE NEW YEAR began with good news. On January 13, 1976, the Gallup poll released its list of the twenty women most admired by the American people. Barbara Jordan ranked fourth.

Respondents in the annual survey chose from a list of eighty-six names submitted by the Gallup pollsters. Ahead of Jordan was the president's wife, Betty Ford, who was first in the poll. Rose Kennedy ranked second, followed by President Ford's chief of protocol, Shirley Temple Black. Behind Jordan in fifth place was the former Israeli prime minister Golda Meir. Jacqueline Kennedy Onassis ranked tenth, and Queen Elizabeth II was twentieth on the list.[1]

Another honor came Jordan's way in February when *U.S. News & World Report* named her one of eight "young builders of America who have made their mark."[2] With these honors and dozens of others, Jordan had every reason to feel good about her career. And because of her weight loss, she was even getting compliments on her appearance. But the weight loss worried her mother. Arlyne thought she was beginning to look like a scarecrow. "People will think you're sick," Arlyne told her. Jordan was pleased with her looks, however, and complained that her mother "can't get a handle on it. I think that's a black thing, looking big and healthy. She simply can't understand it."

Yet all was not well—either with her health or with her feelings about the Congress. The long hours and high stress contributed to the fatigue she had felt throughout 1975, and the fatigue might have contributed to the quick succession of multiple sclerosis attacks that year, each one leaving her slightly more debilitated than before. The numbness in her feet had become permanent, and a "foot drop" sometimes caused her to stumble or trip. The repeated interruptions in brain impulses and signals through the multiple sclerosis–damaged myelin sheaths that connected her nerves had already begun to weaken both legs. Because the muscles were getting weak, they became tight and caused a jerkiness in her walking motion. Also, she had periods when she was unsure of her balance. Jordan resisted using a cane; instead, she felt she could control her movements by concentration and focus. The long walks between her office in the Longworth Building and the Capitol, however, were becoming increasingly difficult. It required enormous concentration to put one foot in front of the other without stumbling. As a result, she rarely smiled or spoke to anyone she saw, keeping her eyes either straight forward or even downcast to discourage greetings or conversation.

Her grim manner on those walks, brought on by her fear of falling, began to reinforce her reputation for being aloof and distant. Some House members and Hill staffers complained about her snobbery or arrogance because of her unwillingness to stop and chat while going to or from her office and the House chamber. When this criticism showed up early in 1976 in newspaper stories, she was hurt. Her solution was to get Bud Myers to drive her the few hundred yards from her office to the Capitol. He would pick her up at the Longworth Building's basement service entrance and drive her across the street to the lower-level entrance under the steps on the east side of the Capitol, where she had to climb eight steps and walk a short distance to an elevator that would take her to the House chamber. By now she had a noticeable limp, and when some of her colleagues asked her about it, she would either joke about her "bum knee" or stare them down in icy silence. She was determined to keep the illness secret, even at the risk of being misunderstood. She did not want pity or sympathy. She did not seek to be "understood" or admired for being sick. She felt her disability was nobody's business, and she intended to keep it that way. "I don't want to become the poster child for the Multiple Sclerosis Society," she told her friend Nancy Earl.

By early spring Jordan felt that she might be in the wrong business. For the first time there was a rip in the web of her enchantment with political life. It was becoming clear to her that the programs and policies she cared most about had little chance of success because of President Gerald Ford's ready use of his veto power. She worried most about the escalating unemployment rates in 1976. Twenty percent of all young men under age twenty-five did not have jobs. Forty percent of young black men were unemployed. She was seeing the effect on her own community. Although people in the Fifth Ward had always been poor, now there seemed to be a growing desperation. No jobs meant no hope, and that was an ominous sign for "her people." Jordan supported the package that liberals in Congress had put together for a $3.7 billion public works program to create three hundred thousand new jobs. It had enough Republican support to pass both the

House and Senate, but Ford vetoed the bill. He also vetoed a bill to provide federal funding for day care for children. Jordan's own cosponsorship of a bill creating a new consumer protection agency was blocked by the president's veto threat, even though it had passed. Ultimately, Ford vetoed twenty bills before the session ended, and Congress was able to override his veto only four times. Jordan was so dispirited by these events that she admitted to a reporter, "Some days I just don't feel there's any use going to work because it appears futile. Those are the days when Ford—a most unimaginative leader, by the way—vetoes a big public jobs bill. You think, why should I bother going to work? All it takes to set policy in this country is a President and one more member than a third of Congress. That makes it impossible to override his veto. You think of all those people in Boston, Detroit and New York struggling to survive and what one of those jobs would have meant to them. You relate all of this to them."[3]

Bickering between Congress and the president continued throughout the session. The federal deficit reached a then-record of $66.5 billion, pumped up by double-digit inflation and the nation's deepest postwar recession. The sharp antagonism between Ford and the Democrats blocked almost every solution. Jordan faulted Ford for his failure to exert moral leadership on the issues she felt should be addressed by government, and she believed the gridlock on progressive legislation should not be blamed on Congress, but on the president. "It is the President who must set the moral character of the government. Congress is the voice of the people reacting."[4]

But Jordan was not particularly happy with her Democratic colleagues in Congress either. She felt that the pettiness of members' egos, their pride and hypocrisy, invaded every aspect of congressional operations like a seeping slime. "I admire and respect people who will level with you and tell the truth about things, not fuzz the issue," she said. "I've found only a few people in Congress who are forthcoming about what is political talk and what is real talk. It's more difficult for a politician to put aside that other thing and level with you."[5]

Jordan was also bothered by the newly aggressive behavior of Washington's press corps. Buoyed by the success of uncovering Watergate, reporters adopted a missionary zeal to ferret out the misdeeds of public officials. And, of course, they found them. Journalists uncovered a House payroll-sex scandal that brought down a powerful Democratic leader: Administration Committee chairman Wayne L. Hays of Ohio. Hays's staff aide, Elizabeth Ray, created a national sensation when she told news reporters that she had been hired mainly to perform sexual favors for the congressman. The affair created public demand for congressional reform, but House members could not agree on any of the ethics reform proposals before them.

Although Wayne Hays had been one of those powerful Democratic congressmen whom Jordan had befriended during her first term, she was disgusted by the whole affair. National journalists, fascinated by the "sex for hire" story in Congress, were trying to dig up other juicy stories implicating members of Congress. Jordan's Texas colleague Jim Wright remembered being with Jordan when she was approached by a young woman reporter from the *Washington Post* who had the task of interviewing the sixteen female members of Congress to see whether any had been subjected to amorous approaches by their male colleagues. The reporter caught Jordan just as she was about to enter the House chamber, and she put the question rather bluntly: Had Jordan ever been sexually propositioned by one of her male colleagues? "Barbara pulled herself to full height as she stared at the young journalist in disbelief," Wright said. Finally, "in that full-throated contralto voice . . . she answered the query in one indignant word: AB-SURD! With that, she turned scornfully on her heel and walked through the doors of the House chamber. The girl reporter was left trembling."[6]

Jordan's impatience with Congress was typified for her in June when the House took up debate on Representative Henry Hyde's amendment to prohibit federal funding for abortion. The House and Senate fought almost the entire year over the funding ban, holding up final action on a $56.6 billion appropriations bill for the Departments of Labor and Health, Education, and Welfare. The key vote was in the House on June 24. The Hyde amendment applied primarily to the Medicaid health program for the poor, which paid for almost three hundred thousand abortions a year at a federal cost of about $45 million. Anti-abortion supporters of the funding ban argued that no tax dollars should support a procedure that they considered the equivalent of murder. Pro-choice opponents argued just as vehemently that the amendment would discriminate illegally against the poor, who would be forced to seek unsafe abortions. The House voted 207–167 for the Hyde amendment, ending the federal payments and jeopardizing financial survival for family planning clinics all across the nation. Jordan, for whom a woman's right of "choice" was embodied in a principle of equity under the law, was appalled at the antics of some of her male colleagues during the abortion debate.

"I guess the most disastrous arguments I've ever heard on the floor of the House [were in] that abortion debate," she said. "It was awful . . . the people who got up and sermonized. It was a super mess. We, the sixteen women in the House, were trying to orchestrate the whole thing, and we had these clowns on the floor talking." Jordan was particularly incensed when one male representative stuck a pillow under his suit jacket to simulate pregnancy. "He was ranting around . . . and I couldn't take any more of it. I told one of my female colleagues: 'I'm going to the ladies' lounge and read a book, and if you need me in this debate that's where I'll be.' And I just left."

Representative Pat Schroeder remembers that the atmosphere was so raucous that she, too, left the House floor—in tears! "The men were making jokes about abortion—like 'Did you get your abortion bill? . . . Well, I paid mine.' They were such hypocrites . . . they just didn't take it seriously, and when we complained, they would say things like, 'You'll get over it.'"

This kind of personal, mocking debate over an issue that Jordan considered to be profoundly serious, plus the policy deadlocks with the president and the misplaced aggressiveness of a scandal-sniffing press corps, created an overall atmosphere of surly cynicism that bothered her, as it did others in Congress. By the end of the session more than thirty members announced they would not seek reelection. For the first time Jordan, too, began to think of leaving Congress. While she didn't have anything else specifically in mind, it was a presidential election year, and the Democrats had begun to feel that they had their best shot at winning the presidency since Lyndon Johnson's 1964 victory over Barry Goldwater. Jordan figured there would be other opportunities available if the Democrats won the presidency. One of them, in fact, had already opened for her.

THE 1976 DEMOCRATIC CONVENTION

In late 1975, Robert Strauss had called Jordan to ask her to chair the Democratic Party's rules committee in preparation for the 1976 summer convention. The Democrats tasted victory. Gerald Ford was facing a surprisingly strong challenge within his own party from then–California governor Ronald Reagan. Strauss figured Ford would be badly weakened by the intraparty struggles, and he wanted to make sure the Democrats were united enough to take advantage of the Republican disarray. He needed someone to chair the rules committee who could handle the Democrats' own inevitable intraparty disputes, which might endanger their chance to win the presidency. But Jordan would have none of it.

"Not on your life," she told him. And just as he had done in his conversation with her about John Connally, Strauss urged her to think about it before she made a decision. Jordan didn't have to think about this one. "I'm not going to think about it, Bob," she told him. "It's not anything I'm going to call you back on this time. I'm not going to serve as chairman of the rules committee, and I know that. Can you imagine all those little factions? I'd be bogged down for the duration."

Jordan had served on a party committee early in 1975, and it had been a miserable experience for her. Democrats had set up the Compliance Review Commission to deal with issues of affirmative action within the party. The group had twenty-five members, six of whom were black. The wrangling, nitpicking, and quarreling were interminable. After attending only a few meetings, Jordan resigned in disgust, infuriating several members of the party's Black Caucus, who expected her to be their spokesperson.[7]

After the beginning of the new year, when Strauss began more detailed planning for the summer convention, which would be held in New York, he came to see Jordan in her House office rather than risk a telephone call. This time he asked her to be one of two keynote speakers at the convention. But not *the* keynote speaker, she wrote caustically three years later in *Self-Portrait*. "He did not feel comfortable having me in the limelight alone. There had been pressure from some of his advisers to even things up."

Strauss said he "needed a man and a woman and a black to give the keynote. This had to be a healing convention." After the disastrous and divisive party conventions in 1968 and 1972, Strauss was determined to create party unity. "I went to John Glenn first because he was a national hero, and then I went to Barbara." Strauss told Jordan that the "newness of an astronaut, plus the newness of a black woman," would be an "unbeatable combination." "All right, I'll do that for you," Jordan told him.

All through the spring, a little-known southern governor, Jimmy Carter of Georgia, had been marching through the Democratic primaries, astounding the party professionals with his string of victories. He won all the primaries from February to April, beginning with New Hampshire and continuing in Pennsylvania. By the time the convention convened in July, Carter was so far ahead in the delegate count that he was assured of the nomination. He had even won a hefty majority of the Texas delegates over a slate pledged to support the favorite-son candidacy of Senator Lloyd M. Bentsen Jr.

Jordan had watched the unfolding of the spring primaries with great interest. She was not particularly excited about any of the Democratic contenders and did not endorse anyone—even though she was pressed to do so. Early in the primary season, she specifically declined to endorse the candidacy of Georgia's attractive young African American state senator, Julian Bond, who wanted to put together a coalition of black and liberal delegates to have some leverage in the eventual selection of the party nominee. Jordan was openly disdainful of the effort, describing it as a "quadrennial exercise" of the black community.[8] Georgia's most prominent black officeholder, Andrew Young, did not support Bond's candidacy either. He was solidly in the camp of Jimmy Carter.

By early June, when it was apparent that Jimmy Carter had enough convention votes to secure the Democratic nomination, speculation turned to the vice presidential spot. Carter campaign staffers had circulated a list of fourteen potential candidates for vice president, with Senator Walter Mondale of Minnesota and Senator Edwin Muskie of Maine as the leading contenders, along with Senator Frank Church of Idaho and Congressman Morris Udall of Arizona. Barbara Jordan, too, was on that list. Yet the writer Garry Wills, in an op-ed piece in the *Washington Star*, dismissed her as an "exotic." Wills believed that "an exotic or two always turns up in this kind of speculation, but is rarely chosen—with good reason. Candidates for President do not want to take chances." Wills thought the vice presidential nomination should be an instrument for cutting risks rather than increasing them—unless one is politically suicidal, like Barry Goldwater in 1964. "More important, Carter has regularly won the black vote during the primary season—and the vice-presidency should woo those not already on board."[9]

Jordan did not let herself get caught up in the speculative balloons, or their deflation. By the week before the Democrats were to meet in New York for their convention, Carter had whittled his list of vice presidential prospects to five names, and Jordan was no longer among them. The *ABC News* reporter Sam Donaldson asked Jordan whether she thought Carter had ever been serious about her prospects to begin with.

"Sam, I never thought he was serious about that, if, in fact, Governor Carter had anything to do with my name appearing on that list of fourteen to begin with," she told him. In fact, she told Donaldson, no one from the Carter camp had even said anything to her about it.[10] Yet she bristled noticeably on the ABC Sunday program *Issues and Answers* when the correspondent Bob Clark asked her whether she would *like* to be vice president. "I don't think that is a question I have to answer at all," she said. "Why would I have to deal with something so 'iffy' and ethereal and far-removed?" Clark persisted, however, telling Jordan that his other guest on the morning news show, Governor Wendell Anderson of Minnesota, who was the chairman of the Democrats' Convention Platform Committee, had answered the question. Why wouldn't she?

With a hint of bitter irony in her voice, she told the reporter, "That question might be asked of Governor Anderson. It is not going to be asked of Barbara Jordan, at least not tomorrow or the next day." Ever the political realist, Jordan was irritated by the question. She was black. She was a woman. Why pretend she had a chance to be nominated when she clearly knew she did not, and everyone else knew it, too?[11]

Jordan had been absolutely correct in her analysis. While Carter staffers had put her name on the original list of fourteen vice presidential possibilities, Carter himself took note only of the two black *men* who were on the list: Mayor Thomas Bradley of Los Angeles and Mayor Coleman Young of Detroit. After the convention, when Jesse Jackson complained to Carter that it would have been nice—if only symbolically—to have included a black among the five finalists who came to Plains, Georgia, to be interviewed, Carter was taken aback. Then he admitted that he had decided quite early on that he needed someone "from Washington" on the ticket and that was why he had not included the two black mayors among the final candidates.[12] Carter apparently had hardly noticed that there was a black female member of Congress on his original list. Barbara Jordan had never quite made it into Jimmy Carter's line of vision, and she knew it.

While the vice presidential talk was PR puffery, the keynote address was quite real. Jordan spent a lot of time thinking about what she would say. She told her old Houston friend Jake Johnson that she wanted to do something different from most keynote speeches. "Traditionally, the keynote speaker fires up the faithful, but I just don't think I can do that," she said. "I don't think I'm going to criticize Nixon or Ford, because the country's already gone through too much trauma. We have to heal. We really do have to heal."[13] As part of that healing process, she felt that Democrats had to admit their own mistakes and excesses. She knew she wanted to say something about that in her speech, too.

Since Watergate, Jordan had been thinking about America as a national community, symbolized for her in the motto, *e pluribus unum*—from many, one.[14] She believed that the diverse people of the nation had to be united by a common belief in the tenets of the Constitution, and by the values of liberty and equality. The dissension and partisan bickering in the Congress so strained unity, however, that she believed there had to be a renewal of commitment to the ideal of a national community and to a vision of the American Dream for poor as well as rich, for black as well as white. She believed that Americans had to develop a new consensus about what constituted their common good, and she wanted her keynote address to provoke that consensus. In ruminating over how it might be done, she realized that although her keynote focus would be on the need for a national community, the common good starts at the local level. "You have to first develop a sense of local community which then fans out . . . to a national community," she said.[15]

Jordan was prepared when she went to New York the weekend before the convention was to begin. She had lost more than sixty pounds since she started her diet some nine months earlier. Her new clothes featured softer, pastel colors, including the lime green silk dress she would wear for her speech. She had a limousine at her disposal and a suite of rooms at the Statler Hilton Hotel, across the street from Madison Square Garden. Because she had so much room, she invited her Texas friends Stan McClelland and Nancy Earl, as well as her aide Bud Myers, to stay with her.

"I wanted to take them out to dinner Sunday night, but virtually nothing was open, except the Sign of the Dove. So that is where we went. Barbara had never been there before, and she was excited," McClelland remembers. Jordan asked him to read her speech while they were at dinner. McClelland was not initially impressed. "Quite frankly, it was the night before, and I didn't want to suggest any major changes, but . . . it just wasn't too much. It started off the way she did at the convention, saying that a hundred and some-odd years ago the Democrats met in convention for the first time, and . . . 'what is different is that I, Barbara Jordan, am speaking.' And I thought, my God, there are a lot of people who will take that wrong. And the speech kind of went on from there, and I thought

Barbara can probably pull this off, but there is nothing real special about it. Frankly, I was scared to death about it."

Bob Strauss was also not impressed when Jordan showed him parts of her speech during a rehearsal in Madison Square Garden the next day. "She showed me one or two paragraphs of her speech, and I didn't think too much about it," he said. The Monday afternoon rehearsal produced other problems and tense moments for Strauss—and for Jordan. Strauss had planned for Jordan and John Glenn to walk to the podium after their introductions from their respective state delegations on the convention floor. He envisioned a kind of grand entrance "from the people" amid cheers, music, and banners and balloons. But Jordan vetoed that idea immediately. "Look, Bob, I've got this bad knee," she told him. "There's this cartilage which is damaged, maybe permanently. I don't need to be walking through the crowd on this knee."[16] Of course, the truth was that Jordan *couldn't* walk that distance, and she was still determined that no one would be told the reason why. The "bad knee" excuse became her standard response to observations about her decreasing mobility. And it worked. For the most part, people accepted her explanation, as did Bob Strauss, who altered his plans and agreed to bring Jordan onstage from behind the podium. John Glenn would make his entrance from the floor, as originally planned, and he would speak first. Strauss had a TelePrompTer set up for convention speeches, and he expected Jordan to use it. She refused, however, telling him she wanted to be able to turn the pages of her speech herself.

A little before eight o'clock that evening, Jordan, along with Stan McClelland, Nancy Earl, and Bud Myers, rode in her limousine to Madison Square Garden. "They allowed two limousines into the Garden, Barbara's and Mayor Daley's," McClelland recalled. "I guess they thought someone would try to kill Daley, but Barbara just couldn't walk that distance. She had to lean on me when we walked to the greenroom, and I just handed her over to Strauss. If you didn't know what to look for, you would just think this was a gentlemanly thing to do."

McClelland left the greenroom behind the stage to go to the convention floor at the beginning of Glenn's speech to see what it would be like for Jordan. He was appalled. More delegates were milling in the aisles talking and laughing than were in their seats listening to Glenn. In fact, between the huge steel scaffold holding the television cameras and the podium, most of the seats were empty.

"John Glenn was droning on, and nobody was listening," McClelland remembered. "All the television reporters were interviewing delegates, people were standing in the aisles, and I thought it was going to be disastrous."

Strauss, too, was worried about the noise and confusion on the convention floor. "I remember that night so vividly," he said. "Glenn read his speech, and he couldn't quiet them down. I was really worried." While her introductory film was being shown to the darkened hall, Jordan was waiting back behind the stage and below it, ready to climb the six steep steps up to the podium. Strauss got everyone else away from her.

"Barbara, I want to tell you something," Strauss said. "As you know, there has been some criticism of my selecting you. People wanted an established national figure. Several governors were unhappy. Barbara, every chip I have is on you. Every Democratic Party chip is on you. Don't let Glenn's experience disturb you. I don't think you can quiet the crowd, and if you can't, just ignore the bastards. Speak into the camera. Remember the television audience. But, if you *can* get them quieted down, then speak into the crowd."

Jordan glared at Strauss with a look of disdain he would never forget and told him, "Bob, if *you* can get me up the damn steps, *I* can make the damn *speech!*"

Strauss did as he was told, almost bodily lifting her up the steps. By the time the lights went up after her introductory film, Jordan was on the stage. The crowd began cheering at the sight of her. And when she started talking, the crowd hushed immediately. "I felt like I'd given birth. I never wanted it to end," Strauss recalled emotionally.

Once she began, Jordan, too, knew it would be different. "I looked up," she said, "and people were not milling around . . . the response was startling, as startling to me as that first standing ovation I got from the Harris County Democrats. Everything had been dullsville at the convention up to then, and I just thought: This is the way it will be."

The beginning, which Stan McClelland thought would be presumptuous, startled the delegates into silence, then tears, and finally, cheers.

> It was 144 years ago that members of the Democratic Party first met in convention to select their presidential candidate. Since that time, Democrats have continued to convene once every four years to draft a party platform and nominate a presidential candidate. Our meeting this week is a continuation of that tradition.
> But there is something different. There is something special about tonight. What is different? What is special?
> I, Barbara Jordan, am a keynote speaker.

That line brought Democrats to their feet. As they cheered, many wiped tears from their eyes.

> A lot of years have passed since 1832. It would have been most unusual for any national political party to have asked a Barbara Jordan to make a keynote address . . . most unusual. But tonight, here I am. I feel that notwithstanding the past, my presence is one additional bit of evidence that the American Dream need not forever be deferred.

Stan McClelland was beside himself. "Nancy and I were standing right there in front of the podium . . . and Barbara is so dramatic . . . different . . . special . . . and the audience goes nuts; they go wild. And from that point on you could hear a pin drop. . . . Barbara electrified everyone, and I just started bawling."

After her dramatic introduction, Jordan began to define what the Democratic Party was all about. After the divisiveness of Vietnam and Watergate, after the massive social and cultural changes of the 1960s, after the scandals and cynicism about government, she seemed to understand what most Americans were feeling.

> *We are a people in a quandary about the present. We are a people in search of our future. We are a people in search of a national community. We are a people trying not only to solve the problems of the moment—inflation, unemployment—but on a larger scale, we are attempting to fulfill the promise of America. We are attempting to fulfill our national purpose; to create and sustain a society in which all of us are equal.*

After sustained applause, she resumed speaking and began to connect the values of the Democratic Party to the promise of America.

> *Throughout our history, when the people have looked for new ways to solve their problems and uphold the principles upon which this nation rests, many times they have turned to the political parties. They have often turned to the Democratic Party.*
>
> *What is it . . . what is it about the Democratic Party that makes it the instrument that people use when they search for ways to shape their future? Well, I believe the answer is our concept of governing. Our concept of governing is derived from our view of people. It is a concept rooted in a set of beliefs that are firmly etched in the consciousness of all of us.*

Jordan described those beliefs:

> *First, we believe in equality for all and privileges for none. This is a belief that each American, regardless of background, has equal standing in the public forum . . . all of us. Because we believe this idea so firmly, we are an inclusive rather than an exclusive party. . . . Let everybody come. . . .*
>
> *. . . We believe that the people are the source of all governmental power; that the authority of the people is to be extended rather than restricted. . . . This can be accomplished only*

by providing each citizen with every opportunity to participate in the management of government. They must have that, we believe.

We believe that the government which represents the authority of all *the people, not just one interest group but all the people, has an obligation to* actively *seek to remove those obstacles that block individual achievement . . . obstacles emanating from race, sex, and economic condition. The government must remove them.*

We are the party of innovation. We do not reject our tradition, but we are willing to adapt to changing circumstances when change we must. We are willing to suffer the discomfort of change in order to achieve a better future.

We have a positive vision of the future founded on the belief that the gap between the promise of reality and the promise of America one day can finally be closed.

This, my friends, is the bedrock of our concept of governing. This is part of the reason why Americans have turned to the Democratic Party. These are the foundations upon which a national community can be built. Let us understand that these guiding principles cannot be discarded for short-term political gains because they represent what this country is all about. They are indigenous to the American idea. They are not negotiable.

Jordan then did the unthinkable for a politician. She apologized for her own party's mistakes.

We have made mistakes. We admit them. In our haste to do all things for all people, we did not foresee the full consequences of our actions. And when the people raised their voices, we did not hear. But our deafness was only a temporary condition and not an irreversible one. Yet, even as I stand here and admit that we have made mistakes, I still believe that as the American people sit in judgment on each party, they will realize that our mistakes were mistakes of the heart. They'll recognize that.

As she began to bring her remarks to a close, she honed in on her theme of a national community.

Now, we must look to the future. Let us heed the voice of the people and recognize their common sense. If we do not, we not only blaspheme our political heritage, we ignore the common ties that bind all Americans. . . . The great danger America faces is that we will cease to be one nation and become instead a collection of interest groups—city against suburb, region against region, individual against individual, each seeking to satisfy private wants. If this happens, who then will speak for America? Who then will speak for the common good? This is the question to be answered in 1976.

Are we to be one people bound together by a common spirit, sharing in a common endeavor, or will we become a divided nation?

. . . We must address and master the future together. It can be done if we restore the belief that we share a sense of national community, that we share a common national endeavor. It can be done. There is no law that can require us to form a national community. This we must do as individuals. There is no president of the United States who can veto that decision.

As a first step we must restore our belief in ourselves. We are a generous people, so why can't we be generous with each other? We need to take to heart the words spoken by Thomas Jefferson: "Let us restore to social intercourse that harmony and affection without which liberty and even life are but dreary things."

. . . I have confidence that we can form a national community. I have confidence that the Democratic Party can lead the way. I have that confidence.

. . . It is hypocritical for us to exhort the people to fulfill their duty to the Republic if we are derelict in ours. More is required. We must hold ourselves strictly accountable. We must provide the people with a vision. If we promise, we must deliver. If we propose, we must produce. If we ask for sacrifice, we must be the first to give. We must be.

. . . What we have to do is strike a balance between the idea that the government can do everything and the belief that the government should do nothing. Strike a balance.

Let there be no illusions about the difficulty of forming this kind of national community. It's tough, difficult, not easy. A spirit of harmony can only survive if each of us remembers that we share a common destiny. If each of us remembers.

I have confidence that we can form a national community. I have confidence that the Democratic Party can lead the way. I have that confidence.

Finally, the woman who had enunciated the "non-negotiable" principles of the Democratic Party concluded her speech by quoting a Republican president.

Now, I began my speech by commenting to you about the uniqueness of a Barbara Jordan speaking to you on this night. I am going to conclude my speech by quoting a Republican president and ask you to relate the words of Abraham Lincoln, relate them to the concept of a national community in which every last one of us participates: "As I would not be a slave, so I would not be a master."

Applause began before she could finish the quotation. She waited for it to subside and concluded, slowly and very seriously, still quoting Lincoln:

"This expresses my idea of democracy. Whatever differs from this, to the extent of the difference is . . . no . . . democracy."[17]

Democrats in Madison Square Garden rose to their feet and roared their approval, affection, and homage.[18] The band began playing "The Eyes of Texas," and delegates started waving the banners of each state. It was the first demonstration of the convention, and it went on for almost five minutes. Members of the Texas delegation were cheering wildly, waving the flag of the Lone Star State. Delegates from Florida and South Carolina came over to join them in their frenzy. The television cameras panned the floor of the Garden, holding their lenses on a beaming Maynard Jackson, one of Jordan's study group friends from Boston University law school, who was now the mayor of Atlanta. Hubert Humphrey, who was sitting with Rosalyn Carter, was on his feet cheering. Mayor Richard Daley of Chicago was telling a news reporter that Jordan's speech was one of the finest he had ever heard. Bob Strauss, knowing that Jordan had created the feeling of unity he so badly wanted, finally bowed to the demands of his delegates on the floor and brought her back to the platform for another bow.

A *New York Times* editorial the next morning captured the joyful irony of the moment when it described Jordan and Strauss as the two unlikely Texas heroes of the national Democratic Party. "There on the platform stood two Texans taking the cheers: the son of a Jewish small businessman and the daughter of a black preacher. If the women's movement hadn't made it something of an offense to repeat, we know what we'd say to the Democrats: You've come a long way, baby."[19]

Barbara Jordan had spoken for almost twenty minutes, and had been interrupted twenty times by applause. She deviated repeatedly from her prepared text, fed by the enthusiasm of the crowd. The New York newspaper columnist Jimmy Breslin described her as the "boss of the high density livers . . . the ones who are out on the streets hurling language into the night air. Here she came, and she knew exactly how to bring this big motley hall into order and send a chill through the nation."[20]

Barbara Jordan had created the emotional rationale for the unity the party so desperately needed and wanted by penetrating the special-interest arguments and baroque barriers that had been built up over time. The clarity of her speech, with its range of instrumentation, pacing, pauses, repetitions, swells, and crescendos, conveyed a meaning that did not rely solely on words. On paper, the keynote address, like many of Jordan's speeches, was rather passionless—intellectually interesting but uninspiring, as both Stan McClelland and Bob Strauss recognized when they read it. Jordan's speeches, like most poetry or librettos, were indeed lifeless on paper without the accompanying sound of her voice. They had to be heard to be felt. Her music-laden voice shot her words into individual hearts; the emotional connection she made that night with her listeners in Madison Square Garden, and across the nation, was deep and lasting.[21]

For the remainder of her life, Jordan continued to receive praise, adoration, even love, from Americans who had been touched by the emotional experience she gave them that July evening in Madison Square Garden. Her speech seemed to dislodge old patterns of thinking and feeling and allow something new to take their place. That evening the same new feeling triggered a "Barbara Jordan for Vice President" boomlet, even before the cheers died down. Many delegates echoed the feeling of the New Yorker Arthur Goodman, who said he would "enthusiastically support" Jordan for vice president. "Sooner or later this country is going to have to face reality. We keep saying we're almost ready for a black, or a woman, or both, as vice president, and somebody is going to have to do it."[22] The speech had the same impact on its television audience. The Pulitzer Prize–winning photographer Brian Lanker said that as he sat in front of his television screen he thought, "Why isn't she running for president? She was the person I wanted to see in the White House."[23]

Barbara Jordan felt the electricity in the hall that evening, too. When Stan, Nancy, and Bud joined her back in the greenroom after the speech, McClelland said, they saw that she "realized that she had hit a home run." Along with party officials, they huddled in front of the television set to see former Republican presidential candidate Barry Goldwater telling reporters that he had been going to political party conventions for thirty years and "this is the most electrifying speech I've ever heard." He told ABC News reporter Howard Smith that if Barbara Jordan had given that kind of keynote speech for him in 1964, "I would have been president."

A phone call from the Democratic nominee-apparent Jimmy Carter was the first to reach Jordan after she finished her speech. He asked for her support if he won the nomination three days hence, and she assured him he would have it.

"Barbara was just ecstatic," McClelland remembered. She was also exhausted and drained. The exertion of mounting the steps to the podium *twice* during the evening left her fatigued and in pain. Although few people noticed in the confusion, she had used a cane for the first time publicly that evening.

When a happy but debilitated Jordan got back to her hotel suite with Stan, Nancy, and Bud, they realized that none of them had eaten since midday; Stan ordered room service. The telephone was ringing constantly. Members of the news media from all over the country wanted interviews. Congressional colleagues were calling, as were old friends from Houston. The Democratic Party doyenne Pamela Harriman finally managed to get through the jammed hotel switchboard to ask Jordan whether she and her husband, W. Averell Harriman, could come up to the room to pay their respects. When they came, McClelland recalled, "it was all very proper. He was very, very old, and they just sat there and chatted with Barbara. They said they were fans of hers, and Barbara really enjoyed it."

Jordan was too keyed up to sleep after the Harrimans left. "I was very fired up by giving the speech and by the audience response and it took just a little while to come down enough to sleep a couple of hours," she said.[24] She finally got to bed around 2:00 A.M., but the phone continued to ring until almost three. Once Jordan had gone to sleep, McClelland turned down all the requests for interviews, including those for early Tuesday appearances on ABC's *Good Morning America* and NBC's *Today Show.*

Early the next morning, hundreds of telegrams were delivered to Jordan's hotel suite, and the telephones were jammed in both her congressional office in Washington and her home office in Houston. While she slept, the spontaneous vice presidential boomlet arising from the floor demonstration for her the night before had turned into a serious move to put her name into nomination. Members of the Black Caucus were at the forefront. A few weeks earlier, when her name had appeared on Carter's list of fourteen vice presidential prospects, several Caucus members had urged Jordan to allow her name to be put into nomination. She had declined, but the floor demonstration Monday night prompted some of her congressional colleagues to urge her to reconsider. They were spurred on Tuesday morning when every major newspaper in the country carried her photograph and glowing accounts of her speech on their front pages. The *Washington Star's* story said, "The Democratic Party, which has been at this convention business for one hundred forty-four years, never had an opening night like this before, and never will again."[25] Sandy Grady of the *Philadelphia Evening Bulletin* wrote, "The Democrats were losing to boredom 1–0 last night when they had the good sense to bring Barbara Jordan off the bench. Miss Jordan, as the ballplayers say, took it downtown. She tore it up. Grand slam. Jimmy Carter, watching the Democrats' lovefest on TV in his Americana Hotel suite, could only feel lucky he won't have to follow Barbara Jordan's act for three days. Getting on the same podium with Miss Jordan is like trying to sing along with Marian Anderson."[26] Ellis Cose of the *Chicago Sun-Times* said it was "generally conceded that Jordan may well be the best orator the Democrats have. She is certainly the most widely heralded black politician in the nation."[27]

"Barbara Jordan for Vice President" buttons showed up on Tuesday. Even Lillian Carter, the governor's mother, was wearing one. Jimmy Carter had also been inundated with telegrams and phone calls urging him to name Barbara Jordan as his choice for the vice presidential nomination. As the morning wore on, Jordan realized that the effort was getting out of hand. She had Bud Myers call Carter's press aide, Jody Powell, to let him know she would issue a press statement to stop the groundswell, which she did shortly after noon. Her written press statement of "disinterest" also expressed her skepticism. "It is improbable that Carter would take the bold, daring, unconventional and un-southern move of naming a black or a woman as his running mate. Certainly not both at once." She added that she did not wish to be a token or symbol. When her name went before a national convention, she said, she wanted it to be for the purpose of electing her to a post, not just to raise issues. "It is not my turn. When it's my turn, you'll know it," she concluded.[28]

Some black leaders, like Basil Patterson, vice chairman of the Democratic National Committee, and Jordan's friend California representative Yvonne Burke, understood and accepted her decision. But two others, who were more active in promoting the nomination, Representatives John Conyers of Michigan and Ron Dellums of California, were "irked."[29] They were the point men for the militants in the Congressional Black Caucus, and their frustration over Jordan's ties with powerful white Democratic leaders often spilled over into the press, although each never allowed himself to be identified publicly as one of her critics. Nevertheless, they did openly express their anger over her refusal to let her name be put into nomination. They couldn't understand why she did not want to continue to break traditions by being the first black woman to be nominated for vice president.[30] But Jordan was adamant. She reiterated that she had just set a precedent by being the first black woman to ever deliver a keynote speech to a major political party. "I ended 144 years of discrimination last night," she said. "Now give me a breather."[31]

Jordan got her breather. Despite the protestations of Conyers and Dellums, some members of the Congressional Black Caucus were relieved that Barbara Jordan's vice presidential boomlet was over. One well-known black politician, who refused to allow his name to be used, told the Chicago reporter Ellis Cose that it was "just as well" because, even though he recognized Jordan's formidable political and oratorical gifts, he didn't like it that she was closer to the established Democratic leadership than to the Congressional Black Caucus. Cose wrote:

> *The black Democratic leaders tend to consider her as something*
> other *than black. They take her at face value when she says she is*

a "pragmatic" politician . . . and they would have supported her
candidacy. To not support her, they reasoned, would have mystified
the whites while shattering the attempt to portray black unity. It
would also have mystified many of the black delegates who tend to
not be as aware as the leadership of who is in which club.[32]

This rather candid assessment revealed the dilemma of the black caucuses, both in Congress and within the Democratic Party, in relation to Barbara Jordan. She was not "one of them." She held herself outside of their reach, influence, and control. The problem for them was that their constituents—hundreds of thousands of African American Democrats—loved her and saw her as *their* leader. She had a direct connection to the African American public that most ordinary African American politicians and members of Congress did not.

The late Mickey Leland, who succeeded Jordan in Congress in 1979, understood the psychological connection Jordan established with ordinary black men and women, beginning in the 1960s and culminating in the 1976 Democratic convention keynote address. "If a person is eloquent and articulate, they are on the top of the heap in the black community," he said. Leland believed that Jordan's manner of speaking was a more important symbol of having arrived than any material gain. "She cut through so many of the prejudices and barriers that we had to face. This may sound crazy to you, but Barbara Jordan proved that not all blacks are stupid."[33]

Writer Paula Giddings took Leland's analysis a step farther.

To blacks in general, Barbara Jordan is the serious politician who
gets things done with a minimum of empty rhetoric and
ostentatious posturing. She plays the game the way it is played,
without apologizing for it, without amoral excesses, and with a
great deal of success. She is the kind of woman we all have known
in our lives—her eye on the sparrow, taking care of business. And
her manner of speaking probably holds more significance to Blacks
than Whites.[34]

No black politician could risk challenging Barbara Jordan without, at best, confusing black voters or, at worst, risking their ire. Jordan's Houston friend Judge Andrew Jefferson learned the danger firsthand one time when he simply remarked that one of Jordan's speeches did not reach her usual high standard. He was inundated by calls and complaints that he had dared to criticize Jordan.

Jordan knew that she was valued by ordinary men and women—"her people." It reinforced her feeling of independence and power, just as it also made other prominent black politicians uneasy. Vernon Jordan, who was then president of the National Urban League, observed that politicians—

black or white—could often be petty in their assessments of each other. But within the Congressional Black Caucus, "it was clear that the pettiness was aimed at the most prominent leader—Barbara. Leadership, prominence, and good press usually add up to a little sniping."

Three days after the keynote addresses, the Democrats selected Jimmy Carter as their nominee, as well as his choice for vice president—Minnesota senator Walter Mondale. It was the most harmonious convention the Democrats had had in years. On the last evening, the canny Bob Strauss called all of the party's stars to the stage with the nominees to join in singing "Happy Days Are Here Again," which, after the success of the convention, Democrats truly believed. When Jordan came onto the stage with Martin Luther King Jr.'s father—"Daddy" King—the convention delegates again went wild, chanting, "We want Barbara." The convention ended on a high note, and Barbara Jordan was one of the reasons.

"The convention was wonderful," a proud Bob Strauss gushed. "It launched the campaign. . . . It propelled Carter into the presidency. There was no greater favor I could have done the Democratic Party or her. It was best for the Democrats, and it was best for her that she gave that speech. I thought I was the smartest fellow in the world because that speech launched her, made her a national figure."

Yet, on the night of her speech, Strauss had said something to Jordan that profoundly disturbed her. While still on the podium and glorying in the applause and adulation of the crowd on the floor of Madison Square Garden, Strauss told her how glad he was that he and Edward Bennett Williams had not "messed her up for all time" by having her testify for Connally. Jordan was shocked. "I felt doubly used . . . to discover that he had seriously thought it might damage my career but had asked me anyway. I was angry that he had not leveled about what reservations he had." Jordan had known she was being "used" when she testified for Connally. It was part of the game, the realpolitik she thought she understood. But she hadn't realized that Strauss and her friend Frank Erwin had been willing not only to use her but to *sacrifice* her to save John Connally. She, Barbara Jordan, different and special as she was, was still a woman and a black. She was expendable. She did not like how it felt to be outmaneuvered by political operatives in a system she thought she had penetrated, mastered, and been accepted into. The scene of her greatest public triumph—the 1976 Democratic convention—thus also reinforced the tension festering inside her about her role in the American political system. It was one more tear in the web of her enchantment with political life. The final ripping of that web would not be long in coming.

THE CAMPAIGN

Jimmy Carter's lead in the polls did not last long. The race had tightened by September, and in October Carter and Ford seemed to be running even.[35] The Democrats' main hope of putting Carter in the White House was a heavy black vote in the South and in the inner black core of the nation's largest cities. Bob Strauss directed his party's get-out-the-vote efforts in the nation's key black voting precincts. The civil rights leader Jesse Jackson plunged into the effort, as did Georgia congressman Andrew Young and other national black leaders. But it was Barbara Jordan who drew the crowds.

When Jimmy Carter had called Jordan to ask her personally to be part of his election effort, she told him, "You've got my help. Just tell me what it is you want me to do. I will help as much as I can with your campaign, consistent with my own efforts, as I am running for reelection at the same time." Jordan did have a Republican opponent in November, but she believed he was of no consequence. He had issued a release that he was going to run against Barbie Doll. It was all kind of a joke.[36] So Jordan, in fact, felt completely free to campaign for the Democratic ticket. She had decided to help Carter because, in her two terms in Congress, "I had Richard Nixon and Gerald Ford, and I thought: One experience that you ought to have is to serve in the Congress with a Democratic President."

Jordan enjoyed making the speeches, and she reveled in the crowd's reaction to her. "When all of it was over, I remember saying to Bud and Nancy that I don't know whether Carter ought to thank me for campaigning for him, or I ought to thank him for sending me to these places to campaign because I was having a ball. The reaction to me was what turned me on. I really enjoyed that."

When a student at Ohio State University stood to ask her a question at the end of one of her speeches, he said, "You know, you're telling me to vote for Jimmy Carter, and I guess I will, but I sure would feel a lot better if I was voting for Barbara Jordan for president." Jordan recounted the story with glee, because the student's comments brought the crowd to its feet to cheer her on. "Those speeches didn't hurt me at all, and I think they helped Mr. Carter. I'm sure they did."

Yet, throughout the campaign, she remained unimpressed by Jimmy Carter. After the first of three debates between Carter and President Ford, Jordan had written a letter she imagined the American people writing to the candidates.[37] She used it on some of her campaign stops, and it reflected, in the simple day-to-day language of ordinary people, how she felt about the 1976 campaign.

Dear Mr. President and Mr. Carter,
How are you? I watched you debate last night. You both looked very nice. You are certainly smart. You know a lot of big numbers.

My problem is I can't figure out what all those numbers have to do with me.

I don't ask for much. I want the people who represent me to be fair and honest in all they do. I want to feel safe in my home and secure in my job. I want to be free to speak my mind and I expect my government to keep me free. I want to feel good about my life, my future and my country.

Mr. President, Mr. Carter . . . whichever of you two gentlemen can take care of that, I'll vote for you on November 2.

Don't bother to answer. You'll hear from me first.

Best wishes,
The American Public

Jimmy Carter won the November 2 election with a bare majority—50.1 percent. Black voters provided the margin of victory in thirteen key electoral states, and Carter carried four of the six states where Jordan had campaigned for him, including Texas, where he got an estimated 97 percent of the black vote.[38] In each of those states, the black turnout was the critical element in his victory.

Barbara Jordan was also reelected to a third term in Congress, with 90 percent of the vote. The Democrats regained control of the U.S. Senate, and the national elections ended eight years of divided government, with one party controlling the presidency and the other controlling Congress. Democrats now held it all, winning lopsided majorities in both chambers of Congress. Jordan was hopeful. Surely, political life would be easier now.

THE APPOINTMENT PROCESS

Cabinet member? Supreme Court justice? Attorney general? United Nations ambassador? What did Barbara Jordan want to do in the new Democratic administration? It would have appeared that she could have her pick. She was on everyone's short list for a top appointment in the Carter administration. She could not pick up a newspaper without finding her name on some politician's speculative list of possible Carter appointees, and she began to think seriously about the possibilities.

She had no trouble focusing on the jobs she *didn't* want to do. "I didn't want HEW [Department of Health, Education and Welfare]; a black woman head of HEW couldn't do a thing that would be of interest. I was not interested in the UN at all, not at all. There was nothing I had ever done that would show an interest in foreign policy initiative."

Late in November, President-elect Carter called Jordan at her Washington apartment to ask whether she would be interested in talking about a position, or would prefer to stay in Congress. Jordan was somewhat taken aback by the form of the question. "An either-or question like that is not exactly an offer of a position," she said. She told Carter that she would certainly talk to him about a position, and they made arrangements to meet when Carter came to Washington the first week in December. How the question was posed, however, should have foreshadowed future problems.

The Urban League's Vernon Jordan, an Atlanta native who was serving on Carter's Personnel Advisory Group to recruit high-level minority appointees for the new administration, knew Carter well. He recalled that Carter had a way of saying, "Do you want to be in my cabinet?" in such a manner that "you knew the answer should be no." Jordan explained that Carter then "could say with some legitimacy that he had offered you the opportunity to go into the government, but it had not been a sufficient enough request to make you think he really wanted you." Because Vernon Jordan had worked closely with Carter over the years, he understood the nuances of the former governor's questions. Barbara Jordan plainly did not.

In preparation for her meeting with the president-elect, she called old friends and family to seek their advice. "We finally decided, my friends and I: Look, you're a lawyer and if you do anything it ought to be in your field, and you ought to be head of it. What we came to then was that if the position of attorney general was offered, I would consider that. But nothing else. And that's where we stood, although I knew that making that decision was like saying I was not going to be a member of the Carter cabinet."

Ben Barnes, her mentor in the Texas Senate, felt that Jordan's friends had steered her wrong. "She had a lot of hangers-on who might have encouraged her. And Barbara could have had *something*, but not that. I told her that she needed to go do something else—go be ambassador to the UN or something like that." Barnes understood that the one cabinet position in which loyalty should matter most to a president would be the attorney general. "It should be someone the president knows well and trusts, and who will protect the president. You can't hand over the powers of the Justice Department to someone you can't trust. So, I told Barbara, 'You can't be appointed attorney general. That's not going to be. Anybody who's telling you that is wrong. Your work on the Judiciary Committee got a lot of national television exposure, but Jimmy Carter's not going to appoint you attorney general.'"

"She should have talked to Strauss," Barnes said. "Strauss would have told her the truth."

But Jordan did not talk to Bob Strauss, whom Carter had asked to stay on as chairman of the Democratic Party. After Strauss's offhand remark to her about the Connally testimony at the Democratic convention, Jordan felt that Strauss's advice might not necessarily be based on what was best for *her*. So she avoided talking to the one Texan who probably had the best understanding of what the Carter people were thinking about possible cabinet appointments.

"She never asked me about it, and I was deeply involved in the transition," Strauss said. "People told me that she wanted to be attorney general, but I didn't think she had a chance in hell, and I would have told her if she had asked me. She just didn't know Jimmy Carter well enough. If she had, she would have known that he would have never considered her. Hell, he would have never considered me," Strauss laughed. "He considered me a political person, and he was looking for experts. He divided people into political animals and experts, and she would have been considered a political person. Carter was looking for an experienced legal person, a judge or legal scholar."[39]

Jordan did talk to other Texas politicians, but it was clear she had already decided that attorney general was the only post she would consider. Congressman Jim Wright said that he had a discussion with her about the appointment, but that he was not very direct with her. "I didn't want to say, 'Barbara, you're not qualified to the extent that someone else might be.' I didn't want to tell her that she had her expectations too high, because that's hard to deal with for anyone."

Her expectations were indeed high. She was receiving letters of encouragement from all over the country. Oscar Mauzy said Jordan called him the day before she was to see Carter at Blair House in Washington. "She asked me if she should take the attorney general's position if Carter offered it to her. I said, 'Well, of course, take it. But, Barbara, they're not going to offer you AG.' " Jordan told him, "Well, I hear that they're seriously considering it." Then she asked him about the ambassadorship to the United Nations, and Mauzy advised her not to take it if offered. "It just doesn't lead anywhere," he said.

There is no doubt that the Carter transition team had seriously considered Jordan for a top spot in the administration. The young Georgia men who had handled the vice presidential interview selection process had been criticized in the press for not taking Jordan seriously as a vice presidential candidate in July. Hamilton Jordan, Carter's top campaign aide and coordinator of personnel during the transition, was determined not to make that mistake again.[40] Yet on the eve of her meeting with the president-elect, top Carter aides let several key Texas Democrats know that she was his choice for UN ambassador—a job Carter had decided would go to a black as a way of dealing more effectively with the African and Asian nations. Some of the Texans Carter's staff interviewed raised questions about Jordan's experience and propensity for the administrative and managerial responsibilities required of a cabinet member. That would present no problem, however, with the UN position. Yet the day before Jordan was to meet with Carter, her friend Congressman Charlie Wilson said she still expected to be offered either secretary of HEW or attorney general.[41]

It was cold and rainy when Jordan went to Blair House to meet with President-elect Carter on Friday, December 10. The meeting did not go well. To begin with, Jordan was ailing. Because dampness and high humidity often trigger symptoms of a multiple sclerosis attack, she was having a particularly difficult time getting around that day. Bud Myers drove her to the meeting and had to help her up the steps to the official guest house. Once inside, she had to wait until the president-elect emerged from another meeting. When they finally sat down to talk, Carter delayed any discussion of an appointment until he could be joined by Hamilton Jordan and Vice President–elect Mondale. The impatient, direct, get-down-to-business congresswoman was frustrated by ten minutes of what she felt was awkward small talk. When Hamilton Jordan arrived, Barbara Jordan took an instant dislike to him.

Hamilton Jordan was the brilliant young political strategist from Georgia who had guided Jimmy Carter through the convoluted Democratic primary system and on to victory in the November election. Jordan shared his boss's contempt for Washington lobbyists and insiders but lacked Carter's charm and diplomacy. His southern pride was concentrated in a chip on his shoulder as big as Georgia's Stone Mountain, and he seemed to delight in making non-Georgians feel uncomfortable. Hamilton Jordan was known for humiliating staff members in the presence of outsiders and for snubbing members of Congress and other high government officials by refusing to return their telephone calls or hurling verbal barbs their way. The Democratic congressional leader Tip O'Neill thought he was so rude and obnoxious that he called him "Hannibal Jerkin."[42] After experiencing the full force of Hamilton Jordan's personality, Barbara Jordan did not like him either.

The young man had always pronounced his last name as if it were spelled *J-e-r-d-e-n*. The national press had made much of his insistence on the unconventional pronunciation during the campaign. When he came rushing into the meeting with President-elect Carter and Barbara Jordan, whom he had never formally met, he teased her in an overly familiar way by telling her she "didn't even know how to pronounce her own name." Jordan was not amused. Her fine screen for humor and her immense sense of dignity were violated by this apparently innocuous joke. She considered it a disrespectful dismissal of herself and all she represented by a brash young man in the presence of the next president of the United States. Before she had time to react, however, Jimmy Carter was asking her to give him some guidance about what she wanted. "Is there something you think you can do for the people?" he asked.

"Well, the one thing I believe I am qualified for is attorney general," she replied.

"Oh, no. Not that . . . not that," Hamilton Jordan interrupted. "That's Griffin Bell."[43] Although there had been no announcement, Carter had indeed already decided to give the post to Bell, a fellow Georgian, federal judge, and onetime law partner of Carter's best friend, Charles Kirbo.[44]

Barbara Jordan did not think there was much more to say after that.[45] She left the meeting, silent and grim. She refused to talk to reporters, who immediately began to speculate that the meeting had gone badly. The *Washington Post* ran a photograph of her leaving Blair House, looking both sick and angry; a front-page *Dallas Morning News* article stated that she had left the meeting with a "cold, fixed expression" because the "meeting did not go well."[46] Carter aides fueled speculation that there was something amiss by letting reporters know that the meeting had ended earlier than planned and that Carter was "irritated" because Jordan would consider only an "appointment consistent with her background."[47]

Jordan called her friend Jake Johnson in Houston immediately after the meeting and described what happened in some detail. "Let me tell you, she felt it was insulting," Johnson remembered. "Carter had some brash, insensitive handlers, and this was one of the very few times since I had known her that she ever said anything negative about someone, and even then she didn't say a lot. But she was not pleased with Hamilton Jordan. I'm sure nothing personal was intended, but obviously she was just not in the mood right then and there to experience any kind of put-down."

Jim Wright, who was a big fan of Jimmy Carter's, nevertheless had a great deal of empathy for Jordan's situation during the encounter. "Some of us, I included, have had my feelings hurt because people didn't come recruit me for a job. I had never offered myself for a job, except for majority leader. I would always wait until they came around . . . it was probably pride. But the reality is that in political life if you want something you must ask for it, and I think it might have been embarrassing for someone like Barbara to have gone to ask for a position, only to have it go to someone else. So I can understand how Barbara might have psyched herself up to the point of going and asking for this, and then, finding it denied, feeling crushed."

Jordan was frustrated and angry when she described her immediate reaction to her Houston friend Jake Johnson. But in *Self-Portrait*, published three years later, a more temperate account emerges. "There was nothing secret about that meeting," she wrote. "It started out with just the two of us initially. He said: 'Now, you know I need some guidance, Barbara. I'd prefer it if you would give me several things that you would be interested in.' And I told him my feeling. I said: 'I would like to be able to give you several things but I don't have them, Mr. Carter. There is just one thing that I would consider. I wouldn't consider anything else but Attorney General.' And then we chatted around about that, and he felt me out about some other things anyway. Did I have an interest in the United Nations. I said: 'I have no interest.' He asked me about Solicitor General—he's the lawyer who brings the Government's cases, who's under the Attorney General—and I told him that I didn't have enough trial practice experience to be Solicitor General. Besides, it was under the Attorney General. He didn't broach the matter of HEW."

Jordan wrote that when Hamilton Jordan and Vice President–elect Mondale joined them, "Carter stated my position to them on Attorney General to let me know that he understood exactly what it was. And I considered that it was absolutely perfectly understood. Then we chatted about other people that he was thinking about appointing to various other things, and the meeting was concluded. The story came out that our meeting ended earlier than it was scheduled for—well, that's because there wasn't much to talk about. Then a further story came out saying that we were not comfortable with each other, that we didn't get along, and the Black Caucus people got very upset because they thought some of the Carter people were trying to do me in with those stories. Carter called to say he had heard all this complaining and that he didn't have anything to do with those stories. And I said: 'I didn't either, Mr. Carter.'"

Unnamed Carter aides were quoted in various Washington news stories after the meeting. One said, "Miss Jordan couldn't make up her mind what she wanted to do. First she was determined to be attorney general, although other things being equal she might have accepted the UN post, if Jimmy had given in to her ambitions. But regardless, she wanted to reserve the right to quit the Cabinet in 1978 and run for the Senate against Tower. That means she would have left after about eighteen months on the job, maybe less, because of the possibility of a primary fight for the Democratic Senate nomination, and Jimmy would have been left looking for someone else to take over." Moreover, the aide said, "Carter is unalterably opposed to anyone's using the Justice Department as a springboard to further political office, which is what Jordan might have done."[48]

Frustrated Texas liberals, angry with Jordan over her friendship with Ben Barnes, her oil and gas votes, her determined independence, and, of course, her testimony for Connally, made sure Carter's top aides knew that Jordan was not *their* top choice for a cabinet appointment, and they were probably responsible for the subject of Jordan's future ambitions being injected into the appointment equation, although the notion of a race against Senator John Tower was pure speculation. Jordan herself did not bring it up in the meeting with Carter.

The *Washington Post* reporter Walter Pincus wrote that "Jordan's chances for Attorney General had been hurt by opposition from some congressional and Texas Democrats." He quoted one anonymous Democrat who said, "Barbara's real character and interests have been obscured by her charismatic public image," which covered up her "negative problems."[49]

Paula Giddings wrote later:

Whatever took place in Jordan's meeting with Carter, her once rapidly ascending political star seemed to have been braked, at least temporarily. Within twenty-four hours, the politician who had seemed above criticism was being criticized by both colleagues and the press. Her alleged poor relationship with the Black Caucus, her unpopular alliance with Texas oil interests, and charges of her political opportunism were discussed. Even her brilliance in the legal field began to be challenged. Suddenly it was remembered that she had actually had very little experience as a lawyer. In fact, it was said that when Thurgood Marshall was in Houston recently, he cited her inexperience in explaining his view that she would not have been the best choice for either Attorney General or the Supreme Court.[50]

Jordan's cabinet aspirations were over. After Christmas, when members of the Congressional Black Caucus went to Plains, Georgia, to talk to Carter about the appointment of African Americans to various positions, she declined to make the trip. Originally scheduled to be part of the group, she said, "I'm not going to Plains to talk about anything. I felt that if half a dozen members of the Black Caucus were going, there was no necessity for one more voice to say the same thing. And certainly Plains is not the easiest place in the world to get to. Besides, I had decided: If Carter wants me, he can call. So that was how I was not in the Carter cabinet."[51]

Jake Johnson believed that Jordan never talked about it again. "If you could call her back from the dead, I don't think she'd say much about it. But let me tell you something, after that it was all downhill."

Her close friend Stan McClelland agreed. "I think she never really liked Carter very much after that," McClelland said. "They just didn't have a very warm meeting, and I just don't understand it because Jimmy Carter today is very warm. They just didn't hit it off. And the things they talked to Barbara about were the kinds of things they would just offer a black. And I know Barbara didn't want that. She just felt like she had earned better than that."

CHAPTER 17

DECISIONS

WHEN SOMETHING WAS over for Barbara Jordan, it was over. It was as if she could simply dissolve the emotion or hurt from an unpleasant experience, or at least reduce it to some infinitesimal and remote molecule of memory that she never evoked again.

Jordan did not talk about her experiences with Jimmy Carter and his aides. If she ruminated about them privately, no one knew. Maintaining silence about emotional events was one of the patterns of her life. She *never* let on that she might have been wounded or betrayed by a personal or political slight. That was a level of emotion she either could not or would not reveal. Perhaps it was the stoic pride she learned from her father, or the protective reserve that she developed in reaction to him. Perhaps it was her own sense of dignity, which did not allow for verbalized remorse or whining complaints. Perhaps it was "just Barbara," which is what her friends would say when they could come up with no other plausible explanation for her behavior.

Her silence did not derive from passivity or bland acceptance of life's blows with equanimity. When she was angry, she expressed it. When she was in the presence of stupid behavior, she called it. When she needed help, she asked for it. When the moment of anger or pain passed, however, she did not dwell on it. She moved on. She seemed to have an uncanny ability to react to the high or low point of the moment and then let it go, never speaking of it again. She was adamant, however, that no offer had ever been made to her by Jimmy Carter, and she wanted to set the record straight on that. While making a speech in Texas, she told news reporters who questioned her about turning down a job in the Carter administration, "The President-elect, the President, the Governor of Georgia, the former Governor of Georgia, no one named Jimmy Carter *ever* offered me any job."[1] And she was smiling when she said it.

While she occasionally criticized the *political* performance of President Jimmy Carter, she never discussed her Blair House meeting with him again. She could even joke about the man who got the job she wanted—Griffin Bell, who turned out to be Carter's most controversial appointee, stirring opposition from civil rights and minority groups because of his poor civil rights record as one of the fifteen judges on the Fifth Circuit Court of Appeals.

When Jordan made a speech to a group of educators in Texas shortly after the U.S. Senate had confirmed Bell for his cabinet post, she quipped, "Mr. Bell is a nice man. I had breakfast with him Wednesday morning . . . we had grits. Mr. Bell will probably make a good Attorney General in spite of himself."[2]

Jordan's ability to joke about Griffin Bell indicated that her strong sense of self was still intact when she began her third term in 1977. It was an undivided self that did not plunge into uncontrollable anxiety or despair because life was not turning out as she had planned. Robert Grudin, in his book *Time and the Art of Living*, could have been describing Barbara Jordan when he wrote:

> *The person of integrity is no superman; he will be, from time to time, defeated, frustrated, embarrassed and completely surprised. But neither is he the common and regular dupe of circumstance, compelled (like some tourist with a pocket dictionary) to consult conscience and emotion at each new turn of events.*[3]

Barbara Jordan did not need a pocket dictionary to chart her course after the disappointment of not being appointed attorney general of the United States. Her understanding of her strengths and weaknesses was so complete that she could absorb her disappointments and learn from them, rather than let them paralyze her with doubt or despair and prevent her from moving on to the next course of action. What she had learned from her Carter experience was this: to never go where she was undervalued. That lesson became etched in her psyche as deeply as the lesson from her unsuccessful legislative campaigns in the 1960s, when she determined that she would never place her destiny in the hands of others, particularly the Texas liberals. The Carter experience taught her that some of her congressional colleagues disliked her enough to try to keep her from getting a major appointment. She learned that her friends and staff were not always in touch with the realities of hardball politics and that their advice always had to be weighed with that in mind. She also recognized that her days of uncritical press attention might be over. The news media reveled in conflict, and despite her accomplishments, she was no more sacrosanct in its collective view than

Wayne Hays or other hapless politicians whenever anonymous "enemies" might try to bring them down. As she began her third term in Congress, she became more detached from the sycophants, the back-slapping politicians in Congress—including many of the Texans—and from members of the working press. In 1977 Jordan rarely gave interviews. When one reporter asked her whether she was deliberately keeping a "low profile," she was quite forthright when she responded, "There is a part of me who enjoys to speak when I have something to say. And if I don't have anything that I feel needs to be said, then I don't say it. . . . This is a quiet time."[4] She *was* out of the limelight, but it was her own choice. She had also vowed never to be deceived again by others, or even by herself.

As a result, when supporters began pressing her to challenge Republican senator John Tower's reelection in 1978, she made a much more sanguine assessment of the possibility of the race than when she sought to be appointed attorney general. Despite what her friends, local supporters, even newspaper editorial writers were telling her about how wonderful she would be in the Senate, she knew the truth in her gut this time. With no self-deception or hubris, she calmly assessed a reality she could not change. Yet she went through the motions of getting advice from all of her old friends and touching all of the political bases that had to be included in such a decision.

One of those she called was Oscar Mauzy. "I think I might be able to get the Democratic primary nomination, but I'm worried about the fall election," she told him. Mauzy agreed; he recalled later that he told her, "Barbara, I just don't think Texas is ready to elect a black woman senator. I'm sorry to say that, but that's what I believe to be the case." She seemed relieved. "Thank you very much for saying that, Oscar. Most of my friends won't tell me that, so I appreciate your honesty. I really do."

Jordan was almost certain that she would not make the race for the Senate. Although she made no public announcement to confirm her decision, she all but ruled it out publicly when she told the *Dallas Times Herald*, "I'm not interested in any more token efforts. I'm forty-one and I don't need to do any more symbolic things."[5]

For the moment, Jordan simply tried to focus her energy on the House of Representatives.

THE NINETY-FIFTH CONGRESS

A deceptive calm had settled over Washington after the 1976 elections. For the first time in eight years, both the White House and Congress were in Democratic hands. There were no assassinations, Watergate investigations, or foreign wars to tear them apart politically.[6] Yet within a short time it was apparent that most members of Congress had no better relationship with

President Carter than did Barbara Jordan. Except to make speeches, Carter rarely visited the Capitol, and neither did his closest advisers, most of whom had no experience in dealing with Congress, or with the Washington insiders who knew how to operate within its intensely complex system. As a result, nothing happened—at least nothing that mattered to the key members of the election coalition that had put Jimmy Carter in office. As early as February 1977—only a month after the president had been sworn in—some of them began to express their dissatisfaction . . . publicly.

Representatives of African American organizations and the Congressional Black Caucus were among the first. Even though Carter had made a few high-profile appointments of African Americans, there was no high-level black staff person in the White House, and there were no initiatives coming from the White House on civil rights issues. When the Urban League held its national convention in Washington, D.C., in February, its president, Vernon Jordan, denounced the new administration's poor beginning. "Carter had to be reminded about the guys who made the difference in his election, and I reminded him of that," Jordan said. Barbara Jordan had not taken part in the meeting and had been careful not to criticize President Carter publicly, but, as he recalled later, she sent Vernon Jordan a note after his speech telling him she thought what he had done "was just fine."

Jimmy Carter was not responsible for everything that turned sour in Congress in 1977. Both houses were under new leadership. Tip O'Neill of Massachusetts had replaced the retiring Carl Albert as Speaker of the House. When the Democrats captured a majority of the Senate, Virginia's Robert C. Byrd became the Senate majority leader. The membership of the new Congress was different as well. The "good old boys" with whom Jordan had developed an easy camaraderie were fading away. The new reformers who took their places were rather humorless and less willing to compromise. Anti-government rhetoric had become stronger and more specific ever since the presidential contender Ronald Reagan injected it into the 1976 Republican primary contests. Many of the new members of Congress who had been elected to "govern" clearly hated government. Jordan was appalled by their rigidity and willingness to slash programs that helped her constituents. The newly formed political action committees (PACs), the funding tool developed by special-interest groups to circumvent recent reforms in campaign financing laws, had also had their first real impact on the 1976 congressional elections. More than twenty-five hundred special-interest PACs had contributed to members of Congress, many of whom began to feel more beholden to them than to their own political parties. Party discipline and control by congressional leaders began to break down. Deals made at high levels often could not hold at low levels. Republican legislators were more aggressive in their attacks and less willing to compromise. Now in the minority within their own party, many conservative Democrats began to

Above, Barbara with her parents, Arlyne and Ben Jordan, shortly before Ben Jordan died in 1972. *Right*, Barbara with her family in front of her mother's Campbell Street home in the Fifth Ward. *Left to right:* Uncle Wilmer and Aunt Mamie Reed Lee, Barbara, Bennie, Arlyne, Rose Mary and John McGowan. *Below*, Barbara with her sisters, Bennie Creswell (left) and Rose Mary McGowan, after winning the Democratic Congressional nomination in 1972.

Above, President Johnson greets a joyous Barbara Jordan at a fund-raising dinner in 1972. *Above right*, Frank Erwin was a fund-raiser for Governor John Connally, a close political ally of President Lyndon B. Johnson, and a friend of Barbara's while she was in the Texas State Senate. *Right*, John Connally, former governor of Texas, secretary of the navy and secretary of the treasury under President Richard M. Nixon. Barbara was a character witness at Connally's trial for bribery, which resulted from investigations of the Special Prosecutor on Watergate in 1974.

Below, Barbara with Vernon Jordan and President Lyndon B. Johnson at a civil rights symposium in December 1972.

Above, Barbara Jordan and Congressman Charles Rangel of New York conferring during proceedings of the House Judiciary Committee during the Watergate hearings in 1974. *Below*, the House Judiciary Committee debating the possible impeachment of President Richard M. Nixon. Barbara is second from left.

Left, Barbara with Congressman Charlie Wilson (left), who also served with her in the Texas Senate, and Speaker of the House Carl Albert of Oklahoma, during Barbara's first session in Congress, 1973. *Above*, Barbara gave the commencement address at Harvard University in June 1979 and met one of her heroes, Marion Anderson.

Above, President Gerald R. Ford signs the extension of the Voting Rights Act of 1975 as Representative Fr. Robert Drinan, former dean of the Boston College Law School, Barbara, Representative Ted Kennedy of Massachusetts, and Senator Charles Mathias, Jr. of Maryland look on.

Barbara just prior to her speech at the 1976 Democratic National Convention in New York. Behind her is DNC chairman, Bob Strauss.

[Courtesy of AP/World Wide Photos]

Barbara with Democratic presidential nominee Jimmy Carter at the podium after Carter's acceptance speech at the Democratic National Convention, July 16, 1976.

[Courtesy of AP/World Wide Photos]

Ill and frustrated, Barbara Jordan left the Blair House meeting with President-elect Jimmy Carter in December 1976.

[Courtesy of AP/World Wide Photos]

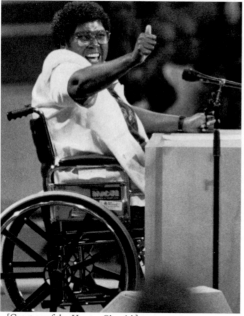

[Courtesy of the *Houston Chronicle*]   [Courtesy of the Barbara Jordan Estate]

Above left, Barbara gives a thumbs-up after delivering the keynote address at the 1992 Democratic Convention, which nominated Bill Clinton for president. *Above right*, Barbara and Nelson Mandela in South Africa in 1991. *Below*, Barbara with Texas governor Ann Richards. Governor Richards named Jordan to her Special Counsel on Ethics in 1990.

[Courtesy of Governor Ann Richards]

[Courtesy of Reni Newsphotos, Inc., *Meet the Press*, NBC News]

Above, in 1987, the U.S. Senate confirmation hearing on President Ronald Reagan's nomination of Judge Robert Bork to the U.S. Supreme Court drew Barbara back to Washington, D.C., where she forcefully opposed Bork's appointment. She even debated Bork supporter Senator Orrin Hatch (R-Utah) on *Meet the Press*. *Below*, Barbara and friends at the White House in 1994 to receive the Presidential Medal of Freedom. *Left to right*, Darrell Teaver, Stan McClelland, unidentified woman, John McGowan, Rose Mary McGowan, Nancy Ear, Hillary Rodham Clinton, President Bill Clinton, Bennie Creswell, Terry Tutchings, Sharon Tutchings, Azie Tayor Morton, Marilyn Allen, Gerry Rapp.

[Courtesy of Sharon Tutchings]

Above, former Texas governor Ann Richards speaking at Barbara's Houston funeral. President Bill Clinton, seated, also delivered a eulogy. *Below*, Texas Honor Guard at graveside burial services at the Texas State Cemetery in Austin. Barbara's family is seated in the front row, with Governor Richards and Stan McClelland (obscured) standing behind them to the left.

join with Republicans to block legislation they did not like. Speaker O'Neill complained that the House sometimes teetered out of control. "You just don't have the discipline out there," he said.[7]

Congressional Democrats were also increasingly embroiled in their own fights with the White House. There was little coordination between the White House and Congress, and the president even vetoed several pet projects favored by Democratic leaders. In addition, the House was awash with new scandals. More than a dozen former or current House members were accused of various criminal offenses. Charles C. Diggs Jr. of Michigan, the first chairman of the Congressional Black Caucus, resigned from his seat after being censured by the House for padding his House payroll account and accepting kickbacks from some of his employees. And when FBI agents posed as Arab sheiks and attempted to bribe various members of Congress in the "Abscam" sting operation, five House members and a senator succumbed and were eventually convicted. In the meantime, the economy had not recovered from its 1976 slump, and both interest rates and unemployment continued to rise. The "united" government under the control of the Democrats could do no more to solve the problems than the previous year's "divided" government split between the Democrats and Republicans. When the first session of the Ninety-fifth Congress ended in December, its only significant action was approval of an increase in payroll tax rates for Social Security, the beginning of a trend in regressive tax shifts to middle-income taxpayers.

Jordan's frustration with both the Democratic president and her colleagues in Congress grew as the months wore on. She had stopped going to many of the political receptions and dinners. She did not have the genial and close camaraderie with her colleagues in Congress that she had enjoyed with members of the small Texas Senate. Neither did she have the supportive group of women friends in Washington that she had had during her last two years in Austin. Although she did have the wonderful retreat on Onion Creek in Austin, she didn't get to spend nearly enough time there because she still felt obligated to spend at least one weekend a month in Houston with her constituents. Her major problem now, however, was that she was sick. Multiple sclerosis had continued its "slow burn" through her system. The use of a cane, which she had shunned before, was now a necessity.

Jordan could no longer hide her illness, only the name of it. Her colleagues were aware that her disabilities—whatever their origin—were limiting her actions. "She changed," Congresswoman Yvonne Burke believed. "It was just so difficult for her to get around, and she was not as free and easy as she had been before. Politics—and life—had dealt her a blow. She had a lot to offer that was never used. So I always felt she was really disappointed." Colorado representative Pat Schroeder also noticed the change at the beginning of Jordan's third term. "Barbara used to be able to go on and on. She would stay up late going to all the receptions and social events and then get up early the next morning and make all the meetings. But then she couldn't do it." People in Houston noticed it, too. Otis King, Jordan's debate partner from Texas Southern University, thought that Jordan had reached a turning point. "There was the question of her health, of course, but sometimes you can plug on through to other things even if you do have problems. Would her health have been in such a state if she had not been so disappointed?" he wondered. Schroeder expressed what many of those who admired Jordan felt: "I got to where I felt sorry for her because of her decreasing mobility."

The last thing in the world Barbara Jordan wanted was for anyone to feel sorry for her—especially her colleagues in Congress. She specifically did not want people to focus on her illness. "While Barbara was a very public person, in a wholly different sense she was totally private," her friend Stan McClelland believed. "I think she felt like being sick was 'her business' and not something the public necessarily needed to know about her." Oscar Mauzy had noticed Jordan's use of a cane when she went to the podium for her Democratic convention keynote speech. Trying to be solicitous, he asked her what was wrong. She brushed off his question by telling him it was "nothing serious." Mauzy had several clients who had multiple sclerosis, and he thought he recognized some similarities in Jordan's unsteady gait. He suggested that she contact a specialist at Southwestern Medical School in Dallas who was familiar with multiple sclerosis. "I don't have anything like that," she snapped, and refused to say another word to Mauzy, allowing their conversation to end in total silence.

Jordan realized there were times when she was rude to people who simply wanted to help. "I'm not long on patience," she admitted. "Sometimes I'm more abrupt with people than I ought to be. I always regret it afterward."[8]

As difficult as her congressional life was becoming for her, Jordan tried to keep her focus on two issues that the civil rights community still deemed important. She pushed for legislation to extend the Civil Rights Act's Title VI nondiscrimination provisions to all federal programs, including the major federal-state revenue-sharing programs and the anti-crime programs renewed under the Law Enforcement Administration Act (LEAA). Jordan said she "would no longer acquiesce when federal money was used by state or local governments to discriminate."[9] Her bill allowed the attorney general to file suit to cut off federal funds for state programs in which minorities were discriminated against, and it also authorized individuals to sue state and local governments for violations of civil rights protections in federally funded programs. Her bill expanded the definition of prohibited activities to include discrimination because of sex, age, or handicap.[10]

Even more important than the civil rights guarantees, however, in the eyes of the NAACP's Legal Defense Fund, was Jordan's role in preventing a damaging breakup of the federal Fifth Circuit Court of Appeals, which had been enforcing most of the key civil rights and integration decrees in the South. Because of the extremely heavy federal court workload, a recommendation had been made by a prestigious commission on the revision of the federal court appellate system to split up the Fifth Circuit and create a new Eleventh Circuit Court of Appeals. When it passed its courts bill in February, however, the House made no change in the Fifth Circuit because many members, especially Barbara Jordan, worried that dividing the circuit would weaken the stands that it had traditionally taken in favor of civil rights.

However, while the Senate bill authorized new judgeships to combat the heavy caseload, it also split up the Fifth Circuit, largely at the insistence of Mississippi's Democratic senator James Eastland. NAACP leaders believed Eastland, chairman of the Judiciary Committee, was determined to reconstitute the Fifth Circuit in order to diminish enforcement of civil rights and integration decrees, if not halt them altogether. The NAACP Legal Defense Fund and other civil rights groups were unalterably opposed to the Senate bill. They enlisted Barbara Jordan's help.

"Barbara blocked it single-handedly in the House," asserted Elaine Jones, the NAACP's Legal Defense Fund lawyer who worked on the legislation. "She was the backbone. This was her circuit, and she understood the issues clearly. So she was willing to take on Senator Eastland in the conference committee. This was her one issue. It was also Eastland's one issue. She sat across the table from him, and she stood him down. She held up all the federal court appointments in 1977 until this was settled. And it was Barbara who came up with the strategy that finally allowed us to settle it," Jones remembered.[11]

As finally approved, the bill provided that any appeals court with more than fifteen active judges could divide itself into more than one administrative unit, complete with separate staff and facilities.[12] The net effect was to keep the liberal Fifth Circuit essentially intact. Jordan also fought for and won a provision in the bill calling for the consideration of women and minorities for the newly created judgeships. "I am fully aware of the smallness of that victory," she told a women's group. "But it *was* a victory, and it just might make a difference."[13]

As with so many other actions in her life that were of significance to the civil rights community, Jordan never talked much about her role in the Fifth Circuit court fight. It was critical, however, to ensuring another decade of pro–civil rights appellate court decisions in the South. "It was her last big fight," Elaine Jones observed. "She had to do most of it herself. She couldn't delegate it to staff because it had to be worked out member to member." Several years later, when the Leadership Conference on Civil Rights gave Jordan its Hubert H. Humphrey Civil Rights Award to celebrate the twenty-fifth anniversary of the passage of the 1964 Civil Rights Act, Elaine Jones, by then the national director/counsel of the NAACP Legal Defense Fund, introduced her at the event. Jones recounted the Fifth

Circuit battle to the audience and bragged that Jordan "held firm when Senator Eastland and others wanted to gerrymander the Fifth Circuit." Jones told the group that Eastland "couldn't go *around* her, *over* her, or *through* her. He had to come *to* her."[14] Jordan, by then in a wheelchair, leaned over and thanked her for remembering. "There are not very many people who know about that," Jordan told her.

ANOTHER LIFE

How many times do you repeat these performances? That question, Barbara Jordan said, kept creeping into her thinking. How many times "do you keep presenting a bill and getting it passed and getting the President to sign it? How many pens do you want?"

Not many, was the answer she kept coming up with.

"Although I was still very junior in the Congress, I had begun to feel very senior," she wrote at the time. "I felt more of a responsibility to the country as a whole, as contrasted with the duty of representing the half-million people in the Eighteenth Congressional District. I felt some necessity to address national issues." Ten years later she was much more frank: "I got bored with the Congress of the United States. I didn't want to do this anymore."[15] It was no longer interesting, intriguing, or *necessary* for her to be the consummate political insider. She now had other options.

Barbara Jordan had always focused on the positive aspects of her life. By 1977, when she felt frustrated by Congress, disappointed by Jimmy Carter, used by her powerful Texan friends, criticized by the liberals whose causes she had championed, and carped at by the Congressional Black Caucus for being the brightest black star on the horizon, she knew she would be doomed if she allowed herself to be swallowed up by all of the negative forces that swirled around her. She began to look at her situation differently. Millions of Americans looked to her as a moral leader, a standard-bearer for excellence, a guide to public ethics, and a truth-teller who could rise above political poppycock. Perhaps it was time she began to see herself that way, too.

"I could read that I was a national figure and not flinch, because I *was* a national figure, and people had heard about me all over the country. So what had to be considered was: What does one do now?"

She was invited to give the commencement address to the Harvard University class of 1977. Jordan had given many commencement speeches in her eleven-year public career, and she had already been awarded twenty-two honorary doctoral degrees. Harvard was different, however, and she wanted to give full attention to her speech. "While I worked on this matter it occurred to me that . . . I didn't need to be an elected public official in order to say those things, or address those problems in any national or global way. That, as a matter of fact, being an elected public official took time away from the time I would otherwise have to think about other problems and address specific problems, because it was easy to become bogged down in the minutiae of committee meetings and settings and roll-call votes and quorum calls."

As Jordan sorted through the reasons to stay in Congress and the reasons to leave, the internal compass on which she had always relied was clearly pointing in the direction of home, away from Washington, away from political power and a lifetime of ambition for public office. Former House Speaker Jim Wright believed Jordan's growing frustration in Congress was similar to what Texas senator Lloyd Bentsen Jr. felt when he left the U.S. House after serving three terms to return to Texas to go into business. Wright said he asked Bentsen once if he missed being in the House. Bentsen told Wright, "Well, of course I missed it. But I didn't want to continue being a member of the thundering herd."[16] Wright speculated "that might have been a feeling Barbara shared. When the bell rings and it's time for a vote, they do come rushing into the House chambers like a thundering herd."[17]

Jordan clearly did not want to be part of the thundering herd. As she withdrew from almost all of the ancillary activities that come with being a member of Congress—the ceremonial functions, receptions, photographic opportunities, caucus and committee meetings—her thinking became more clear. "I believed that in order to free myself to move fully in a new direction, I would of necessity have to leave elected politics and pursue the platform wherever I could find it. And I was thinking at that point, working on the Harvard speech, that the platform would be presented to me, that it wouldn't be difficult to find."

She had already been offered one such platform. In May 1977, without any public notice or announcement, she had signed a book contract with Doubleday to tell her life story, to set the record straight.

"All of the stories that appeared about me in the press were about Barbara Jordan the public person. And I had read what I considered inaccurate characterizations of Barbara Jordan the person, the private person. And I said to myself, 'Why don't I then tell my story about myself the way I see myself?'" Jordan said that when she read in articles that she was "as cozy as a pile driver," or that she had "the personality of slate rock," or that she was "cold, calculating and callous," she had to ask, "Who in the world are they talking about?" She wanted to reveal that she was "warm and caring and has a sense of humor and is loving and just all of those good things I feel about myself."[18]

Jordan had never liked to write, however. Even letter-writing was a chore for her. She knew she would need a collaborator when it came to putting the details of her life on paper. On the recommendation of mutual friends, she interviewed, selected, and shared her book contract with the

Austin-based novelist Shelby Hearon to help produce a book. Hearon had already published five well-received novels and become something of a Texas literary celebrity. After testing each other in a conversation alone at the Onion Creek retreat, the two women decided they liked each other and could work together. The book was not to be ghostwritten. Rather, Hearon conceived the book as a dialogue between the two of them, a collaboration through conversation. As she planned the book, Hearon said that Jordan's "voice, as she told the story, remains hers; mine, as I have reconstructed the world's perceptions and conceptions of her, remains mine."[19]

When Jordan made her speech at Harvard in May, Hearon was there to report it in detail for their book. Harvard was a pinnacle for Jordan. It was perhaps the last remaining institution in which she sought to be accepted, to be "let in." She picked up that refrain in her remarks, making it somewhat reminiscent of her 1968 speech to the Texas Press Association, when she had asked the question, "What does the Negro want?" and answered, "He wants to be let in." At Harvard, she told the graduates of her faith in ordinary American people. "People. The people want in," she said.

> How much longer, how much longer will people tolerate a network
> of illusions and vacuous rhetoric? How much longer? . . . The
> people do not want to be outskirters. They want to be insiders on
> America. We want to be in control of our lives. Whether we are
> jungle fighters, craftsmen, company men, gamesmen, we want to be
> in control. And when the government erodes that control, we are
> not comfortable. We're not comfortable at all. I submit to you that
> the re-inclusion of the people in their government would be
> recombinant of predictable and laudable results. It would be a
> return of a right which we once considered unalienable.[20]

At the end of her ceremonial day at Harvard—where in addition to becoming the first black woman to make the commencement address she also received an honorary degree, along with the singer Marian Anderson and the novelist Eudora Welty—she reflected on the occasion's meaning for her.[21] Shelby Hearon, Nancy Earl, and Bud Myers had accompanied her to Boston, and she told them: "Sometimes I just stare in the mirror and look at myself and I say: 'Barbara, by golly, you've done okay. It wasn't easy, but you've done okay.' Tom Freeman told me I'd never get to Harvard, not to apply. But here I am. I did get in. Right now here I am. I'm in."

After Harvard, working on her book initially seemed to provide a diversion from Congress, as well as to help put her life in broader perspective, as if to prepare for its next—and different—phase. As she toiled in conference committee meetings on the courts bill, however, the Washington summer heat and humidity in 1977 was taking its toll, bringing on another wave of multiple sclerosis symptoms, including recurring problems with her right eye. The attacks had so weakened the muscle that controlled her eye that her vision was affected, and her right eye movement was sporadic.

By fall she was almost certain that she did not want to be in Congress anymore. Her remaining doubts had vanished by October when the political writer Myra MacPherson published a hypercritical article about her in the *Washington Post*. The headline read, "Looking Over Jordan—Black, Women's Groups Complain as the Eloquent Texan Goes Her Own Way." The second paragraph set the tone of the article: "The beneficiary of adulatory media coverage which overstated her power at the time, Jordan now is in an anticlimactic lull, becoming a victim of that past instant stardom. People are beginning to ask the one question politicians loathe above all: 'Whatever happened to . . . ?' "[22]

MacPherson quoted anonymous sources who had nothing good to say about Jordan, including "a leading Democrat on the Judiciary Committee" who said, "She's just not around much and therefore you get little continuity. I'd give her a C in effectiveness." A White House aide said, "She seems to have withdrawn. It hasn't occurred to us to go to her on anything." And Congressional Black Caucus member John Conyers "sputter[ed] his discontent by innuendo: 'Look, I can't talk about this. If I was going to retire, I'd tell you what I think.' "[23] The gist of the criticism, however, was what it had always been: Barbara Jordan was too ambitious and arrogant, too cautious, too friendly with the white southerners, too moderate, too much of a Texan, and on and on. The difference this time, however, was that all of the anonymous criticism was wrapped up in one big story in a mainstream newspaper that was read and quoted by Washington insiders as the bible of American politics. Yet not one of Jordan's critics allowed his or her name to be used.

MacPherson wrapped up her story by saying that no one expected Jordan to stay in the House, and she quoted Jordan as having said, "with crisp finality: 'I don't think I came here to make it my life's work.' " Yet MacPherson admitted that even Jordan's detractors believed that because she was a moderate she could conceivably someday win a vice presidential nomination as "a safe black female." MacPherson added that Jordan "plays her cards so close that not even her friends know what she will do."[24]

That fall, when Jordan hinted to reporters that she might not run for reelection, the resulting news stories set off speculation that she might be appointed to the Supreme Court, but she quickly dispelled that rumor. She said that while she realized that a seat on the Supreme Court was supposed to be the dream of every lawyer, "I would have to think about whether I want to find myself locked off in a black robe for the rest of my life. Do I want to mute my voice and the opportunity to speak out on the issues? Supreme Court justices do not develop issues that they go around and make speeches about." Besides, it would be President Carter's appointment to make, and Jordan was not about to put herself through his selection process again. There was also speculation that she might make a U.S. Senate race against John Tower. She brushed that aside, too. "If I even had some tentative feelings about that [Senate race] I'd be ready to announce."[25]

Jordan was finally coming back full circle in her life, realizing that her real power was in her voice and that her future could be built upon its strength, not on her deal-making and parliamentary expertise or her backroom relationships. She also was facing the reality that she just couldn't handle the physical stress of being in Congress anymore. "Back then, they didn't have any kind of wheelchair access," her friend Stan McClelland remembered. "If you looked at her office situation . . . how she had to walk and go on those underground 'subs,' it was just too hard. It was a chore." Jordan had finally accepted the fact that she was disabled—but only in her legs, not in her brain or in her voice. The voice—she still had the gift of voice—gave her the power that mattered.

Finally, on December 10, 1977, Jordan called a news conference in her district office in the federal courthouse in Houston to announce that she would not be a candidate for reelection in 1978. "For reasons predicated totally, and I need to underscore totally, on my internal compass directing me to do something different . . . I shall not seek elective office in 1978," she said.

> This decision is made now—rather than two or four years hence—because I think it would become increasingly difficult for me to change course. There is, I believe, an inverse relationship between duration of tenure in the Congress and the ability to shift gears.
>
> What course I shall pursue in 1979 when my current term expires, I do not know. Whether in the public or private sector, I do not know.
>
> I do know that my decision will not be made in haste. My experience in elective office has not caused me to become cynical, nor discouraged, nor frustrated about the viability of our political institutions, particularly as they are influenced by the will of the people. There it has been enhanced. It should surprise no one that our political institutions are cumbersome. Nor can it be otherwise when the Board of Directors number over 200 million and their desires are establishment of justice, insurance of domestic tranquility, provision for common defense, promotion of general welfare and securement of liberty.
>
> My gratitude to the people of the 18th Congressional District is boundless. Many supported me when I was more likely to be a loser than a winner. The support and confidence of the people I represent have been sustaining and will never be forgotten.[26]

While there had been speculation for several weeks that Jordan would bow out, her constituents reacted with stunned disbelief. One of Houston's black newspapers, the *Informer*, said the announcement was like a "multi-megaton bomb, sending radioactive rays into the black community."[27] Barbara Jordan had been not only the first black representative from Texas since Reconstruction, but also the only African American behind whom the Houston black community was totally united. Her departure from Congress would end a political era. News reporters found it hard to believe her repeated assertion that she had no plans for her future. "I don't have a hidden agenda, believe it or not," she said during ten minutes of skeptical questioning. She also denied that she had a health problem. When asked whether she had consulted with President Carter about her decision, she replied, "He doesn't consult with me about my future, but he probably *should* consult with me about *his*."[28]

Jordan was in a good humor and laughingly told a reporter from Philadelphia who came to see her a few days later that she did not plan to "fade quietly away. You couldn't do without me," she joked.[29]

She was absolutely honest about having no plans. She really didn't know what would be next for her. "I have never been successful in orchestrating my political future," she told one reporter. "I have tried to be ready and available for opportunity whenever opportunity presents itself. Now I need to think about the options available to me."[30]

The first option was to relax. It was a relief to have it over. No longer did she have to please her father, her constituents, the news media, political party leaders, the Congressional Black Caucus, or anyone else. Only herself. When Congress resumed in January 1978, the smiling, genial Barbara of old seemed to reemerge. She joined with other female members of Congress to fight for and win the extension of the ratification process for the Equal Rights Amendment for women. She worked on her book with Shelby Hearon, accepted offers to make speeches all across the country, and shuffled her congressional staff assignments to begin the transition to private life. Bud Myers moved on to a new job, and Bob Alcock became her chief administrative aide. Nancy Earl moved to Washington for the last few months to take over Alcock's speechwriting chores and to help Jordan close down the office. More importantly, Jordan began to prepare for her new career. Within a few weeks of making her announcement that she intended to leave Congress, she knew what it would be.

One of her old liberal colleagues from the Texas Senate, Don Kennard of Fort Worth, had left the Senate to work on an environmental research project at the Lyndon B. Johnson School of Public Affairs at the University of Texas in Austin. When he heard the news that Jordan would not be running for reelection, he suggested to the LBJ School dean, Elspeth Rostow, that she try to recruit Jordan for a faculty position. Rostow, a presidential historian and erudite lecturer who had come to Austin at the end of the

Johnson administration with her husband, Walt Rostow, President Johnson's national security adviser, immediately made the call. Jordan was intrigued with the idea of becoming a professor. It would be a role compatible with her desire to speak out on national issues. It would allow her to live in Austin at her beloved Onion Creek getaway. She would be able to read and think and further develop her ideas about the Constitution, the national community, and the role of government. And it would be far enough away from Washington that she would be free of the political gamesmanship she now found so wearying. After thinking about it for a few weeks, she decided that teaching public policy to serious graduate students would be a perfect fit for the more relaxed life she wanted to lead. And, yes, there was one more factor in her decision: her affection for Lyndon Johnson.

"I thought back to the time when Lyndon Johnson was alive," Jordan said. "Lyndon Johnson used to talk about the Washington scene. He said, 'It really kind of gets me, Barbara, that all of these people up here are the Assistant Secretary of this and the Deputy Secretary of that, and all of them got their degrees from *Haa–vaad* and Stanford. I know that we can develop talent in Texas, and we can develop young minds, and they can be so good that they will be able to come here to Washington and be the Assistant Secretary and the Deputy Secretary, and the Heads of all of these departments. And when I get out of here, I am going to have a school that is going to educate young people to come up here and do these jobs.' I could hear Lyndon Johnson's words ringing when Elspeth Rostow offered a position. . . . I thought, now what better thing could I do than to go there, to the University of Texas, to the LBJ School, and help those young people become the bright leaders of government as Lyndon Johnson so wanted?"[31]

In the few weeks immediately after her announcement, Jordan had received more than two dozen offers or "feelers," but most were from law firms that would have been happy to just have her prestigious name printed on their stationery. Since she had practiced law only briefly before she started her political career, she didn't want to be a figurehead, ensconced in a fancy office. Teaching, on the other hand, would allow her to use her own experience as a base for speaking and instruction. Jordan told Elspeth Rostow she was interested. Although no announcement was made until June, Jordan began extensive reading to prepare for her first course: teaching graduate students about the ethics and reality of "intergovernmental relations," a course title that hardly described what Jordan wanted to teach. Rostow assigned one of the LBJ School's star students, DeAnn Friedholm, to be Jordan's academic assistant and help organize her course. Jordan would finish her term of office in December and take up her new post in January 1979.

As Jordan neared the end of the congressional term, newspapers in Houston and other Texas cities began to run various retrospective articles about her career. The litany of her "first" accomplishments was repeated again and again. Only one newspaper, however, the all-black Houston *For-ward Times*, was able to tap into Jordan's personal feelings about her career as an elected official. When asked what she thought her greatest accomplishment as a member of Congress had been, she said she was proud of some things she had done legislatively for "my constituency in Houston." Then, in a rare public breakthrough of emotion, she asked: "Do you want to know what I *really* think? At this point in time, my single greatest accomplishment is, and I mean this quite sincerely, . . . it is representing hundreds, thousands, of heretofore nameless, faceless, voiceless people. . . . The letters I enjoy most are those who write and say, 'For the first time I feel there is somebody talking for me.' If I've done anything, I have tried to represent them, and I've done that to the best of my ability. I consider that as the best accomplishment."[32]

PART IV

Life is full of challenges. And we often measure ourselves and our success in life by how we meet those challenges. . . . Challenge validates our aliveness and often disturbs the order of our lives.

—BARBARA JORDAN (1990)

CHAPTER 18

WITHDRAWAL AND RENEWAL

BARBARA JORDAN HAD spent twelve years in the public eye. Now she was out of it, or wanted to be. She felt she had done all that she was capable of doing as a public official.[1] She was the most admired black woman in America, and she was still young—only forty-three years old. Yet in her mix of geniality and reserve, there was still an unreachable quality about her. Who really knew her? Was she all that she seemed? Was she *only* what she seemed?

The paradox of Barbara Jordan was that she both gave so much of herself to her public life and yet held so much back from her public. Now she seemed to want to remove herself entirely from its grasp. In January 1979, her desire for privacy pervaded every aspect of her life, as did an almost equal yearning for normalcy. Since she had gone to Boston University in 1956, and then into public service, every act, every entrance into a new domain, every accomplishment had been extraordinary. As her fame had grown, however, so had the intensity of her detractors, although they were almost entirely out of public view, nipping at her heels in fits of jealousy or frustration because she would not do or be what they wanted. When she began her first week of classes at the University of Texas's LBJ School of Public Affairs, she felt relieved that all of it was behind her.

Yet, on January 17, her second scheduled class day, the *Dallas Morning News* ran a front-page copyright article that said that Jordan had left Congress because she had an incurable illness—multiple myeloma, a malignant disease of the bone marrow.[2] The story cited Jordan's dramatic weight loss as evidence of her illness and quoted Washington sources as saying that she had been treated for the disease by government doctors. The Associated Press picked up the story, which ran in newspapers all across the country the next day, along with a hastily prepared statement issued in Jordan's name by the University of Texas. The message was brief, and its tone was angry: "The story is inaccurate. It is true that I walk with a limp and use a cane. This is a medical difficulty, but I do not suffer from any terminal illness. My weight loss was voluntary, and I wish I could be congratulated for it rather than viewed with suspicion of grave illness." Jordan hoped that would be the end of it, but she was besieged by reporters. University officials quickly arranged for a press conference.

Stan McClelland was with Jordan for the press conference, and she leaned on his arm for support when she walked into the room where reporters had assembled. She did not want them to see her using her cane, but she could no longer walk without assistance. Nancy Earl was there, along with LBJ School dean Elspeth Rostow and other university officials. Nancy and Stan were the only ones who knew the true nature of Barbara's illness, and they surmised that one of her Texas congressional colleagues had leaked the story to the *Dallas Morning News* after piecing together various bits of information. Although the *News* reporters had the time and place of the original diagnosis correct—Bethesda Naval Hospital in 1973—they had misnamed the illness, calling it multiple *myeloma* rather than multiple *sclerosis*. While both diseases were serious and debilitating, there were vast differences between them. Multiple myeloma was a form of malignant bone cancer that could ultimately be fatal. Multiple sclerosis was a progressive neurological disorder that could limit mobility and cause other problems but was rarely fatal in itself. Jordan was determined to put an end to press inquiries about her health once and for all.

"There was considerable hullabaloo yesterday created by an inaccurate news story," she began. "I wrote a denial, which was released by the university. The essence of my denial statement was: (1) that the news story contained inaccuracies, (2) that my right knee doesn't work like that of most folks, (3) that I am not terminally ill. I would add to my statement of yesterday that I do not have, nor have I ever had, the illness described in the news story. My knee has for some three or four years received more attention than my mind, heart or soul . . . I am regretful that my malfunctioning knee has greatly inconvenienced and interrupted what we, at the LBJ School, are all about. I have now, and still have, nothing more to say about my malfunctioning knee. And I have no more to say about the unfortunate news story of yesterday. For better or worse, my knee is mine. Finally and more importantly, I accepted an affiliation with the LBJ School to teach and to work with students. This is the only reason I am here. And I do not wish to be diverted, and I will not be diverted by irrelevances that have nothing to do with the reason I'm here."[3]

She refused to take further questions about her "knee" or about her health, and her formidable presence was intimidating enough to prevent any from arising. Yet she told reporters that she would be happy to talk about anything else. After a moment of tense silence in the crowded room, one reporter finally asked her whether she missed Washington. Jordan's laughter broke the tension. "Do I miss Washington? No." Then she told reporters how she wanted and expected her life to be now that she was no longer a public official.

"I recognize that people have certain things they would like to see me do. *They* have certain plans that they would like to see me fulfill. . . . Well . . . this is a time for Barbara Jordan to do what makes Barbara Jordan happy and . . . the people out there who really care about me, the person, will be happy if I am happy. And that is still the way I see it."[4]

When a reporter asked her whether she would be accepting any speaking engagements, she told him, "Very, very, very few. You may add an additional 'very.' I've done that. I have made more speeches than I can count. . . . People still want me to speak, and I appreciate that and I applaud it because they think I am still great, good, kind and wonderful, and I like that. But . . . if I am going to be a professor of the first rate, which I fully intend to become, I can't spend my time running, making speeches every weekend of my life or more."

Jordan's comments were met with skepticism by the group, and one reporter challenged her: "Why do you want to limit yourself to being a professor? . . . It sounds like you've just quit being a politician."

"I don't think I will ever quit being a politician," she shot back, "because it's sort of a part of what I am. What I *am* going to quit being is one politician who engages in active, political life. . . . If a political opportunity were presented to me on this day, January 18, 1979, I would express a total lack of interest."

When the press conference was finally over, Stan and Nancy felt that a crisis had been averted. Barbara's secret was intact.

Why was Barbara Jordan so adamant that no one know the nature of her illness? Why, when she had once gloried in press attention, was she now so reticent about revealing anything remotely personal or private about her existence?

The obvious answer is that she did not consider her private life the public's business. And like much else in Jordan's life, the obvious answer may be the truest answer. She also did not want to be pitied. So much of her pride—the essence of her dignity—was wrapped up in her independence and strength. She was the "miracle" woman, the young black woman who had overcome virtually every obstacle to rise to the top. Multiple sclerosis threatened both her independence and her strength, the qualities she valued most in herself. If she revealed the nature of her illness, she knew that people would watch her and wait for the signs of physical demise and dependency, which was repugnant to her.

Instead, Jordan insisted on absolute privacy. This privacy protected her vulnerable beliefs and feelings, her inwardness, and, most important, her lifelong sense of being different from everyone else. Her ability to control the flow of information about her life prevented her from being transparent, predictable, or pitiable.

Yet Jordan also seemed to realize that by keeping her illness a private matter, she might be able to diminish its importance in her life. This did not seem to be the kind of classic denial that many seriously ill patients exhibit, nor was it a pathological refusal to deal with reality.[5] Jordan *was* willing to come to terms with multiple sclerosis, but it would be on *her* terms. She intended to do everything she could to minimize its impact on her and to take whatever treatments or medications might be available to help her cope with it. But she would not let it obscure her focus on what was important in her life. For now, three goals were important to Jordan: to promote her new book, to become a good teacher, and to figure out how to build a new life that would allow her to overcome her physical limitations. That was all.

A SELF-PORTRAIT

Part of Jordan's plan to control the flow of information about her life was to tell her story the way she wanted it told. The book she had worked on during her last year in Congress—*Barbara Jordan: A Self-Portrait*—was released in February 1979. Jordan embarked on a limited tour to promote the book in New York, Chicago, Cleveland, and Los Angeles as well as Dallas, Houston, and San Antonio.

Prior to publication, Jordan's co-author Shelby Hearon had described the book to reporters as a "psychobiography." But when a reporter at her university press conference had asked Jordan about that label, she turned to LBJ School dean Elspeth Rostow, who was standing next to her, and joked, "Dean, I don't know what that is."

The discerning Rostow stepped in to stop what she considered a misleading interpretation. "It is a straightforward account of the life of Barbara Jordan. . . . It is not an effort to try to probe beyond the events of her life to extract deep meaning or significance to the events."[6]

In the book, the coauthors tell essentially the same stories in different voices in alternating sections. More than half of the book covers events before Jordan's public career ever began. While Jordan's stories about her upbringing are indeed fascinating, the book glosses over her public life, particularly the years in Congress. And the offhanded and pithy dismissal of important events had the effect of making Jordan come across as a woman who glided across the surface of her life, driven only by her own ambition; her accomplishments and attributes seem almost commonplace. Her political insights, her biblical sense of justice and judgment, her understanding of the nature of power, her personal relationships, and her disappointments are downplayed, if not completely hidden. Her growing physical incapacity is barely mentioned.

While *Barbara Jordan: A Self-Portrait* was politely received and reviewed, it did not break new ground or set sales records. Political insiders who hoped for some insight into Barbara Jordan and her career were plainly disappointed. The political reporter Carolyn Barta, who reviewed the book for the *Dallas Morning News,* complained that Jordan "skirted the high points" of her life, just as she had skirted questions about her possible illness and the reasons she left Congress.[7] Susan Kelly-DeWitt in the *Sacramento Bee* felt the book presented Jordan less as a civil rights leader and "more as an able woman who has lifted herself by force of will to equality."[8]

Some of Jordan's closest political friends saw the book in still another light. Jake Johnson said that when he read the book he was disgusted. "I waited two or three weeks because I didn't want to write her a scathing letter. Finally, I said, 'You do not tell it like it is, and therefore there is going to be a different view by historians about what you are.'" Jordan asked Johnson what he meant. "I'm talking about the insults—all the way from Dorsey Hardeman, Curtis Graves, to the Jimmy Carter stuff," he said. And she just laughed. "Jake, people don't want to hear that stuff. It's only for us to know. There were things left out of the book—things I judged best unsaid. Those of us who know, know. I thought that was enough at this time."[9]

Stan McClelland thought the whole idea of writing an autobiography was really in conflict with how Jordan approached her life. "It was like, 'Well, I'll write an autobiography, but I don't have to tell everything I know. . . . It was unenlightening."

When the book tour was over, Jordan put the book behind her. Several years later, she gave permission to the singer Dionne Warwick to produce a made-for-television "movie of the week" based on her life, but the project fizzled. Still later, however, when Jordan was offered an option by Creative Artists Agency for film and television rights to *Self-Portrait,* she declined, even though a contract had been negotiated by Hearon's literary agent. She did not care to relive the public part of her life.[10]

OUT OF SIGHT

Barbara Jordan almost disappeared from public view from mid-1979 to 1982. Although she made occasional speeches and continued to show up on magazine lists of "most admired women"—including a *People* magazine survey in March 1980 that revealed she was the nation's top choice for the first woman president—she was serious about withdrawing from public life.[11] In October 1979, when Texas Democrats put together a list of prominent Texans who would be supporting President Carter's reelection more than a year in advance of the election, Jordan would not allow her name to be used.[12] She also made no endorsements or public appearances on behalf of the Democrats in the 1980 elections. When one of her students asked her why she had campaigned hard for Jimmy Carter in 1976 but not in 1980, she replied sarcastically, "I'm busy now. I wasn't busy in 1976. I was serving in Congress."[13]

From the beginning of 1979, when she began her new career as a college professor, Jordan's primary focus was on work and health. As usual, she applied all of her attention and drive to her immediate tasks, and she took her teaching responsibilities extremely seriously.

"She just wasn't going to spend the hours telling war stories," Stan McClelland said. "But until she got her course well-designed, I think it was a struggle for her. She would read stuff on every end of the continuum. . . . Barbara never felt unsure of herself, but she didn't have a Ph.D., and it was part of her competitive nature to be the best. She would *never* do anything second-rate."

Also teaching at the LBJ School was Lyndon Johnson's former postmaster general, John Gronouski, the father of the zip code, and Wilbur Cohen, former secretary of health, education and welfare, who was the father of Social Security. They, along with Jordan, represented the kind of political practitioner that Lyndon Johnson wanted students to be able to learn from. There was always a tension, however, between them and the tenured academic faculty.

Jordan had to put together two classes for her first semester: one on intergovernmental relations and the other on political values and ethics. She called the first "a practical course" because it dealt with the inner workings of government at many levels, and she wanted her students to understand "some of the frustrations that will be theirs as 'the feds become a big daddy for them.' " But Jordan's real interest centered on her course in ethics. She had always believed there were "no clear-cut answers to ethical questions" in politics, and she wanted to create in her students an "ethical sensitivity" to their own as well as others' behavior.[14] "Ethical sensitivity does *not* presage saintliness," she wrote in her first syllabus. "It does presage an awareness of action which violates generally accepted norms of civil conduct."

Designing and developing her first two seminars from scratch was difficult for Jordan. It required a shift in her thinking and in her very way of *being*. To become the teacher and mentor that she believed her professorial role required, Jordan had to put other people first in a direct, personal way, and that was a brand-new experience for her. Teaching also required that Jordan reflect on her readings, discussions, and actual experiences to help her students understand their meanings, and as a result, she became more reflective herself. She worked hard to make the transition from a doer to a thinker and teacher, and once she got into it, she was surprised that she did not find it drudgery. "I actually find it enjoyable," she said. "The students and I are learning together."[15]

Jordan went to Harvard's Kennedy School to observe how certain courses on ethics were taught, and her student aide, DeAnn Friedholm, had collected reading lists on ethics from college professors all over the country to help Jordan organize her course. Jordan plunged into the reading with gusto. She, who had never taken the time to be reflective or introspective, now became both. Jordan began to interpret and give meaning to her own experiences in a different way, and it marked the beginning of a transformation for her.

"I consider myself very fortunate that I can read and learn and retrain," she said. "That's going to serve me well, as it has in the past. I want to be a scholar. I want to be able to write the way some of the things I read are written. That will take time."[16]

Her reading choices were eclectic, reflecting both the gaps in her education and the reach of her intellect. She outlined the Federalist Papers as if she were a college student.[17] She pored over Aristotle's *Ethics*, de Tocqueville's *Democracy in America*, Walter Lippmann's *Public Philosophy*, Hannah Arendt's *Origins of Totalitarianism*, and John Rawls's *Theory of Justice*. Reading John Rawls helped refine her own deeply held views on truth and justice. "Our system seeks to guarantee that each citizen gets justice and that justice is denied no one. What is justice? Justice is fairness. It is the first virtue of all human institutions. It is an endemic value in our democracy," she came to see.[18] Sissela Bok's book *Lying: Moral Choice in Public and Private Life* had just been published, and Jordan incorporated its insights into her thinking. She also reread a book that had influenced her thinking much earlier, Reinhold Niebuhr's *Moral Man and Immoral Society*, and she agreed with Niebuhr's ideas about the "nature of man."

"Niebuhr identified greed, will-to-power, and other forms of self-assertion—I would include self-interest and special-interest groups—as natural impulses," she told her students. "If you agree with that view then you do not despair when veterans' groups, organized labor, or oil and gas interests try to cut for themselves the best legislative deal possible. That is in the basic nature of man. There is cause for despair only when the politicians accede to the interests of these groups without any effort to appeal to reason, or the basic rationality of man, which Niebuhr also identifies as a natural force. It would be ideal if the politician could recognize the contest between natural impulses and natural forces as an opportunity to adjust interest to interest for our common good and the general welfare."[19]

Jordan had come to believe with Niebuhr that there would always be a conflict between man's finer instincts and the collective impulses of society. Niebuhr "states that the highest ideal for the society is justice and the highest ideal for the individual is selflessness. After presenting those laudable goals he proceeds to argue that neither is attainable and that the best one can hope for is a peaceful coexistence. Successful implementation should assume that an ethic of pure disinterestedness is not possible, but that *enlightened* self-interest is. However, the requirement for justice as a component for implementation is not negotiable. The surest way to ensure program failure is to have the population perceive that the program and its proposals are not fair."[20]

While Niebuhr and Rawls had a strong intellectual appeal for her, she was emotionally drawn to Judge Learned Hand's "Spirit of Liberty" speech. Judge Hand's words to 150,000 newly naturalized citizens in New York in 1944 connected Jordan's early religious teaching with her belief in the rule of law. She memorized the speech and began to incorporate a section of it into her lectures and speeches.

> *The spirit of liberty is the spirit which is not too sure that it is right; the spirit of liberty is the spirit which seeks to understand the minds of other men and women; the spirit of liberty is the spirit which weighs their interests alongside its own without bias; the spirit of liberty remembers that not even a sparrow falls to earth unheeded; the spirit of liberty is the spirit of Him who, nearly two thousand years ago, taught mankind that lesson it has never learned, but never quite forgotten; that there may be a kingdom where the least shall be heard and considered side by side with the greatest.*[21]

Jordan's practicality continued to assert itself, even with Learned Hand. "Let's not be too smug about this," she warned. "The rule of law does not ensure justice. Nor does it allow us the easy pastime of avoiding our consciences by just 'following the law.' Rather, the rule of law exemplifies and reinforces the spirit of liberty precisely because it constrains our choices and then forces us to choose. What are those constraints? They are principally two: universality—that is, an indifference as to the status of the parties, whether they are rich or poor or powerful or meek; and a certain logic—that is, the application by inference of similar rules in similar cases. Following the rule of law means not just giving reasons for what is done, but reasons that fit these two rigorous requirements. Are laws passed to protect the rich and powerful? Of course they are. In some sense, the rich and powerful have more to protect and more to protect it with. Do laws and legislatures favor the mainstream and penalize the marginal? You bet. And that is not right. Liberty places law above government. That hierarchy should ever remain in the interest of universal order and civility."[22]

Once Jordan began her intellectual journey, it seemed to take her back to her deepest religious beliefs. She sought out the writings of Howard Thurman, the Boston University preacher and theologian who had shaped her religious thinking some twenty years earlier. Thurman had written extensively about the meaning of love and had repeatedly used the phrase "the ethic of love," which Jordan began to incorporate into many of her lectures. For Thurman, there were "no types or stereotypes, not classes and no masses . . . in the presence of love."[23] This religious sentiment was identical to Jordan's belief in the need for universality in the law. In the presence of either love or justice there could be no discrimination based on skin color, gender, economic condition, or any other artificial barrier that separated people. Thurman's views on Christian love reinforced her belief in conciliation and the practice of an "ethic of love" in public policy, and it seemed to resurrect an earlier idealism that her practice of the realpolitik of the Texas legislature and Congress came close to obliterating. "People should count more than money," Jordan emphasized to her students. She admitted, however, that sophisticated politicians would chuckle at such a statement and mutter: "How naive. Doesn't she know that we are on the threshold of the twenty-first century, whose watchwords are 'compete and win'? There is not enough time for love and sharing and caring." Jordan said she would respond to those skeptics simply by repeating: "People matter. People count."[24]

Jordan had always been enamored of the notion of "the people." It was a unique American concept, she felt. She called on her favorite Republican president, Abraham Lincoln, to provide some depth to her belief. "Abraham Lincoln gave us a trilogy we use as a definition of democracy," she said. "But my problem with Abraham Lincoln's trilogy is that we put emphasis on the wrong words. The trilogy is: *of, by, for* the people. When we recite the trilogy we say '*of* the people, *by* the people, *for* the people.' You know how we should recite that? We should say 'of the *people,* by the *people,* for the *people.*' This is a government which has as its base, people. This is a republic which says: here the people will govern. . . . Without the consent of the people, the government fails. In order for the government then to be sustained and remain viable, the people have to support it."[25]

She was proud of her new intellectual attainments, as well as her rediscovered idealism. "I'm in the books," she said. "My students are in the books. We have to know what we're talking about. I don't just come into class and sit down and reminisce and pontificate."[26] Jordan told friends that when she completed a class, she was so high she was "on the ceiling, and all I want to do is talk about what went on in class and how my students responded."[27] The rewards of teaching were so gratifying that she could not help but compare them to her congressional career.

"When you teach students you can see an immediate result of your efforts. You are sitting in a class and you are posing questions and you are exchanging ideas and when you see it all, you say, 'Well, I got that across.' In the political arena, as I was out there for twelve years . . . you do things and you don't know how long it will take for them to bear fruit, if ever."[28]

She joked that it was the "preacher in me that makes me enjoy it so much."²⁹

Jordan applied what she considered to be the Socratic method to her teaching. "She asked our opinions about atomic bombs, balanced budgets, equal opportunity, and other public issues," one student said. "She was no academic tyrant out to embarrass her students or, worse yet, force her opinions on them. Rigorous, yes. Demanding, absolutely. In fact, she seemed harder on women and black students, as though she were trying to toughen them. But her goal seemed to be to inspire debate, not obedience or conformity. She encouraged us to develop informed opinions, argue and defend them well, and modify them, if that was called for. Jordan's own grasp of the issues and her high expectations made us ashamed to offer half-baked ideas."³⁰

She taught that there are seven core values that provide the framework for the American system of government: equality, liberty, freedom, justice, independence, respect for others, and opportunity. She expected her students to wrestle with them as they came to terms with the "inherent nature of man." She wanted students to understand how views of human nature shape the fundamental laws and principles adopted by government. She forced them to grapple with the question: What is the prior principle— liberty or equality? She wanted them to debate notions of distributive justice and the common good and expected them to be prepared to defend their own core values and ethical principles—"even when they appear to collide with the practicable, the utilitarian, and/or the public will." She warned them: "If your thinking about your beliefs is fuzzy, it is likely that the quality of your defense will be equally fuzzy." Her advice was to "think clearly, argue persuasively—in that order."³¹

One of her students warned that "a conscientious student would never consider walking into her class unprepared. If you have to go without food, go without sleep, you go without in any way you can, but you don't take a gamble that this particular time you will be overlooked."³² When asked why it was so important to be prepared in Jordan's class, one student said, "I want her approval. I want to go out and excel because of her." Still another student said that Jordan provoked such admiration in the classroom because "her idea of social commitment and social consciousness and the fact that we have to, in a sense, pay rent for space we occupy is really a driving force." One young man summed up Jordan's classroom impact, saying, "I've never met a person who believed so strongly that we can actually change the world, and that gives me confidence that we really can."³³

Jordan counseled her students, most of whom would have careers in some form of public service, that they had to assume greater responsibility than individuals in other careers. "Are we holding the public servant to a different standard than those in business or marketing or sales or manufacturing?" she asked. She insisted that the answer was, "Yes, a different standard, a tougher standard, a higher standard. Is it fair? Of course it is fair. A public trust must be handled and must be managed by those who are motivated by the public interest. Those who hold the public trust must adhere to the highest ethical standards there are. The job requires it, and the public must demand it."[34] To Jordan it was simple: If you see government service as a noble calling, then ethics are important. If you don't, then they are not.

Jordan demanded this higher standard from her own students and friends, and she could be particularly tough on them when they didn't live up to her expectations. One of her protégés was Rodney Ellis, the affable son of a gardener and a maid who grew up in the Fifth Ward and eventually was elected to Jordan's old Texas Senate seat. Ellis had applied for a job in Jordan's congressional office immediately after he graduated from Texas Southern University. Although Jordan didn't give him a job, she spent an extraordinary amount of time counseling him on his future, which he hoped would be in politics. She told him to go to law school and establish himself financially before running for office so he would not be tempted to trade votes for his future gain. Ellis took Jordan's advice and got a law degree from the University of Texas, as well as a master's degree in public affairs from the LBJ School, and he stayed close to Jordan even after he became the top administrative aide to Houston's Mickey Leland, who succeeded Jordan in Congress.[35] Later Ellis became a public finance bond lawyer and for the first time in his life began making a lot of money, but he was still interested in becoming a politician. In 1990, when it looked like an open race would develop for Jordan's old Senate seat, Ellis sought her advice again. He was surprised when she told him that if he ran for office, he had to get out of the bond business.

"Rodney," she boomed. "You have to decide what you really want to do. You cannot make money and be in politics at the same time. You cannot serve two masters."[36]

Ellis recalled that Jordan told him that he had what it took to go all the way in politics—"whatever that might mean for a black person today— and that I could make all the money I wanted after I left politics, but I shouldn't do it as long as I held public office. So I took her advice— gradually. I got out of the bond business, got my business out of Texas, even got out of the country," he recalled. "But I did get a juicy little contract thrown my way to lobby for NAFTA on behalf of the Mexican government, and I got jumped on all over the place by the press and other politicians when I took it. So I went back to Barbara to get her advice again." This time Jordan "jumped" all over him, too.

"You missed my first premise, Rodney," she said. "You did not listen to me. I told you that you *cannot* make money while you're in politics—*any-time, any*place!"

"She treated me like a rough teacher would treat a bad student," Ellis laughed. He endured her tongue-lashing, however, and later joked to a friend that "Barbara Jordan gave real helpful political advice to her friends, and it was to *go broke*! Someone must have told her I said that because she called me and really pulled my chain over it." Ellis believed that Jordan retained some affection for him and even had hope for his eventual redemption. "She gave me a real boost one time with the Houston business community. She was speaking to the Houston Chamber of Commerce, and someone asked her who she saw as the upcoming black leaders of the next generation, and without hesitation she said, 'Rodney Ellis.' It was a real compliment, better than any paid commercial I could have bought. Her public approval was like being anointed."

Throughout her lectures, personal counseling, heavy reading, and ponderous thinking, Jordan managed to keep her sense of humor, as did the students who had to compete in a lottery to win admission to her classes. A west Texas cowboy did not feel so lucky on his first day in class when Jordan's stern gaze fixed him in her sights and her booming voice asked, "What does freedom mean to you?" He squirmed for what seemed like an interminable moment before he blurted out, "I guess freedom's just another word for nothing left to lose." Other members of the class gasped in horror as they recognized the lyrics from Janis Joplin's soulful rendition of the song "Me and Bobby McGee." Jordan kept her frown as long as she could and then broke into gales of laughter, much to the relief of the blushing student. "That's not too bad," she said. "Not too bad."[37]

For Barbara Jordan, the adjustment to life away from Washington was "not too bad" either.

THE PRIVATE SECTOR

Jordan's withdrawal from Washington and politics was a withdrawal from public life, not from life itself. She did make a few public appearances, but they were limited to showing support for causes she considered worthy. She appeared on the platform when the Freedoms Foundation in Valley Forge, Pennsylvania, honored Aleksandr Solzhenitsyn, Mamie Eisenhower, and Hubert Humphrey in 1979. In 1980 she joined with the television producer Norman Lear and the Reverend William Howard, president of the National Council of Churches, to become a cofounder of People for the American Way.[38] And in 1981 she went back to Washington to testify before the House Judiciary Committee on still another extension of the Voting Rights Act. She told the committee that the 1975 Voting Rights Act had "changed politics in Texas . . . you can measure it in the number of newly registered minority voters—about 420,000 . . . and there is a 22 percent increase in minority officeholders."[39] Jordan also pointed out that many city councils had changed from at-large to single-member districts to allow greater minority participation, including San Antonio, Houston, Waco, and other

Texas cities. To Jordan, the Voting Rights Act was worth a trip to Washington, D.C. She made few other public appearances, however. There were other things she wanted to do.

Early in 1979 Jordan took advantage of several offers to join the corporate world. While part of her interest came from wanting to learn something new, Jordan also wanted a new source of income. She had taken a pay cut to teach at the LBJ School, where her base salary for her first year was $45,000, $10,000 less than her congressional salary. Corporate board work seemed to provide the way because directors were paid handsome fees for attending meetings and frequently received stock options in their companies as a reward for service that, theoretically at least, provided overall direction for the company and exercised fiduciary responsibility on behalf of shareholders.

Great wealth, specific expertise, and influence over other business or financial institutions were usually the criteria for selection of corporate directors. In 1979 corporate directorships represented the business elite of the nation. There were few women who served on boards, unless they were members of the families that held stock ownership in the firms, and there were virtually no African Americans. Barbara Jordan would be one of the first. Ironically, it was Texas Republican George Bush who opened the door for her first corporate board post.

Bush had been asked to serve on the board of the Mead Corporation, one of the nation's largest suppliers of paper products. Mead owned two paper mills and a printing plant in Dayton, Ohio, and wanted to add a Texan to its board. Bush declined because he was getting ready to make a run for the Republican presidential nomination in 1980, and he suggested Barbara Jordan as a substitute. Mead's chairman, James W. McSwiney, and general counsel, Jerry Rapp, were so taken with the idea that they flew to Washington to invite Jordan to be on the board while she was still in Congress. She was interested but decided she would not go on the board until her congressional term was over. Mead waited and officially elected her as a director in April 1979.[40]

It was Jordan's entry onto her second board, however, that was the major coup for her. Texas Commerce Bank was the flagship financial institution of establishment Houston. Its board members were white, wealthy, and, by 1979, mostly Republican including former president Gerald Ford, although Lady Bird Johnson was also on the board. To be invited to serve on the holding company board of Texas Commerce was to be invited "inside" the halls of economic power in Texas. For Texas Commerce's CEO Ben Love, who had gotten to know Jordan when she was in the Texas Senate, her appointment was a pioneering venture. When she joined the board in 1979, Jordan became the first African American to serve on a major bank board in the nation.

"After she decided to leave Congress, but before she actually left, I invited her to be on the board," Ben Love said. "But before I talked to her, I wanted to be sure there was no controversy." Love went to see Howard Creekmore, head of the Houston Endowment, one of the nation's largest philanthropic foundations. "When I told Howard I wanted to put Barbara on our board, he said to me, 'Well, if you don't do it, it's possible one of the other banks might. Then, if you want a black person, there is no second black, no one is equivalent to Barbara Jordan. So you better do it now.'" Creekmore made calls to other Texas Commerce directors, some of whom worried that they would be criticized in their country clubs for adding a black person to their inner circle. "But on the whole, they thought it was worthwhile," Love remembered.[41]

More corporate board offers came her way, and later in the year she joined the board of the *Washington Star,* the newspaper recently acquired by the Houston banker and publisher Joe Allbritton.[42] "She loved those boards," a close friend remembered. "You'd think she personally owned those companies. They would fax her mounds of material and she would read everything. She would talk about buying and selling this or that. She just loved it."

"Barbara was subjected to tokenism a bit on those boards," George Christian believed. "But that didn't seem to bother her. She liked those board fees. But she wasn't just a passive member. She would really get involved. And I think she got a solemn kick out of the way a lot of white people dealt with her. She was so sought after. They just pawed at her."

PHYSICAL LIMITS

While teaching and her new board work took up most of Jordan's time in 1979, her physical condition continued to worsen. She had been taking the corticosteroid drug prednisone off and on since 1973. It had triggered infections of her sweat glands, which caused debilitating swelling and terrible skin irritations and rashes. She was also taking medication to control a tendency toward diabetes. In addition, she had a series of gallstone attacks and had to have her gallbladder removed. Multiple sclerosis attacks had so weakened the muscles that controlled movement of her right eye that her vision was now impaired.[43] But the biggest problem was that her legs had become so weak that her ability to walk was precarious. As a result, she had several falls, one time breaking her collarbone, and another time injuring her wrist. By 1980 her balance was so unstable that her cane was no longer sufficient to help her get around. She swallowed her pride and began to use a walker. One student commented that it was now taking almost twenty minutes for her to walk from her office to her classroom with the aid of her walker. "I don't exactly know what she's got, but I know it's terrible."[44]

It had become so difficult to get around that there were times when she even succumbed to using a wheelchair. Although she still had some mobility, the wheelchair made it easier and faster to get from here to there. And for Jordan, impatience to move quickly finally beat out her pride. Houston attorney Ken Wall, who was one of Jordan's students at the time, drove her home from class every week and remembered how difficult it was becoming for her. "Although she never mentioned it and would change the subject if someone else mentioned it, Barbara Jordan didn't move around very well anymore. She needed assistance in standing and sitting, in getting in and out of a car. And even with assistance, the movement was not without difficulties. Indeed, almost all physical movement for Barbara was an effort, a tremendous effort. Yet during all the excursions we made together, not only from school to her home, but to various speaking engagements and dinner parties, I never once heard her utter a complaint or express any irritation or frustration with me or her conditions. And no matter how much trouble she and I had getting her into and out of a host's home or private plane, and most of these transactions were not flawless, I could always count on two things: her determination and her appreciation."[45]

Jordan's unwillingness to complain did not mean that she accepted her condition. Her frustrations were enormous, and she decided she would try anything to halt the progression of the disease. In 1980 she began a series of experimental treatments. There were plenty to try. Because the cause of multiple sclerosis was unknown, every year or so there seemed to be a new treatment of choice. Many of them were fads: snake venom, blood transfusions, even vertebral artery surgery. Others were untried remedies that were clearly promoted for profit. Some MS patients believed they could be genuinely helped by taking hyperbaric treatments—immersing themselves in a hyperbaric oxygen chamber, where the high-pressure release of oxygen replaced the nitrogen bubbles in their blood. The rationale was that breathing oxygen under increased pressure in a specially constructed chamber would improve the conduction of signals through the central nervous system and perhaps even "refire" dormant cells. Patients seemed more agile and alert and had a feeling of euphoria immediately after the treatment, and Jordan wanted to see whether she, too, could be helped by the treatments. But her condition remained unchanged.[46]

One experimental treatment that Jordan tried might have actually slowed the MS progression, but it was ultimately more damaging to her system. For years she took the powerful synthetic drug Cytoxan.[47] Cytoxan was believed to slow the progression of multiple sclerosis and to reduce the relapse rate. But it greatly increased the risk of cancer and was profoundly damaging to the bladder, and few physicians would prescribe it. Because it was a global immunosuppressant drug—it suppressed not just one target but the entire immune system—it was the equivalent of dropping a bomb on the body. Jordan was willing to take a chance, however. A Houston neurologist prescribed it for her.

Cytoxan gave Jordan hope that she could stop the "slow burn" of multiple sclerosis that was ravaging her body. Within a short time, however, she began to experience repeated urinary tract infections that virtually destroyed her bladder, and eventually she had to have an indwelling catheter. When that happened, she had to have regular help changing the catheter and a succession of therapists and helpers became part of her daily routine. She also needed the regular attention of an Austin physician, as well as her Houston neurologist. And her Austin doctor became one of her closest friends.

Dr. Rambie Briggs's gentlemanly manner and attention to detail endeared him to Jordan quite early in their relationship. He earned her trust by respecting her wishes for total confidentiality about her ailments. He was so careful that he did not keep her medical records in his office files with those of other patients. Nor did he allow his office assistants to transcribe his notes on her care. After each visit, Briggs made handwritten notations about Jordan's condition for her medical records and then took them home with him so no one else would ever see them.

"I guess I was in awe of her. . . . She began to show up periodically, and I began to see her about twice a year. At some point she just decided I would be her family practitioner, but she was still going to Houston for her neurological work. I basically took care of everything else—urinary tract infections and those skin infections. It took us a while, but we got to be close."

By 1980 Jordan was using a wheelchair more frequently, although she still had some limited mobility. "I just resigned myself to moving around without the expenditure of so much energy by getting in a wheelchair and letting people push me around," she said.[48] Nancy Earl had not signed on to be Barbara's nursemaid, however, and was not going to push her all over their house. She bought a motorized scooter/wheelchair that Barbara used at home. Nancy rearranged the furniture so Barbara wouldn't bump into things as she buzzed around. The scooter had a basket in front where she could keep her books and cigarettes, or a drink. She still liked her Cutty Sark in the late afternoons. Many days she would sit in her scooter on the back patio overlooking the wide expanse of lawn. She would read or simply stare off into the trees bordering the creek bank, or just look up at the sky. The vista seemed to fill her up and give her energy and peace. So did just being at home. "I think she would have been content just staying there all the time," a close friend said.

Jordan insisted on regular rituals that provided a framework for her days. In the morning she took a swim in the pool on the east side of the house. Sometimes she would put an Aretha Franklin tape on the stereo and belt out "R-E-S-P-E-C-T" in her best voice as she made her way, with her walker, to the pool. If she left the house to teach or do anything else in Austin, she always wanted to be home by 5:30 P.M. to watch the national news, followed by local newscasts and the *McNeil-Lehrer Report* on PBS. During the evenings she would watch television or a movie on video, or read, and be in bed by 11:00 P.M. Once in bed, she had to have all of her night necessities around her—a glass of water, reading material, the television remote control, paper and pens, and her Sony Walkman and music tapes, which she would listen to as she drifted off to sleep. Sometimes Nancy would put fruit by Barbara's bed in the morning so she would have something to eat before her caregivers arrived to help her begin the morning regime. Barbara had a good relationship with most of the young men and women who over the years became her helpers, and who saw her at her greatest degree of physical vulnerability. Once again, her ability to compartmentalize her life seemed to allow her to preserve her internal pride and privacy, while somehow disassociating her "core being" from her body, which needed the assistance of others to function.

Jordan slept in a king-size bed, covered during the day with an earthtone paisley spread. Over the bed was a Georgia O'Keeffe poster featuring a gnarled oak tree in blues and browns. She could lie in her bed and look south through the floor-to-ceiling windows to the creek and woods in the distance. Facing her bed was a fieldstone fireplace with a bookshelf on one side, crowded with her favorite books and mementos. Here she kept the biographies she read of famous Americans: Adlai Stevenson, Ulysses S. Grant, John Marshall, Judge Louis Brandeis, and later, Taylor Branch's epic work on Martin Luther King Jr. and the civil rights movement, *Parting the Waters*. And of course, she had Lyndon Johnson's book about his presidency, *The Vantage Point*. Johnson had given Jordan the fourth imprint of the book, with the first three going to his wife and two daughters, to whom he had dedicated his book. His inscription to Jordan read, "For another first lady, with affection and deep admiration."[49] A. Philip Randolph had also inscribed a biography of his life for Jordan, telling her he appreciated "all you have done and will be in the struggle for the liberation of all people." And she had a copy of the autobiography of her favorite minister, Howard Thurman of Boston University. For relaxation, she liked to read whodunits and legal thrillers by Scott Turow and John Grisham.

When Jordan began to use her wheelchair more frequently, her bathroom had to be remodeled and the doorway widened. These adjustments made her surroundings more serene than ever, and Jordan was content to spend much of her time in the rambling stone house. So self-contained had she become that she didn't seem to need the company of others. But there were certain friends she was always glad to see.

Stan McClelland was at the top of her list. Always polite, yet witty and irreverent on occasion, Stan often imitated Barbara's booming voice and could make her laugh—even at herself. He would tease her by using phrases from her famous 1976 Democratic convention keynote address, pointing out how "different" and "special" she had become. Sometimes she responded with a parody of herself: "I, Barbara Jordan, different and special as I am, want the first slice of roast beef." They would all take turns making up silly things for the "different and special" Barbara to do. Stan was devoted to Barbara, and after he became a high-ranking executive with Valero Energy Corporation, a natural gas exploration and development firm headquartered in San Antonio, he frequently made Valero's airplane available to her to assist in the logistics of her travels. He was also available to travel with her anytime she needed an escort, or even just someone to push her wheelchair. Jordan once told a friend that Stan was probably the only man she ever knew whom she could have married, because he was smart, funny, and rich and he always knew just what to do and how to do it.

Jordan trusted Stan McClelland and Nancy Earl, and her LBJ School secretary, Sharon Tutchings, who for the last nine years of Jordan's life protected her from anyone who attempted to intrude on her time or life.[50] Most of the people Jordan did see regularly were people whose demeanor matched her own: they were polite, reserved, thoroughly mannered, and always appropriate men and women who did not expect or demand any intimacy not offered by her. They could also be counted on to be discreet about revealing their friendship with her. Jordan stayed close to Azie Taylor Morton over the years, and after Morton moved back to Austin from Washington, where she had been the U.S. treasurer under President Jimmy Carter, they saw each other frequently. Jordan's friend Pat Heard and her neighbors, Billye Brown and Betty Thomas, who were both nurses, were regular visitors, as was her physician, Rambie Briggs. Two students from her first year as a professor remained friends: DeAnn Friedholm and Susan Rieff, who would on occasion bring pizza and beer to Jordan's on Friday nights and sometimes watch movies with her. Jordan liked to go to Elspeth and Walt Rostow's dinner parties, where the conversation was always topical and witty. She also spent long hours in philosophical discussions with the University of Texas law professor Philip Bobbitt, who was a constitutional scholar and a nephew of Lyndon Johnson. She was also fond of her LBJ School colleague Dagmar Hamilton, who had been a staff attorney on the House Judiciary Committee and who had worked for Supreme Court justice William O. Douglas. And Jordan was always happy to do *anything* President Johnson's widow, Lady Bird, asked of her: cut a ribbon, make a speech, or come to dinner.

Jordan did get out on a regular basis to attend the women's basketball games at the University of Texas. "Once I attended my first game, I was hooked," she said.[51] She became such a fixture at the games that she sat on the sidelines with the team and was named honorary coach. After she had been in Austin a few years, she began to open her home several times a year for large parties. She usually invited the women's basketball team and boosters, and at least once a year she entertained her students at the LBJ School. She and Nancy continued the tradition of Fourth of July parties they had started when the Onion Creek home was built. Sometimes Jordan even sang, to the delight of her guests. Although the multiple sclerosis had so weakened her hands that she could no longer play the guitar, it had not affected her voice, which could still belt out "Money Honey," "Saint James Infirmary," or "Amazing Grace."

When Barbara had settled into her Austin life, she talked to her sisters Rose Mary and Bennie every week and saw them frequently. Shortly after Barbara left Congress, her mother, Arlyne, had begun a rather rapid descent into Alzheimer's disease, and Bennie and Rose Mary took turns caring for her in their homes in Houston. Although Arlyne was barely aware of her presence, Barbara began spending the Christmas holidays in Houston with her mother and sisters and her aunt Mamie and uncle Wilmer Lee.[52] They would all attend services at the Good Hope Missionary Baptist Church. She also stayed in touch with the Justice sisters, her childhood friends, and they, along with Rose Mary and Bennie, would come to Austin every year for the Fourth of July party. With a group of friends she felt she could trust and with whom she was comfortable, and with her enjoyment of teaching and the corporate board work, Barbara Jordan gradually began to adjust to her new life. She even came to count its blessings.

Jerry Rapp of the Mead Corporation had become part of Jordan's small circle of friends, and he made arrangements for her to get away from Austin's summer heat and humidity and stay in the Durango, Colorado, home of his close friend, the Democratic Party activist Sam Maynes. Maynes's wife, Jackie, had multiple sclerosis, and they were both active in the National Multiple Sclerosis Society. The home was fully equipped for a wheelchair patient because Jackie Maynes no longer had the muscle capability to hold herself erect and had to use a reclining wheelchair that could support her upper body. The trip was an eye-opener for Jordan. For the first time, she realized just how disabled she might become, and it seemed to reinforce her natural instinct to focus entirely on the present. When she got back to Austin, she told Sharon Tutchings, "I'm so lucky. You should see what Mrs. Maynes has to endure."[53] Jordan did feel lucky. She could move, she could think, she could work, she could travel, and for the first time in her life she had enough money to do anything she wanted. And she was beginning to want to do more. "I discovered that my physical impairment did not diminish my thinking or the quality of my mind. And it did not impact my capacity to talk."[54]

REENTRY

The wheelchair and the catheter, plus the regular assistance of physical therapists, liberated rather than confined Jordan. Without the recurring bladder infections, and without having to struggle to take each step, her energy seemed to return. She taught on Monday and Tuesday and had the remainder of the week free. She would fly to Houston once a month for her Texas Commerce Bank board meetings, and Mead would send its corporate jet to pick her up in Austin to take her to Dayton for its meetings. Little by little, she began taking on more speaking engagements, and she joined the board of the Public Broadcasting Service. Also in 1982, for the first time since she had left Congress, Jordan spoke out publicly on a political issue. She blasted President Ronald Reagan at the annual Lyndon B. Johnson Lecture at Johnson's alma mater, Southwest Texas State University. First, she asserted that Ronald Reagan's economic policies had wreaked havoc in the lives of millions of Americans. Then she charged that Reagan had failed to uphold the duties of his office and that his hostility to government was just plain wrong.

> *There are some things that government must do. The reciprocal duties between the people and their government make ridiculous, meaningless, and empty such a slogan as "Get government off our backs," because government has some work to do for us. . . .*
> *When a president faithfully executes his office, he does not pursue economic policies which are so strange and different that no known economic theory applies and a new name has to be developed to label it—Reaganomics.*

Jordan was perhaps hardest on Reagan on the issue of race.

> *We black people know that whenever Republicans have been in power we don't fare terribly well. . . . We have not lost faith in this country . . . because what you probably don't know is that black people can stand a great degree of suffering because black people always have. A lesser people—I mean people of weaker constitution and fortitude—would have given up on this country long ago. But we didn't. We are going to force this country to live up to what it is supposed to be about or we'll die in the attempt.*

Jordan concluded by saying that Lyndon Johnson was "the last president I had. I am still looking for another."[55]

This speech marked the reemergence of Barbara Jordan as a political figure. But it was a new Barbara Jordan. Humbled by illness, strengthened by solitude, unencumbered by political ambition, and reinvigorated by reading and reflection, she was stronger than ever. But the "new" Barbara still expected the respect and decorum which the "old" Barbara felt she deserved.

When the Houston federal building and post office was to be renamed in her honor at the instigation of her successor in Congress, Representative Mickey Leland, Barbara almost threw a monkey wrench into Leland's carefully planned ceremony. People were always telling Leland, "You've got mighty big shoes to fill, young man." And Leland, always one to find humor in any situation, would reply, "You ought to quit talking about Barbara Jordan's feet." The day before the ceremony in downtown Houston, Leland's then-aide Rodney Ellis called Barbara to confirm the arrangements. "Is everything in order?" he asked her. "It certainly is *not*, Rod-ney!" she replied, drawing out his name. "I want to talk to the congressman." She implied that she might not go to the ceremony if Leland did not call her immediately. "Mickey called her and she chewed his ass for the 'big feet' jokes and he apologized profusely. Only then did she agree to attend the ceremony," Ellis said.

A NEW PUBLIC LIFE

By 1982 the public began to get regular glimpses of Barbara Jordan again. She had put back on some of the weight she lost earlier, and she had let her hair go natural, cutting it very short and letting it frame her face in tight little ringlets. She was a woman thoroughly at ease with herself who had adjusted to her limitations and found peace in her new life. Her ready smile reappeared. Her gaze was less forbidding and her humor less restrained.

By 1984 she had allowed herself to be drawn back into the political campaign orbit. During the Democratic primary contests, she had presided over a presidential candidates' forum in New York that featured the major Democratic contenders: Senators Gary Hart, John Glenn, and Alan Cranston, Governor Ruben Askew, and Vice President Walter Mondale. Although she did not attend the Democratic Party convention that nominated Walter Mondale and Geraldine Ferraro, she enthusiastically supported the ticket. She went to New Jersey to campaign for the reelection of Senator Bill Bradley, and she helped the Texas Democratic nominee, Lloyd Doggett, in his unsuccessful effort to unseat Senator Phil Gramm. After the election, congressional leaders invited her to Washington to be the keynote speaker for the National Prayer Breakfast, where President Reagan, fresh from his reelection victory, would also be speaking.

The event drew more than three thousand people from the ranks of the U.S. Senate and House of Representatives, ambassadorial and other representatives from one hundred nations, and people from every state in the union. To them, Jordan gave a preview of her new, more thoughtful self.

She talked about the soul and the innate nature of man. She discussed Reinhold Niebuhr's view of man's duality, and of what she believed were the requirements for justice and selflessness. And she probed theological questions probably never addressed before in a national prayer breakfast.

> *Shakespeare asks in one of his sonnets, what is your substance, whereof are you made? That's a big question. . . . The answer is not very simple. Most of us would quickly retire to the Old Testament and say we are made in the image of God, and we would intone those words. But that response leaves too much unexplained. If we are made in the image of God, what is the source of our love of money? What is the source of our love of power? Profit? Wherein does greed and avarice and bitterness lie if you are made in the image of God? How do you explain your despoliation of the earth and propensity to rule over other men? How do we explain, if indeed we are made in the image of God, our capacity to extinguish mankind?*
>
> *We are very complex beings and we seem to be bifurcated between an outer self and an inner self. . . . For me, our inner self seems to be in touch with God and communicating with Him regularly. This inner self is likeable, caring, compassionate. The instincts of the inner are right ordered, well ordered. The outer self appears to be dominant, and the outer self seems extraordinarily willing to negotiate those basic fundamental principles which arise from within.*

Jordan then described the "whole" person as one who has managed to merge her inner and outer beings. "That person who is whole has a non-negotiable set of principles. . . . If we are whole people, there are some very old words which will be used to define us, words like truth, virtue, honesty. Our political and policy decisions will reflect them and be released once we are old. Our political and policy decisions will be released, can be released, for ethical analysis and hold up wonderfully, with a good conscience our only sure reward, with history the final judge of our deeds."[56]

Speeches like this earned Jordan the Best Living Orator Award in 1984, presented by the National Platform Association, an organization of professional speakers. The veteran political observer Theodore H. White described Jordan's oratory as "a flow of Churchillian eloquence, or resonance, boom and grip so compelling as to make one forget to take notes."[57] The syndicated newspaper columnist Sandy Grady carried the Churchill analogy even further, asserting that Jordan's power as a speaker could make a listener believe that "Winston Churchill had been reincarnated as a black woman from Texas."[58] But had Barbara Jordan become *only* an orator? Did that fully explain the significance of her impact on those who heard her?

If Jordan's oratory was only an "ornament of speech," in the words of the media critic Neil Postman, then it would have been only "pretentious, superficial and unnecessary."[59] But as she got older, Jordan's oratory, like that of the Sophists of fifth-century Greece who invented the rules of rhetoric, was more than a mere opportunity for dramatic performance. It was a means of organizing evidence and proofs in order to communicate *truth*. When she delivered her most eloquent speeches, her audiences felt they did indeed hear the essence of truth. They were uplifted, perhaps transformed momentarily, into better versions of themselves. "It wasn't only her Olympian voice that awed people," Sandy Grady believed. "It was her ferocious insistence that justice wasn't only for the rich and powerful."[60]

The *Time* magazine essayist Lance Morrow once said that Barbara Jordan had the "gravitas" factor, which sometimes announces itself as eloquence and sometimes proclaims itself as a silence, a "suspension full of either menace or Zen. . . . Gravitas is a phenomenon of power."[61]

In her withdrawal from public life, Jordan found both a new purpose and new opportunities for her talents—and a new sense of her own power. In her reentry, she was discovering that the joy—and meaning—of her life as a teacher came from the variety and depth of her experiences rather than from using them as a means to get something else. The new experiences she now chose were unrelated to any distant ambition, and they were attractive to her solely because of their inherent interest. She wanted to pack as many of them as she could into her new life.

"In my *other* life, I was in the spiral to get ahead," she said. "I was propelled by a driving force and was leading what I now consider to be an unbalanced life. I was forty years old before I decided I really could turn my head and look in another direction. . . . It is not a sin not to work twenty-four hours a day. I began including things that were enjoyable and pleasurable and found that it's not all one way or the other," she said.[62]

In her new life, Barbara Jordan also had learned another lesson. "I live a day at a time," she said. "Each day I look for a kernel of excitement. In the morning, I say: 'What is my exciting thing for today?' Then I *do* the day. Don't ask me about tomorrow."[63]

CHAPTER 19

AMERICAN PATRIOT

WHAT MAKES AN American hero? Or any hero?

The adjectives we use to describe a hero are varied: brave, intrepid, daring, gallant, persistent, noble, lofty, larger-than-life, fearless, relentless, unshrinking, uncowed, adventurous, superior. It follows that an *American* hero would employ most of those qualities in the pursuit of something unique or fundamental to the meaning of America. For Barbara Jordan, three ideals encompassed what she thought of as fundamental to America: liberty, justice, and equality. For her, the pursuit of those ideals was encompassed in the rule of law, the Constitution. Yet until her Watergate experience, she held such a narrow view of herself that her pursuit of those ideals went no further than using them as "ornaments" in her rhetoric. Before Watergate, all she wanted to be was a politician—not a statesman, or a moral leader, or a guardian of government ethics, and certainly not a civil rights leader. After Watergate, Jordan added one more label to describe herself: patriot. She considered the U.S. Constitution her *personal* charter for freedom.

"To say that the Constitution has influenced my life is an understatement. I have an extraordinary reliance on and almost personal attachment to the Constitution. . . . The basic freedoms guaranteed by the Bill of Rights and the Fourteenth Amendment allowed me to become the best I could become without the specter of suppression and restraint. As a young lawyer starting a new law practice in Houston, I knew that I was not consigned to practice law in the ghetto forever. If I could prove to others my competence as a lawyer, there were no limits to the goals I was free to pursue. The Constitution personally and professionally gave me a solid platform for achievement."[1]

"Barbara understood that the law was the fabric of democracy," believed Elaine Jones, director counsel of the NAACP Legal Defense Fund. "Barbara was saying that the law applies to us all—presidents or paupers. She was saying this document, the Constitution, has a process whereby she came into this system."

The early Barbara Jordan—before Watergate and multiple sclerosis, and before leaving Congress—was an interesting symbol of progress in the nation's tortured march to equality. Yet even then, as she struggled to come to terms with her role in American politics, all of the heroic qualities of her character were present as tiny buds awaiting the proper conditions for flowering. Watergate was their first significant nourishment. But Jordan's withdrawal from public life and the process of coming to terms with her physical—and political—limitations provided the conditions that allowed her heroic traits to bloom. Only then did she begin to see more clearly what her most important role could be: not just the first of her race to break so many barriers, but the spokesperson for American idealism. She began to craft for herself a new persona as a patriot-teacher whose classroom was not just for college students but for the whole nation.

The Barbara Jordan who reentered public life in the mid-1980s had become the woman the American people perceived her to be. She was unencumbered by ambition, free from the constraints of public opinion, solid in her core beliefs in liberty, justice, and equality, and unwilling to give in to the physical constraints her body imposed upon her. When she spoke publicly, her words were so connected to the most deeply held American values that they seemed fresh in the midst of a rising American cynicism.

"I am a born optimist," she said. "I find that if you can just cut off the layers, the rhetoric, the superficiality, and get to the inner core—the heart [of a person]—that you will find a responsible human being, and that is destructive of cynicism."[2]

Cornel West has written that African American leaders usually fall into three categories: race-effacing managerial leaders, race-identifying protest leaders, and race-transcending prophetic leaders.[3] For the first part of her public career, Jordan was a race-effacing managerial leader of the highest order; she *managed* politics to the degree that the most ardent segregationists in the Texas legislature and the U.S. Congress came to disregard her race and accept her for her skills. But after 1982, during the second part of her public career, Jordan moved in the direction of becoming a race-transcending prophetic leader. Her integrity, political savvy, moral vision, prudent judgment, courageous defiance, and organizational patience made the transition possible.

"There is no reason why a country as large and powerful as we are should not occupy the highest moral position possible in relation to other countries," she believed. "The core of morality is to do unto others as you would have them do unto you. . . . . I believe each individual should have a principled core of his or her being that cannot get negotiated out. That has served me well."[4]

Some of the responsibilities Jordan took on in the mid-1980s helped develop this new sense of her role. In 1985 she accepted her first international assignment by becoming the only American on an eleven-member United Nations panel examining the impact of transnational corporations doing business in South Africa and Namibia. The panel, appointed by UN Secretary-General Javier Perez de Cuellar, spent a year probing corporate influence, direct or indirect, on apartheid in both countries. The purpose was to find a way for the world's major corporations to put pressure on the South African government to end apartheid. Individuals on the panel did not represent specific countries with specific political agendas, and it was hoped that their independent approach might bring the problem closer to resolution.[5]

Jordan's horizons expanded with her participation on the UN panel. She grew quite fond of her fellow panelist Annie Jiagge of Ghana, who opened her eyes to the reality of apartheid and poverty for blacks, not only in South Africa but all over the world. "I developed a new consciousness of how bad things really are . . . and a new feeling that we, the United States of America, ought to do more to bring about an end to this. . . . Human rights is not a temporary or transitory political issue. We have got to respect the humanity of each other and know that no one has the right to rule over others."[6]

The panel surprised many people because it did not recommend general disinvestment in South Africa by the world's multinational corporations, only a moratorium on new investments and reinvestments. There was a practicality in the reports that Jordan felt reflected her own influence. "My strength [on the panel] was in clarifying things when some seemed hell-bent on obfuscating things."[7] The panel advised the one thousand transnational corporations doing business in South Africa to "confront the apartheid system in two ways: to refuse to supply the military, the police or other security forces with material that could be used to enforce apartheid," and to challenge South African labor laws directly by "abolishing any remnants of apartheid within their own organizations in South Africa."[8] Jordan thought the recommendation was the right way to go. "You phase divestiture in. You want to get apartheid out immediately, but you also want the country to be able to survive."[9] Jordan's role on the panel eventually led her to make a trip to South Africa to meet Nelson Mandela, who praised her United Nations work. Mandela's daughter later traveled to the United States to present Jordan with the first Nelson Mandela Award for Health and Human Rights, established by the Kaiser Family Foundation in his honor.[10]

Largely as a result of the United Nations panel and other public appearances connected to issues with morally fervent advocates, Barbara Jordan's prestige continued to grow. She appeared with some regularity on her favorite television news shows: the Sunday morning public affairs shows and the PBS *MacNeil/Lehrer NewsHour*. When there was a scandal or controversial issue in the news, newspaper editors sent their reporters to get her opinion. They, too, encountered the new Barbara Jordan. She was relaxed, fresh, humorous, and less defensive than she had been during her last few years in Congress. She was also quite willing to state her opinion on just about anything, and usually with broadcast-quality pithiness, delivered with a smile. When Ronald Reagan nominated the federal appeals court judge Robert Bork, who had been Richard Nixon's solicitor general, for a seat on the Supreme Court, Jordan thought it was a bad idea. She said so. In fact, she testified for almost two hours against Bork at the Senate Judiciary Committee hearings in September 1987.

THE BATTLE OVER BORK

Jordan's testimony against Judge Robert Bork proved there was still power in her mere presence. Texas Supreme Court justice Rose Spector said, "I knew it was all over for Bork when I saw Barbara Jordan wheel into the committee room to testify against him."[11]

Jordan took an uncharacteristically high profile during the Bork hearings, which were televised live in September 1987. She even debated Utah's Republican senator Orrin Hatch on the CBS Sunday program *Meet the Press*. Defeating the Bork appointment was important to Jordan because his views on the Constitution and the role of the federal judiciary were diametrically opposite to her own. More importantly, her old friends in the Washington civil rights community convinced her she could make a difference in the outcome of the confirmation hearing. Indeed, black opposition to Robert Bork was the key element in his rejection by the U.S. Senate. Few political struggles since the peak of the civil rights movement testified to black political power as persuasively as the Bork confirmation fight.[12]

The nation's liberals—especially in the civil rights community—had thought of the federal courts as their special protectors.[13] Yet President Reagan's appointment of conservative judicial activists was threatening to tip the balance in the federal judiciary from those who saw the courts as protectors of minority rights to those who were determined to reverse decades of liberal court decisions on civil rights. The appointment of a conservative ideologue who advocated wholesale change in the judicial role galvanized the nation's liberal organizations into action. The Leadership Conference on Civil Rights, which represented almost two hundred minority organizations, joined with the NAACP, People for the American Way, Common Cause, the AFL-CIO, the National Organization of Women,

Planned Parenthood, and dozens of other liberal organizations in an offensive against Bork.

Massachusetts senator Edward M. Kennedy, the ranking Democrat on the Senate Judiciary Committee, led the fight against Bork's confirmation in the Senate. The strategy emerged to have three prominent African American leaders serve as the leadoff witnesses against Bork: former transportation secretary (under Gerald Ford) William T. Coleman Jr.; former congressman Andrew Young, now mayor of Atlanta; and Barbara Jordan.

To help her prepare for her testimony, Elaine Jones of the NAACP's Legal Defense Fund had sent Jordan copies of Bork's writings and speeches, as well as his court opinions as an appellate judge. Judge Bork had left a massive paper trail, and Jordan studied it with the intensity she had applied to the Watergate transcripts. "She wanted all the practical stuff," Jones remembered. "You could talk about doing the 'right' thing or the 'moral' thing, but she wanted the statistics, the memos, the arguments, the reasons. She was a lawyer, and she understood all the legal issues, and the 'right' thing was only the starting point. She wasn't going to get there until she had the rest. She had to make up her own mind, but once she made it up, what an ally!"

Jordan's testimony followed an impressive presentation by Coleman, one of the nation's leading black Republicans. While Coleman's testimony was intellectual and convincing, Jordan's was personal and emotionally charged.

> *I am opposed to the confirmation of Robert Bork to the Supreme Court of the United States. My opposition is not a knee-jerk reaction of followership to the people or organizations whose views I respect. My opposition is a result of thinking about this matter with some care, of reading the White House position paper in support of Robert Bork, of reading the Judiciary Committee's point-by-point response to that position paper, discussing the matter with friends and people I respect, reading some of Judge Bork's writings. But more than any of that, my opposition to this nomination is really a result of living fifty-one years as a black American born in the South and determined to be heard by the majority community.*

Then she recited the specific Supreme Court cases that had allowed her—a young black woman—to succeed in politics, and she quoted Bork's opposition to those very cases: the famous *Baker v. Carr* one-man-one-vote case that changed apportionment; the cases that eliminated the poll tax, which Bork had said were wrongfully decided. "When you experience the frustrations of being in a minority position and watching the foreclosure of your last appeal and then suddenly you are rescued by the Supreme Court of the

United States, Mr. Chairman, that is tantamount to being born again," she told the committee. If the "Borkian" view had prevailed when those cases were decided, she declared, she would "right now be running my eleventh unsuccessful race for the Texas House of Representatives. I cannot abide that."

She also took Bork to task for his views on the right to privacy and covered the whole range of court cases on the issue, from *Griswold* to *Roe*. She thought that the presence of Bork's point of view on the Court placed "at risk individual rights. It is a risk we should not afford. . . . I do not want to see the argument made that there is no right to privacy . . . and the only way to prevent it being made is to deny Judge Bork membership on the Court." Perhaps her most devastating attack on Bork came in her discussion of his firing of Watergate special prosecutor Archibald Cox when Nixon's attorney general and deputy attorney general had resigned rather than do so.

> *All I can say to you is that on the day and at the time that Robert Bork fired Archibald Cox, there were rules and regulations in place, viable, alive, with the force and effect of law. They were violated, and, to me, that means the solicitor general acted illegally. . . . For you to confirm Robert Bork to the Supreme Court I think sends the wrong message. I believe that such a confirmation would indicate that it is all right with you for a person to sit on the Supreme Court who has utter disdain for the Office of Special Prosecutor. . . . A new justice should help us stay the course, not abort the course.[14]*

Members of the Senate Judiciary Committee, Republicans as well as Democrats, were deferential to Jordan when she testified. Republicans Strom Thurmond and Orrin Hatch were effusive in their praise of her. She was thoroughly at ease and accepted it all graciously, as if it were her due. Even when New Hampshire's right-wing Republican senator Gordon Humphrey tried to argue with her, she acted like she was amused rather than angry during their hard-hitting verbal sparring. At one point, Humphrey told her, "You're very good. . . . I cannot get anywhere. Although I think I could get a lesser person really over a barrel, I cannot get you over that barrel."[15] The exchange between Senator Humphrey and Barbara Jordan was useful, as well as sharp, because it got to the "nub" of the conflict over Bork: the question of whether the federal judiciary had a special and unique task to protect minorities and people who needed protection. For Barbara Jordan, the answer was yes.

On October 23, the Senate rejected the nomination of Robert Bork to the U.S. Supreme Court by a vote of fifty-eight to forty-two. Polls of American voters showed that they, too, would have rejected Bork, or any prospective Supreme Court candidate who had criticized recent civil rights gains or revealed a reluctance to acknowledge a constitutional right to privacy.[16]

Barbara Jordan believed that the fight over Bork's nomination was a battle over the direction of the American court system, and the future of the nation itself. The legal and political changes that so offended Bork and the Reagan conservatives were the very changes that had allowed Jordan to succeed. The conservatives rejected the notion of American pluralism, and they did not want the court to lead the way in extending and protecting the rights of women, racial minorities, the poor, and the politically unorthodox in order to allow them to participate fully in society. For conservatives like Bork, society's openness to diverse groups and belief systems had come at the expense of traditional values and generated an overall moral and social chaos.[17] For Jordan, the American ideals of liberty and equality could be achieved only with the continued push toward pluralism, which allowed for an inclusion of all—poor as well as rich, black as well as white, liberal as well as conservative, nonconformist as well as conformist, female as well as male, gay as well as straight, radical as well as reactionary. When the opportunities for liberty and equality were restricted, as they had been when she was a child, someone would always be left out of the American Dream, and that was not Jordan's vision of America. "The community within pluralism requires that my difference be seen and acknowledged; and if not accommodated, at a minimum tolerated," she believed. "What is the problem? Why do we see an apparent resurgence of racism across the face of America? What's wrong? White America, what's bugging you? . . . This country made some grandiose promises. We promised liberty, freedom, and equality to everybody. *No one* was to be excluded from the blessings of liberty."[18]

THE PUBLIC LIFE

Like the civil rights community, Barbara Jordan seemed to be reenergized by the Bork fight. She enjoyed being in the fray again, and she began accepting more invitations to speak or to be interviewed than she had at any time since she left Congress.

She gave a weeklong lecture series at her law school alma mater, Boston University. She participated in a public dialogue with the poet Maya Angelou on the subject of "Facing Evil" at a conference that Bill Moyers filmed for television. She became an active member of the Kaiser Family Foundation board, which focused on health care issues. She wrote an essay for *Time* magazine on the successes of the women's movement. She introduced a topic each week on a regular radio public affairs series called *The New American Gazette,* which featured guests like the Harvard economist John Kenneth Galbraith, former first lady Rosalyn Carter, Senator Warren

Rudman of New Hampshire, and Representative Barney Frank of Massachusetts. In 1987 she received a gold medal from the National Conference of Christians and Jews for her "courageous leadership in governmental, civic and humanitarian affairs." Honors were even *named* for her. In 1988 the Hollywood Women's Political Committee began giving an annual Barbara Jordan Award to honor persons for political courage and commitment. The billionaire Ross Perot gave $100,000 to the LBJ School of Public Affairs to fund a scholarship program in her name—on the condition that Jordan herself pick the recipients whose full cost of education would be paid for. Jordan's first choice was a young woman from the Fifth Ward who was a graduate of Texas Southern University.[19]

By 1988 Jordan had developed an entirely new kind of public life, yet her love of politics was still at its core. In 1988, when fellow Texan Ann Richards became the second woman to make a keynote address at a Democratic convention, Jordan—the first—appeared live on television with ABC's Peter Jennings and David Brinkley to comment on the speech. Two nights later, she seconded the nomination for vice president of another Texan—Lloyd Bentsen Jr.

Jordan put her prestige on the line in supporting Lloyd Bentsen for vice president. Jesse Jackson had made a surprisingly strong second-place finish to Massachusetts governor Michael Dukakis in the Democratic presidential primaries. Jackson expected to be offered the vice presidential spot, and when he was not, many party leaders worried about what he would do and where the sizable black constituency of the party would go. Bentsen's request for Jordan to second his nomination was an effort to reach out to the civil rights community and to reassure it that Bentsen, conservative Texan that he was, would be with them on civil rights issues. Jordan was happy to take on the challenge. She had never been a fan of Jesse Jackson's style of protest leadership. In her convention speech she cited Bentsen's early opposition to the poll tax and his vote against the confirmation of Robert Bork, and warned convention delegates: "It is a mistake for you to label Lloyd Bentsen."[20]

Democrats had greeted Jordan with thunderous applause when she appeared on the convention stage in her wheelchair. It was the first time many of them had seen her this way, and because of the television coverage, it was also probably the first time her fans across the country were aware of the extent of her disability, which news reporters described as a "muscle disorder."[21]

"She had just a little bit of time to gather her thoughts before her speech," Stan McClelland remembered. Jordan had been pushed in her wheelchair several blocks in the ninety-degree heat from her hotel to the Omni convention center, and she was wilted and drained by the time she got on stage. After the speech, rather than spend the night in Atlanta, McClelland flew her back to Austin. "We didn't get in until three or four in the morning, and I was supposed to go out to the LBJ Ranch with her that Friday evening for a birthday party Mrs. Johnson was giving for Philip Bobbitt.[22] Because I knew she was tired, I tried to talk her out of it, but she insisted on going. . . . When we headed for home after midnight, we were both utterly exhausted."

McClelland was getting ready to see Jordan again on Saturday and turned on his radio while he was dressing. "I heard on the radio that she had been found in her swimming pool, floating facedown and lifeless."

Barbara Jordan was near death in an Austin hospital.

THE LIMITS OF THE BODY—AGAIN

Nancy Earl had gone shopping for groceries on Saturday morning, July 30. The temperature was almost 100 degrees Fahrenheit and Barbara wanted to take her daily swim. Her practice was to never swim alone, so she waited until Nancy returned home around noon to place herself into a hydraulic lift that had been installed to lower and raise her from the pool. Nancy was still putting the groceries away some ten minutes later and had gone out to the garage when she spotted Barbara's lifeless body in the pool. She ran to the pool and jumped in to grab her. Barbara had no pulse and was not breathing. Nancy pulled her to the shallow end of the pool and held her head up while she reached for the portable telephone to dial 911. Eight minutes later, two paramedics and six emergency technicians from the rural Manchacha volunteer EMS unit were able to revive Barbara, but she was still unconscious when they flew her by helicopter to Austin's main emergency facility, Brackenridge Hospital, where a team of physicians immediately began working to save her. She was in shock and suffering from pulmonary edema, or a buildup of fluid in her lungs.

"I thought she was dead when I got to the hospital," Dr. Rambie Briggs said. "She was totally unconscious and they were pumping lots of water out of her lungs." But within an hour, the medical team got her stabilized. She was put on a respirator and given medications to rid her lungs of excess fluid. Jordan remained in a state of respiratory distress, however; she had "aspiration" pneumonia. She also was experiencing cardiac arrhythmia—rapid and irregular heartbeats—and had a ruptured lung. Blood tests showed that she was anemic. "Her blood platelets were low, and we thought that was due to the Cytoxan," Dr. Briggs said. "But we didn't have a clue about what happened to cause the accident. My hypothesis is that it was a heart arrhythmia."

Barbara's sisters, Rose Mary and Bennie, rushed in from Houston to be with her. And dozens of Austin residents flocked to the hospital to await news of her condition. "It seemed like the whole town came," Rambie Briggs remembered. By Saturday evening, the news was surprisingly good.

Although she had had a very "close call," Jordan would survive with no brain damage. By Monday, Brackenridge's pulmonary specialist, Dr. William Deaton, said that Jordan still needed supplemental oxygen, "but she can talk, complain, and boss us around on her own." And then Dr. Deaton revealed more personal information about Jordan than anyone had admitted to in years. "She's emotional," he said, "and a little bit teary-eyed some of the time, knowing what she's been through and how close she came to a real catastrophic event."[23]

Unwittingly—and finally—Dr. Deaton also gave a public name to Jordan's neurological disabilities, revealing the secret she had kept for fifteen years. He told reporters that Jordan suffered from a type of multiple sclerosis that had caused her to "lose nerve functions in her lower extremities." He predicted that the multiple sclerosis would likely "cause more problems in her recovery because her muscle strength is not as good. Her breathing muscle strength is not normal."[24] When the *New York Times* ran the story on August 2, it was the first time Jordan's friends and fans all across the country knew the real cause of her disabilities. But when Jordan broke all of her own rules against holding mass press conferences by inviting the press into her hospital room on August 5, Texas news and television reporters were so happy to see her alive that none even brought up the subject of multiple sclerosis. Neither did she. Yet the secret was out.

Although medical tests were inconclusive, Brackenridge physicians believed, as did Jordan's personal physician Rambie Briggs, that the incident was more than a simple pool accident. She had suffered cardiac arrest, but it could not be determined whether her heart had stopped after she lost consciousness or the heart arrhythmia had been the event that caused her to lose consciousness. Jordan did not remember what happened—only that she got in the pool and woke up in the hospital. She thought she had just "blacked out." It was well known that most multiple sclerosis patients are affected by heat, and Jordan had always had to be extremely careful when she was out in the Texas summer heat. Friends remember seeing her go completely limp after being outside on a hot day. She would slump in her wheelchair, and whoever was with her knew they had to get her into the air-conditioning quickly.

No one knows for sure whether Jordan had a heart attack, but the incident was a turning point in her health—and in her life. She had repeated lung problems after 1988 in the form of recurring pulmonary emboli, or blood clots in her lungs. She had given up her beloved cigarettes, and she became totally dependent upon her wheelchair. For all practical purposes, she could never maneuver again without it. Yet she remained undaunted, even philosophical, as she was forced to contemplate her own death for the first time.

"I believe that I have a spirit that is not going to disappear," she told her friend Liz Carpenter, who had been Lady Bird Johnson's press secretary and had remained close to the extended Johnson family. "[I believe] that my body will die and disintegrate, but there is that basic law of physics, that matter is neither created nor destroyed. Now the skin and bones will go back to dust, but the spirit of that individual, the presence of 'isness' of me, I feel will *live*."[25]

Jordan also decided how she wanted to live the rest of her life. "For the rest of the time I have on this planet I want to bring people together. . . . We, as human beings, must be willing to accept people who are different from ourselves. I must be willing to accept people who don't look as I do and don't talk as I do. It is crucial that I am open to their feelings . . . to their inner reality."[26]

CHAPTER 20

FINAL ASSIGNMENT

BARBARA JORDAN'S BRUSH with death in the summer of 1988 seemed to compel her to return to the public arena to *preach* as well as teach. Sometimes she even sounded like one of the Old Testament prophets who could see the folly of her people's endeavors and point out the error of their ways. By fall, when the presidential campaign was in full swing, she brought down the wrath of her Godlike voice on Vice President George Bush.

Jordan had agreed to be one of the co-chairs of the Dukakis-Bentsen campaign in Texas.[1] By mid-September she had recovered enough from the near-drowning incident to make speeches for the campaign in Texas and elsewhere. It was something she was eager to do because she was furious over what she saw as the racist implications of the 1988 Republican campaign. Incensed by the "Willie Horton" television spot, she thought the commercial represented the "darker side of the hollow politics of George Bush."[2] She thought "the Bush campaign has gone out and whacked the Bill of Rights on its head. . . . With code words and 'hot' symbols like the Willie Horton commercial, the vice president has created a divisive campaign with subliminal messages which evoke fear. For civil rights advocates, the Bush campaign is an echo of previous campaigns against the spirit of inclusiveness that permeates the Constitution."[3]

Jordan blamed the tone and tenor of the Republican campaign on "a virus of narrow thinking in some elements of the Republican Party that has viewed the Bill of Rights as an unnecessary attachment to the Constitution.[4]

" 'One nation, under God, indivisible.' We want to be *one*. We want to be a single people working toward a single end, goal or purpose . . . the common good. What a great day it would be if all could suppress—even for an instant—our preoccupation with self; private wishes; private gains; profit desires; I . . . me . . . and instead, think of the public interest, the commonweal; the *community*."[5]

Both during the campaign and during President Bush's term in office from 1988 to 1992, Jordan's speeches reflected an almost brooding concern about the growing divisiveness and racism she saw spreading in the country and the sense that the American nation had failed to live up to its ideals.

"We are a divided people," she lamented. "The wholeness we seek appears to be even more elusive. People come to power who seem to exacerbate our divisions rather than heal them. If we are the inclusive society and government we say we are, then all people—individually and collectively—should have a say. There should be no exclusion from the paths of power of individuals or groups for reasons of status, income, gender, or any of that extraneous litany of traits which have historically, traditionally, and/or customarily consigned individuals to positions inferior to those available to the majority. We refuse to admit, in fact we deny that we as a people have difficulty living up to our creed of inclusiveness, i.e., liberty and justice for all. But reality gives the lie to our denial."[6]

Jordan thought the nation had once accepted the idea of a common good as its political philosophy. But she believed that by the 1980s Americans had adopted the metaphor of the "lifeboat ethic": Only a few could—or should—survive and prosper.[7] And she did not like it one bit. She still held on to the idea of *e pluribus unum*—from many, one. "Divisiveness, diversity; middle-class, underclass; homeowner, homeless; gay, straight; the aged, the young. . . . Can't we reinvigorate the American spirit and renew a sense of the common good?" she pleaded.[8] It was not just the exclusion of the poor or minorities that she decried. She was also troubled by the new strain of black nationalism and the emphasis on placing racial or ethnic identity above the common identity of being an American. She even declared herself an "un-hyphenated American."[9]

"I believe there is a common philosophy, a public philosophy which holds Americans together. It has its genesis in the Bill of Rights, our Constitution, our Declaration of Independence. . . . We cannot consider ourselves hyphenated as a people. We are one. Is that naivete? I don't think so."[10]

"Speaking for myself, I wish that we would get past all the hyphenations that seem to be dividing our society. We must let all Americans be Americans regardless of where their ancestors were born. Social cohesion requires it. Public policy should support it."[11]

Jordan was not ready to give up on the American experiment in democracy. She worried that the words *multiculturalism* and *political correctness* were code words for a new reality in which separateness and ethnic chauvinism were to be promoted. For Jordan, the commitment to democratic ideals and constitutional principles had the power to unite "an extraordinary range of ethnic and religious backgrounds."[12] And she loathed anything, *anything*, that divided or separated one group from another. Sometimes she was as tough on her black colleagues as she was on George Bush.

One of her targets was "black English." So precise and perfect was she in her own use of language, and so convinced that her ability to speak forcefully and correctly had been the key to her entry into the world beyond the Fifth Ward of Houston, Texas, that she lectured young black children and teenagers on the proper use of English. She believed it was *their* key, too, and part of the whole process of "Americanization," which she was committed to. She even admonished adults when they did not meet her standards of proper speech. Once at the Texas governor's mansion, when then-Governor Ann Richards hosted a luncheon for Georgia governor Zell Miller, Jordan cornered a prominent black elected official from Houston who had been one of the luncheon guests. "You'd be much more effective if you didn't slur your words," she told him. Taken aback and temporarily speechless, the official later shrugged off the exchange by telling another guest: "It's just the same old bossy Barbara!" Bossy or not, Barbara did not like it when smart, educated black men or women did not live up to her own standards of excellence and adopted the language or behavior of the ghetto. She was both embarrassed for them and angry at them.

Jordan had moved so easily in the white-dominated world since she entered the Texas Senate in 1966 that she sometimes forgot that it might not be so easy—or even desirable—for others. After she had become famous for breaking so many barriers, white people clamored to be around her; after Watergate, she was often the object of their fawning attention and favors. Even after she left the Congress, doors to wealth and privilege opened for her that were still sealed shut for most African Americans. It was as if there were times when Jordan underestimated her own unique drive, intelligence, and power, as well as the opportunities they continued to bring her. Her almost "preachy" admonitions to other, less well-situated African Americans were not always appreciated.

NEW INTERESTS

By 1990 Jordan had been invited to join even more corporate boards, at a time when only 2 percent of business board memberships in the country were held by African Americans.[13] When she joined the board of Burlington Northern Santa Fe, one of the nation's largest rail lines, she was one of only thirty-four African Americans who served on the boards of three or more Fortune 1,000 companies. She also became a member of the board of the Federal Home Mortgage Loan Corporation, the public-private corporation known as Freddie Mac.[14] Jordan bought stock in many of the companies on whose boards she served, and as the stock market exploded, the value of her holdings soared, making her a wealthy woman with assets of over $2 million by 1994.[15] But even with her growing wealth, Jordan's old insecurity about money persisted. To the amazement of her secretary and friends, she kept several hundred thousand dollars in a checking account. "Barbara was raised poor, and she had clearly decided early on that she didn't ever want to be poor again. I think she was afraid that she would wake up one day and it would all be gone," her friend Stan McClelland believed.

In 1990 Jordan also got involved in Texas politics again. She broke her long-standing rule against endorsing candidates in the Democratic primary and supported then-State Treasurer Ann Richards, who was running for governor. Jordan and Ann Richards had known each other since Jordan's early days in Texas politics. Richards's former husband, David Richards, was a noted civil rights and labor lawyer who was involved in some of the Texas redistricting court cases that had paved the way for Jordan's entry into politics. In those days, both women shared an affinity for Frank Erwin, the hard-drinking, quirky John Connally power broker who was the nemesis of the political left in Texas. And Richards, like Jordan, was a political liberal who moved to the center as she developed her skills as a consensus-building politician. When Richards was selected to make the Democratic Party's keynote speech at the 1988 convention in Atlanta, she called Jordan for advice.

The 1990 Democratic primary for the gubernatorial election was brutal, even by Texas standards. Jordan wanted to help. "I knew Ann was in a very tough race, and that if my name was going to make any difference, when difference really did count, then I needed to break that long-standing policy . . . and make the endorsement and do everything that I possibly could to ensure her success."[16] Richards won the bruising primary, but she had been so cut up in the process that she entered the general election campaign twenty-seven points behind her Republican opponent. Jordan again got behind her, agreed to be co-chair of the campaign, and traveled the state to rouse African American voters on Richards's behalf.[17] After Richards won her upset victory in November, Jordan consented to be the new governor's special—unpaid—counsel on ethics. In her first "state of the state" address, Richards joked with Texas legislators about Jordan when she urged them to pass a strong ethics bill that "had some teeth and authority. Because if you don't do that," she said, "I am going to have to answer to Barbara Jordan. And I'm happy to face any of you any day before I have to deal with Barbara Jordan."[18]

Jordan took her role as Richards's counsel on ethics quite seriously. The Texas political reporter Dave McNeely said that Jordan's new role signaled that she was "back" as a force in Texas politics, and that she was the "pure blue light of ethics standards" for government officials. Jordan herself seemed delighted with her new responsibility. "This is a role which I can do, and am pleased to do because I feel so strongly about ethics and public service. It's an extraordinarily important matter, and it has a high priority with the governor."[19]

Richards made more than three thousand appointments to state boards and commissions during her four-year term of office, and she instituted the first ethics training for appointees ever held in Texas. Jordan spoke to each group of appointees over the four-year period and personally interviewed dozens of Richards's highest-level appointees—particularly those being considered for judicial appointments.[20]

Many of the most highly esteemed lawyers in Texas who wanted to be appointed to vacant judgeships made the pilgrimage to Jordan's LBJ School office at the University of Texas. Jordan grilled them relentlessly to determine their ethical sensibility. Jordan's secretary, Sharon Tutchings, remembers how nervous most of them were as they shuffled their feet or papers waiting to see Jordan. Jordan would ask all the candidates certain questions as a way to draw them out, but she always saved the most important question for last. "If Governor Richards decides to appoint you, what will you owe her in return?" Most of the office seekers usually paused, trying to figure out what Jordan wanted them to say. Some told her that they would be loyal to the governor. That was not the answer she was looking for. One candidate even said that she would make a very large financial contribution to the governor; Jordan immediately struck her from the list. There was only one correct answer, Jordan would patiently explain to those candidates who came close to her ideal. "You owe the governor nothing. But you do owe the people of Texas your total, ethical commitment to excellence in your public service."[21]

Jordan was so proud that Texas had a female governor—and one committed to extending the gains of the civil rights movement by appointing unprecedented numbers of women and minorities to key state posts—that she felt that the energy Richards "brought to the government of the state of Texas needs to be sustained, and there must not be a black mark that surfaces in a Richards administration. The success of her administration is too important for that."[22] But two years into the Richards administration, it was discovered that one of her highest-level appointees, who was then running for statewide office, had listed a college degree on her résumé when she did not have one.[23] Jordan—to the consternation of some Richards loyalists—called on the woman to withdraw from the race. Cold-eyed and clear, she was merely practicing what she preached. Her loyalty was not to her friend, the governor, but to the people of Texas, and she believed the people deserved better representation.

THE NEW DEMOCRATS

Jordan's allegiance to the Democratic Party had been one of the mainstays of her life. Every time she spoke *of* the party or *to* the party, she helped shape its idealistic edge. She gave the keynote addresses at the only two national Democratic conventions over a thirty-year period whose nominees went on to become president—Jimmy Carter in 1976 and Bill Clinton in 1992. It was probably no coincidence. In each of her speeches, she articulated themes dear to the hearts of Democrats, and her clear focus on the fundamental values of liberty and equality gave rank-and-file Democrats the inspiration they needed to go all out for their candidates. In 1976 she had handed the Democrats the high moral ground after Nixon and Watergate. In 1992, when nominee-apparent Bill Clinton asked Jordan to make one of three keynote addresses, she handed the Democrats another theme that resonated with voters: the centrality of the ideals of community and responsibility to the American Dream. She fused that theme with the traditional Democratic message of concern for the poor and minorities.

> *The American Dream is not dead. True, it is gasping for breath, but it is not dead. However, there is no time to waste because the American Dream is slipping away from too many. It is slipping away from too many black and brown mothers and their children; from the homeless of every color and sex; from the immigrants living in communities without water and sewer systems. . . .*
>
> *We should answer Rodney King's haunting question, "can we all get along?" with a resounding YES. We must profoundly change from the deleterious environment of the Eighties, characterized by greed, selfishness, mega-mergers and debt overhang to one characterized by devotion to the public interest and tolerance. And yes, love . . . love . . . love.*
>
> *We are one, we Americans, and we reject any intruder who seeks to divide us by race or class. We honor cultural identity. However, separatism is not allowed. Separatism is not the American way. And we should not permit ideas like political correctness to become some fad that could reverse our hard-won achievements in civil rights and human rights. Xenophobia has no place in the Democratic Party. We seek to unite people, not divide them. And we reject both white racism and black racism. This party will not tolerate bigotry under any guise. America's strength is rooted in its diversity. Our history bears witness to that statement. E pluribus unum was a good motto in the early days of our country, and it is a good motto today. From the many, one. It still identifies us—because we are Americans.[24]*

As the 1990s wore on, Jordan worried about the increasing income gap between rich and poor, and she articulated the liberal Democratic view when she discussed it. "We see an inherent unfairness in the unevenness of America's prosperity. For that reason, we Democrats continue to assault the stubborn poverty of the left-out, locked-out, and forgotten. That effort does not seek to re-create the 'liberalism' of the sixties. No. We fully recognize that there is no free lunch, and if the idea of inclusion is to be actualized, our job is to expand opportunity. That is—we are determined to make the American Dream available to everyone willing to do whatever is necessary to attain it."[25]

Although the word *liberalism* had faded from use by Democrats and become a pejorative word hurled at them in derision by Republicans, Jordan still remained one of the nation's most respected spokespersons for New Deal–Great Society principles. She had always believed in a strong national government. It had been the federal—not state or local—government that had allowed her to enter fully into the public life of her times and to emerge as a whole human being. "The federal government has to be involved because it has the greatest capacity to organize a national response, raise the adequate resources, and to see that these resources are fairly distributed among areas of this vast country with uneven needs and endowments."[26] When she talked about the role of government, she always returned to her emotional attachment to Lyndon Johnson, particularly as time passed. She believed the Great Society legacy of Lyndon Johnson enriched lives because it rested on two principles: liberty and justice. "He saw the enemy, and the enemy was *not* government. The enemy was ignorance, poverty, disease, ugliness, injustice, discrimination. He believed that it was the duty of government to defeat the enemy."[27]

Although the 1992 campaign—until its last days—tracked more centrist themes, Jordan came to feel almost a motherly affection for Bill Clinton as he weathered one crisis after another. She was delighted when he defeated President Bush, and she immediately accepted when he invited her to be his special guest at the inauguration. President-elect Clinton had also asked Jordan to give a scripture reading at the midnight prayer service the day before his inauguration. After the service, one young African American boy, who was about seven years old, brought her a Bible to sign, which she dutifully did. When the crowd finally left, Stan McClelland asked Jordan why the little boy had asked her to sign his Bible. Without a moment's hesitation, she said, "Well, Stan, I can only conclude that he must have thought I wrote it."[28]

The next day, Jordan had a good seat for the inauguration, although members of the Marine honor guard had to carry her wheelchair up the Capitol steps because there were no ramps. She also had an appointment to be interviewed by Bill Moyers and Bernard Shaw at the CNN television studio immediately after the swearing-in ceremony, and she was in high spirits as she and Stan, along with their van driver, Jim Bouchillon, drove to the studio.

Jordan's CNN interview was soft and smooth until right before the break, when Bill Moyers brought up Zoe Baird, the corporate lawyer whom Clinton had nominated to be his attorney general. "Do you think she should be confirmed?" he asked. Jordan paused before answering, and then said bluntly: "Zoe Baird should not be confirmed as attorney general of the United States." As the cameras cut away for the station break, Moyers instructed his director to get the word out that Jordan had just called for the rejection of the nomination of Zoe Baird. By late afternoon, the news media and Democratic dignitaries were buzzing, and within seventy-two hours the nomination had been torpedoed. Zoe Baird became the first U.S. cabinet nominee in 120 years to withdraw her name from consideration.[29]

Only days earlier, Baird had freely admitted to administration officials and to the senators on the Judiciary Committee who would vote on her confirmation that she had hired undocumented workers and had not paid Social Security or unemployment taxes on their wages. They had generally brushed it off as an "honest mistake." The important issue for Jordan, however, was that Baird had broken the law. The Immigration Reform and Control Act of 1986 had made it illegal to hire undocumented aliens. To Jordan, it was unconscionable for a woman of Baird's income, education, and professional standing to be excused for violating a law that other working women, with far fewer means and less education, obeyed.[30]

As it turned out, Jordan was more in touch with the mood of the American people on the issue than President Clinton and his advisers. Senate offices were flooded with thousands of calls from people who resented the fact that the corporate lawyer Baird and her law professor husband, with a net worth of over $2 million, had failed to pay the Social Security and other taxes they owed because of "bad legal advice." The story came across as an issue of people who play by the rules versus those who do not and get away with it. One of Barbara Jordan's most sacred tenets was that all should play by the same rules.

The failure of the Baird nomination was one of many setbacks in the first weeks of the Clinton administration, and Barbara Jordan had played an important role. Stan McClelland jokingly warned her, "Barbara, you've just ended your short honeymoon with this administration." But no one from the Clinton camp ever said anything to her about Zoe Baird, and President Bill Clinton obviously remained a fan of Barbara Jordan's. In 1993 Jordan and the president even had several conversations about the possibility of a U.S. Supreme Court appointment, although the talks were never specific and no offer was tendered to her. "They had some calls back and forth," Nancy Earl remembered. "The indication from Clinton was that he might be interested if *she* was, although no formal offer was ever made. Barbara thought about it, but she didn't have to think about it long." Jordan was not interested in becoming a member of the Supreme Court, but she did accept another important assignment from her president.

THE U.S. COMMISSION ON IMMIGRATION REFORM

Immigration was one of the trickiest and most emotional issues in the 1990s, with odd alliances cutting across political lines. An estimated eight hundred thousand foreigners immigrated to the United States legally every year. In addition, four million illegal immigrants already lived here, and another three hundred thousand a year entered illegally or overstayed their visas. More than 70 percent of the nation's legal and illegal immigrants lived in six large, voter-rich states—California, Texas, Florida, Illinois, New York, and New Jersey.[31] The issue was particularly volatile and ready-made for the scapegoat, stir-up-the-voters, scare-tactic television ads that were so popular—and effective—in campaigns in the 1980s and early 1990s. The immigration debate was always clouded by labels and stereotypes. Those who supported reform of the system were generally characterized as anti-immigration, while those who opposed reform were characterized as pro-immigration. But that was not necessarily the case. Many civil rights organizations thought the immigration system was abusive and unfair, and they wanted it changed, albeit in a different way from those who wanted to halt or severely restrict immigration altogether. As people got locked into the labels and hyperbole, however, it became increasingly difficult to reach a middle ground.

The Immigration Act of 1990 created the nine-member Commission on Immigration Reform to monitor and evaluate immigration reform, and only the president had the power to appoint a chairperson. The Clinton White House had been notoriously slow in making many appointments during its first months in office, and only got around to asking the commission's staff to put together a list of potential candidates for chair during the summer of 1993. The executive director of the commission, Susan Martin, believed that the "chair had to be someone whose intelligence and moral authority is so strong that if he or she says a strategy makes sense, it will be considered seriously."[32] Martin had only been in elementary school when she heard Jordan's Watergate testimony, but she had followed Jordan's career ever since. "Barbara articulated something at that hearing that restored faith for people in our constitutional system. And in subsequent speeches over the years, she added to that. Her ability to talk about equity and fairness gave a human face to issues that were sterile to most of us," she believed.[33] She put Barbara Jordan at the top of the list.

"We had an extraordinary telephone conversation," Martin remembered. "She started off by saying there was no way she would agree to do it. But I pressed her, telling her that the immigration debate was becoming mean, and we needed someone like her to prevent an anti-immigrant hysteria from developing. I told her that she could make the same difference on the Immigration Commission that she had on the Voting Rights Act by prevailing on the inclusion of Hispanics."

As the women talked, the role Martin laid out seemed to be an extension of the patriot-teacher role that Jordan had envisioned for herself. She began to see that someone of stature had to keep the country from "going overboard" on the issue, that the ultimate solution to the problem would not be resolved by either the anti-immigration extremists or those who spouted lofty ideals, but by practical and principled individuals who had "flexible negotiating skills and sensitive interpersonal relationships," as well as the ability to factor in the "cold calculation of who wins and who loses."[34] She felt that she had mastered the skills to do just that.

Jordan finally told Martin she would consider taking on the responsibility if the commission's meetings could be worked around her teaching and board meeting schedule. Martin immediately made the arrangements to do so and notified the White House that Barbara Jordan would accept the appointment to be the chair of the U.S. Commission on Immigration Reform.

The reaction to Jordan's appointment was favorable on all sides. "She's neutral, she's evenhanded, she's an independent broker and she has great moral authority," said Dan Stein, head of the Federation for American Immigration Reform, a group that favored reducing legal immigration.[35] And on the other side, Celia Munoz, an analyst at the National Council of La Raza, a Hispanic advocacy group fighting anti-immigrant hysteria, also hailed Jordan's appointment. "We have faith in her; she represents fairness and concern for civil rights."[36]

As Jordan prepared for her first meeting and pored over the latest data about immigration, including statements by members of Congress, she was surprised and appalled at the negative tone of the immigration reform debate. "There is no credible basis for the anti-immigrant sentiment which appears to be so pervasive," she said. "The way to counter emotionalism is with facts. Look at the numbers. What is the reality of the financial impact on schools, health care, the criminal justice system? We hope to bring a light of rationality on claims that have no factual basis."[37] That is what she hoped to do first: lay out the facts.

The first meeting of the commission that Jordan attended was in Miami in February 1994. Much of the testimony concerned the thousands of Haitian refugees who had been arriving on Florida beaches in rickety boats after fleeing their country's brutal dictatorship. As a candidate, Bill Clinton had denounced President Bush's policy of sending the Haitians back to the harsh conditions on their island, but as president he had continued the same policy. Jordan wanted to see the policy changed so that the

Haitians could be protected rather than punished, but the commission was not ready to take action, so she made a plea as a private citizen. She told the White House, "I don't want to criticize the President by going public with a statement, but I do want his ear on this."[38] A month later, the president reversed his policy and agreed to let the Immigration and Naturalization Service (INS) grant asylum interviews to potential Haitian refugees. By then, Jordan had turned her attention to the work of the commission itself.

The nine-member Commission on Immigration Reform was a highly partisan "nonpartisan" group. Jordan was the only member appointed by the president, and the only woman. The other members had been selected by the leadership of the Democratic and Republican parties in both the House and Senate.[39] One of the Republican appointees was Harold Ezell, who was a coauthor of California's controversial Proposition 187, the ballot initiative that would take away public benefits, including public schooling, from illegal immigrants in the state.[40] The other members included a Brandeis professor, a corporate lawyer, a private foundation official, a newspaper editor, an immigration lawyer, and others.

"Those eight men were as awestruck and intimidated by her as was our staff," said Susan Martin. And Jordan's stature loomed just as large on the Hill. Once when she was to meet with members of the Senate Judiciary Committee, there had been a mixup on the time of the meeting, and Jordan arrived almost twenty-five minutes early. To accommodate her, Senator Edward Kennedy began the meeting early. When Republican Alan Simpson came into the room at the original appointed time, Jordan was already speaking, and without breaking her rhythm, she said, "Good morning, Senator, we're so pleased you could join us." Simpson looked like a reprimanded schoolboy and apologized profusely, telling Jordan he was so sorry and promising "never to be late again." Jordan just laughed because she genuinely liked Simpson, who, she told commission staffers, "listened and asked good questions," and more important, "had a good sense of humor."

Jordan's reputation had impressed even Vice President Al Gore. When she was leaving the White House one time after a briefing, Gore spotted her. He was on crutches because he had broken his leg, yet he hurriedly hobbled over to Jordan and stuck out his hand. "Barbara, I'm Al Gore," he gushed. "I know who you are, Mr. Vice President. How are you?" she replied.

Barbara Jordan knew how to make the respect and awe others felt for her work to her advantage. When she accepted the position of chair, she decided that she did not want straight up or down votes because she wanted `no major splits that could weaken the commission's eventual recommendations. Instead, she would try to reach a consensus on all the important issues. She felt her first task was to get members to agree on some core principles of immigration policy before they even began looking at specific issues. She articulated the essence of those principles in her simple, straight-forward manner: "People who *should get in,* do get in . . . people who *should not get in,* are kept out . . . and people who are judged deportable are required to *leave.*"[41]

Under her leadership, the commission arrived at three key principles for immigration reform: First, illegal immigration is a violation of the rule of law and undermines America's tradition as a nation of immigrants; second, if properly regulated, legal immigration serves the national interests; and third, we must pay attention not only to admissions policy but also to what happens to immigrants after entry. It is perhaps in this third principle that Jordan's influence on the commission was most directly felt. She wanted to ensure that the nation's new immigrants understood and developed a commitment to the American values of liberty, democracy, and equal opportunity. Jordan did not want to shy away from the term "Americanization." In fact, she wanted to find ways to help integrate and absorb immigrants, and yet ameliorate the harm people felt by the presence of so many immigrants.

"There is a word for this process: Americanization," she claimed. "That word earned a bad reputation when it was stolen by racists and xenophobes in the 1920s. But it is our word, and we are taking it back. Americanization means becoming a part of the polity—becoming one of us. But that does not mean conformity. We are more than a melting pot; we are a kaleidoscope, where every turn of history refracts new light on the old promise."[42]

"Professor Jordan tried to set a tone for the debate on immigration that recognized the importance of our immigration tradition while addressing weaknesses in our immigration policies," Susan Martin wrote. "She decried hostility and discrimination against immigrants as antithetical to the traditions and interest of this country. At the same time, she disagreed strongly with those who labeled any efforts to control illegal immigration or regulate legal admissions as being inherently anti-immigrant."[43] Martin said that Jordan was "patient and persistent, but her own ego was not involved. She didn't mind saying, 'I don't know,' when she was unsure, and she set such broad parameters in our discussions that we could talk about anything." Martin and the staff were also amazed at how graciously she treated them. "She helped build my confidence in my ability to lead our staff, and she always pushed me forward to get recognition for our work," Martin said.

Jordan did the same with people who did not have titles or positions of power. Ever since the mid-1980s, when she began to come back to Washington for speeches and other events, she had needed help in getting around the city. She had hired driver Jim Bouchillon, whose van service could accommodate her wheelchair. They had become friends over the years, and once she took on her responsibilities for the immigration commission, he was at her service on a regular basis. Jordan had always taken Bouchillon to her Washington dinners and receptions, insisting that he be treated like a guest instead of "hired help." That continued when she started going to the White House on immigration matters. Once when she was scheduled to meet with President Clinton, she insisted that Bouchillon come inside the White House with her.

"I was standing along the back of the wall with some of the other aides, you know, pretending we weren't even there," Bouchillon remembered. "When the meeting was over, she motioned for me to come to her. 'Mr. President,' she said, 'I want you to meet the man who's been driving me around for ten years.' So I got to meet the president and have my picture made with him. No one else ever treated me the way she did," he said. "She would talk to me, ask my opinion, ask about my family, tell a few jokes. When you were with her, she was present with you and paid attention to you."[44]

Barbara applied the same kind of charm and one-on-one attention to each member of the commission. "I could sense where people were and how far they would go on a given issue, and I also knew their limits—I knew where people would not go," she explained. "You stop where you have gone as far as people will go—you don't try to push them beyond where you know they want to go. I enjoyed working with people with different political ideologies and getting them to turn around because one thing I knew when I was in politics is that there is a basic human dimension in people and no matter what the bluff of the exterior is, if you can get through that, you might find a genuine human being who is rational."[45]

Commission staff members thought Barbara was "masterful" in guiding members to a consensus. In every report issued during Jordan's tenure as chair, nearly all of the recommendations were unanimous.

When the commission's first report was ready for release in the summer of 1994, it called for better management of the nation's borders to prevent illegal entries; better work-site enforcement to verify the legal status of immigrants; restriction of public assistance—except on an emergency basis—for illegal immigrants; detention and removal of criminal aliens; using American foreign policy more effectively to help curtail unlawful immigration from the nations that provided the largest numbers of illegal immigrants; and improving the data collection on immigration so that the financial and social impact could be more accurately assessed.[46] The basis for Jordan's support for cracking down on illegal immigration was her lifelong belief in the rule of law. Because illegal immigrants broke the law, she believed the government had a responsibility to find a safe and humane way to deal with them.

The most controversial provision in her report called for the use of a national computer registry with a listing of Social Security numbers to help employers verify the legal status of potential workers: were they citizens, legal immigrants who had work permits, or undocumented workers who were in the country illegally? Some civil liberties groups, including the National Council of La Raza, which had initially hailed Jordan's appointment, and the Mexican American Legal Defense and Education Fund, which she had worked closely with on the Voting Rights Act, were appalled. They were vehemently opposed to any kind of national registry because they believed the next step would be a national identity card, which they considered both a violation of civil liberties and a means to discriminate against citizens of Hispanic origin. Opposition to the national registry was widespread. Conservative groups like the Cato Institute and liberal groups like the American Civil Liberties Union also opposed anything like a national registry of workers because it smelled like an "unwarranted intrusion by Big Brother government" into the private lives of Americans.[47] The furor over the possibility of an identity card led many people to believe the commission had actually proposed such a card, and that was not the case.

"I am *not* for a national identity card," Jordan had to repeat on numerous occasions.[48] She would patiently try to explain that because American jobs remained a magnet for illegal immigrants, a centralized computer registry would help neutralize that magnet. Current law already required employers to check for a potential worker's Social Security number, but because Social Security cards could be so easily forged, the system did not work. "With a computer registry to back them up, forgery would be more difficult," Jordan believed. The report called on the president to establish some pilot projects to see whether such a registry would work.

Before the report was released publicly, Jordan had gone to the White House to brief the president's chief of staff, Leon Panetta, a former member of Congress from California. After she explained the recommendations and the commission's rationale for issuing them, she told Panetta: "I'm not expecting the White House to say 'yes' or 'no' to this report, but I just don't want to see a headline in the *Washington Post* that the White House rejects the report without knowing about it first." Nevertheless, the day after the report was released, just such a headline appeared, implying that the White House was rejecting the recommendations of the commission. Jordan was not happy. If the White House disagreed, she felt that Panetta should have told her first. She told Martin she would never brief Panetta on anything again. When Martin relayed the message to Panetta, he called Jordan to apologize and indicated that neither he nor other top aides had leaked the story. He told Jordan that the *Post* got its information from "low-level" White House staff. "Well, if you can't control them any better than that, you've got real problems," she retorted.[49]

Jordan felt that the commission's 1994 report gave the administration a chance to seize the initiative on immigration reform, but administration aides kept sending conflicting signals on how the president would respond.[50] Nevertheless, the relationship between Jordan and the president remained cordial, even affectionate. During the summer of 1994, he presented her with the nation's highest civilian honor, the Presidential Medal of Freedom.[51] Clinton gave Jordan the award, established in 1944, for having "dramatically articulated an enduring standard of morality in American politics," and he said she had "captured the nation's attention and awakened its consciousness."[52]

"I think she was as proud of that honor as anything she ever got," Stan McClelland said. "It seemed apparent to me that both the president and the first lady took special pleasure in her award." Jordan had a grand time at the ceremony and afterward at the reception. She took eleven people with her to the White House for the ceremony, and her guest list included the people she felt closest to, and who were most involved in her daily life: Nancy Earl; Stan McClelland; her sisters, Bennie Creswell and Rose Mary McGowan, and Rose Mary's husband, John;[53] Azie Taylor Morton, former treasurer of the United States; Mead Corporation's former general counsel, Jerry Rapp, and his friend, Marilyn Allen; Jordan's secretary, Sharon Tutchings, and her husband, Terry; and her caregiver and travel aide, Darrell Teaver. The Texans went outside after the ceremony and asked the Marine Corps Band to play Texas songs. They all sang "The Eyes of Texas."

Jordan was still getting dozens of awards each year, but the Medal of Freedom for her was special, and it provided a pleasant interlude during a very intense year of work on immigration.[54] The work became even more intense when the Republicans swept the 1994 congressional elections and took control of both the House and Senate. Jordan felt that the task of forging a middle ground on immigration was going to be more difficult. Immediately after the election, Senator Alan Simpson and Representative Lamar Smith offered bills that not only cracked down on illegal immigration but promised to reduce the number of legal immigrants as well.

By then, however, Jordan was also feeling repeatedly frustrated by the Clinton administration. To her, administration officials were "all over the place" on the issue. She would forge a consensus on the commission on an issue, and then White House officials would move in a totally different direction. She feared the administration would cut the rug out from under her on the final report.[55]

In June 1995, when the second report was to be released, Jordan insisted on personally briefing the president. "The meeting was fantastic," Susan Martin remembered. "They were on the same wavelength on the principles. And the president's only major concern was the commission's recommendation to stop the legal immigration of unskilled workers. When Barbara explained that if you looked at the whole problem of unskilled workers in the light of proposed welfare reform measures, which would force welfare recipients into the workforce, they would simply not be able to compete against unskilled immigrant workers. So if the president wanted welfare reform to work, the country had to stop the flow of both legal and illegal unskilled workers. The president agreed and rewrote the White House press release himself to reflect his agreement." The commission's report had recommended that legal immigration be gradually reduced by one-third, to about 555,000 a year, reinforcing the Republican bills in Congress.

Still reeling from the devastating congressional election results when he met with Jordan, Clinton surprised his own staff when he issued the press release endorsing her report, including the cuts in legal immigration. The *New York Times* said the endorsement stunned top aides, including Chief of Staff Panetta and INS chief Doris Meissner. Both had advised the president to make a more studied response.[56] Barbara Jordan's presence and power of persuasion obviously swayed the president on the spot, because several months later, when Jordan no longer headed the commission, he reversed himself on the report and opposed provisions to cut legal immigration.[57]

Jordan did not get to see the completion of her work on the Commission on Immigration Reform.[58] While preparing for the final push before Congress in early 1996, her body began to fail her once again.

"I'M GOING TO DO WHAT I WANT TO DO UNTIL I CAN'T DO IT ANYMORE"

Since her near-drowning incident, Jordan had suffered repeated bouts of chest pain and pneumonia. Dr. Briggs worried that instead of pneumonia, Jordan was suffering from recurring pulmonary emboli—or blood clots—in her lungs. He wanted to put her on a blood-thinning medication, but when he consulted heart and lung specialists, they hesitated to recommend any change in her current treatment. Briggs brooded about what to do, and one evening after a dinner party with Barbara, Stan McClelland, and others, he confided his worries to Stan. Stan joked that he wasn't surprised that none of the other physicians would make a recommendation on a new treatment for her. "Briggs, nobody wants to kill Barbara Jordan!"[59] Briggs said that was when he realized that because he was Barbara's friend as well as her physician, he had to assume full responsibility for her care, as well as all the risks it entailed. The next day he put her on Coumadin, a common blood-thinning medication, and she never had another problem with blood clots in her lungs.

Briggs continued to monitor Jordan on a regular basis. In 1994, she began to have another series of respiratory problems. Briggs ran a series of tests, which revealed an abnormality in her blood count. He had worried for years that Barbara's long-term use of Cytoxan would cause cancer. A bone marrow biopsy in June 1994 confirmed his fears.[60] Barbara had leukemia. Although she had quit taking Cytoxan in 1988 after it had already destroyed her bladder, it was only now that the other major side effect of the drug manifested itself. Briggs said he knew after the bone marrow biopsy that Barbara would have some bad days ahead of her. "We knew then that the evolving leukemia would kill her."

"She would have made a great poker player," Briggs said. "We were sitting on her bed at home. When I told her that she might have leukemia . . . well . . . she never blinked. Nancy might cry, or at least turn pale, but with Barbara, you could never tell. She just looked at me and said, 'Okay.' And then she declared, 'I'm going to do what I want to do until I can't do it anymore.' " At this point, only Barbara, Nancy Earl, and Rambie Briggs knew that her days were numbered.

Instead of slowing down, Jordan seemed to pick up the pace, adding more and more activities to an already hectic schedule. She made frequent trips to attend board meetings. She campaigned for the reelection of Governor Ann Richards. In addition, she was teaching her seminar on ethics once a week, making several out-of-town speeches each month, and going to Washington every month for the immigration commission. She even went to the Dominican Republic and Mexico City to meet with government officials to get their perspective on the wave of immigrants flooding across the border into Texas, Florida, Arizona, and California.

The Mexican trip was particularly hard on her, however. When immigration commission staff members were setting up meetings and appointments in Mexico, they stressed that every site had to be "wheelchair-accessible" in order for Jordan to participate. But when she went to meet the finance minister, she learned that the Mexican officials' notion of wheelchair accessibility was to provide four strong men to carry her up twenty steep steps into the government ministry. It was a harrowing experience for her—and the staff, who were frantic about the possibility that the carriers would drop the chair—and Jordan! Jordan herself was nervous, a rarity for her in situations like this. Yet the near-disaster in Mexico did not deter her from future trips.

None of Jordan's travels were easy. She always had to have someone with her to help her in and out of the wheelchair, on and off airplanes, and to deal with all of the complexities of helping her change the indwelling bladder catheter. Prescriptions would have to be called in to pharmacies all over the country. Bathrooms in her hotel rooms had to be wheelchair-accessible. Sometimes Sharon Tutchings went with her, or one of her former students, DeAnn Friedholm or Susan Rieff; other times she was accompanied by one of the regular travel aides or caregivers—Darrell Teaver, Diane Knesek, Joy Davenport, or Joyce Harris, who probably traveled with her over the longest period of time. Sometimes it was Nancy Earl or Stan McClelland. Whatever the arrangement, Jordan would not give up travel even when she was sick.

Rambie Briggs believed that she approached this time of her life as if she were some aging opera singer and "did not want to miss a single performance." When he advised her against making a trip, she would question him extensively and usually talk him into approving her plans. "I was never a very authoritarian-type person. But finally she would tell me that if I *really* didn't think she should do it, she wouldn't." Once in 1995, however, she went to a meeting of the immigration commission in Washington when she had pneumonia and became very sick while she was there. "Finally, after that, she allowed me to cancel things," Briggs said. The travels were a distraction for Jordan, and they seemed to keep her from dwelling on the amount of time she had left to live. She even seemed driven about it. She wanted no empty spaces in her life, and who is to say that this kind of diversion was not preferable to facing what she did not want to face: her own now-sure end, prefaced by an ever-increasing physical deterioration.

Once Jordan's leukemia had been diagnosed, Briggs monitored her blood count every few weeks. "Every time I'd get a good white blood cell count, I'd tell her we were okay until the next time. That went on for over a year."

"Barbara never missed a beat during that year," Stan McClelland believed. "She had such an uplifting attitude, a totally unshakable faith in God. Barbara's vision of God was that it was somebody that was right there with her, and I think it kind of helped her get through the hard stuff. If you were out there for supper, you'd hold hands and pray. But it was different from going through the formalities of religion."

Jordan had once given a speech in which she said that the way to realize our humanity is to ask of ourselves the recurring biblical question: What manner of men shall we be? The challenge, she felt, was to identify our options and then to "choose among them, not blindly, but with a discerning, understanding eye."[61] Jordan had identified her options when she learned that the leukemia would limit her days. And the manner of woman she wanted to be demanded that she go on.

She also talked more frequently about the power of love and community, posing the questions she addressed in her speeches and in a discussion she once had with the poet Maya Angelou.

JORDAN: Maya, do we dare to love each other? Love is such a powerful emotion. Love can really help us to understand evil. Love can help us to overcome all of the bad stuff we do to each other. Do you think we have it within us to love each of us?

ANGELOU: Yes. Oh, I love that question! I use the word *love* and I
           believe that this is how you mean it, not meaning mush or
           sentimentality but that condition in the human spirit so
           profound that it encourages us to develop courage.
JORDAN: Yes . . . yes.[62]

Jordan needed that spirit and courage to go on. By the fall of 1995, her
blood count looked troubling to Briggs, and he cautioned her to slow down.
But in early December, she went to a scheduled meeting of the immigration
commission and became very sick while she was in Washington. At first, it
appeared to be another bout of pneumonia. Two weeks later, however, she
still had not recovered. Briggs ran more tests and realized that her leukemia
was no longer "evolving": it had taken over. "She knew she was going to die
then, but she didn't know it would be so soon—and neither did I," he said.
Nancy Earl said she, too, found it hard to believe that Jordan had only a
little while to live. "I thought that no matter what the blood looks like, no
matter what . . . no matter what . . . this is not just *anybody*. She will
defeat it, like everything else that ever stood in her way."[63]

Jordan felt well enough to go to Houston for Christmas, as she did
every year. She was worried about her mother, who seemed listless and
dehydrated. Jordan made the arrangements to put her mother into the hospital, and she stayed in Houston until Arlyne had improved enough to go
home. When Jordan got back to Austin, however, she was so exhausted she
could barely move, and Briggs put *her* in the hospital. She couldn't get any
rest there, however, because so many hospital attendants were coming into
her room to get a look at their famous patient. She persuaded Briggs to let
her go home. By Monday, January 15, she was so weak she realized she
might have to cancel her first class for the spring semester, which began the
next day. Never in her seventeen years of teaching had she canceled a class.
For the first time, she told a few people about her leukemia. She confided in
the LBJ School dean, Max Sherman, and in Sharon Tutchings. She told
Sherman that she still planned to give the commencement address in May
to commemorate the twenty-five-year anniversary of the founding of the
LBJ School, but she doubted that she would be around to start classes in the
fall. She seemed resigned to her death—almost. When she told Sharon
Tutchings that the doctors did not give her long to live, Sharon asked her
what could be done. Jordan replied: "They say nothing . . . but that is
unacceptable!" Yet Jordan had instructed Rambie Briggs not to make any
heroic efforts to revive her in the event of a medical crisis. Being on a
respirator and staying alive for another week or so wasn't going to make the
leukemia go away. Barbara Jordan, above all, was a realist.

She wanted to attend the LBJ School faculty meeting on Tuesday,
January 16. On that morning, however, she was having extreme difficulty

breathing, and Nancy called Briggs. "I drove out there, and she was so short of breath that she could hardly move, so I got some oxygen on. But we couldn't make her comfortable at home, and she asked for help. So we called for an ambulance." Austin Diagnostic Medical Center, the hospital where Briggs practiced, was about a fifty-minute drive from Jordan's house. Briggs knew her lungs were filling rapidly, and, afraid she would not survive the ride to the hospital, he stayed with her until she was settled into the intensive care unit.

By late afternoon, Jordan was generally unresponsive, and it was clear that her death was near. Nancy began to call on friends to think about what they should do. Jordan's lawyer, William Hilgers, Max Sherman, and her neighbors Betty Thomas and Billye Brown began to notify family and friends about Jordan's now-imminent death. Nancy and Betty Thomas spent Tuesday night at the hospital with Jordan, who was awake off and on during the night. When Rambie Briggs went to the hospital early Wednesday morning, he stood at her side and held her hand. "Barbara, I'm here," he said. She smiled at him. Then she drifted into a deeper sleep. She stopped breathing at 9:15 A.M.

"Right before she died she told me, 'Nothing is a secret anymore,'" Briggs said. "But when a reporter called me and asked what had caused her death, I couldn't tell him. I had been protecting her for seventeen years, and I just could not break the habit."

ENDINGS

On January 20, 1996, Barbara Jordan's life was celebrated at the Good Hope Missionary Baptist Church in Houston. It was cold and rainy. Thousands of her friends and fans came: members of Congress and the cabinet, mayors and judges, dignitaries from the civil rights movement, local and state officials, former students, labor leaders, bankers and corporation executives, precinct workers and neighbors, ministers and club women, and men and women from Houston's Third and Fifth Wards—her people. Her body was in an open casket, and she had been dressed in a black suit with gold braids around the collar and sleeves. Her Presidential Medal of Freedom had been draped around her neck. Her family and close friends sat in the front pews, and the church was packed, with thousands of people standing outside in the rain to listen to the funeral service over a loudspeaker.

President Clinton gave a moving eulogy, as did former Texas governor Ann Richards and the actress Cicely Tyson, as well as Jordan's old debate coach Tom Freeman. Her Delta Sigma Theta sorority sisters, members of the Top Ladies of Distinction, and Good Hope Baptist's leaders paid her tribute. Aretha Franklin sent a floral wreath in which the flowers spelled out R-E-S-P-E-C-T. A few days later, at a memorial service in Washington,

D.C., Senator Alan Simpson paid an eloquent tribute to her at the Kennedy Center and Odetta performed a song in her honor. At another service in Austin, Bill Moyers said that the universe must have been getting ready for Barbara Jordan because on the day she died, scientists announced the discovery of forty billion new galaxies deep in the inner sanctum of the universe. "It will take an infinite cosmic vista to accommodate a soul this great," he said.[64] Newspapers all across the nation ran articles and editorials celebrating Jordan's life and accomplishments. Old friends wrote op-ed pieces about their experiences with her. New schools and city streets were hastily renamed in her honor. She was called a "national treasure," "an American original," a "heroic champion of justice," a "liberator" in the tradition of Harriet Tubman and Sojourner Truth, a "monument" to liberty, a "rare spirit," and on and on.

It was her pastor, a Good Hope preacher and orator who understood her roots and her spirit, who managed to transform all of the memorial rhetoric into a simple rhythmic eloquence that captured the meaning of Barbara Jordan's life. The Reverend D. Z. Cofield held the dignitaries and famous leaders enthralled when he talked about what this Fifth Ward woman, this lifelong member of the Good Hope Missionary Baptist Church, had meant to her people.

> I like to think that if Dr. King was the conductor of the orchestra,
>> Barbara would be in the first chair.
> If Dr. King opened the doors of segregation,
>> She taught us how to walk in and hold our heads up high.
> If he allowed us to sit at any table and eat where we wanted,
>> She taught us how to act at the table.
> So we leave here today focused in our minds
>> That we can be the best we can be
> Because she was the best she was.[65]

Barbara Jordan's body was buried on a hillside in the old State Cemetery in Austin only a few feet away from the founding father of Texas, Stephen F. Austin, who led a band of settlers into Texas in 1820 and precipitated a war with Mexico that led to Texas independence and eventual entry into the Union. Her burial in the State Cemetery came twenty-seven years after she had written a bill to outlaw segregated cemeteries in Texas. On one side of her final resting place was the daughter of Colonel James Fannin, one of the defenders of the Alamo, and on the other side was Brigadier General Ben McCullough, a Confederate war hero who fought to preserve slavery. While her cemetery desegregation law would have allowed others to rest in that hallowed ground, Barbara Jordan, in death as in life, was the *first* to garner enough power to make it happen. In 1996, one hundred and thirty-one years after the end of slavery, thirty years after she entered the Texas Senate, and twenty-four years after she became the first African American woman elected to Congress from the South, Barbara Jordan became the first black person to be buried in the State Cemetery in Austin, Texas, the United States of America—her home. *E pluribus unum* at last.

BARBARA JORDAN
1936–1996

ACKNOWLEDGMENTS

THE ASSISTANCE AND advice of many people have made this book possible. *Texas Monthly* writer Jan Jarboe first suggested to my agent Jim Hornfischer that I undertake the task of writing about Barbara Jordan's life. Jim's knowledge and skill helped turn the project into reality, and I am grateful both for Jan's confidence and Jim's support. My editor at Bantam Books, Katie Hall, also believed in the possibilities of this work, and her encouragement, advice, and sensitive editing have been invaluable. Once the project was under way, two people were responsible for opening the doors that allowed me to enter into the life of Barbara Jordan. Nancy Earl, executor of the Barbara Jordan Estate, was generous with her time. Her keen intelligence and fine humor provided a filter for Jordan's life, without which this book could not have been written. Jordan's attorney, William Hilgers, who arranged her business affairs while she was alive, and who settled her estate after her death, was always helpful. The cooperation of Earl and Hilgers encouraged other individuals who were close to Jordan to agree to be interviewed; however, at no time did either Earl or Hilgers attempt to guide or control the direction of the book. Jordan's sisters, Rose Mary McGowan and Bennie Creswell, were generous and forthcoming anytime I asked for information and I am grateful for their assistance.

Two key friends helped me with tips, ideas, arrangements, research, and a lot of plain old hard work. The book could not have been completed without them. My administrative assistant at the LBJ School of Public Affairs, Sharon Tutchings, had been Jordan's assistant for the last nine years of her life. Because she kept Jordan's schedule, traveled with her, dealt with students for her, and in general helped Jordan's life run smoothly, Tutchings provided information that would have been impossible to ferret out of libraries, museums, correspondence files, or news clips. She was always available to find an important photograph, document, or speech. Ruthe Winegarten, one of the foremost historians about the experiences of African American women in Texas, made herself available to me for major—and minor—research assistance. Winegarten was so familiar with historical sources and available data that her help and ideas played a large role in shaping the book. I was incredibly lucky to have both Winegarten's and Tutchings's help and, more importantly, their friendship.

My dear friend, the poet and editor Betty Sue Flowers, read the manuscript at various points along the way and was generous with her time and insightful advice. Max Sherman, former dean of the LBJ School of Public Affairs, supported and encouraged the project from the beginning. Susan Rieff, a former student and close friend of Jordan's, became an encouraging sounding board for my ideas. The late Billy Ramsey, a wise veteran of Houston's political wars, was my early guide to key players and events. I am grateful to Harris County commissioner El Franco Lee, who drove me around Houston's Fifth Ward and interpreted the significance of the key places and neighborhoods where he grew up and lives today, and which Jordan represented in the Texas legislature and in Congress. Houston state senator Rodney Ellis, as well as former Texas governor Ann Richards, provided key introductions for me that made several important interviews possible. Shannon Stewart, a former LBJ student of mine, assisted with some key research in Washington, D.C., and my friends, Don Temples and Sam Smith, opened their home to me when I conducted my research there. Carl Richie helped me understand the strength of the African American church in sustaining people through difficult times. Dr. John Silber, chancellor of Boston University, generously provided information about Jordan's time in law school there. I appreciate Pat Heard's careful reading of the manuscript and Amon Burton's legal assistance at key points. Conversations with a number of people added insight and depth to my research: Philip Bobbitt, Martha Coniglio, Ernesto Cortes Jr., James A Galbraith, Dagmar Hamilton, Charles Miller, Mary Sanger, Judge Rose Spector, Ellen Wartella, and the incomparable Polish Group.

I am indebted to almost a hundred people who allowed me to interview them for this book, and particularly to several individuals whose personal experiences with Jordan helped flesh out her story: Stan McClelland, Dr. Rambie Briggs, Nancy Earl, Jake Johnson, and Oscar Mauzy.

I received the generous assistance of numerous scholars, librarians, archivists, and reference staff workers from many institutions: Janet Humphrey and David Humphrey; Sandra Parham and Helen Hamilton, Texas Southern University; Anne Douglass, Houston Public Library; Stephen Luttrell, LBJ School of Public Affairs; Philip Scott, LBJ Presidential Library and Museum; Nancy Mirshah, Gerald R. Ford Library; Joan Carroll, Wide World Photos; Michelle Jaconi, *Meet the Press*; Katherine Staat, director of Texas Senate Media Services; Jo Gutierrez, *Houston Chronicle*; Ben Sargent, *Austin American Statesman*; and numerous individuals at the Center for American History at the University of Texas at Austin.

Finally, my family encouraged me throughout the project. My son Billy Rogers and my daughter Eleanor Rogers Petterson are my biggest boosters and closest friends. Eleanor and her husband Mark began their family at about the same time I began my research, and they presented me with two wonderful granddaughters—Lauren and Lindsey—before the book was finished. My sisters and brother, nieces and nephews, and my aunts whose lives span the century—all of my wonderful close-knit family cheered me on during the process. And, of course, my parents, to whom this book is dedicated, continued to give me the unconditional love that is the foundation of my life and work.

APPENDIX

Barbara Jordan
1936–1996
Curriculum Vitae

Education:
L.L.B.   Boston University, 1959
B.A.   Texas Southern University (political science and history), 1956
Honorary Doctoral Degrees: 31—including Harvard University, Princeton
               University, the University of Notre Dame, Brandeis University,
               the College of William and Mary, Wake Forest University, and
               the Tuskegee Institute

Experience:
1982–1996   **Lyndon B. Johnson Centennial Chair in National Policy,** The
               Lyndon B. Johnson School of Public Affairs, The University of
               Texas at Austin

1979–82   **Lyndon B. Johnson Public Service Professorship,** LBJ School
               of Public Affairs

1972–78   **United States House of Representatives,** Congresswoman from
               the 18th District of Texas
               Member: House Committee on the Judiciary; House Committee
               on Government Operations; Steering and Policy Committee of
               the Democratic Caucus
               Major Legislative Achievements Enacted into Law:
               Amendments to the Voting Rights Act which expanded its
               coverage and provided for the printing of bilingual ballots; repeal
               of federal authorization for state "Fair Trade" laws, which
               sanctioned vertical price-fixing schemes; detailed mandatory civil
               rights enforcement procedures for the Law Enforcement
               Assistance Administration and the Office of Revenue Sharing

1966–72   **Texas Senate:** elected as Senator to the Texas State Legislature
               1972—President Pro Tempore, Texas Senate
               1972—"Governor for a Day"—first black woman "Governor" in
               United States history

1960–66   **Private Legal Practice,** Houston
               Administrative Assistant to the County Judge of Harris County

Professional Organizations:

American Bar Association
Fellow of the American Bar Foundation
State Bar of Texas
Massachusetts Bar
District of Columbia Bar

Publications:

Barbara Jordan: A Self-Portrait, with Shelby Hearon (Doubleday, 1979).
"Individual Rights, Social Responsibility," *Rights and Responsibilities,* November 1978, pp. 9–17.
The Great Society: A Twenty-Year Critique, edited with Elspeth Rostow (Austin: The LBJ Library and the LBJ School of Public Affairs, 1986).
"Reflections on the Constitution," *The Houston Lawyer,* Sept.–Oct. 1987, vol. 25, no. 2, pp. 8–10.

Corporate Boards:

The Mead Corporation, member of the Board of Directors
Texas Commerce Bancshares, Inc., member of the Board of Directors
Federal Home Mortgage Loan Corporation (FREDDIE MAC), member of the Board of Directors
Burlington Northern Santa Fe, Inc., member of the Board of Directors
Northrop-Grumman Corporation, member of the Board of Directors

Advisory Boards:

Chair, Immigration Reform Commission
Founder and member of the Board of Directors, People for the American Way
Member, Presidential Advisory Board on Ambassadorial Appointments, 1979–81
Hearings Officer, National Institute of Education Hearings on Minimum Competency Testing

Awards and Honors:

Recipient of Harvey Penick Award, 1995
Recipient of Sylvanus Thayer Award, West Point, 1995
Recipient of Sara Lee Corporation Frontrunner Award, 1994
Recipient of Seton Hall University School of Law, Sandra Day O'Connor Medal of Honor, 1994
Recipient of Presidential Medal of Freedom, 1994
Recipient of Joseph Prize for Human Rights, 1993
Selected "one of the most influential American women of the 20th century," by a survey for the National Women's Hall of Fame, 1993

Recipient of the Nelson Mandela Award for Health and Human Rights, 1993

Inducted into the African-American Hall of Fame, 1993

Recipient of the 77th NAACP Spingarn Medal, 1992

Recipient of the Eleanor Roosevelt Val-Kill Medal, 1992

Recipient of the National Civil Rights Museum Freedom Award, 1992

Recipient of the Bess Wallace Truman Award, 1992

Recipient of the Tom C. Clark Equal Justice Under Law Award, 1991

Recipient of the Elmer B. Staats Public Service Careers Award, 1990

Inducted into the National Women's Hall of Fame, 1990

Dedicated in her name, the 1990 edition of the *Annual Survey of American Law* by New York University School of Law

Recipient of the Harry S. Truman Public Service Award from the Harry S. Truman Scholarship Foundation, 1990

Recipient of the 21st Charles Evans Hughes Gold Medal of the National Conference of Christians and Jews, March 5, 1987

Appointed by the Secretary-General of the United Nations to serve on a panel to conduct hearings on the role of transnational corporations in South Africa and Namibia, September 1985

Recipient of the Eleanor Roosevelt Humanities Award, State of Israel Bonds, 1984

Voted "Best Living Orator" by the International Platform Association, 1984

Elected to the Texas Women's Hall of Fame, Public Service Category, 1984

Selected by *World Almanac* in 1986 as "One of the 25 Most Influential Women in America" (for the twelfth consecutive year)

Hosted a PBS television series entitled "Crisis to Crisis with Barbara Jordan," which premiered in July 1982

Selected by the editors of *Ladies' Home Journal* as among the "100 Most Influential Women in America"

Selected as first choice in a poll conducted by *Redbook* magazine on "Women Who Could Be Appointed to the Supreme Court," October 1979

Presented keynote address at the National Democratic convention, 1976 and 1992

Selected by *Time* magazine as one of the "Ten Women of the Year," 1976

ADDITIONAL HONORS

The Hall of Honor for Congress in 1993 made an effort to identify the top one hundred members of Congress, out of 11,397 individuals who had served from the beginning of the Republic. Barbara Jordan not only made the top one hundred but was on the cover of the book: Val J. Halamandaris, ed., *Heroes of the U.S. Congress* (Washington, D.C.: Caring Publishing [National Congressional Trust]), 1994. Others on the list included John Quincy Adams, John C. Calhoun, Frank Church, Henry Clay, Everett Dirksen, Sam Ervin, Benjamin Franklin, William Fulbright, Barry Goldwater, Sam Houston, Thomas Jefferson, Lyndon B. Johnson, James Madison, Claude Pepper, Jeannette Rankin, Sam Rayburn, and Daniel Webster.

NOTES

INTRODUCTION

1. House Judiciary Committee, "Debate on Articles of Impeachment," hearings, July 24–30, 1974.
2. Adrienne Rich, *What Is Found There: Notebooks on Poetry and Politics,* (New York: W. W. Norton & Company, 1993) p. 83.
3. Ibid., p. 84.
4. Barbara Jordan, keynote address, Democratic National Convention, New York, July 12, 1976.
5. Studs Terkel, "Celebrating Our Heroes," *Life* magazine, May 1997, p. 8.
6. David Levering Lewis, *W.E.B. Du Bois: Biography of a Race, 1868–1919* (New York: Henry Holt and Co., 1993), p. 199.
7. Miscellaneous correspondence files, Barbara Jordan Archives, Texas Southern University, Houston.
8. Author's interview with George Christian, Austin, Texas, September 6, 1996. All subsequent quotations from Christian are from this interview, unless otherwise noted.
9. Author's interview with Dr. Rambie Briggs, Austin, Texas, August 7, 1997. All subsequent quotations from Briggs are from this interview, unless otherwise noted.

CHAPTER ONE

1. Barbara Jordan and Shelby Hearon, *Barbara Jordan: A Self-Portrait* (New York: Doubleday, 1979), p. 22.
2. Kathy Russell, Midge Wilson, and Ronald Hall, *The Color Complex: The Politics of Skin Color Among African Americans* (New York: Anchor Books/Doubleday, 1992), p. 38. The authors believe that the "color complex" is a psychological fixation about color and features that leads African Americans to discriminate against each other. Because the color complex has long been considered unmentionable, the authors call it the "last taboo" among African Americans (p. 2).
3. Jordan and Hearon, *Self-Portrait,* p. 62. All quotes from Barbara Jordan are taken from this source, unless otherwise noted.
4. Russell, Wilson, and Hall, *The Color Complex,* p. 41.
5. Ibid., p. 23.
6. Ibid., p. 25.
7. Paula Ancona, "Do Twice as Much, Jordan Tells Dunbar Students," undated article from Dayton, Ohio, c. 1980, Barbara Jordan Office Files, LBJ School of Public Affairs, now at Barbara Jordan Archives, Texas Southern University.
8. Ibid.
9. Ibid.
10. Barbara Jordan, "The Supply Side of Race," remarks at Urban League Banquet, Austin, 1981. Public Affairs Library, LBJ School of Public Affairs, University of Texas at Austin.
11. Jennifer Res, "Jordan Shares Experiences About Racial Harmony with Texas Teens," *On Campus,* February 14, 1994, Center for American History, University of Texas at Austin.

1. Lawrence D. Rice, *The Negro in Texas, 1874–1900* (Baton Rouge: Louisiana State University Press, 1971), p. 35.
2. The exact departure date of federal troops from Texas is unclear, but it probably began around 1871 with the shutdown of the Freedman's Bureau. By 1874 most federal troops had left Texas, but it was 1877 before all federal troops had left the South: Alwyn Barr, *Black Texans: A History of African Americans in Texas, 1528–1995,* 2d ed. (Norman: University of Oklahoma Press, 1996), pp. 41–52.
3. Lawrence Goodwyn, *Democratic Promise: The Populist Movement in America* (New York: Oxford University Press, 1976), p. 278.
4. *Houston Telegraph,* October 10, 1875, quoted in Rice, *The Negro in Texas,* p. 23.
5. Rice, *The Negro in Texas,* p. 127.
6. Ibid., p. 45.
7. Quoted in Lawrence Goodwyn, "Populist Dreams and Negro Rights: East Texas as a Case Study," *American Historical Review* 76, no. 5 (December 1971): 1435–56.
8. Aldon Morris, "Centuries of Black Protest: Its Significance for America and the World," in Herbert Hill and James E. Jones Jr., eds., *Race in America: The Struggle for Equality* (Madison: University of Wisconsin Press, 1993), p. 42.
9. Information about Edward A. Patton is taken from his entry in *The Handbook of Texas,* vol. 5 (Austin: Texas Historical Association, 1997), p. 94. Additional information comes from Merline Pitre, *Through Many Dangers, Toils, and Shares: The Black Leadership of Texas, 1868–1900* (Austin: Eakin Press, 1985). In addition to the poll tax, Patton had some *limited* legislative success on education issues. He was able to secure $98,000 for the state's only all-black public college, Prairie View State Normal School. Patton's conservative demeanor had allowed him to be relatively effective on the two issues that mattered most to him during the four-month legislative session.
10. *Galveston Daily News,* February 21, 1891.
11. Nicholas Lemann, *The Promised Land: The Great Black Migration and How It Changed America* (New York: Vintage Books, 1992), p. 9.
12. Rice, *The Negro in Texas,* pp. 260–62.
13. Hill and Jones, *Race in America,* p. 24.
14. The two versions of the name, Patton and Patten, are used interchangeably in the census records of 1880, 1890, and 1900, resulting in some confusion. An Edward Patten, listed in the 1870 San Jacinto County census, is probably one and the same as the Edward Patton who served in the legislature. Barbara Jordan's sisters, Bennie Creswell and Rose Mary McGowan, confirmed that some of their relatives from Evergreen spelled their name Patton, rather than Patten, as did their maternal grandfather, John Edward. Neither Mrs. Creswell nor Mrs. McGowan, like their sister Barbara, knew that Edward A. Patton, their great-grandfather, was a member of the Texas legislature. After looking at available records, which are scant, I am convinced that the stories of "Grandpa" Ed Patten match the tales of Edward Patton, and that because there were only between fifty and one hundred people who lived in Evergreen, the known facts indicate that the Edward A. Patton who lived there was John Ed Patten's father.
15. Pitre, *Through Many Dangers, Toils, and Shares,* p. 62.
16. Joe R. Feagin, *Free Enterprise City: Houston in Political-Economic Perspective* (New Brunswick, N.J.: Rutgers University Press, 1988), p. 17.
17. Howard Beeth and Cary D. Winty, eds., *Black Dixie: Afro-Texan History and Culture in Houston* (College Station: Texas A&M University Press, 1992), p. 17.
18. Rice, *The Negro in Texas,* pp. 260–62.
19. Barr, *Black Texan,* p. 41.
20. Beeth and Wintz, *Black Dixie,* p. 88.
21. Ira Bryant, *Barbara Charline Jordan: From the Ghetto to the Capitol* (Houston: D. Armstrong Co., 1977), p. 6.
22. Beeth and Wintz, *Black Dixie,* p. 96.
23. Quoted in Jordan and Hearon, *Self-Portrait,* p. 4.

24. "Race Riot of 1917 Was Black Mark in History," Emancipation 100th anniversary edition, *Forward Times* (Houston), June 15, 1963, Houston Public Library.

25. Beeth and Wintz, *Black Dixie,* p. 161.

26. Feagin, *Free Enterprise City,* p. 251.

27. In 1982 Houston mayor Kathy Whitmire appointed African American Lee Brown to the position of police chief. Brown later was chief of police in New York City and directed President Clinton's war on drugs. In November 1997, Brown was elected the first African American mayor of Houston.

28. Will Hogg, the son of former Governor Jim Hogg, was among the prominent Houstonians who advocated racial segregation. His father's first term coincided with the service of Edward A. Patton in the Texas legislature. Governor Hogg completed the restoration of the Southern Democracy, and his family made a fortune from their landholdings in the east Texas oil fields. Governor Hogg's son Will presented a plan to Houston's city fathers to end the racial "scattering" of blacks throughout the city by setting aside certain areas for blacks and restricting their access to other areas. Will Hogg later developed Houston's premier and exclusive River Oaks residential area, home to Houston's most wealthy white citizens.

29. Beeth and Wintz, *Black Dixie,* p. 161.

30. The account of this incident is from Jordan and Hearon, *Self-Portrait,* pp. 13–21.

CHAPTER THREE

1. The Good Hope Baptist Church building constructed under Cashaw's direction was totally destroyed by fire on February 21, 1997. Although it had been vacant for twenty-five years, plans were under way, and money had been raised, to remodel the building and turn it into a Barbara Jordan memorial and community center. The Federal Bureau of Investigation immediately began an investigation to determine whether the fire might have been arson and related to other fires that destroyed African American churches in 1996 and 1997. As late as 1998, no report had been released, however.

2. Quoted in Jordan and Hearon, *Self-Portrait,* p. 35.

3. Author's interview with Rose Mary McGowan and Bennie Creswell, Houston, August 23, 1996. All subsequent quotations from Jordan's sisters are taken from this interview, unless otherwise noted.

4. Jordan never knew the source of the quotation.

5. Quoted in Jordan and Hearon, *Self-Portrait,* p. 32.

6. Evelyn Brooks Higginbotham, *Righteous Discontent: The Women's Movement in the Black Baptist Church, 1880–1920* (Cambridge, Mass: Harvard University Press, 1993), p. 188. Higginbotham details the impact and meaning for women of the search for respectability (p. 205).

7. Ibid., p. 190.

8. "Experiences of the Race Problem, by a Southern White Woman," *Independent* 56 (March 17, 1904), quoted ibid., p. 190.

9. Quoted in Jordan and Hearon, *Self-Portrait,* p. 46.

10. Bryant, *Barbara Charline Jordan,* p. 2.

11. Ibid., p. 31.

12. For a discussion of businesses run and owned by African American women, see Ruthe Winegarten, *Black Texas Women: A Sourcebook* (Austin: University of Texas Press, 1996).

13. Beeth and Wintz, *Black Dixie,* p. 92.

14. Ibid., p. 91.

15. Ibid., p. 55.

16. C. Eric Lincoln, ed., *The Black Experience in Religion* (Garden City, N.Y.: Anchor Press/Doubleday, 1974), p. 3.

17. Ibid., pp. 187, 14.

18. A commemorative program for Lucas's funeral identified him as a "race pride" man. And in an interview with the author, Reverend William Lawson (Houston, February 20, 1997), also a Baptist minister in Houston and a longtime civil rights leader, said that Lucas was clearly the leader of the black ministers in Houston during his tenure at Good Hope.

19. Cheryl Coggins Frink, "A Bastion of Hope: Black Church Still Has Faith in Social Change," *Austin American Statesman*, March 6, 1989.

20. Michael L. Gillette, *The Rise of the NAACP in Texas*, p. 409. While Lucas may have been the kingpin, several talented women, like Lula B. White and Christia Adair, were superb organizers, and they were also responsible for the growth of the NAACP in Houston.

21. Mike Kingston, Sam Attlesey, and Mary G. Crawford, *The Texas Almanac's Political History of Texas* (Austin: Eakin Press, 1992).

22. Gay Elliott McFarland, "Barbara Jordan's Houston," *Houston Chronicle*, February 5, 1979.

23. William Broyles, "The Making of Barbara Jordan," *Texas Monthly*, October 1976.

24. Ibid.

25. Liz Carpenter, "Barbara Jordan," *Family Circle*, 1977.

26. Ibid.

27. Ibid.

CHAPTER FOUR

1. Quoted in Jordan and Hearon, *Self-Portrait*, p. 42.

2. Quoted ibid., p. 33.

3. Gay Elliott McFarland, "Barbara Jordan's Houston," *Houston Chronicle*, February 5, 1979.

4. Bryant, *Barbara Charline Jordan*, p. 5.

5. Edith Sampson was also the first black woman appointed as a judge in Illinois and the first black person to hold an appointment with the North Atlantic Treaty Organization (NATO). She was in great demand as a lecturer, and she traveled extensively throughout the Middle East, Scandinavia, Europe, and South America. She was as active in public service in Chicago as she was in national activities, holding the offices of assistant corporation counsel, associate judge of the municipal court, and judge of the Cook County Circuit Court. Sampson was born in 1901 in Pittsburgh and died in 1979 in Chicago, the year Barbara Jordan retired from Congress.

6. Author's interview with Otis King (dean of the Thurgood Marshall School of Law, Texas Southern University), Houston, October 3, 1996. All quotations from King are from this interview, unless otherwise noted.

7. Charlotte Phelan, "State Senator Barbara Jordan Wins Her Battles Through the System," *Houston Post*, May 24, 1970.

8. McFarland, "Barbara Jordan's Houston."

9. Mark V. Tushnet, *Making Civil Rights Law: Thurgood Marshall and the Supreme Court, 1936–1961* (New York: Oxford University Press, 1994), p. 127. All of the Thurgood Marshall quotes in this paragraph are taken from *Making Civil Rights Law*.

10. Irwin Ross, "Barbara Jordan—New Voice in Washington," *Reader's Digest*, February 1977.

11. Tushnet, *Making Civil Rights Law*, p. 127.

12. Ibid., p. 132.

13. Ibid., p. 147.

14. Neil Sapper, "The Fall of the NAACP in Texas," *Houston Review* 7, (no. 2 1986): 53–68.

15. Ibid.

16. For a full discussion of the early days of TSU, see Ira Bryant, *Texas Southern University: Its Antecedents, Political Origins, and Future* (Houston: Ira B. Bryant, 1975).

17. Paula Giddings, *In Search of Sisterhood: Delta Sigma Theta and the Challenge of the Black Sorority Movement* (New York: William Morrow, 1988), p. 43.

18. Jordan and Hearon, *Self-Portrait*, p. 78.

19. Quoted ibid., p. 79.

20. David Montejano, *Anglos and Mexicans in the Making of Texas, 1836–1986* (Austin: University of Texas Press, 1987), p. 275.

21. For a thorough discussion of the impact of anti-Communism on race and politics in

Texas, see Don E. Carleton, *Red Scare!: Right-wing Hysteria, Fifties Fanaticism, and Their Legacy in Texas* (Austin: Texas Monthly Press, 1985).
22. Oberlin College, in Ohio, was also open to all races when it was founded in 1833.

CHAPTER FIVE

1. Kathleen Kilgore, *Transformations: A History of Boston University* (Boston: Boston University Press, 1991). All information about Boston University comes from this book, unless otherwise noted.
2. Ronald E. Marcello, interview with Barbara Jordan, Austin, Texas, July 7, 1970, University of North Texas Oral History Collection, Denton, Texas.
3. Kilgore, *Transformations,* p. 250.
4. Taylor Branch, *Parting the Waters: America in the King Years, 1954–1963* (New York: Touchstone/Simon & Schuster, 1988), p. 6.
5. Howard Thurman, *The Luminous Darkness: A Personal Interpretation of the Anatomy of Segregation and the Ground of Hope* (New York: Harper & Row, 1965), p. 38.
6. Branch, *Parting the Waters,* p. 124.
7. Anne Spencer Thurman, ed., *For the Inward Journey: The Writings of Howard Thurman* (New York: Harcourt Brace Jovanovich, 1984), p. 188.
8. Ibid., p. 184.
9. Ibid., p. 187.

CHAPTER SIX

1. Feagin, *Free Enterprise City,* p. 93.
2. Joe Feagin calls the Suite 8F crowd the most powerful elite group in Houston's history because of its cohesion and distinctive personalities, as well as its corporate networks and national and international resources. Although the actual membership fluctuated from the 1930s to the 1960s, the core of the group included Jesse H. Jones, Herman and George Brown, James A. Elkins Sr., Gus Wortham, and James Abercrombie. Herman and George Brown's ties with Lyndon Johnson have been well documented. Elkins was one of the founders of the Vinson and Elkins law firm, where John Connally would one day be a partner. Elkins also headed Houston's largest bank at the time, First City, and had a major interest in the South's largest insurance company, American General Insurance. Gus Wortham was the founder of American General and helped build Houston's cultural institutions, supporting local colleges and art facilities. James Abercrombie was an oil entrepreneur who started Cameron Iron Works, which became one of the world's leading oil tool manufacturing firms, with plants in Europe and Asia as well as Houston. One of the few women welcomed by the Suite 8F crowd was Oveta Culp Hobby, who owned the *Houston Post* and a major television station. Mrs. Hobby was head of the Women's Army Corps during World War II and served in President Eisenhower's cabinet in the 1950s. She was the widow of a former Texas governor, and her son, William P. Hobby Jr., would serve as Texas lieutenant governor for eighteen years, in the 1970s and 1980s.
3. "One in Five Residents Called 'Poor,' Churches Attack Poverty," *Houston Post,* July 3, 1965.
4. According to the Texas State Bar Association, the other two African American female lawyers were Charlye O. Farris of Wichita Falls, a graduate of Howard University, who passed the Texas bar in 1954, and Hattie Briscoe of San Antonio, a graduate of St. Mary's University Law School, who passed the Texas bar in 1956.
5. Phelan, "State Senator Barbara Jordan Wins Her Battles."
6. Author's interview with Chris Dixie, Houston, February 21, 1997. All subsequent quotations from Dixie are from this interview, unless otherwise noted.
7. Phelan, "State Senator Barbara Jordan Wins Her Battles."
8. Advertisement, *Forward Times* (Houston), June 15, 1963, Houston Public Library.

9. Christopher Lasch, *The Revolt of the Elites and the Betrayal of Democracy* (New York: W. W. Norton, 1995).

10. Saul Friedman, "Determined Negro Bloc Spoke with Single Voice," *Houston Chronicle*, November 8, 1964.

11. "Profile of the Houston Negro Community with Special Tribute to Barbara Jordan," Harris County Council of Organizations, 1967, Houston Public Library.

12. "A Conversation with Miss Jordan," *Texas Observer*, May 27, 1966.

13. Molly Bowers, "Attorney Advocates Effective Use of Ballot," *Houston Post*, August 28, 1965.

14. Richard West, *Richard West's Texas* (Austin: Texas Monthly Press, 1981), p. 133.

15. Chandler Davidson, *Race and Class in Texas Politics* (Princeton, N.J.: Princeton University Press, 1990), p. 159.

16. Ibid., p. 162.

17. Malcolm Boyd, "Where Is Barbara Jordan Today?" *Parade*, February 16, 1986, pp. 12–13.

18. Willis Whatley served in the Texas legislature until 1969. In 1966 he briefly considered switching to the Republican Party with a number of conservative Democrats, including then–state representative W. R. "Bill" Archer, who would become a powerful Republican congressman and chair of the U.S. House Budget Committee in 1994 under Speaker Newt Gingrich. Whatley died in 1989 at the age of sixty-one.

CHAPTER SEVEN

1. "If Mom Told Me Once . . . ," *Houston Chronicle*, August 4, 1968.

2. Helen Parmley, "Jordan: Why Carter Didn't Call," *Dallas Morning News*, January 9, 1977.

3. Jordan continued to indicate throughout her early career that she might consider marrying, but she reaffirmed her career objective in 1974 when she told the *Christian Science Monitor*, "Politics is all-consuming, almost totally consuming. I definitely do not discount marriage, but a good marriage requires that one attend to it and not treat it as another hobby." Joann Levine, "Impact in Congress," *Christian Science Monitor*, March 18, 1974.

4. Molly Bowers, "Attorney Advocates Effective Use of Ballot," *Houston Post*, August 23, 1963.

5. Barbara Jordan, "His Presence Speaks for the Negro," *Austin American Statesman*, June 16, 1968.

6. Saul Friedman, "Houston, a Backwater of the Civil Rights Movement," *Texas Observer*, November 1963.

7. Ibid.

8. James Haskins, *Barbara Jordan* (New York: Dial Press, 1977), p. 46.

9. The African American school board member Mrs. Charles White had been able to win her election in 1958 because of several favorable circumstances that did not apply to the legislative races Jordan was undertaking. First, the school district's boundaries were smaller; the district did not include some of the white suburbs, which had their own independent school districts. Second, the nonpartisan school elections never attracted the large number of voters who turned out for the Democratic primary elections, and a well-organized bloc of African American voters could have a greater impact. Third, the elections were decided by a plurality of the voters, not a majority. In a race with three or more candidates, Mrs. White's small but committed hard-core bloc of votes put her in the lead, while white voters were split among a number of other white candidates.

10. The four Texas members of Congress who voted for the Civil Rights Act of 1964 were J. J. "Jake" Pickle of Austin, Henry B. Gonzalez of San Antonio, Abraham Kazen of Laredo, and Albert Thomas of Houston. Senator Ralph Yarborough voted for the measure in the Senate.

11. Broyles, "The Making of Barbara Jordan."

12. Author's interview with Oscar Mauzy (former state senator and former Texas Supreme Court justice), Austin, Texas, August 12, 1996. All subsequent quotations from Mauzy are from this interview, unless otherwise noted.

13. Molly Sinclair, "Miss Jordan Aims to Serve," *Houston Post,* March 7, 1965; and Dick Raycraft, "Barbara Jordan Quit Legal War to Battle for Houston Needy," *Houston Chronicle,* April 25, 1965.

14. Haskins, *Barbara Jordan,* p. 44.

15. "Profile of the Integration Movement in Houston," Harris County Council of Organizations (1967): p. 47, Houston Public Library.

16. Phelan, "State Senator Barbara Jordan Wins Her Battles."

17. The Twenty-fourth Amendment, ratified in 1964, outlawed the poll tax in federal elections and primaries leading to federal elections. At the time four states, including Texas, still required a poll tax in state elections.

18. Chandler Davidson, "The Voting Rights Act: A Brief History," from *Controversies in Minority Voting: The Voting Rights Act in Perspective* (Washington, D.C.: Brookings Institution, 1992), p. 26.

19. Montejano, *Anglos and Mexicans in the Making of Texas,* p. 277.

20. Quoted in Jordan and Hearon, *Self-Portrait,* p. 131.

21. Ibid.

22. Haskins, *Barbara Jordan,* p. 54.

23. "Whitfield Questions Opponent's Conflict of Interest; She Denies It," *Houston Chronicle,* March 20, 1966.

24. "A Question of Today," *Texas Observer,* April 29, 1966.

25. Ibid.

26. Charlie Whitfield wrote Jordan after seeing her on television during the House Judiciary Committee hearings on Watergate in 1974, and he apologized for the tone of their 1966 race. He said that he thought Jordan had always been gracious to him, and that he wanted to remain her friend. Correspondence files, Barbara Jordan Archives, Texas Southern University.

27. The last African American Texas state senator in the nineteenth century was Walter Burton, who served from 1876 to 1883.

28. Haskins, *Barbara Jordan,* p. 56.

CHAPTER EIGHT

1. Mary Rice Brogan, "Seating of Sen. Barbara Jordan Proud Day for Her, Her People," *Houston Chronicle,* January 1, 1967.

2. In 1996 Texas Republicans reestablished themselves as a dominant party by winning control of the Texas Senate for the first time since Reconstruction.

3. Author's interview with Mauzy. Mauzy recounts this tale of his visit to the late state senator George Parkhouse, who represented Dallas County for many years in Austin.

4. Ibid.

5. Quoted ibid.

6. Walter Mansel, "Barbara Jordan Has No Fears About Serving in State Senate," *Houston Chronicle,* May 22, 1966.

7. As a result of investigations related to Watergate, Claude Wild was indicted in 1978 for making almost $7 million in illegal campaign contributions on behalf of his employer, Gulf Oil.

8. Broyles, "The Making of Barbara Jordan."

9. Molly Ivins, "A Profile of Barbara Jordan," *Texas Observer,* November 3, 1972.

10. Barbara Jordan, "How I Got There," undated, unidentified clip from Barbara Jordan's personal scrapbook, Barbara Jordan Archives, Texas Southern University, Houston.

11. Hardeman was an "old guard" conservative Democrat, and he resented Connally's brashness and willingness to raise taxes for public services. The power struggle between the two men began when Hardeman busted a Connally appointment to the University of Texas Board of Regents. (Gubernatorial appointments must be confirmed by the Senate.) Hardeman continued to oppose Connally's programs and made Connally's life so difficult that the governor singled him out in a speech as an "obstructionist." In their biography of John Connally, the Texas journalist Jack Keever and the historian Ann Fears Crawford say there

was an "undeclared war" between Connally and Hardeman. The Texas publisher Houston Harte once arranged a truce meeting between the men, and Hardeman was charming, but the very next day on the floor of the Senate he called Connally "arrogant" and "made for power." But Connally got his revenge. Crawford and Keever report that Connally personally intervened in the Senate redistricting process to pair Hardeman in a district with the former legislator W. E. "Pete" Snelson of Midland, who ended Hardeman's thirty-one-year legislative career by defeating him in 1968. Ann Fears Crawford and Jack Keever, *John B. Connally: Portrait in Power* (Austin: Jenkins Publishing Co., 1973).

12. Raymond Brooks, "With Hardeman Defeat Legislative Era Ends," *Austin American Statesman*, May 9, 1968.

13. David Anderson, "Hardeman Leaves, Microphones Arrive, Texas Senate Loses Two Traditions in Day," *Fort Worth Press*, July 8, 1968.

14. The post-Reconstruction Texas Constitution of 1867 severely limited the powers of the governor and vested most power—but not too much—in the state legislature. The legislature could meet only every other year, and then only for four months. But for those four months, old-timers used to say, "no Texan was safe from harm." Texas governors derived their only power from some key appointments to boards and commissions, plus the threat of a veto of legislation passed by the House and Senate. By sheer personality and bravado, some governors have been able to dominate the legislature. But most often, the state's most powerful officeholders have been the lieutenant governor, who is the presiding officer of the Senate and elected statewide, and the Speaker of the House, who is elected by members.

15. Ivins, "A Profile of Barbara Jordan."

16. Author's interview with former state representative Jake Johnson, Houston, August 22, 1996. All subsequent quotations from Johnson are taken from this interview, unless otherwise noted.

17. Ibid.

18. "First Speech Made by Negro Senator," *Dallas Morning News*, March 16, 1967.

19. Senator Barbara Jordan, press release, March 17, 1967, Texas Senate Files, Barbara Jordan Archives, Texas Southern University.

20. Quoted in author's interview with Mauzy.

21. Greg Olds, "The Babe and Charlie Show—A Harbinger of Better Days?" *Texas Observer*, March 31, 1967.

22. Corrine E. Crow, interview with Dorsey Hardeman, February 27, 1975, East Texas State University Oral History Program, East Texas State University, Commerce, Texas, in the Texas Legislative Reference Library, Austin, 923.2764, #217 I.

23. Jordan assigned Patrick Dobel's book, *Compromise and Political Action* (Savage, Md.: Rowman & Littlefield Publishers, 1990), in her course on ethics at the LBJ School of Public Affairs. She took seriously Dobel's admonition: "Serious political morality flows from what I call the effectiveness imperative. Individuals of integrity enter politics to accomplish good. Their moral convictions and commitments define the nature of the good. For a conscientious person, these commitments generate imperatives to act and bring about enduring good as defined by their conceptions of right and to engage obstacles to achieve these results. Armchair moralists and contentedly otiose consciences never need compromise. But once persons begin to act to achieve purposes derived from integrity, if they fail by ineptitude, negligence, laziness, or inattention to results, they violate the effectiveness imperative" (pp. 41–42).

24. Greg Olds, "What Minimum Wage Bill?" *Texas Observer*, March 31, 1976.

25. George Bush to Barbara Jordan, March 23, 1967, Texas Senate Correspondence File, Barbara Jordan Archives, Texas Southern University, Houston.

26. Author's interview with Vernon Jordan, Dallas, Texas, May 15, 1997. All subsequent quotations from Jordan are from this interview, unless otherwise noted.

27. Ivins, "A Profile of Barbara Jordan."

28. Rick Casey, "The Jordan Blend: Intellect, Impishness," *San Antonio Express News*, January 18, 1996.

29. Ibid.

30. Jordan, "How I Got There."

31. Quoted in author's interview with Mauzy.

32. Levine, *Christian Science Monitor*, 1974.

33. State Senator Barbara Jordan, newsletter, January 19, 1969, Barbara Jordan Archives, Texas Southern University.

34. "Club President Angry over Negro Ban Fuss," *Houston Chronicle,* May 5, 1967.

35. "Sen. Barbara Jordan Makes Realism Pleas," *Houston Chronicle,* April 23, 1967.

36. Christina Goggio Banks, "Where Have All the Leaders Gone?", unpublished article based on a 1993 interview with Barbara Jordan. Dr. Banks, a senior lecturer at the Haas School of Business, University of California at Berkeley, provided the article to the author after the death of Jordan in 1996.

37. William S. McFeely, *Frederick Douglass* (New York: W. W. Norton, 1991), p. 244.

38. Ivins, "Profile of Barbara Jordan."

39. Walter Shapiro, "What Does This Woman Want?" *Texas Monthly,* October 1976.

40. Ronald Marcello, interview with Barbara Jordan, Austin, Texas, July 7, 1970, University of North Texas Oral History Collection, University of North Texas, Denton.

41. Howard Thurman, *Luminous Darkness,* p. 3.

42. Anne Spencer Thurman, *For the Inward Journey,* p. 210.

43. Barbara Jordan, remarks to the Women's Day Committee, Metropolitan AME Zion Church, Hartford, Connecticut, April 14, 1981, Barbara Jordan Archives, Texas Southern University.

44. Ibid.

CHAPTER NINE

1. John Hope Franklin, *From Slavery to Freedom: A History of Negroes in America,* 5th ed. (New York: Alfred A. Knopf, 1980), p. 448.

2. In 1966, David Dinkins, a future mayor of New York City in the 1990s, was first elected to the state assembly in New York. Future Los Angeles mayor Tom Bradley was elected to the Los Angeles City Council. Future Cleveland mayor Carl B. Stokes had been elected to the Ohio state legislature. Charles Rangel of New York had just defeated Adam Clayton Powell to win the Democratic Party nomination to represent Harlem in Congress. He won in November, at the same time that Richard C. Hatcher became the mayor of Gary, Indiana. Several African Americans who would soon become well-known elected officials started their careers a few years earlier. They lived in areas where large African American populations were in the majority. In 1966, future congresswoman Shirley Chisholm was already serving in the New York Assembly, as was future Manhattan borough president Percy E. Sutton. Sutton was originally from San Antonio, Texas, and his brother G. J. Sutton was the first African American elected to public office in Texas in the twentieth century. In 1948, G. J. Sutton had been elected to the board of the San Antonio Union Junior College District. He later served in the Texas legislature, and was succeeded after his death by his wife, Lou Nelle Sutton.

3. Harry McPherson, *A Political Education: A Washington Memoir* (Austin: University of Texas Press, 1995), p. 355.

4. Ibid., p. 356.

5. Ibid., p. 357.

6. For information on the impact of President Johnson's civil rights and antipoverty efforts in the South, see Lemann, *The Promised Land.*

7. President's schedule, briefings, memos, and miscellaneous information relating to meeting with civil rights leaders, February 13, 1976, President's Appointment File and Diary Backup, box 55, Lyndon B. Johnson Presidential Library, Austin.

8. Roland C. Hayes, interview with Barbara Jordan, March 28, 1984, Oral History Project, LBJ Library, Austin.

9. Ibid.

10. Rowland Evans and Robert Novak, "Guests Chosen Carefully," *Washington Post,* February 24, 1967.

11. Lemann, *The Promised Land,* pp. 179–80.

12. Joseph A. Califano Jr., "Jordan Knew How to Help Others Soar Toward Goals," *Austin American Statesman,* January 27, 1996.

13. Hayes's interview with Jordan.

14. Author's telephone interview with James Muldrow, Houston, February 22, 1997.

15. Lemann, *The Promised Land,* p. 183.

16. Crawford and Keever, *John B. Connally,* p. 404.

17. In addition to George Christian, Bob Strauss, Ben Barnes, and Frank Erwin, Connally's bright young men included Will Davis, later a powerful insurance lobbyist and progressive leader for public education in Texas; and Larry Temple, who became a respected banking lawyer and champion of the University of Texas. Loyalty to Connally and to Johnson was key to their success. One of those on the fringe of the Connally-Johnson boys was Jake Jacobson, who would turn on Connally, becoming the government's main witness in Connally's trial for bribery in 1975 (see chapter 14).

18. Crawford and Keever, *John B. Connally,* pp. 236, 152.

19. Former Texas governor Ann Richards used the term "oscillating fan" to describe Ben Barnes in action when she roasted him at a gathering in Texas in the late 1980s.

20. Author's interview with Ben Barnes, Austin, Texas, November 7, 1996. All subsequent quotations from Barnes are from this interview, unless otherwise noted.

21. Author's interview with Robert Strauss, Dallas, Texas, April 16, 1997. All subsequent quotations from Strauss are from this interview, unless otherwise noted.

22. Kaye Northcott, "Amidst the Wreckage," *Texas Observer,* September 6, 1968.

23. Ibid.

24. Author's interview with Nancy Earl, Austin, Texas, June 18, 1997. All subsequent quotations from Earl are from this interview, unless otherwise noted.

CHAPTER TEN

1. Barbara Jordan, "Who Speaks for the Negro?", remarks to a conference, "The Role of the News Media and Race Relations," sponsored by the Texas Daily Newspaper Association and the Texas Association of Broadcasters, Austin, Texas, May 27, 1968, reprinted in *Austin American Statesman,* June 16, 1968.

2. Marcello interview with Jordan, pp. 45–46.

3. Kaye Northcott, "Weak Wage Bill Passed," *Texas Observer,* June 20, 1969.

4. After the 1966 elections, all senators, including the newly elected Jordan, had drawn lots to determine the length of their term of office, either for two- or four-year terms. This was necessary because the 1966 redistricting process forced all senators to run again, no matter what their original term of office. Jordan had drawn a two-year term, so she had to run again for a full four-year term in 1968. Her new term would not expire until the end of 1972.

5. Sam Kinch and Ben Proctor, *Texas Under a Cloud: The Story of the Texas Stock Fraud Scandal* (Austin: Jenkins Publishing Co., 1972), p. 82.

6. It would be former congressman Lloyd M. Bentsen Jr. who took on and defeated Yarborough in the 1970 Democratic primary. Bentsen then went on to victory over the Republican nominee, George Bush.

7. Marcello interview with Jordan, p. 39.

8. John Connally had opposed earlier efforts to enact a state minimum wage. When he was governor, he had entangled Barnes and then–attorney general Waggoner Carr in a public relations fiasco when he took them to an impromptu meeting on the Austin–San Antonio highway to meet Mexican American farmworkers who were marching across Texas to call attention to their dismal working conditions and to advocate a state minimum wage. The meeting had turned into a hostile confrontation, in which Connally came off as arrogant and insensitive. In the 1966 U.S. Senate race, liberal Democrats took revenge on Attorney General Carr for his role in the episode when they voted en masse against Carr, ensuring the reelection of Republican senator John Tower. The farmworker confrontation was so distressing and dangerous politically for Barnes that he was looking for ways to repair the lingering damage.

9. The workers' compensation reform bill also lengthened the payment periods for partial disabilities and raised the amount of attorneys' fees that could be recovered.

10. Greg Olds, "Outlook Good for Comp Bill," *Texas Observer,* February 21, 1969.

11. Marcello interview with Jordan, p. 45.

12. Dobel, *Compromise and Political Action*, p. 64.

13. Scott Williams, "Jordan Praises Stockman," *Daily Texan*, November 23, 1981.

14. Boyd, "Where Is Barbara Jordan Today?"

15. "Political correctness" is the term used most commonly in the 1990s to describe a form of political purity that rigidly follows prevailing views, conventional thought, or the ideology of true believers of any cause—liberal or conservative, religious or secular. The very notion of partisan or ideological purity or "political correctness" was anathema to Barbara Jordan.

16. Some of the key lobbyists who lined up votes for the food sales-tax bill included Frank Erwin, who was on the board of regents of the University of Texas; James Nance, who represented DuPont, Houston Lighting and Power, Pennzoil, and Union Carbide; Ted Read of the Licensed Beverage Distributors; B. M. Brittain, who represented some leading pipe-line companies; and L. P. Sturgeon, who represented teachers' organizations ("Smith's Role," *Texas Observer*, September 12, 1969).

17. "The Taxers' Gyrations," *Texas Observer*, September 12, 1969.

18. At the Alamo, William B. Travis had drawn a line in the dirt floor of the Alamo mission and asked those who were willing to sacrifice their lives in the upcoming battle with Mexican general Santa Anna to step across it. The scene is legendary in Texas history. In contrast to Travis, however, Ben Barnes asked only the defectors in his food tax fight to step across his imaginary line on the carpet.

19. "The Senate Fight," *Texas Observer*, September 12, 1969.

20. Broyles, "The Making of Barbara Jordan."

21. In 1960 Henry B. Gonzalez became the first Mexican American elected to Congress from Texas, after serving as the first Mexican American on the San Antonio City Council and in the Texas Senate from 1956 to 1960. Gonzalez generated pride among Mexican American voters in San Antonio comparable to the feeling Barbara Jordan generated among black voters in the Fifth Ward. In 1997, at age eighty-one, Gonzalez announced that he would not seek reelection in 1998. At the time he made the announcement, he was the ranking Democrat on the House Banking Committee.

22. Bill Archer succeeded George Bush in the safe Republican House seat in Houston in 1970 after Bush ran for and lost a race for the U.S. Senate. Bush's original target was the liberal Democratic senator Ralph Yarborough. But conservative Democrat Lloyd M. Bentsen Jr. defeated Yarborough in the Democratic primary in May and went on to beat Bush in the November general election.

23. Searcy Bracewell at one time represented Harris County in the Texas State Senate—when the county had only one senator. He knew Austin politics and the Houston business community, and the Suite 8F crowd relied upon his advice in making political decisions. His law firm represented not only some of the most powerful industries in Houston, but also the Houston Independent School District and other public entities.

24. By the mid-1970s, Texas Commerce Bancshares would become the largest bank in Houston with more than $6.6 billion in assets. In the 1980s, TCB merged with Chemical Bank of New York. Another merger in the 1990s with Chase Manhattan Bank resulted in a name change: Chase Bank of Texas.

25. Author's interview with Ben Love (retired chairman and CEO of Texas Commerce Bancshares), Houston, February 19, 1997. All subsequent quotations from Love are from this interview, unless otherwise noted.

26. Texas voters approved the Equal Legal Rights Amendment to the state constitution by a four-to-one margin in 1972. In 1973 the Texas legislature became the first in the South to ratify the federal Equal Rights Amendment.

27. Ruthe Winegarten, interview with Frances "Sissy" Farenthold, Austin, June 12, 1995, Archives and Research on Women and Gender, University of Texas at San Antonio.

28. Farenthold was the leader of a band of liberal reformers in the House known as the "Dirty Thirty." The group was agitating for ethics reforms in the lower house as the result of a banking-legislative bribery scandal involving special favors to the Sharpstown Bank on the edge of Houston. House Speaker Gus Mutscher was convicted of bribery and served a prison sentence for his favors to Frank Sharp and the Sharpstown Bank. Governor Preston Smith and the state Democratic Party chairman, as well as a number of other state representatives

and senators, were implicated in the scandal. Although Ben Barnes's image was tarnished by the scandal because it occurred during his watch over the Senate, he was never implicated in any wrongdoing. As a result of the scandal, the House of Representatives in the 1973–74 session selected a reform-minded speaker, changed its procedural rules, and adopted new ethics legislation.

29. Haskins, *Barbara Jordan,* p. 103.

30. Author's interview with Stan McClelland, San Antonio, Texas, November 19, 1996. All subsequent quotations from McClelland are from this interview, unless otherwise noted. McClelland became the U.S. ambassador to Jamaica in January 1998.

CHAPTER ELEVEN

1. Broyles, "The Making of Barbara Jordan."

2. Glen Castlebury, "Sen. Jordan's Chances for Congress Are Good," *Austin Statesman,* April 26, 1972.

3. One police officer was killed in the shooting melee at TSU, although later investigations could not confirm whether he had been hit by a bullet from another policeman's gun or one from a TSU student firing back at police officers. The incident forced a brief closing of TSU in order to repair the extensive physical damage, and 448 students were arrested after the police attack. It was by far Houston's most serious racial incident of the 1960s.

4. Paula Giddings, "Will the Real Barbara Jordan Please Stand," *Encore American and World-wide News,* May 9, 1977.

5. Broyles, "The Making of Barbara Jordan."

6. Quoted in Jordan and Hearon, *Self-Portrait,* p. 156.

7. "Blacks in Office to Increase in 1972 Elections," *Houston Chronicle,* April 15, 1972.

8. Paul Slater, "Freedoms Attacked, Senator Tells Meet," *Corpus Christi Caller-Times,* May 14, 1970.

9. "Incumbents Victorious," *Texas Observer,* undated clipping, 1972, author's files.

10. Susan Kent Caudill, "Getting Things Done," *Houston Post,* May 5, 1972.

11. Henry Holcomb, "Sen. Jordan Takes Oath, First Black in Governor's Chair," *Houston Post,* June 11, 1972.

12. Broyles, "The Making of Barbara Jordan." Many of the first women who ran for public office in the 1970s and 1980s had to deal with "underground" or "whisper" campaigns about their sex lives. Usually, the "gossip" hinted that they were lesbians, but often it involved charges that they were sexually promiscuous in their relationships with men. Sometimes both rumors were circulated about the same woman. Although these campaigns of innuendo almost never showed up in any written materials, many women who have run for office have experienced one or the other of the charges.

13. "Blacks in Office to Increase in 1972 Elections," *Houston Chronicle,* April 15, 1972.

14. Broyles, "The Making of Barbara Jordan."

15. Barnes never ran for political office again, becoming John Connally's partner in various real estate deals that eventually ended in bankruptcy. Barnes became a successful lobbyist and an active national Democratic Party fund-raiser. Jordan understood at the time that the Democratic Party in Texas needed someone like Barnes, or her beloved Lyndon Johnson, who would be able to keep the money people inside the party while making room for new leaders like herself from the minority communities. While Briscoe had a personal fortune, he had few linkages to Houston or Dallas bankers or industrialists, and their interests and money began to flow into the Texas Republican Party, with a few exceptions, for the remainder of the twentieth century.

16. Marcello interview with Jordan.

17. Mary Rice Brogan, "Sen. Jordan First Black Elected to Pilot Any Legislative Body," *Houston Chronicle,* April 29, 1972.

18. Holcomb, "Sen. Jordan Takes Oath."

19. Ibid.

20. Ibid.

21. Ibid.
22. Jordan and Hearon, *Self-Portrait*, p. 173.

CHAPTER TWELVE

1. John Herbers, "It Seemed So Very Long Ago," *New York Times*, December 17, 1972.
2. Ibid.
3. David Herbert Donald, *Lincoln* (New York: Simon & Schuster, 1995), p. 375.
4. Barbara Jordan, "Looking for a Vision for the 1990s," remarks at a Great Society Roundup, LBJ Presidential Library, Austin, Texas, May 5, 1990.
5. Former congresswoman Burke later became a Los Angeles County supervisor. Alan Steelman of Dallas represented the new breed of southern Republicans swept into office on President Nixon's coattails, and William Cohen of Maine was a moderate Republican and independent intellectual cut in the mode of his state's venerable senator Margaret Chase Smith. Cohen would later serve in the U.S. Senate; in 1997 President Bill Clinton appointed him secretary of defense.
6. James A. Galbraith, John Kenneth Galbraith's son, who later was a faculty colleague of Jordan's at the LBJ School of Public Affairs, was a college student at the time. He remembers a wide-eyed and clearly excited young Barbara Jordan coming to his parents' home for dinner, along with the other "Head Start" fellows.
7. Author's telephone interview with Yvonne Braithwaite Burke, June 30, 1997. All subsequent quotations from Burke are from this interview, unless otherwise stated.
8. During Reconstruction, twenty African Americans served in the House of Representatives, and two served in the Senate. All were from the southern states, where white Confederate soldiers had been disfranchised and federal troops protected the ballot.
9. The original members were all Democrats: Shirley Chisholm of New York, William Clay of Missouri, George Collins of Illinois, John Conyers of Michigan, Ron Dellums of California, Charles Diggs of Michigan, Parren Mitchell of Maryland, Charles Rangel of New York, Augustus Hawkins of California, Robert Metcalf of Illinois, Robert Nix of Pennsylvania, and Louis Stokes of Ohio. They were joined by Walter E. Fauntroy of Washington, D.C., who was elected a nonvoting member of Congress on April 19, 1971.
10. Marguerite Ross Barnett, "The Congressional Black Caucus," *Focus* (Joint Center for Political Studies), October 4, 1977.
11. Charles L. Sanders, "Barbara Jordan, Texan, Is a New Power on Capitol Hill," *Ebony*, February 1975.
12. Quoted in Jordan and Hearon, *Self-Portrait*, p. 179.
13. Peter W. Rodino Jr., "A Tribute to Barbara Jordan: The Voice of 'We the People,'" *Annual Survey of American Law* (New York: New York University School of Law, 1989).
14. Sanders, "Barbara Jordan."
15. Molly Ivins, "Whither the Democratic National Committee?", *Texas Observer*, December 1, 1972.
16. Crawford and Keever, *John Connally*, pp. 411–12.
17. Author's interview with Rufus "Bud" Myers, Washington, D.C., September 18, 1996. All subsequent quotations from Myers are from this interview, unless otherwise noted.
18. Charitey Simmons, "In Her Own Words: Barbara Jordan, the Private Person," *Chicago Tribune*, February 25, 1979.
19. Author's interview with former House Speaker Jim Wright, Fort Worth, Texas, October 24, 1996. All subsequent quotations from Wright are from this interview, unless otherwise noted.
20. Simmons, "In Her Own Words."
21. Ibid.
22. Griffin Smith Jr. and Paul Burka, "The Best, the Worst, and the Fair-to-Middling," *Texas Monthly*, May 1976.
23. Lemann, *Promised Land*, pp. 156–57.
24. Smith and Burka, "The Best, the Worst."
25. Ibid.

26. Ibid.

27. Rena Pederson, "The Wilson-Jordan Camaraderie," *Houston Chronicle,* June 24, 1973.

28. Sanders, "Barbara Jordan."

29. Jo Ann Levine, "Impact in Congress," *Christian Science Monitor,* March 18, 1974.

30. Sanders, "Barbara Jordan."

31. Giddings, "Will the Real Barbara Jordan Please Stand."

32. Levine, "Impact in Congress."

33. The female members already serving in Congress were: Ella Grasso of Connecticut, Patsy Mink of Hawaii, Margaret Heckler of Massachusetts, Martha Griffith of Michigan, Leonore Sullivan of Missouri, Bella Abzug of New York, Shirley Chisholm of New York, Edith Green of Oregon, and Julia Butler Hansen of Washington.

34. Sissy Farenthold of Texas was the first president of the National Women's Political Caucus.

35. Author's telephone interview with former representative Patricia Schroeder, June 26, 1997. All subsequent quotations from Schroeder are from this interview, unless otherwise noted.

36. Another of Jordan's fellow Texans, Sarah Weddington, was the attorney who successfully argued *Roe v. Wade* before the Supreme Court.

37. *Congress and the Nation, Congressional Quarterly* 4 (1973–76): 2.

38. Haskins, *Barbara Jordan,* pp. 136–44.

39. *Proceedings and Debates of the Ninety-third Congress, First Session, Congressional Record,* vol. 119, April 18, 1973, p. 13170.

40. Ibid. A U.S. district court also came to that conclusion and ruled that Nixon's dismantling of the OEO was an unconstitutional infringement on congressional power.

41. *Proceedings and Debates of the Ninety-third Congress, First Session.*

42. Ibid.

43. The resolution presented by freshmen members was signed by Edward Mezvinsky, John Breaux, Bill Gunter, Barbara Jordan, Wayne Owens, Gerry Studds, Ray Thornton, Ike Andrews, Jaime Benetiz, David Bowen, John Breckinridge, Yvonne Burke, Ron de Lugo, Bo Ginn, Elizabeth Holtzman, James R. Jones, William Lehman, Jerry Litton, Gillis Long, Clem McSpadden, Dale Milford, John Moakley, Charles Rose, Leo J. Ryan, Patricia Schroeder, Fortney H. Stark Jr., Charles Wilson, Antonio Won Pat, Andrew Young, and Lindy Boggs.

44. Jim Wright, *Balance of Power: Presidents and Congress from the Era of McCarthy to the Age of Gingrich* (Atlanta: Turner Publishing, 1996), p. 202.

45. Most of the LEAA funds were used to improve correctional facilities, hire staff to reduce case backlogs, and develop programs to reduce crimes against the elderly and numerous other programs that state and local communities developed to reduce crime, which was becoming a serious safety and political issue.

46. Karen Elliott, "Black Star over Washington," *Parade* (Texas edition), April, 1974.

47. "Watergate Scandal: A Senate Search for the Truth," *Watergate: Chronology of a Crisis,* vol. 1, *Congressional Quarterly* (1973), p. 3.

48. Barbara Jordan, remarks to the American Society of Newspaper Publishers, Washington, D.C., May 2, 1972, in Public Affairs Library, LBJ School of Public Affairs, University of Texas at Austin.

49. Wright, *Balance of Power,* p. 215.

50. Haskins, *Barbara Jordan,* p. 143.

51. Jacqueline Trescott, "Representative Barbara Jordan," *Houston Post,* special section, October 1974.

52. Mary Lenz, "Rep. Jordan Predicts Recession," *Dallas Morning News,* December 2, 1973.

53. Author's interview with Robert Alcock, Washington, D.C., September 18, 1996. All subsequent quotations from Alcock are from this interview, unless otherwise noted.

54. Even today, the causes and the nature of multiple sclerosis remain unclear. The most recent research suggests that an attack on the myelin sheath around nerve cells may be only part of the problem. Using laser-scanning microscopes, researchers have observed the severing of nerves in the brains of patients with multiple sclerosis cells, presumably by chemicals in the brain. The research also suggests new strategies for treatment, including experimental

drugs that could prevent nerve cell death. See Gina Kolata, "Study of Brains Alters the View on Path of M.S.," *New York Times,* January 29, 1998.

55. The source of most of this information on multiple sclerosis is the National Multiple Sclerosis Society, which provides information about the latest research and treatment for the disease. The National MS Society maintains a Web page (info@nmss.org) and a toll-free number (800–344–4867). Other information is from Louis J. Rosner, M.D. and Shelley Ross, *Multiple Sclerosis: New Hope and Practical Advice for People with MS and Their Families,* updated edition (New York: Fireside Books Simon & Schuster, 1992). With the introduction of magnetic resonance imaging (MRI) in the mid-1980s, an earlier and more certain diagnosis of multiple sclerosis can now be made.

56. Current MS research is focusing on new treatments designed to slow or halt disease progression, as well as finding agents that will repair the nerve and promote remyelination, or at least promote more efficient electrical conduction through demyelinated nerves. See National Multiple Sclerosis Information Resource Center and Library, *Compendium of Multiple Sclerosis Information (CMS),* rev. ed. (New York: National Multiple Sclerosis Society, c. 1992).

CHAPTER THIRTEEN

1. Barry Schwartz discusses the psychological process of how an individual can rise to meet a challenge to greatness in *George Washington: the Making of an American Symbol* (New York: The Free Press, 1987).

2. Barbara Jordan to Frank and Eleanor Freed, January 4, 1974, Barbara Jordan Archives, Texas Southern University, Houston.

3. "Barbara Jordan Returns to Work," *Houston Post,* December 11, 1973.

4. Peter W. Rodino, foreword to *High Crimes and Misdemeanors: Selected Materials on Impeachment* (New York: Funk & Wagnalls, 1974), p. 2.

5. B. J. Phillips, "Recognizing the Gentleladies of the Judiciary Committee," *Ms.,* November 1974.

6. Greater Washington Educational Telecommunications Association (GWETA), *Summer of Judgment—Impeachment Hearings,* film documentary produced by WETA–Washington, D.C., narrated by Charles McDowell, 1984.

7. Ibid.

8. Carolyn Raeke, "Jordan Sees 'Further Delay,'" *Dallas Morning News,* April 11, 1974.

9. The additional areas of allegations were: the ITT case, the dairy industry fund, the Howard Hughes donation, and Robert Vesco's contribution. Ultimately, the House prepared articles of impeachment on only six of the allegations. A number of excellent books detail the circumstances and specific charges that formed the basis of the House Judiciary Committee's inquiry on impeachment. The memoirs of Special Prosecutor Leon Jaworski are helpful to understand the legal case against the president. See Leon Jaworski, *The Right and the Power: The Prosecution of Watergate* (New York: Reader's Digest Press, 1976).

10. Levine, "Impact in Congress."

11. Ibid.

12. Barbara Jordan to John W. Wilson (editor of the *Daily Cougar,* University of Houston), May 1, 1974, Barbara Jordan Archives, Texas Southern University, Houston.

13. Levine, "Impact in Congress."

14. Rodino, *High Crimes and Misdemeanors,* p. 9.

15. GWETA, *Summer of Judgment.*

16. Barbara Jordan, "The Great Society and Its Meanings" (keynote address), LBJ Library, April 18–19, 1985. The title of the symposium was "The Great Society: A Twenty-Year Critique."

17. Barbara Jordan, remarks during a television interview by Tom Snyder, Los Angeles, March 14, 1995.

18. Barbara Jordan, "The Relation Between Liberty and the Rule of Law," *New York University Survey of American Law,* April 26, 1990.

19. House Judiciary Committee, "Constitutional Grounds for Presidential Impeachment," report of the staff, *Hearings,* 93d Cong., 2d sess., book 2, p. 17.

20. GWETA, *Summer of Judgment.*

21. For a full explanation of the naming of President Richard Nixon as an unindicted co-conspirator, see Jaworski, *The Right and the Power.*

22. Phillips, "Recognizing the Gentleladies."

23. Unattributed, undated transcript of interview by "A.R." (unknown) with Barbara Jordan, Barbara Jordan Office Files, LBJ School of Public Affairs, now in the Barbara Jordan Archives, Texas Southern University, Houston.

24. John Pierson, "Barbara Jordan's Star Reaches Dizzy Heights for House Sophomore," *Wall Street Journal,* February 6, 1975.

25. Levine, "Impact in Congress."

26. GWETA, *Summer of Judgment.*

27. Bob Woodward and Carl Bernstein, *The Final Days* (New York: Touchstone/Simon & Schuster, 1976), p. 281.

28. GWETA, *Summer of Judgment.*

29. House Judiciary Committee, "Debate on Articles of Impeachment," p. 60.

30. Ibid., pp. 110–13.

31. Dagmar S. Hamilton, "Barbara Jordan: Constitutional Lawyer," *Texas Journal of Women and the Laws* 5, no. 153 (Summer 1996).

32. Henry E. Petersen was an assistant attorney general in charge of the Justice Department's probe of the Watergate break-in until a special prosecutor was appointed in May 1973.

33. The letters quoted in this chapter, as well as most of the several thousand letters Jordan received after her Watergate testimony, are in the Barbara Jordan Archives, Texas Southern University, Houston.

34. Walter Brueggemann, *Hope Within History* (Atlanta: John Knox Press, 1987), pp. 60–65.

35. Broyles, "The Making of Barbara Jordan."

36. Ibid.

37. GWETA, *Summer of Judgment.*

38. Quoted in Jordan and Hearon, *Self-Portrait,* p. 182.

39. GWETA, *Summer of Judgment.*

40. House Judiciary Committee, "Debate on Articles of Impeachment," pp. 204–5.

41. GWETA, *Summer of Judgment.*

42. Phillips, "Recognizing the Gentleladies."

43. Snyder interview with Jordan.

44. "A.R." interview with Jordan.

45. I am indebted to Professor Dagmar Hamilton, one of the two female staff lawyers who worked for the House Judiciary Committee's inquiry into the impeachment of President Nixon, for bringing Jordan's reasoning on this particular vote to my attention. Professor Hamilton, who teaches at the LBJ School of Public Affairs, was a colleague and good friend of Barbara Jordan's.

46. Schwartz, *George Washington,* p. 14.

47. Howard Gardner, *Leading Minds: Anatomy of Leadership* (New York: Basic Books, 1996), p. 15.

CHAPTER FOURTEEN

1. Broyles, "The Making of Barbara Jordan."

2. Ibid.

3. Ibid.

4. In January 1975, House Democrats approved a number of changes in the rules and procedures governing the operation of their party, resulting in changes in the House itself. The changes transferred the task of making committee assignments from the conservative Democratic members of the House Ways and Means Committee to a group controlled by the Democratic leadership. The Steering and Policy Committee was authorized to nominate

chairmen at the beginning of each session. Then all nominees were subject to a secret ballot vote of the entire caucus. This paved the way for the defeat of three veteran Democratic chairs: F. Edward Hebert (Louisiana) of the Armed Services Committee, Wright Patman (Texas) of the Banking, Currency, and Housing Committee, and W. R. Poage (Texas) of the Agriculture Committee. In 1974 and 1975, Barbara Jordan was the only woman and only minority member of Congress on the Democratic Policy and Steering Committee.

5. Meg Greenfield, "The New Lone Star of Texas," *Newsweek*, March 3, 1975.

6. Pierson, "Barbara Jordan's Star Reaches Dizzy Heights."

7. Greenfield, "The New Lone Star of Texas."

8. Energy industry officials promoted natural gas deregulation as a way to channel more natural gas into interstate sales from the intrastate markets, where federal price controls did not apply. In 1975, when natural gas was sold within the states where it was produced—primarily Texas, Oklahoma, and Louisiana—it sold for prices three or four times higher than the top federal regulated interstate price of 51¢ per 1,000 cubic feet.

9. Giddings, "Will the Real Barbara Jordan Please Stand."

10. Ibid.

11. Pierson, "Barbara Jordan's Star Reaches Dizzy Heights."

12. Paul Duke, "Washington Straight Talk," interview with Barbara Jordan, NPACT, WETA-TV, March 24, 1975, transcript, Center for American History, University of Texas at Austin.

13. Banks, "Where Have All the Leaders Gone?".

14. Duke interview with Jordan.

15. Sanders, "Barbara Jordan."

16. Ibid.

17. Author's interview with Strauss.

18. Samuel Dash, *Chief Counsel: Inside the Ervin Committee—The Untold Story of Watergate* (New York: Random House, 1976), pp. 229–30.

19. Jaworski, *The Right and the Power*, pp. 263–67. Connally always believed the indictment was orchestrated by both Republicans and Democrats who wanted to keep him off the Republican presidential ticket in 1976. He put the blame for his indictment on two prominent individuals: Republican Richard Cheney, who Connally felt was waging a campaign against him with President Ford, and who later became President George Bush's secretary of defense; and special Watergate prosecutor Leon Jaworski. "To this day," Connally wrote, "I am at a loss to explain the animosity that he [Jaworski] felt against me, other than the rivalry between our competing law firms." Connally felt that Jaworski's close friendship with Ambassador Ed Clark, one of the Johnson insiders who never liked Connally and who was a friend of Connally's Texas nemesis, liberal former U.S. senator Ralph Yarborough, might have influenced his opinion. Jaworski disqualified himself, however, in all aspects of the milk fund investigation because his law firm was representing the Independent Milk Producers in an antitrust suit against AMPI, accused of making a payment to Connally. When Connally was governor, he had appointed Jaworski to serve as chairman of a special governor's committee on education. Jaworski took no part in the investigation or subsequent decisions to indict and prosecute Connally. See John Connally with Mickey Herskowitz, *In History's Shadow: An American Odyssey* (New York: Hyperion, 1993), pp. 284–86.

20. For details about the investigation and trial, as well as the relationship among Connally, Jacobsen, and Lyndon Johnson, see James Reston Jr., *The Lone Star: The Life of John Connally* (New York: Harper & Row, 1989).

21. Ibid., p. 273.

22. Connally and Herskowitz, *In History's Shadow*, pp. 273–74. Connally said that what Jacobsen had suggested was "that this money was available, and I could control who received it to enable me to gain some influence with Congress. I told Jake when he brought it up I couldn't do that, and wouldn't. I was a Democrat in a Republican administration. I didn't want to be out raising money for the Democrats while I was secretary of the treasury, and at the same time I didn't want to be raising campaign money for the Republicans, or against members of my own party. That was all there was to it. Jake concocted an elaborate story."

23. Michael Tigar later became a successful trial attorney on his own, mixing defense of unpopular clients with his role as a professor at the University of Texas School of Law in

Austin, where he and Jordan occasionally saw each other socially. In 1997 Tigar would defend Terry Nichols against charges that he participated in the plot with Timothy McVeigh to blow up the federal building in Oklahoma City in 1996.

24. Reston, *The Lone Star,* p. 532.

25. John B. Connally to Barbara Jordan, June 3, 1975, Correspondence Files, Barbara Jordan Archives, Texas Southern University, Houston.

26. Broyles, "The Making of Barbara Jordan."

27. Correspondence Files, Barbara Jordan Archives, Texas Southern University, Houston.

28. Reston, *The Lone Star,* pp. 532–33.

29. Giddings, "Will the Real Barbara Jordan Please Stand."

30. Myra MacPherson, "Looking Over Jordan," *Washington Post,* October 30, 1977.

31. Barbara Jordan, keynote address to the Southern Africa Grant-Makers Affinity Group, Council on Foundations, Chicago, April 21, 1991.

32. Greenfield, "The New Lone Star of Texas."

CHAPTER FIFTEEN

1. Barbara Jordan, "A Fundamental Right," remarks to Planned Parenthood Federation of America, Dallas, Texas, October 18, 1990.

2. The seven southern states subject to the pre-clearing, or section 5, requirements of the original Voting Rights Act of 1965 were Louisiana, Georgia, Alabama, Mississippi, Virginia, North Carolina, and South Carolina. If these states made any change in law or procedure which might affect the rights of minority voters, they had to request approval for the changes by the U.S. attorney general or by the federal district court for the District of Columbia.

3. Changes in laws in any of the following activities had to be submitted to the Justice Department for approval: annexation, at-large elections, bilingual materials, home rule charters, multimember districts, polling places, political parties, precinct lines, redistricting, referenda, registration and voting methods, requirements for running for office, special elections, and staggered terms of office. The purpose was to prevent vote dilution which occurs when election laws or practices diminish or cancel the voting strength of the minority group. At-large elections, for example, can dilute minority voting strength because the minority vote would never be large enough to elect a minority candidate. This was the system that prevented Barbara Jordan from being elected when she ran for the Texas legislature in 1962 and 1964. But the impact of minority voters can also be diluted by annexation or de-annexation of certain geographical areas.

4. Testimony by Eddie Williams, director of the Joint Center for Political Studies, *Hearings on Extension of the Voting Rights Act before the Subcommittee on Civil and Constitutional Rights of the Committee on the Judiciary, House of Representatives,* 94th Cong., 1st sess., on H.R. 939, H.R. 2148, and H.R. 3501, serial no. 1, pt. 1, p. 115.

5. House Judiciary Committee, Subcommittee on Civil and Constitutional Rights, Barbara Jordan testimony, *Hearing on Extension of the Voting Rights Act,* 94th Cong., 1st sess., serial no. 1, pts. 1 and 2, February 25–March 25, 1975, p. 77.

6. Duke interview with Jordan.

7. House Judiciary Committee, Aaron Henry testimony, *Hearings on Extension of the Voting Rights Act,* pp. 675–76.

8. Duke interview with Jordan.

9. House Judiciary Committee, *Hearings on Extension of the Voting Rights Act,* p. 82.

10. House Judiciary Committee, Jordan testimony, *Hearings on Extension of the Voting Rights Act,* p. 76.

11. House debate, *Congressional Record,* June 3, 1975, p. 16284.

12. Texas congressmen Jack Brooks of Beaumont, Abraham "Chick" Kazen of Laredo, and Richard White of El Paso came to Gonzalez's assistance when they spoke for his amendment. The only member of the Texas delegation to come to Jordan's defense and speak for the bill was Democratic representative Bob Krueger of New Braunfels. Krueger was a Shakespearean scholar who came close to defeating Texas senator John Tower in 1980. Governor Ann Richards appointed Krueger to the U.S. Senate seat to fill the vacancy left when Lloyd

Bentsen became secretary of the treasury in January 1993. Jordan enthusiastically endorsed Krueger's bid to win election to the seat in 1994 and specifically referred to his support of her on the Voting Rights Act. "Only one other Texan . . . stood up and said I want to support that amendment, too, because I believe democracy includes everybody. That one other member of the Texas congressional delegation who stood with me and said let's make democracy real—that Texan was Bob Krueger." ("Krueger's Appointment Draws Enthusiastic Crowd," *New Braunfels Herald,* January 6, 1993.) Krueger was defeated by Republican Kay Bailey Hutchison in the general election.

13. Cragg Hines, "Jordan Gets Both Her Wishes—Voting Act and Ford Cards," *Houston Chronicle,* August 7, 1975.

14. This legislation was identified by the misnomer of "fair trade laws." Jordan repealed the federal authorization that allowed states to make antitrust exceptions by giving manufacturers the right to set a minimum price below which a retailer could not sell an item. Jordan estimated that her repeal of the fair trade laws would save consumers about $3 billion a year by allowing prices to be set by market factors rather than by manufacturers acting in concert. She introduced her bill in January 1975. It passed in December, was signed into law by President Ford, and became effective in March 1976.

15. "Barbara Jordan Reports to the People of the 18th Congressional District of Texas" (newsletter), February 1976, Houston Public Library.

16. Barbara Jordan, "The Media: Improving the Human Condition," address to Hollywood Chapter of Media Women, Los Angeles, November 2, 1975.

17. Sanders, "Barbara Jordan."

18. Ibid.

19. Barbara Jordan, remarks at benefit for Ron Dellums, Los Angeles, October 4, 1975.

20. In 1975 there were few restrictions or reporting requirements on outside income.

21. Bryant, *Barbara Charline Jordan,* pp. 13–15.

22. Micah 6:8, Authorized (King James) Version.

CHAPTER SIXTEEN

1. George Gallup, "Betty Ford Is 'Most Admired Woman,'" Gallup poll press release, January 13, 1977, Barbara Jordan Archives, Texas Southern University, Houston. The top twenty women in the poll, in order of their ranking, were Betty Ford, Rose Kennedy, Shirley Temple Black, Barbara Jordan, Golda Meir, Lucille Ball, Mamie Eisenhower, Barbara Walters, Joyce Brothers, Jacqueline Kennedy Onassis, Coretta Scott King, Pat Nixon, Kate Smith, Rosalyn Carter, Shirley Chisholm, Lady Bird Johnson, Margaret Mead, Bella Abzug, Carol Burnett, and Queen Elizabeth II.

2. "Young Builders of America—8 Who Have Made Their Mark," *U.S. News & World Report,* February 9, 1976.

3. William L. Chaze, "Barbara Jordan: A Little Dramatic, a Little Aloof, a Lot of Clout," *Dallas Times Herald,* July 11, 1976.

4. Lois Landis, "The Twice and Future Congresswoman," *Cincinnati Inquirer,* June 13, 1976.

5. Chaze, "Barbara Jordan."

6. Wright, *Balance of Power,* pp. 242–43.

7. Haskins, *Barbara Jordan,* pp. 172–73.

8. "Rep. Jordan Thinks Ford Won't Run," *Houston Post,* March 20, 1975.

9. Garry Wills, "Udall Would Be the Best Running Mate," *Washington Star,* June 16, 1976.

10. ABC *Issues and Answers,* with correspondents Bob Clark and Sam Donaldson, July 11, 1976, Barbara Jordan Office Files, LBJ School of Public Affairs, later incorporated into Barbara Jordan Archives, Texas Southern University, Houston.

11. Ibid.

12. Peter G. Bourne, *Jimmy Carter* (New York: Scribner's, 1977), p. 334.

13. Quoted in author's interview with Johnson.

14. The Latin phrase *e pluribus unum* was adopted by the new U.S. government as its official motto in 1777. The phrase was first found on the title page of the *Gentleman's Miscellany* in January 1692. The exact meaning is "from many, one," although many Americans have

always assumed the phrase means "united we stand." See William Safire, *Safire's Political Dictionary: An Enlarged, Up-to-Date Edition of "The New Language of Politics"* (New York: Random House, 1978), p. 758.

15. Robert Schwab, "Jordan Discusses Black Interests," *Waco Tribune Herald*, September 7, 1976.

16. Jordan's *Self-Portrait* co-author, Shelby Hearon, wrote of this incident that Jordan "did not need to confide to him [Democratic Party chairman Bob Strauss] that surgery had been suggested, or that if she hadn't got so heavy to begin with it would never have got in that shape. It took enough pride to mention the matter to him at all, a matter that he should have perceived for himself, seeing her hobble on that leg" (p. 229). Jordan never disclosed her multiple sclerosis to Hearon during the year they spent working on the book together.

17. Barbara Jordan, keynote address, Democratic National Convention, New York, July 12, 1976.

18. Martha Angle, "Barbara Jordan Fires Up Democrats," *Washington Star*, July 13, 1976.

19. Quoted in Jordan and Hearon, *Self-Portrait*, p. 234.

20. Jimmy Breslin, column, *Washington Star*, July 13, 1976.

21. The poet Diane Ackerman explains how a great orator like Jordan is able to work on the senses: Some sounds, particularly musical sounds that surround certain tones, engage the whole body. "Our pupils dilate and our endorphin level rises . . . and there is a healing quality to it." Ackerman believes the sounds of some music actually send shivers of delight through the listener. "Tingles usually start at the back of the neck, creep over the face and across the scalp, dart along the shoulders, trickle down the arms and then finally shiver up the spine." The shiver is real; the emotional wallop affects the body. We feel it as the lump in the throat, or the tear in the eye, or the smile on our lips. Our blood pressure can soar, or settle. And we remember in a general way the experience, even if we cannot recall the details. For more information, consult Ackerman's book *The Natural History of the Senses* (New York: Random House, 1990), pp. 207, 178, 219.

22. Angle, "Barbara Jordan Fires Up Democrats."

23. Brian Lankar, *I Dream a World* (New York: Stewart, Tabori & Chang, 1989), p. 10.

24. Stan Hinden, "Jordan a Little Weary Following Her Big Night," *Los Angeles Times*, July 14, 1976.

25. Angle, "Barbara Jordan Fires Up Democrats."

26. Quoted in Jordan and Hearon, *Self-Portrait*, p. 232.

27. Ellis Cose, "Touch of Irony in Great Acclaim," *Chicago Sun-Times*, July 18, 1976.

28. Quoted in Jordan and Hearon, *Self-Portrait*, p. 234.

29. Norman Baxter, "Congresswoman Barbara Jordan: A Hero for All Times," *Houston Chronicle*, July 18, 1976.

30. Ibid.

31. Ibid.

32. Cose, "Touch of Irony."

33. Giddings, "Will the Real Barbara Jordan Please Stand."

34. Ibid.

35. Ford's running mate was Senator Bob Dole of Kansas, who would be the Republican presidential nominee who lost the presidency to Bill Clinton in 1996.

36. Sam Wright was Jordan's Republican opponent in the Eighteenth Congressional District election in November 1976. He was given no chance of election, and neither Jordan nor the Houston news media took him seriously. His major campaign act was to write a guest column for the *Houston Chronicle* complaining that his "opponent's every word and action is splashed across the newspapers and his own candidacy is ignored. To date, few people could probably tell you whom Jordan is running against" (quoted in Jordan and Hearon, *Self-Portrait*, p. 236).

37. The letter in Jordan's handwriting was attached to her basic 1976 campaign stump speech, Barbara Jordan Office Files, LBJ School of Public Affairs, later incorporated into the Barbara Jordan Archives, Texas Southern University, Houston.

38. Joint Center for Political Studies, *The Black Vote—Election '76* (Washington, D.C.: August 1977), p. 11. The states where black votes made the difference for Carter were Alabama, Florida, Louisiana, Maryland, Mississippi, Missouri, New York, North Carolina,

Ohio, Pennsylvania, South Carolina, Texas, and Wisconsin. In each of those states, the black votes for Carter exceeded his margin of victory. In Louisiana, Mississippi, New York, and Ohio, black votes for Carter were two or three times greater than his winning margin. The relatively monolithic 5.2 million black votes for Carter—some 90 percent of the total black votes cast—amounted to more than three times his popular vote margin of 1.7 million. In the six states where Jordan campaigned for the Democratic ticket, Carter carried four—Texas, New York, Ohio, and Pennsylvania—and lost two, Indiana and California.

39. After the election, President Carter appointed Robert Strauss his special trade representative. Strauss also became an informal counselor to the president. At one point when Carter's relationship with Congress had deteriorated, Strauss brought four veteran Democratic lawyer-lobbyists—Lloyd Cutler, James Rowe Jr., Harry McPherson, and Lloyd Hackler—to see Carter's friend Charles Kirbo to get him to convince Carter to deal with Washington insiders in order to be able to work more effectively with Congress. Strauss's political skills were valued by Republicans as well as Democrats. In 1990 President George Bush appointed Strauss ambassador to the Soviet Union to watch over American interests during the breakup of the Soviet empire.

40. Walter Pincus, "Jordan's Expectations Likely to Go Unfulfilled," *Washington Post*, reprinted in *Houston Chronicle*, December 16, 1976.

41. Author's interview with former representative Charles Wilson, Washington, D.C., September 18, 1996.

42. Martha V. Gottron, ed., *Congress and the Nation, vol. 5, 1977–1980* (Washington, D.C.: Congressional Quarterly, 1981), p. 3.

43. Quoted in Jordan and Hearon, *Self-Portrait*, p. 245; author's interview with Jake Johnson.

44. Carter named Griffin B. Bell as his choice for attorney general on December 20. He was the most controversial of Carter's initial cabinet appointments, stirring opposition from civil rights and minority groups as well as public interest advocates. The opposition to Bell stemmed from his poor civil rights record as one of the fifteen judges on the Fifth Circuit Court of Appeals. Carter filled two positions where loyalty counted most with Georgians he knew and trusted. In addition to his appointment of Bell to the attorney general's post, Carter named Bert Lance, his chief fund-raiser, as director of the Office of Management and Budget. See Bourne, *Carter*, p. 367.

45. This account of the meeting was relayed to Jake Johnson by Barbara Jordan immediately after it was over. Jordan apparently told few other people, even her close friends, about her perceptions of the meeting. In fact, she seems to shrug it off entirely in her *Self-Portrait*, published just three years later.

46. Helen Parmley, "Jordan: Why Carter Didn't Call," *Dallas Morning News*, January 9, 1977.

47. Pincus, "Jordan's Expectations Likely to Go Unfulfilled."

48. "An Open Question—How Did Barbara Jordan Lose Her Way to Carter's Cabinet?" *Houston Chronicle*, December 26, 1976. Griffin Bell did not serve a full term as attorney general. He resigned on August 16, 1979, to return to private practice.

49. Walter Pincus, "Barbara Jordan Caught Up in Hardball Politics," *Washington Post*, December 16, 1976.

50. Giddings, "Will the Real Barbara Jordan Please Stand."

51. President Carter named two African Americans to his cabinet: Patricia Roberts Harris became secretary of housing and urban development, and Andrew Young accepted the post of ambassador to the United Nations. One other woman was also named to the cabinet: Juanita Morris Kreps became secretary of commerce. Young was forced to resign his ambassadorship in July 1979 in the wake of protests from some members of Congress, the Israeli government, and others who were upset because he had made "unauthorized" contacts with the Palestine Liberation Organization.

CHAPTER SEVENTEEN

1. News and Information Service, press release, University of Texas at Austin, February 16, 1977.
2. Debra Nagle, "Participation in the Political Process Best Way for Blacks to Find Equity," *Dayton Black Press,* May 1, 1979.
3. Robert Grudin, *Time and the Art of Living* (New York: Ticknor & Fields, 1988), p. 51.
4. Bruce Nichols, "Rep. Jordan, at 41, Considers Political Future," *Dallas Times Herald,* November 27, 1977.
5. Ibid.
6. Gottron, *Congress and the Nation,* p. 3.
7. Ibid., p. 4.
8. Pierson, "Barbara Jordan's Star Reaches Dizzy Heights."
9. Office of Representative Barbara Jordan, "Jordan Civil Rights Bills Advance" (press release), undated, Barbara Jordan Archives, Texas Southern University, Houston.
10. Jordan was appalled at the government's lack of efforts to enforce Title VI nondiscrimination requirements. When she introduced her bill, she cited facts that showed that all Title VI agencies throughout the federal government had commenced only nine administrative fund termination proceedings against recipients, exclusive of those against local school districts, and that only five cases had been referred by agencies to the attorney general for litigation. She wanted the attorney general to be able to initiate enforcement action without waiting for referral from bureaucratic federal agencies, and her bill mandated that federal agencies suspend payments to a recipient within forty-five days after the attorney general had filed a civil action alleging discrimination. Her legislation also gave the Executive Office of the President the power to coordinate the activities of Title VI agencies.
11. Author's telephone interview with Elaine Jones (director/counsel, NAACP Legal Defense Fund), July 10, 1997. All subsequent quotations from Jones are from this interview, unless otherwise noted.
12. These new units could act as an entire appeals court and hear cases either in panels of three or by sitting together. At the time the law was enacted, the language applied only to the Fifth and Ninth Circuits.
13. Barbara Jordan, remarks to the National Federation of Democratic Women, Washington, D.C., April 29, 1978, Barbara Jordan Speech File, Public Affairs Library, LBJ School of Public Affairs.
14. Elaine R. Jones, introduction of Barbara Jordan at Leadership Conference on Civil Rights awards dinner, Washington, D.C., May 19, 1989.
15. Barbara Jordan, "Why We Teach," *Center for Teaching Effectiveness Newsletter* 10, no. 3 (February 1989), Barbara Jordan Archives, Texas Southern University, Houston.
16. Quoted in author's interview with Wright.
17. Ibid.
18. Simmons, "In Her Own Words."
19. Jordan and Hearon, *Self-Portrait,* p. viii.
20. Barbara Jordan, commencement address, Harvard University, Cambridge, Mass., June 17, 1977.
21. Also receiving honorary degrees at Harvard that day were the financier Albert Gordon, the botanist Paul Mangelsdorf, the lawyer-historian Paul Freund, and the Oxford scholar Sir Richard Southern. Derek Bok was president of Harvard at the time.
22. Myra MacPherson, "Looking Over Jordan—Blacks, Women's Groups Complain as the Eloquent Texan Goes Her Own Way," *Washington Post,* October 30, 1977.
23. Ibid.
24. Ibid.
25. "Jordan to Discuss Plans for Future," *Dallas Morning News,* December 10, 1977.
26. Office of Representative Barbara Jordan, press release, December 10, 1977, Barbara Jordan Archives, Texas Southern University, Houston.
27. George McElroy, "Rep. Jordan's Retirement Top News Story in 1977," *Informer and Texas Freeman,* January 7, 1978.

28. Bill Curry, "Jordan Won't Seek Fourth Term, Is Undecided on Future Plans," *Washington Post*, December 11, 1977.

29. Hans Knight, "My Mother Said I Always Talked This Way," *Philadelphia Sunday Bulletin*, April 16, 1978.

30. "Jordan to Discuss Plans for Future," *Dallas Morning News*, December 10, 1977.

31. Jordan, "Why We Teach."

32. Ed Wendt, "The Word from Barbara Jordan," *Houston Forward Times*, December 17, 1977.

CHAPTER EIGHTEEN

1. Nagle, "Participation in the Political Process."

2. Charmayne Marsh and Stewart Davis, "Barbara Jordan Fighting Greatest Battle," *Dallas Morning News*, January 17, 1979.

3. Barbara Jordan, remarks at press conference, transcript, LBJ School of Public Affairs, UT News and Information Service, University of Texas at Austin, January 18, 1979.

4. Simmons, "In Her Own Words."

5. Rosner and Ross, *Multiple Sclerosis*, pp. 148–50.

6. Barbara Jordan, press conference, University of Texas at Austin, January 13, 1979.

7. Carolyn Barta, "Barbara Jordan from There to Here," *Dallas Morning News*, February 13, 1979.

8. Susan Kelly-DeWitt, "Barbara Jordan—She Reached Equality by Force of Will," *Sacramento Bee*, March 18, 1979.

9. Author's interview with Johnson; Barbara Jordan to Jake Johnson, March 30, 1979, Barbara Jordan Archives, Texas Southern University, Houston.

10. If viewed as the most complete set of interviews Barbara Jordan ever gave, the text of *Barbara Jordan: A Self-Portrait* provides valuable information about what she thought about certain events in her life. During the year they worked on the book together, Hearon got to know and understand Jordan as few individuals had done. However, because she, too, did not want to "rehash" old stories, Hearon declined to be interviewed for this book. Correspondence related to the proposed licensing of film and television rights between Jordan and Dionne Warwick, and Jordan and the Julian Bach Literary Agency, as well as Creative Artists Agency, can be found in the Barbara Jordan Archives, Texas Southern University, Houston.

11. "Jordan Top Pick to Head Nation," *Austin Citizen*, March 20, 1980. In the *People* magazine survey, Jordan received more votes than any other woman. The second choice was President Jimmy Carter's wife, Rosalyn, and third place went to Barbara Walters. The survey question was, "What woman would you support for president?"

12. Brian Dunbar, "Texas Leaders Endorse Carter," *Daily Texan*, October 30, 1979.

13. "Barbara Jordan, College Teacher," *Newsweek*, August 3, 1981.

14. Helen Tacket, "Barbara Jordan: A Woman of the Decade," *On Campus* (University of Texas at Austin), October 22–28, 1979.

15. Ibid.

16. Ronald Ozio, "Barbara Jordan: Collegians, Not Congress, Hear That Elegant Delivery Now," *Corpus Christi Caller-Times*, March 25, 1979.

17. Jordan's handwritten outlines of her assigned reading material can be found in the Barbara Jordan Archives, Texas Southern University, Houston.

18. Barbara Jordan, "The Law and Lawyers: Democracy's Bulwark" (remarks), William O. Douglas Award dinner, Los Angeles, March 18, 1989.

19. Barbara Jordan, remarks to the Council of Foundations, 1980, Public Affairs Library, LBJ School of Public Affairs, University of Texas at Austin.

20. Barbara Jordan, "The Common Good: A Framework for Discussion and Consensus," Southwest meeting of the American Assembly, Austin, May 11, 1990, Public Affairs Library, LBJ School of Public Affairs, University of Texas at Austin.

21. Gerald Gunther, *Learned Hand: The Man and the Judge* (Cambridge, Mass.: Harvard University Press, 1994), p. 549; see, for instance, Barbara Jordan, "Is Ethics a Component of

Government?", remarks at the University of California at Santa Barbara, September 22, 1990, Public Affairs Library, LBJ School of Public Affairs, University of Texas at Austin.

22. Jordan, "Is Ethics a Component of Government?"

23. Anne Spencer Thurman, *For the Inward Journey,* p. 191.

24. Barbara Jordan, "The Obligations of Intergenerational Justice," commencement address, Kenyon College, Gambier, Ohio, May 21, 1989.

25. Barbara Jordan, "The Importance of Public Service," remarks to IRS employees at the Austin Compliance Center, April 5, 1988.

26. Simmons, "In Her Own Words."

27. William K. Stevens, "Commanding Presence, Political Past," *New York Times,* February 13, 1979.

28. Undated, untitled article in *Daily Texan,* c. 1982.

29. Barbara Jordan, guest column, *The Advocate* (Texas State Teachers Association), February 1986.

30. Brett Campbell, "More than a Voice: Barbara Jordan, the Teacher," *American Educator* (Spring 1996).

31. Barbara Jordan, "Political Values and Ethics" (syllabus), LBJ School of Public Affairs, Fall 1995.

32. Harry J. Middleton, introduction of Barbara Jordan, Hofstra University, April 10, 1986.

33. Ibid.

34. Barbara Jordan, remarks at the University of Texas at Austin, February 22, 1991.

35. Leland was killed in a plane crash in Africa in August 1989. When then–state senator Craig Washington won Leland's congressional seat in a special election, there was a vacancy in the eighteenth senatorial district, which Rodney Ellis ran for and won in 1990.

36. Author's interview with State Senator Rodney Ellis, Houston, October 3, 1996. All subsequent quotations from Ellis are from this interview, unless otherwise noted.

37. This incident was described by Jordan's good friend and former aide DeAnn Friedholm when she spoke at a memorial service for Jordan at the University of Texas at Austin, January 28, 1996. The singer and actor Kris Kristofferson actually wrote "Me and Bobby McGee."

38. In 1980 Jordan also made a campaign television spot for an anti–gay discrimination ordinance campaign in Houston and allowed a Texas group to use her likeness on a three-inch bronze medal given annually to individuals whose contributions benefited handicapped persons. David Deming, a professor of art at the University of Texas at Austin, designed the bronze medal. He would later win a commission to design Jordan's tombstone. She also accepted a three-year-term appointment on the national advisory board for the George Foster Peabody national broadcasting awards.

39. Barbara Jordan, testimony before the House Judiciary Committee, Subcommittee on Civil and Constitutional Rights, June 18, 1981, Barbara Jordan Office Files, LBJ School of Public Affairs, University of Texas at Austin.

40. Although George Bush paved the way for Jordan to become a member of the Mead Corporation's board of directors, she did not let that stop her from criticizing him during his campaign for president. She was also a frequent critic of some of his policy decisions after he was president.

41. Author's interview with Love. In 1987 Texas Commerce Bancshares merged with Chemical Banking Corporation, which in turn merged in 1997 with Chase Manhattan. In 1998 Texas Commerce changed its name to Chase Bank of Texas.

42. In 1994 *Ebony* magazine named Jordan one of the nation's top black corporate directors. African Americans held only 2 percent of corporate directorships in the United States; she was one of only thirty-four African Americans who served on the boards of three or more Fortune 1,000 companies. Others at the top of the list were: Vernon Jordan, Washington lawyer/lobbyist; Sybil C. Mobley, dean of the Florida A&M School of Business; Louis Sullivan, M.D., Morehouse School of Medicine; and the former member of Congress William Gray III, CEO of the United Negro College Fund. See "Jordan Named Among Top Black Directors," *Austin American Statesman,* September 24, 1994. For a listing of Jordan's corporate board directorships, see Appendix.

43. *Strabismus* is the medical term for wandering eye movement. Although it occurs in only about 2 percent of the population, it is not uncommon among patients who have disorders of

the central nervous system. See Margaret Eckman and Nancy Priff, eds., *Diseases*, 2d ed. (Springhouse, Penn.: Springhouse Corp., 1997), pp. 113–15.

44. Susan Stewart, "Barbara Jordan: A Very Private Citizen," *Dallas Times Herald*, May 3, 1981.

45. Ken Wall, "Barbara Jordan Still Has Her Hold on Us," *Houston Chronicle*, August 12, 1988.

46. Controlled studies of hyperbaric oxygen treatments on MS patients revealed no significant improvement, and the practice faded from use. See Rosner and Ross, *Multiple Sclerosis*, p. 112.

47. Cytoxan, or cyclophosphamide, was a widely used, last-stage drug in chemotherapy for cancer patients and is now considered for use by MS patients only in the rare situation of rapid downhill progression.

48. Ancona, "Do Twice as Much, Jordan Tells Dunbar Students."

49. Private collection, Estate of Barbara Jordan, Austin, Texas.

50. All of Jordan's secretaries or assistants over the years learned to protect her privacy. Prior to Sharon Tutchings, her secretaries at the LBJ School of Public Affairs were Alice Romberg and Susan Martin.

51. "People" (column), *Newsweek*, April 15, 1988.

52. Although Arlyne Patten Jordan was still alive at the time of Barbara Jordan's death in January 1996, she was not aware that it had occurred. Mrs. Jordan died October 31, 1997, at eighty-seven.

53. Author's conversations with Sharon Tutchings, Austin, Texas, 1996–97.

54. "Meet the Five Outstanding Speakers of '95," *Toastmaster* (December 1995).

55. Bob Lloyd, "Reagan 'Distrusts' Government—Barbara Jordan Takes President to Task for His Economic Politics," *Fort Worth Star Telegram*, November 7, 1982.

56. Barbara Jordan, remarks at the National Prayer Breakfast, Washington, D.C., February 2, 1984.

57. "Meet the Five Outstanding Speakers of '95."

58. Sandy Grady, "Barbara Jordan Wouldn't Fit in Today's Spitball Congress," *Biloxi Sun Herald*, January 24, 1996.

59. Neil Postman, *Amusing Ourselves to Death* (New York: Penguin Books, 1985), p. 22.

60. Grady, "Barbara Jordan Wouldn't Fit."

61. Lance Morrow, "The Gravitas Factor," *Time*, March 14, 1988, p. 94.

62. Boyd, "Where Is Barbara Jordan Today?", pp. 12–13.

63. Ibid.

CHAPTER NINETEEN

1. Barbara Jordan, "The Constitution: Perspectives on Contemporary American Democracy," remarks to the Close-Up Foundation, 1986, Public Affairs Library, LBJ School of Public Affairs, University of Texas at Austin.

2. Liz Carpenter, "Barbara Jordan Talks About Ethics, Optimism, and Hard Choices in Government," *Ms.*, April 1985.

3. Cornel West, *Race Matters* (Boston: Beacon Press, 1993), pp. 39–40.

4. Boyd, "Where Is Barbara Jordan Today?"

5. Serving with Jordan on the UN panel were: Malcolm Fraser, former prime minister of Australia and chair of the group; Gamani Corea of Sri Lanka, former secretary-general, UN Conference on Trade and Development; Dame Judith Hart, member of Parliament of Great Britain; Annie Jiagge, a former judge in Ghana and former president of the World Council of Churches; Stanislav M. Menshikov, adviser of the International Department of the Central Committee of the Communist Party of the Soviet Union; Adolfo Perez Esquivel, Nobel Peace Prize winner from Argentina; Germanico Salgado, member and coordinator of the board of the Andean Pact and former minister of industry in Ecuador; Janez Stanovnik of Yugoslavia, former executive secretary of the UN Economic Commission for Europe; Layachi Yaker, ambassador, Foreign Affairs Ministry of Algeria; and Konstantin Kolev, counselor, Permanent Mission of Bulgaria to the UN.

6. Helen Tackett, interview with Barbara Jordan, UT News Service, University of Texas at Austin, December 16, 1985.

7. Ibid.

8. *Transnational Corporations in South Africa and Namibia: United Nations Public Hearings,* vol. 1, *Reports of the Panel of Eminent Persons and of the Secretary-General* (New York: United Nations, 1986), p. 5.

9. Tackett interview with Jordan.

10. Jordan's 1991 trip to South Africa was arranged by the Kaiser Family Foundation, which directs its resources to programs that improve health care for disadvantaged people, including $12 million in South Africa for worker training, programs for children with disabilities, and other health care innovations. Jordan became a member of the Kaiser Foundation's board in 1985.

11. Author's conversations with Judge Rose Spector, Austin 1997.

12. Ethan Bronner, *Battle for Justice: How the Bork Nomination Shook America* (New York: W. W. Norton, 1989), p. 285.

13. Ibid., p. 60.

14. Remarks of Barbara Jordan, Senate Judiciary Committee, *Hearings on the Nomination of Honorable Robert H. Bork to Be Associate Justice of the Supreme Court of the United States,* Washington, D.C., September 21, 1987.

15. Ibid., remarks of Senator Gordon Humphrey.

16. Bronner, *Battle for Justice,* p. 348.

17. Ibid., p. 349.

18. Barbara Jordan, "How Do We Live with Each Other's Deepest Differences?", remarks, Dayton, Ohio, June 28, 1990, Public Affairs Library, LBJ School of Public Affairs, University of Texas at Austin.

19. Enedelia J. Obregon, "Perot Foundation Awards $100,000 for LBJ School's Jordan Scholarships," *Austin American Statesman,* October 8, 1988.

20. During the 1988 presidential campaign, Jordan told a National Press Club gathering that "Jesse Jackson can help this ticket if he wants to. . . . He was very reluctant to do that because . . . Jesse Jackson never realized quite that he was defeated for the Democratic nomination, and carried forward as if he was somehow a co-nominee with Michael Dukakis. And we know there is no such thing." See Cragg Hines, "Jordan Blasts Jackson," *Houston Chronicle,* undated clipping, c. fall 1988, Barbara Jordan Office Files, LBJ School of Public Affairs, University of Texas at Austin. For an explanation of Jackson's role in the 1988 campaign and his hurt feelings over being summarily dismissed as a potential vice presidential candidate by presidential nominee Michael Dukakis, see Marshal Frady's excellent biography *Jesse: The Life and Pilgrimage of Jesse Jackson* (New York: Random House, 1996).

21. Kenneth F. Bunting, "Crowd Cheers Jordan for Speech Cheering Bentsen," *Fort Worth Star Telegram,* July 22, 1988.

22. Philip Bobbitt, a professor of constitutional law at the University of Texas School of Law, was part of Jordan's close circle of friends. After Jordan's death, Nancy Earl, who is executor of Jordan's estate, gave Bobbitt the palm-size copy of the Constitution that Jordan always carried with her. In 1997 Bobbitt moved to Washington to become director of intelligence for the National Security Council.

23. Grace Lim and Monty Jones, "Jordan Listed Critical After Near Drowning," *Austin American Statesman,* July 31, 1988.

24. Ibid.; Fred Bonavita, "Jordan Taken Off Critical List," *Houston Post,* August 1, 1988.

25. Carpenter, "Barbara Jordan Talks."

26. Barbara Jordan, "All Together Now," *Sesame Street Parents,* July/August 1994, Barbara Jordan Office Files, LBJ School of Public Affairs, later turned over to the Barbara Jordan Archives, Texas Southern University, Houston.

CHAPTER TWENTY

1. There were a number of co-chairs for the 1988 Democratic presidential campaign in Texas. They included, in addition to Jordan, Representative Mickey Leland, Houston's Texas

Commerce Bancshares chairman Ben Love, and State senator John Montford from Lubbock.

2. Barbara Jordan, "Protecting the Bill of Rights," guest column, *Washington Post,* November 4, 1988, Barbara Jordan Office Files, later turned over to the Barbara Jordan Archives, Texas Southern University, Houston. Jordan submitted this op-ed piece to the *Post* after she had seen the television commercial, which featured a visual of a black man moving through a revolving door, purported to represent his exit from prison on a furlough authorized under state law during the tenure of Massachusetts governor and Democratic presidential nominee Michael Dukakis.

3. Ibid.

4. UPI, "Jordan Chides Bush's Frequent Misstatements," Washington, D.C., undated, unidentified clipping, Barbara Jordan Office Files, LBJ School of Public Affairs, University of Texas, later turned over to the Barbara Jordan Archives, Texas Southern University, Houston.

5. Barbara Jordan, "One Nation Indivisible: True or False, Rhetoric or Reality?", remarks to symposium on "Cities in Transition: Policies for the 1990s," LBJ Presidential Library, Austin, October 6, 1988, Public Affairs Library, LBJ School of Public Affairs, University of Texas at Austin.

6. Ibid.

7. Barbara Jordan, remarks to the Council on Foundations, New York, N.Y., June 1980.

8. Barbara Jordan, "Compassion Versus Tough Love, or Mother Teresa Versus Marie Antoinette," remarks to the Federation for Community Planning, Cleveland, Ohio, March 20, 1992, Public Affairs Library, LBJ School of Public Affairs, University of Texas at Austin.

9. Barbara Jordan, remarks while participating in a panel discussion with Peter C. Goldmark Jr. and Antonia Hernandez, Investment in Excellence Award dinner, Denver, November 8, 1995.

10. Barbara Jordan, interview, *The Late Late Show with Tom Snyder,* March 14, 1995.

11. "Focus: Legal Immigration/Naturalization," *CIR News* (newsletter of the U.S. Commission on Immigration Reform) 2, no. 1 (February 1995).

12. Ibid.

13. "Jordan Named Among Top Black Directors," *Austin American Statesman,* September 24, 1994.

14. Richard W. Stevenson, "The Velvet Fist of Fannie Mae," *New York Times,* April 20, 1977. Other government-created, shareholder-controlled financing mechanisms that serve a public interest are the Federal National Mortgage Association (Fannie Mae), the Federal Home Loan Banks, the Farm Credit System, and the Student Loan Marketing Association (Sallie Mae).

15. At the time of Jordan's death in January 1996, the value of her estate was set at over $3 million. Estate of Barbara C. Jordan, Deceased, Inventory, Appraisement, and List of Claim, Probate Court No. 1 of Travis County, Texas.

16. Dave McNeely, "Jordan: Richards' Right Arm of the Law on Ethics," *Austin American Statesman,* March 31, 1991.

17. Jordan's other co-chairs were former San Antonio mayor Henry Cisneros, who later became secretary of housing and urban development under President Bill Clinton, and William P. Hobby, then–lieutenant governor of Texas.

18. McNeely, "Jordan."

19. Ibid.

20. In Texas all state court judges—from the county and district levels to the appeals court and the Supreme Court—are elected. However, the governor has the power to appoint judges at each of these levels when there is a vacancy. Because there are more than seven hundred elected judges in Texas, during a governor's four-year term there could be more than one hundred appointments to fill judicial vacancies.

21. Governor Ann Richards's general counsel, David Talbot, sat in on all of the meetings Jordan had with potential judicial appointees and reported these conversations to the author, who was chief of staff for Governor Richards at the time.

22. McNeely, "Jordan."

23. In 1991 Richards appointed State Representative Lena Guerrero of Austin to a vacancy

on the state's Railroad Commission, a powerful agency that regulated the oil and gas industry in Texas, as well as intrastate transportation. The commission was composed of three members who were elected statewide for four-year terms. In 1992 Guerrero was running for election to the post to which Richards had appointed her. She lost her bid for statewide elective office.

24. Barbara Jordan, "Change: From What to What?", keynote address, Democratic National Convention, New York, July 13, 1992.

25. Barbara Jordan, "The Democratic Party—What Now?", remarks to College Democrats of America, San Antonio, February 4, 1995, Public Affairs Library, LBJ School of Public Affairs, University of Texas at Austin.

26. Barbara Jordan, "Stewardship and the Public Trust," remarks to the Council on Foundations, Atlanta, March 30, 1987, Public Affairs Library, LBJ School of Public Affairs, University of Texas.

27. Barbara Jordan, "The Great Society and Its Markings," keynote address to a symposium on "The Great Society: A Twenty-Year Critique," LBJ Presidential Library, Austin, April 18–19, 1985, Public Affairs Library, LBJ School of Public Affairs, University of Texas at Austin.

28. Quoted in author's interview with McClelland.

29. Nancy Gibbs, "Thumbs Down," *Time,* February 1, 1993.

30. Jeffrey Rosen, "Good Help," *New Republic,* February 15, 1993.

31. Eric Schmitt, "Milestones and Missteps on Immigration," *New York Times,* October 26, 1996.

32. Maria Puente, "Familiar Voice Leads Way in Reform Effort," *USA Today,* July 14, 1994.

33. Author's interview with Susan Martin, Washington, D.C., September 20, 1996.

34. Jordan, "One Nation Indivisible."

35. Puente, "Familiar Voice Leads Way."

36. Ibid.

37. Ibid.

38. Quoted in author's interview with Martin.

39. The members of the U.S. Commission on Immigration Reform appointed by the Senate Republican leadership were: Richard Estrada, associate editor of the *Dallas Morning News;* Harold Ezell, president of the Ezell Group; Robert Charles Hill, a partner in the law firm of Jenkins and Gilchrist; and Dr. Michael S. Tetelbaum, program officer of the Alfred P. Sloan Foundation, elected by his fellow commissioners to be the Republican vice chair of the commission. The members of the commission appointed by the Senate Democratic leadership were: Dr. Lawrence H. Fuchs, professor of American civilization and politics at Brandeis University, and the Democratic vice chair of the commission; Warren R. Leiden, executive director of the American Immigration Lawyers Association; Nelson Merced, chief executive officer of Inquilinos Borcicas En Accion/Emergency Tenant Council; and Bruce A. Morrison, partner in the Morrison and Swaine law firm.

40. Proposition 187 was approved by California voters in November 1994, but, as late as 1998, it had not yet been implemented, because of legal challenges.

41. U.S. Commission on Immigration Reform, "U.S. Immigration Policy: Restoring Credibility," report to Congress, Washington, D.C.: September 1984.

42. Barbara Jordan, "The Americanization Ideal," *New York Times,* September 11, 1995, op-ed page.

43. Susan Martin, "The Practitioner's Corner," *LBJ Journal of Public Affairs* (Spring 1997).

44. Author's interview with Jim Bouchillon, Washington, D.C., September 18, 1996.

45. Christina Goggio Banks, "Where Have All the Leaders Gone?", unpublished article based on an interview with Barbara Jordan conducted by Banks in 1993, and provided to the author by Banks in May 1996.

46. U.S. Commission on Immigration Reform, "U.S. Immigration Policy: Restoring Credibility."

47. Tessie Borden, "Registry Would Slow Illegals, Jordan Says," *Houston Post,* October 12, 1994.

48. Ibid.

49. Quoted in author's interview with Martin.

50. Schmitt, "Milestones and Missteps."

51. In addition to honoring Jordan in 1994, President Clinton also awarded the Medal of Freedom to Herbert Block, the Pulitzer Prize–winning *Washington Post* cartoonist known as "Herblock"; Arthur Flemming, former chairman of the Civil Rights Commission and the White House Conference on Aging, and a past secretary of health, education and welfare; James Grant, executive director of the United Nations Children's Fund (UNICEF); Dorothy Height, civil rights activist; Lane Kirkland, president of the AFL-CIO; U.S. Representative Bob Michel, a Republican from Illinois who was House minority leader; and Robert Sargent Shriver, former U.S. ambassador to France, the first director of the Peace Corps, and director of President Johnson's War on Poverty. The award was also given posthumously to the late Cesar Chavez, founder of the United Farm Workers of America.

52. Michele Kay, "Clinton Honors Jordan, Chavez with Medal of Freedom," *Austin American Statesman,* August 9, 1994.

53. John McGowan died in January 1998.

54. Another prestigious award that Jordan received was being listed as one of the ten most influential American women of the twentieth century by the National Women's Hall of Fame. Also on the list, in order of their perceived influence, were: Eleanor Roosevelt (1884–1962); Jane Addams (1860–1935); Rosa Parks (1914–); Margaret Sanger (1883–1966); Margaret Mead (1901–78); Charlotte Perkins Gilman (1860–1935); Betty Friedan (1921–); Jordan; Helen Keller (1880–1968); and Alice Paul (1885–1977). See Bob Dart, "Barbara Jordan Named Influential Woman of the Century," *Austin American Statesman,* March 13, 1993.

55. Author's conversations with Susan Martin, Nancy Earl, Sharon Tutchings, and others with whom Jordan discussed the work of the commission.

56. Schmitt, "Milestones and Missteps."

57. "Clinton Opposes It . . . ," *Washington Post,* March 20, 1996.

58. Congress and the president finally compromised on a massive overhaul of immigration laws in the summer of 1996. Some key recommendations of the commission were adopted, but others were not. The most glaring conflict between what the commission recommended and what Congress and the president agreed upon was the linkage of citizenship to eligibility for public assistance in welfare reform. The commission had specifically opposed such a link, recommending against a categorical denial of eligibility to legal immigrants. The commission argued that a distinction should be made between illegal aliens and legal immigrants.

59. Quoted in author's interview with Briggs.

60. Cytoxan (cyclophosphamide) limits white blood cell activity and in so doing limits T-lymphocyte activation. The presence of excess T-cell activity is evident in most multiple sclerosis patients. However, studies of cyclophosphamide in the 1990s indicated that close monitoring of bone marrow and liver function were necessary because of potential damage. Literature made available by the National Multiple Sclerosis Society advised that these kinds of drugs should not be used indiscriminately on MS patients who have ongoing disease activity. Jordan never had a multiple sclerosis episode after 1989.

61. Barbara Jordan, commencement address, Laurel School, Shaker Heights, Ohio, June 6, 1991, Public Affairs Library, LBJ School of Public Affairs, University of Texas at Austin.

62. Paul Woodruff and Harry Wilmer, eds., *Facing Evil: Light at the Core of Darkness* (LaSalle, Ill.: Open Court, 1988), p. 41.

63. Author's interview with Nancy Earl, Austin, Texas, June 18, 1997.

64. Bill Moyers, remarks at the memorial service for Barbara Jordan, University of Texas, January 28, 1996.

65. D. Z. Cofield, remarks at the funeral service for Barbara Jordan, Good Hope Missionary Baptist Church, Houston, January 20, 1996.

BIBLIOGRAPHY

BOOKS

Ackerman, Diane. *The Natural History of the Senses*. New York: Random House, 1990.

Barr, Alwyn. *Black Texans: A History of African Americans in Texas, 1528–1995*, 2d ed. Norman: University of Oklahoma Press, 1996.

Becker, Ernest. *The Denial of Death*. New York: Free Press, 1985.

Beeth, Howard and Cary D. Wintz, eds. *Black Dixie: Afro-Texan History and Culture in Houston*. College Station: Texas A&M University Press, 1992.

Bok, Sissela. *Secrets: On the Ethics of Concealment and Revelation*. New York: Vintage Books/Random House, 1989.

Bourne, Peter G. *Jimmy Carter*. New York: Scribner's, 1997.

Branch, Taylor. *Parting the Waters: America in the King Years, 1954–1963*. New York: Touchstone/Simon & Schuster, 1988.

Bronner, Ethan. *Battle for Justice: How the Bork Nomination Shook America*. New York: W. W. Norton, 1989.

Brueggemann, Walter. *Hope Within History*. Atlanta: John Knox Press, 1987.

Bryant, Ira B. *Texas Southern University: Its Antecedents, Political Origins, and Future*. Houston: Ira B. Bryant, 1975.

———. *Barbara Charline Jordan: From the Ghetto to the Capitol*. Houston: D. Armstrong Co., 1977.

Buenger, Walter L., and Joseph A. Pratt. *But Also Good Business: Texas Commerce Bank and the Financing of Houston and Texas, 1886–1986*. College Station: Texas A&M University Press, 1986.

Butler, Addie Louise Joyner. *The Distinctive Black College: Talladega, Tuskegee, and Morehouse*. Metuchen, N.J.: Scarecrow Press, 1977.

Carleton, Don E. *Red Scare!: Right-wing Hysteria, Fifties Fanaticism, and Their Legacy in Texas*. Austin: Texas Monthly Press, 1985.

Carter, Stephen L. *Integrity*. New York: HarperCollins, 1996.

Connally, John, with Mickey Herskowitz. *In History's Shadow: An American Odyssey*. New York: Hyperion, 1993.

Crawford, Ann Fears, and Jack Keever. *John B. Connally: Portrait in Power*. Austin: Jenkins Publishing Co., 1973.

Crick, Bernard. *In Defense of Politics*. New York: Viking/Penguin Books, 1982.

Dash, Samuel. *Chief Counsel: Inside the Ervin Committee—The Untold Story of Watergate*. New York: Random House, 1976.

Davidson, Chandler, ed. *Minority Vote Dilution*. Washington, D.C.: Howard University Press, 1984.

————. *Race and Class in Texas Politics*. Princeton, N.J.: Princeton University Press, 1990.

Dobel, J. Patrick. *Compromise and Political Action: Political Morality in Liberal and Democratic Life*. Savage, Md.: Rowman & Littlefield Publishers, 1990.

Donald, David Herbert. *Lincoln*. New York: Simon & Schuster, 1995.

Egerton, John. *Speak Now Against the Day: The Generation Before the Civil Rights Movement in the South*. Chapel Hill: University of North Carolina Press, 1995.

Feagin, Joe R. *Free Enterprise City: Houston in Political-Economic Perspective*. New Brunswick, N.J.: Rutgers University Press, 1988.

Frady, Marshall. *Jesse: The Life and Pilgrimage of Jesse Jackson*. New York: Random House, 1996.

Franklin, John Hope. *From Slavery to Freedom: A History of Negroes in America*. 5th ed. New York: Alfred A. Knopf, 1980.

Gardner, Howard. *Leading Minds: Anatomy of Leadership*. New York: Basic Books, 1996.

Giddings, Paula. *When and Where I Enter: The Impact of Black Women on Race and Sex in America*. New York: Bantam Books, 1984.

————. *In Search of Sisterhood: Delta Sigma Theta and the Challenge of the Black Sorority Movement*. New York: William Morrow, 1988.

Goodwyn, Lawrence. *Democratic Promise: The Populist Movement in America*. New York: Oxford University Press, 1976.

Gottron, Martha V., ed. *Congress and the Nation*. vol. 5, 1977–1980. Washington, D.C.: Congressional Quarterly, 1981.

Grofman, Bernard, and Chandler Davidson, eds. *Controversies in Minority Voting: The Voting Rights Act in Perspective*. Washington, D.C.: Brookings Institution, 1992.

Grudin, Robert. *Time and the Art of Living*. New York: Ticknor & Fields, 1988.

Gunther, Gerald. *Learned Hand: The Man and the Judge*. Cambridge, Mass.: Harvard University Press, 1994.

Haskins, James. *Barbara Jordan*. New York: Dial Press, 1977.

Higginbotham, Evelyn Brooks. *Righteous Discontent: The Women's Movement in the Black Baptist Church, 1880–1920*. Cambridge, Mass.: Harvard University Press, 1993.

Hill, Herbert, and James E. Jones Jr. eds. *Race in America: The Struggle for Equality*. Madison: University of Wisconsin Press, 1993.

Jaworski, Leon. *The Right and the Power: The Prosecution of Watergate*. New York: Reader's Digest Press, 1976.

Jordan, Barbara, and Shelby Hearon. *Barbara Jordan: A Self-Portrait*. New York: Doubleday, 1979.

Kilgore, Kathleen. *Transformations: A History of Boston University*. Boston: Boston University Press, 1991.

Kinch, Sam, and Ben Proctor. *Texas Under a Cloud: The Story of the Texas Stock Fraud Scandal*. Austin: Jenkins Publishing Co., 1972.

Lasch, Christopher. *The Revolt of the Elites and the Betrayal of Democracy*. New York: W. W. Norton, 1995.

Lemann, Nicholas. *The Promised Land: The Great Black Migration and How It Changed America*. New York: Vintage Books, 1992.

Lewis, David Levering. *W.E.B. Du Bois: Biography of a Race, 1868–1919.* New York: Henry Holt and Co., 1993.

Lincoln, C. Eric, and Lawrence H. Mamiya. *The Black Church in the African American Experience.* Durham, N.C.: Duke University Press, 1990.

Lippmann, Walter. *The Public Philosophy.* New York: New American Library, 1955.

Livingston, William S., ed. *The Legacy of the Constitution: An Assessment for the Third Century.* Austin: Lyndon Baines Johnson Library and the Lyndon B. Johnson School of Public Affairs, 1987.

McCollough, Thomas E. *The Moral Imagination and Public Life.* Chatham, NJ: Chatham House Publishers, 1991.

McFeely, William S. *Frederick Douglass.* New York: W. W. Norton, 1991.

McPherson, Harry. *A Political Education: A Washington Memoir.* Austin: University of Texas Press, 1995.

Margalit, Avishai. *The Decent Society.* Cambridge, Mass.: Harvard University Press, 1996.

Montejano, David. *Anglos and Mexicans in the Making of Texas, 1836–1986.* Austin: University of Texas Press, 1987.

Norrell, Robert J. *Reaping the Whirlwind: The Civil Rights Movement in Tuskegee.* New York: Alfred A. Knopf, 1985.

O'Connor, Patricia Ann, ed. *Congress and the Nation,* vol. 4, 1973–1976. Washington, D.C.: Congressional Quarterly, 1977.

Pitre, Merline. *Through Many Dangers, Toils, and Shares: The Black Leadership of Texas, 1868–1900.* Austin: Eakin Press, 1985.

Postman, Neil. *Amusing Ourselves to Death: Public Discourse in the Age of Show Business.* New York: Penguin Books, 1986.

Prather, Patricia Smith, and Bob Lee. *Texas Trailblazer Series.* Houston: Texas Trailblazer Preservation Association and Texas Commerce Bank, 1996.

Reston, James, Jr. *The Lone Star: The Life of John Connally.* New York: Harper & Row, 1989.

Rice, Lawrence D. *The Negro in Texas, 1874–1900.* Baton Rouge: Louisiana State University Press, 1971.

Rich, Adrienne. *What Is Found There: Notebooks on Poetry and Politics.* New York: W. W. Norton & Company, 1993.

Rodino, Peter W. *High Crimes and Misdemeanors: Selected Materials on Impeachment.* New York: Funk & Wagnalls, 1974.

Rosner, Louis J., M.D., and Shelley Ross. *Multiple Sclerosis: New Hope and Practical Advice for People with MS and Their Families.* Updated edition. New York: Fireside Books/Simon & Schuster, 1992.

Russell, Kathy, Midge Wilson, and Ronald Hall. *The Color Complex: The Politics of Skin Color Among African Americans.* New York: Anchor Books/Doubleday, 1992.

Schwartz, Barry. *George Washington: The Making of an American Symbol.* New York: Free Press, 1987.

Scott, Emmitt. *The Red Book of Houston: A Compendium of Social, Professional, Religious, Educational, and Industrial Interests of Houston's Colored Population.* Houston: Houston Public Library, Metropolitan Collection, 1915.

Thurman, Howard. *The Luminous Darkness: A Personal Interpretation of the Anatomy of Segregation and the Ground of Hope.* New York: Harper & Row, 1965.

————. *With Head and Heart: The Autobiography of Howard Thurman.* New York: Harcourt Brace Jovanovich, 1979.

————. *For the Inward Journey: The Writings of Howard Thurman.* Anne Spencer Thurman, ed. New York: Harcourt Brace Jovanovich, 1984.

Tushnet, Mark V. *Making Civil Rights Law: Thurgood Marshall and the Supreme Court, 1936–1961.* New York: Oxford University Press, 1994.

West, Cornel. *Race Matters.* Boston: Beacon Press, 1993.

West, Richard. *Richard West's Texas.* Austin: Texas Monthly Press, 1981.

Winegarten, Ruthe. *Black Texas Women.* Austin: University of Texas Press, 1995.

————. *Black Texas Women: A Sourcebook.* Austin: University of Texas Press, 1996.

Woodruff, Paul, and Harry Wilmer, eds. *Facing Evil: Light at the Core of Darkness.* LaSalle, Ill.: Open Court, 1988.

Woodward, Bob, and Carl Bernstein. *The Final Days.* New York: Touchstone, Simon & Schuster, 1976.

Wright, Jim. *Balance of Power: Presidents and Congress from the Era of McCarthy to the Age of Gingrich.* Atlanta: Turner Publishing, 1996.

PUBLIC DOCUMENTS

Congressional Record, Proceedings and Debates of the 93d Cong., 2d sess. Vol. 120, part 22, August 16, 1974, to August 22, 1974, pp. 28675–30170. Washington, D.C.: U.S. Government Printing Office, 1974.

Congressional Record, Proceedings and Debates of the 94th Cong., 1st sess. Vol. 121, part 13, June 2, 1975, to June 5, 1975, pp. 16237–17480. Washington, D.C.: U.S. Government Printing Office, 1975.

Congressional Record, Proceedings and Debates of the 94th Cong., 2d sess. Vol. 122, part 16, June 18, 1976, to June 24, 1976, pp. 19067–20506. Washington, D.C.: U.S. Government Printing Office, 1976.

House Judiciary Committee. *Impeachment Inquiry: Hearings.* 93rd Cong., 2d sess., books I–III, January 31 to July 23, 1974. Washington, D.C.: U.S. Government Printing Office, 1975.

House Judiciary Committee. *Debate on Articles of Impeachment: Hearings Pursuant to H.Res. 803, a Resolution Authorizing and Directing the Committee on the Judiciary to Investigate Whether Sufficient Grounds Exist for the House of Representatives to Exercise Its Constitutional Power to Impeach Richard M. Nixon, President of the United States of America.* 93rd Cong., 2d sess., July 24–27, 29, and 30, 1974. Washington, D.C.: U.S. Government Printing Office, 1974.

House Judiciary Committee, Subcommittee on Civil and Constitutional Rights. *Extension of the Voting Rights Act: Hearings.* 94th Cong., 1st sess., February 25, 26, March 3–6, 13, 14, 17, 20, 21, 24, and 25, 1975, serial no. 1, parts 1 and 2. Washington, D.C.: U.S. Government Printing Office, 1975.

House Judiciary Committee, Subcommittee on Monopolies and Commercial Law. *A Proposal to Divide the Fifth Circuit: Hearings.* 95th Cong., September 21, 27, and October 19, 1977. Washington, D.C.: U.S. Government Printing Office, 1978.

Transnational Corporations in South Africa and Namibia: United Nations Public

Hearings. Vol. 1, *Reports of the Panel of Eminent Persons and of the Secretary-General.* New York: United Nations, 1986. Publications sales no. E.86.II.A.6.

MISCELLANEOUS PUBLICATIONS

"Barbara Jordan Dedication," *Annual Survey of American Law,* 1989. New York: New York University School of Law, February 1990.
Current Biography, 1974, s.v. "Jordan, Barbara."
The Handbook of Texas. Vol. 5. Austin: Texas State Historical Association, 1997.
Joint Center for Political Studies. *The Black Vote—Election '76.* Washington, D.C.:
Last, John S. *Texas Southern University: From Separation to Special Designation.* Undated pamphlet, Heartman Negro Collection, Texas Southern University, Houston.
Watergate: Chronology of a Crisis. Vol. 1. Washington, D.C.: Congressional Quarterly, 1973.

FILM DOCUMENTARY

WETA Television, *Summer of Judgment—Impeachment Hearings.* Narrated by Charles McDowell. Washington, D.C.: Greater Washington Educational Telecommunications Association, 1984.

INDEX